The publisher and the University of California Press Foundation gratefully acknowledge the generous support of the Barbara S. Isgur Endowment Fund in Public Affairs.

Badges Without Borders

Badges Without Borders

HOW GLOBAL COUNTERINSURGENCY
TRANSFORMED AMERICAN POLICING

Stuart Schrader

UNIVERSITY OF CALIFORNIA PRESS

University of California Press
Oakland, California

© 2019 by Stuart Schrader

Library of Congress Cataloging-in-Publication Data

Names: Schrader, Stuart, author.
Title: Badges without borders : how global counterinsurgency transformed
    American policing / Stuart Schrader.
Description: Oakland, California : University of California Press, [2019] |
    Series: American Crossroads ; 56 | Includes bibliographical references
    and index. |
Identifiers: LCCN 2019004095 (print) | LCCN 2019006628 (ebook) |
    ISBN 9780520968332 () | ISBN 9780520295612 (cloth : alk. paper) |
    ISBN 9780520295629 (pbk. : alk. paper)
Subjects: LCSH: Counterinsurgency—United States—History—20th
    century. | United States. Agency for International Development. Office
    of Public Safety—History. | Racial profiling in law enforcement—United
    States—20th century. | Social control—United States—20th century. |
    Militarization of police—United States—century.
Classification: LCC U241 (ebook) | LCC U241 .S37 2019 (print) |
    DDC 355.02/180973—dc23
LC record available at https://lccn.loc.gov/2019004095

Manufactured in the United States of America

26 25 24 23 22 21 20 19
10 9 8 7 6 5 4 3 2 1

To my mother, Jane Marie Schrader,
and
In loving memory of Phyllis Waller, Erica Vallario,
Gail Moody, and Mike Stoddard

CONTENTS

List of Abbreviations ix

Introduction 1

1 · Rethinking Race and Policing in Imperial Perspective 27

2 · Byron Engle and the Rise of Overseas Police Assistance 52

3 · How Counterinsurgency Became Policing 79

4 · Bringing Police Assistance Home 113

5 · Policing and Social Regulation 142

6 · Riot School 166

7 · The Imperial Circuit of Tear Gas 192

8 · Order Maintenance and the Genealogy of SWAT 214

9 · "The Discriminate Art of Indiscriminate
Counter-revolution" 235

Conclusion 259

Acknowledgments 275
Notes 281
Selected Bibliography 343
Index 363

ABBREVIATIONS

ADST	Association for Diplomatic Studies and Training, Foreign Affairs Oral History Project
AID	Agency for International Development
ARPA	Advanced Research Projects Agency
CIA	Central Intelligence Agency
CORDS	Civil Operations and Revolutionary Development Support
CRDJA	*Civil Rights during the Johnson Administration,* online database
CREST	CIA Records Search Tool
CSA	California State Archives, Sacramento, CA
CSTI	California Specialized Training Institute
DDRS	Declassified Documents Reference System, Farmington Hills, IL
DOJ	Department of Justice
E	Entry
FBI	Federal Bureau of Investigation
FRUS	US Department of State, *Papers Relating to the Foreign Relations of the United States*
GPO	Government Printing Office
HIA	Hoover Institution Archives, Stanford, CA
IACP	International Association of Chiefs of Police
IAPA	Inter-American Police Academy

ICA	International Cooperation Administration
IPA	International Police Academy
IPG	Interagency Police Group
IPS	Internal Defense and Public Safety
JFKL	John F. Kennedy Presidential Library, Boston, MA
KCMNC	Kansas City Municipal Library Mounted Newspaper Clippings, Missouri Valley Special Collections, Kansas City, MO
KCPHS	Kansas City Police Historical Society Missouri Valley Special Collections, Kansas City Municipal Library, Kansas City, MO
LAPD	Los Angeles Police Department
LBJL	Lyndon Baines Johnson Presidential Library, Austin, TX
LEAA	Law Enforcement Assistance Administration
MSU	Michigan State University
MSUA	Michigan State University Special Collections, East Lansing, MI
NACCD	National Advisory Commission on Civil Disorders (Kerner Commission)
NACLA	North American Congress on Latin America
NARA	National Archives and Records Administration, College Park, MD
NLF	National Liberation Front for South Vietnam
NRA	National Rifle Association
NSAM	National Security Action Memorandum
NSC	National Security Council
NSF	National Security File
OIDP	Overseas Internal Defense Policy
OISP	Overseas Internal Security Program
OLEA	Office of Law Enforcement Assistance
OPS	Office of Public Safety

PCLEAJ	President's Commission on Law Enforcement and Administration of Justice (Crime Commission)
PDB	President's Daily Brief
POCC	Police Operations Control Center
PP	Personal Papers
PSN	*Public Safety Newsletter*
RG	Record Group
RMNL	Richard M. Nixon Presidential Library, Yorba Linda, CA
RRL	Ronald Reagan Presidential Library, Simi Valley, CA
RWK	Robert W. Komer
SCAP	Supreme Commander for the Allied Powers
SEADOC	Senior Officers Civil Disturbance Orientation Course
SGCI	Special Group (Counter-Insurgency)
SORO	Special Operations Research Office
TAPP	*The American Presidency Project*
TNA	The National Archives, Kew, United Kingdom
TPC	*The Police Chief*
TTU	Vietnam Center and Archive, Texas Tech University, Lubbock, TX
USD	Richardson Collections, University of South Dakota, Vermillion, SD
WHCF	White House Central File
WHTRT	White House Telephone Recordings and Transcripts

Note: All emphases in quotations are in the original.

Introduction

IMAGINE A LARGE-FORMAT PHOTOGRAPH with a prison looming in the foreground. The print renders the building in impeccable detail. Sunlight glints off the razor wire. You can count the bars on the windows and make out the piercing eyes of guards in the towers. What's more, you can see a new wing of the building, now under construction, which will transform the site into a Justice Complex, integrating corrections, courts, and police. A state-of-the-art training facility for police officers will be built next door. You spy the helmeted welders and bricklayers. Off to the side are the elected officials planning the ceremonial ribbon-cutting. They will congratulate themselves on fulfilling campaign promises to be tough on crime. Prison officials, police chiefs, and criminology experts will be in the audience, satisfied that their own advocacy of "law and order" has paid off. This picture also illustrates the most important aspect of the prison: people peering from behind those barred windows, locked up. They are parents stolen from children, children stolen from parents. Their lives have been shortened and depleted.

Look closer and you realize that this photograph is not the work of a single artist. It is a collage of different moments, and it is the work of activists, journalists, and scholars who have transformed a movement for racial justice into a new way of understanding the history of the United States. This collage puts the prison at the center of the social and political history of the past four decades, if not the past fifteen. And the prison is really a broader agglomeration of punitive policies that depend on aggressive policing, extravagant sentences, and court-mandated surveillance and pecuniary penalties.[1]

The effects are far-reaching. Almost 2.3 million people in the United States are locked in jail or prison on any given day, with another 4.5 million on parole or probation. Jails and prisons are unhealthy places, and these levels of incarceration are among the reasons why the United States has lagged behind other wealthy countries in growth of its average life expectancy in recent decades. Black men overall lose 3.09 years of life expectancy to prison or jail, Latino men 1.06 years, and white men 0.50 years. For women, these subtractions from life expectancy average 0.23, 0.09, and 0.05 years, respectively. Around nineteen million Americans have a felony conviction record, and many more a record of arrest, making them ineligible for multiple types of employment and civic benefits, including voting rights in some states. Interactions with this system start at age twelve on average among Black youth. These interactions almost invariably begin with police.[2]

Yet this detailed illustration of the prison complex and its effects in the photograph's foreground sits against a background that remains hazy. Its structures and shapes are indistinct. From the existing rendering, it is unclear how pathways that disappear into the horizon connect with the police and guards in the foreground. This background is an imperial project. It is the US effort to assure its national security by assuring the internal security of countries across the globe. To look at that background is to grasp that although the history of policing and prisons within the United States appears grotesque, the true extent is worse. This US apparatus has encircled, and encaged, the globe.

This book re-imagines the collage, clarifying its nebulous background. *Badges Without Borders* shifts figure and ground, bringing into focus that imperial project.[3] This simple movement reveals that the growth and empowerment of cops and cages beginning in the 1960s was not independent of that imperial background, but has been intimately tied to it. The ideas and people essential to the background were ideas and people essential to the foreground. They were one and the same. To look at these policymakers and their maneuvers to bolster law enforcement around the globe after World War II is to understand who the builders of the carceral state were, how they crafted this policy, and why they did it. Racially invidious policing and incarceration within the United States, which many have worked so hard to bring to public consciousness, do not represent the sum of state-building in the name of law and order. A close look at the collage's background reveals that many of the law-enforcement leaders who stewarded the rise of this new penal apparatus had already been engaged in a program of deterritorialized state-building. They crafted policy designs and rationales overseas. They deployed technical expertise to any country that would have them, helping endow these states with up-to-date repressive capacities and bolstering authoritarianism. And they then policed American streets like "foreign territory."[4]

Black radicals at the time understood, named, and condemned the interrelationship this book excavates, sometimes calling it "internal colonialism." Although some have questioned the concept's utility for analyzing political economy, its undisputed strength was its focus on policing. As the objects of countersubversive policing, Black radicals mounted critiques of US policy overseas by refracting it through their experiences back home, situating the United States in the world and the world in the United States.[5] Bobby Seale of the Black Panther Party for Self-Defense, for example, declared in a prescient 1967 article: "The racist *military* police force occupies our community just like the foreign American troops in Vietnam."[6] An occupying military was unaccountable and vicious; residents could not reason with it. Police in Black neighborhoods were the same. Seale predicted the "long hot summer" that began with small uprisings against police in Tampa and Cincinnati, followed by massive ones in Newark and Detroit. Police then redoubled efforts to upgrade their own technologies, training, and techniques. New Left radicals with organizations like the North American Congress on Latin America and the Institute for Policy Studies who studied these projects confirmed the links between war overseas and repression at home using every government document they could obtain.[7] Before it became a topic of scholarly inquiry, Black radical intellectuals like Seale highlighted the centrality of policing and prisons to American political development, while also connecting repression of freedom movements at home to repression of anticolonial efforts overseas. Personal experience with police taught them counterinsurgency's first principle: it is not only insurgents or criminals who must be pacified, but entire populations.[8] This book's inquiry into the development of the carceral state as racialized social control stands on the foundation these thinkers built, taking their political analyses seriously and matching them with extensive new archival research, using records unavailable at the time. This research shows that the relationship that made the policing of Seale's Oakland neighborhood feel like colonial occupation depended on longstanding personal and institutional connections across borders.[9]

The Black Panther Party attempted to forge a new liberation politics adequate to the challenge of the intertwinement of the military-industrial complex and the prison-industrial complex. *Badges Without Borders* wagers that to realize these elusive politics today will require reckoning with the extensive connections US security agencies built across borders after World War II—and continue to intensify now. Racial formation, and racial oppression, took shape locally, through histories of slavery, settlerism, and segregation. But these also took shape globally, through histories of colonial occupation, dispossession, and extraction. At the center of both these efforts was police power, and this book demonstrates the vigorous global transit of police ideas and personnel.

Following domestic political unrest in the 1960s, officials in Washington, DC, as well as state capitals and city halls, decided that the way to prevent future outbreaks was to upgrade policing. This allocation of resources was not inevitable. Proposals that confronted the problem but did not put police at the center also came from establishment sources, like the National Advisory Commission on Civil Disorders (NACCD), better known as the Kerner Commission, after its chair, Illinois governor Otto Kerner. President Lyndon B. Johnson appointed the NACCD in July 1967 to investigate the causes of unrest in twenty-three US cities—and to devise prophylaxis against future unrest. In its bestselling *Report,* issued on February 29, 1968, the commission offered recommendations to alleviate racial and economic inequality, urging a vast federal spending program on jobs, education, and housing to address the socioeconomic conditions underlying the political unrest.

President Johnson spurned this proposal, but most of the subsidiary recommendations the Kerner *Report* delivered on how to transform policing were adopted. Security came first. And the way to assure security was to reform its technical apparatus. Police chiefs, national security officials, and social scientists concurred. This coalition helped produce some federal legislation in 1965 and a huge bill in 1968 that put federal money in cops' hands. Elected officials offered this "war against crime" to concerned voters as a way to control political unrest.[10] What it actually did was offer resources to police and prisons to enhance their capacities and repertoires, laying the stony foundations of the carceral state: aggressive policing, mass incarceration, and the engulfing of the state's welfare capacities by penal demands.

Accounts of the rise of the carceral state have emphasized conservative ire, liberal frustration, and shifting voting blocs, but this commitment to reforming law enforcement won popular support because it had police support. The War on Crime was not only the result of white electoral backlash against the gains of the civil rights movement, or concerted organizing among elites to prevent those gains.[11] By the late 1960s, attempting to ensure social peace by means of police reform was already the US approach in dozens of countries in Africa, Asia, and Latin America. The carceral state had bipartisan origins. Its proximate catalyst was the demand to reform policing. And this demand was consonant with the prerogatives of the national security state, the most bipartisan aspect of US politics in the post-1945 period. The expansion of incarceration and policing that began at home in the late 1960s grew out of an expansion of policing capacities around the globe that the United States stewarded to prevent communist revolution. New endowments for police training and equipment were the product of US imperial governance, which during the Cold War conferred purpose, coherence, and political acumen on law-enforcement actors to expand their power and prestige back home. Racism, movements to counter it, and their repression have, of course, existed throughout US history. The War on Crime, however, emerged specifically in the context of an effort to use police to manage global decolonization.[12]

Examining how recommendations on revamping policing practices reached the Kerner Commission opens a window on a set of actors surprisingly excluded from the history of the growth of prisons and policing, namely, those who would themselves be tasked with waging war on crime. It turns out that many police leaders at the time already saw themselves as global actors. One stands out among them: Byron Engle, who testified to a globe-spanning career's worth of law-enforcement expertise in his appearance before the Kerner Commission on September 20, 1967. The NACCD copied several of the ideas in Engle's brief statement nearly verbatim into its *Report*.[13]

Engle recommended the use at home of lessons learned overseas: "The Communists have had long experience in utilizing disturbances, riots, terrorism, as political action tools. As a consequence, we ... have put a lot of emphasis on nonlethal riot control. We have found there are many principles and concepts which apply, whether it is [in] Asia, Africa, or South America. Perhaps those same principles would apply in the United States."[14]

He was an obscure figure, except to subscribers to *The Police Chief,* the monthly magazine of the International Association of Chiefs of Police (IACP), and staff of the National Security Council (NSC). Few of the millions who read the paperback NACCD *Report* would have noted Engle's name among those of more famous witnesses who testified. But he was one of the most consistent and influential voices in professional circles of law enforcement around the globe. His testimony demands the perspectival shift from the foreground of the domestic development of aggressive penal policy to the background of its international development.

Although Engle's testimony came in a setting of heightened political attention, it signaled a process that had actually been ongoing since the 1940s, with Engle at its center. When he said perhaps the principles used overseas might apply at home, he was being coy. In fact, his entire career, and those of his influential collaborators, who constituted the leadership of law-enforcement modernization, had been dedicated to mounting a single border-crossing war on crime and left-wing radicalism that utilized the same practical techniques and technologies and similar policies overseas and at home. Not simply individual police officers, but rather the milieu of professional policing as a whole envisioned itself as situated on an unruly globe that inexorably posed dangers requiring police intervention, from chaotic roadway congestion in extensively and intensively urbanizing regions to armed anticolonial insurgencies and narcotics trafficking. For law-enforcement modernizers like Engle, the professionalization schema they applied to Third World police forces applied just as readily to many police forces across the United States. By the 1960s, professional policing did not possess two repertoires, one for deployment at home and one for deployment abroad. Rather, it possessed a single repertoire, which experts vigorously attempted to institute wherever they could.

Over the previous six years, Engle had developed a close personal and professional relationship with the NACCD's associate director of public safety, Arnold Sagalyn, who invited him to testify. In a wink to the Office of Public Safety (OPS) that Engle directed in the Agency for International Development (AID), Sagalyn named his section of the Kerner Commission, charged with investigating all aspects of the control of disorders, the Office of Public Safety.

OPS was a small outfit with a large impact.[15] For the purpose of counterinsurgency, it assisted police forces in at least fifty-two countries, and officers from seventy-seven countries attended its training academy, funded either by AID, the countries themselves, or the Central Intelligence Agency (CIA).[16] The goal of this police assistance effort was to prevent communist revolution and crime. Public safety advisors, as OPS technicians were called, reckoned that these were never distinct from each other. OPS would create the "first line of defense" against subversion, its advocates often remarked. During two decades, US public safety assistance reached over a million police officers around the globe in some way.

Engle's testimony constituted cutting-edge security expertise. Sagalyn ensured that the ideas of their cohort—a transnationally mobile ensemble of reformist law-enforcement experts—carried the day. To police the tide of revolution, this vanguard would revolutionize policing. The Departments of Justice and Defense reconfigured crowd-control guidance based on the NACCD recommendations, affecting nearly every police officer, soldier, and National Guardsman in the United States over the coming decade. This

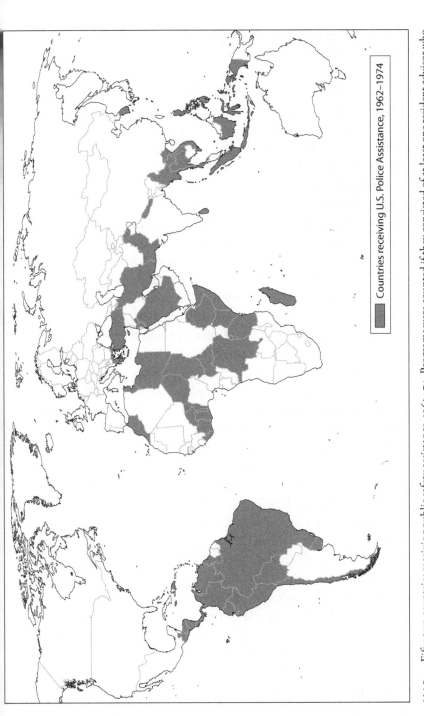

MAP 1. Fifty-two countries receiving public safety assistance, 1962–74. Programs were counted if they consisted of at least one resident advisor who stayed beyond an initial survey period. In the 1950s and 1960s, advisors conducted program surveys in other countries, like Argentina and Cambodia, that never received long-term technical assistance, and countries like Barbados, Gambia, India, Iraq, Malaysia, Paraguay, and Zambia sent trainees to the United States in the absence of an advisory program.

Countries receiving U.S. Police Assistance, 1962–1974

upgrading of "riot control" was a single phase of a far broader effort to transform law enforcement in response to crisis. These reforms recognized how integral policing practices were to state legitimacy. The technical refinement experts shepherded across borders aimed to shed any institutional confirmation of slapstick stereotypes of oafish, corrupt cops. To protect police power and insulate it from external control, reform was crucial. The key argument for the reformatting of law enforcement that these experts led from the 1950s into the 1970s was that what was needed to fight communist subversion was simply routine police work.

The public safety advisors under Engle's direction were woven into a powerful organized constituency of law-enforcement voices that was able to push President Johnson and Congress to act. This vanguard aimed to renew and redeem policing after years of Southern cops' complicity in lynchings of African American people and brutal crackdowns on civil rights protest, apparent nationwide inability to stanch rising crime rates, and, most recently, violent responses to Northern urban protest that transformed it into destructive unrest. The resulting federal War on Crime funneled federal money to the states to enhance, upgrade, and strengthen police, prisons, and courts. Self-interested, this constituency cohered institutionally and attained prominence through the Cold War battle against communism, which it waged at home and abroad.

Elites pushed, but law-enforcement professionals also made demands. Elite approval of cops' demands in turn shaped cops' own capacities to respond to legislators. Constituencies created doctrinal programs, and programs hailed constituencies.[17] The field of law enforcement was contested and changing, but the vocabulary of "law and order" originated with law-enforcement figures themselves. They were the ones who advocated a War on Crime, and they would wage it. Their easy assent to the use of the metaphor of "war" for their objectives shows that the territorial borders of the United States did not enclose their work.[18] These historical actors developed the political resources and institutional coherence to transform policing at home through their work on behalf of the national security state. As the War on Crime took shape, law-enforcement experts were already working hand in hand with liberal elites under the sign of counterinsurgency. At the close of the Johnson administration, an internal assessment declared that OPS's program across the globe contributed "the international dimension to the Administration's War on Crime by assisting police institutions to carry out their role as the first line of defense against those influences which seek to destroy free societies through the erosion of public order."[19]

Civilian policing met the demand for security against internal threats, or exogenous threats that manifested as subversion, both at home and overseas. The personnel, technologies, ideas, and repertoires that enabled the extension of policing overseas were the very same ones that reformed it at home. The elevation in prominence of a professionalized form of policing in both domains led to the domestic creation of new bureaucratic infrastructures, police training regimens, police technologies, and intellectual frameworks that transformed the state's coercive capacities. Engle, Sagalyn, IACP director Quinn Tamm, and other security experts discussed in this book participated in a multiyear effort to transform a key instrument of US foreign policy, the counterinsurgency program of police assistance to Third World countries, into a key instrument of domestic policy. Through a relentlessly comparative framework, the experts who developed the protocols and techniques of assuring order sanctified the foreign-domestic divide in assessing the seriousness of threats. Yet their practical recommendations obliterated it. US policing's leaders were insistently transnational in their orientation, outlook, and formation. Not incidental, occasional, or fleeting, overseas experiences shaped the marrow of US policing practices and institutions.

The centerpiece of the anticrime efforts of the Johnson and Richard M. Nixon presidencies was the Law Enforcement Assistance Administration (LEAA), created in 1968 by the Omnibus Crime Control and Safe Streets Act. It was a loose domestic analog of OPS. Thanks to Sagalyn, the overseas model of police assistance became the blueprint for the War on Crime. From April 1961, his primary responsibility was to oversee training and coordination for the Treasury Department's law-enforcement officers, and in this capacity he collaborated with OPS. This global perspective inspired him when he contacted Lyndon Johnson's aides to present a novel idea for resolving the apparent crisis of policing signaled by urban unrest in the summer of 1964. Sagalyn argued for the creation of federal grants to local law enforcement to upgrade capabilities for crime and disorder control, separate from funds for poverty alleviation. The goal was to empower law-enforcement agencies at the smallest scales, while not infringing on their autonomy. He invoked OPS efforts abroad as the model. Counterinsurgency bequeathed a skeletal bureaucratic form to achieve social order amid protests against racist social structures. Devolutionary assistance at arm's length would upgrade local law enforcement, funded by a centralized purse. The Frankenstein of fiscal federalism would be zapped to life. With expensive reform efforts proliferating, many police executives hankered after federal dollars, though they were reluctant to risk diminishing their local discretion. Organized by the nationwide IACP and in many individual statewide professional associations, they lined up to support a federal declaration of war against crime. A vocabulary honed through inflation of the communist threat would be unleashed on the crime threat. Legislators listened. This cohort perceived modern policing expertise not only as the cutting edge of state power, but also as a means of transforming it. Cold War national security policy was the acme of this approach, but its lineaments were already apparent in the Red Scare of 1919–1920, Prohibition, and the New Deal.[20]

National security had no essence, only motility. By the end of the 1940s, given the alarming possibility that the globe's loyalties might sway toward the communist camp, national security considerations transcended the practice seen in the two world wars. In those, after congressional consultation, the country had gravely declared war, with a concerted mobilization of science and industry. Now, waging the Cold War would entail the creation of the multifaceted national security state, shaped by executive-branch prerogative. It relied on a steady business outlook cemented by tentative compromises between capital and labor, underwriting national and international prosperity, "military Keynesianism" or "the warfare-welfare state."[21] Upon this foundation, the president and the NSC, guided by the CIA, made discretionary decisions to use coercive force. Not like the two big wars, those outliers of US history, the United States now returned to a pattern of war-making that preceded the country's founding and also characterized its relations with the world across its shifting borders in the late nineteenth and early twentieth centuries. The United States once again became a fighter of small wars. This approach amounted to the adoption of a police posture in foreign relations, the creation of a discretionary empire. To foster the welfare of a globally integrated system of states and ward off threats to capital accumulation, the United States' discretionary police power at the interstate level took the form of policing at the intrastate level.

Overseas, technical police assistance encapsulated President John F. Kennedy's New Frontier posture, a foreign policy no longer restricted to mutually assured destruction in the form of massive atomic retaliation. It was a policy newly attentive to the birth of new nations, within which differing approaches to socioeconomic development vied for adherents. Soviet premier Nikita Khrushchev had pledged support for "wars of national liberation" a mere fortnight before Kennedy's inauguration, which the new president interpreted as an incendiary taunt.[22] Kennedy's administration immediately set to work on the problem of insurgency. In this changing world situation, prevention of communist subversion was paramount. Modern, well-equipped, disciplined, and fair police forces were to be a tool of democracy, not tyranny. Police professionalization was the surest way for the United States to guarantee that the first line of defense against subversion would be strong, resolute, unafraid, honest, and innovative. The result, however, would be more efficient, individually structured, and molecular tyrannies.

Liberal politicians placed great faith in police assistance as a cheap, flexible, small-footprint instrument of US geopolitical power and suasion. President Dwight D. Eisenhower's preferred combination of strategic air–atomic defense and covert action steadily lost its appeal between the CIA-sponsored coups in Iran in 1953 and Guatemala in 1954 and the disaster of the Bay of Pigs invasion of Cuba in 1961—plus the concomitant unraveling of the French colonial empire, first in Indochina and then in Algeria. The story of overseas police assistance in its classic form, and therefore the story of this book, runs from 1954, when the NSC created the predecessor to OPS, to 1974, when Congress shut down OPS, a decade on either side of the Civil Rights Act of 1964. It was the two-decade period after *Brown v. Board of Education* and approximately between the Asian-African conference in Bandung and the proposal for a New International Economic Order. These decades saw the intertwining and enthronement of Keynesianism at home and developmentalism abroad. In a new global situation of decolonization and self-determination, up-to-date policing techniques would be the means to contain revolution; the same would be true of a domestic situation of implacable Black freedom demands met with attempts at legislative containment.

The professionalized form of policing became dominant both at home and abroad by the mid-1960s. Its hegemony derived from the laboratory of professionalization Third World countries offered, with lessons transmitted across national borders and across scales of government through institutions like the IACP and the LEAA, and later the Police Foundation and Police Executive Research Forum. These lessons appeared in professional periodicals and textbooks and would be taught in growing numbers of criminology schools. Professionalization of policing entailed specific recruitment standards, formal training, remuneration that allowed full-time and career-long service, and supervision according to a ranked system. Professionalizers often additionally aspired to introduce "functional specialization of personnel, use of modern technology, neutrality in law enforcement, responsible use of discretion, and a measure of autonomous self-regulation."[23] At a more basic level, professionalization meant new uniforms and new technologies, the routinization of everyday tasks as guided by data collection and research, the eradication of the graft that had long made up for cops' low pay, and the expectation that police be accorded the autonomy and respect expected by any other skilled professionals. Professionalization also created complex bureaucracies, with differing structures of accountability, which promoted street-level discretion while insulating command officers from responsibility for the situational despotism that resulted. Lessons learned confronting foreign subversive forces were not just repatriated to the United States as up-to-date domestic policing techniques, they had been developed all along in a comparative framework, constantly alert to the imminence of the appearance of new foreign threats at home and domestic alliances with foreign subversive forces.

At the apex of the machinery of US statecraft, invested in the practical and intellectual management of a new global dispensation after World War II—of the management of the contradiction between newly won political sovereignties and the unshakeable necessity of their rejection of communism—stood a cohort of security practitioners, educators, and theorists who made no strong distinction between how this management should proceed overseas or at home. The narrative nucleus of this book is the OPS public safety program, but this cohort's institutional and professional reach extended well beyond it. OPS was one key node in the global movement to professionalize policing. Before voters latched onto the phrase "war on crime," the public safety advisors who staffed OPS readily adopted it, an effort AID would internationalize.[24] For advocates of police modernization, security was equally unfinished at home and abroad. Security's assurance demanded both the martial "police action" and the peopling of security forces across the rapidly growing conurbations of distant lands, as well as the far reaches of the global countryside, with well-trained and -equipped professional constabularies on a US or "Anglo-Saxon" model. Contingencies of locale and rooted political structures would inevitably shape particular permutations, subject to an endless ongoing assessment of aid recipients' fitness for advancement to equality, but it has been a mistake of retrospective analysis to assume that territorial borders constrained the prospective vision these historical actors mobilized. If US streets could suddenly appear to those charged with pacifying them like foreign territory, expert pacification methods had already been developed according only one globe-spanning vision of security. The professional itineraries of public safety advisors as counterinsurgents, which crisscrossed oceans and state agencies alike, were integral to their identities as experts. Many political commentators have tossed around variations on the metaphor "global policeman" in both positive and negative evaluations of US geopolitical power without realizing that security experts in the post-1945 era ensured that the United States used beat cops to police the globe.

. . .

The Kennedy administration popularized the term "counterinsurgency." The neologism was barely a couple years old at Kennedy's inauguration. Its meaning was unsettled. Histories of counterinsurgency's elevation during the Kennedy years often center on preexisting rural approaches involving Army special forces, small-unit Marine Corps operations, or CIA covert infiltration tactics.[25] But these military approaches were not novel during this period, and, despite the resources devoted to them, they saw limited application.[26] Police assistance, which focused on the urban domain, had more extensive reach. *Badges Without Borders* demonstrates that counterinsurgency was a police-led, less-lethal, preemptive, and anticipatory approach to challenges to the state's legitimacy and its monopolization of means of violence. Despite the variegated institutional pathways to the enactment of security that existed historically, from cloak-and-dagger espionage to tanks to ballistic missiles, one in particular—police-led counterinsurgency—rose to prominence in the minds of key policymakers and strategists in the period this book covers.

How to achieve counterinsurgent goals was an object of intense bureaucratic and intellectual contestation. Arguments involved the CIA, the Pentagon, the NSC, and a bevy of social scientists, not to mention strong personalities who had the president's ear, including his brother Robert and advisors like Roger Hilsman and Maxwell Taylor. Lessons learned from comparisons with other empires' experiences, or in US war-making against Japan, seemed apposite to some of these officials. Practically, however, these figures drew upon the opportunities created and institutional knowledge held by the likes of Engle and his greatest ally and defender on the NSC, Robert W. Komer. They were the winners of these contests over the shape of counterinsurgency. Attorney General Robert Kennedy indicated his commitment to counterinsurgency by visiting OPS's Inter-American and International Police Academies. Kennedy loyalists later took these visits as evidence that the brothers would not have escalated the war in Vietnam, because of a commitment to the less bellicose approach constituted by public safety assistance.[27] But, at the time, Robert Kennedy's visits showed that the administration increasingly conferred the internal-defense mission on Engle's shop, with Komer at the helm. Engle and Komer supported police assistance around the globe before Kennedy's arrival in the Oval Office, and they kept it going for years after his assassination. They took advantage of Taylor's interest in a new, flexible defense posture, which Kennedy adopted, to create a strong institutional foundation for police assistance. What would keep the Cold War from becoming hot in Europe was counterinsurgency in Third World countries: uncompromising police, professionally trained and equipped on a US model. Keystone Kops could not catch communists.

The term "counterinsurgency" was a misnomer, because the insurgency to be countered was one that had not yet occurred. Counterinsurgency did, however, refer to specific practices that joined security imperatives to controlled uplift through economic development. In this sense, it embodied an older, plenary sense of the police power of the state, articulated to twentieth-century police institutions. Counterinsurgency was directed at a wide target—"the people"—and aimed to prevent civil violence, meaning symbolic and other violence against people and property that was organized, collective, and addressed to capital and state.[28] Such prevention occurred by investing the people in their own security through calibrated penalties and rewards. Yet this procedure often sparked the activities labeled insurgency. Atrocities commonly associated with counterinsurgency flowed from failures to achieve pacification.

Counterinsurgency was imperial. It occurred in dozens of countries that fell into the national-security purview where no US troops ever fired a gun. The behemoth national security state would weave together intelligence gathering and covert action with unhampered military outlays. The covert action component was originally intended to be "a small capability that could be activated when and where needed" according to "discretion," rather than a "large-scale continuing" operation in perpetuity.[29] Police assistance in the end allowed both. And it would economize, whereas military assistance and projections of military power remained costly and of dubious effectiveness. Direct US military action in South Vietnam was a short-lived, though devastating, deformation of and departure from the civilian, police-led, proxy-dependent thrust of the US counterinsurgency effort undertaken across the globe in over fifty other countries. Unlike blunt aerial bombings, police assistance enabled more surgical arrests, killings, and disappearances. Despite the expansion of US special forces, in practice counterinsurgency was marked by its joining of civilian development and security objectives and its delicate attempt to use surrogacy to avoid neocolonial maternity. To empower the police of often-weak allied regimes against internal challengers was also to prevent the United States from falling into older colonial patterns of direct rule. This effort had profound domestic consequences.

. . .

How is it possible to study these itineraries, and why have scholars occasionally assumed them but not substantiated them? State archives are divided according to the canonical separations this study is historicizing. "Foreign" and "domestic" are not ontologies. They are contested outcomes of social, political, and economic processes. By holding them together in a single analytic frame, *Badges Without Borders* takes the multifaceted connection between foreign and domestic as its case, rather than focusing on police in a particular city.[30] This book tracks the policies, people, and processes that crossed the divisions of civilian and military, foreign and domestic. This analysis demands more than metaphor and analogy—the analytic tools of these historical actors—including the construction of a bespoke new archive. It is the archive left in the restless tracks of counterinsurgent knowledge, a state-legitimating form of expertise, both scientific and experiential, that distilled the task of governance into the problem of maintaining order. This archive tracks motion across multiple divides, based on often declassified federal and state records, professional and popular publications, social-scientific studies and reports, oral histories and memoirs, and many other sources. Put another way, this is the archive of the police power, external to the place-bound records of individual police institutions, yet also inherent in the circuits of their connection. To examine this archive is to confront a security apparatus that declared the imminence of chaos, the necessity of its protection from chaos, and the moral rectitude of its protective tools. This archive must be analyzed cautiously, with an eye to the tensions it reveals, as the exorbitant violence of security methods cannot but ooze from the edges of the energetic efforts to portray them as reasonable and exacting. This methodological imperative calls for a new theorization of the police power attentive to its expanding scales of activity and routes of travel, where mismatches appear. It is found in the perceptive explanation of the US "concept" of police by a Bolivian official, at the First Inter-American Conference of Uniformed Police in Lima, Peru, in 1966, facilitated by OPS: "This concept states that . . . 'police' has no ascertainable limits. Everything that tends to promote the public welfare is a matter for the police and for that reason its objective is extraordinarily difficult to establish and extends to such extremes that its definition presents insuperable obstacles."[31]

The public safety program therefore offers a unique vantage on the troublesome relationship between the classic concept of police power and its expression in the everyday institutions we refer to as the police. Historically, police once addressed the most domestic of state functions: the maintenance of order and prosperity within a delimited jurisdiction. Canonically, for William Blackstone in the middle of the eighteenth century, police concerned "the due regulation and domestic order of the kingdom," focusing on "the minutiae of social life."[32] Police narrowed throughout the nineteenth century into the early twentieth century to the constabulary functions of coercive preemption of social disorder and apprehension and punishment of the disorderly, to produce the image of the local police officer who spent a lifetime on the beat in a given town or city. Even among those advocating a geographic extension of crime-fighting expertise, these place-bound conceptualizations have prevailed, typified in the idea, promulgated through US overseas police assistance, that professional police officers had to be service-oriented. In this way, dealing with crime for only a small fraction of the day or night, and with violence for an even smaller fraction, the police officer's work became concerned with small-scale social regulation.

At the heart of the expansive and the narrow variants of police is a presupposition that police is defined by its prudential ability to identify emergent threats to present order and future prosperity that may not be known in advance of their occurrence, and accordingly to decide how best to manage, squelch, or otherwise overcome such threats.[33] It is insistently downscaled and downscaling in its concerns, which find resonance in US ideologies and institutions of localized, devolved state power. Police's self-understanding consists of its productive ability to transform uncertainty into risk, which is quantifiable, measurable, predictable, manageable, and profitable.[34] The name for this complex of actions or inactions is discretion. But it also suggests limitlessness to police's range of objects. Police enumerates its concerns as they arise, with their enumeration always ending with an ellipsis.[35]

What Byron Engle's cohort achieved above all was the conjugation of technocratic, modernizing reforms of individual constabularies across the globe to an extension of the sovereign police power of the United States. The national security apparatus would determine if threats beyond borders were arising and devise tools to anticipate them and manage the threats they posed. In this sense, the police power—not trade, markets, raw materials, finance, or

FLOW CHART
DOCTRINE

AID/W
Office of Public Safety

| OPERATIONS DIVISION | TRAINING DIVISION | TECHNICAL SERV. DIV. |

INDUSTRY

POLICE FORCES

EDUCATIONAL INSTITUTIONS

DOCTRINE COMMITTEE

OTHER AGENCIES

IPG

THRU DOCTRINE CHANNELS EXPERIENCE

PUBLIC SAFETY ADVISOR USAID/COUNTRY X

FIGURE 1. Doctrine flow chart, June 1963. This OPS-produced chart shows the development of doctrine to be taught at the International Police Academy, illustrating flows across borders from "Country X" to experts within the United States. "AID/W" indicates the Washington, DC, headquarters of OPS. National Archives and Records Administration.

labor power—determined the form of the imperial project. All these other duly important drives depended on and presumed the ground-clearing, the formatting of social order, and the diminution of impediments to the realization of capital investment that the police power entails. The police power of the state inhered in the prerogative to determine where threats existed; the police function that public safety advisors fashioned was the result of the decisions policymakers above Engle made according to that prerogative.

The capacities of the state constrained police, but police reform reconfigured state capacities. The dispersion and repatriation of modalities of rule under the sign of police professionalization required and created discontinuous routes of state-formation, as well as chutes and ladders. Capacities and competencies to maintain order that developed in one setting arose in others, including domestically (fig. 1). Doctrine would be modified reflexively, based on experience on the ground, with transfer and translation going in multiple directions. The actual personnel behind these irruptions and the mechanics of these connections were not exceptional. They were central to the advancement of law-and-order politics and the rise of the carceral state. It was not simply that state capacities grew automatically through overseas escapades and then, via further automated turns of the imperial gears, reverberated domestically.[36] The active progenitors of state-formation can be tracked, along with how transfers across borders unfolded, and what the specific media and outcomes of the attendant transformations of the state were.

· · ·

Overseas police assistance took shape over decades. From President Theodore Roosevelt's day, with US interventions from the Philippines to Haiti to Nicaragua, and expanding greatly upon the occupation of Japan, where US officials developed the blueprint for Cold War police assistance, this quintessential form of US empire was decentralized and devolutionary. Global policing operated by proxy to self-consciously modernize other states' capacities, while extending the administrative concerns of state power to the control of the unknowable. Even before the postwar occupations, the Federal Bureau of Investigation secretly trained and equipped police in Latin America during World War II, while also gathering copious intelligence on both leftists and Axis-aligned targets.[37] Truman's creation of the CIA in 1947 pushed the Bureau out of police assistance. As early as 1948, a top Indonesian police official appealed to the State Department for help in maintaining "law and order" and "reducing Commies," which led to transfers of equipment like jeeps and uniforms, as well as "free ride" training visits for officers to the United States.[38] In the first half of the 1950s, US police who traveled abroad as advisors often did so under CIA, or sometimes Army or Treasury Department, auspices. The CIA trained 150 foreign police from 1951 to 1955 on an ad hoc basis, mostly in a modest Virginia farmhouse.[39]

In late 1954, the NSC called for a continuing police assistance, or public safety, program. First named 1290d, it was then branded the Overseas Internal Security Program in 1957. The Mutual Security Act funded it, not without snags. While on temporary duty in recipient countries, advisors often referred to the program as the Public Safety Division, as they had first called it in Japan. Its Washington office was the Civil Police Division of the Foreign Operations Administration. That outfit was renamed the

International Cooperation Administration in 1955 and finally reorganized as AID in September 1961. The IACP held a subcontract for training officers visiting the United States from 1955 until May 1963. AID's Inter-American Police Academy in the Panama Canal Zone opened its doors in July 1962 and closed them in April 1964; its Washington replacement, the International Police Academy, was inaugurated in December 1963. Via the high-level Special Group (Counter-Insurgency), OPS officially came into being in November 1962 and lasted until 1974; the lights were finally turned off in its academy in Washington the next year. The termination of OPS was the result of internationalist, anti-imperialist, left-wing organizing, exactly what OPS had been designed to thwart.

Most police reforms the United States exported to aid-recipient developing countries were Janus-faced. Counterinsurgency was their past and future purpose. Looking forward to proactive policing on a globe facing the tumult of anticolonial upheaval, the standard US big-city police techniques that police advisors took abroad with them after World War II had themselves been imported from the theater of colonial counterinsurgency on the Tropic of Cancer at the turn of the century, if not the so-called Indian Wars and the counterguerrilla campaigns of the Civil War. Some were capital-intensive. For example, the intelligence databank, containing population and crime statistics or crucial identifying characteristics, including fingerprints, of known criminal suspects was an innovation consciously repatriated from colonial counterinsurgency approaches. Also repatriated were telecommunications that linked dispersed police units to a centralized command. The very institution of centralized professional command and geographic divisions of patrol, which was crucial for professionalization to break the linkages between political ward bosses and police officers in their wards, drew on Army counterinsurgency, particularly in the Philippines. Labor-intensive patrol itself, the most recognizable feature of modern policing, had to be invented. The concentrated, data-driven approach to patrol, including across great distances using horses or bicycles and then eventually automobiles, was an inheritance of counterguerrilla warfare. Modern patrol merged labor- and capital-intensive versions of police reform. The most essential component of technical police assistance, a focus on rigorous training for new officers and in-service retraining for veterans, including in the use of firearms, was a novelty that defined professionalization of domestic policing after it had defined professionalization of soldiering in the colonies. The disciplined police officer on the beat in Los Angeles or Louisville was the progeny of the disciplined soldier or marine in Luzon or Las Segovias. When public safety advisors visited these same regions in the 1960s to upgrade police officers, they repatriated palimpsestic institutional knowledge that had passed through the way stations of metropolitan police departments. Mid-twentieth-century professionalized policing, which became the US bequest to world law enforcement, already had a colonial etiology.[40]

OPS possessed no enforcement powers of its own overseas. But extenuating circumstances did occur. Advisors coordinated protection of US dignitaries visiting aid-recipient countries, for instance. And sometimes stopping and frisking someone on the street was the best way for an advisor to train his advisees how to do it. Public safety advisors officially were not to usurp locals' roles and patrol the beat themselves. Instead, police assistance consisted of three primary domains: technical assistance such as help setting up telecommunications, crime laboratories, surveillance units, or prisons; material aid, by providing guns, tear gas, vehicles, radios, file cabinets, binoculars, or cameras; and training, either on-site, in the United States, or occasionally in third countries. Training included logistics, riot control, marksmanship, surveillance, and record-keeping. The ethos was one of "training trainers," so that the lessons imparted were sure to be replicated in other countries. "Regardless of what color policemen are, the suits they wear, what they call themselves, they are all the same," one OPS executive argued. "They are the same for the simple reason that a policeman exists in society as a behavior control mechanism. The basic principles of what is done, how it is done, and why it is done are the same."[41] He illuminated both sides of the shift from peer-to-peer diplomacy and cultural fellowship to interoperability and technical universalism that police assistance enacted from the 1950s into the 1970s.[42]

Everyday policing was an integral part of the fabrication of order in multiple states, in a heterogeneous mosaic of locally distinct situations that were nonetheless consonant with US global security and economic development imperatives. What united these situations of discretionary empire under US hegemony was not simply an extensive web of commercial and political relations across borders, but the very experience and expertise of security and development officials, who hopscotched from, for example, Wisconsin to Pennsylvania to Indonesia to Turkey to Brazil, compared situations compulsively, and enacted refinements and modifications based on what did and did not work in each setting.[43] OPS peaked in size by 1969, with over five hundred advisors, around a hundred of them based in Washington, DC. Of these, 68 percent had meritorious civil police experience of an average 13.5 years, with

12 percent possessing additional technical skills in areas such as telecommunications or motor-vehicle maintenance. The remainder had military police or special warfare experience. Over fifty advisors had prior experience teaching police administration or police science at the college or university level.[44] Tiny Walnut Creek, California, supplied several public safety advisors, after the police chief there, Leigh Brilliant, persuaded a cluster of his officers to join him overseas. This recruitment chain led to the oft-repeated claim that the "cement police" of middle-class Walnut Creek were ill-equipped to advise "rice paddy cops." Yet among this cluster of Walnut Creek officers were men with backgrounds in overseas counterintelligence and special warfare.[45] Almost three-fourths of 125 recruits to OPS in the eighteen months after February 1, 1965, already possessed "international" experience.[46] And, in any case, even Walnut Creek experienced the type of events that concerned public safety advisors overseas: in January 1968, and again 366 days later, bombs exploded outside Walnut Creek's police station.[47] US cops were not all parochial.

Like more familiar contingents of doctors without borders, these police who carried badges without borders aspired to a form of humanitarianism too. Where a mismatch erupted between classroom conditions and the settings of practical application, between prescriptions and perceived pathologies, the task of public safety assistance was to modify conditions on the ground so that they would adhere more closely to diagnostic criteria. When technical assistance succeeded, self-congratulatory OPS highlighted the protests that did not result in massacres. When technical assistance failed to achieve its goals, this result did not issue from inherent cultural incompatibility but was rather the outcome of political struggle, even by apparently willing recipients of US foreign aid, including reactionary representatives of the ancien régime hoping to maintain their comfortable sinecures. They could not take the money and run, but instead received pistols, motorcycles, handcuffs, teletypes, and flashlights—plus reams of translated training manuals based on widely available US policing textbooks.[48]

. . .

A multi-sided story of policing, race-making, and empire unfolds in the following chapters, beginning with a grounded theoretical exploration of the changes—propelled by post-1945 US empire and concomitant domestic freedom struggles—in the relationship of policing and racism. Chapter 1 recasts the Cold War as a US-superintended effort to maintain hierarchy and social order on a decolonizing globe. A discourse of modernization would combine with the practice of devolutionary policing by proxy to mark the contours of this new global arrangement. While situating these shifts in relation to a long history of imperial governance challenges the United States first faced in the Indian Wars, this chapter's discussion outlines how technical reformism and developmentalism in policing did not supersede racism but became the engine of a reformatted liberal racial covenant at home and abroad.

Byron Engle was one standout figure among a broad complement of law-enforcement professionalizers active in the 1940s and 1950s, the subject of chapter 2. Across the twentieth century, there were two generations of these reformers. One was active during the 1920s, led by August Vollmer, and a much more extensive second one achieved its strongest effect during the 1960s, influenced by Vollmer's protégé Orlando W. Wilson. This ecosystem already tended toward globalism. After Engle's start overseas in occupied Japan, which conferred lessons in how to decentralize the police power from a centralized governing node, he spent over a decade working at the border between overt and covert action. Robert Komer, a bureaucratic infighter, then lashed the work of police modernization Engle and his colleagues were already supervising to the urgency of Kennedy's New Frontier. As chapter 3 details, in 1961 and 1962, Komer guided Engle into a bureaucratic safe harbor, creating OPS in AID, while putting police assistance at the center of the global counterinsurgency mission.

Around this time, Engle met Sagalyn and empowered him. Sagalyn, in turn, brought his knowledge of OPS to Lyndon Johnson's aides who were concerned with devising a War on Crime in 1964. The eventual shape of the LEAA, after legislative twists and turns, bore a striking resemblance to Sagalyn's blueprints, as chapter 4 explains. Sagalyn also successfully urged reliance on OPS experts to help professionalize underprepared police at home. As organizations like OPS and the IACP spread the professionalization orthodoxy across borders, overseas implementation in turn shaped the orthodoxy's development at home.

Chapter 5 details the everyday experience of police advisors overseas, how public safety was crafted as part of a commitment to counterinsurgency, bringing together political repression with positive forms of social regulation. This chapter reveals the frequent contradictions between the public safety mission of reform, de-escalation, and professionalization and the actuality of policing unruly zones and confronting revolutionary activity. It ranges from death squads and forced disappearances to OPS adherence to the mandate for political participation in community development.

Chapters 6, 7, and 8 go on to illustrate the global fraternity of policing and how overseas assistance affected reforms at home, including the competition among various personalities and institutions for leadership in law enforcement. Over the nearly decade and a half of OPS operations overseas, advisors traveled back and forth across borders, met and corresponded continually with law-enforcement leaders at home, and developed new techniques and technologies that would become widely adopted, including most directly in riot control. At the same time, other police leaders, social scientists, and hangers-on became deeply interested in trying to translate overseas experience into domestic practice, which exceeded but also replicated some of the work OPS was doing. Centralized emergency-response training, the deployment of the chemical weapon or "tear gas" CS, and the emergence of the Special Weapons and Tactics unit all relied on OPS efforts. Riot-control training realized the imperatives of the War on Crime's federalism, involving OPS, Army facilities, and California's Specialized Training Institute (chapter 6). Widespread use of CS in South Vietnam, particularly to "flush" people out from hiding, shaped new reliance on the weapon at home. New formulations and delivery methods of this chemical replaced the bayonet and buckshot in crowd control (chapter 7). And from Los Angeles, with its internationally mobile police department, William Parker and Daryl Gates pitched their expertise in maintaining order to wide audiences (chapter 8). As the intensity and duration of unrest worsened throughout the 1960s in the United States, civilian and military leaders adopted the recommendations of the internationalists who advised other countries. Almost overnight, riot-control orthodoxy at home departed from old dogmas, to embrace the new orthodoxy propagated abroad. Intelligence-led deployments and preemptive tactics became routine in training, if not always in practice. The fear of losing mass loyalty, which characterized US counterinsurgency theory, also shaped US policing's commitment to reformism. Training, technologies, and tactics for emergency situations grew from overseas counterinsurgency and became integrated into everyday policing in the United States, recalibrating racialized social control.

Meanwhile, continual crises demanded constant rethinking of counterinsurgency practice. Engle, Komer, and OPS remained centrally involved with new demands imposed by emergent situations on the ground in places like South Vietnam, but their work had also already devised answers to situations of disorder that intellectuals later tried to tackle. Chapter 9 examines social-scientific debates around counterinsurgency and crime. OPS practice prefigured contending positions in intellectual debates around so-called rational-actor or cost-benefit counterinsurgency. These highly coercive tactics would filter into domestic policing practice in guise of "broken windows" policing.

In conclusion, amid scandal and focused protest, Congress terminated overseas police assistance. The targets of OPS's public safety program defeated it. Many public safety advisors sought new law-enforcement careers, as police chiefs, prison wardens, riot-control trainers, private eyes, or traffic consultants. The OPS counterinsurgency mission also became internalized within new crime-control agencies, including the LEAA and Drug Enforcement Administration, which continually identified novel international criminal threats.

Badges Without Borders outlines how the national security state has shaped everyday life on American streets by enrolling local constables in the limitless project of assuring global security. Given the suturing of foreign and domestic spheres that police enabled, at stake is the question of what a transformative politics will look like, and how it will address a global map of policing. Insights into the depth of these connections necessitate new questions, new organizational forms and tactics, and new solidarities. Simply put, this book demonstrates that to dismantle the carceral state, the national security state will also have to be dismantled. If police reformers have understood their task to be refining policing so as to disarm revolutionary exhortations and neutralize radical movements all over the globe, then the purpose of reformism at home becomes clearer. To weaken the hold of police reform on the imagination, in response to every outrageous encounter between police and policed, contemporary police reform as a global project of US power will have be constrained. More broadly, the discretionary empire the United States built after World War II has been the precondition of the empire of discretion that police enforce daily on US streets. It has provided experience, resources, and legitimacy for the continual expansion of police power. The lives of the racially marginalized and economically vulnerable in the United States are shaped by dragnet identity checks and street stops, computerized databases of population information, SWAT raids, "nonlethal" weapons like tear gas, uncompromising restraints on political protest and agitation, and the constant suspicion that complaint about these circumstances is less politics than incipient criminality. The roots of these conditions and these apparatuses lie in the national security state's efforts to bring law and order to the globe. Those efforts took the form of counterinsurgency because, beneath superpower rivalry, millions of people around the world tried to forge a new path to freedom. The United States could not fight a hot war against all of these everyday people who took up the mantle of revolution, but its security thinkers tried mightily to figure out how to stymie these efforts. It turned out that halting revolutionaries actually meant stopping and frisking their neighbors.

Across the globe, counterinsurgency was policing. At home, policing was counterinsurgency.

ONE

Rethinking Race and Policing in Imperial Perspective

IN 1944, THE INTERNATIONAL CITY MANAGERS' Association enlisted a midwestern police chief, Theo E. Hall, and an anthropologist of Pacific island cultures, Joseph E. Weckler, to coauthor a report titled *The Police and Minority Groups: A Program to Prevent Disorder and to Improve Relations Between Different Racial, Religious, and National Groups*, which focused on urban unrest. Historically a white mob attack on Black people, "rioting" was now becoming a form of Black protest and self-defense, as in Harlem in August 1943, a "precursor" to unrest of the 1960s.[1] In the former type of riot, police failed to protect Black populations from white mobs; in the new form, police violence against Black people spurred unrest. Given that riots were extremely difficult to manage once they exploded, Hall and Weckler argued, they needed to be prevented. This idea would become public safety orthodoxy, and Hall became the acting director of the overseas police assistance program in the 1950s, prior to its consolidation as the Office of Public Safety. During the June 1943 riots in Detroit and Los Angeles, Hall and Weckler observed, "minority peoples" could not depend on police for "protection." Such "intergroup" clashes, the contemporary term for racial violence, were not only a problem at home, they had the potential to bring about intergroup clashes of a different order: "Such disorders . . . undermine our influence with millions of our non-white Allies and neutrals and give our enemies material for effective propaganda against us."[2] The pamphlet recommended a number of professionalizing reforms pertaining to police training, organization, and tactics in unrest. Published around the same time as Gunnar Myrdal's landmark study *An American Dilemma: The Negro Problem and Modern Democracy* for the Carnegie Corporation, "The Police and Minority Groups" entered police training curricula across the country, distributed by the

International Association of Chiefs of Police. Sometimes trainers paired it with Myrdal's work.³ The short pamphlet and the extensive study both outlined a new governing approach to civil rights in the United States that situated the challenge in a global context. Events soon proved them prescient.

In 1946, a white mob in Georgia gunned down George Dorsey, a Black veteran of World War II, and three companions, galvanizing new Black demands for rights and freedom. How could a man who had fought against tyranny abroad not be spared from it at home? A dozen years later, the Congress of Racial Equality lobbied the US secretary of state on behalf of a Black man named Jimmy Wilson, condemned to death in Alabama after a conviction for a small theft. The secretary's attention, like that of the National Association for the Advancement of Colored People, focused on how world opinion, particularly in West Africa, interpreted this sentence. These stories are central to the narrative of Cold War civil rights: the superpower clash between the Soviet Union and the United States spotlighted US racial injustice, particularly in the South, which compelled diplomats and statesmen to take up the cause of civil rights, lest racist brutality give the Soviet Union a competitive advantage in garnering adherents among the "darker nations," in the phrase of W. E. B. Du Bois.⁴

The analysis of Cold War civil rights hinges on a mismatch. Racial inequality at home did not comport with a US foreign policy drained of racism, newly attempting global stewardship without recourse to racist ideology. Racial hierarchy as the principle of global organization and mode of managing interstate relations was supposed to conclude with the defeat of the Axis powers, the ongoing dissolution of European imperialisms, and the rise of the United States to leadership of a multilateral global system of sovereign states. In place of racial development, economic and political development would be the ordering principle and objective, with US technical assistance as the means of enlarging and refining state and communal capacities.⁵ But domestic racism undermined this new leadership role, making its elimination a geopolitical necessity. Myrdal's *An American Dilemma* defined this liberal approach. In contrast, a dissenting analysis emphasizes how anticommunism that comported with Myrdal's thinking constrained Black freedom movements and how Black voices highlighted US hypocrisy and built solidarities among victims of racism at home and imperialism abroad.⁶

Between elites and the grassroots, though, stood the first line of defense: cops. The centrality of US police experts to this reshaped world-system suggests the need for a closer look at the police role in reshaping race on a global scale. The story of Cold War civil rights might also begin with technical police assistance, "the most far-reaching" of all types of technical assistance "in its effect on the lives of people of the free world," a high-ranking official boasted.[7] Not only the foreign-policy elite, but police too were acutely sensitive to how racist violence at home would be perceived overseas. The very police institutions where these experts learned their trade, from Kansas City to New York City, Los Angeles to Greensboro, NC, were frontline enforcers of the US racial order—an uneven distribution of civic participation, citizenship, commerce, property, and sexual intimacies. World War II swept many of these cops off their beats to far-off lands, and after it ended, they would take responsibility for race management at home and abroad, suturing the two domains. Race management entailed preserving racial hierarchy, preventing outright rebellion against it. Working with and for the State Department, however, these security experts were aware that they would be judged based on how they managed grassroots revolts at home and abroad. They aimed to transform subjectivities for the prevention of disorder by reforming policing. In the process, the meaning of race itself would be transformed. World War II did not usher in a solution to what Du Bois called "the social problem of the twentieth century," namely, "the relation of the civilized world to the dark races of mankind."[8] What would race management entail in a postcolonial world-system consisting not of European empires but of sovereign states and international institutions? Myrdal's *American Dilemma* contemplated the overcoming of racism at home and in international affairs, according to a putatively race-neutral discourse of development, but Theo Hall's global travels as a policing expert indicated that the machinery of race management would not vanish as quickly as its ideology.

For security experts, the challenge of the post-1945 era was how to effect "internal defense" exogenously, to maintain rule while creating sovereign, self-governing power in a multilateral system. At home, police institutions were soon attempting to liquidate the appearance of bias in their ranks. Police forces controlled by partisan political machines had been instruments for the social advancement of minoritized European ethnic groups, but professionalization efforts weakened this control. Now, Hall and Weckler advocated hiring more African American, Mexican American, Puerto Rican, and other darker-skinned cops. Overseas, the solution was to delegate responsibility for security to a stratum of the subject population, who might better achieve legitimacy with US technical assistance, a strategy that had long structured small wars. The arrival of foreign police officers on US shores for training purposes alerted police professionalizers to the need to achieve order other than by outright racial repression. Strategies for overcoming racism within the institutional matrix of policing went hand in hand with strategies for overcoming the appearance of racism by police. Pressure to end the appearance of racism *by* police resulted in efforts to end the appearance of racism *within* police institutions.[9]

Before World War II's end, it was difficult to predict how US national-security thinkers would come to rely on police in the coming decades, favoring efficient and diligent constabulary forces to ensure order in far-flung but strategically important former colonies in Asia and Africa and the republics of Latin America. Du Bois and thinkers like him realized that even if the United States did not replicate prior colonialisms, the challenges to existing forms of domination posed by popular anticolonial insurgencies were likely to modify US racial hegemony.[10] Decentralized US technical assistance would constitute an imperialism without imperialists that did not require staffing distant jurisdictions with white supremacist colonial officers, because local police would protect the emergent discretionary empire. This new situation matched the fortunes of white supremacy at home, which would be slowly remolded toward a "racism without racists": persistent patterns of inequality no longer legitimated by open avowals of bigotry.[11] The American Century was supposed to usher in a new epoch of peace and freedom, with European tyrannies vanquished, but Du Bois and others observed that the United States, the rising steward of a remade global order, was itself captive to its own color line, which prevented it from achieving "rational and progressive" democracy.[12]

Police, who had been so deeply responsible for enforcing the color line, would now, after 1945, become the instruments of the spread of a color-blind Americanism abroad. In his Philadelphia ward, Du Bois recalled, the "police were our government," not guarantors of the safety of Black people.[13] The same had been true of the European colonies, too, and would be of US client states. But this enrollment of the police apparatus into a new imperial situation of social hierarchy not necessarily determined by color changed the relationship of police activity and racial formation, modulating the dimensions of rule, while also requiring renovation of the apparatus itself. Sheer racial repression and subjugation would be combined with more subtle and constructive forms of pacification and subject formation. These efforts relied on the conscription of darker peoples into their own racial management.

In 1948, CIA analysts also saw race and decolonization as shaping the predicament US global power faced. A CIA paper, "The Break-Up of the Colonial Empires and Its Implications for US Security," argued that the European colonial system had emerged from World War II badly damaged and was likely to disintegrate further, creating "a power vacuum in the Near and Far East" that the United States would not necessarily be able to fill. Obstacles to the formation of alliances between the United States and Europe's former colonies were manifold. The new nations would likely align politically to act along coalition lines, based on ethno-religious solidarities and shared economic aspirations. Among the chief hurdles to easy conciliation between the new nations and the United States was "racial antagonism": Japan's successes in the Russo-Japanese war and World War II had "punctured the myth of white superiority," and "a deep-seated racial hostility of native populations toward their white overlords" had "taken the form of a reaction against 'white superiority.'" This reaction was to the advantage of the Soviet Union, which maintained "an assimilative racial policy" and could "represent itself to colonial peoples as largely Asiatic," thereby avoiding "the resentment of colored toward white peoples." In contrast, "US treatment of its Negroes, powerfully played up by Soviet propaganda, embarrasses the US on this issue."[14]

After fostering an ideology of self-government, Washington risked charges of hypocrisy if it supported European powers struggling to hold on to their remaining colonies, the CIA analysis cautioned. "US encouragement of colonial self-determination and economic development may itself incur the charge of US imperialism and run the risk of alienating the colonial powers," but "the US may be unable to afford to let its policy on colonial issues be swayed by the colonial powers if such support of its allies tends to alienate the dependent peoples and other non-European countries."[15] A generation of political leaders and intellectuals in the new nations confirmed this CIA analysis, among them Kwame Nkrumah and Walter Rodney.[16]

The CIA recognized the need for policymakers to understand the interconnections among peripheral nations, and how postcolonial solidarity and institutional coalitions would make use of emerging fora, especially the United Nations and the new Organization of American States, formed amid violent upheaval in Colombia a few months earlier in 1948. Too robust and aggressive a posture would create antagonism; too flimsy a security apparatus would be easily outsmarted and outgunned. Stability, security, and political deference to the United States were unlikely to be achieved by direct US intervention. Yet in trying to fashion a favorable global integument, US security assistance often landed in furrows already plowed by prior colonial powers, strengthened authoritarian militaries, and bolstered caudillos, tycoons, and compradors.

Robert Komer, a CIA analyst for fourteen years, from the time of the agency's founding until he entered the Kennedy administration in 1961, took note of this 1948 paper, which was the only document from his early days at the CIA that he left behind amid a disorganized jumble of personal papers.[17] He would devise the Special Group (Counter-Insurgency), and the Office of Public Safety that it oversaw, to work within the difficult parameters the CIA analysis outlined.

POLICE ASSISTANCE AND THE TANGLE
OF RACIALIZATION

"Anywhere you go, a cop is a cop," public safety advisor John F. Manopoli declared. "There is an odd kind of professional brotherhood."[18] Manopoli spoke French (albeit with a Bronx accent), which was helpful in achieving a rapport with police in Burundi, the Congo, Chad, Côte d'Ivoire (Ivory Coast), Rwanda, and South Vietnam, if not so much in Liberia and Nicaragua.

Yet beneath that fraternal feeling a risk calculus unfolded, as did a practical assessment of security capabilities to contain risk. The calculus was inscribed, for example, in the dry technical reports outlining each nation's limitations that preceded the initiation of a police assistance mission. Writing these reports was Manopoli's professional specialty. Equality, ever provisional, was still subject to risk analysis. Inequality registered as a criminalized threat to equality, but also as an impediment to the necessary technical upgrading of police institutions. One such impediment was, for example, "the temperament of Latin people."[19] Not all advisors were convinced that a universal police science was possible, even as they nurtured the global fraternity of police. There was a "vast difference in thought processes between oriental and occidental minds," one declared. Prepackaged lessons might be "wasted" or even "counterproductive." "What might placate an American mob might infuriate one in Bangkok, Saigon or Djakarta."[20] Officers' fellowship was riven by anxieties about the development of state capacity, which advisors often scripted through racialized metonymy as the personal capacities of advisees.

The public safety program had no great ambitions in francophone Africa. As chief of the Congo program, which lasted fourteen years, Manopoli did not expect it to be a "deluxe job." In 1965, basic police tasks were the goal of what became Africa's costliest police assistance effort. A mere decade earlier, as a New York State police officer, Manopoli had witnessed his own agency's rapid modernization, with the advent of cream-and-blue police cars, festooned for the first time with sirens and flashing lights, patrolling the Dewey Thruway, the new highway across New York State. Police horses were put out to pasture, spurs and riding breeches were retired. The .38 special revolver replaced the old Colt .45 as the troopers' standard firearm.

Though recently achieved, the standard set by New York State was not Manopoli's benchmark. "We are not trying to turn out criminologists, or give them polygraphs, or laboratories, or fingerprint files. We are just trying to get a functioning police force," Manopoli explained about the Congo program. The line between basic functioning and higher-order police science was blurry, however. It would be redrawn according to exigencies on the ground. In this flexibility inhered the volatility of the risk calculus of racial ascription that would no longer herald itself in racial terms. A global police brotherhood confronted a globally active but locally embedded threat. But it was not simply that racially demarcated dishonor became alchemized into criminal disposition; suspicions fell on foreign police themselves. The anticommunist bulwark that the United States needed around the globe could be permeable if it remained underdeveloped. Although the police might lag among the suite of governing institutions afforded US technical assistance, and, as Manopoli confirmed, be ineligible for the most advanced approaches, the local police apparatus had to serve societal modernization. US national security depended on it.

An even more explicitly suspicious version of risk-aware fellowship could be found as late as 1963 in *Police* magazine. Ruminating on police training in the "Far East," an experienced military police operator named Frank Tenny lamented that the public safety advisor had to confront the problem of convincing "the local police that what he is teaching them is truly the practical; the sensible; the successful way." Nevertheless, "a goodly number of men—Malay, Sino, Caucasian," even if though sometimes from strata with criminal propensities, were demonstrating that "modern, honest law enforcement" was possible. When it came to the white cop's advisory burden, it was as yet still uncertain whether "Kipling was right," Tenny observed cryptically. Capacity for progress remained impaired by a frequent tendency to be refractory toward it.[21] The involvement of cynical cops like Tenny in the discretionary project of US empire strained its liberal scaffolding.

These assessments illustrate three strands of the relationship of policing and race in this period of reformulated international relations. The braiding tightened even as it was rewoven. The familiar, widespread critique of police turns on its historical connection to racial oppression.[22] Police grew alongside chattel slavery as an institution in the United States concerned with preventing rebellion, self-emancipation, and even basic Black sociality. It blossomed into a profession due to ruling-class demands for the control of restive minoritized groups with the advance of industrial capitalism and Jim Crow racial segregation. Police enforced both legal and extralegal racial rule directly, unaccountable to those at their mercy. Discretionary despotism defined policing. That was the first strand. But police and race-making were braided in other ways.

White police institutions attempted to achieve racial rule by inviting select Black and brown men into the fraternity.[23] That was the second strand. Early efforts at professionalization recognized that police legitimacy and public compliance with police might be enhanced if the cops enforcing order resembled the people they were policing. In 1900, however, the overall number of Black police officers in the country was nearing its post-Reconstruction nadir—Du Bois counted only sixty-two Black police officers (among over four thousand) in Philadelphia in the late 1890s, none of whom ranked higher than patrolman.[24] Nationally, police integration was uneven, halting, and tentative throughout the twentieth century, and it remains incomplete to this day.

African-American veterans of the Spanish-American War were, however, recruited to municipal police forces. One of the first Black officers in Kansas City, Missouri, was Lafayette Tillman, who had been a member of a segregated Army infantry regiment responsible for pacification in the Philippines. Black officers like him primarily, but not exclusively, patrolled Black sections of town.[25] The next limited surge of police integrations occurred after World War II, particularly in certain Southern jurisdictions, relying on Black veterans. A greater surge followed in the 1960s, marked by Secretary of Defense Robert McNamara's Project Transition, meant to place Black veterans of the US war in Vietnam on police forces.[26]

Police institutions were subject to external social pressures and retorted with professionalizing attempts to solidify their legitimacy and appearance of accountability. Professionalization might have alleviated racism internally, but it actually gave it new purchase. Black officers often faced vicious abuse from their white counterparts. The end of hiring via patronage could have helped dampen inequality, with new rigorous civil-service standards for hiring as the substitute. Instead, these hiring standards provided new terms of racial disqualification and exclusion. Insofar as professionalization efforts often aimed for a consolidated command structure, which recommended ending patrol apportionment and supervision according to ethnicity, the effect was to narrow the already limited opportunities for Black and brown officers to be hired or to rise in the ranks. And everyday bigotry and abuse within departments never disappeared. These professional arrangements did not overcome white primacy; they reconfigured it.

The enrollment of Black veterans of imperial excursions highlights a third aspect of the relationship of police and race-making: police reform simultaneously aimed to bolster the legitimacy of the institution and rehearse new modes of regulating and producing social order. Imperialism heightened the social tensions police at home faced by changing the demographic composition of the United States, while fomenting subaltern solidarities across borders. Imperial efforts at social control variously rewrote, undermined, and upheld racial distinctions overseas. Political demands of the era of decolonization and the communist confrontation, though, shifted the terms of the security calculus at home. White business and political leaders relied on police to stymie Black political organization and radical demands, even though racist brutality undermined the global goodwill Washington sought in the ideological battle against Moscow, Beijing, and Havana. Like the elective bonds of atoms, constantly in motion, police power continuously tangled with racial difference. The challenges racial otherness posed had to be confronted in the act of policing and managed in the institutional matrix of police. Social difference rent the institution itself at home and abroad. The US national security state's project of attaining global hegemony needed police proxies, but it would be caught in the reconfiguration of racial relations on a global scale even as the compound of crime and subversion formed the axis of racialization.

The public safety program developed different strategies to cope with the difficulties of using white cops to train darker proxies. Training police in their own countries was one option, but many nations lacked the specialized facilities needed—indeed, had they possessed them, they would not have been receiving US police assistance in the first place. Another approach was to use a centralized academy overseas. AID operated the Inter-American Police Academy (IAPA) in the Panama Canal Zone for police from around Latin America for a few years. Training facilities for Latin American military, including the predecessor to the School of the Americas, were adjacent.[27] Holmes Alexander, a syndicated columnist, noted that a "very tough cop" employed by the IAPA was trying to change the Latin American police mentality to minimize "brutality." This Latino advisor, formerly a Los Angeles county narcotics officer, "clearly enjoyed" his job and punctuated his lecture with "a wicked-looking riot stick."[28] The lessons' tone and even the expert publications distributed were coarse and sometimes taught forensic techniques considered obsolete domestically, like the typology of facial features called "Bertillonage."[29] After destructive unrest in Panama in January 1964, which included attacks on IAPA instructors and damage to the school's buildings, the academy needed to relocate. Public safety officials were already searching for a new location, not least because attendees were subject to "emotional and inflammatory anti-US propaganda" on the radio and when they met ordinary Panamanians. OPS director Byron Engle suggested moving the IAPA to an Air Force base in Harlingen, Texas. "About 50% of the people in Harlingen are of Mexican/American extraction and speak Spanish," he noted. "The City Manager advises that there is absolutely no discrimination and all facilities are completely integrated, including people with Negroid features or of Negro extraction."[30]

The need to train officers from sub-Saharan Africa magnified the problem. The solution was to train African and Afro-Latino cops in Washington, DC, sometimes called "chocolate city." Some public safety advisors were fluent Spanish speakers, especially those from Arizona, California, New Mexico, and Texas, and those who had begun their law-enforcement careers with the Border Patrol. When it came to sub-Saharan Africa, though, none of the advisors resembled the trainees. The requirement that new advisors possess a minimum of five years of prior command experience, meaning lieutenant rank or higher, limited the pool of Black recruits. Racial prejudice that African trainees might face if dispersed around the country was one reason AID opened the International Police Academy (IPA) in the nation's capital in a decommissioned Georgetown trolley barn. Prior to the academy's opening, the IACP facilitated visits of foreign trainees to the United States for tours of police facilities, ride-alongs, and specialized classes. Dark-skinned police officials on training junkets to US station houses were not always assured a warm welcome. "Participants from many of the African Republics should be kept out of the South," a reviewer of the IACP program warned in 1962. He also cautioned against "sending an officer from an Arab country" to New York City's police department, with its "good proportion of Jewish personnel."[31] One advisor reported complaints he heard about visiting police, such as: "My God, I've got these damn 'Gooks' coming out my ears." A colleague scolded him for recording this quotation in writing, but AID eventually adopted his recommendation of a centralized academy as a way to deal with the problem.[32] Centralized training in Washington not only resolved problems of organization and systematicity but also fended off potential encounters with racial prejudice.[33] Moreover, there was a degree of reciprocity. "We learn from them, too," a New York City police officer told a journalist, speaking of trainees from around the world.[34] Racial clashes tempered by conviviality highlighted the contradictory position of foreign police assistance on a globe undergoing racial upheaval.

The contrast between the public safety mission of upgrading police capabilities and local fears of street crime in Washington, DC, fueled congressional attacks on foreign aid. In a 1963 hearing of the House Subcommittee on Inter-American Affairs, Representative H. R. Gross (R-IA) used the threat of crime to berate the Kennedy administration's foreign policy. Hoping to justify cutting the foreign aid budget, Gross asked Byron Engle whether Latin American officers trained in the Panama Canal Zone might be brought to Washington to deal with "the situation we have here." Why, he wondered, "should we be training police down in Panama to curb lawlessness and subversion," considering the problems "unfolding in the District of Columbia"? Foreign police were probably not "impressed . . . with our inability to curb lawless elements right here." Armistead I. Selden Jr., a segregationist Democrat from Alabama, who led the subcommittee, expressed envy that unlike police at home, police in Latin America did not have to adhere to "certain court decisions," concerning suspects' procedural rights. Engle tried to assuage the representatives' worries that the training program was insufficiently dedicated to countersubversion and too focused on fighting crime, noting that the "principles of good police management and good investigative techniques" were meant to be "applied to control of subversives."[35]

Although applications from qualified US policewomen occasionally arrived in Washington, female public safety advisors were out of the question.

FIGURE 2. Byron Engle and a Nigerian official, Malam Ibrahim Nock, February 2, 1971. Although OPS did not mount an advisory mission in Nigeria, the country received a $3.4 million loan for the construction of a police college, guided by OPS. Keystone Pictures USA / Alamy Stock Photo.

In 1959, an internal newsletter edited by Theo Hall, the expert on intergroup relations, asked advisors in the field to indicate whether countries receiving aid needed female US advisors, adding: "A negative answer is requested."[36] The first woman to attend the IPA, Superintendent Gladys Philip Gathoni, from Nairobi, Kenya, arrived to some fanfare early in 1972.[37]

WHAT RACISM DOES

Counterinsurgency, policing, and law enforcement were not static in the Cold War period; they were in the throes of upheaval themselves due to anti-colonial movements overseas and their analogs at home. Shaped by super-power deadlock, instability was the Cold War's crux: decolonization bred a new arrangement of formally color-blind interstate equality and de facto economic and political inequality, whose effects were labeled crime and sub-version.[38] The home situation was the mirror, with post-1965 formal equality of US citizens but persistent, racialized inequality in housing, education, jobs, and healthcare. Police in this situation were not passive recipients of demands from above, but actively made demands on lawmakers and fought political battles against limits on their activities. They shifted the meaning of crime itself through reference to emergent forms of social and political protest. Yet police also treated crime as presocial and constant. They bracketed other forms of state intervention, insisting crime would fall only thanks to the focused efforts of expert policing. Law-enforcement leaders described themselves as reactive, when they were insistently proactive, shaping political signifiers. Crime, and its constant companion in this period, subversion, became the political vocabulary and governing grammar through which unequal property relations within, and grafted upon, a matrix of racial difference would be understood, justified, and reproduced. Race constituted not a substance or an essence but "a discourse of vacillations," and there was an intrinsic relation between this flexibility and the police power of the state, the highly flexible, unlimited, vacillating, sticky, and proactive set of actions taken to ensure the current well-being and future prosperity of the population.[39] Police power relied on two static reifications, crime and race, which became mutual surrogates. Construed as a fungible activity intended to achieve security, policing was an engine of intertwining discourses and practices of criminalization and racialization.[40]

Typically, in relation to policing, race is understood as cause, when it should be understood as effect. The transposition of US policing practices overseas, through training and technical assistance, to countries with dramatically different histories of inequality highlights this paradox. Most social analysts recognize race not to be grounded in biology, nor directly associated with any objective difference in ability or other attributes. Yet common analyses understand police (or prosecutors, judges, and juries) to use racial demarcation as a decision-making surrogate. Racial difference signals a threat of insecurity. This racist thinking fixes on existing group characteristics and mobilizes these to activate invidious social consequences. Racial demarcation, in this understanding, reinforces racial stratification. Such explanations, however, struggle to theorize how race came to exist in the first place without resorting to discredited scientific accounts of racial origins, or without positing an infinite regress to identical antecedent conditions. They also are inadequate to explain how policing might work similarly in contexts without the specific US experience of racism and policing. Still, it is important to recognize that the prospective use of race in policing has pertinent effects, layered on histories of racism. Yet a problem arises for analysts who use this interpretation when they know race is not real, but presume the condition it wrongly indexes is. Racial difference is not real, but insecurity is.[41] Widespread criticisms of policing in the United States argue that police should not "profile," treating racial characteristics as probable cause or as "a factor in discretionary decision making," as allowed by the Supreme Court decision *United States v. Brignoni-Ponce* (1975).[42] The criticisms turn on whether race is an effective proxy for insecurity. To critics, it is a gross and misleading index of criminality. To advocates, it is as good as any other and perhaps better. A different theoretical account might break this see-saw, by understanding race and insecurity as coproduced.

An alternative approach theorizes race as a product of racism.[43] Ruth Wilson Gilmore's definition of racism as "state-sanctioned and/or extralegal production and exploitation of group-differentiated vulnerability to premature death" is useful here.[44] Emphasis on the processual, ascriptive production and exploitation of vulnerabilities implies that the groups are not static. Rather, they are also always in the process of creation and destruction in the realm of discourse, ideas, state projects and strategies, and cultural forms. As Nikhil Pal Singh proposes, "to answer the question, 'What is racism?' one needs to begin not with the presumption of existing groups that are the victims of sanctioned harm, but with an account of the formation and institutionalization of structures and situations of protection and vulnerability for which post hoc description of dishonored groups serves as a form of rationalization or justification."[45] Vulnerability to premature death thus does not begin with the group, but the group begins, extends, and coalesces as an object of state and extralegal interest that is subject to violence. Previous experience of vulnerability is a heuristic of future vulnerability. Race is a probabilistic technology. Race is not a predefined matrix of meaning for intervention, but the unstable material product of that relational matrix over time and space. In this sense, race is a social form par excellence in Marx's sense of social form: "Social forms are expressions of 'the reciprocal relations between social individuals,' but they are ... 'autonomous vis-á-vis their conscious will and actions,'" Sonja Buckel observes. Such forms are persistent: "social relations congeal into a materiality imbued with its own dynamic." (This characteristic "obfuscates the fact that they are social relations.") Moreover, inasmuch as they "allow for the perpetually regulated repetition of a particular practice by virtue of their autonomization," social forms have structural effects that shape their own political contestation.[46] Race is not racism's predetermined object;

it is what racism produces. The occlusion of this fact is intrinsic to race's autonomization. Racism produces the benefit from state projects of race-making, including police discretion, which has been called whiteness. Blackness, as a category of practice, is resistance to enclosure, categorization, and differentiation conducive to premature death.[47]

Although it has become common today to acknowledge that race is not biological, the retention of an absolutist notion of race pervades the apologia that disclaim any racial basis of international order in the post-1945 era.[48] Widely shared understandings of this international order as no longer racially organized rely on strictly biological definitions that insulate it from antiracist critique. Cold War global projections of US power, and the enthronement of security as the priority of governance, constituted less a global war between pregiven, stably categorized races, as previous imperial adventures might be characterized, than a war to re-racialize the globe, to hierarchize territories anew in the absence of such stable referents and without direct political subjugation. The United States fought a race war in Vietnam, but its objects did not constitute a "race" outside their subjection to this violence. Further, if race is the relationally articulated condensation of the "two exes" of capital accumulation, expropriation and exploitation, into distinct and durable social forms, then security is nothing more than the active guarantee of these processes.[49] This violent process constructed stable referents—the Third World, communist insurgency, guerrillas—rather than only responding to them. It took the form of war occasionally: discretionary, counterrevolutionary police actions; more commonly, as the discretionary actions of police against revolution. That US policing expertise was the instrument of this ordering process contradicted claims that the new global order would be nonracial.

Within the realm of knowledge production, race mediated the continually emergent disjuncture in US development practice in Third World countries between universality and particularity. Modernization entailed the ideologies and practices of accelerated development processes that would rush other lands to a stage of US likeness. As a dominant national discourse, however, modernization also conferred upon the United States the exceptional, self-justifying capacity to be the overall arbiter of other lands' closeness of fit with its model. In a contest between universality and particularity, the United States would be the judge, since *it* was the bearer of universality.[50] Counterinsurgency, as policing, was the gritty practice ensuring that the model of modernization applied, even as it also projected or enforced nonsynchronousness, rather than innocently encountering it, by offering diminished or obsolescent versions of modernized facilities and techniques, as in Manopoli's efforts in the Congo or IAPA lessons in Bertillonage. Anticolonial racial assertion, therefore, as radical political practice in the counterinsurgency era, consisted of varied forms of resistance to the processes of classification and differentiation inherent in modernization, and in counterinsurgent knowledge and practice, that were conducive to group-differentiated premature death. In this sense, anticolonial racial assertion has aimed not for an affirmation of race, but for the abolition of it as the precipitate of the processes of racism.[51]

In diagnoses of threat, security experts offered analogies and comparisons across borders. So too did radicals attempting to analyze and defeat this logic of imperial state power. Racial distinction was propagated through comparison.[52] Police and military enacted comparative gestures and were subject to them, often attempting to make sense of imperial subjects through an empirically ill-fitting frame that misdiagnosed the situation.[53] One reason was that modernizers and police professionalizers who took development of overseas lands as their responsibility were conscious of the deep, abiding cleavage within US history that was anti-Black racism. Its eradication was development's goal but also its impediment, because this cleavage's persistence suggested that it might not be amenable to development.[54] But it was important to try, because if development elsewhere were possible, so might the eradication of this cleavage at home be possible—and vice versa. That is why Hall and Weckler's pamphlet *The Police and Minority Groups* so effortlessly prefigured modernization's objectives. Remedying the problem at home was necessary for the export of modern Americanism; the successful export of Americanism could signal resolution of the "American dilemma" at home. The tools of the eradication of racial fracture at home were the tools of development abroad in this period: police professionalization, participatory community development, economic assistance, education, and so on. The comparative compulsion among expert researchers was an endlessly recursive form of cross-border analysis that was at the anxious heart of counterinsurgent knowledge production. It underwrote the examination of the social problems of Third World countries in terms of US racial schism while simultaneously proposing solutions to US racial schism through lessons learned in attempts to modernize foreign lands. For foreign policy, comparison was incorporated into conceptualization.

No one exemplified this anxious frame of mind better than the modernization theorist Walt W. Rostow. As a key member of President Lyndon

Johnson's team, Rostow's advice spanned the mutable map of metropole and periphery. He was alert to the differing constituencies and audiences the administration addressed, but he was also conscious of parallels and similarities. It was at the nexus of development and security—always central to modernization theory and its implementation, and always a moving target—that he was most clearly able to express this globe-encompassing vision. While the smoke of the July 1967 rebellion was still rising from Detroit streets, Rostow sent a remarkable memorandum to Johnson, after the president had given a prime-time television address about his appointment of the Kerner Commission.[55] The address was resolutely domestic in subject matter, marked by the inward-looking, soul-searching temperament Johnson displayed when confronted with seemingly inexplicable unrest despite "the depth of our concern" manifest in the Great Society: "the Model Cities Act, the Voters Rights Act, the Civil Rights Acts, the Rent Supplement Act, Medicare and Medicaid, the 24 educational bills, Head Start, the Job Corps, the Neighborhood Youth Corps, the Teacher Corps, manpower development and training. And many, many more acts too numerous to mention on television tonight."[56] Rostow, however, heard the remarks in a different light. "I was struck—in your excellent address last night," he wrote Johnson, "by the parallels between your formulation of domestic policy and those you have applied to foreign policy." With alacrity, he rattled off the parallels: "At home your appeal is for law and order as the framework for economic and social progress. Abroad we fight in Vietnam to make aggression unprofitable while helping the people of Vietnam[—]and all of Free Asia—build a future of economic and social progress. The equivalent of domestic law and order on the world scene is that nations forego the use of violence across international frontiers." He devised a tabular summary of the domestic parallel of each of the key elements of Johnson's foreign-policy agenda (see table 1).

Rostow and other social scientists envisioned and produced the mutual constitution of foreign and domestic spheres. This type of comparative sentiment was not new, but it gained purchase after World War II. Extant empires fell and the nonterritorial, discretionary empire of the United States reached its apogee. With differing politics, Hannah Arendt, Aimé Césaire, Jean-Paul Sartre, and Michel Foucault all described the "boomerang effect" of colonial forms of rule: how techniques of power deployed in far-off lands by imperial rulers tend to be repatriated for domestic use.[57] Armed with this analysis, critics of US empire, however, often fail to grasp the specificity of US empire

TABLE 1 Walt Rostow's foreign-domestic comparison, addressed to
Lyndon Johnson, July 28, 1967

Abroad	At Home
Deterrence of Aggression	Law and Order
Economic and social progress	Economic and social progress
US partnership with regional organizations	Federal partnership with the States
Reconciliation among nations postured in mutual hostility	Reconciliation among all groups in our own society

and unreflexively analogize it to European empires, as if policymakers in Washington did not attempt to learn from other empires' mistakes.[58]

Key aspects of post-1945 US empire were its fetishization of security as the primary value and object of governance, its dependence on a normative discourse of equality that exceptionalized difference as anything that threatened those norms, and the tendency of managerial approaches to insecurity to travel back and forth across borders.[59] Technocrats confronted foreign and domestic situations with the same tools of political management and delegation to local authority. This management tended to ascribe dependency to the governed, while disparaging how dependency gave evidence of a lack of self-control. Tutelary prescriptions veered between admitting the necessity of uplift and frustrating its possibility. Many of the actors discussed in this book were much less constrained by biologistic determinations of race than we might assume. Older scientific racisms incubated in the prior imperial era are unhelpful guides to this process. Instead, as Rostow's table shows, US social scientists deployed flexible, performative analogies that sought to rationalize and minimize differences.

Though never far removed from conversations about inherent capacities, policing internationalists believed in tutelage and the crafting of common paths to universal outcomes. For them, racial difference was less a guide for action than a heuristic, a self-exculpating explanation for the failure of their actions. Byron Engle's own recourse to racial explanations flitted into view early on, but he largely suppressed it for most of his career. "The Japanese are not a criminally inclined people," he noted in 1948.[60] How much stock he put in the sentiment is difficult to assess. It sounds like boilerplate. Development became his colleagues' prevailing racial vocabulary, shorn of race references. If reports of US racial abuse in international news media impeded US efforts to win support in the darker nations, then racial strife at home also served as a tangible example of what was at stake to policing experts on the ground trying to ensure order.

The export of counterinsurgent knowledge developed within a US racial idiom meant that whatever the actual singularity of that historical experience was, it had to become mobile and flexible when used as a guide for practice. Left-wing and anti-imperialist solidarity movements during the Cold War recognized and built capacious political platforms. Internationalist organizations like the Black Panthers, Revolutionary Action Movement, Revolutionary Union, Student Nonviolent Coordinating Committee, Third World Women's Alliance, and Young Lords issued insistent, persistent demands for freedom and equality and for protections from state violence, as well as for what Black Panther leader Huey P. Newton conceptualized as an "intercommunalism" exorbitant to the nation-state.[61] These led to the apparent necessity of formulating security imperatives across the divide of foreign and domestic. Cross-border threats were what most alarmed counterinsurgents, whose strategic vision was dramatically sensitized to racial appeals and racial fractures. The archives of US foreign relations are not arid domains of cold, bloodless reason; they are saturated with race-thinking, with awareness of how racism both compelled and blocked the achievement of US geopolitical hegemony. For this reason, among others, counterinsurgency would be delegated to indigenous forces close to the population responsible for coercion, lest the rising tide of color against white world supremacy, as the eugenicist Lothrop Stoddard had once put it, overspill its national containers.[62]

COUNTERINSURGENCY BEFORE THE COLD WAR

What, then, was the relationship of counterinsurgency and race-making prior to World War II, when the United States did acquire colonies, and how did it inform the post-1945 situation, when it sought new forms of long-distance rule? If counterinsurgency is defined by its "economy of force," as the political theorist Patricia Owens argues, why is economizing on force necessary?[63] To economize on force is to proclaim an ideological commitment to civilization, bolstering the rationale for imperial rule. In the words of Frank E. Walton, a former Los Angeles Police Department deputy chief who helped supervise police assistance in South Vietnam, "Recognizing that the battleground here is PEOPLE—how do we attack this problem? There are only three broad ways: (1) kill all of them; (2) jail all of them; (3) control them." Walton continued: "Foremost among the measures which must be taken is the provision of security and protection to the citizen."[64] Moreover, thinking through the limits of international law in relation to counterinsurgency applied to "savage tribes," Elbridge Colby declared in 1927 of any combat field commander's judgment, which necessarily prevailed beyond those limits, "It is good to be decent. It is good to use proper discretion." Law might sometimes apply, and to be civilized was to know the difference. But for Colby the discretionary decision to act within or outside the law—to economize on force or not—was insufficient in the face of an implacable enemy, knowable only as unknowable threat. Instead, the unknowable threat had to be systematically excluded from legal protection. As Colby discussed "poisonous and toxic" chemical weapons, and the killing of "'non-combatants'—if there be any such in native folk of this character," he concluded, "The inhuman act thus becomes actually humane, for it shortens the conflict and prevents the shedding of more excessive quantities of blood."[65]

Kill, jail, control: these are the discretionary options policing contains. The imperial mode clarified this choice for Walton after an illustrious career at home. Police refers to governance through the downscaling of state violence, and to the discretionary decision to enact this violence. Control is the preference. In the 1920s, while Elbridge Colby investigated where law ended and policing began on a global scale, the police as a US institution was undergoing permanent, epochal transformation through professionalization. Policing had once been performed by irregular forces of private citizens and police power grew from a conception of household management, but policing was now subject to the state's "claims" to a monopoly on the instruments of violence, which had to be taken from other contenders.[66] Moreover, as French pacification experts had already realized, policing entailed all measures, whether destructive or constructive, taken to preempt threats to general welfare.[67] According to the legal scholar Quincy Wright, Elbridge Colby's primary interlocutor, France apparently regarded "the activity of her forces" in post–World War I Syria—including aerial bombing of defenseless people—"as police measures outside of international law."[68] For Colby, policing as control was not enough. For Wright, policing as unrestrained violence against criminals was too much. Paradigmatically, the US war in Vietnam, particularly under the oversight of Elbridge Colby's own son William, who was influenced by earlier generations of French pacification experts, proved them both correct. Policing is in essence the indeterminate, irreducible substrate of governance in a world beset by insecurities, many of them produced by police's own institutionalization.

Although policing bridged the historical hiatus of World War II, as a mode of governing a global order, global police power realized its full potential only after 1945, institutionalized by men who wore its badge. In Elbridge Colby's time, the League of Nations' Permanent Mandates Commission had already decided not to oppose French efforts to restore order in its newly acquired Near Eastern colonies, which included bombing civilians.[69] Policing accepted by the League included the suppression of elements whose legitimacy fell below the level of international law's regulatory schema. In the atomic era, police power came to define the legality of all wars enfolded within that regulatory schema, because it was impossible for major powers to wage war except as police actions against so-called bandits, brigands, dissidents, insurgents, and separatists. World War II was a climacteric. It interwove, particularly in the Pacific theater, total mobilization for big war between nations with small guerrilla and counter-guerrilla campaigns—and its resolution took the form of mass annihilation by atomic inferno. Furthermore, in the twilight of European imperialism, the horizon of political formation became the nation-state, with its formal militaries, and revolutionaries perforce directed their efforts toward or away from this terminus.[70] Imperium was shifting discursively and politically, if not militarily. Modernization—a self-understood counterrevolutionary process of revolution—soon became the order of the day. John F. Kennedy personified its internal contradiction: in his initial appearance on *Meet the Press* as a junior congressman in 1951, he argued for US support for the independence struggle of the Vietnamese against the French, but as president, he oversaw a very different form of US support to the government of South Vietnam. Begun under his predecessor, Kennedy increased not only police assistance but military assistance as well, laying the foundation for the massive, disastrous US intervention that followed under his successor.

In the racial regime that emerged between the end of World War II and the end of the US war in Vietnam, what Elbridge Colby had called "savagery"—meaning the exclusion of groups from legal protection, as evidenced by subjection to unfettered violence—became an individually chosen political condition. Inasmuch as it created a new form of rational-actor subjectivity, the economy of force was at the center of this transformation, compelling potential victims of violence to make a cost-benefit calculation: what were they willing to sacrifice?[71] The practical form of this economizing was policing.

The professionalization of policing aspired to the perfection of the force economy, which meant allowing and enabling the policed to make a cost-benefit calculation. Unreasonable and unpredictable, pre-professionalization policing allowed no such calculus. In turn, the most mundane and routine failure to submit to the discretionary despotism of the police power remained the justification for a full unleashing of brutality, both directly—all "the law in the end of a nightstick"—and indirectly, through courts, jails, and prisons.[72] The economy of force resided in the legitimacy it conferred on wholesale destruction but also in its compelling of cost-benefit calculations. Unheeded warnings, whether from the cop who says "move along" or in the aerially dropped leaflet in advance of firebombing, evidenced ineligibility for more civilized exertions of force. Destruction resulted in this liberal imaginary, not from stereotype or prejudice, but rather from evidence given of political choice made according to a cost-benefit calculus. Unreason was no longer a regrettable racial inheritance but became a conscious choice. These were the contours of the gift of freedom bestowed upon the unfree. At the heart of the American creed sat a new ideology and legal apparatus of civic equality to release the racialized from the shackles of prejudice. Now the racialized would face violence, possibly destruction, because they had chosen to face it. Not pre-judged capacities (prejudice) but volitional evidence would determine one's fate. Not status, but behavior, as the rational-choice framework would concretize through "broken windows" policing (see chapter 9). Because of political radicalism or implacable criminality, or some combination of the two, the destroyed had chosen to be destroyed: killed extrajudicially in exigent circumstances, injured in the course of resisting despotic authority, or jailed or imprisoned according to the application of due process of law. In times of so-called peace, the American way of governance would remain counterinsurgency.

The aspiration to create rational actors who would make cost-benefit calculations when facing unlimited capacities for violence was the aspiration of counterinsurgency as policing. In counterinsurgency, the necropolitics of violent containment and liquidation have been yoked to a pastoral biopolitics of social improvement. This tethering of practices was another crucial dimension of the economy of force, typically labeled pacification. The tutelary practice of preparing subjects for self-government often followed massive violence. It was intended to clear the social field of those who would not be amenable to self-government. Or it preceded violence, as refractory behavior indicated ineligibility for tutelage. But because pacification required affective intimacy and spatial proximity, it implied the very structuring phobia of revenge present throughout the revolutionary American settler tradition. This conferral of the arts of self-control on the eligible was the dimension of freedom accompanying the destructiveness of the revolutionary tradition.[73] Always conferred or granted, rather than ever considered pregiven, it remained a peculiarly heteronomous freedom. What caused this combinatorial approach, rather than a simple, unalloyed exterminationism? It was not the discretionary kindness or chivalrousness that Elbridge Colby identified as the occasional application of the decency of international law to "savage tribes." Rather, it can be attributed to political frailty, the structure of small wars.

The vulnerability of colonial rule always encumbers occupiers. Fabricating legitimacy can be difficult amid a dearth of cultural and technical competencies. Like racial integration of police forces at home, the delegation of responsibilities for pacification to swaths of subject populations beyond borders has been the recurrent solution. The animus attributed by Colby to "savage tribes" was not primordial. It was historical, the outcome of contingent tactical decisions in the project of expansionism. Through the climax of the Indian Wars west of the Mississippi in the 1870s, the razing of villages, destroying of foodstuffs, and killing of leaders and women and children noncombatants alike went hand in hand with the taking of captives who would become guides and "scouts," as well as indigenous servant laborers with little left to lose and nowhere to return.[74]

The structuring principle of US empire has been its dependence on local proxies to manage the challenges of rule. The Cold War US police assistance program entrenched this form upon the dissolution of older imperialisms. And Lyndon Johnson's War on Crime reinvigorated federalism for the purpose of the control of disorder. The persistence of the imperial mode within domestic borders appeared in the centrality of this delegated form as the mechanics of social control linking federal, state, and local authorities. It used local labor guided by local discretion, empowered by a distant purse. That this form became concretized legislatively and bureaucratically at the very moment of at-last achievement of legal equality among the races, with the initial introduction of federal anticrime support to lower-scale governments in 1965, indicates how it recapitulated but renovated racial rule in a haunting echo of the exigencies of the colonial situation, even as police techniques and tactics themselves also drew upon a reservoir of knowledge honed in occupation and overseas emergency.

Racial demarcation composed all points on a historical pendulum's arc of the identities of colonized subjects: from expendable to indispensable, from needed expert guides to needing expert guidance. But the trail from this set of practices to the War on Crime becomes indistinct, however, when zoom-ing in on practices applied to specific populations in, for example, Haiti or the Philippines. Instead, over a winding and tortuous path, this reliance on proxies became the primary mode of US counterinsurgency, earning even greater political importance insofar as it might confer legitimacy on the project of counterinsurgency in the post-1945 era of decolonization, when direct colonial rule was becoming anathema in emergent international fora like the United Nations. With reliance on delegated police assistance, the United States implemented an approach to pacification that looked back toward earlier lessons from frontier and colonial campaigns and looked for-ward toward a new international settlement characterized by discretionary empire. The way it would shape latter-day policing was not so much in its nominalist, concrete mobilization of difference, however, as in its realization of this principle of arm's-length support from a centralized authority (and purse) to a decentralized, autonomous, and discretion-enabled local enforce-ment mechanism.

At home, especially, but not only, among law-enforcement experts, an emergent conflation of crime, racial difference, and communism became the singular protean construct of the preeminent social problem to be managed, entailing newfound foreignness. At the very moment racial particularity in the form of insufficiency for full membership in a national polity was liqui-dated by civil-rights legislation, it became reinscribed as criminal propensity that was at once incapable of rising to the level of politics and also excessive to typical political wrangling in its subversive predilection. It thus demanded bipartisan, apparently nonpolitical consensus in its management. The tool-kit for this management came in the form of a prospective and multifaceted technical expertise. Now it had tested itself worldwide under the aegis of modernization's universalism, in an arena of competition structured by the postcolonial abstract equivalence of nation-states, guided no longer by explic-itly racial qualifications for self-governance. In this way, the experience of police assistance overseas in the moment of US geopolitical hegemony could adequate itself to a restructured social formation at home now marked less by heritable forms of dishonor than ostensibly chosen ones: crime, delin-quency, deviance. The new domestic infrastructure for spreading this techni-cal knowledge arose alongside but quickly came to submerge the modest state social-welfare apparatus that took the mitigation of these forms of dishonor as its object. To conflate crime with subversion meant treating the political dedication of revolutionaries as the permanence of crime and the incorrigibility of criminals.[75] It also meant denying any structural or social causality, including policing practices themselves. According to multiple Pentagon-funded analyses, incidents like "racial friction in schools" or "a dramatic rise in the crime level" were indicators of the "pre-mobilization phase" of civil unrest. Crime was tantamount to insurgency, but insurgency was not based on legitimate grievance. It was instead social pathology, or "virus."[76] This lesson was counterinsurgency repatriated. Like the limitless threats to global order posed by communist subversion, such pathologies now became fixed features of the social firmament, amenable only to risk management, not eradication. If demands for freedom exceeded the geography of the nation-state, so, too, did law enforcement's responses to them.[77]

TWO

Byron Engle and the Rise of Overseas Police Assistance

IN 1940, KENNETH WHERRY, a future Republican senator from Nebraska, uttered a prophecy of ascendant US global power, declaring: "With God's help, we will lift Shanghai up and up, ever up, until it is just like Kansas City."[1] Yet it was not God who catalyzed the modernization mission. Instead, its bearer was a more earthly being: the beat cop. And "Kansas City" was not mere synecdoche. This city bequeathed to the world a new Americanism not only in the form of the badge, woolen uniform, pistol, and club, but in the form of the classroom, crime laboratory, and shooting range. Although no street plaque in Kansas City, Missouri, commemorates Byron Engle, the municipal police prodigy who made Wherry's vision a reality, every US city street memorializes his legacy.

US policing, insistently local in self-conception, came of age on a global scale. The modernization, professionalization, and reform of policing by experts—fundamental to US state-formation in the twentieth-century from municipality, to state, to nation—was a transnational project, even though it nestled in an arc-like corridor west of the Mississippi River, from St. Louis to Kansas City to Wichita. The stereotype of the Midwest as isolationist is unhelpful. Policing expertise developed a resolutely transnational field of operations while still retaining its Norman Rockwell ideal of the service-oriented cop helping a wayward child to safety.

Engle's cohort inhabited a professional policing ecosystem that only expanded with the rise of Cold War counterinsurgency. These experts did not function like architects, sitting at a drafting table designing a fully formed "first line of defense," as they called it, against crime and subversion from afar. Nor were they like early astronomers who gazed upon the firmament and traced coherent constellations about which they could tell compelling tales from disparate points. Rather, these men, and their institutions, were themselves the mobile bodies constellating the formation. They were bricoleurs who picked up bits of useful knowledge along the way and modified them in relation to what they already knew. Modernization as an intellectual paradigm provided a very basic map, but mostly their route-finding occurred as they went along, dashing from emergency to crisis, which they or their allied agents had often helped to create. There was for them no certain, safe Archimedean point from which to understand and map what they were trying to create—US hegemony.

These security experts defined the problems they were to solve as newly global in extension, called into being by the efflorescence of formerly colonized, newly independent nations. These problems were not amenable to direct US intervention. Though they were certain of US goodwill and purity of intentions, the projections of US power abroad that Engle and his colleagues oversaw were remarkably chaste and pragmatic, aware of their own limitations, and by extension, aware of their country's limitations. Engle and Robert Komer (the subject of the next chapter) reconfigured state capacities by insisting on the utility of expert law enforcement to the management of a range of social problems. They persevered in internecine bureaucratic battles. By tracing their milieu, their interpersonal connections, and the way these men's advocacy married opportunism with calibrated alarmism, this analysis registers the historical through-lines of policing against the radically new dispositions it came to inhabit. As the United States became the global policeman, it relied on these global policemen.

Engle trafficked ideas overseas drawn from his early experience in police reform in the Midwest. His time on the force in Kansas City bestowed a method rather than an essence. It was a reformist bearing, made explicit in a review, issued at the close of the Johnson administration, of the overseas program he oversaw: "In the field of police administration it may be stated there are no 'developed' countries—all should be developing. *It is not*, however, *solutions to social problems which should communicated* to other cultures, but *rather the methods and techniques for solving problems.*"[2] Engle's initial experience abroad, administering police reforms in occupied Japan after World War II, confirmed some of what he had learned in his early career but also equipped him with tools to realize the relationship of police reform to US state power on a much grander stage: law enforcement was the leading edge of state power, but it could also be a medium of the transformation of the mechanics of the state, including the reconfiguration of relationships among formally sovereign entities—the United States and Japan, in the case of Engle's early career—or among levels within a sovereignty—local, state, and federal governments. This unending reconfiguration entailed using centralized state authority to decentralize state functions. That dialectic of state-formation was enmeshed in a broader struggle over the intensive and extensive application of the most fundamental prerogative of liberal governance, the police power: the congeries of techniques and rationalities used to preemptively identify and mitigate threats to the general health and prosperity of a population, which also defined the terms and conditions of health and prosperity by declaring who was in or out of the population.

BUFFALO, ROAMING

A search for the inner motivation hidden from view, for the heretofore secret personal story that propelled Byron Engle to become the father of modern US foreign police assistance, to oversee a major phase of the US prosecution-by-proxy of the Cold War across the globe—such canvassing will turn up little. Unlike a police investigator in the present, the analyst of the past can discern psychological motivation only from how it took practical expression. The historian must go on available evidence. As actors who shape history go, the available evidence on Engle the person is scanty. The geopolitical reasons to create new national security bureaucracies were beyond his ken, but once tasked with mobilizing them, he excelled.

Engle was a cop, an exceptionally good cop, who believed that to make other cops good cops they needed to be properly trained. For Engle, innate ability went only so far. The bulk of what made a man exceptional in law enforcement was training. According to Engle's worldview, it mattered little that he had worked in a butcher shop before he became a Kansas City police officer.[3] What mattered most were personal connections and the localized yet also geographically extensive milieu of police professionalization in which he labored.

Engle was born in 1910, in the small town of Buffalo, Missouri, some seventy years after the town's founding. American bison, its namesake, might still be seen in the town's Ozark environs between prairie and woodland when it first buildings went up and its street grid was mapped. Buffalo became the seat of Dallas County in 1844, renamed from its original 1841 appellation, Niangua County, for James K. Polk's vice-president. Niangua or Neongwah, the Sioux name of a nearby river (Ni- or Ne-, meaning water or river), had

LIEUT. BYRON ENGLE
Director of Police Academy

FIGURE 3. Byron Engle, lieutenant and director of Kansas City Police Academy, ca. 1943. Missouri Valley Special Collections, Kansas City Public Library, Kansas City Police Historical Society Collection, Kansas City, Missouri.

been difficult for white settlers to pronounce. Residents today inaccurately recall Niangua meaning, "I won't go away."[4] This was as untrue of the Sioux as it was of Buffalo's most important son. Engle never returned to Missouri for long after leaving in 1946, until he was interred in Benton Branch Cemetery, northeast of Buffalo, in 1990, where his name shares a headstone with that of his wife and constant companion, CIA officer Geraldine "Jerry" L. Jelsch Engle.

After receiving a 1957 commendation from the International Cooperation Administration (ICA), the predecessor to AID, for his "outstanding competence in initiating and operating a totally new and complex world-wide program for technical cooperation, the Civil Police Administration program," he allowed that the award, bestowed in Washington, DC, at a ceremony attended by Secretary of State John Foster Dulles, was "a nice thing they did for a country boy in a big town."[5] There was another country boy in a big town who mattered to the possibility that Engle would be swept across the globe from police training facilities in Kansas City: Harry S Truman, the president who oversaw the initial construction of the Cold War national security state. Truman hailed from Jackson County, which includes Kansas City. He owed his political fortunes to that minor metropolis and its Democratic machine.[6]

There seems to have been little to Engle's life beyond law enforcement. Perhaps he left behind so few papers unrelated to the bureaucratic details of countering insurgency because there was little else to say. No oral history, no memoir, no diary. A smattering of mundane personal letters from very early days. There are a few stray newspaper mentions of a first wife and a daughter never otherwise discussed.[7] It was not his inner life that rated as consequential. No rhetorical chicanery hid his ideas. There was barely any prose flair buried in the thousands of bureaucratic memoranda he signed. Bland writing signaled the intention to universalize prescriptions. Essence matched appearance. Security was his earthly purpose. His high forehead, broad nose, prominent ears, and bulbous chin contrasted with his thin, tight lips. Exaggerated features balanced by a mouth easily kept shut—his was the very visage of US empire.

Engle's passion was shooting. He was a gun aficionado and a hunter. Yet he did not grow up shooting. Before becoming a cop, he had never fired a gun. His passion was inextricable from his profession, from training. Within a couple years of joining the Kansas City force in 1940, he scored the highest marks in a pistol-shooting competition in Oklahoma.[8] Some of his future colleagues in overseas police assistance were cops he had met at shooting contests.[9] Throughout their overseas deployments, advisors made time for game-hunting. Memoranda to Engle included updates on their quarries. Almost four decades after learning to shoot in Kansas City, Engle was still winning shooting competitions, even if now he competed in the "Senior" category. In New Mexico, he won using "his .357 Colt Python presented to him by staff when he retired from OPS." His wife Jerry also had a knack for shooting; in one competition, she "beat everyone in sight, including the male chauvinists."[10] In retirement, the Engles lived in an apartment in Bethesda, Maryland, and kept in close contact with other former public safety advisors. One visited for "tea and crumpets" and reported that their home was "a veritable museum," chockablock with "medals, cups, ribbons, elephant tusks, antlers, heads of innumerable animals, tiger skins, zebra skins, leopard skins, and various animal trophies."[11]

OPS would assiduously teach foreign police trainees the value of marksmanship. Instructors expected even high-ranking executives, unlikely ever to need to fire their guns, to use the state-of-the-art firing range OPS built in its

FIGURE 4. Marksmanship training at the International Police Academy, 1964. National Archives and Records Administration.

training facility in Washington, DC. For OPS, the ability to strike a target as necessary could actually prevent the flagrant use of gunfire, which was likely to endanger bystanders and inflame political tensions. Advisor John Manopoli proudly informed Engle that five of the six members of South Vietnam's shooting team were OPS-trained National Police, who brought home one gold and four silver medals (more than half the nation's total count in all events) in the Sixth South East Asia Peninsula Games, held in Malaysia in late 1971. The team's coach was OPS's Dudley Britton, a burly Texan. From this shooting instructor came an important lesson for police: skill had to be matched by discretion. "It is as important to know when to shoot as it is to know when not to shoot," Britton noted. "Police problems are the same the world over."[12]

Engle retired in 1973, a year before Congress terminated OPS. Advisors were fiercely loyal to him and spoke of him with great admiration. Most advisors referred to each other by last name in internal correspondence, but Engle addressed his men in writing by first name. As one scholar who interviewed many advisors writes, Engle "was reputed to get whatever he wanted for his organization, and could always ram police aid proposals through the AID bureaucracy, regardless of who objected."[13] Another emphasizes that Engle impressed colleagues as "a 'masterful bureaucrat' and 'compulsive modernizer.'"[14] Yet records of the intense efforts made by Robert Komer and others to keep OPS alive and well-funded during the mid-1960s indicate that Engle's bureaucratic finesse extended down, but not up, the chain of command. NSC staffer Harold H. "Hal" Saunders warned his supervisor, "frankly Byron's biggest problem is that he has antagonized many people in AID," from the deputy administrator on down.[15] In OPS, those below him were, in many cases, men he had recruited personally. Recruitment was never an easy task, but Engle had a knack for it, going back to his days in Kansas City. In 1945, he attended a course in Los Angeles on "training and analyzing personalities," which proved helpful when it came to "fitting men to jobs."[16] As Engle traveled the globe, logging 1.5 million miles by the time he retired, recruitment was always on his mind.[17] When he passed back through the United States, he would stop and visit his mother in Kansas City, but he would also visit criminology schools, such as at Northwestern University or the University of Iowa, where potential recruits enrolled.[18]

"A Jim Crow town right down to its bootstraps," Kansas City became a centerpiece of police reform toward the end of the fourth decade of the twentieth century.[19] There, Engle benefited from the tutelage of Lear B. Reed, a maverick police reformer who rebuilt Kansas City's venal, politically partial force from the ground up, through purge upon purge. His agenda was simple: "Police plus politics equals parasites, in Kansas City or anywhere else. The sooner municipalities become convinced of this, appoint, train and assign officers on a basis of their character, education, knowledge and fitness, the sooner law enforcement throughout the nation will rid itself of the deadheads, political nincompoops, pot-bellied pinheads, allies of the underworld, grafters, chiselers, enemies of society, catspaws for ward heelers and dishonest incompetents of other stripes and caliber."[20] Ending Jim Crow was not on the agenda, though. Reed left the police department under a cloud of bad press. A state-level investigation examined departmental malfeasance, spurred by "an indignant Negro populace" that, as reported in *The Crisis,* was "tired of being kicked and beaten"—and shot in the back.[21] Reed was later reputed to have urged on the assassins of President Rafael Trujillo in the Dominican Republic while stationed there with the CIA in 1960, and he continued meddling there while a private citizen, to the State Department's annoyance.[22] Six-foot-seven, a former marine and disciple of J. Edgar Hoover, the director of the Federal Bureau of Investigation (FBI), Reed was proud that the reformed Kansas City force was called the "little FBI." At a men's club meeting, less than three months into his tenure, he announced the strides the force was now making. "The local police department is the first line of defense," he declared. No longer would "criminals and logheads," unfit "men who could not read or write their own names," who thought "arson" was "some kind of a poison," be allowed to bear the responsibility of safeguarding "children and the public property."[23] Engle typified the new type of officer he was hiring, and in just a few years Engle would supervise the hiring of hundreds of new Kansas City officers in his own mold.

Reed was nothing if not self-promoting. The urgent need for police reform in the face of creeping subversive threats demanded it. His blustery memoir bore the grandiose title *Human Wolves; Seventeen Years of War on Crime, in Which Is Told, for the First Time, the Dramatic Story of the Rebuilding of Kansas City's Police Department—and the Return of Law and Order to the Heart of America*. In it the former FBI agent detailed how he reformed the Kansas City police force and introduced new technologies. Reed also described his prescience in identifying the threat to "internal security" of "subversive activities by the representatives of foreign dictatorships." Of "advocates of foreign 'isms'" who complained of violations of their civil liberties, he declared that liberties were not their goal. "What they want is license. They are all rats. I know 'em. I've been slugged by 'em and shot at by 'em. I've put on a false mustache and sat in on their meetings." The fake mustache signaled Reed's belief that political radicalism was endemic among recent European immigrants. He imparted such FBI tactics of subterfuge against radicals to the municipal force. Kansas City was the first in the nation to set up an "Internal Security Unit," he claimed, though police campaigns against those labeled seditious and against labor radicals had a long history there. Reed offered rebarbative thoughts on "Negro" and Jewish susceptibility to communist exhortations and demanded that communists be interned in "concentration camps." Such accusations led the Kansas City African American newspaper *The Call* to sue him for libel. Reed's officers' alacrity in gathering meticulous records on Kansas City's inhabitants would become a hallmark of Engle's teachings with OPS, capabilities, however, continuously amplified with each year's latest surveillance technologies. Law and order might have returned to the heart of America, as his memoir's nostalgic fantasy had it, but it was exported from there too.[24]

Engle adopted Reed's outlook on internal security as he worked his way up the ranks, advancing with startling rapidity. He also took to heart lessons on reform and an emphasis on police work as "public service."[25] Reed emphasized training. Kansas City police practiced shooting in all manner of situations, at different targets, using multiple types of guns. Reed also required police to train regularly with tear gas, including "entering a gas-filled building, with and without gas masks, and running through clouds of tear gas."

Reed also established a new division of labor within the department. Five new branches were created for communications, traffic safety, motor equipment, record-keeping, and police training.[26] Professionalization of Kansas City's police consisted of three major fields: ongoing training, which entailed keeping high standards; up-to-date technology, including communications and investigatory tools, as well as meticulous record-keeping and inventory of police property to prevent theft or loss; and coordination to make all the pieces work together, even as new divisions of responsibility were introduced.

In 1943, having risen to the rank of captain, Engle traveled east for a course at the FBI National Academy. J. Edgar Hoover reported Engle's successful graduation to the *Kansas City Star*.[27] In 1944, Kansas City's training operations, which Engle oversaw, became formalized as a school, still open today. With Richard L. Holcomb, Engle co-authored a standardized test for promotion in rank, circulated nationally in a policing textbook.[28] Holcomb went on to teach university-level police science, consulted with the overseas police assistance program through the 1950s, and continued to publish policing textbooks. In devising Kansas City's training division, Reed took inspiration from the FBI academy, calling the institution "one of John Edgar Hoover's greatest contributions to mankind."[29] This division, and the force generally, focused on public relations, disseminating information about police accomplishments, as OPS would decades later. Soon Engle would travel beyond Kansas City, to Iowa, for instance, to teach officers evolving techniques of policing. Riot control was Captain Engle's specialty.[30]

Planners in Washington feared that World War II's end would entail chaos and disorder. US police became essential to peace. Engle took a leave from the Kansas City police force in 1946 when General Douglas MacArthur asked him to come to Japan, as one of six administrators, and work under the auspices of G-2, or intelligence, with the Supreme Commander for the Allied Powers (SCAP). The charge was to rebuild Japan's police forces in every dimension. SCAP chose "Engle, in particular, for his knowledge and experience in reforming police by training."[31] Other recruits were delegated to reconstruct areas like maritime policing, communications, and records. Of the six, Engle was the youngest. With prior experience as high-ranking police, journalists, and army officers, some of these men—Arthur Kimberling, Edward Bishop, Johnson Munroe—remained Engle's colleagues in police assistance for decades.[32] He also met Jerry Jelsch in Japan, where she was working for the American Red Cross.[33] Engle was soon to become a CIA officer, deployed next to Turkey under official cover, and his wife Jerry also joined the CIA.

Engle renewed his leave from Kansas City's police force regularly for seven years. During that time, local leaders considered him for the job of police chief. But after he failed to renew his leave officially in 1953, the board of police commissioners "dropped" him from the ranks.[34] Yet Kansas City remained interested in, and informed of, his exploits overseas. Radio Moscow dubbed him "Killer Engle," but he denied to a local newspaper columnist that he taught the "American method" of torture by electric shock in Turkey.[35] Years after OPS disbanded, he told a scholar that the foundations of his work in training police around the world had been laid in Japan, "the best laboratory that anyone interested in organization and administration could have been involved in."[36] However, he informed his admirers back home that many of his ideas for reforming Japan's police came from Kansas City. To modernize the look of Japanese officers, for instance, he sent his Kansas City uniform to be used as a template. Save for the color of the fabric, the new Japanese police dressed like officers back home, even with rain gear designed for visibility such as his former colleagues wore. He introduced nightsticks and substituted handcuffs for the rope with which Japanese police were accustomed to restraining prisoners. The training schools in Japan were modeled on Kansas City's, only larger. The measure of Engle's success, he reported, was that instead of genuflecting before authoritarian police, now, thanks to this work, Japanese citizens would relate to their cops the way any American would: "The cop on the corner is everyone's favorite. People go to the police for help, for advice and for friendly conversation to pass the time of day. That's one phase of the new democracy in Japan."[37] This new democracy in Japan was to be a bulwark of US economic and political power in Asia.

In Turkey, a US Police Advisory Group blurred narcotics control, espionage, and everyday policing. As chief advisor there in 1951–1952, Engle instituted training in record-keeping and traffic enforcement, among other practices. He helped Turkish police executives secure membership in the International Association of Chiefs of Police (IACP), whose lapel pins quietly announced to other US agents their trustworthiness in a delicate situation where underworld and nationalist actors for different reasons loathed the US presence. Most important, with the blessing of Turkish officials and the zealous director of the US Federal Bureau of Narcotics, Harry Anslinger, Engle created Turkey's first police section dedicated to narcotics control, led by an English-speaking officer. The fruit of these labors included fine-grained intelligence reports, detailing the yields of illicit crops of opium poppies and seizures of the product, as well as disputes among Turkish government agencies, which landed on Anslinger's desk monthly.[38] In Turkey, working alongside Anslinger's deputy Charles Siragusa, Engle helped the Bureau of Narcotics initiate source control, an approach that has blended US national security imperatives, rural counterinsurgency, and domestic panic about narcotics for almost three-quarters of a century now, without ever succeeding.[39] One Bureau of Narcotics official lamented that it was difficult to raise Turkish competence in suppressing narcotics to the levels of Turkish competence in suppressing communism.[40] In practice, the two approaches fitfully converged, enveloping a country that did not easily submit to Washington's dictates within the folds of US hegemony.

Engle hopscotched from the first to the second of the models for US modernization thinking. As Japan went, so might go the East Asian new nations. As Turkey went, so might go the West Asian new nations. When Turkey turned to military rule after a 1960 coup, some US theorists of political development updated their ideas to be less wary of authoritarian routes toward noncommunist modernization.[41] After Turkey, Jerry and Byron Engle returned to Japan, where he continued his work, assigned for a few years to the Army's provost marshal. In 1955, the Engles moved to Washington, DC, to work at CIA headquarters, where Jerry became a liaison between the CIA and the ICA's predecessor to OPS, a post she held through OPS's formalization and until she and Byron retired from the world of police assistance.[42] After Byron left the CIA and became an overt, civilian, executive employee of AID, Jerry thus formally remained a principal connection point between the US intelligence apparatus and the professionalization of policing across the globe that her husband oversaw.

MIDWESTERN MEASURES

The history of the municipal police forces in the trans-Mississippi West records many discontinuities of corruption and reform, home rule and external control. Reformist police leaders in this area came under the influence of J. Edgar Hoover, and geographic proximity linked the midwesterners who would lead overseas police assistance with the most celebrated figures in the mid-century professionalization of US law enforcement: August Vollmer and O. W. Wilson.

Kansas City was not the only midwestern city that played an important role in the refinement of US policing. St. Louis and Wichita counted too. St. Louis's unique position in the history of American law enforcement dates to the Civil War, where in 1861 in a generally pro-Union city the police force was reconstituted under Democratic, pro-Confederacy, state-level control. The newly state-superintended St. Louis Metropolitan Police Department was to address the disorder of a border city in wartime by clamping down on Black life, and German enclaves too, lest rebellious ideas fester. A paramilitary police force, with secret squads to ferret out the seditious, kept the city tightly controlled through the war years.[43] State supervision of St. Louis's police force lasted until September 1, 2013.[44] The broader question of local autonomy for law enforcement, as against control by higher levels of government, aired first during the Civil War, would persist generally for a century and shaped Lyndon Johnson's efforts to institute a federal War on Crime. In St. Louis, it was indelibly a question of racial power, and state supervision maintained white control over a police force in a city growing increasingly Blacker.

St. Louis was the site where the founders of what would become the IACP first met, in 1871. Chief James McDonough had successfully lobbied Missouri's governor to support this convocation of police chiefs. Among his reasons: St. Louis was then home to an experiment that McDonough wanted colleagues from near and far to witness. He was proud of his city's program of legal and municipally regulated prostitution, with registration of women and buildings involved in the trade.[45] Attendees included 113 delegates from the District of Columbia and twenty-one states and territories, including Wyoming Territory and the Indian Territory. Among delegates' discussion points were "the effects of the Civil War"—the abolition of slavery, the spread of wage labor, and westward expansion—"upon the increase in crime."[46]

The police of Kansas City, like their counterparts in St. Louis, also operated under state-level control by a board of governor-appointed commissioners. Almost sixty years of that control came to an end in 1932, however, when a Missouri State Supreme Court decision enabled police home rule. This switch empowered Thomas J. Pendergast, a "hard-boiled, tin tack, extremely practical, undisputed boss," who since 1925 had controlled much of the Democratic Party in the city. Home rule enabled him to ensure that men loyal to him employed cops loyal to them. Before home rule, Kansas City's police had not been impervious to corruption. Rather, they were "the last real organized unit of GOP patronage in the city." The overturning of state control marked a "crushing blow" to the Republican Party's leadership: "The police represented their last line of defense, although much to the chagrin of many Republicans, they were not nearly active enough politically. Pendergast's police would be far more active. Pendergast's political power was considerable enough to warrant a 1932 meeting with Franklin Roosevelt, who sought Boss Tom's support, and hence that of the Missouri delegation, at the Democratic convention. Pendergast did "not greatly care" who was president of the United States "so long as he can nominate his local ticket." His top concern was parochial: "Police commissioners mean a lot more in his life."[47] The votes, and the money, rolled in. After Roosevelt became president, he rewarded Kansas City with federal patronage.

After 1932, however, Johnny Lazia, a young gangster allied with Chicago's Al Capone, obtained "broad powers in the municipal police department," including the ability to recruit new officers, many of whom had criminal records. On Pendergast's watch, cops received intentionally small paychecks, encouraging them to take bribes. Officers would often be hired simply because they had written a letter pledging loyalty to the Democratic machine. Beyond bootlegging, racketeering, and protecting fugitives, Lazia's criminality included likely blessing, and then, in a semi-official capacity, investigating, the so-called Union Station massacre, which killed four officers and one underworld acquaintance of Lazia's. The imbroglio strengthened Hoover's FBI. Two of his men were shot in the incident, bolstering his fear-mongering about escalating crime.[48] Reflecting on this period, whose conclusion he oversaw, Kansas City's police chief Lear Reed called the corruption of the city's police under Pendergast a "reign of terror."[49] Reed's campaign of thoroughgoing police reform could occur only when home rule over the force was eliminated in July 1939, the day he took over. Pendergast, formerly among the century's most powerful chieftains of an urban political machine, soon found himself locked up. Before that, though, Harry S Truman, a former Missouri official, relied on Pendergast's counsel and support to win office as one of the state's two US senators.[50] Pendergast's well-known criminality later nearly prevented Truman from becoming Franklin D. Roosevelt's final, and most consequential, vice-president. But even Roosevelt knew that Truman's need to secure solid chunks of voters on the Democratic line, like his own, could not easily be dismissed. Later, incensed by Truman's push to create the CIA, which J. Edgar Hoover considered an encroachment on his turf, the FBI funneled derogatory information about Truman's Pendergast links to his Republican opponent in the 1948 election, Thomas Dewey.[51]

Across the river in Kansas was Fort Leavenworth. Home to the Army's graduate school, Leavenworth trained numerous US military leaders as well as foreign officers. Leavenworth also was home to a federal prison, where Pendergast spent fifteen months while Reed dismantled the police force that had operated as his foot soldiers. Earlier, in the aftermath of the Russian and Mexican revolutions and the Palmer Raids, Leavenworth had held radicals, trade unionists, and subversives from three continents, caught in the webs of surveillance, intrigue, and simple crime control set interdependently by local red squads, the border patrol, the General Intelligence Division of the Bureau of Investigation, led by Hoover, and the War Department's Military Intelligence Division, led by Colonel Ralph Van Deman, the sorcerer of countersubversion who repatriated techniques of surveillance and intrigue from the Philippines to the United States in the early part of the century.[52]

Two important figures for overseas police assistance had ties to Wichita, not far from Kansas City. Howard W. Hoyt worked in a supervisory position for Michigan State University (MSU) as it trained police in South Vietnam. In May 1955, he was among the first of that university's advisors to arrive in Saigon.[53] Hoyt got his start wearing a badge in Wichita, where he spent eleven years.[54] In the 1930s, Wichita already was attracting international attention: two officers from Afghanistan, for instance, visited to experience US police professionalization firsthand.[55] In addition, Theo E. Hall, who would oversee US police assistance in the late 1950s as Engle's confederate, spent time on the force in Wichita in the 1930s. Hall linked midwestern law enforcement with the broader field of social-scientific research through his relationship with Joseph Weckler. These two men were professional acquaintances of New York City's police commissioner Lewis J. Valentine, whose plans for reforming police in postwar Japan Engle would be assigned to implement. Valentine helped Hall and Weckler produce their 1944 report on controlling unrest and racial violence. Also aiding them was Kansas City's city manager, who must have known Engle, the city police force's rising star.

Nonwhite allies and neutrals were at the center of these experts' thinking, with racial ideologies that their work was supposed to make obsolete never far from the surface. In 1943, Weckler published a widely circulated report on Polynesia for the Smithsonian Institution, intended to inform US citizens about the Pacific islands, which had suddenly become crucial to the US war effort. He spent most of his subsequent career studying Pacific island peoples, though he continued to publish on US race relations and law enforcement.[56] Hall also went overseas. After the war, he worked in denazification and the reorganization of the German police, as did Hoyt.[57] A number of Nazi police and soldiers became US intelligence assets and trainers who worked alongside public safety advisors in, for instance, South Vietnam and Nicaragua.[58] A US official decreed that in Germany, police could decide at the local level whether to hire former Nazis, but the US military government's national policy banned hiring a police applicant with communist sympathies.[59] In US-occupied Korea, in violation of new strictures, former "collaborators" with the Japanese empire remained employed in the police force, which retained the structure and mission of opposition to the Left that Japan had created.[60] In 1957, Hall conducted a survey of Iraq's police forces and offered advice once he learned that a US architecture firm had won a contract for the design and construction of a new civilian prison in an outlying area of Baghdad called Abu Ghraib.[61] US military and intelligence operatives, five decades hence, would brutally torture detainees on that site. Underpinning that torture was a cavalcade of racial tropes about what could compel compliance, which bore affinities with the race science underpinning US policing before the era of professionalization.

Orlando W. Wilson was Wichita's police chief for eleven years, beginning in 1928, and mentor to Hall and Hoyt. This boomtown's police force was corrupt and brutal. Wilson reformed it, focusing on both a preventive tactical approach to crime and managerial changes, like eliminating ethnic patronage in recruitment. He instituted professional standards of education and specialization of tasks and introduced up-to-date technologies such as two-way radios and a mobile crime laboratory. Together with Hall, Wilson conducted research that revolutionized police patrol. The resulting recommendation was for motorized patrol with a single officer per car, even at night. That way the police could cover more ground, were more likely to be cautious while alone, and were unlikely to become distracted. Cops tended to hate the one-man-patrol reform, but the technique swept the nation. Combined with this tactical reform was a statistical analysis that began to craft predictions on where crime would occur, a proactive approach that would only grow more robust in subsequent decades.[62] Public safety advisors continually refined Wilson's patrol guidance. One even published an article on it in *The Police Chief* while on duty in the Philippines.[63] Wilson also favored a semi-military appearance for police officers: instead of blue uniforms, Wichita's cops wore khaki. Kansas City adopted this uniform standard under Reed in 1939. When one of Reed's successors wanted to phase out khaki uniforms six years later because he believed they made police invisible by looking too much like soldiers, Engle headed the committee to procure new uniforms. Wartime shortages made obtaining khaki cloth challenging anyway, but blue cloth was easier to find.[64] In direct and indirect ways, the war shaped policing at home.

Wilson was the prize student of August Vollmer, the police chief in Berkeley, California, considered the grandfather of US police professionalization, who lectured at the University of California. Vollmer got his first taste of law enforcement in the Philippines, after enlisting in 1898. His participation in counterinsurgency there included ensuring that local scouts were equipped and reliable. He referred to his experience in the Philippines repeatedly during his illustrious subsequent career.[65] Later, his expert reforms in Berkeley provided a model for other cities. Berkeley was the first city to develop a mobile police force, with cars available to every officer, after earlier experiments with bicycles. In between, a test of motorcycles resulted in too many injured officers.[66] Kansas City brought in Vollmer as a consultant to survey reorganization needs in 1929, just what OPS advisors would come to do in dozens of countries before initiating active institutional relationships. But Vollmer's menu of reforms could not take hold until Pendergast was out of the picture. Vollmer became president of the IACP in 1926. He found that the test of his techniques would be their wide applicability. The modernism of his methods derived from their mobility. Vollmer's fortunes rose, and numerous city leaders sought his counsel. "For years, ever since Spanish-American War days, I've studied military tactics and used them to good effect in rounding up crooks," he told a Los Angeles Police Department (LAPD) audience. "After all we're conducting a war, a war against the enemies of society and we must never forget that."[67] He was thinking tactically, about a current scourge of bank robberies. Soon after recommending professionalizing reforms to the LAPD, Vollmer journeyed to a city that would pay a higher salary than any other for his services: Havana. There he instituted reforms like bicycle-based patrol, as tested in Berkeley, and new technologies like the teletype. These were easily replicated policy innovations.

Despite his martial rhetoric, Vollmer was more socially liberal than many who received his advice, more attuned to trends in social science. He focused on transforming policing into a community service that would address local social needs alongside the war against crooks. He urged that the police officer be considered a "social worker." Officers "must engrain themselves in the community, recognize the needs of individuals in the neighborhoods they police, especially the needs of juveniles, and work toward providing and coordinating the necessary social resources to improve the individual and the quality of life in each neighborhood."[68] In this expansive sense, the Vollmer-counseled peacetime rule of the Cuban dictator Gerardo Machado y Morales, a developmentalist avant la lettre, extended wartime practices of combining social uplift with strict security criteria. Within six years of his first trip as a policing consultant, Vollmer had journeyed across the globe, carrying with him lessons from Berkeley and Havana. From the Pacific Rim to western Europe, his expertise found audiences, and, in turn, several countries began to send their police officials to the School of Criminology Vollmer had founded at the University of California.[69] There they rubbed elbows with students who would go on to become Cold War public safety advisors and trainers at the International Police Academy.[70] Informal social connections combined with formal training, and it became possible, in tentative outline, for security experts to imagine how the United States might ensure the security of its global realm without necessarily putting its own troops on the ground.

Occupied Germany and Japan were test cases for a new dispensation of security and development that would marry US technical expertise to local labor, unencumbered by ongoing insurgencies, as the United States had been, for instance, in the Philippines and Nicaragua. Vollmer's Berkeley colleague Howard E. Pulliam was in charge of the Public Safety Division in occupied Japan. Pulliam was a rabid anticommunist who felt police reform and decentralization should not lead to Japan being turned over "to the pinks and reds."[71] To him, a potential insurgency lay hidden just beneath the wrecked surface of postwar Japanese society. His extremist views and viceroy-like behavior made him unpopular with the public and with Japanese officials. When the Japanese magazine *Ryoki* published a bawdy satirical article about his wife, the authorities prosecuted the editor, but a million copies of the issue sold.[72]

Engle arrived in Japan in mid-1946. MacArthur invited Engle to Japan on the recommendation of Major General O. P. Echols, a central figure in catalyzing the development of US air power in World War II, who was Wilson's supervisor in occupied Germany. Wilson and Hall likely brought Engle to Echols's attention.[73] Though an anticommunist like Pulliam, Engle, in an early address at Pulliam's behest to a conference of the Far East Command in Tokyo organized by the provost marshal, described the work of police more expansively as "essentially, *the regulation of human conduct.*" The work depended on police legitimacy, which consisted of the "*willingness of the people to accept regulation*" and the ability to convince "the subjects of regulation" of "the need for such regulation." If regulation went undefined here, it was implicitly anticommunist in orientation, focused on disciplining and constructing subjectivities through as wide a range of activities as "the enforcement of moral regulations and traffic control." Engle admitted that 95 percent of the people police encountered were not "criminals." Police dealt with the criminal 5 percent by eliminating "conditions conducive to crime," eliminating "the opportunity to commit crime," regulating conduct from vice to automotive traffic, and apprehending offenders. Though Pulliam had been Vollmer's man, Engle's address exhibited Vollmer's understanding of police work. But his practical recommendations in this address referred less to police philosophy than to a narrow technics of educational, aptitude, and physical requirements for officers; training regimens; and organizational orientation toward planning, supervision, and delegation of responsibility.[74] His catechism was beginning to congeal.

In Italy first and then postwar Germany, O. W. Wilson played a supervisory role much like Engle played in Japan, reorganizing and democratizing the police force. Wilson helped draft the *Public Safety Manual of Procedures: Military Government of Germany*, a compendium of guidelines on rebuilding the police, based on his principle that Adolf Hitler's centralization of police was "odious." To "reinitiate local control" was the first priority.[75] Engle recalled that in Japan he had ordered the experimental testing of "Wilson's pattern . . . in an oriental atmosphere."[76] Wilson brought Hall from Wichita to Europe, along with Ray Ashworth, another Wichita officer, who later became a leading police expert in traffic management and spent many years working for the IACP. Vollmer briefly joined Wilson in Germany too. Wilson had attended the new School of Military Government before leaving for Europe, where he was the only expert in policing among the students and faculty. Though nominally a student, Wilson ended up teaching seminars on law enforcement. He believed that structural reforms would lead to the professionalization of policing. Wilson required military-style discipline, an unbending chain of command, minute specialization of tasks within a rigid division of labor, and ongoing training. To professionalize policing was to militarize it, not in the sense of weapons or tactics, but through the construction of an institutional framework, the inculcation of a military bearing, and the cultivation of codified internal relationships. Army experience, with the untrammeled power to institute such reforms, confirmed his ideas.[77] The success of his approach in Germany legitimated its further deployment back home and elsewhere. This type of professionalization was highly replicable. OPS would carry it overseas. Engle's cohort disseminated it domestically as well.

Wilson gained prominence in the United States after he followed in Vollmer's footsteps. Recruited to the University of California, he became the first dean of Berkeley's School of Criminology, from 1950 to 1960. He published the most popular policing textbook of the period, *Police Administration*, first officially issued in 1938, and subsequently reissued over a half-dozen times in the coming decades, for a total publication run of over 100,000 copies. The versions published in the 1960s contained precepts his acolytes were already putting into practice and inscribing in manuals for police in countries like South Vietnam. Included among his writing and editing collaborators were several public safety mavens, including Theo Hall, Richard L. Holcomb, Howard Hoyt, John A. Lindquist, and Jeter L. Williamson. Wilson also produced other textbooks, *Police Records* and *Police Planning*. The very idea of a textbook to teach officers how to police reflected a reconceptualization of the task, an inward-looking, ascetic approach that placed the achievement of order in the hands of police, not in a broader social field. One prominent police historian evaluated Wilson's textbook as uninspiring: "Essentially a how-to book, it is written with all the passion of a car repair manual, focusing on issues like filing systems and inventory control."[78] That was the point. Although Vollmer early in his career may have brought to US policing an extension of and variation on lessons from counterinsurgency in the Philippines that treated social uplift through public works as the antidote to disorder, by the time his pupil Wilson surpassed him in influence in the profession, Vollmer too had come around to Wilson's approach. The demand for interventions in the welfare of the populace, and his belief that police shared much in common with social workers, became muted as Vollmer's career progressed. Wilson's yen for technical mastery and utmost discipline in crime suppression represented one pole in the constant oscillations within policing; Vollmer's more extensive approach to crime prevention was the other. Over his career, Vollmer voiced both, but he eventually adhered to the ethos Wilson and Engle both would advocate: police would achieve the requisite level of social intervention by focusing on intervening among their own ranks, pruning responsibilities and disciplining officers.

After leaving Berkeley, Wilson became Chicago's police commissioner. But he retained a global perspective. In 1958, Hall hired Wilson, his old mentor, as a consultant to review the ICA police assistance program.[79] In 1962, AID identified two of Wilson's textbooks as meriting top priority for translation into multiple languages and worldwide distribution.[80] "It looks like the name of Wilson will go down in Arabic annals with the name of Lawrence,"

Hall assured Wilson when an Arabic translation of *Police Administration* became available for Iraq and Saudi Arabia.[81] Wilson was among the most important bridge figures between the first generation of police professionalizers, active after World War I, and the second, active after World War II. Truman's Democratic administration ushered in the mandate of professionalization through its early attempts to assure racial equality, specifically the President's Committee on Civil Rights, which saw "professionalization of state and local police forces" as key to "racial progress."[82]

Engle called himself a "country boy," and that might have been true once, but he was faking provincialism even before OPS came into being. The midwesterners who piloted professionalized policing—Reed, Engle, Hoyt, Hall, Wilson, and others—were no rubes. Professionalized policing evolved through overseas encounters. Kansas City met Tokyo met Ankara met Saigon under the aegis of Engle's incipient vision of modernized, professional, well-trained, proactive, countersubversive police. National borders could not hem in this vision, because subversive and criminal threats to democracy perforce thrived on the porosity of borders. Policing expertise codified in the doctrines of professionalization that OPS imparted, and institutions like the IACP broadcast and taught, was neither simply exported from Japan nor imported from Missouri. Comparing situations compulsively, enacting context-specific refinements, navigating inherited conditions and preceding empires' institutional palimpsests, it took the globe as its domain of operations. It was locally grounded, because police had to patrol a beat. It was also forever expansionary, ever seeking the next nation in need of development and modernization, the next imperiled by radicalism. It sought the nooks and crannies of villages or growing metropolises where subversion and crime, or some novel configuration in combination of the two rooted, germinated, and blossomed. What these men took with them overseas, however, cannot explain what they achieved overseas, nor what they carried back home. Instead, the extraterritorial domain opened the possibility to achieve what was impossible back home. It was an opportunity to be seized, even if what its seizure would entail was not knowable in advance.

THE EDGES OF EMPIRE

Wilson ensured there was a stable security flank, policed on a US model, in West Germany, at the edge of eastern Europe. On the Pacific Rim, Engle secured the western flank. In Japan, he used the centralized power of SCAP to decentralize Japanese policing, to purge unwanted elements, and to institute protections that would neutralize political influences on the force. It was the only path out from authoritarianism, the only way to use the police as a device of democratization.[83] Engle designed police forces to fight the political war of counterinsurgency: when subversives sought to influence or wrest political control over social and cultural institutions and the state, the antidote was an apolitical, technically adept, and corruption-free police force. In effect, the reforms his mentor undertook in Kansas City to extract the police from the tentacles of a corrupt political machine were exactly what would insulate police overseas from communist subversion. To accomplish the task of developing this technocratic, politically insulated instrument, Engle instituted his particular method of police training, which potentiated the reach of lessons by focusing on training trainers to teach down the ladder of rank. This method was eventually adopted everywhere OPS operated and within the United States. Vollmer himself had tested this method, training only sergeants when he visited Kansas City in 1929.[84]

After SCAP ended, the prehistory of OPS was marked by a series of decentralized efforts to institute police assistance and devolve countersubversive functions to local authorities across a wide swath of the globe. Each effort, however, was less decentralized than the prior one, until OPS at last became a centralized locus for the initiative—which, nonetheless, retained a quasi-federalized, functionally decentralized modus operandi. A sort of shell game, a subterfuge, a feint, was necessary to avoid direct rule, but it was the means not the end. Order was the end.

Unlike the later programs Engle oversaw, the first post-1945 US police assistance program, in Japan, had no need to hide its purpose. Direct rule was temporarily necessary. The Allies had defeated Japan, and the goals were straightforward: first, to liquidate the remaining strains of authoritarian state power to prevent the rise of another government like the one that had bombed Pearl Harbor and attempted to control the Pacific; second, to monitor communist activities on the Pacific Rim, with Japan as a new US-supported bulkhead, which became even more important after Mao Zedong's revolutionary success in China. SCAP viewed Japan as having been a police state, and its reforms sought a precarious balance. The Allies needed to preserve the state's ability to gather intelligence on subversives and networks of illicit entrepreneurs, but SCAP also had to prevent this police power from regaining its authoritarian hue. The Public Safety Division's work in

Japan consisted of democratizing and pluralizing the police there by breaking up their centralized authority structure, abolishing militarized special forces, and then purging militarists and nationalists in other branches. Where once a massive police force integrated into a central hierarchy had reigned, now, without losing the ability to maintain internal security, Japan's police forces would operate on a more federalized model. Officially, it was a "revolutionary change of the police system," which would dismantle a "vast, powerful institution for suppressing essential human freedoms."[85] Occupation overseers believed that prewar centralization of security forces in Germany and Japan had inexorably founded those regimes' totalitarianism, expansionism, and, especially in the German case, exterminationism. They compared these integrated state structures to dispersed US federalism, but willfully ignored the reality of the US counterpoint: the decentralized despotism of policing that for African Americans in particular amounted to thousands of everyday micro-fascisms.

For SCAP, policing was a demonstration of how democratization, a modernization of state capacities friendly to US interests, could unfold. In practice, however, Pulliam's obsessions prevented sober assessment of local political realities. He inflated the subversive threat and then manipulated crime statistics to show decreases.[86] His inflexibility allowed other SCAP officials to outmaneuver him by building relationships with Japanese counterparts.[87] These kinds of problems would plague police assistance for decades. The reform of Japan's police had to be seen as "implanting the democratic ideal and principle in the Japanese police force," in the words of the longtime New York City police commissioner Lewis J. Valentine. MacArthur invited Valentine to visit Japan in early 1946 to make initial recommendations on reform. Pulliam's Public Safety Division set the framework for recommendations Valentine's team of New York officers could make, but, in light of his status as an exemplary mid-century US police reformer, it is little surprise that Valentine thought it was necessary to institutionalize "local democratic control" and to eliminate "many extraneous functions, including press censorship, supervision of health, sanitation and welfare, and fairly wide judicial functions."[88] In line with the professionalizing ethos, aimed at making police impervious to corruption, that Wilson advocated, Valentine's team called for "improvement in the policeman's position and qualifications" and a corresponding increase in pay.[89] These were recommendations that, devised in near-complete ignorance of Japan, would prove applicable in many locales, including throughout the United States.

The occupation of Japan offered crucial lessons for all future US police assistance; the occupation of Germany offered crucial personnel. Valentine, the urban policing expert, was one of two American police commissioners initially brought to Japan. The other was Oscar G. Olander, chief of the Michigan State Police, headquartered in East Lansing, near MSU's campus, but traditionally focused on sparsely populated rural areas.[90] In line with this orientation, Olander's recommendations during his four-month stint in Japan concerned its rural forces. In Michigan, Olander had refined the state police concept. First instituted in Pennsylvania in 1905, inspired by the US colonial government's Philippine Constabulary, the Keystone State's police agency recruited 80 percent of its initial officers from veterans of counterinsurgency in the Philippines, Cuba, and China.[91] Less beholden to political machines than their municipal counterparts, state police emphasized professionalism. Autonomous from local parties and staffed by men from across a given state, they often would be used to control labor disputes that municipal forces were unable to resolve. Olander's Michigan State Police not only assisted municipalities in emergency situations but also held a centralized repository of criminal identification and record-keeping and standardized training for all forces statewide.

Michigan, in turn, became an important base for US overseas police assistance, particularly after Mao Zedong seemed to propose a blueprint for a new rural route to communist revolution. East Lansing's municipal police chief was Arthur F. Brandstatter. After a stint as a cop in Detroit during World War II, he assumed a Military Police assignment in occupied Korea, where he devised a police reorganization plan. "I'd never heard of Korea," he later recalled. He soon afterward journeyed to occupied Germany to promote police reforms.[92] After his return to East Lansing, Brandstatter was appointed in 1947 to direct MSU's Department of Police Administration, the first degree-granting policing program, renamed in 1956 the School of Police Administration and Public Safety. Olander called it "Police West Point." One of Brandstatter's early initiatives was a training program at MSU specifically for West German police. He became a nationally renowned figure in police training.

From 1955 to 1962, under ICA sponsorship and with secret CIA funding, MSU operated a public-administration technical assistance mission to the Ngo Dinh Diem regime in South Vietnam.[93] Diem had befriended MSU professor Wesley Fishel, who facilitated the contract. Brandstatter helped evaluate the country's administrative needs soon after the Geneva accord of

FIGURE 5. Ceremony for the presentation of 100 new Jeeps to the Vietnamese Civil Guard from MSU, May 28, 1957. Michigan State University Archives & Historical Collections, Vietnam Project Records.

1954 formally ended the disastrous French occupation.[94] The biggest portion of the MSU consultation effort was police assistance, dwarfing finance and agriculture components, for example. Olander's rural patrol model was the basis for Diem's Civil Guard, which MSU advisors hoped would control ordinary crimes in the countryside. At first treated "like a bast—d at a family reunion by certain top functionaries of the Vietnamese government," it became a paramilitary police agency central to countering the rural insurgency that flared in South Vietnam beginning in 1957.[95]

The MSU group boasted 146 man-years of domestic police experience, including by some luminaries.[96] Howard Hoyt had become police chief in Kalamazoo, Michigan, where, in 1948, his officers confronted steel workers, joined on a picket line by sympathizers, who blocked roads, overturned cars, and burned a milk truck (a headline in the *New York Times* called them terrorists).[97] Hoyt subsequently headed MSU's police assistance operation in Saigon for several years. In 1963, after returning home, he parlayed his experience into new advisory roles, in Fort Worth, Texas, and Meriden, Connecticut.[98] Ralph F. Turner, the MSU forensics professor who succeeded Hoyt in South Vietnam, got his start in the Kansas City police department under Lear Reed. Turner supervised the Kansas City criminalistics laboratory at the time when Engle was overseeing the training division. Well-liked and a torchbearer in the field, he taught forensics for over three decades and co-founded the American Academy of Forensic Sciences. One of his early star students was Frank Walton of the LAPD, who then went to Vietnam to coordinate the ICA division that would supersede the MSU police assistance effort and become OPS's largest branch. Walton, a tough and unsentimental cop, clashed with Brandstatter, who complained to Turner about him. But Turner defended Walton.[99] They both saw the writing on the wall and anticipated the future under Engle.

Problems in Washington, Saigon, and East Lansing brought the MSU police assistance program in South Vietnam to an abrupt conclusion. Faculty chafed. The educational value of the program was questionable, and dangers were palpable. Diem was enraged when MSU professors wrote unfavorably about his regime in the *The New Republic*. MSU faculty consistently worried that their mission of technical assistance was impotent, particularly as an isolated Diem, bunkered in Saigon, tried to use the Civil Guard to control distant provinces and to employ other police agencies, including the Sûreté investigatory bureau, to clamp down on dissidents. Jack E. Ryan, a former FBI agent, reported that Vietnamese police trainees had "heard about our Negro problem," and worried that "we would treat them exactly as we treat Negroes down South."[100] Diem complained of US ambitions to impose a universal police dogma on his security forces. "This is not Brazil, Argentina, France, or Michigan," he caviled.[101] Suspicions at multiple levels, the proliferation and overlap of internal security and police agencies in South Vietnam, factionalism, and clashes between military and civilian command structures all hampered and confounded US assistance. Repression increased apace.[102] Engle's efforts to expand police assistance also competed with MSU for recruits, while the small size of the MSU operation was inadequate for the more than tripling in police force strength that advisors recommended. Engle also wondered whether MSU's operation was up to the task of helping secure the countryside, resistant as it was to the military weaponry the United States was supplying to the Civil Guard. Embedded but autonomous CIA officers must have raised similar questions. In turn, Ryan complained about furnishing cover for the CIA, condemning "'bubble head' Truman" for removing FBI "laddies" from the business of police technical assistance. He believed the FBI was far more capable in this domain than the CIA.[103] Among MSU staff, infighting and sniping, as well as Fishel's imperiousness—a political scientist should not be telling cops how to teach fingerprinting, went one of Hoyt's complaints—all challenged the advisory mission.[104] Engle and others in Washington easily perceived that putting police assistance under more direct control might be necessary.

Once MSU closed up shop, Diem acceded to US requests that he consolidate some police agencies into a single central command, which made training and technical assistance easier. One successful aspect of the reorganization was the transformation of the Sûreté, descended from the French colonial secret police, into the Vietnam Bureau of Investigation, or VBI, modeled on the FBI but embedded in the National Police. Yet the decreed reorganization also proved Engle's own thesis, applied in Japan, that too centralized a police apparatus could be undemocratic. Further repression of urban opposition ensued, aided by US matériel, which popularized the rural insurgency and undermined Diem's already fragile rule.[105]

Engle would never again have as free a hand as he had had in Japan, and he was obliged to walk the knife-edge between democratization and security—or, as Pulliam once put it, reflecting on reforms in Japan in comparison to the League of Nations' shortcomings, the conflict between "mawkish sentimentality over the individual rights of man" and "practical considerations in a world of eternal conflict."[106] This balancing act echoed the work of Reed in Kansas City. Engle carried it with him on his peregrinations across the globe, as he assessed internal security situations and indigenous police and paramilitary capabilities.[107] The US experience in occupied Germany set precedents for the longer-lasting occupation of Japan. Yet the lessons the experts learned in each setting, with their particularities, also proved useful at home and for further rounds of export. Engle would address the failures of the MSU effort, which Brandstatter and Turner bitterly and amply recorded, in subsequent programming that was fully under his control.[108] He constantly sought the right combination of reforms. In February 1956, a US advisor contacted British officials in Malaya on Engle's behalf about sending police instructors from Cambodia, Vietnam, and Laos to Kuala Lumpur to use British facilities as "training for trainers," though he recognized that police personnel from countries whose legal systems were shaped by French imperial inheritances might not benefit.[109] These extraterritorial experiences, and the constant interimperial and cross-cultural comparisons they evoked, enhanced state capacities and provided testing grounds for new ways to take advantage of them. They were crucial moments of state-formation. Tokyo may not have been Shanghai, but it became like Kansas City. And Kansas City would become like Tokyo, a crucible of police experimentation for decades.

．．．

Engle held a steadfast commitment to a particular modernizing vision of the police, of police as malleable, not static, to be used to shape social formations undergoing the turbulence of rapid development. Engle's citation for excellence, when he called himself "a country boy" in an interview with a Kansas City reporter, illustrated how the malleability of police would be measured at a global scale. Engle knew the audience he was addressing there, and how his achievements would be received. He did not want to seem to have forgotten his roots, even though Kansas City was in his rear-view mirror once he had decamped for Japan. Engle's citation, however, was also noted by the monthly magazine for police executives *The Police Chief,* which paid close attention to US police advisory work overseas (each group of advisors stationed across the globe received a subscription to it, plus *Police, Public Management,* and *The Journal of Criminal Law, Criminology, and Police Science*).[110] Domestic and foreign interosculated. The professionalization of US policing proceeded through its relations with a world not constrained by national borders. It was a world this action constructed. The professionalizers' ambition was for that world—*a* US-centered world—to become *the* world. The professionalizers' ambition was to make the world a US-centered one.[111]

Before the Engles retired to their life of African safaris and shooting competitions, the United States was afflicted by the same conflations of subversion and crime, communism and racial difference, that had propelled police-led campaigns for order across Africa, Asia, and Latin America. A wide array of critics of the policing of American city streets at the time used the term "occupation" in signifying their disgust and organizing political opposition. Whether undergoing reform or not, policing in Black neighborhoods was despotic. James Baldwin famously likened Harlem to "occupied territory," and the white police officer there to an "occupying soldier in a bitterly hostile country"; the sociologist Robert Blauner called the police in the Watts section of Los Angeles an "army of occupation."[112] Significantly, the police practices condemned as "occupation" had been learned and tested through occupations on the edges of US empire, first tentatively by Vollmer in the Philippines and then more firmly by Wilson in Germany and Engle in Japan.

THREE

How Counterinsurgency Became Policing

IN 1963, OPS, THE US OFFICE OF PUBLIC SAFETY, produced a didactic film titled *First Line of Defense* to use as a training tool for the police officers from across the globe who attended its academy in Washington, DC. A film could be dubbed, as this one was, in French, Portuguese, and Spanish, which was easier for US personnel than lecturing in a foreign language. Some foreign officers even starred in the film. *First Line of Defense* was produced in the Panama Canal Zone, with Latin American cops playing the roles of the subversives and the angry mobs they incited. It depicted the stages of unrest a civilian police force could expect to encounter when communists attempted to destabilize a country. Benign-seeming political agitation, such as any liberal social formation might be expected to witness, was one of those stages, and it should not be overlooked, given its potentially catalytic effect in developing countries. One tool of such agitation was the daubing of walls with political exhortations. In the film, a cryptic graffito reading "O/PS" appeared in the background of many shots. This was an inside joke: O/PS was the routing term for communications within the Department of State and AID hierarchy to the Office of Public Safety, which aimed to guarantee that Third World nations would be capable of creating their own first line of defense against subversion, backstopped by US money, materials, and know-how. For leaders of industry, the state was capital's last line of defense, expected to intervene if markets went haywire as a result of subversive agitation. In the law enforcement view, however, subversion would not develop if well-trained, professional police nipped agitation—and crime—in the bud.[1]

There is another way interpret the O/PS graffiti in the training film, however. OPS, and the Special Group (Counter Insurgency; hereafter SGCI) that oversaw it, were the results of a low-intensity battle within the US government. These institutions represented three unpopular positions: a turn toward counterinsurgency, a shift away from prioritizing the military to wage counterinsurgency, and the centralization of oversight of counterinsurgency into one council. Robert W. Komer was the greatest advocate of OPS, and of these three positions. He was nothing if not an agitator. Komer overturned orthodoxies, consequences for the reputations of his superiors and social proprieties among Washington insiders be damned. And in so doing, he and Byron Engle created the institutional space within the state for a remaking of the state itself, which would put crime prevention as the social goal above all others. They transformed counterinsurgency into policing.

In Komer and Engle's view, if anything stymied the rise of police-centric counterinsurgency, it would be inertia and sclerosis in the bureaucracy, not guerrillas, terrorists, gangsters, or revolutionaries. Komer took the eradication of such impediments as his primary task. He was a vocal activist, pushing, manipulating, and even teaching those around him, including prominent intellectuals like Walt Rostow. Engle, in contrast, relied on what he saw as the self-evident importance of his own subordinates' practiced expertise and the routines of professionalized policing, rather than on a nimble assessment of the specific problems to be managed in Washington. His attention was focused on Saigon, Kinshasa, and Tegucigalpa.

Engle's cop cohort figured their project of police reform as a global one. It was a project that reconfigured itself—policing, the state's first line of defense—as it reconfigured its object—crime, subversion, a globe in the throes of revolution. It sought to adequate itself to an unknowable, seemingly metastasizing threat by producing expertise, reshaping lines of bureaucratic authority, and affirming the necessity of programmatic adherence to codes and procedures. Engle might have remained in the shadows if Komer had never joined the National Security Council. It was far from inevitable that Komer would succeed in creating OPS. Many powerful men did not believe policing should be the essence of counterinsurgency, and Komer had to disprove and outlast all of them. Key to his effort was his anxious appraisal of recent history, his concurrence with the CIA's analysis in "The Break-Up of the Colonial Empires and Its Implications for US Security," and his aversion to recapitulating direct colonial rule. Without Komer's relentless labors and exquisite success in achieving his goals, the effort to construct the first line of defense might have petered out, unraveling in a mire of deflected responsibility, rather than tightening in an ever-stronger spiral of centralization of state administration to decentralize state functions.

"First line of defense" was a term to describe the beat cop that migrated from J. Edgar Hoover's lexicon to other Washington venues. In Komer's hands, its intensity ratcheted up and its applicability widened.[2] It was spelled out in October 1955 in an address by CIA Director Allen W. Dulles to the IACP in Philadelphia: "The importance of police and other internal security forces in this work has become more and more evident in many parts of the world. . . . Where countries are subject to communist subversive tactics, the internal security forces must generally be the first line of defense."[3] The term "first line of defense" proclaimed the project's own necessity: in its absence there was no defense but US-Soviet thermonuclear stalemate.

THE FUNCTION OF THE FIRST LINE OF DEFENSE

There was a certain functionalism to this understanding of the first line of defense. Underpinning it was the certainty that problems of rule arose with disruption of the "differentiated and harmoniously integrated functioning society" that was, in the dominant social-scientific thinking of the time, "the normative standard for identifying social health and pathology."[4] The first line of defense aimed to preserve this homeostatic standard. As one indispensable node in the functional system, the police played a leading role in their ability and duty to preserve harmony. Yet in the post-1945 period, contradictions troubled the very framework. For one thing, "functionalism was famously unable to account for change." When the leading US sociologist Talcott Parsons, its best-known advocate, "began more explicitly laying the groundwork for a modernization-theoretical account of historical change, history was constrained to follow a path that flattened it out."[5] The NSC under President John F. Kennedy was enthralled by modernization, committed to keeping history on this path. Counterinsurgency was the means, according to Walt Rostow, of ensuring that modernization was not channeled into extremist appeals to redirect this revolution, inasmuch as "scavengers of the modernization process" aimed to capitalize on discontent and disarray.[6] Although structural-functionalism had little to say about revolution or insurgency, or their prevention, in Rostow's view, insurgency was necessarily related to disequilibrium. Infiltrating revolutionaries and subversives took advantage of disequilibrium ushered into Third World social life by the frenzy of modernization, which entailed urban migration and new sociospatial morphologies, technological change and novelties of consumption, emergent mass sources of information, reconfigured gender relations, the endowments and expectations of sovereign citizenship, and the dissolution of customary economic ties via capitalist-oriented commerce and labor relations. Theorists of this transformation substituted the outcome of homeostatic modernity for what was the uneven and relentless churn of capitalist social relations and their encounter with and transformation of noncapitalist social, political, and economic forms.[7]

Modernization theory inherited counterinsurgency from structural-functionalism.[8] Modernizers imagined the process of modernization in broadly functionalist terms, with institutions playing specified roles in maintaining functional integration of a social formation itself in flux, and with their failure to do so retarding or imperiling modernization. Yet even among less explicitly structural-functionalist interpretations, the relationship of insurgency and counterinsurgency within the modernization paradigm turned on the problem of disequilibrium. When disequilibrium occurred, as it necessarily had to, the most potent risk was that of externally triggered insurgency derailing the modernization process. To right it demanded counterinsurgency. In fact, in Rostow's punchy directive to create an "Institute of Modernization Studies," he argued of the "internal defense" of "emergent nations" that "encouraging the forward thrust of these societies, and anticipating and preparing them against the tension and resistance generated by modernization, are two sides of the same coin."[9]

Modernizers keenly appreciated that the construction of order implied cracking extant order, even if they underestimated the instability at the level of everyday life that market dependence and proletarianization entailed. New physical infrastructures, land reform, urbanization, industrialization, and the adoption of consumer-oriented lifestyles would unsettle settled modes of living, they believed, leaving many susceptible, in the disarray and confusion of ongoing social upheaval, to the appeals of revolutionaries, who would tilt public sympathies away from the West, away from capitalism, away from democracy. The necessary encounter with difference that modernization represented produced recalcitrant new social subjectivities, scripted as avatars of crime and subversion. "Change itself causes stress," OPS's second and final director suggested. "If it gets out of hand, it can frustrate progress."[10]

Theorists hoped to devise what the United States lacked in comparison to communists: doctrine, personnel, and institutions to predict, prevent, ameliorate, and resolve the disarray of the modernization process. Rostow championed the sweeping away of traditional social relations. He believed, however, that communists possessed ready doctrine, ready personnel, and ready institutions at hand to take advantage of the social disarray of this process. In the functionalist schema, disruptive forces always originated exogenously from a bounded social system, which fed into security planners' worries about border control, smuggling, subversion, and social alterity. Insurgency's occurrence, meaning that communists had taken advantage of dislocations to redirect loyalties and aspirations, necessitated counterinsurgency. Insurgency was "an attempt to change all or part of the power subsystem of a society, or if necessary the entire social system," a Defense Research Corporation workbook observed. Counterinsurgency aimed "to maintain the system in the status quo or to restore it."[11]

For some observers this view toward the status quo underwrote the countersubversive police assistance program, particularly in its support of repressive and authoritarian regimes.[12] Calibrating the "right kind of revolution" implicit in modernization was difficult.[13] Komer sought to discard the notion of maintenance of the status quo—which was in fact underdevelopment. Far from defending this situation, security forces had a multifaceted mission to "help governments deal with the dislocations inherent in development in an orderly way."[14] But the inescapable paradox of prioritizing security as a precondition for development was that the institutions called upon to effect such orderly change, whether military or civil police, tended to defend entrenched interests and resist institutional transformation, although US assistance was intended to transform them. Counterinsurgency truncated the menu of political options available in aid-recipient countries, even in the absence of active guerrilla insurgency.

Throughout the 1960s, officials vacillated and ultimately failed to resolve whether counterinsurgency as national security policy meant opposition to social transformation and regime change tout court. For example, a member of the State Department's Bureau of Intelligence and Research questioned the description of counterinsurgency as "freezing the status quo" that Kennedy's deputy under secretary for political affairs U. Alexis Johnson offered in a lecture. The goal was modernizing reform, but if a government refused to reform, "would not our effort be aimed at getting it at least to yield constitutionally to a reformist government if one were elected?"[15] Nikita Khrushchev zeroed in on this "challenge" to Kennedy directly at their 1961 summit in Vienna, when he is quoted as saying that "the Soviets are the automatic allies of those seeking change of the *status quo*."[16] This critique rattled the Kennedy administration. Development aid could not be timid in the face of this challenge.

Yet Rostow had to be convinced of the importance of police assistance to counterinsurgency. Komer took persuading him as his task. Unlike Komer, Rostow, along with many others in the Kennedy administration, believed counterinsurgency could be waged actively. US specialists, and the indigenous groups or mercenaries they would enlist and train, could adopt the guerrilla guise. In this sense, though, US-trained guerrillas who attacked guerrillas purportedly backed by Moscow or Peking were themselves disruptors of social equilibrium. Komer's "first line of defense" replaced this model of counterinsurgency. Although modernizers lavished support on the romantic idea of fighting guerrilla warfare with guerrilla warfare of their own, Komer's far less flashy vision ultimately accorded with the functionalism underlying their intellectual framework. It would be a mistake, of course, to assume that exogenous US aid, even for policing to maintain orderly social homeostasis, did not reshape social relations. Insofar as social formations were functionally integrated, autonomous, and bounded wholes, the imposition of aggressive counterinsurgency measures or even more benign forms of community-development aid disrupted the smooth operation of these countries' institutions. Counterinsurgency, some social scientists warned, might have "unforeseen effects. . . modifying the whole social system."[17]

What modernization theory sought to derive, and also to prescribe for heads of state, was a universal rheostat that would first develop and then maintain functionally integrated and balanced yet semi-autonomous subsystems within new nations. But the everyday details were difficult. For on-the-ground police and paramilitary advisors, the prescription read: no carrot in an environment that required the stick. Though endlessly reinvented, recalibrated, and rebalanced, there was little margin of error for the carrot, as backsliding into a situation of insecurity was a constant threat. Heavy, frequent reliance upon the stick ensued. OPS was Komer's quiet realization of promises of modernization thinking, which meant slowly discarding the vision of the renaissance-man covert military operator and replacing it with the more familiar but now professionalized, homogenized beat cop. How Komer achieved this transformation was to act like a plucky guerrilla himself, disrupting the entrenched, self-propelling, seemingly homeostatic bureaucracy from within, taking the interdependence of its parts not as writ but as a challenge.

After 1945, US overseas police assistance occurred on an ad hoc basis. In December 1954, however, dissatisfied with the covert, reactive approach, the Eisenhower administration initiated a formal program for undertaking proactive police assistance in the maintenance of internal security, called National Security Council Action 1290d. Soon thereafter, the administration established the International Cooperation Administration. A working group consisting of representatives from State, the Pentagon, ICA, and CIA convened to investigate how to fulfill the mandate of 1290d. Their initial list of forty-four endangered countries to research was soon halved, which led to more intense investigations and a resulting ranking in terms of threat of subversion in these twenty-two countries. At the top of the list were Laos and Vietnam, but Indonesia was the first country to receive police assistance under the new arrangement, with Vietnam next. The Eisenhower administration determined in December 1955 that ICA would house the overt 1290d program in its regional and local bureaus. Formal police assistance had commenced, consisting of the training and equipping of indigenous police and paramilitary forces for crime and riot control, counterguerrilla action, and surveillance of potentially threatening individuals and organizations.[18] Though the term "counterinsurgency" did not yet exist, this effort was its chrysalis: addressing the broad population to immunize it against political militants (countersubversion) and protect against active guerrillas (counterguerrilla warfare).

From the start, a lack of centralized coordination hampered the effectiveness of the program. Under Secretary of State Herbert Hoover Jr., one of the prime movers behind 1290d, bemoaned the program's lack of interagency coordination to CIA representatives Byron Engle and Jerry Jelsch.[19] In March 1957, 1290d was rechristened the Overseas Internal Security Program (OISP), but it never gained a strong, centralized organization. The various interested agencies, including State, Defense, ICA, and CIA, often competed with each other. They duplicated responsibilities. Or they punted. Each attempted to use OISP for its own purposes, selfish tendencies encouraged because the program was dispersed across the globe in execution and management. Within ICA, many officials viewed police assistance as a distraction from economic aid. Heated arguments erupted over whether police assistance should consist of supplying mortars and machine guns to recipient countries or placing police advisors alongside CIA mercenaries in combat operations, for example.[20] ICA officials derided the program as "running guns to cops."[21] Though Theo Hall came to take charge of the OISP, there was no single defender of the mission who was empowered to hone a specific public safety vision. Compared to the goals that would guide OPS, the goals of OISP were at once narrower, due to limited capacities, and more ambitious, due to a lack of codification and the influence of the totalizing example SCAP in Japan had provided. Most important, OISP was not a great success because there was no single budget for police assistance. Advisors had to compete for allocations in each ICA mission.

Despite having tried to institutionalize it, Eisenhower's NSC did not prioritize police assistance. It was always considered at best an adjunct to military assistance, which drew greater interest throughout the 1950s. Halfway through Eisenhower's second term, however, the Military Assistance Program came under scrutiny, and a partisan reorientation commenced. Democrats in Congress, among them Senator John F. Kennedy, saw a critique of military assistance as a way to score points against Republicans. They were hoping to articulate a new vision of foreign policy that would emphasize development in poorer countries and the prevention of the spread of communism, while shifting the focus away from nuclear stalemate.[22] The shift was from defense to offense, from the Northern Hemisphere to the Southern. The key apparatus for this shift was the President's Committee to Study the Military Assistance Program, or Draper Committee, an Eisenhower-approved inquiry into military assistance launched in November 1958. Led by General William H. Draper Jr., the committee issued a massive report in August of the next year. The Draper Report set the stage for the elaboration of what General Maxwell D. Taylor called the doctrine of "flexible response." Taylor would become Kennedy's chief military advisor, largely on the strength of his caustic criticism of the Eisenhower status quo of massive retaliation and its accompanying reduction of tactical ground-force troop levels throughout Eisenhower's administration. For Taylor, flexible response offered a way to sneak troop mobilizations around the demobilizing thrust of atom-age paralysis.

While the OISP was in operation, several incidents of urban unrest around the globe, exactly what the program was designed to help prevent, caught the attention of counterinsurgency experts, as well as members of Congress. Clashes between protesters and security forces across Latin America during Vice President Richard Nixon's 1958 tour of the region were the most prominent of these. Angry, expectorating crowds met Nixon in nearly every country he visited. When, in his words, "a weird-looking char-acter," "one of the most notorious Communist agitators in Lima," spat in his face, Nixon kicked him in the shins.[23] A protest in Japan scuttled President Eisenhower's planned visit on the day a new United States–Japan mutual security pact went into effect, leading a week later to the prime minister's resignation. This and other protests in Japan, many led by student radicals, marked the inception of the global New Left, well in advance of its US phase. The irruption on the Pacific Rim was the opening salvo of the 1960s period.[24] In years to come, experts and elected officials repeatedly invoked these events as models for communist-led urban unrest, both in cautionary and tactical terms. James O. Eastland, the arch-segregationist senator from Mississippi, soon headed a congressional hearing that took note of Nixon's difficulties in Latin America and tied them to a need for better countersubversive action to prevent urban unrest.[25] But the intensity of these clashes also seemed to high-light how military assistance, which took the form of creating arsenals geared toward external aggression, was inadequate to fighting insurgency. Such aid, moreover, was tarnishing the image of the United States abroad. It was also possibly empowering authoritarian regimes: on this point later New Left critics and the advocates of police assistance agreed.

Nixon's visit to Latin America occurred within the broader context of an ongoing debate in foreign-affairs circles about US obligations of economic and military assistance with a view to Third World modernization and devel-opment. Eisenhower appointed William Draper, an Army general who had participated in the occupation of Germany and advised in that of Japan, to lead a committee meant to mollify his partisan critics.[26] The Draper Committee's findings supported Eisenhower's approach and insisted that military and economic aid were equivalent and interchangeable, however, which emboldened the critics.[27] Still, Democrats in Congress had trouble agreeing on the best method, with some, like J. William Fulbright, arguing that foreign economic aid should be considered a separate objective from military aid. Ultimately, a new approach would attempt to rejigger the bal-ance, toward economic aid while maintaining a strong focus on security. That approach coalesced out of findings buried within the pages of the Draper Report. Three topics stood out: "civic action," a term the counterinsurgency impresario Edward G. Lansdale had introduced to the committee, meaning the use of military forces to promote and carry out projects in education, public works, health, sanitation, agriculture, communications, and other dimensions of development; reliance on well-trained and -equipped indigenous forces to carry out these projects; and recognition that communist tactics were shifting "from direct military challenges to subversion, propaganda and economic offenses."[28] The approach also was contained in messages conveyed to the Draper Committee's investigators, even if they did not wholeheartedly adopt them. One such message came from Komer of the CIA: "for what it's worth, my own personal opinion is that OISP ought to be increased, and offered to each new underdeveloped country. And if anyone had the guts to do so, OISP could be used to reduce the demand for military aid, especially in countries where internal security is the primary mission."[29] Komer did not get his way on police assistance at the time, but he did under Kennedy, when he joined the NSC. If Engle was the father of US police assistance, Komer was both its midwife and godfather. He consolidated the first line of defense.

KOMER'S GLOBAL FUNDAMENTALS

Flexibility became a watchword of Kennedy's foreign policy. The "New Frontier" Kennedy championed meant breaking free of the mutually assured superpower deadlock. It directed attention to the nonaligned, the neutral, and, most important, the nationalist. Police assistance, with its wide applicability to emergent problems along the New Frontier, proved an exemplar of flexibility. Intellectuals who adhered to the modernization paradigm, whom Kennedy admired, thought of modern police as a presupposition of modernization, a central ingredient of liberal governance. Foreign police reform had support within intellectual circles at a time when foreign-policy officials were trying to develop a set of guidelines for the US role in the world that were consonant with the leading scholarly approach. Yet flexibility was not wholly new. In an interview with David Apter, a key modernization theorist, in 1955, General Maxwell Taylor articulated his view that nuclear deterrence was insufficient in a world beset by "local aggressions." Taylor amplified this view in his 1960 book *The Uncertain Trumpet,* and it came to shape the counterinsurgency era of the Kennedy and Johnson administrations. Taylor told Apter that "the question of how best to resist local aggressions, or limited wars—how to deal with situations in which neither side will wish to engage in the unrestricted use of [nuclear] weapons" was fundamental. It called for "a flexible system of defense, capable of meeting various degrees of aggression with appropriate degrees of force."[30]

NSC 68, issued under the authority of President Truman and Secretary of State Dean Acheson in 1950, was the origin of the "flexible response" posture.[31] This proposal articulated in explicit terms the globalization of the Cold War that was embryonic in the Pacific Rim occupations. Paul H. Nitze, its primary author, intended the policy statement to shift away from reliance on atomic arms toward conventional forces. The novel threat NSC 68 diagnosed, which required the United States to assume "world leadership," was "the absence of order."[32] The Eisenhower administration, in contrast, moved in a different direction, atomic deterrence. Flexibility, therefore, bore the Democratic Party's imprimatur. The Eisenhower administration's position was shifting, but Kennedy beat Nixon while painting him as wanting to maintain Eisenhower's posture. The new administration immediately went to work developing the New Frontier's approach. The second Kennedy National Security Action Memorandum (NSAM) exhibited the new flexible stance, "placing more emphasis" on counterguerrilla forces. Even the term "action memorandum" signaled a shift from what the new administration had perceived as an ossified national security apparatus during the prior one. "A mobile, substantial, and flexible US capability for operations short of general war is essential to meet the threat of limited aggression, which is likely to assume increasing importance in the years ahead," insisted an early statement of priorities from Secretary of State Dean Rusk to Secretary of Defense Robert McNamara, issued a day after NSAM 2.[33] Taylor's excoriation of Eisenhower in his book, and Kennedy's adoption of the flexible-response posture, evinced a return to Cold War fundamentals, which for Komer, orbited around the question not of communism per se but of nationalism in decolonizing zones, and to what uses it would be put.

To understand this return to fundamentals, which the Kennedy administration portrayed to voters as a drastic change of course, it is necessary to look more deeply at Robert Komer, who grew up as an outsider, the son of a Jewish merchant family from the outskirts of St. Louis, but rose to prominence in the National Security Council, his trademark pipe always in hand as he counseled multiple presidents.[34] He was Engle's primary defender during the Kennedy and Johnson presidencies. Komer took it upon himself to realize what SCAP's reforms in Japan had indicated. His work on behalf of the national security state centralized to decentralize. He also insisted that law enforcement would be the means of ensuring order on the state's behalf while also acting as a vanguard for the transformation of inherited bureaucracy. To achieve flexibility in national security, the state itself had to become flexible. This work was visible in the operation of the SGCI, in the formation of OPS, and, finally, in Civil Operations and Revolutionary Development Support (CORDS), the directorate for pacification in South Vietnam that Komer came to oversee. Komer showed that police could be both the instrument of state power and the means of transforming the state. The benchmark, however, would be nothing less than dozens of new nations' achievement of independence and self-determination and their simultaneous fealty, it was hoped, to US interests.

When Komer joined the Kennedy NSC, having studied the work of Engle and others in police assistance throughout the 1950s, he became a most vociferous proponent—"the chief pusher," as he described himself to Robert F. Kennedy—of extending police assistance as counterinsurgency across the globe.[35] Such aid should go "to each new underdeveloped country," as he had explained to the Draper Committee. Komer insisted that police assistance had been remarkably successful in spite of its status as a neglected "orphan child" within the foreign-affairs bureaucracy.[36] After Kennedy's inauguration, he ascended to his NSC post as an assistant to National Security Advisor McGeorge Bundy. Though much of the Kennedy reputation rests on the administration's approach to international development, security had to be its precondition. Among intellectuals, the idea that security must precede development quickly traveled from the Foreign Policy Research Institute on the anticommunist right in 1959 to the mainstream among liberal intellectuals in a couple years. Its embrace by security experts smoothed this shift, and the Draper Report gave it a voice.[37] Early in Kennedy's term, NSC staffers began to investigate how to help a country "develop adequate security forces" and how such help "might foster the country's economic development."[38] Komer was positioned perfectly: to a receptive audience he brought experience and knowledge on what nonmilitary internal security assistance could achieve in the field of political and economic development. In essence, such assistance could enable the construction of an environment of security that would allow development to proceed, while also managing the tumult rapid development would unleash. This congeries was Komer's vision of counterinsurgency.

A list US officials who gave purchase to the newfangled term "counterinsurgency" would include CIA officer William Colby, State Department analyst Roger Hilsman, diplomat U. Alexis Johnson, Marine Lieutenant General Victor Krulak, CIA officer Ed Lansdale, Deputy National Security Advisor Rostow, and General Taylor. Among these men were veterans of jungle warfare and partisan efforts to repel occupations during World War II.

President Kennedy and his brother Robert, the attorney general, were crucial, with the administration issuing at least twenty-three NSAMs concerning counterinsurgency in three years. At the top of the list, however, should be Komer. He joined the Kennedy White House after a fourteen-year career in intelligence at the CIA.[39] Counterinsurgency theory was unsettled and contested in this moment. Komer was for a brief time at the vanguard of its practical rethinking. Modernization theory often cemented together these figures' conceptualizations of desired outcomes, threats to those outcomes, and their remedy. But Komer himself aimed to modernize the incipient US fight against insurgents. He insisted that two obsessions shared by Colby, Hilsman, Krulak, Lansdale, and the Kennedy brothers were outdated: the phantom of Mao-indoctrinated rural warriors and the deployment of specially trained forces in response who would fight guerrillas as guerrillas themselves. No, Komer insisted, civil policing and development programming must counter insurgency preemptively. It would occur largely in cities. For Komer, this new campaign could not be fought with the old weapons these combat veterans shouldered. The lessons of occupation veterans like Engle, Hall, and Hoyt prevailed.

No other figure better typified, or more rigorously enacted, the resolute commitment to US security on an ambitiously global scale through a devolved, combinatorial approach of development assistance yoked to civilian-based countersubversive policing. Komer adopted a "worm's eye point of view," as he put it;[40] intelligence collection and policing were the soil in which US global power would be grow, permitting political and economic alignments favorable to US interests to flower. He understood that the Cold War against the Soviet Union was unlike previous wars, because it would be a war fought mostly on the terrain of recently decolonized countries, among and for peoples not eager to accept a new dispensation of dominion. Not simply a matter of repelling Soviet arms, this war entailed competing visions of a global covenant. Halting Soviet visions of modernization was not enough, however. Loyalties to the US vision had to be won.

Compared to Eisenhower's, Kennedy's administration adopted a less hierarchical approach to its management of foreign affairs. Komer was the hub of a "broad network throughout the bureaucracy which he had developed during his service in the CIA." He solicited input from lower-rung experts who focused on the budget, economic development, or military issues. He also spent time in Kennedy's Oval Office "almost daily." Komer was a dynamo: pugnacious and short-tempered, with "little regard for stepping on people's toes or for any protocol requirements."[41] But he was loyal to a fault and unfailingly persistent, persistent, persistent. More so than anyone in the NSC environs he inhabited, Komer almost invariably got his way. That may explain his relentless optimism, a characteristic that made him look like a fool in the eyes of many US news audiences after the US war in Vietnam appeared lost. He valued flexibility, leadership, and grit. Rostow quipped that Komer "lets no grass grow under his feet."[42]

Komer's nickname was Blowtorch. He acquired it when he offered unvarnished assessments of how the policy decisions of Ambassador Henry Cabot Lodge Jr. were failing to generate success in South Vietnam. Blowtorch Bob—listening to his cajoling about the war's progress could be like sitting atop a blue flame. Yet what does a blowtorch actually do with its heat? A blowtorch is not a cutting tool; rather it applies heat in preparation for reshaping, or for completing modest reconfiguration through soldering and brazing. Komer was a master of the national security state. He was a driver, a navigator, and a mechanic working beneath the hood. He understood its chassis and knew that tweaks would improve performance. He applied the initial heat that would make possible the joining or splitting a more concentrated application of heat, by, say, the president or McGeorge Bundy, would then enable. This catalyzing was Komer's work on behalf of US national security. He frequently got his way because Lyndon Johnson trusted him and believed his word. It helped that Komer described his work as an extension of partisan politics, having once assured Johnson that he was "a lifelong Democrat."[43] While stationed in Vietnam, Komer was so sure of imminent success that prior to the Tet Offensive he told Johnson that he did not expect Vietnam to play a major role in the 1968 election. At a party of US elites in Saigon on the eve of that Tet holiday—invitations bedizened with the phrase "Come see the light at the end of the tunnel"—Komer showed up dressed in an orange, flame-retardant suit, an ironic reference to his blowtorch moniker.[44] The light came in the form of mortar rounds and satchel charges. Komer's reputation was destroyed. His loyalty to Johnson and dedication to seeing his promises kept clouded his judgment. He had had a good many years of successful, if irascible, advisement before then, though. The way he used his acerbic tongue was not impartial or disinterested. From his early days in intelligence work, Komer developed a vision of how the state worked and what reconfigurations of its capacities would be necessary for it to take on the massive, difficult, delicate, and unpopular task of superintending a global system.

FIGURE 6. Robert W. Komer and Lyndon B. Johnson in the Oval Office, February 1, 1966. LBJ Library, photo by Yoichi Okamoto.

Born in Chicago in 1922, Komer attended Harvard University as part of a growing crop of outsiders to its usual elite, Protestant pedigree. At Harvard, Komer excelled. He studied history, a point of personal pride that he occasionally raised when speaking with academic advisors to the Johnson administration. Komer told Bernard Fall, a preeminent French expert on Vietnam, that he had once been a "soi-disant military historian."[45] US entry into the war in late 1941, when he was almost twenty years old, interfered with Komer's studies. He was already pursuing a Master's degree in business at Harvard when he was called up from the Army Reserve in 1943. Komer's demanding father had been an officer in the US Army. The son referred to him as Major.[46] He followed in his father's footsteps, like so many, into the military in World War II. Military intelligence was his assignment, and he put his experience studying history to work drafting analyses of "lessons learned" in past operations. According to Komer's biographer, "this encounter with the historiography of the Army's role in the governance and civil administration of liberated and occupied areas would later influence his thinking," including in Vietnam.[47] At war's end, after completing his interrupted studies at Harvard Business School, he did not relish a return to Missouri. He had been lined up to inherit the family business, but his sights were set far beyond St. Louis. Working for his father seemed like small potatoes. When Army buddies informed him of job opportunities in the newly formed intelligence agency, he jumped at the chance. It took some time for his career in intelligence to take off, but the appointment of a former Harvard professor of his to lead the CIA's new Office of National Estimates in late 1950 gave him scope to shine. As was the case for Engle, though of a different tenor, the connections Komer had made early in his life would later afford him the opportunity to demonstrate his dedication, perseverance, and aptitude.[48]

A generation of commentators argued that ignorance of the specificities of Southeast Asia led the Johnson administration to disaster. Neil Sheehan mentioned, for example, that Komer had little knowledge of Southeast Asia before his assignment to head pacification for Johnson.[49] His expertise was in the Middle East, India, and Europe. The administration had access to the most sophisticated, up-to-date, and robust expert knowledge on Southeast Asia, however. The problem was that policymakers ignored this information.[50] Komer's correspondence with Bernard Fall indicates this access. Ignorance was not the problem. Rather, it was the breach into which the United States stepped: what the CIA had called the break-up of the colonial empires. The nascent US national security state's ambitions were worldmaking. Its officials felt nationalism in decolonizing areas could thwart a global Pax Americana.

In 1960, just weeks before Kennedy's election, Komer recapitulated the 1948 analysis of "The Break-Up of the Colonial Empires and Its Implications for US Security" in a memorandum titled "Focus."[51] Komer was attempting to remind his CIA colleagues that they had once known better how to understand the world. Insurgencies that the earlier analysis had feared were now roiling the Gray Areas, a term he took from Thomas K. Finletter, secretary of the Air Force under President Truman (indicating an affinity with the last Democratic administration, rather than the current Republican one).[52] Too frequently, though, intelligence officers analyzed the unsettled situations in new nations in isolation from one another, as static islands, with independent and autonomous causal motors. Analysts were too easily separating part from whole and succumbing to what social scientists today would call "methodological nationalism," the naturalization of the nation-state as the adequate unit of analysis for sociopolitical processes. This polemical critique of CIA interpretations circulating at the time called for intelligence to reconsider its methodology and to make its analyses appropriate to the expansive reach of US geopolitical power—and vice versa. It argued that "Laos, Cuba, the Congo, the Offshore Islands, and even Berlin" were significant insofar as "they are as manifestations of much broader trends." The crisis in the Congo was "merely symptomatic of the whole sweep of the nationalist revolution in Africa, superimposed on a much larger social revolution as this backward area of the world propels itself from tribal society into the 20th century." The same could be said of Castro's revolution in Latin America. "Yet we write primarily about the crises … in terms of their local significance; we don't write enough about the larger trends which essentially cause these local eruptions."

This analysis was not a brief for retreat or timidity. Instead, it called for proactive work, not mere crisis response. Rather than putting out fires, as seemed to be US prerogative, what was needed was a long-term eradication of tinder. But Komer worried that the national security apparatus was misdiagnosing the world situation, conferring a lack of focus. The analysis showed a certain grudging respect for, or even jealousy of, Moscow and Beijing, governments that seemed to be playing a long, if inflexible, game. These powers were "disciplined" in "the marshalling of power" in pursuit of long-term goals. Shifting toward a long-term approach was difficult, he admitted, but at the very least, intelligence could try to "analyze the problem *before it is upon us*" and "set it in its larger context." That context was widespread anticolonial feeling amid urbanization and technological and social changes. The memorandum concluded with a lament that intelligence assessments tended to write about "national entities" as "piece of real estate" that either "stay firmly in our camp, lean toward neutralism, or are absorbed by the Bloc." These alignments mattered, "but it is only part of the story, and in an era of revolutionary change not always the most important part."

What Komer meant by "focus" was not laserlike narrowing of vision on a specific piece of real estate. He wanted analysts to step back, to look at the relationship between foreground and background, to appreciate their inter-relationship. He addressed this analysis to General Charles P. Cabell, deputy director of the CIA, who would be responsible in part for the Bay of Pigs invasion and then forced to resign. If Cabell and others in his cohort had taken such an analysis to heart, that fiasco might have been prevented. Its aftermath, in the form of further widespread support across the globe for Fidel Castro's project, confirmed the analysis. Between nationalism and "nuclear stalemate," war could no longer be the "arbiter of disputes." More broadly, however, this perspective compelled a diffuse, wide-ranging, flexible, and proactive program of security. It was the counterinsurgent police assist-ance program Komer shepherded, which reached maturity under President Johnson, and which Komer repeatedly protected from budget-tightening legislative threats. The CIA's failure in Cuba, on a mission set into motion under the prior administration, chastened President Kennedy and side-lined a generation of officers, opening the space for Komer to take hold of the situation.

In essence, what the CIA of 1948 understood, what Komer in 1960 under-stood, and what liberation-movement leaders bent on self-determination understood, was that successful anticolonial revolution in one place would breed anticolonial fervor elsewhere. Reciprocally, the imposition of what Ghana's President Kwame Nkrumah called neocolonialism would threaten the trust and goodwill the United States might have enjoyed in other places. And yet, as "The Break-Up" had diagnosed, the two places where nationalism seemed most volatile, and the threat of communist revolution most alarming, were by 1960 the countries in which the United States had spent the most money on maintaining European colonial control, Vietnam and Indonesia. Where the 1948 CIA analysis was wrong, dreadfully wrong, was in its prog-nostication that new nations in the grip of nationalist demands for self-determination "militarily . . . will be unable to withstand any major power."[53]

"AN INSURANCE POLICY AGAINST AN UNLIKELY CONTINGENCY"

In the years after his NSC service for Kennedy and Johnson, Komer reflected on his having been appointed in March 1966 by Johnson to oversee "pacifica-tion" in South Vietnam—Johnson: "I'm going to make you my man on the other war in Viet Nam"—as if it had been a complete surprise. A reshaping of US war-fighting infrastructure was Johnson's last-ditch attempt to win the war, culminating a year later in Komer's appointment as pacification czar and his deployment to Saigon. It was revolutionary. Komer would have a direct line to the president. Civilian efforts would have access to Pentagon funding. Military personnel would fall under civilian supervision. Domestic agencies attached to Johnson's Great Society would send experts to Indochina. Komer, feigning ignorance: "Mr. President, what's the other war in Vietnam? I thought we only had one." He had heard Johnson discuss the "other war," geared toward "ending poverty" in South Vietnam in a meeting with congressional leaders the previous month.[54] Johnson: "Well, that's part of the problem. I want to have a war to build as well as to destroy. Your mandate will be an extensive one. In fact, I wrote it myself."[55] But Komer had been writing his own mandate for half a dozen years by then, preparing for such an assignment since the outset of the Kennedy administration, if not earlier. Even without knowing the details, he foresaw a debacle and believed that splicing development initiatives together with expert law enforcement would resolve it.

To become "the high panjandrum of pacification," as Komer called it, in 1967 required that he be given extensive authority and direct access the president.[56] A link to the Oval Office had been established under Kennedy in creating the SGCI and OPS. Now it would be extended across the ocean. Komer became the sole manager of the "other war," overseeing CORDS, which had no budget of its own but could draw on and redirect the massive reserves of Military Assistance Command Vietnam. CORDS was less an organization than a political method of focusing specialized resources without relying on the slow adaptation of large, ossified infrastructures. With the SGCI, OPS, and finally CORDS, all dedicated to the single mission of preventing communist revolution, Komer attacked the national security bureaucracy itself.

Komer was one of the inventors of the other war, because he had never wanted the US war in Vietnam, or in any of the other Gray Areas, to be fought by the military. He knew such a war could never be won, and the US military simply could not get involved in all the globe's trouble spots that seemed ripe for insurgency. Instead, covert action, police work, and development aid would wage war indirectly. Richard Nixon is today remembered for "Vietnamization," the replacement of US fighting forces with indigenous ones, but before his predecessor's introduction of ground troops in 1965, the US war in Vietnam was "Vietnamized" and fought by locals. But even indigenous military involvement tended to exacerbate tensions rather than lessen them. Unlike the military, police were nimble. They were close enough to local networks of patronage and dispute resolution to gather intelligence, identify problems before they occurred, and manage criminal or other elements susceptible to recruitment by extremists. The police's mission was "to restore order, not destroy the enemy."[57] The "other war" was a term that could make sense only when Johnson deviated, by sending soldiers and pilots into battle, from his administration's own prior global counterinsurgency strategy of using civilian proxies in the form of development and law-enforcement agencies. The other war had been Vietnamized all along.

Komer is best remembered for his role as pacification czar, overseeing CORDS in South Vietnam in the waning years of Johnson's presidency. Yet his official assignment in the NSC, focusing on the Middle East and South Asia, cannot explain how he ended up in Saigon. His biographer devotes great attention to his savvy as a strategist of US national security, which is accurate as far as it goes, but still does not capture the deep (and strategy-oriented) connection between his early work for Kennedy and his late work for Johnson. Here the record is amended.

Upon entering office, Kennedy immediately set into motion the requisite processes for new state initiatives: investigations that would produce recommendations that could in turn be implemented. He even had his NSC replicate the Draper Committee's investigation internally, with Komer in charge.[58] At each juncture, when recommendations on the Gray Areas were to become policy, Komer prepared a tart, sharply worded spur that would redirect the recommendations. He shared talking points with those who had Kennedy's, and then Johnson's, ear—Rostow, Taylor, Bundy. They frequently amplified Komer's message as if it were their own. When Vice President Johnson visited the Middle East in August 1962, Komer accompanied him, which cemented their friendship and Johnson's faith in Komer's judgment on foreign affairs. More important, for Komer, it countered the Kennedy insider line on Johnson, that he was out of his depth overseas. Johnson was sensitized to the issues and a quick learner.[59] Yet Komer's actions in 1961 and 1962, before that trip, were not focused on the Middle East per se so much as on developing a strategic capacity and institutional method for problem-solving that would apply as much in his geographic region of specialization as elsewhere.

The CIA's Richard Bissell headed the first task force on countering guerrilla warfare, which Komer had spurred in February 1961. Bissell soon began to fall out of favor in the aftermath of the Bay of Pigs fiasco in April 1961. He was a strong defender of militarized approaches to fighting guerrillas, including the use of elite special forces, who would act like guerrillas themselves and train indigenous forces to do the same. Bissell's frequent yearning for drastic action drove Komer nuts.[60] The task force was supposed to be a bulwark against Pentagon initiatives, but Bissell undermined that purpose.[61] "In all the talk about countering guerrilla warfare and subversion no one seems to be paying much attention to about the only relevant program which is already a going concern," Komer opined, almost as soon as the task force convened, in a memorandum to Rostow (who provided intellectual ballast) titled "Let's Not Forget the OISP." Komer worried that the Eisenhower-era program was "in bad odor," but amid the "general din" about guerrilla warfare, it would be a mistake, "for Pete's sake," to "dismantle a going concern of major value" in addressing insurgencies. "If anything, this program should be beefed up and raised to office level"—exactly what did come to pass. The reason was simple. US police, not soldiers, had to be the ones training foreign police. The Pentagon lacked the requisite experience and would confer "far too much of a military flavor" on the effort. His argument was sensible: "Here is, in existence, a major instrumentality for carrying out our counter-subversion aims. Let's factor it in to the total program instead of letting it wither on the vine."[62]

Rostow and Komer were in constant communication at this time. Rostow was preparing his definitive statement on the relationship between modernization and counterinsurgency, a speech at Fort Bragg, the US Army Special Warfare School. Prior to that point, the majority of students at Fort Bragg were foreign soldiers, but Kennedy's drive was changing the composition to include many more US troops.[63] Komer hammered away at the necessity of minimizing military participation in counterinsurgency and at the folly of Fort Bragg's conflation of guerrilla and antiguerrilla warfare. Rather than training US soldiers to fight like guerrillas, Komer thought an emphasis should be placed on "training *locals* in these tasks." For Komer, the overwhelmingly rural framework of Fort Bragg's lessons ignored its urban "counterpart": "the OISP program of beefing up police force counter-subversive capabilities."[64] By the time Rostow gave the speech to the graduating class of sixty-three foreign and seventeen US soldiers at Fort Bragg in late June, its emphases were all Komer's, particularly the notion that the modernizing society that was facing insurgency was itself responsible for managing the threat, with a healthy dose of US assistance.[65] Komer was behind one of Rostow's most frequently cited texts, widely thought to exemplify the importance of security concerns to modernization theory.

The notion that US Army Special Forces, and indigenous mercenaries whom they and the CIA trained and armed, were the antidote to communist insurgency intoxicated many powerful officials. It would not be dispelled in Washington meeting rooms, no matter how forceful Komer's arguments were. In March 1961, Bundy called on the Pentagon and CIA to launch new, or expand ongoing, offensive guerrilla operations in "Viet Minh territory."[66] A host of men who possessed experience with the Office of Strategic Services in the Pacific theater offered Kennedy powerful, romantic tales of jungle-warfare derring-do. For example, Roger Hilsman, who directed the State Department's Bureau of Intelligence and Research, was highly influential with President Kennedy and his brother Robert. Hilsman advocated the training of US forces in offensive guerrilla techniques, not simply defensive counterguerrilla techniques. Ed Lansdale did too. At Kennedy's behest, Lansdale published an article in the *Saturday Evening Post*, using the byline "An American Officer," that lauded an irregular force of Vietnamese villagers said to have thwarted "Viet Cong" intrusions and then undertaken their own guerrilla raids, claiming that they received no US support, which could not be given "legally" to irregulars.[67] The president urged distribution of this article to ambassadors in Asia and Africa and to Military Assistance Groups in Latin America. Komer identified his adversaries as those who had the president's ear and believed in rural counterinsurgency using military special forces—as opposed to his own plan to use urban police.

Top Kennedy advisors vacillated as to whether guerrilla warfare was positive or negative for US geopolitical goals. Roger Hilsman captured this perspective in the first lines of his major recommendations to Kennedy, published as the Bureau of Intelligence and Research's "Internal Warfare and the Security of the Underdeveloped States," which began, "The key to fighting guerrillas is to adopt the tactics of the guerrillas themselves." Buried inside the report was an appraisal of public safety assistance that called police forces "instruments of self-rule." It reiterated what Komer and Engle insisted, saying police were better able to "spot trouble and gather needed intelligence on subversive activities than a military force."[68] One NSC colleague of Komer's found Hilsman's lengthy analysis lacking in anything new. It was a rehash, missing updated information based on new research being conducted outside the Bureau of Intelligence and Research.[69] Deputy Assistant Secretary for International Security Affairs William P. Bundy later dismissed Hilsman's pro-guerrilla approach more bluntly, saying: "That never worked."[70] Many articles in the professional military literature further elaborated the pro-guerrilla notion, which justified the Army's new emphasis, overseen by Kennedy, on training Special Forces to be "hunter-killers," "small, mobile, semi-independent units which can seek out and destroy the enemy wherever he is operating."[71] After visiting Fort Bragg, an Israeli expert in counterinsurgency observed, however, that Army training for "World War II jungle warfare with new weapons"—exactly what Hilsman and others thought was needed—"is not geared to your problem."[72]

For all their close reading of Mao and Vietnam's Vo Nguyen Giap, what these men could not comprehend was that guerrillas infiltrating North Vietnam were doomed to fail, because they would lack the local support that Mao always insisted was crucial for guerrilla success. Hilsman's World War II experience in Burma was not one of training offensive guerrillas to invade, much less of himself fighting as a guerrilla. The Japanese military were the invaders, and partisans repelled them as such. The CIA was scarcely any more sophisticated. William Colby remarked that the "black entry tactic" could be seen as deriving "essentially from World War II experience."[73] The agency had encouraged the French to undertake such efforts as far back as 1951.[74] Not only liberals like Hilsman, but right-wing intellectuals in the Foreign Policy Research Institute advocated such offensive guerrilla operations. But when CIA-trained offensive guerrillas and mercenaries attempted missions in North Vietnam beginning in 1958 and throughout the next decade, they were slaughtered, sometimes at rates of 95 percent.[75] The Bay of Pigs invasion was another such catastrophe. Even when Colby came to urge restraint in such tactics because his agency's own trainees had been unsuccessful, Marine General Victor Krulak persuaded Lyndon Johnson to continue similar programs, laying the groundwork for the Gulf of Tonkin incident in 1964. Moreover, the CIA weaponized ethnic difference in Indochina by arming proxy militias of, for example, mercenary Montagnards, upland Southeast Asia's historically recalcitrant, culturally and linguistically separate peoples. That effort conflicted with later attempts at US nation-building in South Vietnam by constructing a polity that could accommodate ethno-religious difference. Worse, as NSAM 162 ordered, this dangerous model was to be exported around the globe.[76] If the notion that fighting guerrillas with guerrillas, subversion with subversion, was dispelled, it happened individually, amid muck, blood, agony, and screams, as proxy guerrillas lay dying.

Still, Komer worked to reorient the fight. Kennedy had come into office calling for a pragmatic reevaluation of the Military Assistance Program. This reassessment led US military assistance in Latin America to be directed toward the "internal rather than the external threat," with the consequence of dirty wars and military repression throughout the hemisphere. In many countries, police and military were unified; where they were not, the State Department urged assistance directed at aiding collaboration.[77] US-supplied military weapons and gear consistently made their way into police hands, even if public safety advisors recommended otherwise. Komer advocated against overmilitarization from the first meeting of the Bissell task force on, emphasizing that the urban threat was more worrisome than the rural one, and OISP was the best way to answer it.[78] In the summer of 1961, after Bissell circulated a draft of his task force's report on guerrilla warfare, Komer's arguments still fell on deaf ears, but he was able to get Rostow to redraft part of the Bissell report, originally written by the CIA's James Eliot Cross.[79] He continued to feed ideas to Rostow, playing along with one of the latter's foibles by highlighting the importance of "knitting a resistant social fabric" and suggesting a new section of the report emphasize "sealing off the disease" of communism.[80]

With Rostow heeding his advice, Komer turned his attention elsewhere, higher up the chain, to Maxwell Taylor. He played down the forthcoming Bissell report, noting that it would represent only a first step, with more work still to be done. Komer continually refined his argument. To Taylor in August 1961, he distilled three points he would continue to regard as key: practice preventive medicine; focus on urban dissidence, "rather than guerrilla warfare in the boondocks";[81] and avoid overmilitarization: "Political, economic and social measures are equally essential. And the first line of active defense is usually *the police* rather than the military." On the same day, a State Department official sent Taylor his positive assessment of the Army Special Forces counterinsurgency training curriculum.[82] Komer reminded Taylor about the OISP and forwarded background information on it.[83] The battleground was the bureaucracy.

Knowing that Bissell was bent on a military approach to the guerrilla problem, Komer returned to the debate about military assistance that given rise to the Draper Committee. Echoing what he told Taylor, he admonished Bissell that military assistance geared toward overt aggression was off-target: "In effect we are like a man who bought an insurance policy against an unlikely contingency, but one which cost roughly 70 per cent of his income and permitted him barely enough to keep alive with what was left." Assistance should, instead, be aimed at internal threats. And it should emphasize, not undercut, "social and economic viability" through development, "which is essential to creating a hostile environment to subversion and guerrilla war.

Nation building is an indispensable corollary of counter-subversion and counter-guerrilla programs."[84] He could not resist beating the police assistance drum. Compared to military assistance, he asked, "Which buy[s] more for our money?" Over the next few months, the Bissell report would be finalized. Despite Komer's efforts, it underscored "offensive countermeasures" and paid scant attention to policing. An interim draft report disparaged the OISP as misdirected, toward "civic and administrative police responsibilities rather than to the violence threat to internal security." Komer incredulously scribbled in the margin: "preventive medicine?" The task force, he felt, had fundamentally misunderstood what police assistance was meant to accomplish.[85] Yet the Bissell report, along with other advice Kennedy received around the same time from Robert McNamara, was successful in reconfiguring the bureaucracy toward the creation the "single, high-level locus," one of Komer's chief goals.[86] This move empowered him further. As he had told Taylor, "Perhaps the greatest lack is institutional." There needed to be a single point of focus to analyze and address all dimensions of urban and rural subversion. "We need a more sophisticated doctrine, suitable overall policies, and an integrated, comprehensive program."[87] Because Taylor could be the leader of this new institutional outfit, he agreed.

REWIRING THE BUREAUCRACY: "INSURGENCY CRITICAL"

The White House established the Special Group (Counter-Insurgency) by issuing NSAM 124, originally drafted by Komer, on January 18, 1962.[88] Komer boasted about this new body, "It was my idea."[89] The SGCI was a high-level alternative to the NSC, an institution that, despite its resculpting by Kennedy, retained too many engrained interests to exhibit the requisite flexibility. Once in place, the SGCI eclipsed the NSC throughout the Kennedy administration and until the Senior Interdepartmental Group replaced it in 1966. The SGCI drew from across the federal agencies working overseas: Defense and Joint Chiefs of Staff, CIA, State, AID, and the US Information Agency. It invited guest speakers, ranging from CIA officers to important figures outside government who could contribute to its goals, like Walter Reuther, leader of the United Automobile Workers union.[90] Other meeting attendees varied, depending on topics to be covered. As such, the SGCI was action-oriented—"pushing, needling, prodding, and coordinating"—and it consistently expanded its coverage geographically and practically.[91] At the outset, it was to be concerned with Vietnam, Thailand, and Laos. Colombia was on the penultimate list of countries but was cut, only to be added back in June 1962, because it merited the status Taylor named "Insurgency Critical."[92] The SGCI sent investigators abroad to assess security situations. Draper, of the eponymous Committee, went to Brazil during the Cuban missile crisis on the SGCI's behalf.[93] By the end of 1964, the Special Group was monitoring twelve countries directly. By April 1965, via OPS, its concern extended to at least thirty-six countries.[94] Komer was emphatic that the usefulness of police assistance and counterinsurgency efforts under the SGCI's guidance was limited to the prediction and prevention of insurgency's eruption. Once widespread rebellion took hold, counterinsurgency efforts were gravely limited in what they could achieve. (Komer's own later experience in Vietnam overseeing "the other war" proved him right.) By 1966, he even argued that the three countries initially placed under the SGCI's watch should be in a separate category as they already were experiencing ongoing insurrectionary movements. The counterinsurgency coordination infrastructure instead should focus, he thought, on those countries requiring preventive measures to "forestall any Vietnams occurring in the first place."[95]

The SGCI's major accomplishment in its first year was issuing a formal statement that prioritized counterinsurgency, the Overseas Internal Defense Policy (OIDP).[96] This 34-page document, drafted chiefly by Charles Maechling Jr., enshrined overarching guidance for counterinsurgency that united civilian and military agencies. It predated many Pentagon formulations of doctrine on counterinsurgency, meaning that the military had to play catch-up to civilian agencies in this field. The Joint Chiefs had published a guidance document in April 1962 that called for a "'fully integrated, mutually supporting and concurrently applied' mesh of political, military, and socioeconomic programs," but only the SGCI had the participation of the agencies that could enable this push, detailed in the OIDP.[97] Marked "Secret," though widely distributed, the OIDP made explicit the replacement of nuclear deterrence with counterinsurgency as the primary concern of US national security. It placed the SGCI's civil-military combination at the foundation of counterinsurgency policy and insisted on the importance of police to preventing subversion. The OIDP bore the imprint of Rostow's characterization of the relationship of insurgency to modernization. It predicted: "Rural people crowd into the strange environments of cities that lack for them a satisfactory pattern of living. . . . While the institutions required for modernization are in process of being created, this revolution contributes to arousing pressures, anxieties, and hopes which seem to justify violent action."

Consonant with Komer's view of the importance of enabling indigenous forces to act as the front-line actors of US counterinsurgency strategy, the OIDP emphasized that all US agencies, civilian and military, had to lend support to incumbent regimes. It was careful to remark, however, "The US does not wish to assume a stance against revolution, per se, as an historical means of change." For one historian, this aspect of the OIDP was its greatest flaw: if "indigenous authorities" could not adequately address socioeconomic inequalities and political strife and insurgency were the result, "what confidence could the United States have that it would be able to persuade these very same people to adopt American-proffered reforms?"[98] One solution to this conundrum of devolved responsibility for internal security the OIDP offered was clandestine destabilization, which could lead to a change in regime. If incumbent leaders refused reforms, strengthening "other elements of the society which are willing and able to contribute to sound development" might be necessary. Covert action was built into the policy. Another solution was what Komer would label "leverage-oriented mechanisms": conspicuously withholding aid to convince rulers of the need to implement reforms.[99] "Let's face it, Dave," Komer jeered to AID's David Bell, a cabinet-level agency chief, "a high proportion of our aid total is for such purposes as buying political leverage, baksheesh, buoying up feeble regimes, preclusion and the like—hardly 'constructive' purposes. But these are essential (though overused) instrumentalities of our cold war policy, and as insurance against worse they are probably worth the cost in gross terms."[100] Despite his acid tongue, Komer conceded the practical challenge of empowering weak regimes and hoping their police could uphold the first line of defense, a term the OIDP also invoked. The United States did selectively withhold aid in South Vietnam for programs it did not like, but the major risk was undermining the already weak government of South Vietnam by showing it to be incapable of standing on its own, if not causing its collapse entirely. Looking back in 1999 with chagrin on his role in drafting the OIDP, Maechling called it "the most interventionist statement of American policy ever promulgated."

The SGCI brought together powerful figures, representing agencies with formidable constituencies, to attempt to solve a highly intractable challenge. The group did not technically possess power to issue policy, only to make recommendations. A major difficulty was rendering its weekly pressure-cooker meetings productive while not causing the interagency stew to explode. Taylor was the group's first leader. Bundy occasionally attended the meetings, held Thursday afternoons, though he had hedged on the formation of the SGCI. He felt that a "single steering committee" with varied responsibilities across different regions was of doubtful utility and might usurp other decision-making structures, including his own authority.[101] But, at Komer's urging, he also favored a centralization of attention on counterguerrilla activities. The SGCI's remit in practice combined an extremely wide set of geographical interests with fine-grained analysis and debate of counterinsurgency efforts. Ultimately, the SGCI came to be characterized above all by Komer's insistence that it focus on potential threats rather than areas already perceived to be under Soviet or Chinese influence or control. Komer read the SGCI meeting agendas and minutes carefully and advised Bundy how to respond. Special group recommendations, in turn, frequently became policy when issued as NSAMs that Bundy signed. Before long Komer was attending some of the meetings, as was Engle, but Komer recognized that with many cooks in the kitchen, he would have to promote his agenda obliquely.

All participants knew that one man's attendance indicated the president's keen interest in the SGCI's mission: that of his brother, Attorney General Robert Kennedy. The SGCI was not the first "special group." That term migrated from the Department of Justice's fight against organized crime, to which Robert Kennedy had been devoting his energies. In SGCI meetings, he was forceful, truculent, impatient, and, according to Maechling, surprisingly uninformed and inarticulate.[102] When Taylor was tapped to lead the Joint Chiefs, the name of a career diplomat was floated as a possible new leader of the group, but the diplomat was an unknown quantity to the Kennedy family. Robert Kennedy instead suggested himself for the job. But CIA Director John A. McCone, who recognized that Kennedy was a neophyte and a hothead, delicately pointed out that the executive branch's "image would be damaged" if news leaked that the attorney general was diverting his attention toward directing "an important committee wholly unrelated to his office."[103] Bundy and Taylor personally reassured Kennedy that McCone was wrong, but, in the end, Under Secretary of State U. Alexis Johnson replaced Taylor. Robert Kennedy did not like Johnson, who was Dean Rusk's "protégé," and Averell Harriman, a consummate Washington insider and former governor of New York, soon replaced him.[104]

Despite the rotating cast of leaders and attendees, the SGCI's consistent focus was Robert Komer's agenda. A centralized, empowered directorate of counterinsurgency across the globe was Komer's dream come true. The SGCI enabled in-depth review, as well as the collection of enough expert information to make policy recommendations that, as Komer had put it in the "Focus" memo, took account of "larger trends which essentially cause these local eruptions." Perhaps to reassure observers that President Kennedy's overseas commitments would not waver despite several setbacks, the White House allowed the *Wall Street Journal* to reveal the SGCI's existence in June 1963, heralding its wide-ranging accomplishments according to a unified set of goals, from road-building and supplying barbed wire in Southeast Asia to "special riot training" for police around the globe.[105]

With the SGCI in place, Komer continued his campaign in 1962. He fought with all the tenacity and connivance of an experienced guerrilla—after all, he was subverting the principles and command structures put in place by his elected and appointed superiors—to elevate foreign police assistance to a prominent role in the rapidly globe-encircling counterinsurgency campaign. At the first meeting of the SGCI, AID and CIA representatives agreed to report back in a couple of weeks' time on the status and progress of police assistance.[106] With the creation of AID by the end of the summer of 1961, the OISP had become fragmented, left to a few individual advisors in regional bureaus, with no coordination. Washington's neglect did not deter the advisors still in the field, but they were handicapped. Komer set to work warning Bundy and others that AID was already cutting budgetary allocations for police assistance. The cuts were unacceptable. From the high for OISP of $14.2 million in fiscal year 1958, spending had declined by at least $3 million in four years, Komer determined. "Having some familiarity with police-type programs," he pronounced, offering cost-benefit analysis, "*dollar for dollar we get more for our money from these in terms of 'preventive medicine' than from any other single US program.*" The police, Komer assured Bundy, were "almost invariably the first line of defense against subversion, demonstrations, riots, and even local insurrections." The solution was to give the police program separate and "quasi-independent" authority within AID and perhaps separate budgeting.[107] In February 1962, Bundy sent a letter to the president, authored by Komer, relaying that he and Taylor thought that police programs, "a crucial element in the counter-insurgency effort," were being allowed to fall by the wayside. They wished "to halt this alarming trend." Taylor and Bundy then shared a "hortatory chit" by Komer, which Kennedy could use to urge AID's administrator, Fowler Hamilton, to evaluate how to strengthen police assistance within AID and allow it a measure of autonomy.[108] Five days later, Kennedy issued a version of this Komer letter to

Hamilton as NSAM 132, "Support of Local Police Forces for Internal Security & Counter-Insurgency Purposes."[109] Punching above his weight, Komer was succeeding. With Komer applying heat, the SGCI, as a new bureaucratic tool, catalyzed further restructuring of the bureaucracy.

THE FORMATION OF OPS

A year after the Bay of Pigs disaster, on April 20, 1962, the SGCI called for an investigation, on the President's behalf, into whether training police in cities of "newly emerging countries" could assure the maintenance of order "without the excessive use of violence." The SGCI also asked whether such technical assistance should fall under AID's jurisdiction. AID was already planning to open the Inter-American Police Academy in the Panama Canal Zone, with the first class commencing July 2.[110] The study was also to include "an examination of the police techniques in the United States, in France, Italy and other selected countries," to ascertain what the latest developments were.[111] U. Alexis Johnson won the assignment to conduct the review of police assistance. He gathered a committee that first met on April 27. At the meeting, Johnson "spoke almost verbatim from my script," Komer bragged.[112] Johnson initiated subcommittees to conduct research, including one headed by Byron Engle, then still with the CIA, and another headed by Komer.[113] At last, Komer and Engle were formally paired in the effort to elevate foreign police assistance.

Johnson's committee was supposed to report back to the president in six weeks. Even before the first meeting, Komer confided to Bundy that he figured he, not Johnson, would have to be the one to write the final report. Alexis Johnson was a careerist who lacked the requisite specialized knowledge and Komer's tenacious desire to see the government's lines of authority rewoven. After making "fitful progress," Komer, not Johnson, informed the president on June 11, 1962, that the task of thorough review and recommendations was likely to take at least a month longer than planned. It was already clear that Johnson was the leader of the effort "in name only."[114] Komer and Engle plugged away. A reason for the delay was that Engle's technical Subcommittee found that "deficiencies" in the OISP resulted from "a lack of organization and management." As such, the subcommittee took on the task of assessing management problems as well.[115] Komer worked on the financial aspects of reorganization, insisting that "central direction" of foreign police assistance was crucial, and that such centralization would, in fact, save money. The Pentagon, he noted, was spending the same amount on paramilitary-support programs, which emulated the OISP's material assistance, in six countries (Costa Rica, Iran, Nicaragua, Panama, the Philippines, and Vietnam) as the OISP spent in twenty-six countries. Putting all such assistance in one shop, within AID, would cut costs and achieve the goal of retaining a civilian character.[116]

The transformation of the OISP into a more centralized and well-funded operation would not entail a reconceptualization of what it did, only of how it did it. The operational blueprint was already sound. Engle submitted to Johnson a lengthy coauthored report on the basis of his subcommittee's research, which entailed interviewing numerous OISP advisors (men he already knew well), FBI agents, leaders of the IACP, CIA officers, and others. The recommendations of Engle's report became OPS orthodoxy: countries' police capabilities to counter subversion, enforce the law, and maintain order "with the minimum use of violence" would be developed only "through teaching, technical assistance, and equipment." Engle couched the mission of police assistance in terms of its importance to "economic and political development." The report emphasized that the United States possessed a different "police concept" from "the less developed and newly emerging Free World countries," which often found themselves amid "the natural confusion and emotional imbalance incident to new-born independence." But the report declared that "a well-defined police concept" was a necessity for a country "to flourish economically" and "withstand the menace of Communist subversion." The point, therefore, was not to impose US organizational models but instead "to accept and understand differences, and to concentrate on helping recipient nations to make the best use of their resources." To convince a skeptical audience of development professionals within AID, Engle downplayed the violence of policing and adopted a culturally liberal perspective. The report briefly acknowledged the "limited number of CIA personnel" who assisted "investigative units combating subversion." CIA presence was one major reason AID officials were leery of the program. They worried about it gaining further independence. But the current "management difficulty" of police assistance was that it was "fragmented, diffused, and diluted by varying objectives in the agencies contributing" to it, or tugging on it. What police assistance needed was "greater autonomy." It was an objective police assistance would consecrate for police agencies themselves.

Meanwhile, countries in the SGCI's purview were experiencing continuing security threats. Or rather such threats were becoming visible thanks to the SGCI's expanded cognizance. The camera produced the landscape its film captured. Public support for Ngo Dinh Diem was waning, according to a new Working Group report on South Vietnam.[117] Thirteen countries, from Cameroon to Nepal, Guatemala to Burma, were, according to the State Department, now "sufficiently critical to warrant the specific attention" of the SGCI. A CIA assessment of eleven of these countries concurred.[118] The SGCI heard a briefing on Colombia, where "violence in the tradition of the 'Old West'" was constituting a "real problem" with "subversive potential," even if it was not exactly insurgency yet.[119] So construed, these threats demanded professional preventive policing.

In July, over a weekend, Komer and his deputy Hal Saunders drafted the final report of U. Alexis Johnson's Committee on Police Assistance Programs. Tired of Johnson's hemming and hawing, Komer shoved the committee toward a resolution, which meant spurning Johnson's desire to run the recommendations past a variety of agency heads. "Most agency principals couldn't care less," Komer quipped. AID administrator Hamilton was likely to go along with whatever the committee recommended, "so long as he doesn't have to hear the word 'police' again for a while."[120] The report and its cover letter to the president, unsurprisingly, adopted all of Komer's favorite language. Police assistance was "preventive medicine," because police coped with urban (and rural) dissidence "before it reaches major proportions." Its cost was low "in comparison to the potential return." The management of police assistance had to be "civilian in character." Police assistance should remain within AID and be granted "funding autonomy." But, "in view of the anomalous nature of the problems involved," it should have an organizational structure different from typical AID programs and be led by a "senior qualified professional with direct access to the Deputy Administrator," allowing also for the "highly profitable" ongoing "covert personnel, advice, training, logistical, and equipment support" from the CIA. Overall, foreign police assistance had to be expanded, and its mission extended from the "conventional tasks" of police toward "greater emphasis" on quelling subversion. Thirty-five countries needed increased police assistance or close monitoring of their internal security conditions; current levels of assistance should be maintained for fifteen countries. The budget for police assistance needed to be roughly doubled in the next fiscal year, with a target of $50 million by 1966.[121] The report was pithy and persuasive.

US overseas police assistance was ongoing, trapped in a holding pattern. New at the time was the Pentagon's mushrooming devotion of resources to specialized military training. But Komer made it clear that if countering insurgency was to be the paramount foreign policy goal, the priority should not shift away from police. He offered a cogent rejoinder to a problem that Bissell, and the military, could not quite overcome. In the Maoist conceptualization of guerrilla warfare, insurgents' success arose because they drew succor and cover from local inhabitants, and Komer noted that police, unlike military forces, "live among the people." Rather than training forces to act like guerrillas and subvert unfriendly regimes, police assistance could fight insurgents on their own social terrain. Preempting threats would ensure that "the vital process of growth" would remain uninterrupted. On August 7, after the attorney general's review and anointment by the SGCI, the report's list of major recommendations became, with little modification, NSAM 177. Two weeks later, Dean Rusk ensured that the report and Komer's cover letter were cabled to every US ambassador or chief of mission in the Gray Areas.[122]

The Office of Public Safety would now be a reality, and no longer just an idea in Komer's head. Owing to foot-dragging within AID, another few months elapsed before the inauguration of OPS on November 1, with Byron Engle as its director.[123] Robert Kennedy was responsible for lighting the last bureaucratic fire needed to finalize the creation of OPS, pushing AID to act.[124] To make sure the message was clear, all AID staff received notification that they were to give "full cooperation" to OPS.[125] But foreign assistance was always, even at the height of President Johnson's power, potentially on Congress's budgetary chopping block, which could have shuttered the public safety program. In 1965, after an outside review of AID's programs by the consulting firm Booz, Allen & Hamilton found no justification for retaining OPS as part of the civilian development agency, Komer argued to AID's deputy administrator that the consultants did not understand the stakes. He pleaded, "Protect my baby."[126] Two years later, when Engle received word that a new command structure in South Vietnam was on the horizon, he begged Komer for help ensuring that CORDS would prioritize police assistance. On his most formal stationery, Engle appealed to their long-standing bond: "You will recall that a guy named Bob Komer kept" police assistance "from being entirely junked" years earlier. Engle thought another command structure would slash public safety operations. Komer offered his personal reassurance in pen, "Byron—*I'll* be running this program, so don't worry."[127]

In fall of 1962, the Cuban missile crisis was the most significant event in US foreign policy. It augured shifts in the prosecution of the war for the Gray

Areas, including further reliance on preventive medicine in the form of civilian policing. Yet on the day after the issuance of NSAM 177, calling for the formal creation of OPS, Robert McNamara recommended the experimental initiation of crop destruction in South Vietnam via chemical defoliants, with the goal of "forcing the Viet Cong out of the target area."[128] While many nations would now receive vigorous civilian police assistance, the showcase nation for this project until that point was undergoing a shift toward the overmilitarization Komer dreaded.

· · ·

Komer's revolt against bureaucracy had its own built-in alibi for failure. If the on-the-ground results were insufficient, calcified bureaucracy itself was to blame. In the years after Johnson's presidency, while employed as an analyst for the RAND Corporation, Komer attempted to exculpate himself, and CORDS, for the administration's failure to achieve success in South Vietnam. The problem had not been his vision of civilian-led, proxy-dependent counterinsurgency via police and limited developmental uplift, but the entrenched interests and the personalities within the massive US and South Vietnamese bureaucracies, who did not hew to his action-oriented strategy. They would not relinquish control over their particular domains and chains of command.[129] Even Engle himself sometimes seemed to lack the perspicacious eye Komer demanded.

Komer was, in a sense, a failed revolutionary. He was not put up against the wall and executed for treason. But if Nixon's fateful trip to Latin America was one bookend to Komer's counterinsurgency career, his own reprise of it was the other. Komer's last act for Lyndon Johnson was to become US ambassador to Turkey. Soon after arriving, he visited an autonomous university. Hundreds of students protested, overturning and torching his limousine, after allowing his African American chauffeur to flee to safety. Komer lasted less than six months in Ankara.[130]

FOUR

Bringing Police Assistance Home

THANKS TO THE INDEFATIGABLE ROBERT KOMER, professionalized policing became a most crucial component of US national security strategy with little fanfare. It would soon also become the centerpiece of a new domestic political reconfiguration, as both political parties committed to law and order in response to Black political insurgency. Abroad, US security, the public safety program declared, depended on the internal security of the Gray Areas of the globe. Local cops in cities and villages overseas, trained and equipped by the United States, would, through their unremarkable routines, assure US security by proxy, as its surrogates. The enormous budgets of the Air Force and Navy dwarfed the puny new AID budget for police assistance. A single airplane could cost more than sending dozens of public safety advisors around the globe. But cops could achieve what napalm could not. The fight was to ensure that nationalist struggles amid modernization's ferment did not result in the transmutation of US assistance for self-help into wide-ranging, upscaling self-determination. Jose Lukban, the J. Edgar Hoover of the Philippines and an OPS asset, warned in 1965 that it was imperative to thwart "the slimy tentacles of the greatest threat to peace—COMMUNISM AND CRIME," which were "slowly but surely fastening a stranglehold on such neighbor nations as Laos, Vietnam, Cambodia, India and Burma."[1]

Political negotiations over the management of this dangerous cocktail on American streets led to the creation in 1968 of the Law Enforcement Assistance Administration (LEAA) to federally fund law enforcement. OPS provided a model. Arnold Sagalyn, the director of the Treasury Department's Office of Law Enforcement Coordination, drew the example of OPS to the attention of the Department of Justice (DOJ) and Lyndon Johnson's domestic aides in 1964. Sagalyn was attempting to find solutions to "lawlessness," his own term conflating communism and crime. US overseas police assistance inspired Sagalyn to advise the DOJ on reformatting local-level policing after a crisis of civil unrest. Sagalyn was as progressive a law-enforcement expert as could be found during the period. He desired a greater federal role in local law enforcement, but he recognized existing constraints. Sagalyn addressed a turbulent law-enforcement world, buffeted by the organized pressure of the civil rights movement. He limned the parameters within which the War on Crime would be declared, aware of this pressure and of the proclivities of police themselves. Not only did he derive the War on Crime's shape from the blueprint OPS provided, he favored a distinction between social-welfare assistance aimed at the underlying causes of crime and assistance meant to upgrade policing. This distinction was novel and consequential. Contingent personal connections allowed the War on Crime to draw on overseas experience, but the field of professional law enforcement was in internally and externally imposed upheaval, which shaped its reconfiguration through professionalization, even as it reconfigured the broader political landscape of the 1960s and beyond.

Sagalyn was one among many law-enforcement actors trying to shape the field. Law and order was not internally fixed in the period of its ideological ascendancy. Law-enforcement practice was undergoing dramatic revision and renovation, with intense struggles among its practitioners and expert counselors over what it should look like, where its limits should be, and even whether it was in self-imposed crisis or the solid pole around which a tempest of social crisis was unfolding. To create an apparently unbiased policing apparatus underpinned the professionalization efforts at the heart of the new approach to law and order.[2] In short, police themselves were key actors who put crime on the national political agenda and benefited from this shift. Professionalization had long demanded political autonomy for police from local partisan machines, but their very autonomy from local politics empowered organizations like the International Association of Chiefs of Police nationally, as more effective policing led elites to take their demands seriously. Cloaked in the mantle of local prerogative, police decried federal encroachment, but they craved federal dollars. Police were the primary recipients of federal funding from the LEAA during its first decade, receiving 79 percent of its block grants in 1969, versus 8 percent for courts and 13 percent for corrections. In 1977, police got 41 percent, versus 26 percent for courts and 33 percent for corrections.[3] This incremental redirection of federal dollars toward jails and prisons, in turn, jump-started mass incarceration.

At home, concrete evidence of Lukban's conflation of crime and communist subversion seemed to burst forth out of nowhere—or more accurately, out of Harlem, the centerpiece of and metonym for Black urban life in the North. Five days of protest there followed the killing of a 15-year-old Black boy, James Powell, by an off-duty white police lieutenant, Thomas Gilligan, in mid-July 1964. Initial intransigence by the authorities, a refusal to heed Black demands for justice, spurred larger and larger mobilizations. Police attempts at crowd dispersal grew violent and wanton. The protests mobilized extant Black political networks. But they had a new flavor, inflected by reactions to US projections of power overseas. Progressive Labor had called the first nationwide rally demanding withdrawal of US personnel from Vietnam on May 2, 1964, which saw over a thousand rally in Harlem, six hundred of whom then marched to United Nations Headquarters.[4] In July, Progressive Labor rallied Harlemites against police brutality. Police responded with bullets and truncheons.

The vicious police response worsened the unrest. In contrast, Byron Engle's generation of reformers desired measured, scientific policing tactics, and his public safety program built the infrastructure to implant these overseas. What happened in Harlem was anything but measured. It demanded a reformist response. Moreover, the connections radicals were drawing between their efforts at home and those overseas encouraged perceptions of law enforcement as necessarily global in scope, leading to the further domestic internalization of the professionalizing ethos. US policing professionals identified an underdeveloped area that needed their help, namely, their own police forces, in which law enforcement was delegated to ill-equipped, incompletely trained, undereducated, poorly paid, politically partial men, most of whom were white. The effort to modernize policing at home was the essence of the War on Crime. But professionalization also unleashed police, allowing them to become advocates of the War on Crime. With old ties to partisan political machines sundered, police became self-interested, unaccountable political actors unto themselves. Law-enforcement leaders' political objective was to keep their local prerogative sacrosanct while inviting fiscal and technical help from the federal government. Local chiefs who did not want to be forced to retool or modify their officers' routines were able to limit the transformative power of the War on Crime on the craft of policing.

Komer and Engle built institutions to ensure that policing would be at the forefront of the fight to achieve internal security in Third World nations. The use of law enforcement to exercise but also to sharpen state power reverberated at home in this period as well. Growth of imperial institutions of law and order preceded the mainstream adoption of the political discourse of law and order. But new domestic professionalization efforts were not separate from overseas initiatives, particularly as foreign police officials visited the United States to observe and then copy these efforts. National security called for fungible initiatives, and US experts introduced standardized, portable, context-independent methods and technologies. Police professionalization was inseparable from the turn to counterinsurgency, with shared personnel, a single transnational field of technical expertise and, most important, but thus far most underappreciated, parallel devolved, federalized structures of responsibility and funding for the renovation of law enforcement.

That radical, anti-imperialist exhortations like those issued on Harlem's streets after the killing of James Powell would be met with a War on Crime was not preordained. Nor was it necessarily clear to members of the elite bloc promoting the transubstantiation of Black freedom dreams into white nightmares of Black lawlessness that the result would take the form of federal support for professionalized policing. Most law and order advocates did not desire federal intervention in local affairs, seeing it as opening the door to diminution of discretion, including that of racial discrimination. Yet a focus on the mutable object that was law-enforcement knowledge in the period and on the globe-spanning, counterinsurgent itineraries of the entrepreneurs of these transformations allows us to comprehend how these coordinating bodies—the Special Group (Counter-Insurgency), the Office of Public Safety, and the International Association of Chiefs of Police—fixed on common objects, vocabularies, and grammars that were not deployed solely overseas but through their work of coordination were able to travel across borders.

Moreover, the effort to scale down the fight against crime and subversion through empowerment of local police with new knowledge and skills meshed perfectly with two locally scaled political imperatives that both contended and cohabited in this period. One was the Right's vision of local autonomy. The other was the Left's vision of grassroots community development. The first sought to maintain a rigid, uneven distribution of political power. The second hoped to redistribute political power but lacked the capacity to upend entrenched hierarchies, including the one that had downscaled political contestation to the local in the first place. The local was the terrain of police violence, inadequate school facilities, usurious white shopkeepers, and slumlords' rat-infested, overpriced housing: the very targets of Black political mobilization in Harlem and elsewhere in this period, aside from the demand for the vote.[5] But it was not the terrain on which these injustices could be addressed. Fractions of capital and police tried to prevent federal-level interference that would endow actors at this scale with greater resources. Malcolm X and Progressive Labor's Bill Epton, organizer of protests in New York City against police violence and US militarism in Vietnam, understood that local conditions had extralocal causes. They created and invited affinities and solidarities at scales greater than the nation. Injustices were highly localized, but their distant analogs provided lessons. Chiefly, the lesson was that these analogs were actually connected. A web of stretched relations, composed of slowly moved and rusty chains, anchored local injustices. It was for this reason that they could explain police brutality in Harlem as an instance of imperialism. So too would be its remedy.

LAW ENFORCEMENT'S FEDERALISM

The defining difficulty Lyndon Johnson faced overseas was not so different from the difficulty he faced domestically: how to exert leadership without undermining the sovereignty of those over whom leadership was exerted, lest it provoke rebelliousness. Persistent pressure from below, regardless of political persuasion, was the most powerful countervailing tendency both pushing and thwarting Johnson's designs. The problem was essentially geographic: the spatial configuration of state power was at the heart of any solution, both as impediment and expedient. Abroad, Komer's police assistance program fit the bill, attempting to skirt violations of state sovereignty through the provision of knowledge and funding, rather than boots on the ground. At home, Johnson's two major legislative initiatives of 1964 aimed to reduce abject poverty and outlaw racial discrimination. To their critics, both pieces of legislation entailed federal vitiation of the autonomy of smaller-scale governments, the states and municipalities. During the very summer months in which the Civil Rights and Economic Opportunity Acts crossed Johnson's desk for his signature, however, a new front of racial discord opened, which was exactly what these initiatives were intended to prevent. This new territorial front, too, would require a novel approach.

The historical geography of the advent of the War on Crime was multidimensional. The spatial forms of governance signaled by adherence to a principle of federalism were not fixed but were objects of active contestation, including by police themselves. A growing expert consensus that intergovernmental funding needed to be rethought was not transformed into action until the specter of crime, and the model of delegated enforcement drawn from counterinsurgency, outlined a path. To mount what became the War on Crime required tentative, iterative, and contested steps to reconfigure the inherited spatiality of state power in the United States. Chief among these reconfigurations was the scalar hierarchy, which had inserted a division between the higher-scale federal government and lower-scale state and municipal governments. Encroachment on the part of the federal government on lower scales was supposed to be disallowed by the law of the land. To many, this encroachment could signify only constriction of white racial prerogative. J. Edgar Hoover's own incessant incantations against usurping local authority through the creation of a federal police force gave chiefs and sheriffs cover. Not long before White House action to create an instrument of domestic police assistance began, Hoover told an interviewer: "I am inclined toward being a States' righter in matters involving law enforcement. That is, I fully respect the sovereignty of State and local authorities. I consider the local police officer to be our first line of defense against crime, and I am opposed to a national police force.... The need is for effective local action, and this should begin with whole-hearted support of honest, efficient, local law enforcement."[6] Hoover used this inclination as a way to resist deploying FBI agents in the investigation of crimes against civil-rights workers or of allies in the business world involved with organized crime. Johnson agreed that law enforcement was an eminently local concern. He did not intend to violate its sanctity from Washington. He mentioned this commitment repeatedly, even as he signed bills extending federal capacity.[7] Yet changes were afoot. Law-enforcement leaders themselves wanted greater resources. Long-standing reform tendencies were busting budgets. Trends in crime and political unrest seemed to indicate that police needed help.

Federalism, the both overlapping and mutually excluding distribution of authority between and among scales of government, shaped the contours of the attempt to upgrade policing capabilities during the period of legislative achievement of Black civil rights. The police power downscales by transforming societal disorder into individualized and discontinuous police interaction with members of the public, but in this period law-enforcement actors fought to create and exploit national-level structures to ensure local autonomy. The ideological sanctity of local authority mandated by federalism had been a bulwark against reform, enabling all manner of repressive policing and wanton violence to go unchallenged. It also sanctioned passivity amid lynchings and other racist outrages. Southern states and municipalities were beacons of federalism, both in their law-enforcement agencies' refusal to enforce prior civil-rights legislation and in their active violation of Black people's rights. The argument used by mainly Southern white officials to resist federally mandated racial integration of public space and accommodations turned on the rights of lower jurisdictions to autonomy and control over how they would conduct themselves. Local custom was imagined to supersede legal determinations issued at the federal level. Police across the country benefited from an insulation made legitimate by the ideology of federalism. The invocation of states' rights was not ideological flimflam or mere rhetorical cover for strengthening police. The localism of states' rights was a police project through and through. Police did not want "the Federal government to peer over the shoulder of every local law enforcement officer and drastically punish him if he does not conform to the concepts of a Federal official far from the scene."[8] The jurisdictional arrangement of semiautonomous locality enabled large pockets of "massive resistance," in the phrase of Senator Harry S. Byrd of Virginia, to the national-scale project of formal, legislated racial equality.

As the possibilities for resistance to civic racial equality waned within the existing state-spatial framework due to changes in law and custom, and, above all, pointed political protest, the project of law and order then recapitulated the architecture of local autonomy. This state project would refashion the unity and coherence of rule by pioneering a new federalism within the very structures of the nascent federal program of law-enforcement assistance, which enshrined local autonomy by vesting it with resources from the federal government. In the context of new civil-rights legislation, police could reinvigorate traditions of racially invidious practice on the newly forged ground of outlawed de jure discrimination because their local prerogative remained insulated.

The federal War on Crime expanded state-, county-, and municipal-level capacity without diminishing local autonomy. The result was the carceral state, which is not singular and unitary but is composed of myriad overlapping and interlocking jurisdictions, penal systems, and law-enforcement agencies. Still, the Johnson administration's achievement was to unify while preserving separation. It ensured that struggles over the police would be adjudicated at the local level and in state legislatures, while still calling upon and relying on federal money, expertise, and legitimacy. Widely accepted explanations of what shifted over the decade of the 1960s in the wake of the Civil Rights and Voting Rights Acts—white populist backlash, the rise of the New Right, the Great Society built then stalled, and the launching of a War on Crime—cannot account for the spatial form this congeries of political strategies took. The bureaucratic infrastructure that would cohere as the supposed expression of white backlash looked remarkably similar to the bureaucratic infrastructure of Black grassroots achievement. Both preserved local autonomy while also infusing money from federal coffers. But whereas the War on Poverty gave limited decision-making power to local groups of citizens while lodging decisions over the scope of poverty alleviation at higher levels, the War on Crime allowed local police wide latitude in deciding the scope of law enforcement, with few constraints from above. The law-enforcement assistance from higher-scale governments to lower-scale governments that emerged in the 1960s was a creative form of federalism prized by conservatives. It would spread elsewhere later via the block grant and come to eviscerate the legacy of the War on Poverty, which was vulnerable precisely because it relied on targeted interventions within a delimited scope.

The devolutionary thrust of federal assistance, using centralized state infrastructure to decentralize state functions, was baked into the architectures of the wars on poverty and crime. Devolution was not, as one political scientist has claimed, "a managerial response to the administrative dysfunctions and implementation failures stemming from the Great Society."[9] The War on Poverty aimed to "revitalize the federal bureaucracy's capacity to deliver social services and contend with the complex problem of poverty through an institutional reorganization that emphasized decentralization and local control."[10] The Economic Opportunity Act's mandate to alleviate poverty via participation gave it an essential measure of control in terms of design, management, and benefit to the grassroots. In effect, however, this act simply provided what the War on Crime took away. Collective political participation was eroded by law enforcement's new capacities for maintaining order, which individualized disqualification, confronting the economically disenfranchised with a drastically attenuated scope for political participation. The injunction to preserve the local autonomy of law enforcement preceded the creation of a federal infrastructure for the War on Crime, which echoed the War on Poverty's language, substituting "crime" for "poverty" and "law enforcement" for "social services."

The new issue of supposedly rising crime represented a "depoliticization and criminalization of racial struggle."[11] The answer was to go to war:

President Johnson's aides and Congress devised a new policy instrument that would preserve yet "obscure racial power through vocabularies of bland administrative reform," argues Naomi Murakawa.[12] This reform was not ambitious. Both J. Edgar Hoover and Lyndon Johnson believed that although crime was a national problem, confronting it did "not carry with it any threat to the basic prerogatives of state and local governments."[13] The War on Crime sanctified this stance of law-enforcement federalism. A new federal infrastructure analogous to the overseas police assistance program blossomed, but it would not overturn orthodoxies underpinning the police power. Rather, it technically refined and magnified policing's capacities.

Federalism was a managerial tool for maintenance of a kind of status quo, disempowering social forces that had been gaining potency throughout the decade. It formed the bedrock for a politics that "divides democratic participation and state accountability in ways that strengthen existing power differentials and disadvantage those groups already marginalized in the political process," in Lisa L. Miller's words. Federalism, according to this analysis, is an arrangement that "divides and conquers," by allowing single-minded, resource-endowed groups to dominate the policymaking process while constraining the ability of less resource-rich groups and those with more "diffuse" goals to play an equivalent part.[14] The emergent technical instrument of professionalized policing could be wedded to an intentionally demobilizing policy instrument. With the advent of the carceral state, shifts within the bureaucracy could at once transform political common sense about the utility of fomenting racialized fears by invoking the weakening of law and order and freeze in place the jurisdictional relations that would maintain law and order.

This peculiar form of law-enforcement federalism, in light of the work of Engle and Komer and Arnold Sagalyn, their domestic translator, was not a reactionary new invention. Its law-enforcement application at home mirrored its counterinsurgency application overseas. A common refrain in criticism of OPS has been that it failed because it was charged with assisting governments with national police forces, a structure alien to a US ethos.[15] But this ahistorical view demands a reassessment of how a national police bureaucracy could rise within the United States while preserving the veneer that no such thing had been constructed. An inheritance of federalism did not impede OPS's functioning, but confirmed advisors' sense that they were implanting a uniquely American governing ethos abroad. The fundamental aim of police assistance abroad was to redistribute expertise in coercion from a centralized node to far-flung recipients. Little did the advisors realize that the model they were launching would come home to roost as an exquisite realization of federalism. By appreciating the connectedness between police assistance at home and police assistance overseas, this consequential series of events can be understood. Moreover, the experience of wrangling with the federal bureaucracy to link domestic policing expertise to training of foreign police officials was consequential. Particularly among senior IACP officials, it was a bitter experience, but it emboldened them to make demands on Congress and to refuse to take no for an answer.

"A FEDERAL TECHNICAL POLICE ASSISTANCE PROGRAM"

After nine so-called riots exploded in Northern cities and suburbs in July and August of 1964, Johnson's aides cast about for explanations. In light of Johnson's recent legislative victories, and on the cusp of a presidential election, it would have been anathema to explain the unrest in terms of the administration's failures, much less failures of the broader liberal vision the legislation symbolized and enacted—the progressive management of economic and social dislocation through moderate government reform. If anything, they were evidence of the necessity of such legislation. The Economic Opportunity and Civil Rights Acts were still new, and it would take some time for their effects to be felt. Was there a more immediate explanation? Some, including Johnson, reasoned that unrest had to be the fault of subversive instigators. But even J. Edgar Hoover found that explanation unsatisfying. If subversives had played a role, they had probably just exploited the discontent, rather than causing it, according to an FBI investigation.[16]

Instead, Arnold Sagalyn believed the explanation for these events had to include police themselves. The response would be addressed to police as well. He had watched sporadic flares of unrest around the globe and deduced that the severity of the unrest in Harlem, and possibly its ignition, was the result of the inadequacy of the forces of law and order. Police were ill-prepared to handle such civil violence due to failures of training, technology, doctrine, and leadership. In light of overseas experience, this lack of preparation resulted in what should have been avoidable: the unrest's high intensity, lengthy duration, and wide geographic dispersion. The answer was simple. OPS was the proof. An update of police training and capabilities was needed.

A push to upgrade police could have run aground on the same adamantine rock of local autonomy that had hindered the effort to legislate civil rights. "Law enforcement is basically the responsibility of the Governor, State and local officials," Johnson intoned, even before calm had fully returned to Harlem, in response to calls for federal intervention.[17] Law-enforcement experts concurred. Confronting the possibility of a uniform federal speed limit being imposed on interstate highways, for example, the commissioner of the California Highway Patrol had cautioned in 1963 in *The Police Chief* magazine that communists ruled by strengthening centralized police forces and destroying local ones. A slippery slope threatened. "If the federal government moves to control crime at the local level, it will constitute one of the longest steps toward dictatorship of which I can conceive," Commissioner Bradford Crittenden warned. Doing so would weaken local law enforcement and "provide the way to achieve the centralized police that a dictatorship must have to control and to supervise." Professionalization, Crittenden reckoned, might ward off federal intervention, though he neglected to discuss its monetary cost.[18] J. Edgar Hoover, too, was insistent: law enforcement that smelled of centralized authority was rancidly antidemocratic. Police embodied federalism. "The patrolman is the ultimate in the decentralization of municipal service," O. W. Wilson himself declared in his textbook *Police Administration*.[19] The postwar occupations, however, had made law-enforcement leaders like Wilson and Engle comfortable with using centralized authority to devolve responsibility, as was Sagalyn, who was also a strong believer in professionalization.

Johnson's contention that subversives were to blame forced Hoover to act and opened the door to broader federal action. The Bureau could not sit idly in the face of such a threat, though its investigation downplayed the subversion explanation. Johnson's worry about the coordination of civil violence across great distances not only spurred Hoover's involvement. It also called for a new federal approach to what should have been the task of local law enforcement. Additional unrest confirmed the need for innovation. Within a week of the return of uneasy quiet to Harlem's streets, civil unrest erupted in Rochester, New York, following the violent arrest of a Black man, leading authorities to summon the National Guard. Over the next two days, 4 civilians were killed, 350 injured, and 976 arrested.[20] These grim statistics were worse than those tallied in Harlem. In August, Jersey City, Paterson, and Elizabeth, New Jersey, each saw revolts. Then Dixmoor, just south of Chicago. Then Philadelphia, Pennsylvania.[21] Geographically dispersed unrest, and the potential for organizational linkages across space, meant that localities were simply outmatched. The strict federal-local division of labor in criminal justice was faltering in the face of apparently new threats and forms of disorder.

Key law-enforcement leaders gave their blessing for Washington to intervene, strategically reasoning that their agencies and institutions stood to benefit. Federal action concerning new forms of disorder was a response to pushes from police, particularly the IACP. Johnson and his allies in Congress allowed themselves to be pushed. The volume of demands for police professionalization increased in the aftermath of the summer of 1964. Federal officials had to heed the trusted voices of police themselves. Professionalization was the formula for federal involvement.

The idea for how to thread a solution through the interstices of federal-local-state relations originated in two reports submitted in September 1964 by Arnold Sagalyn to Lee C. White, assistant special counsel (who worked on civil rights issues), and S. Douglass Cater, special assistant to the president.[22] Whereas police assistance was a temporizing tool, used overseas to stave off more direct and warlike intervention, at home, it was the infrastructure of the War on Crime. Overseas police assistance was typically an adjunct to economic and political development programs, meant to ensure that they could proceed without interference while also managing the social dislocations they might entail. Similarly, from the outset, Sagalyn considered the modernization of domestic policing to be a companion to, and insurance for, the Great Society. Law and order, as a new frame of governance, did not sprout in opposition to the liberal creed of progressive amelioration of socioeconomic dissatisfaction (which liberals thought conducive to criminality); rather, the two were intertwined vines that arose from the same soil. "While the lawlessness and violence arising out of civil disturbances focus attention today on this aspect of law and order, a basic need also exists to help our police departments cope with increasing crime, and to maintain the standard of law and order in our 'Great Society,'" Sagalyn explained. Riot control alone would not ensure the success of the Great Society. The crisis of unrest demonstrated the need to upgrade a panoply of policing capabilities dealing with ordinary crime. Failure to address police shortcomings "would have a most serious and detrimental effect both on the confidence of United States citizens in the ability of their government to assure law and order, as well as on the image of United States leadership abroad."[23]

Using federal grants to smaller-scale entities of government to reduce crime was not Sagalyn's invention. But he placed the burden directly on police.

Kennedy administration programs to counter juvenile delinquency had initiated a type of federal assistance, building on an Eisenhower effort scotched by conservatives in the House of Representatives.[24] Sagalyn's contribution was to argue that such grants should go primarily to law enforcement, rather than to agencies concerned more broadly with socioeconomic conditions. He also framed his appeal in terms of bolstering police capacity, rather than of correcting racial prejudice, as had prior recommendations from the US Commission on Civil Rights.[25] In doing so, despite acknowledging the inseparability of security from economic uplift, he inserted a division between social-welfare programs and law enforcement that would begin to deflate the modest means-tested US welfare state and simultaneously inflate the carceral state over ensuing decades. This division was not operative for Kennedy administration experts concerned with juvenile delinquency. They believed that addressing root causes of delinquency, which existed on the level of economics and social bonds, would alleviate, though not remove, the need for law-enforcement agencies' involvement. Sagalyn, in contrast, adopted a position that was fundamental to counterinsurgency, influenced by the modernization paradigm: economic uplift and development were impossible in an environment destabilized by insecurity. Armed with this outlook, his experience guided him to the easy next step, which was to attempt to repatriate the key instrument of counterinsurgency overseas, OPS.

Sagalyn worried about how the summer's unrest had overwhelmed local police forces, demonstrating their inadequate preparation. In his initial report, he suggested that one problem was a lack of a centralized repository of expertise. There was nowhere for municipalities to turn for help when unrest erupted, other than the military. "Yet the problems faced by police departments in preventing lawlessness and violence in local communities" differed from those faced by the military overseas. He continued, "For, unlike the objective of the military mission, which in essence is to kill and destroy, the techniques and equipment for dealing with violence and civil disturbances in our cities should employ the minimum force necessary with a humane, non-injurious effect on those against whom they are employed." His language could have been copied from the reports that justified creating OPS.

To address insufficient local preparation would require Washington's intervention, and Sagalyn already knew what such intervention could look like. Unrest that overwhelmed police called for "an assistance program" that would "improve law enforcement capabilities of local and State police departments." Currently, the US government, he explained, was "providing this kind of technical police assistance to many foreign countries as an integral part of our foreign policy to strengthen the capabilities . . . in maintaining law and order and internal security." The "expertise and resources" of OPS "could provide a nucleus" of a "technical police assistance program which could provide local and state communities with the guidance, training, and help they urgently need to meet developing problems." He was arguing for the domestic dissemination of expertise accumulated overseas, fully in line with Komer's design for OPS as an alternative to overmilitarized and unduly violent responses to unrest and subversion.

In a follow-up report issued a week later, Sagalyn focused on funding. He expanded on the initial proposal, which had focused mostly on the dissemination of expertise. Now he argued that the creed of local autonomy in law enforcement had "severely handicapped our police departments," restraining the creation of "capabilities to meet modern day police problems."[26] In fact, "territorial jurisdiction" did not match "the activities of criminals," which "often extend beyond local borders and authority." Among "overtaxed" local police, facing "civil disturbances," there was a need for better-trained personnel, "selected for their outstanding qualities and character." Localism was no answer. "The Federal government can provide leadership, training and other types of assistance without in any way doing injury to the established Federal-state relationships." The way to do so was to issue "police training grants" to police departments, state or local agencies concerned with law-enforcement training, colleges or universities, and other nonprofit organizations. "Grants could be given to develop and demonstrate techniques, weapons, and practices which would provide police forces with the capability to maintain law and order effectively but humanely," he suggested. He reiterated the need for a central repository of expertise and advocated convening a "Presidential Law Enforcement Advisory Council," which could help raise standards and capabilities of law-enforcement agencies. Finally, in addition to the FBI and the Treasury Department's own law-enforcement agencies, he urged reliance on OPS, "which currently provides technical assistance and training support to assist the police forces of a number of countries in South America, Africa and Asia."

Sagalyn created a warrant for the modular domestic reapplication of the skeletal structure of foreign police assistance. It arose between his arguments for granting mechanisms that would be inoculated against accusations of overreach and his invocation of the need to upgrade and professionalize domestic policing. This effort would rely on the geographically extensive domain of police professionalization, utilizing some of the same personnel. Within a few months, Lyndon Johnson appointed the President's Commission on Law Enforcement and Administration of Justice (PCLEAJ, or Crime Commission), for which Sagalyn was a consultant, and it embarked on devising the Law Enforcement Assistance Act of 1965. Johnson outlined these developments in his first major national address on crime in March 1965, which further entrenched a separation between "long-run" welfare-oriented programming and short-term anticrime programming.[27] Sagalyn's ideas, reworked by Johnson's aides, were coming to fruition as the War on Crime.

WHO WAS ARNOLD SAGALYN?

Sagalyn was perfectly situated to introduce new ideas because he straddled professional worlds. His personal connections, Democratic Party loyalties, and background in law enforcement brought him into the Treasury Department soon after John F. Kennedy's inauguration. After growing up in a Jewish family in western Massachusetts, Sagalyn attended Wesleyan University in Connecticut, where, as one of only a handful of Jews, he felt alienated socially. On the recommendation of a professor, he transferred to Oberlin College in Ohio, where he thrived. For a term paper, he decided to research the famed Prohibition agent Eliot Ness (who had organized the crack squad called the Untouchables). Ness was now directing law enforcement in nearby Cleveland. Sagalyn brashly requested an interview with a reporter who had been chronicling Ness's achievements, which led to a meeting with the man himself. Ness took a shine to the unabashed student. After answering Sagalyn's probing research questions, and later reading the resulting paper, Ness offered the young man a job. This position in law enforcement in Cleveland allowed Sagalyn, like Engle, Hall, and Hoyt, to witness the departure of the old guard, as reform-oriented leadership weeded out corruption and inefficiency.

His experience working for Ness, whom he followed to Washington in the early 1940s, combined with what Sagalyn thought was the misfortune of having eyesight too poor to allow him to serve in a combat role, led him to a public safety position in Berlin under O. W. Wilson after World War II's end, working on denazification. One of Sagalyn's colleagues from Cleveland was Wilson's closest subordinate. And Sagalyn's mentor Ness had been an early advocate of Wilson's patrol reforms.[28] Amid rumors of clandestine plots and imminent guerrilla attacks by Nazis hoping to regain power, Sagalyn's role was to assess the risk of insurgency and develop preventive plans. In the end, he felt that economic assistance and the steady liberalization of governance staved off any residual threats. On January 1, 1946, Sagalyn was promoted to captain. He was proud to have Wilson, "a wonderful boss," ceremonially pin the captain's bars on his jacket. After the war, he worked in print and broadcast journalism (aided by the connection made while researching Ness), among other jobs, but he also participated in election campaigns, working on behalf of Eisenhower's Democratic challenger Adlai Stevenson. When Kennedy entered the White House, Sagalyn sought a position in the new administration. He spotted a perfect one in the lengthy list of federal job openings published after each presidential election: assistant to the secretary for enforcement in the Treasury Department. He knew of Treasury's law-enforcement powers from his time working for Ness, and, as luck would have it, the official who interviewed him happened to be a neighbor and a friend of his wife's (Louise Sagalyn had worked with the interviewer in local Democratic political campaigns). Arnold Sagalyn's impressive experience in Germany won him the job.[29]

Situated in Treasury, Sagalyn was now in charge of coordination among seven law-enforcement agencies with domestic and international responsibilities, as well as oversight of training for these agencies' four thousand officers. From controlling narcotics, tax evasion, and currency counterfeiting to protecting the president, Treasury's law-enforcement duties were extensive.[30] In addition, Sagalyn's position entailed serving as the US representative to Interpol (the International Criminal Police Organization), the communications network and depository of crime-fighting intelligence for, at that time, over eighty member nations. Unbeknown to Sagalyn, however, he had stepped into a fast-moving river. Law enforcement was becoming the first line of defense on a global scale.

The United States was poised to use law enforcement to achieve global supremacy, while, in turn, achieving global supremacy in law enforcement. Engle ensured it. Along with Harry Anslinger's right-hand man, Charles Siragusa, the tough and successful deputy commissioner of the Bureau of Narcotics, with whom Engle had worked in Turkey in the early 1950s, Engle maneuvered to make certain the United States filled one of three vice-presidencies of Interpol for a three-year term beginning at the organization's 1961 meeting in Madrid. The head of the Royal Canadian Mounted Police was running unopposed for the position, which would represent North and

South America, but Engle and Siragusa, whom Sagalyn called "forces to contend with," orchestrated a campaign to persuade a majority of the meeting's delegates to vote for Sagalyn.[31] He was new and unknown to Interpol's delegates, and Engle had only just met him in Madrid. But Engle saw something in Sagalyn that inspired his support. Perhaps it was his freshness, his lack of institutional baggage, or maybe it was Sagalyn's background and experience with Wilson, his belief in the power of reform to make law enforcement effective. A majority of Interpol's delegates agreed that the United States, not Canada, should hold an executive seat. Sagalyn won. Over the next three years, he traveled around the globe as a global leader of law-enforcement coordination, while also overseeing such coordination domestically, in the Treasury Department.

Yet that position was not the most salient for this story. After 1961, Engle stayed in touch with Sagalyn. On behalf of the U. Alexis Johnson Committee on Police Assistance Programs, Engle's research subcommittee interviewed Sagalyn—and he, in his Treasury role, was anyway an ex officio overseer of the Johnson Committee (in reality, the Engle-Komer Committee). Buried in NSAM 177, which authorized the formation of OPS, Kennedy directed that AID's administrator, "establish an interagency police group, to be chaired by his designee," which would assist him in "coordination and vigorous leadership of all police assistance programs." Members were to "bring to bear their professional knowledge and agency interests in Police Assistance Programs; be the principal points of contact within their respective agencies on matters relating to Police Assistance Programs; [and] present the needs of Police Assistance Programs to their respective agencies."[32] Engle was the designated leader. At AID's request, the secretary of the Treasury nominated its representative to this new body.[33] There was never any question as to which Treasury law-enforcement official it would be.

This new Interagency Police Group (IPG) acted like a corporate Board of Directors for OPS. It became a vessel for law-enforcement coordination across the foreign-domestic divide. Otherwise ignored in the literature, the IPG enabled an intimate, irregular convocation of law-enforcement and counterinsurgency experts. The IPG initially brought together Engle, Sagalyn, Courtney Evans (FBI assistant director), Abe J. Moses (State Department politico-military officer), Ralph Butchers (Army provost marshal), and Lyle "Ted" Shannon (a leader of CIA covert operations and one-time CIA acting executive director).[34] Its discussions were free-flowing and informal but more fine-grained than those in the SGCI, concerned not only

FIGURE 7. Arnold Sagalyn speaks at the International Police
Academy, ca. 1964. National Archives and Records Administration.

with identifying countries needing attention but also devising how police
assistance in them should proceed and whether the resources marshaled were
adequate. The IPG, in addition, provided a forum for sharing and gathering
expert knowledge across jurisdictions, as well as for coordinating among
agencies.[35] Moreover, given persistent needs to bolster the number of OPS
advisors in Washington and in the field, the IPG enabled OPS to draw upon
the personnel resources of the represented agencies. It helped create a rank
and file of policing experts who traveled widely and wove experience with
typical law-enforcement tasks together with specific intelligence-oriented
expertise. In addition, whereas law-enforcement agencies tended to be limited in their jurisdictions, either inward- or outward-facing (though mostly
the former), Treasury's agents in particular had an expansive purview. At the
level of leadership, the IPG allowed Sagalyn to keep a finger on the pulse on
law-enforcement modernization the world over. Thanks to his participation
in the IPG, Sagalyn and Engle became "good friends."[36] In ensuing years,
Sagalyn joined crucial ventures for the professionalization of policing and the
reformatting of federalism in criminal justice, including the Crime and
Kerner Commissions. He wrote in popular and professional venues and
advised authors of benchmark reformist texts.[37]

Sagalyn brought to the table experience with two organizations that modeled how a new technique of modernizing policing in the United States could
proceed, OPS and Interpol. Though different, both were coordinating
mechanisms without enforcement authority. Instead, both relied on

indigenous police to carry out the street-level operations they orchestrated and aided. The LEAA, which came into existence with 1968's Omnibus Crime Control and Safe Streets Act, similarly had no enforcement powers of its own but instead was tasked with facilitation of knowledge sharing and budgetary allocation from Washington to the states.

THE FEDERAL ORBIT

US law enforcement was fluid in the 1960s, but J. Edgar Hoover attempted to remain steady and unyielding. However, there were events and shifts he could not prevent, that escaped his grasp, or that he simply misjudged. His contemporaries learned to deal with his power and prerogatives. Several transformations in the period occurred in the gap between White House initiative and Hoover's reliable insistence that there would be no federal police force. The actions of the attorney general and Sagalyn joined transnational perspectives to locally scaled action. The FBI's methods of countersubversive policing, which attacked many groups on the Left and some on the Right, would be replicated in public safety training, though the FBI was largely superfluous to the bureaucratic formation of OPS.

Robert Kennedy was a bridge figure, spanning foreign and domestic concerns. Kennedy brought overseas expertise that he encountered in the SGCI to bear on domestic problems like crime and juvenile delinquency, while expatriating his obsessions with these problems and aligning them with the problems counterinsurgency had to manage. What Robert Kennedy lacked in expertise, he possessed in tirelessness and the desire to achieve visible results. Because the attorney general was in the room as his brother's "viceroy," his demands had to be met.[38] Yet, as a brash young official, he occasionally came into conflict with the FBI and Hoover himself, not to mention the other SGCI principals. As a result, when possible, Kennedy tried to help the FBI extend its own influence in some areas, while constraining it in others. The SGCI provided one venue in which he could seem supportive of the FBI, often insisting that the Bureau be consulted. Therefore, though the FBI would frequently assert how the internal security of other nations fell outside its jurisdiction, it nonetheless participated in discussions leading up to the formalization of OPS, via Engle's technical subcommittee. Kennedy insisted on it.[39] Thanks to the insignificant-seeming provision in NSAM 177 to establish the IPG, the FBI was party to discussions of counterinsurgent law-enforcement coordination throughout the 1960s. Yet Kennedy never extended an invitation to any FBI representatives to participate regularly in SGCI meetings.

In the year and a half prior to the formation of OPS, Robert Kennedy's frequent attempts to bring Hoover's FBI on board took shape as the assurance that the Bureau would share resources as needed when it came to counterinsurgency and police training. For example, during discussions led by Rostow on the formation of an institute to teach tenets of modernization and counterinsurgency theory to officials across the gamut of federal agencies, Kennedy insisted that the FBI be consulted. An agent could lead a course on "Communist internal subversive techniques." Courtney Evans, one of Hoover's closest subordinates and soon the FBI's delegate to the IPG, spearheaded the consultation.[40] AID officials were wary of being batted around in a power play between Hoover and Kennedy on the relationship of development and security. And public safety advisors themselves were not fully empowered within AID yet and were trying to tread carefully, lest they incur the displeasure of the agency's skeptics. Although liberal adherents of the development mission might not from today's perspective seem ready supporters of the coercive side of counterinsurgency, the paradox of the moment was that AID's leaders had an easier time convincing their staff of the necessity of police assistance when it was framed in the idiom of countersubversion. If it came to seem that police assistance concerned only public order measures like upgrading traffic control, communications technologies, or crime laboratories, which were less apt to be coercive, AID staff tended to become resistant and consider it a diversion from the agency's development mandate.[41]

The formal creation of OPS preserved long-standing operational and interpersonal ties between public safety advisors and the FBI, though public safety remained under the aegis of the CIA. These ties persisted beneath rivalries at the pinnacle of the executive branch. The FBI, for instance, reserved space within its National Academy classes for English-speaking foreign police in 1963, and some did attend.[42] The International Police Academy, which opened in December of that year, obviated the need for AID to send trainees to the FBI Academy. And the IPA invited participants who did not speak English fluently. Still, throughout the IPA's existence, several participants each year did receive specialized training from the FBI, or toured its facilities.[43] High-ranking foreign police officials visiting the United States also occasionally were afforded the opportunity to meet Hoover in person. He would assert how limited the FBI's powers actually were.[44] The FBI's most demonstrable impact on police assistance came through the hiring of individual active or former FBI agents as public safety advisors. Engle and Hoover met personally on occasion.[45] Several key advisors were former FBI agents, including Edward Kennelly, who directed operations in the Middle East and Africa; Michael McCann, who directed the OPS training division; and Jack Ryan, who started overseas via MSU, occasionally translated during meetings between Ngo Dinh Diem and MSU officials, and then directed the public safety program in South Vietnam. In 1969, some fifteen to twenty public safety advisors were former FBI agents.[46] The route from employment by the FBI to OPS was not always direct. A longtime FBI agent became an instructor at the IPA only after joining the St. Louis Metropolitan Police Department, highlighting the salience again of seemingly intangible Missouri connections.[47] Public safety advisors could also be useful for FBI training. In 1967, the FBI invited one experienced advisor to speak to officers from his home state of North Carolina attending FBI-overseen training on the subject of "International Crime Development and Its Relationship with Domestic Law Enforcement."[48] Still, the public safety program worked much more closely with other federal law-enforcement agencies, particularly those within the Treasury Department.

Rivalry bubbled between the FBI and Treasury law-enforcement agencies, dating to competition decades earlier between Hoover and Anslinger. Unbeknown to Sagalyn in the 1960s, Hoover worried that, as liaison to Interpol, Sagalyn would eclipse the FBI director as the face of US law enforcement globally. The FBI monitored him, even though Sagalyn's official role was to enliven FBI connections with police overseas.[49] In any case, Sagalyn was a behind-the-scenes operator. He had fallen into his leadership position within Interpol only because of Engle's angling. Sagalyn's domestic advice as a catalytic source of federal anticrime legislation would prove even more threatening to Hoover's supremacy. Sagalyn anticipated how Hoover would react to realignments of policing's scalar architecture. In 1964, he noted that the FBI's own attempts to train municipal officers and issue guidance were hampered by Hoover's concern over "initiation of a national police system." As such, "a Federal police assistance program" could respond "to the needs of our local communities and states in a positive and effective way, while at the same time respecting the authority and responsibility of the states in this field."[50] Sagalyn offered the IACP as an example of how it was possible to skirt the obstacle of federalism—noting that it was already conducting a survey of preparedness for "racial disturbances" in every major city in the United States. Hoover had been trying to maintain a tight grip on the IACP. He saw the writing on the wall: an independent IACP could overcome the charges of federal encroachment in national leadership of law enforcement while also pushing the FBI aside.

THE IACP'S POLITICIZATION

The IACP's eight-year contract with the International Cooperation Administration to supervise the training of thousands of foreign police officials empowered it. This experience raised the IACP's profile internationally (and nationally). The contract was worth around $300,000 per year to the IACP. Thanks to this program, by the late 1950s, 15 percent of IACP members came from outside the United States, and the IACP fulfilled its charter duty to "foster and promote the exchange of information and experience among the police administrators of the world."[51] Engle and other police assistance notables were frequent attendees of IACP annual meetings in the 1950s and 1960s, and advisors called upon leading members for guidance, such as in setting up a police athletic league in Bangkok.[52] Even though they were not technically police executives, all public safety advisors became members of the IACP, listed in its massive annual directory of members, and AID sponsored IACP memberships for all graduates of the International Police Academy. *The Police Chief* featured articles that described aid-recipient nations' forces, carried news about police assistance, and published recruitment advertisements. International cooperation in the fight against communism shaped IACP executives' views, as well as legislators' perceptions of their expertise. Exemplifying the resulting consensus, one testified to Congress that IACP members "feel that the unrest and violence outside our borders and that being experienced domestically are definitely not unrelated."[53] Yet once OPS came into existence, Engle's staff determined that it should recalibrate its training efforts and centralize them in an academy, which the IACP lacked. AID terminated the IACP contract.

The IACP's experience working with the federal government provided crucial political lessons. And the organization's leaders found the cancellation of the foreign police-training contract with AID a bitter pill. Quinn Tamm, the IACP's director, fulminated against the cancellation. It seemed to suggest municipal chiefs were ill-suited for the task of modeling leadership, while dishonoring the good work and collective experience of the IACP.[54] The result, Tamm feared, was that the IACP would not win funding for future training endeavors. The money might go to colleges and universities. Michigan State University had been planning to create an International Police Institute within its School of Police Administration since 1959.[55] Or the money could go to municipalities directly, without the IACP as an intermediary. Well-acquainted with Hoover's savvy, Tamm also worried that AID might fund a new FBI training program for police from overseas. The IACP proposed its own International Police College as a way to enhance its role.[56] In the end, funds for training did not end up disbursed the ways IACP officials feared. AID would internalize training expenditures. Professionalizers were aware, however, that the IACP had for years received federal funding to train foreign police at the municipal level. Reliable external sources of funding were not just welcome, they were necessary, whether from Washington or from the Ford Foundation, as MSU staff noted in brainstorming correspondence between East Lansing and Saigon.[57] Though the cancellation of the contract with AID angered Tamm, it was an educational experience. The same had been true for his colleague Arthur Brandstatter with the termination of MSU's subcontract. To obtain external funds for the expansion and improvement of police capacities became these leaders' new mission.

Tamm and his colleagues transformed the IACP by reconfiguring its relationship to Washington, which meant subordinating the demands of some members and stepping on the toes of powerful men like Hoover. Although the IACP was an organization responsible to its members, leaders could decide which members' perspectives would determine its course. Tamm confirmed the organization's professionalizing tack, and it became one of the strongest institutional advocates of the War on Crime. One way to assume the mantle of professionalism was to heed the advice of stand-out police executives whose forces were marked by strong training regimens. The training experience of foreign police visiting the United States in the 1950s indicated which locales took training seriously. Another way to demonstrate professionalism was to speak with a disciplined voice. Many members were skeptical about federal intervention in the fight against crime. And powerful chiefs threatened not to support the federal War on Crime if their concerns went unheeded.[58] By helping to ensure that police chiefs were included in new initiatives, and by choosing not to amplify dissident views, Tamm whipped the organization into line. Like Sagalyn, he stressed the difficulty of maintaining "law and order" when "the crisis" of unrest "has transcended the scope of police responsibility and capability."[59] He and his colleagues repeatedly appeared before Congress or submitted statements (MSU's Brandstatter and Turner among them) and spoke to reporters about the importance of federal anticrime legislation. "It is not a question of whether you should act but rather it is a question as to the price in lives, property loss, and freedom should you fail to act," an IACP representative testifying on the Law Enforcement Assistance Act told Congress in 1965.[60] The IACP was, moreover, the first advocate of distributing surplus military gear from the Pentagon to police forces, as far back as 1965.[61] These cops specialized in apocalyptic language, honed in the fight against communism, and this proactive stance earned rewards.

Tradition-bound US police chiefs were not always receptive to the IACP's new direction, but they were not necessarily sympathetic to the FBI either. Resolutely independent local officials often saw jurisdictional differences in competitive rather than cooperative terms. Many never much appreciated the interventions of more patrician, better-educated, and upwardly mobile outsider federal officials. By helping win passage of both the 1965 and the 1968 federal anticrime bills, which brought much-needed money to small-city police forces, Tamm won the respect and admiration of reluctant conservative chiefs. His efforts helped overcome police officers' defensiveness and resistance to change. The IACP also earned the trust of mayors and other leaders, which police reformers recognized would be necessary.[62] The IACP pushed a scientific tone at its conferences and in its publications, even if the cantankerous Tamm did not himself adopt it. Haphazardly sharing tales of personal experiences, whether with nearby or distant fellow officers, could not substitute for a rigorous, planned, and structured set of lessons and benchmarks. Out with the fishing stories, in with the ichthyology.

As an institutional actor with a unique voice, the IACP helped the profession develop autonomy, building on decades of effort to insert a wedge between partisan politics and policing. Once politically independent and professionalized, police became better able to mobilize as self-interested, decisive political actors who were impossible to ignore. The IACP began the decade receiving money from AID for a contract to help train foreign officers in precinct houses across the United States; it ended the decade, after Congress enacted anticrime legislation, receiving a great deal more federal funding to train US police officers themselves.

The transformation of law enforcement went hand in hand with legislation on civil and voting rights, economic opportunity, and immigration. In the aftermath of the unrest in the summer of 1964, Johnson's aides devised the Law Enforcement Assistance Act, which set up the Office of Law Enforcement Assistance (OLEA) and ushered in the first federal anticrime efforts specifically focused on upgrading law enforcement. The OLEA's acting director was Courtney Evans, once the FBI's representative to the Interagency Police Group, a direct colleague of Sagalyn's. By then Evans had fallen out of favor with Hoover, and his assuming this new position was regarded as an affront to the latter. In the brief lead-up to the signing of the Law Enforcement Assistance Act in 1965, many parties lavished praise on the FBI in congressional testimony, though the FBI itself did not participate in the discussion because Hoover recognized the legislation might encroach on his power.[63] The OLEA issued grants to 359 projects in almost three years of operation, for an expenditure of $20.6 million.[64] Over subsequent years, civil unrest continued to occur and crime rates appeared to continue to rise, though the increase in arrest numbers, for example, can at least in part be attributed to the bolstering of law enforcement. Recorded crime rates increased because police were better prepared to discover and respond to a range of new, as well as traditional, crimes. Increased policing capabilities, including two-way radios and squad cars, enabled better coverage, leading to additional interactions with the public and thus higher rates of police observation or public reporting of lawlessness. New data collection protocols allowed crime to be more accurately reported to the FBI, giving the appearance of increasing crime levels in federal statistics. Police may also have fraudulently inflated crime rates to secure federal or state funding.[65]

The Omnibus Crime Control and Safe Streets Act of 1968 was passed by a shocked and despondent Congress and signed by President Johnson right after Robert Kennedy's assassination.[66] Many police chiefs from smaller municipalities organized by the IACP supported it, but even Tamm noted that Kennedy's murder had pushed Congress to act.[67] An early draft of the bill proclaimed that it would "strengthen our first line of defense—our city police forces."[68] When the bill emerged from its congressional committee reformulation, it rejected giving wide latitude to the federal government or bypassing the states, as had Kennedy's juvenile-delinquency legislation.

Although it did insist on the value of exploring novel approaches, an effort to change social structures in local communities did not whet elected officials' appetites. Instead, the federal purse would be the blunt weapon warring on crime. In its first year, the LEAA, which succeeded the OLEA, spent $63 million. In 1971, it spent $529 million. Appropriations kept increasing. Cumulatively, by 1982, $7.5 billion had been appropriated for LEAA distribution.[69] Throughout the 1970s, the LEAA was the fastest-growing federal outfit, and spending on all aspects of criminal justice tripled between 1968 and 1985, a greater increase than seen in any other budgetary domain. By 1970, at 8 percent, the federal contribution to criminal justice in the United States equaled the federal contribution to education.[70] Meanwhile the LEAA stipulated that states receiving its funds increase their criminal-justice budgets by 5 percent annually.[71]

The Johnson administration initially proposed legislation geared toward comprehensive planning, bolstering police salaries, capital construction projects, and innovative research and development. This version of the bill stalled in Congress. Yet legislators' reluctance to adopt it was not due to disagreement about whether to expand the initial federal anticrime effort the OLEA had begun. It resulted from disagreement about whether these specific objectives were appropriate.[72] The adopted legislation weakened the possibility of comprehensive planning at the regional or national levels and lodged planning at the state level. Moreover, the administration's formulas on capital construction projects and salaries were modified. Additionally, in the political wrangling, conservatives in Congress were able to include two titles that were not fully germane, but that did act as a shot back at the Supreme Court's decision in *Miranda v. Arizona*: confessions would become admissible at trial, and electronic wiretapping would be expanded. The latter title fostered domestic political surveillance, using techniques of cross-border intelligence gathering in the guise of crime control. Chiefs also relished any attempt to push back on the courts, which many believed too protective of defendants. The public blamed increases in crime on police shortcomings, but big-city chiefs thought the courts were culpable.[73]

Republicans and Southern Democrats worried that police forces would become effectively addicted to federal funds. To get their fix they would, one Republican warned, "give up their State and local control over police until they are finally persuaded that law enforcement is a national problem and no longer a State or local responsibility."[74] In one sense, this worry was accurate: federal funding seeded new projects in criminal justice that would otherwise have been impossible, and their expenditures required new revenues. But with the growth in state capacity, there was never a diminution of local responsibility. Instead, addiction to federal funds meant an increase in state and local funding sources as well because of a newly shared commitment to law enforcement as the leading edge of governance.[75] Finally, Southern Democrats worried that the Civil Rights Act would mean that once federal funding became widely available for police, departments would have to racially integrate, or prove they did not practice discriminatory hiring. This was not to be. Section 518 (b) of Title I of the 1968 bill stated that police departments would be eligible for federal funds even if they violated civil rights law by, for instance, refusing to employ African American police. All in all, the solution to a range of problems came in the form of a proposal for the LEAA to issue block grants, with few strings attached at the federal level and disbursement directed by new State Planning Agencies. Conservative members of Congress did insert provisions that set aside large amounts of money for quelling civil unrest, which was consequential for new police training regimens and opened the door to the adoption of military gear, like Big Bertha, Louisiana's LEAA-purchased armored personnel carrier, used in a 1970 raid on a Black Panther Party office. The LEAA also enabled greater experimentation with police aviation, leading to today's ubiquitous urban police helicopters.

As it proceeded through Congress, the bill Johnson would sign lost its resemblance to the one his aides had drafted. Scholars have largely agreed that the unwieldy State Planning Agencies meant to distribute the monies that originated in block grants, designed by a cohort of staunchly conservative congressmen, was the fatal flaw of the Omnibus Crime Control and Safe Streets Act and the reason Johnson had to hold his nose in signing it.[76] Yet the Johnson administration never had much interest in violating the local autonomy of law enforcement. The LEAA created the conditions for increasingly well-funded, -networked, and -armed citadels of localism: fortresses of solicitude for grant reviewers. The effect was to solidify the ongoing association of crime with Blackness, insofar as the defense of white supremacy and the defense of crime-fighting police both rested on the strengthening of locally scaled political power. The discourse of white supremacy relied on protection of small-scale autonomy. This discourse did become less explicit, but the materiality of it remained. This maintenance relied on keeping struggles against it from upscaling, while also strengthening the first line of defense. If, as the administration's critics charged, Johnson's DOJ had not been able to muster a strong and incisive anticrime effort, which created space for its opponents in Congress to sculpt the legislation, then it was nonetheless true that what emerged rested on the firm unelected foundation of itinerant law-enforcement expertise that had grown in preceding decades, beyond the direct control of Johnson's domestic aides.

The peculiar shape of the War on Crime, congruent with the overseas police assistance program, would provide technical assistance and much-needed equipment and training to local police while preserving the distribution of authority inherent in federalism. Moreover, it took advantage of the ongoing flux of law-enforcement expertise by empowering new players and inviting domestic application of technologies and training methods field-tested overseas. If anything, conservative congressional action diluted the federalism injunction by mandating decision-making by state-level appointees in order to prevent direct infusions of cash from the federal level to large urban municipalities, which tended to have Democratic leaderships. And IACP-organized small-town chiefs benefited from the unrestricted block grants, because categorical spending would likely have skipped them. A convoluted "troika" system of LEAA oversight ensured no attorney general would control it. The troika did not streamline law-enforcement assistance. The State Planning Agencies created a massive bureaucracy, and bureaucrats and appointees devised ways to line their pals' pockets with unsupervised flows of federal money.

The block grant represented a conservative dream come true: a way to hasten the demise of the more targeted and planned federal fiscal interventions of the War on Poverty and the participatory, grassroots character of social programming based around "felt needs" of recipients. The Republican Coordinating Committee, on behalf of Richard Nixon, Barry Goldwater, Gerald Ford, and other past and future party powerbrokers, advocated the block grant. This novel instrument explicitly repudiated new grants-in-aid Johnson wanted to issue beginning in 1967, which these Republicans complained were "conditioned upon compliance with Federal dictates on what is to be done and how it is to be done." The block grant's novelty was to take advantage of the federal budget while trying to decentralize control and eliminate "the minute conditions and close supervision accompanying" the tide of money.[77] By the LEAA's final years, in the late 1970s, it had become clear that recipients ignored "federal directives" if funding did not stipulate adherence them.[78]

Upon his resignation as administrator of the LEAA under a cloud of bad press, Donald Santarelli, who had spoken at the International Police

Academy graduation ceremony a few months earlier, wrote to President Nixon that the LEAA had "been the pioneer in implementing your concept of the New Federalism, to assure that law enforcement stays in the hands of state and local government, close to the people. It is an exciting and rewarding experience to play a role in implementing this Presidential mandate."[79] The Nixon administration did use LEAA discretionary funds to bolster law enforcement in majority-Black cities, violating its own principles of federalism because State Planning Agencies tended to lavish money on white rural areas.[80] Nevertheless, Nixon had adopted the inclination to use law enforcement as an instrument to reshape the state, not simply to enact its power. The War on Crime, invented by Democratic law-enforcement officials and legislators, ended up setting the stage for decades of devolutionary dismantling of federal social programming.

· · ·

Federalism was the medium, stake, and outcome of political battles within and for law enforcement. Municipal police stood to benefit from putting law and order on the national political agenda, from compelling elected officials to take up the charge. The very demand for "law and order" gained popularity among police before politicians, with *Law and Order* itself as the name of a monthly magazine for cops in the 1950s and 1960s, edited by a Far Right former chief. Police leaders were active progenitors of change, not merely passive recipients of demands placed on them by elected officials or voters. Police discovered how to protect and serve themselves. Through the LEAA's heavy purse and light planning touch, police reasserted their local autonomy, stoking racialized fears of lawlessness to encourage continued appropriations. The result was a recrudescence, beneath a formally equal veneer, of the discretionary power of policing. In turn, to focus federal attention and resources on crime limited the ability of small-scale, localized groups of civilians, particularly those most intimately involved in the criminal justice system, to affect crime policy. Instead, they became its likely objects. Magnifying resources for punishment and policing rather than other types of state social programming, in a move toward risk management rather than risk eradication, meant that everyday experience with crime would predominate among people least able to affect the social conditions that gave rise to it.

FIVE

Policing and Social Regulation

POLICING THE GLOBE ENGENDERED NEW APPROACHES to governance. The public safety project insisted upon the universality of its approach to crafting the first line of defense, uniting cops from across the United States and across the globe in a single fraternity. Advising police overseas differed from patrolling a beat at home, however. Innovation, flexibility, and patience were essential. The experience affirmed and reinforced police experts' belief in the vital necessity of cutting-edge policing expertise as a bulwark against societal chaos.

Many older public safety advisors retired from law enforcement when they left AID, but around a hundred rotated back into ordinary police positions at home, now with a new outlook.[1] Lee Echols, who initiated the public safety mission to Bolivia in 1957, was elected sheriff of Yuma County, Arizona, in 1960. A campaign ad included endorsements from Office of Strategic Services director William Donovan and OPS's Theo Hall. Echols lost a bid for reelection after one term, during which he spent lavishly and implemented rigorous FBI-led in-service training for his men, in effect imitating OPS-style reforms.[2] This vigor was premature, however—the law and order craze still lay in the future. Echols was obliged to resume overseas advisory work.

After OPS shut down, Adolph Saenz became a prison administrator in New Mexico, recruiting OPS buddies to staff his facility, and Donald Bordenkircher Jr. became warden of the West Virginia State Penitentiary. In the late 1950s, Bordenkircher had been a rising star in prison administration at San Quentin State Prison in California, and he became a public safety advisor in South Vietnam in 1967. He took lessons learned at San Quentin to Vietnam, like the rapid-response "troubleshooting squad" for prison rebellions and the "hole," or solitary confinement, for disciplinary infractions.

Bordenkircher eventually returned overseas, advising prison administration in Iraq from 2005 to 2009.[3] Both Saenz and Bordenkircher put their counterinsurgent knowledge to the test when called on to suppress rebellions in prisons they supervised, earning national news coverage.[4]

The individual itineraries of returned advisors do not suffice to illustrate the domestication of counterinsurgency, however. Instead, the institutions they developed would reproduce the knowledge they created long after they moved on and their names were forgotten. In their travels, advisors designed, introduced, and tested universally applicable policing techniques and technologies. In the context of global counterinsurgency, information collection, sorting, and dissemination were essential, and reliance on new technologies was consistent with the capital-intensive thrust of police reforms that professionalizers of the 1960s adopted. Technologies for surveilling and managing the population encouraged new forms of violence, like forced disappearance. And new weapons and new ways to use them also emerged. Through these developments, global security congealed.

POLICE POWERS

The actions of the police can be decomposed into what have more broadly been called the despotic and infrastructural powers of the state, that is, into destruction and construction.[5] Typically, police are thought to act as a bulwark against demands for change addressed to the state, particularly for the eradication of racial or economic inequality. Police help elites avoid negotiating with social movements and other groups. Repression and discretionary violence meted out against vulnerable and marginalized, or simply incautious, people insulates the state. Those who protest or challenge police activity are likely targets of repression, but it takes many forms and has shifting targets. OPS often helped client regimes repress dissidence. From the mid-1950s, US police assistance was directed toward strict control of labor organizing, rallies, pickets, and strikes. Barred from these forms of politics, militants joined clandestine guerrilla movements, particularly in Latin America, where class composition and labor routines were shifting anyway.[6] OPS was alert to charges that it supported tyranny and taught torture or assassination techniques. In their memoirs, former public safety advisors all both acknowledge and rebut such accusations, often in remarkably similar language.[7] The rebuttals are strident, perhaps particularly so because the charges were so effective in focusing the attention of Congress on OPS, ultimately leading to its closure. The claim that US police assistance backed brutal repression was accurate in some cases—it was notably true, for example, of pre–World War II policing by US marines in Nicaragua, where a weak state and lack of resources stymied constructive US efforts and left only a deeply repressive security force, which would later alarm public safety advisors.[8]

During the Nixon administration, as assistance for the despotic aspects of policing grew, so too did assistance more directly concerned with nonviolent social regulation. For example, even as OPS became entangled in the targeted "neutralization" program (i.e., by capture, induced defection, or assassination) in South Vietnam dubbed Phoenix, it also dutifully reported on its adherence to standards of community participation in economic development. Advisors understood the two as equal faces of a single coin. In this sense, then, looking at OPS can help us step back and analyze police not simply as the organizer of the state's repressive power. Police also encompasses its companion power to produce and shape civil society, the infrastructural power that hails subjects as citizens, constructing the limits of civic inclusion. Not only barriers to change, police institutions reform themselves when organized challenges to their legitimacy arise, which in turn transforms their relations with populations. This disciplining of social subjects corresponds, but is not reducible, to the routines and requirements of the broader regime of capitalist accumulation, shaping "an ensemble of norms, institutions, organizational forms, social networks and patterns of conduct." Together, these "sustain and 'guide'" capital accumulation by promoting "compatibility among the decentralized decisions of economic agents."[9] The police power operates in the conditional gap between the possibility of accumulation and its realization, in the potential of labor power to be a commodity and the actuality of the already disciplined social subject selling labor power.[10] In the traditional way it has been understood, OPS, a facilitator of the modern police institution, was solely oriented toward repression, including torture, on CIA orders.[11] But the police power, if not the police institution, also aspires to transform its own sharp coercions into the semiautomatic, dull compulsions of smoothly functioning markets. To face political crises, aid-recipient states had been endowed with the capacity to squelch contestation not only through repression but through negotiation and calculated capitulation to demands. The legitimacy of police, and the state by extension, rested on the willingness of police to demonstrate a penchant for reformism. Sharp power over civil society and responsive power through civil society came to emanate from a single institutional locus. Linked to development officials, but answerable to intelligence officials, OPS encapsulated this shift. Still, security always came first.

In analyzing the overlapping of the state's productive and destructive power, scholars have focused on what is called "pacification,"[12] a strategy that troubles distinctions upon which liberalism is founded: between foreign and domestic spheres, war power and police power, coercive and consensual policy instruments, destructive and constructive approaches to security, and war and peace themselves. Police assistance was central to facilitating security within the self-described pacification program in South Vietnam, overseen for several years by Robert Komer. This controlled uplift strategy also emerged in other countries. Policing was intended to avoid military engagement, but nonmilitary development efforts to prevent insurrectionary violence relied heavily on local police, who were often linked to higher-level police and intelligence agencies. In Thailand, for instance, the OPS-aided Border Patrol Police used its officers to engage in all aspects of community development, even placing paramilitary officers in a "school teacher platoon."[13]

Civilian policing and participatory economic development programming were not intended to stamp out the threat of insurrection entirely, however much that possibility might have appealed to some officials. Pacification instead recognized that loyalties and allegiances were up for grabs. Central government domination would be replaced by a relationship of economic transaction oriented toward self-help as well as consensus-based investment by development advisors and community members alike. Pacification meant action. William Colby reflected, "We searched around for another name than 'pacification,' because of its connotation that the population was to be forced into quiescence, when the idea was precisely the opposite, to activate the people in the villages."[14] Pacification comprised future-oriented, community-based, civilian-led proactive methods to prevent civil violence and held that ongoing prevention as its goal. The most mobile aspects of pacification were not the most abjectly coercive, but rather those that worked to further political participation and police-enforced rule of law.

Pacification and policing share genetic material. Experts implemented new technologies and repertoires with the goal of strengthening police power against criminal suspects, perceived subversives, and disorderly public gatherings. But they also pursued the goal of regulating the behavior of the broad population, enabling police to be more responsive to complaints and emergencies. As US public safety advisors encountered police forces in new nations previously shaped by Belgian, Dutch, French, Portuguese, and Spanish colonialism, they affirmed the widely held belief that US policing, drawing on Anglo-Saxon traditions, differed from Continental policing because of its public and democratic orientation.[15] They tried to instill this ethos, while nevertheless maintaining capacities for secret, intelligence-led operations.

Policing everyday lives at home and abroad was intended to achieve what such focused deterrence could not. But protests against police compelled them to respond, further reinforcing the expert conviction that these institutions were democratic. Infiltration, disruption, and surveillance of radical groups remained central to the training work of public safety advisors overseas and their colleagues at home, but to achieve legitimacy, security instruments had to be flexible. Intertwined political and economic crises at home and abroad concentrated class, national, and racial struggle on "the terrain of the state," forcing its agencies to change.[16] The experiences of hamstrung postcolonial governments, frequently further weakened in legitimacy by US-directed efforts to shore up their security, were crucial rehearsals for the irruption of instabilities at home. The answer in all these settings was to reformat policing to make state violence simultaneously less blatant but more diffuse and omnipresent.

DISCRETION STANDARDIZED

In classrooms, laboratories, or firing ranges, public safety advisory work tended to be monotonous. Advisors trained their charges to watch out for patterns that matched the subversive blueprint. Whether political violence was an authentic expression of that blueprint remains difficult to discern. Racialized confirmation bias shaped extant archival records, telling of a subversive specter that haunted the alleyways of the bidonville, the favela, and the shantytown. It crouched on the paths between rice paddies. It flitted down the double-track crisscrossing rubber and banana plantations, or sugarcane fields. It graffitied the walls beside the factory gates, pressed leaflets into workers' outstretched hands, and whispered details of furtive organizing meetings. It broadcast exhortations on low frequencies, breaking through the static on transistor radios that entire neighborhoods might gather around. The radios were often manufactured by US companies like Philco, which in the 1960s became a subsidiary of one of the industrial giants central to the extraordinary post-1945 US economic expansion. Philco-Ford eventually diversified.

Selling radios that could broadcast US Information Agency messages or communist propaganda alike was not as lucrative as joining the counterinsurgency effort directly. This company thus mounted social-scientific research ventures, funded by the Pentagon's Advanced Research Projects Agency or by AID itself.[17] Headquartered in Saigon but operating across Southeast Asia, Philco-Ford researchers would seek local assistance, for security, for intelligence, for advice about local customs. And they would encounter public safety advisors, who would tell them about the subversive blueprint. Research reports would dutifully record what social scientists had learned. And public safety deployments would then match the predictions. Send more advisors to northeastern Thailand, the recommendation might be. The specter was just across the border, threatening, or holding up a mirror.

Because of the specter, public safety advisors routinely urged the police of newly independent nations to de-escalate. Use tear gas, not live ammunition. Batons, not bayonets. The fragile legitimacy of the state itself was at stake. The memory of a victim of police violence could become a galvanizing tool of subversive ideology. Among police and intelligence agencies, the usual imperative was kill or be killed. The weapons and riot-control expert Rex Applegate elaborated this ethos in his widely circulated 1943 book *Kill or Get Killed: A Manual of Hand-to-Hand Fighting.* But AID officials by 1963 determined that because it contained "physically and politically" risky details, a Spanish translation was unacceptable as a textbook at the Inter-American Police Academy. Latin American officers might, AID feared, return home armed with "easy methods to kill" and put the responsibility on AID for imparting them.[18] Yet Applegate had lived in Mexico City in the 1950s, training both municipal riot squads and federal secret police there, suggesting that keeping his book out of AID curricula was insufficient to limit the spread of brutal techniques in the hemisphere. US security operations were kaleidoscopic.[19]

Public safety advisory work was comparatively safe and paid up to three times what police work at home did.[20] Fewer than ten advisors were killed in the line of duty, despite deployments to countries where rates of killings of police could be as high as twenty times the contemporaneous rate in the United States.[21] Most violent deaths occurred in Vietnam, either by gunshot, shrapnel, or, in one case, in an airplane "believed to have been shot down by VC."[22] One advisor intentionally shot and killed his supervisor, Jack Ryan, as well as Nguyen Thi Hai, a Vietnamese woman employed by AID.[23] Two advisors died by self-inflicted gunshot, one intentionally in Vietnam, one accidentally in El Salvador. Some got drunk and brandished their guns, obliging other AID employees who were not ex-cops to restore order.[24]

Strictures against killing were set aside if public safety advisors feared for their own safety. The identities of people public safety advisors directly killed remain difficult to trace. For an advisor to usurp the police power of his advisees was to throw a wrench into the program itself, and, by extension, the design of US postcolonial global leadership. But it did happen. In 1966, for instance, one advisor shot a "Viet Cong" named Do Van Gioi from a low-flying airplane, which his superiors rated as "commendable," but "not in his job description."[25]

Advisors could not shirk the paradox of police professionalization, the standardization of an activity defined by discretion. Policing oscillated between craft and science. It was based on cultivated instincts and handed down through fraternal connections, but also subject to routinization, technological refinement, statistical measurement, and analytic assessment. Previously, the police in South Vietnam had followed orders too literally, one advisor noted. "If a man was told to stand on the corner and watch the traffic he'd do just that—watch the traffic. There could be an accident right in front of him and he'd do nothing about it—he had been told to *watch* the traffic!" OPS urged flexibility. "Now, it's entirely different."[26] Such exaggerated accounts were tinged with ethnocentric stereotype, but they reveal how advisors understood their challenge. Professionalizing police overseas meant re-racializing them, firming up the cultural distinction between the police and the policed. To do so, what advisors tried to impose was the technical capacity to confront surprising situations with patterned improvisations, standard protocols, and predictable interventions.

The public safety mission conferred the sense among police in the United States that the global threat of communism was real, insidious, tireless, and growing. In 1965, during the IACP's annual meeting in Florida, a Miami Beach police officer confronted visiting Uruguayan police executives accompanied by OPS's advisor to the newly instituted program in Montevideo. This local lieutenant, visibly drunk, harassed the Uruguayan officials, complaining that the country needed to outlaw the Communist Party. The Uruguayans responded in their limited English, but he was not assuaged. Finally, the Uruguayans' patience ran out when he drew his gun and pointed it at them. One batted the pistol away, and the roomful of police officers pounced. The episode embarrassed OPS. The key witnesses having returned to Montevideo, the Miami Beach cop was never charged.[27] His drunken wish was nevertheless granted: several leftist political parties were soon outlawed in Uruguay, bolstering the ranks of groups like Uruguay's Tupamaros.

The emergence of the Tupamaros was deeply consequential for OPS. These militants reveled in making Uruguayan security forces look hapless and inept, whether through bank robberies or even burglaries of police and military officers' homes.[28] They managed to infiltrate the Uruguayan police, and at least one received OPS training, an embarrassing counterintelligence failure. In 1970, the Tupamaros killed a public safety advisor, Dan Mitrione, claiming that he taught torture. Mitrione became the most famous OPS casualty. His killing set into motion the spiral of public outrage that resulted in the cancellation of the public safety program. In death, OPS gave Mitrione the treatment its advisors warned was a common communist tactic: he became a martyr, a symbol of the turpitude of the enemy. Frank Sinatra and Jerry Lewis performed at a memorial concert in his hometown in Indiana. Routine commemorations of his death followed, including annual masses held in Washington, DC, churches. The *International Police Academy Review* printed frequent reminders of Mitrione's sacrifice.[29] Academy participants across the globe received this quarterly newsletter, published from 1967 to 1975 in English and Spanish, as did criminology schools and other law-enforcement and counterinsurgency experts.[30] The Tupamaros may also have received copies, if so, allowing them to map the internationalist security web for internationalist militants.

Mitrione's kidnappers took advantage of his everyday work routine, abducting him as he commuted to the AID office in Montevideo. In Vietnam's more dangerous provinces, public safety advisors lived in compounds with other AID or military-assistance employees involved in pacification. They convened for morning briefings before splitting up to meet with their Vietnamese counterparts, first at the administrative level and then at lower, operational levels, whether in the fields of security, agriculture, or public administration.[31] But public safety advisors did not always follow predictable routines, particularly in the early years of police assistance during the Eisenhower administration. Some would visit all different parts of a given country, driving battered jeeps down rutted back roads and meeting with local police in distant countryside outposts and border crossings, in ports where harbor or riverine patrols docked, or in provincial capitals. In national seats of power, they would meet with heads of state and high-ranking police, military, and intelligence officials, as well as with veteran and newly recruited police officers. Through training and technical assistance, advisors gathered intelligence on the security capabilities of US allies. These relationships also enabled the collection of intelligence on security threats perceived to afflict these countries, as well as information on the reception of other US aid efforts. Monthly reports advisors routed to Washington reflected this dual purpose. Experience with mundane police reporting on crime at home, familiar to advisors from prior careers, easily meshed with sensitive countersubversive activity abroad.

Walking the beat on US streets was not the worst training for advising on security in foreign lands. The experience nurtured the even disposition advisors were to maintain no matter what surprise they faced. Most advisors were in the middle of their police careers, and they tended to be highly qualified. Only 3 percent of applicants were hired.[32] In the 1960s, before deployment, new advisors would take a two-week class at the IPA on the "art of advising." One remarked that the key to preparing cops to go overseas was "dissipating any tendencies toward parochialism and 'the way we did it in East Podunk is the best' attitude." Success was not inevitable. But advisors often then stayed overseas for so long that they required retraining upon return to the United States, including explanations of new technologies and "new methods of performing old police functions." Reorientation visits to police facilities in the vicinity of Washington, DC, were arranged for returnees, along with lectures and discussions emphasizing, beginning in 1970, "riot control, student disorders and crime rates."[33]

Building trust was crucial for advisors. One AID official, David Jickling, who spent his career working in Guatemala training locals in public administration and community development, recalled how OPS created trusting assets. His friend Desiderio L. Crisostomo, a Guamanian public safety advisor, became the mission supervisor in Guatemala in 1961. Dey, as his colleagues called him, would later be detailed to Brazil and South Vietnam. In Guatemala, Jickling remembered, Crisostomo was the lone recipient of the AID commissary's minuscule quota of Scotch. Though he was not much of a drinker, and he did not speak much Spanish, he employed the Scotch in "an interesting technical assistance technique." It lubricated the flow of intelligence tidbits from Guatemalan police officials, with whom, he reported, "he had very good relationships."[34] For the CIA to do its job, it needed low-level advisors like Crisostomo to raise their glasses with cops around the globe.[35] Imported luxuries like Scotch were authorized supplies for AID officials on temporary duty in foreign countries only if there was a pressing need—but nothing was more pressing than the need for booze if it meant security.

Public safety advisors introduced new tools to fight the subversive threat. Advisors created technologies usable both at home in the United States and across different countries. Communications technologies held high priority, because gathering and then efficiently disseminating information was paramount for counterinsurgency. This information guided local, national, and international security deployments. With the blessing of President Kennedy, the National Security Council, and six Central American presidents, OPS constructed a new regional teletype system country by country, which linked police forces across the region, enabling coordination across borders among police searching for fleeing suspects, controlling circulation of contraband, or monitoring movements of militants.[36] Intelligence agencies' belief that Cuba was saturating the region with mobile subversives on clandestine missions gave this project its urgency. Within given countries, OPS also helped police in capital cities maintain communications connectivity with distant villages, using transmitting equipment engineered for Vietnam. Honduras was one beneficiary.[37] Additionally, aid-recipient countries developed a universal emergency-services telephone number, which debuted in 1963 in Caracas, Venezuela, as a tool of urban counterinsurgency five years before the introduction of the 911 system in the United States.[38] In countries with centralized police systems, this service was easier to implement. At home, the telecommunications industry and the IACP both opposed creating the universal number, the latter because it saw the number's intermingling of multiple jurisdictions and emergency-response agencies as a "hat full of snakes." Public safety advisors learned what worked and what went wrong in Venezuela and shared their lessons at home. Arnold Sagalyn received these briefings and, based on additional research of Lyndon Johnson's Crime Commission, advocated the creation of the 911 system. In the coming decades, it transformed policing by allowing members of the public to initiate service calls more easily. Agents of state power authorized to enact violence would not be a last resort. The first line of defense became the first responders.[39]

OPS also produced specifications for durable, inexpensive, lightweight two-way police radios, which became popular at home and abroad. From AID's perspective, a standardized technology that dropped unnecessary features, if used in all aid-recipient countries, would dramatically cut costs and address prevailing budgetary constraints. OPS distributed over 30,000 of these radios to police forces overseas, which then became dependent on

US-manufactured replacement parts and upgrades. This dependence was one direct way OPS facilitated profit by US corporations. By 1973, nineteen aid-recipient countries had spent over $32 million on additional OPS-recommended commodities.[40] Public safety advisors conversed with law-enforcement experts at home to determine how their specifications could also meet the needs that the Crime and Kerner Commissions identified. One result was the development by OPS of a cheap miniature radio receiver for placement in a "riot helmet," which would enable constant communication among command and operational officers.[41] US manufacturers adopted specifications public safety technicians devised. For example, a Northrup Corporation subsidiary advertised its "hand-command" FM portable trans-ceiver as showcasing advances derived from "the battlefields and extreme environments of Southeast Asia . . . Africa . . . the Middle East" (fig. 8).[42] The company offered this radio to customers in the US marketplace, where many rural and small-town forces were as technologically underdeveloped as those OPS advised overseas. This type of walkie-talkie became as indispensable to a police officer as the badge or handcuffs. The low-cost version OPS devel-oped enabled the walkie-talkie to become ubiquitous far beyond the counter-insurgency theater. By allowing rapid response by mobile police officers, this simple technology, combined with the 911 system, reconfigured the relation-ship of police to populations, creating new consumer-like expectations of police responsiveness.

Professionalization did not always require the latest technologies. Foreign aid allowed the introduction or upgrading of the most fundamental symbols of the profession, like the nightstick, badge, and uniform. But training was essential for taking possession of new technologies, including in basic logis-tics, inventory control, billing, and other procedures. Training dovetailed with assistance in police administration. OPS recommended the reorganiza-tion or formation of specialized divisions like record-keeping or narcotics bureaus and consolidation of unified commands in cities or provinces. Still, the allure of new gadgets was difficult to resist, especially for police executives in aid-recipient countries with suddenly expanded equipment budgets. As one advisor, Jeter Williamson, observed, new technologies were not always better: "I feel rather strongly about the advantages of the nightstick as an excellent weapon, both defensive and offensive, in the control of crowds both orderly and unruly. I feel that too often its importance and usefulness are not fully exploited in our dealings with foreign police agencies." For police around the world who received brochures from weapons manufacturers, the nightstick

FIGURE 8. Private industry adaptation of OPS-designed hand-held transceiver. National Archives and Records Administration.

might seem, as Williamson suggested, like "an anachronism dreamed up by a penny-pinching Public Safety Advisor."[43] Whereas foreign military assistance in the 1960s often introduced pricey high-tech gadgets, police assistance was penny-pinching by design. Excluding South Vietnam, global police assistance cost 5.8 percent what military assistance did in 1968 alone ($28.9 million versus $500 million, respectively).[44] Even modest new funds would allow fulfillment of basic unmet needs. As the assistance program in the Dominican Republic built up steam in 1964, an eager commander requested that OPS forward him catalogs from badge manufacturers in the United States.[45]

Fulfilling basic needs was key to professionalization, but some aid recipients skipped to increasing their status before attending to rote practicalities of policing insecure zones. OPS butted heads with counterpart police executives whose ambitions outstripped their capacities to ensure security. The head of Vietnam's National Police, Tran Thanh Phong, for instance, complained in 1971, to Frank Walton, director of public safety there, about his officers' shabby, cheap white-and-gray uniforms, comparing them to US gas station attendants' attire. Walton reasoned that the white shirts were preferable in Vietnam's climate. He conceded that the standard blue trousers police wore elsewhere could mark an improvement. Phong yearned for his officers to project significant social stature and to be accorded respect. OPS's operational concerns were pedestrian but urgent. Walton left the meeting frustrated. Amid the chaos of war, facing major manpower problems, the top-ranking police official wanted to discuss fabrics.[46]

The promise of respect was a most fundamental purpose of police assistance in the first place. Officers might not be identified with the threat of force at the heart of the police power if they could succeed in shaping popular consciousness about the police as an institution. Yet in an atmosphere dominated by the demand for security, commodity assistance unleashed powers that were difficult to constrain. Walton's conversation with Phong indicated the hazard of supplying whatever materials aid recipients desired, whether traditional or newfangled: diminishing or discrediting the importance of OPS assistance. "Engle himself grumbled that all these countries wanted was an 'equipment drop' and not our advice."[47] Exigent circumstances, however, sometimes did call for an anonymous equipment drop. In 1973, OPS deviated from its typical matériel support to supply thousands of fragmentation hand grenades to Thailand for use against suspected insurgents in its unstable border regions with Laos and Malaysia. To ward off political opposition, AID insisted that its emblem should not appear on the shipments.[48]

At home and abroad, professionalization afforded police vastly increased resources to mobilize in their discretionary actions. Increased appropriations artificially enlarged the magnitude of the problem law enforcement faced. Better equipped and trained, aided by new telecommunications technologies and rethought tactical deployments, police were primed to respond to or observe activity that, with each passing year, came to be more and more likely to be criminalized. Threats magically increased. US assistance consistently expanded recipient countries' police forces, jails, and prisons. The most dramatic expansion was in South Vietnam, from roughly 17,000 to 120,000 uniformed National Police officers in the decade after 1962 (the National Police formed that year, under OPS advisement, combining several smaller forces).[49] Within the United States, the legacy of continually expanding police forces continues, both in the absolute number of forces and their relative size.

DISAPPEARANCES AND DEATH SQUADS

Others police tools were intangible, existing at the levels of technique and disposition. The requisite inclination was something no textbook could convey. Take "disappearing" people, a form of state terror that denies that anything untoward has occurred to produce dread. A targeted individual simply disappears, allowing loved ones no closure and requiring no judicial process, including an autopsy that might reveal evidence of torture. OPS archives tell a new story of forced disappearance in Latin America, a Cold War tactic that originated in the early 1960s in Venezuela, where it was actually a misbegotten product of the rule of law. Venezuelan police officers who killed suspects on the street were subject to obligatory investigatory detention and trial, but with disappearances, there was by definition no corpus delicti. Cops could kill with impunity.[50]

Serving in Venezuela, the public safety advisor John P. Longan observed the investigatory detention of police who killed suspects. Disappearance avoided such detentions. When he subsequently became chief of US public safety assistance for Latin America, Longan disseminated what he had learned across the region. In December 1965, he went to Guatemala, the country where some have thought disappearance originated among Latin American republics. There, three months after his arrival, an interviewer later asked him whether it was true that security officers took "terrorists" and "put them in bags and tossed them in the ocean." "Right," he replied, "and they washed back in and they were found, but that's the same type of people that had been killing their people and kidnapping and extorting a lot of people, and that—that just happened." The "type of people" in question were generally leaders of workers' and peasants' political federations, however, hardly terrorists. The secret workings of this campaign, called Operación Limpieza, would have remained unknown to the victims' loved ones if the bodies had not washed ashore. As to the US role in this operation, whatever happened "just happened." Longan's presence, the presence of other US technical advisory staff, their facilitation of security coordination across the Americas: all of it would be disavowed through a passive construction. Throughout this interview, nearly any time a question about torture or extrajudicial activity arose, the tic "so on and so forth" appeared in Longan's speech. "A philosopher I ain't," Longan laughed. "I am security minded." His task was to "furnish cover for CIA operations," leaving the responsibility for carrying out security measures to local, US-groomed recipients of public safety aid.[51] The year after Operación Limpieza, Longan became a consultant to the Kerner Commission. He shared an account of how Venezuela defeated "urban terrorism" with Arnold Sagalyn.[52] To this day, disappearances continue across Latin America.

The generic term for paramilitary groups that enforce terror on the state's behalf without the clear participation of uniformed state agents is "death squad." Disappearance is a central task of death squads. Originally, a group in Brazil in the late 1960s called itself the Esquadrão da Morte, meaning death squad, before the term came to apply more widely, including to earlier formations.[53] Often, death squads consisted of nominally off-duty or out-of-uniform police or soldiers. Questioned by Senator Frank Church (D-ID) on death squads, a top public safety advisor denied that OPS-advised police played a part in them, while acknowledging that Brazilian press covered the topic extensively.[54] The death squad that formed in the early 1970s in the Dominican Republic, which John Longan visited as a public safety advisor soon after he left Guatemala, was called La Banda. Unidentified agents recruited members from the ranks of the unemployed, offering twice the pay a soldier earned. These recruits invaded university classrooms by day and cleared the streets at night, leaving "tourists and businessmen . . . surprised to find they have the city virtually to themselves after dark." The death squad killed scores of leftists and assaulted, abducted, or disappeared hundreds more. From exile, the Dominican Republic's former president Juan Bosch blamed OPS for La Banda's creation.[55] One director of the public safety mission in the Dominican Republic explained that when political disorder erupted, "foreign capital runs like scared cats."[56]

OPS facilitated connections among security forces in the hemisphere and beyond that enabled the sharing of knowledge. The material infrastructure of connectivity, whether a cross-border communications network, or the *IPA Review*, was a necessary condition for this sharing, which, once initiated, no longer required US personnel, but continued to meet US security demands. Like international police assistance more broadly, operators like Longan not only transmitted security tactics across borders but made them context-independent, functionally useful anywhere, without even the necessity of US presence. Forced disappearance was an acute instance of a broader shift that security practices were undergoing. Disappearance afflicted urban populations, and it was often combined with outright massacres in rural areas. It constituted a swerve of policing, under conditions of US empire, away from the strict reliance on open, avowed, explicitly racist repression, toward less direct, acephalous risk-management.

SOCIAL REGULATION

For counterinsurgency to control behavior required not only violence or its threat but also the shaping of social subjectivity through lessons in civics, meant to impart communitarian investment and a sense of national belonging. Police could not afford to be aloof from this process. In April 1964, Byron Engle shared with colleagues what he had learned from a Brazilian police executive who had recently visited the United States. His police force, in the subtropical state of Paraná, received US assistance, and "the local leftist press" had attacked him for "trading police records for US assistance and commodities." "To dispel this leftist propaganda," Engle reported, the Brazilian police colonel had held a press conference to explain the agreement with AID, which he called "common knowledge." Thanking AID for its "great assistance to the police of Paraná," he had "rented a space in the Public Library, located in the center of the Capital, where he displayed the received commodities and the various types of technical assistance given." Three OPS advisors assisted in staging the exhibit, and over five thousand local residents visited.[57] To be an upstanding citizen of Paraná, and of Brazil, was to welcome US assistance in rooting out subversives.

Advisors aimed to help indigenous forces fight ordinary crime, control unrest, and keep tabs on radicals. No great distinctions were drawn between these tasks, and the techniques for their accomplishment overlapped. Crime-fighting tools were countersubversion tools. In order to create dossiers on radicals, which the leftist press accused the Paraná police of trading in exchange for commodities, the police needed record-keeping and surveillance technologies, plus technical assistance in their use. But relationships between police and the public mattered too. A few years after the display in Paraná, Dan Mitrione initiated another program with similar overt aims elsewhere in Brazil, based on his work in Indiana, bringing some 34,000 school-age children to visit and tour the municipal police station.[58] A CIA advisor embedded with OPS in Thailand explained, from the perspective of his agency, the value of promoting positive relationships with kids through cooperative mentoring and counseling: "schoolchildren are just about the best sources of information around."[59] OPS made it impossible to withdraw the civic component from the coercive edge of the first line of defense.

South Vietnam was the site of the most ambitious and innovative security thinking and garnered the most resources. Police assistance there faced the greatest challenges but also realized the widest programmatic ambitions. The fusion of police's coercive aspects and forms of social regulation typically delegated to other agencies in liberal states was total there. A 1964 textbook titled *The Police and Resources Control in Counter-Insurgency* that OPS used in Vietnam distilled the essence of its recommendations on fighting subversion with crime-fighting methods. Influenced by the British counterinsurgency experience in Malaya, OPS defined "resources control" as regulating "the movement of selected resources, both human and material, in order to restrict the enemy's support or deprive him of it altogether." The focus of the textbook was on "control of the movement of people and goods throughout the countryside," because guerrillas required "a steady supply of food and the basic necessities of life," including clothes and medicine, as well as information and weapons. Theft from government and other sources, secret manufacture, and smuggling across borders were three typical ways to fulfill supply needs, but the most difficult problem was "sympathizers or relatives" who aided the guerrillas, especially juveniles. There was thus a synergy between "protecting life and property" and "protecting the state."[60]

OPS taught how to be good cops. There were quick searches or strip searches ("Only when there is a specific and compelling reason"), vehicle searches at checkpoints, and spot checks of travelers. "The quick search is one in which the searcher runs his hands over a person's body to determine whether any offensive weapons—pistol, hand grenade, knife or other—might be concealed within his clothing. It is the same search that a police officer uses as part of a routine arrest."[61] In other words: stop-and-frisk, recognizable to any beat cop in New York or Chicago. OPS vainly tried to insist that resources control was central to "stringent, *war-time* measures" in Vietnam. It recognized that "such controls are extremely bothersome and time-consuming to local citizens."[62] Yet given its global remit, OPS could not help but argue that the "fundamentals" of such controls "are known and may be uniformly applied in a guerrilla war anywhere in the world, whether it be Vietnam, Malaya, Colombia or Venezuela." Could it really be said that stop-and-frisk policing methods were unique to "situations of national emergency"?[63] OPS advisors knew that to be untrue.

The British pacification experience in Malaya showed OPS that it was difficult to distinguish innocent from guilty in stop-and-frisk searches so advisors introduced a national identity card for everyone in South Vietnam over the age of eighteen. An official card was supposed to allow easy distinctions between innocent civilians and subversives, particularly those who had secretly crossed the border from North Vietnam. These identity cards made total surveillance of South Vietnamese citizens possible. Moreover, the technological advances made in creating a tamper- and forgery-proof, indestructible identity card for South Vietnam proved valuable for corporations in the United States engaged in similar efforts domestically. The national identity card was a mundane modality of subject-producing power, lodged within the responsibilities of the National Police, geared toward quantifying the population, gathering data, collecting taxes, and regulating social interaction. The cards made the innocent appear guilty, however: a lost or damaged card was cause for suspicion. Guerrillas surreptitiously destroyed or tampered with innocent people's cards, which increased the likelihood that police would treat the holder unjustly. Antigovernment sentiment might then set in. The police check of the card forced intimate interactions, allowing officers to intimidate and humiliate denizens, even making them beg for mercy. Such population-oriented counterinsurgency techniques also coerced individuals into relationships with police that made them targets of retributive violence by insurgents. Not only did the card introduce new behaviors, like simply carrying one at all times, it constructed new social relations, by forcing fixed addresses on people who until then might have never had one, because their villages were impermanent.

The identity card, meant to aid police investigations, meshed with a broader effort to compile population statistics. But even these were oriented toward countering crime and subversion. In 1968, South Vietnam's National Identity Registration Project began collecting data on teenagers, including photographs and thumbprints. Adults already had to register all ten fingerprints; photographs and biographic data were collected as well. A police-overseen census noted family relations and collected data on family wealth to enable easy identification of new visitors or pinpoint black market activity. The special branch of the National Police responsible for intelligence, which was its largest component other than the conventional corps of police officers, used "intelligence collection, political data, dossiers compiled from census data, and counter-subversive operations to separate the bad guys from the good."[64] Over the four years before 1972, the National Police produced more than seventeen million index cards containing basic data, along with fifteen million sets of fingerprints and 616,280 wanted notices. Ten times more wanted notices appeared for "criminals" than for "VC."[65] Beyond the practical and intellectual how-to knowledge police assistance produced, policing itself was structured to generate knowledge, statistics, and intelligence about the population on behalf of the state. Via police, populations were constructed, managed, divided, and controlled, with repression reliant on such productive power.

Another important area of OPS police modernization was traffic control. In this domain, social regulation was ubiquitous but invisible. It aimed to foster proper behavior, not simply sanction improper behavior.[66] "I hope we teach these guys more than just how to direct traffic," Attorney General Robert Kennedy quipped while reviewing overseas police assistance.[67] But directing traffic was exactly the sort of thing public safety advisors taught. The expert reply from Engle was that there was a direct "relation between traffic control and crowd control," as evidenced by the 1963 March on Washington for Jobs and Freedom.[68] Engle rendered the policing of subversive threats overseas recognizable by pointing to the control of protest for racial justice. He attached the control of political protest to the quiet regulation of social conduct that traffic control entailed, conflating foreign and domestic realms, policing at home and counterinsurgency overseas. After Charles Sloane, an expert on police dogs, first went to Vietnam with MSU, his hometown newspaper reported his discovery that the "Far East" had a lot in common with Syracuse, NY. Both were beset by the "universal" problem of "traffic jams."[69]

Blending destructive and constructive power through technical police assistance could lead states to destroy what they also tried to build. The contradictions of security were impossible to resolve: risks could not be vanquished, only managed, but expanding the capacity to attempt to vanquish risks destructively undermined capacity to manage them productively. For security thinkers, the impediment to development, or modernization, was insecurity, which also was the evidence of modernization's failure. According to this understanding, pacification would make security, and insecurity would unmake pacification. Insecurity could take the form of strident demands for democracy, but pacification was not allergic to democracy. Rather, it attempted to internalize and constrain it through political participation. The most important vehicle for political participation in development was the legislative mandate written into Title IX of the Foreign Assistance Act, the law governing US foreign aid, in 1966. It required, much like Title II of the Economy Opportunity Act, the Johnson administration's signature domestic legislation on poverty alleviation, "maximum participation in the task of economic development on the part of the people of the developing countries."[70] Democratic participation in the management of foreign aid was integral to the goal of political stability, especially in areas threatened by insurgency and subversion. Participants would play a role in the design and execution of community development, and then they would reap the rewards of such self-help. Participation, through labor and limited decision-making, was the means by which the pacified enacted and made visible their own pacification.

Participation was a prominent, if underappreciated, aspect of counterinsurgency. Even before Title IX became law, pacification experts, including William Colby, Komer's successor in Vietnam, AID advisors on the ground, and others in the circle of the CIA operative Edward Lansdale, believed in the necessity of participation to counterinsurgency's success. In South Vietnam, participation would counter "Communist People's War" tactics and extremist appeals by investing the people in their own betterment to assure their loyalty to the government of South Vietnam. To this end, AID encouraged organizations that would have been at home anywhere within the United States, such as Parent-Teacher Associations, which Colby called "useful vehicles for 'maximum participation' on the part of the population."[71] The Phoenix program itself also fit the mandate. Its targeting of purportedly communist South Vietnamese citizens relied on denunciations and informants. In this way, Phoenix enlisted the population in its own protection.[72] Voilà: participation. Technical police assistance provided novel tools that were grafted onto existing security dispositions, which Title IX renarrated in a US democratic idiom. Destructive institutions worked in tandem with constructive ones on participatory poverty alleviation, even as they could undermine it as well.

The United States' global reliance on policing shows that there were limitations to the project of participation-oriented pacification, which necessarily assumed resistance.[73] Had there been no resistance to liberal property relations and extant political-economic conditions, pacification would have been unnecessary. Social transformation did often lead to disaffection, as inherited political, economic, and spatial orderings of life eroded. Participation would ease restoration of order, but it was unpredictable. One veteran AID staffer who had been in South Vietnam in the 1960s and Central America in the 1970s later reflected: development organized through popular participation "has caused problems, is causing problems and is going to cause problems." AID could intervene to shape outcomes, but "many of our own attempts to 'maintain stability' have touched off explosions."[74] Participation allowed citizens to air grievances and even mobilize and protest around them, but an essential reason for pushing participation was that it was a method for producing the labor force that would undertake small-scale development projects. These were supposed to be designed and implemented by communities through participatory decision-making, with the communities that stood to benefit from them integrally involved in their construction, assisted by development advisors. By affording tools for self-help to these communities, pacification aspired to transform control into loyalty, marking the boundaries of community membership in the process. But not everyone in a given community wanted to be enrolled in such democratically willed but compulsory labor. Resistance that could coalesce through democratic participation made it difficult for development advisors to trust that a program would not fall apart due to security concerns. Police assistance provided the tools to quarantine the recalcitrant. For counterinsurgency experts, development approaches that did not posit and proactively prepare for the possibility of their own failure risked drowning in a sea of insecurity.

The empowerment of ordinary people that Title IX allowed did not protect them from counterrevolutionary forces and may even have made them more susceptible to them. Pacification fused its future orientation to policing by foregrounding coercive and punitive responses to noncompliance with community-development programming, which was itself aimed at preventing insecurity. Vocational training and lessons in hygiene for young people were meant to create legible and pliant subjects and foster heteronormative lifestyles, but those who strayed found that police surveillance was baked into the programming. Tutelary efforts grew alongside penal institutions for those who failed them. Moreover, democratic participation had a tendency to undermine inherited political structures, which could lead to a conflict with overall US strategy, or with the local powerholders whom public safety assistance had equipped with a powerful instrument of repression. Under Title IX, one of AID's programs in Guatemala consisted of identifying and training people who exhibited potential to become local leaders who could advocate on behalf of their villages. It was "the same kind of thing the poverty program was working on in the United States, the same methodology." For approximately five years, these young Guatemalans, mostly schoolteachers, would be handpicked and, using AID funding, sent to Loyola University in Louisiana. There they would spend at least six months learning how to represent and focus the "felt needs" of their constituents and translate them into achievable development goals. Upon return from the United States, "they came back all fired up." Many became mayors and one even became president in 1986. AID studied other outcomes of this training program into the 1980s. The findings were stark: up to two-thirds of the trainees had been killed by security forces well after Operación Limpieza concluded. "They were killed because they were agitators in terms of the powers that be. In terms of development, they were the ideal change agent . . . but that was the kiss of death for them."[75] US police assistance had provided the security apparatus of the Guatemalan state with the tools and expertise to track and kill such agitators, to the tune of $5.4 million from 1956 to 1974. Long after US troops had returned home from Vietnam, pacification continued in Guatemala. When police assistance was outlawed, ongoing military support to Guatemala still went to law enforcement.[76]

The premise of Cold War police assistance was that professional law enforcement could enhance democracy. Such claims were not entirely cynical, but police fell victim to their own propaganda and their instrumentalization by the CIA. The IACP, for instance, bestowed an honorary membership on Carlos Castillo Armas, the CIA-anointed leader of the 1954 coup against an elected government, in recognition of his "unselfish labor for the good of democratic law enforcement in the Republic of Guatemala."[77] He was soon assassinated. Police assistance extended capacities of social regulation, while also increasing capabilities of repression that undermined democratic accountability. OPS strengthened police investigatory capabilities, even if these forces were frontline adjuncts to retrograde and repressive legal systems. By committing to technical upgrades without much sensitivity as to how they would be deployed, some advisors were willfully blind to how their assistance enhanced repression.

Participatory development was not revolutionary. It was one mechanism for constraining political horizons, with security assistance as another. Participation was a tool for enhancing the legitimacy of existing regimes, which public safety advisors took as their key task. Demonstrating the combinatorial character of these approaches, OPS announced in 1969 that according to the Title IX mandate of "democratic institution building and popular participation," it recognized the "vital role of the police as a builder/protector of democratic institutions." After noting the importance of recipient police forces becoming "democratically oriented," the report claimed that police assistance programs helped counterparts "develop a sympathetic identification with the citizenry. The concept of 'public service' in policing, includes the *protection* of people's *right to dissent* within the boundaries of law. . . . This concept is new to most political and police leaders and attitudes must change—and are changing." Molding a new social order was the point of foreign aid, and reshaping the attitudes of foreign counterparts was the most difficult advisory task.[78] When it came to community development, local police could compel participation, but public safety advisors focused on assuring an environment of security and order, which their training identified as a precondition to democracy. At home and abroad policing would remain the cornerstone upon which liberal democracy was built, as well as its greatest fetter.

. . .

During the Cold War, under the rubric of modernization, the United States guided heads of state to insulate the state apparatus from retrograde social structures. US anticolonialism favored untainted outsider figures, like Ngo Dinh Diem, who came from a social sphere alien to that of the elites who had collaborated with prior colonial empires. This choice had the effect of politically sundering the state from social institutions, and uncertainties abounded. These outsider elites faced a deficit of popular legitimacy. Figures like Komer believed these problems could be managed by irenic professionalized policing. He wanted police to effect productive power, assembling an orderly and disciplined population that was insulated from the wrong foreign influence. Despotism insulated leaders from internal influence, however. The weakness of US-friendly leaders also meant that they could not always control the heads of security forces, who were not eager to let go of their own influence and answered to unruly, intimidating constituencies. Thus, preexisting ways endured and reform efforts stalled. US advisors either shrugged, bewildered at their impotence to change the situation on the ground, or innocently denied that the technically advanced methods they introduced might be used to settle old scores or uphold entrenched inequalities. Meanwhile, sometimes working out of the very same shops as public safety advisors, the CIA hired bloodthirsty mercenaries to do the jobs old-line powerholders or newly trained security forces refused, often recruited from the ranks of veterans of the European empires' violent attempts to maintain their integrity.

Ultimately, the history of OPS, ended because of accusations of lessons in torture, shows that despotic power undermines its goal. Rather than protecting a given social order, it strengthens the will and courage of those opposed to it. Attempts to activate constructive power and manage people's conduct without naked repression were the response. Such productive power needs to be understood as dynamically inflected by the police institution, which modified itself in response to social-movement pressures and asserted its compatibility with small-scale democratic participation. The result was a reformatting of the social terrain from which revolutionary impulses and organizations grew. Overall, what policing aimed to do, operating in both destructive and productive registers, was make insurgency impossible. One way was by internalizing critiques of state power, whether by hiring cops from minoritized groups or reforming a repressive agency. Another was by recoding social regulation to narrow horizons of political possibility.

SIX

Riot School

THE SEVERITY OF THE UNREST in Harlem in 1964 would be overshadowed in Watts, Detroit, and Newark in summers to come. These rebellions shared a pattern cemented in Harlem, which was recognizable to counterinsurgency experts. After a precipitating incident of racial violence by police, protesters encountered intransigent state authorities, unwilling to investigate wrongdoing. Ensuing confrontations with these officials, and with mainly white local landlords and retailers, then led to ferocious reactions by the police in the streets in the form of wanton, unrestricted violence toward the local populace, further worsening the unrest. By 1968, in response to this challenge, several institutions had created new training for police in "riot control," with insights of public safety advisors shared among them. Competition among state agencies for primacy in training for riot control not only did not curtail but actually fostered the development of repressive and coercive capacities, underpinning the rise of the carceral state. Enlarging these police capacities aimed to focus, not simply expand, state violence in crisis situations.

As Byron Engle informed the Kerner Commission, a foundational principle of overseas police professionalization was reducing killings by police in situations of civil unrest. The point was to avoid bolstering charges by communists and other radicals about the repressive character of US-backed regimes. In practice, however, aid-recipient governments brutally suppressed demonstrations in Brazil, Iran, Korea, Vietnam, and elsewhere. After the Harlem unrest, it took several years for Engle's advice to take root at home, as part of a broader complex of transformations of policing in response to further unrest from 1964 to 1968. These transformations accelerated longstanding professionalization efforts to a tempo not seen since August Vollmer's heyday of reform in the 1920s. If cops in Harlem spurred Arnold

Sagalyn to act, then the particular failures of riot control that he and Engle observed, marked by police violence that worsened the unrest, resulted in new training efforts to overcome these deficiencies. At the outset of the 1960s, escalation of force in encounters with noncompliant crowds was considered standard procedure, and shooting or clubbing became the instant reaction of many officers charged with keeping the peace. In contrast, new training programs focused on planning, coordination, and operational discipline. Control guidance moved away from escalation of force toward explicit rules, pre-planning, and interagency coordination, as OPS urged overseas. Yet public safety advisors themselves analyzed diverse overseas situations through the prism of US racial strife. Riot control's revamping was among the loudest of the global Cold War's domestic reverberations, but when US experts overseas heard the refrain of rioting, it already sounded like the blues of American streets.

Experts who took a transnational view of the difficulties facing US state power developed responses to this crisis that admitted, in limited ways, that police forces had exacerbated their own lack of legitimacy. They wanted to reformulate policing on a professional model because protests, unrest, and court proceedings had shown that policing needed to be upgraded. Professionalization was a measured crisis-management tool. The crisis was self-inflicted. Both conservative and liberal police experts agreed that reform depended on training, training, and more training. Sagalyn's blueprints for what became federal anticrime legislation were testaments to this position. The severity of civil violence signaled the need to redeem policing. The route to redemption wended its way past chalkboards, classrooms, and libraries. These chalkboards and libraries themselves were not simply conceived and then ready to accept pupils. They had to be won legislatively and bureaucratically, funded, built, advertised, and attended. The IACP, FBI, OPS, Army, and the state of California retooled in-service training. Each took interdependent steps toward a new regime of police training that depended on and came to exemplify the devolutionary thrust of the War on Crime's federalism. Few scholars have credited the role of new in-service police training initiatives and educational requirements for new recruits in the carceral state's emergence. But the OLEA and LEAA funded copious training, including "over one million man-years of college credits" in the War on Crime's early years, plus fellowships for graduate study at institutions like MSU, supervised by border-crossing law-enforcement leaders like Ralph Turner and Arthur Brandstatter.[1] Such figures' advocacy of the War on

Crime bore fruit as federal money became available for new training programs. This funding transformed criminology as a professional-academic field. New college- and university-level programs sprang up. More students meant more money. More students also meant more police and prison guards. But prior institutional identities shaped the programmatic decisions of these players in devising how to ask for, and take advantage of, such funds, especially amid urban unrest. Among new initiatives, training for riot control received the greatest attention.

POLICE PROFESSIONALIZATION IN RESPONSE TO UNREST IN HARLEM

On the evening of a scorching-hot Saturday that saw a rally in Harlem demanding justice after the fatal shooting of the fifteen-year-old James Powell, several hundred people marched to the nearby 28th precinct, where they demanded that the lieutenant who had shot Powell be suspended. The demand went unanswered. Police charged the crowd in an attempt at dispersal. Fighting broke out, and bottles rained from rooftops. Officers quickly ascended to the ramparts of nearby tenements in search of the bottle-throwers. More scuffling, arrests, and bottle-throwing ensued. Word of the fighting reached the crowd that had remained at the site of the earlier rally, where speeches continued. Numbers increased dramatically. It was not long until a police car was set ablaze, which led to the officers' quintessential response: firing their guns wildly.

Gunfire continued into the night. It did not quell the crowds. Rather, it further antagonized them. Feeling threatened by bottle- and brick-throwing Harlem residents, police officers kept shooting and shooting. Officers also swung nightsticks to subdue crowds. Yet the police failed to grasp how this random violence made residents feel besieged. "Why don't you go home?" exclaimed one officer through a bullhorn. "We are home, baby!" came the reply.[2] When one person throwing "debris" was shot on a rooftop, police broadcast word of it on a special frequency to avoid press attention. As Saturday night turned into Sunday morning, the New York Police Department had exhausted its supply of bullets. "Boxloads of .38-caliber rounds were sent by truck from the police pistol range at Rodmans Neck, the Bronx, the *New York Times* reported. "They were then loaded onto a makeshift ordnance truck manned by two men armed with a shotgun and a machine gun. They made the trip through the dark Harlem streets cautiously."[3] Arrests, injuries, daylight, or exhaustion seemed to ease the violence. But unrest soon broke out in Brooklyn.

The White House took notice, and new training programs would be the result. Lyndon Johnson was wary of how a strong federal reaction to Black urban unrest would play politically, including among Black people. On one flank, he worried that using the military, as Eisenhower and Kennedy had in Arkansas, Mississippi, and Alabama, would provoke Southerners in his party. Johnson thus responded to the 1964 crises of the highly publicized Ku Klux Klan murders of civil rights workers in Mississippi and revolt in Harlem by sending in the FBI, rather than the military.[4] On another flank, the president was acutely aware of the Republican challenge. Arizona Senator Barry Goldwater clinched the Republican Party nomination as Johnson's 1964 opponent the very day Powell died on a Harlem sidewalk. Goldwater's ballyhooed assertion that "extremism in the defense of liberty is no vice ... moderation in the pursuit of justice is no virtue," in his peroration accepting nomination as the Republican presidential candidate, was ringing in Johnson's head: he repeated the phrase "extremism is a virtue" with disapproval in a telephone call to New York's Mayor Robert F. Wagner.[5] Racially liberal voters composed a third flank to defend. When unrest in other cities across the Eastern Seaboard and Midwest followed the unrest in Harlem, the administration labored to explain these events as little different from white racist violence across the South. To condemn them specifically might confer a discriminatory image on Johnson. His stratagem was to thread a path between federal intervention and reliance on failing local state power.

The White House was not the only driver of accelerated police reform in response to the unrest. Law-enforcement experts themselves were vocal and active. At least at first, Johnson wanted to rely on their expertise, and more generally on the decentralized character of US policing, instead of the blunt instrument of military response. Too strong a focus on the White House among historians of this moment has obscured how the administration empowered a more hidden echelon of security experts, like Sagalyn, Engle, Quinn Tamm, the Pentagon's head of counterinsurgency research Seymour Deitchman, and others from interstitial domains. Harsh FBI (and CIA and military) action against Black political radicals drew on long-standing traditions. What was novel in the period was the attempt at the federal level to modernize local policing with new training and new technologies—precisely because the unrest highlighted how draconian local policing continued to be.

A conversation between Johnson and J. Edgar Hoover in the immediate aftermath of the Harlem unrest indicated the stakes for the White House. To Johnson, the legitimacy of local police, forged by their reactions to unrest, underwrote his administration's legitimacy. With Harlem in rebellion, Johnson read a constituent's telegram to Hoover over the phone. Though some biographers have described him as capricious, Johnson was exacting here. He deliberately chose this message, from among the deluge his office was receiving, for what it said: "I'm afraid to leave my house.... I feel the Negro revolution will reach Queens.... Please send troops immediately to Harlem." Johnson had no intention of sending troops, and the conversations he had with Hoover on that day concerned whether Hoover himself would visit New York City. The quotation suggests that Johnson was warning Hoover, and perhaps himself, that an incipient "Negro revolution" loomed, the logical extension of increasing crime. Sending Hoover would "contain the political fallout" and "shield the Great Society," in the words of the historian Michael Flamm.[6] The implication is that continued Black unrest and political radicalism ultimately undermined liberal social-welfare programs. But Flamm skips the next part of the telegram that the president read to Hoover, distorting its overall meaning: "For two consecutive nights we've watched with horror as thousands of white policemen have beat up and shot innocent people." The correspondent even quoted Johnson's own lines back to him about using federal authority where local governments failed to prevent white racist violence against Black people in the South.[7] Johnson was a firm believer that policing was a local matter. Hoover was too. But the subtext here was clear: federal intervention *in policing* would be unavoidable without a solution, whether in the South or the North. Johnson put Hoover on notice. The solution soon blossomed—even Hoover had to submit to it—in the shape of new rounds of professionalizing funded federally first through the OLEA and then the LEAA. Rather than a predetermination that Black unrest threatened his legislative program, Johnson perceived police violence as a threat, and he tied the slow-moving War on Poverty to the more immediate assurance of security through enhanced policing. It was not an either/or choice. Increasingly organized politically, reform-minded police themselves were game.

The events of the summers of 1964 through 1967 demonstrated to US policing professionals that their forces were underprepared. This recognition spurred the specific training developed in subsequent years and strengthened the professionalization ethos. Whether the policing response to mass protest, in the form of clubbing and shooting at crowds and bystanders, led to crime or was simply inadequate, as demonstrated by the duration, extent, and spread of the unrest, it was clear that change was necessary. Proactive law-enforcement officials sought ways to manage and moderate externally forced transformation, whether by courts or by social movements, so that external pressure did not disrupt their authority. External, nonprofessional oversight of lawyers or doctors would have been anathema, and reformers wanted police to be seen in the same light. Police were to be appreciated as impartial enforcers of impartial law, liberal criteria that were given the lie with each nightstick blow to a Black person's head, whether in the South or the North.

The redemption of policing through professionalization was partially successful. Heightened educational requirements for recruits and ongoing specialized in-service training accompanied increasing reliance on advanced technologies. This shift was a quiet admission that police had not always been up to the task presented to them by apparently rising crime and social protest. Moreover, it was a response intended further to insulate law enforcement from critique and political pressure. Not only could police executives and elected officials point to increasing levels of rigorous training as evidence of responsiveness to changing needs, the fact of specialized training would foster the image of police officers as highly skilled, commanding abilities, know-how, and repertoires that were not to be questioned by the uninitiated. Budgetary appropriations for policing grew, even as the national economy contracted in the first half of the 1970s. The new training programs for riot control would be captive, however, to the peculiar federalized structure of law-enforcement reformism.

TRAINING THE TRAINERS

Three institutional loci of law-enforcement training stood out in the period: the FBI, the IACP, and the Army's Directorate for Civil Disturbance Planning and Operations. OPS was also crucial. Its academy modeled how training and coordination across scales and jurisdictions could take shape. The FBI was the most parochial institution. Hoover was the preeminent law-enforcement official in the United States, but his exalted position attracted challengers. Defectors, like the IACP's Quinn Tamm, a former FBI assistant director, constituted one type. Aspirants to Hoover's throne constituted another. Hoover's long experience in Washington, however, enabled him to outflank challengers in the contest for budgetary resources. The importance of centralization of training would become the new orthodoxy, but the FBI was not the only operator in the field. The IACP, OPS, the Army, and the state of California, copying the Army, all began centralized training projects in the 1960s. How to make these projects complementary was elusive, especially because no agency principal wanted to cede ground, or funding, to another. In any case, alarmism about unrest meant that emergency initiatives were launched in advance of strategic planning. In its first three years, the LEAA spent $6, $14, and $20 million respectively on controlling disorder. This money funded regional conferences, state-level technical assistance units, a range of educational and community-oriented activities, and equipment including protective armor, cameras, and tear gas.[8] With the ascendency of fiscally conservative federalism, materially instituted via the War on Crime's block grants, a competition for trainees took hold among training projects. Riot-control fervor diminished within a few years, but competition over how to shape the initial training efforts shaped the contours of subsequent programs.

The FBI

Hoover treated the unrest in summer 1964 as an opportunity to direct attention toward the FBI and to invigorate its training programs in riot control. President Johnson agreed. In the aftermath, the FBI took "immediate action": "intensive" in-service training of FBI instructors in mob and riot control. "The importance of preventive action and proper planning will be emphasized," Hoover declared. In addition, more lecture time for the current class at the FBI National Academy would be devoted to the subject, and, as Hoover told Johnson's aide Bill Moyers, "training in mob and riot control has been a regular subject in the FBI National Academy curriculum" and would now receive "additional emphasis" because of "the great national concern over the violence." In 1965, the FBI sent trainers to lecture at 4,239 local police training facilities, attended by over 117,000 officers.[9] In 1967, 6,045 departments hosted these lectures, attended by over 177,000 officers, to little apparent effect on controlling unrest.[10] The Law Enforcement Assistance Act of 1965 earmarked funds for a new FBI academy in Virginia, intended to expand opportunities for attendance sixfold. Hoover further attempted to secure subventions from the OLEA to cover the expenses of room and board for attendees at the academy. Though there was no statutory basis for such a grant to the FBI, administrators were willing to make an exception to appease Hoover.[11] Through such demands the FBI director was throwing his weight around, to show challengers he was the boss of US law enforcement.

In August 1967, after rebellions in Newark and Detroit, Hoover informed Johnson of still more stepped-up training efforts: "all major police agencies in the United States are being invited by this Bureau to send representatives to a mob and riot control demonstration," under the auspices of the Military Police.[12] Journalists observed a demonstration, as did researchers for the Kerner Commission, Sagalyn among them. They found it woefully lacking, not least because it wrongly implied that peaceful political protest led to rioting and that rifles with fixed bayonets should be used in crowd control.[13] The following June, the Omnibus Crime Control and Safe Streets Act became law. It appropriated over five million dollars for FBI training for the next fiscal year and called for a tenfold increase in attendance at the FBI academy.[14] Hoover's connections in Congress, particularly to the conservative Senators John McClellan and James Eastland, leaders of the anticrime charge, enabled the FBI to benefit directly from the 1968 anticrime legislation.

At the beginning of 1965, in concert with the Army, the FBI issued a new set of guidelines titled *Prevention and Control of Mobs and Riots,* further revised in 1967 and subsequently far more widely distributed.[15] This publication was far from the final word on the subject, however. Instead, it spurred other criminology, riot-control, and counterinsurgency experts to weigh in with articles in magazines like *Ordnance, The Police Chief,* and *Police.* In addition, for the development of new disorder- and street-crime–specific technologies and official doctrine on their usage, the OLEA soon awarded grants to research organizations, including many that had already been seeking and receiving grants for counterinsurgency research, such as the Institute for Defense Analyses, which received the OLEA's largest grant in fiscal year 1966: $498,000.[16] Hoover maintained some control, stuck in his old ways, but other agencies were slowly surpassing the FBI.

The IACP

The International Association of Chiefs of Police transformed rapidly under the leadership of Quinn Tamm, executive director of the organization and editor of *The Police Chief.* Prior to 1961, Tamm had been FBI liaison to the IACP. He was Hoover's inside man, reputed to rig elections so that only Hoover-approved police chiefs ascended to IACP leadership positions.[17] But when Tamm left the FBI to direct the IACP's Field Service Division, he was determined to press the IACP to replace the Bureau as the premier training organization for the nation's police, reprising and building on its experience training overseas police before the consolidation of OPS training facilities by 1963. As executive director, beginning in 1962, Tamm staged an insurgency of his own against what he perceived as sclerosis in the IACP at a time when events demanded an aggressive stance by robust leaders of "Free World" law enforcement. He hoped to prove what a top CIA official had once declared at an IACP annual gathering: "As a group the police are among the most anti-Communist of the professional organizations in the free world. There is a natural antipathy between police and Communists."[18]

Tamm ultimately was successful in raising the IACP's profile in riot-control training. The IACP's phones rang often after the summers of unrest, with simple answers sought. The complex recommendations of the PCLEAJ's 1967 report *The Challenge of Crime in a Free Society* frequently fell on deaf ears. One official thus recommended that the Kerner Commission, initiated later that year, develop proactive approaches to convince police of the accuracy of its own findings and the necessity of its recommendations. Only with specific and detailed instructions would it be possible to counter reluctance to change, a communication method at which the IACP excelled.[19] The IACP and DOJ organized four week-long meetings at Airlie House in Virginia in advance of the publication of the 1968 *Report of the National Advisory Commission on Civil Disorders* (Kerner *Report*). Closely watched by the White House, the meetings brought together some four hundred mayors, police chiefs, and other officials from 136 cities across the country to discuss prevention of civil disturbances and responses to them.[20] A former public safety advisor was one of the OLEA's behind-the-scenes planners of these "conceptual" meetings.[21] A key influence on the meetings was Robert McNamara's trusted deputy Cyrus R. Vance, who collaborated with Komer on Vietnam, OPS on recruitment, and the SGCI on unrest in hot spots like Panama in 1964 and the Dominican Republic the next year. This experience primed him for domestic civil-disturbance duties, as the president's special emissary. McNamara credited Vance with restoring order in Detroit in 1967. Vance conveyed his ideas on riot control to the DOJ and Kerner Commission in a secret report. They were virtually indistinguishable from OPS guidance.[22] He urged the use of curfews, discretionary deployment of tear gas, and standardized rules of engagement to avoid indiscriminate gunfire. At the meetings, Sagalyn summarized the Kerner findings, including an emphasis on facilitating positive interactions between police and the public long before angry protest or civil violence occurred. Speakers focusing on riot-control tactics included Army Provost Marshal General Carl C. Turner, in charge of the Military Police, and the LAPD's Daryl Gates. The meetings primed these audiences for the newly developing riot-control orthodoxy that would issue from the Kerner *Report* and other police professionalizers. Ten subsequent one-week meetings in five other states gathered command-level law-enforcement officials to devise operational planning based on the discussions at Airlie House. *The Police Chief* disseminated the new orthodoxy in the coming months and years, emphasizing intelligence and community relations as much as emergency tactics. The IACP recognized the benefits it reaped from facilitating this federal convocation. On the first day of the meetings, the IACP executive board voted to support the omnibus crime bill.[23]

Although Hoover's political ties meant it was difficult to outmaneuver him in battles for resources, Tamm was prescient to appreciate that new federal funding for law enforcement could help fill the IACP's coffers. A decade after the cancellation of the IACP contract for help with overseas police assistance, the organization's leaders were able to build on their good works with the LEAA to rekindle a relationship with AID, inviting foreign police to tour IACP headquarters, for example, and selling IACP training materials to Thailand.[24]

The Army

With the FBI relatively static, if increasingly well funded, and the IACP attempting to marry its own experience with police assistance to the anticrime fervor that was sweeping Congress, the most dynamic operator in the field of law-enforcement training was the Army, whose civil-disturbance training aimed to foster cohesion among state agencies tasked with security. The Army was entering a field from which it had generally been excluded, and it thus suffered from few of the constraints of inheritance. Until this point, Provost Marshal Carl Turner had held the rudder steady, working with Hoover but carefully not stepping on toes. The Military Police, after all, did not have jurisdiction to investigate civilians or enforce the law outside military contexts, except by special executive permission. Turner did advocate for a National Guard role in riot control, drawing on his knowledge of the world situation. Amid confabulation, he confirmed police primacy in confronting internal enemies: "The riots we are experiencing today are caused by groups. In the Philippines they are referred to as *Huks;* and in Argentina, as *Commancheros.* In the United States, they are *criminals.*[25] After Detroit's rebellion in July 1967, when the National Guard responded with unrestrained and wanton violence, such as fusillades from tanks aimed at buildings, it was clear the armed forces would need to change their civil-disturbance posture. (Army soldiers, however, were somewhat more restrained in Detroit.)[26] The FBI itself declared, "We are in a guerrilla war for which our National Guard has not been as adequately trained as it should be."[27]

Professional courtesies mattered among these proud men. Each believed his own experience offered unimpeachable lessons. When Lyndon Johnson publicly called upon the Army to retool its civil-disturbance training, one of Hoover's high-ranking aides insisted that Turner tell the president that Hoover wanted him to acknowledge FBI collaboration.[28] But the Army did not answer to Hoover. It was galvanized by the Kerner Commission's findings. The Army immediately published its manual *Civil Disturbances and Disasters* (FM 19–15), and it produced Garden Plot, an exhaustive civil-disturbance plan that was designed to comport with the Kerner findings and recommendations. Garden Plot also inscribed French counterinsurgency theory into Army disturbance control, adopting David Galula's tripartite division of the population division into the reliably loyal, the neutral or apathetic, and the firmly rebellious, creating a ready template for interpreting complex political dynamics in emergency situations. The well-entrenched Turner did not, however, lead this reform effort. Nor did Army Special Forces maven and former leader of Fort Bragg's training in counterguerrilla warfare, General William P. Yarborough. He had the inclination, given that under Johnson his responsibilities included extensive domestic surveillance operations, aimed primarily at Black radical groups and focusing on Black urban neighborhoods. During unrest that April after the assassination of Martin Luther King Jr., Yarborough declared to his staff, "Men, get out your counterinsurgency manuals. We have an insurgency on our hands."[29] Thanks to his own predilections, these manuals emphasized offensive guerrilla operations, making their guidance inappropriate.

By then, like many high-ranking Army officers during the years of the US war in Vietnam, Turner and Yarborough were falling out of favor, as too old-fashioned and out of touch to lead a reform effort. Already, by disposition, Turner and others from the provost marshal's staff blocked the nimble operation of counterinsurgency organized through the Special Group (Counter-Insurgency). For instance, Turner refused to "concur" with systematic reviews of police assistance, feeling they underplayed his potential contribution. "He does not look favorably upon the AID police program," a public safety advisor reported. "Further discussions with him . . . would serve no useful purpose." He was thus excluded. Turner retaliated by circulating a paper on policing and counterinsurgency in "developing nations," written by a high-ranking military policeman, which barely mentioned OPS; several public safety advisors in turn excoriated it.[30]

Turner then directed his attention homeward. For his final acts, Turner deployed as an on-the-ground liaison to the Army's chief of staff during unrest twice in Chicago in 1968—though other officers felt he was superfluous in this liaison role. He had also been a liaison during large antiwar protests at the Pentagon in 1967. In 1968, Turner reported that Chicago's police had exhibited restraint during the Democratic Party convention, when all evidence pointed to the opposite conclusion.[31] Soon thereafter, he retired from the Army to become one of the many security consultants populating an emergent field. His ambition was to succeed Hoover as FBI director. The DOJ, however, quickly hired him as chief US marshal. After holding that post for only five months, he was forced to resign due to investigations into corruption while he was provost marshal. Yet that investigation was not exactly his undoing. In the second half of 1968, Turner used his Army rank and uniform to compel the Chicago and other police departments to turn over firearms confiscated during unrest and in other investigations to him, saying they would become Army property. He claimed they would be used in civil-disturbance training at the Military Police facility at Fort Gordon in Georgia. But he illegally funneled almost five hundred rifles, shotguns, and pistols to his side business as a firearms dealer, with many of them ending up in the hands of Third World right-wing paramilitaries. When congressional investigators discovered the CIA was likely involved, they relented, but Turner still faced prosecution.[32]

Anticrime political waves unsettled the very ground on which the Army's head policeman had long been standing: 1968 gun-control legislation rendered some dealing in firearms illegal, and Turner also became ensnared in investigations owing to the rival claims of the Pentagon, intelligence agencies, Congress, and the White House during the Nixon presidency. Sentenced to three years in prison, Turner earned parole after one.[33] The position of Army provost marshal general was eliminated entirely in 1974. Meanwhile, a massive retooling of Army civil-disturbance training was under way, aided by an influx of funding from the DOJ.

Like the FBI National Academy and the OPS International Police Academy, the Army's civil-disturbance education program was oriented toward training trainers. Rather than using its resources to reach low-level soldiers and police officers who would be the boots on the ground in situations of urban conflict, the Army targeted mid-level planners and overseers, just as OPS did. The Army's new training program, based at Fort Gordon, Georgia, called the Senior Officers Civil Disturbance Orientation Course (SEADOC), was initially open to FBI agents, state and municipal police executives, and Army and National Guard officers.[34] The LEAA's Civil Disorders Program Division, in charge of ensuring state-level preparedness for unrest, urged civil law-enforcement personnel across the country to attend.[35] The idea behind the SEADOC training program, begun when Garden Plot was becoming the nationwide civil-disturbance plan, was not only to standardize training across jurisdictions and geographic areas but, as much as possible, to train civil police and military representatives from the same regions together so that they would already have shared training and interpersonal connections during deployments. In 1967, before his fall from grace, Turner had already advocated joint police and National Guard exercises.[36] Fort Gordon already sponsored specialized technical training commingling police and military from other countries, such as a course in radio operations that enrolled Venezuelan and Vietnamese police alongside US Army enlistees.[37]

Contingency planning and riot-control operations were the two primary components of SEADOC. A single SEADOC session was one week long, with forty hours of training scheduled over five days.[38] The majority of the course consisted of conference-type presentations and seminars, with additional time devoted to films and guest speakers, plus a full eight-hour day of disturbance demonstrations and practical exercises. Operations training included a range of subjects and demonstrations, including, in a mock urban setting called Riotsville: "Riot control formations, techniques, and equipment ... use of riot control agents, munitions, and equipment; operational techniques and tactics; civil police in civil disturbances; after-action reports and lessons learned in civil disturbances," and so on. Training for contingencies ranged from gathering intelligence by cultivating sources and identifying "professional agitators and leaders of dissident groups" to "mental preparation" to avoid succumbing to panic.[39] SEADOC was designed to be intensive, though at first attendees did not get the message. Many of the initial participants believed Fort Gordon's prime location near the Augusta National Golf Club and other courses meant SEADOC would allow considerable time spent on the green. A Hoover aide recalled, "I got a call from one of the fellas who was running the program, he says, 'Some of these law enforcement fellas think this is a vacation. It is not. We are training them hard.' So we told them not to bring their golf clubs in the future."[40]

There were two iterations of SEADOC. It initially lasted from February 1968 to April 1969, offered multiple times each month. Around 1,300 police, 1,000 National Guard, 700 Army soldiers, 300 reservists, and a smattering of other security officials attended in its first iteration.[41] After the abrupt termination of the initial course, officials developed a revised course. It commenced on May 10, 1970, six days after the Ohio National Guard's killing of young people at Kent State University and a day before unrest in Augusta itself. Although the Army's Directorate for Civil Disturbance Planning and Operations determined deficient training was not to blame at Kent State, National Guard soldiers composed the largest proportion of SEADOC attendees from the military soon after its reopening.[42] It also began to enroll mayors and other officials alongside police and soldiers. The rapidity with which it was reestablished after the Kent State shootings indicated that SEADOC remained a tool of crisis management.

SEADOC's transformation reflected a shift in militant repertoires and protest tactics. The first SEADOC course focused narrowly on riot control, both in terms of preparation and actual operations, but the second iteration of the course was retooled to encompass "mass demonstrations, nonviolent protests, and acts of political terrorism."[43] Riotsville was renamed Maxville, indicating the wide range of emergencies the training might cover. The law-enforcement response to the American Indian Movement occupation at Wounded Knee in 1973 included SEADOC-trained personnel and exemplified its interagency coordination beyond the specific setting of riot control. The new SEADOC lasted through 1978, relocating to Fort McClellan, Alabama, in 1975. In anticipation of new threats, the LEAA also organized workshops at other sites, alongside the new SEADOC, to enable centralized issue-specific training, such as one on improvised bomb detection and disposal, which the Army housed at an arsenal in Alabama. Public safety advisors were permitted to attend as auditors.[44]

The Army's impetus to form SEADOC was the lack of coordination among various agencies, along with the generally disastrous responses of the National Guard in Detroit and Newark. But interagency coordination was no panacea when different agencies possessed varying levels of prior training and discipline. Army restraint in Detroit did not necessarily match municipal police or National Guard approaches. Bertram Levine, an official with the DOJ's Community Relations Service, the office originally housed in the Commerce Department that was charged with overseeing adherence to civil-rights legislation, reviewed SEADOC for the DOJ. He worried that insufficient attention was being paid to "precipitating or aggravating actions by law enforcement authorities, such as over-responding, moving in initially with too little force, improper responses stemming from panic, fear or uncertainty."[45] Concerned primarily with coordination, the Army was not actually addressing why police actions tended to exacerbate destructiveness of civil violence.

SEADOC could proffer but not mandate best practices around coordination and preparation. Interagency training did not deliver doctrine. Military instructors did not command military students, nor were police bound by chain of command to follow military training they received. The seminar-like quality of many SEADOC classes reflected the difficulty of developing a uniform set of guidelines. As the scientific advisor to the commander of British forces in Northern Ireland observed on a visit to SEADOC, with a certain admiration, "The instructors do not really instruct; they set the scene for the discussions and the attendees do almost all the talking."[46] Civil-disturbance training entailed the creation of a physical space of encounter for civil and military authorities to mingle, share past experience (and future intelligence), and gain exposure to the latest thinking and technologies. SEADOC's flexibility, rather than rigidity, and the conversational atmosphere reflected the shifting foundations of the US social order, the imperative of iterative crisis-management, and the general uncertainty of the era provoked by insistent social-movement demands on the state.

At first, the Army intended SEADOC to complement civilian training programs. From the vantage of the DOJ, SEADOC had the potential to "insure against confusion, lack of direction, and ineffective cooperation," as had occurred in Detroit and Newark in 1967.[47] The Army's position was that its training offerings should not overlap greatly with other DOJ or IACP training programs, which were focused on improving relations between police and urban residents. Under Secretary of the Army David McGiffert attempted in early 1968 to have Turner work with Tamm to ensure no overlap occurred.[48] Turner's fall scotched that plan. But Levine, of the Community Relations Service, worried that SEADOC was not directed toward prevention of disturbances or improvement of "community relations." He argued that it was important to establish relationships between military officers and "civil rights and ghetto leaders" during unrest, and he even suggested that SEADOC include a panel discussion by rioters, "to impress the trainees with the fact that while rioting is wrong, rioters are human beings." Levine sought an intermediary between the DOJ and the Army, someone who could provide an expert, independent evaluation of SEADOC, as well as a person who might have instructions to offer on the subject of how military men and "ghetto leaders" might develop rapport. He chose Sidney Rocker, a former riot-control trainer with OPS in Washington, Guatemala, and Brazil, who became an administrator for the OLEA and LEAA.[49] To manage domestic racial strife, the liberal-minded Levine looked to expatriated counterinsurgency expertise.

Ultimately, SEADOC began to attract far larger numbers of attendees than IACP programs did, for example. For these students, who represented a critical mass of US law-enforcement and military personnel, issues of "community relations" did not enter into training on riot control or other specialized emergency situations involving sociopolitical disorder. The alleviation of racism, or even acknowledgment of it as an underlying cause of disorder, became epiphenomenal to keeping the peace. Nonetheless, the second SEADOC prefigured the strategy of proactive negotiated management, which came to replace reactive escalation of force as crowd-control orthodoxy by the 1990s.[50]

During two SEADOC iterations, more than ten thousand police officers, soldiers, and other officials attended.[51] Many of these officers would, in turn, have relayed what they learned to colleagues who did not attend, greatly increasing the diffusion of the training offered. The course was designed for replication, and printed guidance materials ended up on police department bookshelves. In comparison, 5,204 foreign police officers graduated from the International Police Academy from 1963 to 1974 (an additional 3,651 attended but did not graduate).[52] OPS routinely cited the figure of a million police officers around the world touched by its training, technical services, matériel, and other forms of assistance. By 1972, Engle bumped it up to 1.5 million.[53] Even conceding Engle's grandiosity about the impact of OPS, the figure captured the exponential magnification of specialized training of trainers as a method. If fewer than nine thousand trainees translated to a million officers touched by OPS, as those trained then operated training facilities in their own countries around the world, it would not be unreasonable to calculate that SEADOC training touched up to half a million US police officers, meaning nearly all US police, in some way, especially if half of the ten thousand SEADOC attendees were police. Centralized training was designed to spur decentralized training, down the ladder of rank. The Treasury Department began to supersede this model, while expanding beyond riot control, by creating the Federal Law Enforcement Training Center for all federal law-enforcement officers, an idea first drawn up near the end of Johnson's presidency. Eventually consolidated into the Department of Homeland Security, these facilities trained officers directly, rather than focusing on training trainers, but they retained SEADOC's interagency, collaborative model. Some of the first employees of the Treasury Department's new training facility in the 1970s were former public safety advisors.

OPS

SEADOC trained trainers on the national scale, a rescaling of expertise from the aspirationally globe-encircling domain of the US military and police assistance in this period. Police assistance could not remain at the global scale alone, nor was the global an independent domain, detached from localities. OPS connected global and local. It opened the doors of its academy to domestic police. They did not take classes, but they could observe how International Police Academy training might be replicated. The LEAA helped realize the possibility of replication. On the cusp of the passage of the 1968 crime bill, a specialist deemed the lessons for foreign police executives at the IPA "superior to any training offered anywhere in the United States to our domestic law enforcement agencies."[54] The academy offered separate senior- and intermediate-level curricula. One reason to bring high-ranking police to the United States was to convince them to accept the reforms and technical upgrades public safety advisors were bringing to low-ranking officers in their countries.

The International Police Academy combined training in routine police methods and administration, as modeled by O. W. Wilson, the era's leading police reformer, with training in shadowy intelligence-gathering methods. Participants received a copy of J. Edgar Hoover's exploration of communist subversion, *Masters of Deceit*.[55] FBI agents themselves were masters of deceit who specialized in infiltrating radical groups and placing informants. These lessons spread globally. By March 1966, public safety advisors in Saigon boasted, for example, that officers of the US-trained National Police had "penetrated" all Buddhist student organizations involved in recent protests, while controlling traffic efficiently during the demonstrations—and these students were avowedly anticommunist.[56] But public safety advisors also touted the rectitude they instilled. In one bizarre criminal investigation in Cam Ranh, South Vietnam, which featured a US citizen falsely claiming to be enlisted in the US Army, a National Police officer refused a sizeable bribe. OPS determined that his doing so was the result of the standards set by his IPA-participant supervisor.[57]

Overall, riot control was a focal point of IPA training. A point of great pride for OPS was the Police Operations Control Center (POCC), a logistical training center for police officials designed to illustrate, in highly stylized fashion, the imperatives of centralization of command, coordination of resources, intelligence-gathering, and flexibility in countering unrest. Training in the POCC took the form of games: different scenarios that might occur in areas threatened by subversion. The POCC was a mock situation room, with a map covering one wall, depicting the city of Rio Bravos in the Republic of San Martin, a fictional country that bordered Maoland, which was constantly sending subversives to disrupt the tranquility of Rio Bravos.[58] On the map and other screens, combinations of magnets, fluorescent symbols and ultraviolet lights, film projectors, and grease pencils allowed bombings, protests, fires, and robberies to be plotted in different configurations in each game. Trainers circulated mug shots and location photos. They reported events via phone and teletype to trainees, who gathered at a desk before the map. Trainees would determine what the appropriate police response was, based on other lessons. Although the POCC was the first training room of its kind, the logic behind it was to focus on preparedness, not the technology. As one trainer declared, "The Academy emphasizes, in POCC operations, that *training* is important, not equipment."[59]

The POCC encapsulated the complicated and overlapping geographies of police assistance and training in the period, which cannot easily be captured by tropes of US-centric diffusion or repatriation. The POCC's map actually depicted the city of Baltimore, Maryland. The university in Rio Bravos, a hotbed of radicalism shown in photographs during the simulations, was actually Georgetown University, right next to the IPA. Trainees themselves came from Latin America, Africa, Asia, and even Europe. Classes were conducted in French, Spanish, and English, and boards provided information in all three languages during POCC games. The United States supplied the IPA's trainers, and the era's most influential US policing authorities visited to impart lessons. Guest lecturers also included renowned counterinsurgency experts such as Napoleon Valeriano of the Philippines, as well as recent IPA

FIGURE 9. Police Operations Control Center, International Police Academy. National Archives and Records Administration.

graduates who reported on counterinsurgency efforts back home. Moreover, the on-site Reference Center gathered "more than 5,000 books and other publications for use by students and staff of the Academy," in many languages, from around the globe. It was "a nucleus for a repository of professional knowledge ... regarding counter-insurgency generally," including many items from military sources. Rather than a hushed library setting, the Reference Center, like other parts of the IPA, encouraged conversation among police officials from different countries.[60]

Not only was the POCC's map based on a US city, OPS officials explicitly envisioned the POCC as a prototype for situation rooms in cities around the United States and abroad. The POCC model, AID explained, "can be adopted with minimum equipment at low cost, which can be produced locally by any police force."[61] OPS helped Bolivia, Brazil, Chile, Iran, Somalia, and Venezuela build similar facilities. Additionally, Los Angeles, Cincinnati, and other US cities instituted training centers modeled on the POCC.[62] The technology was replicable and transposable, for civilian or military forces. By 1967, an expert discussant at an IACP forum encouraged coordinated training "games" based on the IPA model as a way to improve civil-disturbance training of US police generally.[63] SEADOC followed the IPA lead on simulations, and OPS shared

FIGURE 10. Seminar, International Police Academy, 1964. National Archives and Records Administration.

information with the Army on the company that had constructed the POCC.[64] For the prominent sociologist Morris Janowitz, the unrest of the mid-1960s showed that the bedrock of professionalization, classroom training, and standardized manuals had to be supplemented with realistic participatory simulations.[65] OPS led the way as game-based training came to predominate, superseding less realistic FBI and Military Police demonstrations.

In IPA classrooms, the modularity of US-designed technique encountered the variety of practical Third World experience. Engle's successor likened the space the IPA created for "candid exchanges of ideas" across borders to IACP annual meetings or Interpol conferences. Not all training occurred at the IPA. Foreign IPA participants also frequently attended the Special Warfare Center and School at Fort Bragg for specialized counterinsurgency lessons, where OPS trainers also gave presentations to military attendees. The CIA front company International Police Services (usually called Inpolse), also based in Washington, DC, but outside the formal control of OPS, was another destination for IPA students. In-country and third-country training, which were components as important as attendance at IPA for OPS's overall training scheme, provided other venues. Additionally, IPA attendees could also take technical classes at Fort Gordon, the FBI National Academy, the US Postal Service Scientific Identification Laboratory, the US Coast Guard Training Center, Northwestern University's Traffic Institute, and Southern Illinois University for penology and corrections. English classes were available for Spanish-speaking officers at Georgetown University.[66]

OPS officials insisted to critics that the IPA curriculum aimed to squelch the use of torture or extrajudicial violence. Yet participants studied policing in the Soviet Union at length, which was meant to illustrate totalitarian police repression. Lessons in interrogation without torture, or bomb disposal, allowed participants to fill in the gaps or reverse engineer what they learned. Training beyond IPA doors conferred another layer of plausible deniability. Inpolse, for instance, publicized its innocuous-sounding courses in police records management, which enabled disappearance, torture, and extrajudicial killings across the globe. From the US intelligence perspective, far more important than lessons in how to commit violent acts were lessons in specialized technical knowledge and data management to surveil and target populations, along with supply of filing systems, fingerprinting materials, binoculars, cameras, and other mundane items.[67] Police assistance tried to integrate specialized police intelligence units into broader national command structures, enabling them to build on the everyday police work public safety advisors were professionalizing. Countries where OPS celebrated these bureaucratic changes, like South Vietnam and Guatemala, became sites of severe repression.

Advisors curated a collegial atmosphere, to foster sharing of homegrown techniques among IPA participants. A Senate investigation into OPS uncovered multiple research theses written by IPA graduates that condoned torture. New Left activists tried to pin the blame for these ideas on OPS.[68] Required for graduation, the theses were subject to an oral discussion by a panel, meaning that IPA instructors and participants knew what they contained. US police assistance could simultaneously disavow torture in its efforts at police professionalization and foster the possibility for what today might be called South-South transfer of locally sourced experience and knowledge (both toward and in spite of US geopolitical ends), including torture. Through its collection of thousands of theses in its Reference Center, OPS facilitated contiguity: unpredictable and extrametropolitan circuits of knowledge dissemination. An IPA instructor wrote that graduates' theses were "prepared with full academic freedom," and the IPA assured each student that "his thesis will not be released outside the Academy without his consent."[69] No OPS official anticipated that a senator's staffers would read the theses.

Beyond training, bringing high-ranking police officials from around the world to the United States under IPA auspices enabled their vetting as intelligence assets. Analysts visited the Reference Center to mine the theses for information on the security situation in participants' home countries.

Foreign police officials also met with CIA officers in the free-flowing conversations in the seminar room, at auxiliary institutions, and in casual social gatherings. Most would not even have known who employed these interlocutors, especially at first—some IPA trainers included. When they returned home, newly vetted police officials would become conduits of information, provided that they or their subordinates kept their ears close to the ground. It may be for this reason that "some of those sent abroad for training were looked upon with disfavor upon their return," compromised by their usefulness to US spycraft.[70] The US term "advisor" also irked some foreign police executives, because it subordinated them. The Thai colonel who worked most closely with OPS had studied in the United States at Ivy League institutions; his AID counterpart had not even attended college.[71] By June 1974, 1,787 IPA graduates (44 percent) had been promoted once back home. Within the first decade of the academy's operation, eleven IPA graduates had become the heads of their own countries' national police forces. Of all graduates, 529 (13 percent) had risen to positions in national command structures by 1974, and 1,027 (25 percent) to positions in provincial, divisional, or major metropolitan command. Others ascended later. AID bilateral public safety contracts stipulated that IPA participants be elevated to "key positions."[72] Some did so via coups.[73]

California

As the War on Crime took on its decentralized shape due to the block-grant funding mechanism at the heart of the Omnibus Crime Control and Safe Streets Act, California, under Governor Ronald Reagan's leadership, positioned itself as a vanguard. It created its own statewide civil-disturbance plan and training exercises called Cable Splicer, and it developed its own training school. Centralized federal training of trainers was one side of the coin of federalism; state-level training by California was another. Under the auspices of the California Military Department, which controlled the California National Guard, the California Specialized Training Institute (CSTI) opened at Camp San Luis Obispo in May 1971, enabled by LEAA funds.[74] Its first director was Colonel Louis O. Giuffrida, a trainer at SEADOC until California recruited him.[75] When Reagan became president, he nominated Giuffrida to lead the Federal Emergency Management Agency. At his confirmation hearings on Capitol Hill, Giuffrida emphasized his own allegiance to federalism. He endorsed Reagan's "principle of passing as much of the decision making down to the State and local level and keeping the Federal Government as much as possible out of the pockets of the people doing these actions." This notion was the guiding principle of CSTI. Also in those confirmation hearings, a sordid detail in Giuffrida's background emerged: he had once advocated developing a plan for the mass internment of "American Negroes" in a situation of widespread civil unrest. Over a decade after the initiation of police-focused centralized riot-control training, the racial politics of this training, consistently submerged and disavowed, bubbled to the surface.[76] Given the racial prerogative that it enabled, a repressive apparatus with nearly limitless coercive capacities did not, for him, contradict the ethos of limited government federalism.

The idea behind CSTI was to reproduce SEADOC in microcosm. In practice, however, with the availability of LEAA funds, California's school transcended the limited scope of SEADOC to encompass a broader range of training parameters. Still in existence today, CSTI expanded the range of topics covered within SEADOC's curriculum to more general disaster and emergency situations, including earthquakes, floods, and industrial accidents. It also maintained a focus on unrest and terrorism. As with SEADOC, Reagan's inspiration for developing CSTI was the recognition that failures of interagency coordination and inconsistencies in adherence to guidelines had impeded control of civil disturbances, particularly on university campuses.[77] Or, as a handwritten note recounting a Reagan Gubernatorial Task Force meeting said: "CSTI—Why created[:] Watts, People's Park," referring to the Los Angeles uprising of 1965 and the attempted violent eviction of the occupiers of a park in Berkeley in 1969.[78] Furthermore, to conserve costs, a single training center for multiple agencies would consolidate existing disparate programs, an ambition Reagan's penny-pinching administration possessed from its outset.[79] Throughout the first decade of its existence, CSTI attracted more than twenty thousand attendees, from at least forty-seven states, three US territories, and nine other countries.[80] These included a variety of police officers, from the FBI down to municipalities, college administrators and security staff, California National Guard personnel, and others. A British official concerned with counterinsurgency in Northern Ireland had visited SEADOC in 1972 to study it, and CSTI invited another British official with similar expertise to speak to one of its seminars in 1976 (with Giuffrida in the audience).[81] Although elected and appointed municipal and county officials were able to attend, the institute engineered training to orient their emergency-management techniques toward law-enforcement agencies after "the breaking point" had been reached. CSTI training did not push law enforcement to consider other options, including earlier identification of "racial, religious, or ethnic tensions" and corresponding intervention by other state agencies, as one attendee complained.[82] It was a complaint that echoed the early assessment of SEADOC issued by Bertram Levine of the Community Relations Service.

CSTI funneled a range of law-enforcement and emergency-management agencies and situations into a narrow "hands-on" practical approach that emphasized enhancing agency-specific capabilities while strengthening mutual understandings across agencies. CSTI's first course concerned "Civil Disorder Management," but by 1973, it had expanded to offer a course on "Officer Survival and Internal Security," for example, inspired by "incidents of police officer assaults and killings within the last few years." Not just for cops, it was also open to "firemen, military personnel, and those persons involved in enforcing the laws," for the purpose of "upgrading training to insure officer survival."[83] Additional courses added throughout the 1970s concerned terrorism, investigations of violent crime and robbery, and investigative techniques for dealing with juvenile suspects and victims. The campus of the institute included a mock city for training in how to deal with booby traps, barricaded suspects, and hostages, as well as in other operations.[84] Activists uncovered maps used in CSTI simulations that depicted highly segregated towns like the fictional Santa Luisa, which consisted of white and Black neighborhoods separated by a thin "Chicano" strip, along with an enclave labeled "upper class" in the white area. The implication was that the Black and Chicano areas might be sources of insurgency, but the white area could be protected by dividing Black from Chicano people, using the strip as a racialized spatial and political buffer. A journalist commented on what was at stake: "There is no pretense here that the racial and class aspects are incidental; they are the determining factors."[85] Soon after CSTI was up and running, word of its course offerings reached the International Police Academy. The chief of OPS's Training Division requested further information on California's training in civil disorders from Giuffrida, completing an alphabet-soup circle of inspiration from IPA to Kerner's NACCD to SEADOC to CSTI back to IPA.[86]

Yet CSTI also transformed the field of training by taking advantage of and inhabiting a space created by the funding instruments of the War on Crime. CSTI most fully realized the insistent downscaling, devolutionary thrust of domestic law-enforcement assistance. Reagan was responsible for this replicable marriage of fiscal austerity and crime-fighting. Although it was from the beginning just one training facility among others, as CSTI developed, it fulfilled a programmatic ambition of the emerging new federalism: to view state functions in competitive terms and thereby implant a market-like logic of competition for customers among agencies at the same scale and at different scales. Even as the remit of CSTI was to foster cooperation within California for purposes of emergency management, its external-facing projection was one of zero-sum competition with SEADOC, the IPA (which it outlasted), and the FBI National Academy. The result of such competition was the increased salience and centrality of street-level policing to all forms of emergency response. Competition, therefore, did not result in the development of the best product. It led all customers to buy the same product, as alternatives lost viability. This dispersed monopoly of technique facilitated the reassertion of the legitimacy of the state's monopoly on the means of violence.

. . .

The advocates of the professionalization of policing consciously imagined it as a progressive and linear, if interminable, program. To upgrade competencies in controlling unrest through specialized training was central, going back to the earliest moments of professionalization, when it focused on controlling labor radicalism and managing the changing racial composition of cities. Although the possibility of assessing adherence to desired reforms was embedded in professionalization, unrest on the scale seen from 1964 to 1968 did not occur in the ensuing years, so it was difficult to tell whether the new riot-control training was working. Nixon's aides believed that large cities experienced fewer episodes of unrest after 1968 because of federal spending on riot-control training. LEAA officials agreed, hoping the logical response would be greater appropriations for small cities that continued to be unstable.[87] But newfound police competence in suppressing mass forms of protest led to more scattershot, wildcat, diffuse, and politically ambiguous tactics among radicals during the 1970s. From the outset of the urban unrest the Johnson administration confronted in Harlem through 1968, policing faltered, but failures only gave law-enforcement experts a greater incentive to advocate types of reforms that held externally forced, radical transformations in abeyance. Reformers wanted police to be perceived never to use too much force, because "when this happens, the police end up being the central figure in the disturbance"—as if the disturbance were not so often the result of police abuse.[88] Professionalization justified itself by failing: police officers' excesses meant insufficient professionalization, which required more funding for upskilling the bad apples. Unrest accelerated ongoing professionalization efforts, giving them new urgency and summoning new expertise, including from military figures.

What did professionalization through training achieve? It had two effects. First, it rendered instabilities stable anew, on a different plane. With burning Black neighborhoods as the clearest evidence of a crisis, and a state that gathered legitimacy through its manipulation of racial meanings to propose a progressive narrative that would entail their formal erasure from politics, the global upheaval of decolonization that landed on America's street corners left the state harboring magnificent capacities of security but difficulties in determining how to mobilize them. Professionalization offered a route out of this crisis, since it codified practices, instituted new repertoires and technologies, and, most important, increased the prominence of the police. This increased prominence was the second achievement of professionalization. Yet even as professionalization aimed for codification of routines and predictability of their application, the possibility of formulating new training practices was deeply influenced by the contingencies of personality, as exemplified by Turner and Giuffrida.

Overall, public safety advisors developed a new riot-control orthodoxy that they spread overseas, and in the process, lessons they learned changed the orthodoxy at home. If riot-control training represented the labor-intensive side of police reform in response to unrest, then there was a capital-intensive side as well, which the LEAA's new funding streams enabled. Law-enforcement experts consciously imagined a range of new technologies, particularly for riot control, to be necessary to the redemption, as well as the insulation and upskilling, of policing.

SEVEN

The Imperial Circuit of Tear Gas

FEDERAL LABORATORIES, INC., a manufacturer of tear gas grenades and projectiles, would always have had good reason to try to expand the range of uses of these munitions and thus to increase sales. But one company employee argued in *The Police Chief* in 1961 against using tear gas to flush out "barricaded criminals," because of the "peril" it presented to officers and the public. By 1969, however, Federal Laboratories published new tactical information explicitly illustrating how to use "riot agents" to force "barricaded criminals" out of hiding.[1] The illustration resembled one that MSU experts developed to train South Vietnamese police in the 1950s, which transplanted a suburban two-story American house across the ocean (see fig. 11). Even more aggressive use of tear gas would come to characterize the US war in Vietnam, and overseas experience shaped domestic transformations. Byron Engle was a conduit of this experience.

In 1967, Engle convinced the Kerner Commission that OPS had developed techniques for "nonlethal riot control," using "chemical munitions."[2] Clouds of gas would disrupt and derail mass public protest without causing grievous injury or death. But the use of tear gas in war in Indochina shaped its use at home, transforming repertoires of social contention in the process. Although Engle's recommendations seemed neutral and clinical in their application of best practices to reduce violence, they came in the context of the US war in Vietnam. Despite their technical guise, Engle's recommendations also enabled a recrudescence and recapitulation of the racial inequity that the Kerner Commission demanded be overcome. Envisioned as a way to quell civil violence in Black neighborhoods, chemical munitions became a tool of violence used against Black people outside the setting of political unrest.

So-called nonlethal weapons redeemed US policing after disastrously violent responses of police and soldiers to Black freedom protest in the 1960s.

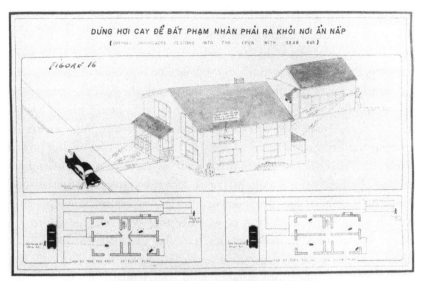

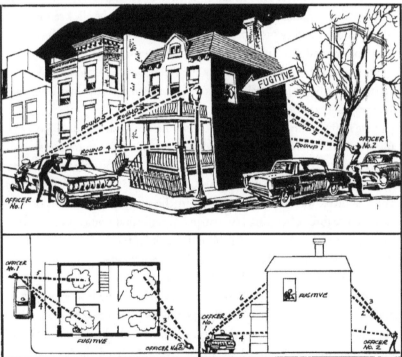

FIGURE 11. Tear gas to flush barricaded persons. Michigan State University Archives & Historical Collections, Vietnam Project Records, 1950s (top), and *The Police Chief,* May 1969 (bottom).

Expert advice to increase reliance on chemical munitions emerged directly from the crucible of police-led counterinsurgency overseas. This shift represented a stark repatriation of counterinsurgent knowledge as domestic policing. From the rank and file to J. Edgar Hoover, police themselves were frequently loath to admit that their own actions might stoke the severity and spread of urban unrest.[3] Yet among producers of counterinsurgent knowledge, such as Arnold Sagalyn, the evidence was clear: white police were brandishing and firing guns too frequently in Black crowd-control and protest situations. Strict rules mandated that federal law-enforcement agencies shoot only in life-threatening situations, but no such rules typically governed local law enforcement, or else cops followed rules that expressly allowed police to kill "fleeing felons" regardless of whether they were armed.[4] Moreover, National Guard soldiers with bayonets fixed had a dismal record of violence against crowds by 1968. Sagalyn's research found that the use of guns was "backfiring" for police. This situation needed to change, and new technologies were likely to address it more quickly than legal and policy reforms. The Office of Public Safety promoted CS—a potent compound first formulated in 1928 but not adopted until the 1960s—which incapacitated its victims by simulating suffocation. Employed by the Army of the Republic of Vietnam and the US military in South Vietnam, CS carried the imprimatur of counterinsurgency experience.

Engle's affirmation to the Kerner Commission that use of CS domestically would be appropriate reassured US crisis managers, among whom he had credibility as the civilian official most directly responsible for spearheading flexible-response capabilities abroad. Employing nonlethal weapons against crowds was a key OPS lesson in the professionalization of Third World police forces, but it had two surprising effects at home: preemptive use of CS made mass street protest more difficult in the United States, sometimes leading to more violent forms of resistance—and, moreover, police often used CS in situations where there were no crowds.

Chemical weapons like CS became prevalent in the domestic policing setting because they epitomized the very redemptive response to criticism that was professionalization writ large: stamped with the politically significant though inaccurate name "tear gas," they conferred the appearance of sensitivity to political criticism, while also enhancing the ability of police to conduct their business of fabricating social order unfettered. President Johnson thus labeled them, and his assent to professionals' taking advantage of them, "measured." But although these tools could substitute for using firearms against crowds, they did not remedy the underlying grievances that led to mass protest.

Nonlethal weapons embodied the search for technical, apparently apolitical, solutions to political problems—counterinsurgency's most sacrosanct, yet most disavowed, liberal principle. Prior to 1964, the term "nonlethal weapon" had been rarely used, and only by specialists.[5] Yet when national security officials debated how to defend US actions in South Vietnam in 1965, they adopted this term with little explanation, as if it were commonly accepted. Soon it was appearing in newspapers—most commonly with reference to CS, which has since become prominent in the law-enforcement arsenal. CS "brought the war home," to use the classic New Left phrase, but Lyndon Johnson justified the use of such chemical weapons in South Vietnam by claiming falsely that they were common tools in the policing of American streets.

CS and other types of tear gas followed a frenzied, to-and-fro itinerary across the foreign-domestic divide. Although this divide regulated how policymakers rendered military and police action toward civilians acceptable in legal and moral terms, these weapons' travel undermined this divide's very regulatory power. The munition categories of "nonlethal" and its cognate "riot control" came into existence through travel across this divide, for mutually supportive purposes of occluding the deployment of weapons of war against civilians, collapsing distinctions the divide might have otherwise allowed. To call CS "riot control agent," as the US military did, was to legitimize its use in Vietnam and make it uncontroversial; to deploy CS domestically was to build on the foundation of experiential and engineering knowledge constructed in Vietnam, where, in fact, CS was not used in riot control as much as in combat. Finally, advocates of these weapons depended on a bait-and-switch tactic. By avoiding naming the agent choking Vietnamese civilians and instead referring to law-enforcement use of the chemical CN, which was not as severe as CS, the Johnson administration hid the use of CS in Vietnam, as well as the panoply of new delivery devices undergoing testing there, which increased its versatility and lethality. The appearance of CS at home became a self-fulfilling prophecy.

CS: NOT A GAS, NOT NONLETHAL

Kerner as Conduit

For the Kerner Commission, or National Advisory Commission on Civil Disorders, certain as it was of the problems of racism, nonlethal weapons were supposed to enable the state to act preventively against civil violence without engendering racist brutality. During the 1960s, as the cycle of civil disobedience waned, when faced with situations of militant protest, police experts found that common riot control methods were counterproductive. Scattershot killing of protesters and/or bystanders was unlikely to restore order. Crowd management and the prevention of various types of protest escalation, including looting and burning, became the priorities instead. Nonlethal weapons married methods to goals, shoring up the state's authority by their ability simultaneously to control mass protest and show the authorities to be responsive to criticism.

The Kerner *Report* gave pride of place to nonlethal weapons. It recommended their wide deployment and urged federally funded research into the development of new nonlethal technologies. Arnold Sagalyn had already been advocating nonlethal weapons before he authored the Kerner *Report*'s chapter "Control of Disorder." Sagalyn's preference for such new technologies stemmed from his relationship with Engle and from his support of US overseas police assistance more generally. Sagalyn initially learned about nonlethal weapons like CS in meetings of the Interagency Police Group in 1963, and he came to collaborate with the primary researcher on the topic for the Institute for Defense Analyses, Joseph Coates.[6] In 1965, as one of the Crime Commission's researchers, Sagalyn urged the commission to take testimony from Engle, but it did not.[7] Though that commission noted the incendiary character of police violence, rioting did not much occupy its attention. But, by 1967, in addition to Engle, at least two other public safety advisors, plus MSU's Arthur Brandstatter, worked with Sagalyn's research unit.[8]

As an instrument of governance, the Kerner Commission was designed to reassert state legitimacy. Sagalyn's task was to figure out how police might help do so, aware that police abuses had been detrimental to it. The Kerner *Report* foregrounded suggestions Engle had offered based on US overseas police assistance, but it modified the reasoning. Rather than conventional firearms, Engle argued, "chemical munitions" were among the "most effective" weapons for suppression of unrest. Agitators were constantly trying to get police to "overreact," so it was imperative to avoid the use of guns against protesters, crowds, and even riots.[9] Seymour Deitchman, the Pentagon's head of counterinsurgency research, confirmed this analysis to Sagalyn privately. Police had to be trained "to discriminate between the instigators of riots and the innocent victims or those swept along by the emotions of the moment and to treat each in an appropriate manner." Deitchman was even more specific than Engle: "one of the objectives of the Black Power militants is to provoke an indiscriminate response."[10] The Kerner *Report* recommended police reform rather than endorsing claims that police killings of protesters were the protesters' fault.

The Kerner Commission's analysis of unrest in 1967 showed riot control methods to have been disastrous. Police and National Guard units had indiscriminately killed Black people during unrest across the United States. "Equipping civil police with automatic rifles, machine guns, and other weapons of massive and indiscriminate lethality is not warranted by the evidence," the Kerner *Report* concluded. "Chemical agents provide police forces with an effective and more appropriate weapon."[11]

The Omnibus Crime Control and Safe Streets Act fast-tracked the distribution of funds for riot control in advance of states' implementation of the comprehensive plans of the Law Enforcement Assistance Administration.[12] Although the yearly percentage of LEAA funds spent on riot-control matériel dropped after 1969, the initial spending spree of around $40 million left police arsenals well stocked with chemical weaponry and other riot gear. Surplus military-grade gas masks became available to police and fire departments at very low prices beginning in 1969, with the LEAA facilitating the transactions. Soon, the LEAA helped lubricate further purchases and ensure legality in questionable cases. LEAA leaders were interested in circumventing restrictions on putting surplus military weapons into police hands. Ultimately, the LEAA helped sell upwards of seventy thousand gas masks to police forces. Other surplus body armor, vehicles, and additional cheap hardware gradually became available, as Washington heeded police chiefs' demands for the amendment of laws on procurement.[13]

Early in 1968, the International Association of Chiefs of Police won a contract to educate police forces around the United States in the use of nonlethal weapons, particularly CS, as part of its new riot-control training.[14] The IACP's Professional Standards Division published a book on these weapons that superseded prior guidance, portions of which were serialized in *The Police Chief* at the attorney general's request in an effort to help disseminate information to civilian police.[15] The IACP recommended that officers become familiar with CS, even if their police department did not adopt it, because "all national guard and federal troops committed to disorder control duty will be equipped" with the agent.[16] Civilian law enforcement did widely adopt CS, however, thanks in part to the development of a versatile delivery system, the multi-purpose grenade, at the behest of OPS. Domestically deployed Army and National Guard units also armed themselves with CS, delivered by the same backpack- and helicopter-mounted systems their counterparts used overseas. Dangerous chemicals mendaciously labeled "nonlethal" thus made their way to American streets by way of Vietnam.

The Development of "Riot Control Agent"

As the Kennedy administration's zeal for counterinsurgency increased, security experts clamored for the use of chemical weapons, which, they argued, might be more humane than conventional weapons and were also less likely to destroy property. "The best way for the free world to guard freedom in South-East Asia is to make use of chemical warfare weapons," one wrote, referring to the British experience in Malaya. "Otherwise there will never be enough counter-insurgency troops to comb every rice paddy." A capital-intensive tool could substitute for labor, which was in any case in short supply. Chemical weapons could create barriers (including even by rendering national borders impassable), destroy hiding spots, and "flush out" guerrillas.[17]

CS was not at that point considered an agent strictly for riot control. In fact, the term "riot control agent" appeared only twice between 1958 and 1965 in articles on chemical munitions in ten military periodicals, according to one analysis. Over the next six years, in the same set of periodicals, twelve of fourteen articles dealing with the use of chemical munitions in South Vietnam used the term.[18] One of the pre-1965 articles that did call CS a riot control agent nonetheless made no reference to its deployment in the setting of urban unrest. Rather, it advocated what would become the primary use of CS in South Vietnam: as a tool to incapacitate guerrillas so they could be more easily killed or captured.[19] Years later, CS became a means of forcing the enemy into "free-fire zones," while defoliants made targets in the zones more observable.[20] The term riot control agent became more prevalent as a description of CS as its use outside riot control expanded. What propelled this shift? Not events in Vietnam, but those in Harlem, Watts, Detroit, and Newark.

The intense but short-lived effects of CS made it appealing. The US Department of Defense first adopted CS in 1959 for training and testing purposes.[21] In August 1960, the National Security Council affirmed that "existing smoke and incendiary agents and agents of the riot control type" could be deployed "as appropriate in military operations, including the suppression of civil disturbances, without prior approval of the President."[22]

Before the introduction of CS, the lachrymator, or tear gas, of choice was CN, which the Pentagon commenced phasing out of its arsenal on May 23, 1963.[23] CS is actually a talcum-like powder, not a gas, and some formulations of it were designed to persist environmentally for weeks or months. It is more potent than CN at the same concentrations, though CN takes effect more quickly. Unlike with CN, a wet cloth held over the nose and mouth does not impede the effects of CS. In the words of the US Army, within twenty seconds of CS exposure, affected individuals experience "severe burning sensation in the eyes with copious tears, coughing and difficulty breathing with tightness of chest. The eyes close involuntarily, the nose runs and moist skin stings."[24] US servicemen inadvertently exposed to large quantities of CS reported that it caused uncontrollable urination and defecation. A journalist who accidentally encountered CS used to clear a tunnel near Da Nang in 1966 said, "I felt as though my whole exposed skin area had been slashed with red-hot barbed wire." The skin later blistered with chemical burns, an effect worsened by sweat. "Next time, I will try hard not to sweat," he quipped.[25]

CS traversed civilian-military divides throughout the 1960s, as well as national borders. British colonial forces first deployed CS tactically in counterinsurgency policing theaters in Cyprus and British Guiana between 1958 and 1961, during the same period that the US military tested it. The first US civilian guidance on CS came from OPS in June 1963. OPS followed the British lead, while the Pentagon began its own CS testing and training. OPS initially noted that because it was stronger than CN, CS should "supplement" it and be used only "at advanced stages of rioting where CN has not been sufficiently effective" in open-air settings. And CS should replace the lachrymator/emetic combination CN/DM.[26] OPS did not recommend the use of CS in confined spaces, with limited fresh air. Soon, Britain was distributing CS to its colonial police forces around the world and to other countries. By April 1965, the US State Department calculated, based on OPS and British sales records, that fifty-four other countries possessed CS.[27] Around the same time that the Pentagon adopted CS, British scientists developed another lachrymatory agent, CR, even more powerful and persistent than CS. Planned for use in Northern Ireland, initial field testing of CR was supposed to use volunteers from the Hong Kong police, until journalists sounded an alarm.[28] The United States and Britain, close allies and competitors, engaged in a geographically dispersed, iterative, step-by-step escalation of the lethality of their nonlethal weapons. Yet most of the professional debate over such agents concerned how enemy forces would react. Would CS use by the United States spur Chinese or Soviet use of lethal and expressly banned chemical weapons? The answer turned out to be no.

White House Actions and Reactions

In March 1965, the Johnson administration was still riding the crest of its electoral success the previous November when it faced a crisis that rattled public perceptions of what it was doing in South Vietnam. News stories claimed that "gases," which seemed uncomfortably close to banned chemical weapons, were being used in Indochina. Blaming misleading enemy propaganda, officials tried to dampen the outcry by saying that the gas in question was merely "tear gas" and, as such, a "riot control agent."

The controversy had a long prehistory. The United States Senate did not ratify the Geneva Protocol of 1925, which outlawed the use of asphyxiating or otherwise poisonous gases after World War I. Still, the United States claimed to adhere to it because of its "general abhorrence of 'inhuman' forms of warfare."[29] The State Department maintained, however, that the Geneva Protocol did not cover "riot control agents." To do so, officials used a range of other terminology, including "nonlethal," "irritating," and "temporary," to describe why riot control agents were exempt. None of these terms, however, appeared in the Protocol's language. In fact, the Protocol did not detail exceptions, though US delegates insisted in discussions prior to its issuance that lachrymatory agents (though not CS, which had yet to be invented) were acceptable for police use to apprehend criminals.[30] Although US police did not, in fact, yet use CS domestically, to justify using CS in South Vietnam, Secretary of Defense Robert McNamara falsely claimed that such agents were employed by law enforcement in the United States for riot control.[31].

News dispatches on March 22 and 23, 1965, alerted the American public to the use of chemical agents in South Vietnam.[32] To avoid exploding incendiary devices where guerrillas and civilians "intermingle," and thus to protect civilians, the Pentagon stated, chemical weapons had been employed tactically, as advocated in the military literature.[33] McGeorge Bundy clarified to Johnson, who was desperate for accurate information in response to the news stories, that there had been three deployments of "riot-control gases." In two of these cases, South Vietnamese troops had used them to rescue US advisors (not Vietnamese civilians), he reported, and the agents in question were "precisely analogous to those used by police forces all over the world."[34] The initial news reports did not name any agents but suggested that a nausea-inciting compound along with a tear gas had been used. In actuality, these had not been the first uses of these agents in combat operations in South Vietnam. South Vietnamese forces had already used CS in December 1964, but General William Westmoreland quietly greenlighted its use by US forces in February 1965.[35]

In response to the "international furor" over what many perceived to be a violation of the long-standing international prohibition of chemical weapons, Secretary of State Dean Rusk held a press conference. He noted that no violation of the Geneva Protocol had occurred because, "We are talking about a gas which has been commonly adopted by the police forces of the world as riot control agents—gases that are available commercially and have been used on many occasions, some in this country and on many occasions in other countries." Police favored these weapons, Rusk argued, because officers "would like to be able to use the minimum force that is required for the maintenance of law and order." He confirmed that an "admixture" (i.e., CN/DM) had been deployed on one occasion. He also implied that some "gases" remained in the South Vietnamese arsenal from "the French days out there."[36] But the shelf-life of French-supplied lachrymatory agents would have long expired by 1965. Humid atmospheric conditions, like those prevalent in Southeast Asia, shortened the time before expiration of chemical munitions. Any recently used effective agents had to be newer. Off the record, Lyndon Johnson told a friendly syndicated columnist, Drew Pearson, that some of the gas was of US origin. He projected a modest, avuncular image, telling Pearson, "I have said I'd be appropriate and fitting and measured," and "I'm being just as measured as I know how."[37]

Johnson weighed in publicly on the issue after a week, even though his permission had neither been sought nor needed for the gas to be used.[38] His discussion conflated different agents to imply that all were equally safe and all were in law-enforcement use. The specialists' usage, calling CS simply "riot control agent" rather than *a* riot control agent, eased the conflation. Johnson claimed that the type of gas used in South Vietnam was common and had been used recently at home. There was thus, he assured the press, no cause for alarm.[39] Earlier, Johnson had declared to Pearson of the munitions in question, "Every police chief in the United States has them." He noted that US Army riot-control units had tear gas. Saigon's police did too. That was true; OPS supplied it to them. "When you start rioting and tearing over the embassy and coming in, rather than shooting people, you give them something that'll upset their stomach or make their eyes blink," he observed. "It's the same kind of gas Chief Murray's got right here" in Washington, DC, he added. "If the Negroes started moving in [on] the White House," the police would use it on them.[40]

Johnson thus saw CS as a tool of racialized social control prior to its widespread deployment for that purpose domestically. CN was the chemical agent of choice. CS was not in police arsenals in 1965, and CN/DM was rare. Neither Rex Applegate nor Raymond Momboisse, two prominent riot-control experts, had recommended CS prior to that point, preferring CN or simple obscuring smoke.[41] National Guard and Army units had used CS in 1964 in Cambridge, Maryland, and in 1962 in Oxford, Mississippi, respectively, to break up angry, racially segregated crowds.[42] During the 1964 unrest in Rochester, New York, municipal police had used CN. Just a few weeks prior to the revelations about gas use in South Vietnam, police attacked civil-rights protesters in Alabama with truncheons and CN grenades on what was called "Bloody Sunday," even firing them into a nearby public housing project where movement leaders boarded with Black residents.

Tear gas, its advocates already insisted, had to be used reluctantly against people who arrayed themselves momentarily against social order, but it would not kill them as bullets would. The modesty of the discourse of "tear gas," however, belied its tactical application. This recognition of human vulnerability, which called for tear gas, also misrecognized the reasons for political protest where police and military forces used it, which were mass political vulnerability and persistent individualized risk of death at the state's hands.

The revelation about US soldiers' use of tear gas in South Vietnam occurred at a time when the administration had reason to be guarded. Rolling Thunder, the bombing campaign against North Vietnam, had commenced only three weeks earlier, and the war was also widening on the ground. The way top officials, including Johnson, discussed the introduction of tear gas in South Vietnam, both conflating multiple different chemicals and foregrounding human fragility, made US policy toward Vietnam seem other than it was.[43]

Johnson explained that tear gas "is a standard item in the South Vietnamese military forces." Moreover, it could be obtained "from open stocks in this country just like you order something out of a Sears Roebuck catalog." He was referring to the Federal Laboratories catalog, which Secretary of Defense McNamara had displayed to reporters in a background briefing. This firm was the chief supplier of tear gas to the governments around the world receiving US police assistance. From the catalog, Johnson suggested, "any of you can order it."[44] A few years later, a professor of bio-chemistry at University of California Berkeley attempted to obtain CS for experimental testing but was unable to do so.[45] It was impossible to buy it on the open market. Nor could members of the public easily obtain the newest chemical weapon on the market, Chemical Mace, a liquid form of CN in a pressurized canister.[46]

CS was far more effective than CN or CN/DM, according to military scientists. Its short-term terror-producing effects derived from the sensation of suffocation it caused, indicating how promising its use in confined spaces would be. In an exquisite act of redefinition that instrumentalized and adapted ostensibly neutral scientific findings to match tactical purposes, the Army Medical Research Laboratory noted that because CS did not affect the central nervous system, no psychological effects could be attributed to it. Irritation itself induced flight responses. Any "irritant agent" would have this physical effect. And because CS was less toxic at the same concentration than CN, it was advisable to use it in confined spaces, where it would be less hazardous than CN.[47] This advice reversed earlier OPS recommendations to avoid using it against people in confined areas.

Engineers soon developed a variety of delivery systems and new formulations of CS in the attempt to overcome the vagaries of environmental conditions. Deploying CS to "flush" people from bunkers and tunnels appeared to be its optimal use. In March 1965, Secretary of State Rusk asserted that there would not be wider use of gas after the initial operations, because it was ineffective. "When the wind blew it away it was dissipated. It didn't achieve the purpose." If further use occurred, it would be "only in those situations involving riot control or situations analogous to riot control."[48] Why Johnson suggested Sears as a possible source of CS is unknown, but his doing so may have been what inspired the Pentagon's Project PROVOST (Priority Research and Development Objectives for Vietnam Operations Support) to develop the M-106 Mity Mite to deliver it. A modified insecticide blower manufactured by Buffalo Turbine Agricultural Equipment based on a model sold by Sears, Mity Mite could pump a total of ten pounds of CS fog in four minutes over distances up to five hundred feet, filling an enclosed space with the chemical at a rate of up to fifty feet per minute.[49] US soldiers used the backpack-mounted Mity Mite, or devices like it, to force people out of hiding in South Vietnam, where CS grenades fell short in the stagnant air of underground warrens. The Kerner Commission obtained the Mity Mite's specifications in its research, but because it was designed for use in cramped spaces like tunnels, not windswept streets, parks, and plazas, it was suboptimal for riot control. Yet that did not keep cops from later experimenting with it, or similar contraptions, on crowds at home.[50]

Several months after the newspaper revelations, at a Tuesday Lunch meeting in September 1965, the Johnson administration finalized its position on the military use of CS in South Vietnam. General Westmoreland had asked for confirmation that CN and CS were acceptable (though technically CN had been already phased out). Johnson's top science advisor pushed to ban CS from military use.[51] McNamara overruled him, despite having previously argued against both CN and CS: "The agents would be used primarily to clear tunnels, caves, and underground shelters in cases where their use will lead to far fewer casualties and less loss of life than would the combat alternatives which involve high explosive or flame munitions. Of particular importance would be the reduction in casualties to civilians who are inevitably mingled with hostile military elements as the result of VC tactics."[52] Bundy and Rusk agreed. Bundy noted that "even the *New York Times* is resoundingly with us on this." No presidential approval for the use of the agents would be needed, as had been the case under Eisenhower.[53] Johnson approved the policy, allowing combat use of CS in Vietnam.[54]

At this point a shift in terminology seemed useful. Bundy, who had referred to riot control agent in recent months, now thought tear gas the best term for CS, and White House Press Secretary Bill Moyers observed that anybody "would prefer to cry from tear gas rather than be killed by hand grenades."[55]

Blanketing South Vietnam

After 1965 the US military used CS in massive quantities in South Vietnam. The Pentagon spent $2.4 and $2.9 million, respectively, on riot control agents in 1963 and 1964. Over the next four years, after 1965's dip in spending on these while protocols and public rationales were devised, purchases increased dramatically. In 1966, spending on them was $16.8 million. It increased only slightly the next year, but in 1968 and 1969, it was $66.3 and $80.5 million, respectively.[56] By August 1967, four US manufacturers were producing 275,000 pounds of CS each month, at a price of $4.00/pound.[57]

One of the first large-scale tests of CS in South Vietnam was Operation Birmingham in April 1966. As an experiment with tear gas, this appellation invoked anti-Black violence. In the words of an after-action report, the operation deployed "an unprecedented amount of riot control agent." Contemporaneous news stories put the figure at 6,500 pounds.[58] In actuality, the total was 24,000 pounds, all dropped from dual-rotor Chinook helicopters, mostly in drums filled with 80 pounds of CS, whose fuse was lit individually before being dropped. Air strikes, artillery, "and/or infantry attacks" followed within ten minutes of the CS drop. The point was to test this delivery method to see whether it effectively incapacitated "VC," in order to kill them more easily with conventional weapons. "In two CS attacks followed up by ground forces, no VC were found in the target areas," the report noted, but it concluded nevertheless: "Massive CS attacks on suspected or known enemy locations are feasible and practical. The application of CS should be approximately 30 drums (2,400 pounds) per square kilometer of target area. This munition is effective for terrain contamination and creates an effective cloud that drifts with the wind."[59] Joseph Coates, the Institute for Defense Analyses expert on nonlethal weapons, wrote, perhaps with resignation regarding what he already knew to be true, "If nonlethal weapons are used to augment lethal tactics or strategy, the principal value of the nonlethal weapons may be lost."[60] After Operation Birmingham's proof of concept, further experiments yielded as many as thirty delivery methods, including an air compressor that could be mounted to a truck or a helicopter.[61] The original formulation of CS caused contamination lasting up to seventy-two hours, but scientists developed longer-lasting CS-1 and the more persistent, water-resistant CS-2, which could contaminate terrain for weeks or months at a time.

In 1969, Matthew Meselson, a Harvard biology professor, reported the results of his research on chemical weapons used in Southeast Asia. By then, he calculated, 13,736,000 pounds of CS had been dropped on South Vietnam, an amount equivalent to a blanketing layer 80,000 square miles in size, 14,000 square miles more than the country's total territory. Additionally, CS would have been used repeatedly in some areas and combined with defoliants. It leached into soil and ground water. The United States effectively teargassed the entire country, and then some.[62]

The primary use of CS in South Vietnam had little to do with riot control. Operation Birmingham and other tests showed that CS would cling to moist jungle foliage, irritating the skin of anyone who touched it. Dense foliage did prevent its even dispersion, which called for its use in greater quantities. When US or South Vietnamese soldiers abandoned fortifications, they would often coat the interiors in CS to prevent anyone else from using them.

FIGURE 12. Lake Erie Chemical Advertisement: CN versus CS. *The Police Chief,* June and August 1968.

The Institute for Defense Analyses proposed corking tunnels and bunkers after they had been filled with CS, to prolong its persistence and render the spaces unusable.[63] Inventive grunts found that hidden caches of rice, corn, or salt could be rendered inedible, though technically not deadly, if mixed with CS powder at a ratio of 100:1.[64]

The wide deployment of CS in Vietnam outside riot control nonetheless came to justify its domestic deployment in riot control. "Things like tear gas, the CS that is being used in Vietnam, have a tendency to find their way into domestic use," one of Meselson's colleagues observed in a hearing on chemical weapons.[65] The circulation went both ways. "Recent experience with crowds, mobs, and riots in the United States has stimulated numerous studies of all aspects of their control. Developments in nonlethal weapons for this purpose have concentrated on exploiting the super tear agent CS," the Institute for Defense Analyses reported the following year. "Many of these developments are directly applicable to low-level combat in cities abroad."[66] By 1968, advertisements in *The Police Chief* were touting the advantages of CS over CN, illustrating how thoroughly CS could incapacitate its targets. Advertisements also cited the authority of the Kerner Commission on CS. Well into the 1970s, the LEAA continued funding Army research on "less-lethal" weapons, with Sagalyn as a consultant.[67]

For its part, OPS was centrally involved in creating travel-ready chemical technologies. From 1964 to 1969, AID was the largest buyer of commercial chemical munitions, which it distributed to countries receiving police assistance.[68] Dissatisfied with existing technologies, OPS issued technical specifications for a tear-gas grenade more suited to law enforcement than the existing military-grade weapons. Engineers with Maryland's Aircraft Armaments, Inc., developed the new multi-purpose grenade, based on OPS designs. This grenade became a favored riot-control weapon both at home and abroad. It was a versatile dispenser of tear gas that could be held in the hand, tossed, or launched from a shotgun. Its fuse length was variable, which also gave its users flexibility. It had a lengthy shelf-life, was cheap (initial cost was double the Army's standard grenades, but with the longer shelf-life, its amortized cost was lower), durable, and resistant to temperature fluctuations. Upon discharge, it did not pose a fire hazard, nor did its body produce sharp-edged fragments, like other tear-gas grenades. Multi-purpose grenades could disperse CN, CN mixed with dye, or CS.[69]

Top-ranking Johnson administration officials' claim that tear gas had already been in use in peace-keeping riot control domestically justified the use of CS in South Vietnam. Its massive combat deployment in South Vietnam, as well as its use elsewhere in riot control by aid-recipient police forces, then encouraged and enabled its use as an alternative to lethal force by professionalized police domestically. Its success in counterinsurgency in South Vietnam owed to its utility, it was originally argued, in the "intermingled" situation of guerrillas and civilians in a single location. Tear gas helped separate the two. The sensible law-enforcement approach, according to OPS, was to use tear gas similarly at home. In situations of domestic unrest, even as the Kerner Commission found explanations reliant on communist and subversive agitation to be incorrect, the need to separate the hardcore rioter from the opportunist or the bystander remained central. CS answered this need because of its history in South Vietnam. Yet this history was not one simply of separating guerrillas from civilians, which Military Assistance Command Vietnam acknowledged was uncommon by early 1968.[70] Instead, it was used to contaminate land, intending to make areas impassable. It was used to create barriers, including at borders with Cambodia and Laos. And it was used to force both guerrillas and civilians out into the open, where they could more easily be killed or captured.

Blanketing American Streets

The Kerner Commission repudiated the guns-blazing riot-control response manifest in, among other locales, Newark and Detroit in 1967. The DOJ's adoption of the commission's recommendation on nonlethal weapons showed the state's malleability in response to the concerted pressure of social movements. After years of intransigence, state managers changed the response to protest about law-enforcement agencies' conduct. Yet the violence of US empire conditioned policing's shift toward nonlethal weapons. Rather than addressing the reasons for unrest, wide and indiscriminate use of CS simply made street-level social control even more palpable.

Given the go-ahead to deploy CS, the Army and National Guard began to use it in vast amounts domestically in 1968. For example, though 23,008 Army and 15,586 federalized National Guard soldiers participated in the control of unrest nationally in April 1968, after the assassination of Martin Luther King Jr., collectively, they fired only sixteen bullets. But they used 5,972 CS grenades. In comparison, the prior year in Newark alone, the National Guard had fired at least 10,414 bullets but used no CS.[71] The Washington, DC, Metropolitan Police Department used both CS and CN in April 1968. Having found that CS broke up crowds more rapidly, it ceased using CN after that. Under Provost Marshal Carl Turner, Military Police had stockpiled large amounts of tear gas in preparation for antiwar protests and sabotage aimed at military bases. In spring 1968, the White House attempted to procure CS for municipal police departments from Army stock, but the Army was unwilling to let much go. It possessed more spare bulk CS than grenades, which many police departments could not easily deliver.[72] But the National Guard could.

In May 1969, a National Guard helicopter doused Sproul Plaza on UC Berkeley's campus with CS during protests over the eviction of the People's Park occupiers. Operating according to mutual-aid procedures under an emergency declaration by Governor Ronald Reagan, 5,600 Guardsmen reinforced 791 police officers. Soldiers and police arrived armed with tear-gas grenades, as well as a backpack dispenser like the Mity Mite. Sheriff's deputies' conventional firearms, buckshot, and birdshot, injured 51 civilians and killed one.[73]

A helicopter dropped CS on New York's Attica Correctional Facility yard in 1971 during the uprising there. As in Vietnam, CS made targeting the incapacitated with gunfire easier. Bullets killed thirty-nine men in the chaos. Many were shot amid the CS clouds. State troopers also tossed the chemical calcium oxide, or quicklime, to subdue prisoners, which caused painful chemical burns.[74] Because it was not affected by the humid climate, Don Bordenkircher, OPS advisor to South Vietnam's prison system, favored quicklime over tear gas for controlling prisoners.[75]

With the use of tear gas in wide-open urban spaces, the ineffective targeting Rusk had lamented overseas was repeated at home. Attempts to prevent looting by creating a barrier cloud of CS in Baltimore in 1968, for example, failed because wind blew away the CS, which enveloped nearby residents.[76] This experience was typical. Bystanders and peaceful crowds in adjacent areas, along with residents, often found themselves choking on CS. The use of tear gas also influenced the gender composition of victims of state violence. Black men had been the most likely to be hit by police gunfire during earlier situations of unrest, but beginning in 1968, the victims of gas tended to include many Black women.

Counterinsurgent policing recommendations to use chemical munitions in Japan and the Philippines in the 1940s, and Latin America, including Puerto Rico, in the 1950s, antedated the domestic military use of these weapons.[77] Yet far from meeting the chaste expectations of liberal US law-enforcement professionals, the results of chemical weapons' use to suppress domestic unrest in 1968 in fact conformed to Army experience in Southeast Asia. Seymour Deitchman had warned Sagalyn in 1967 that nonlethal weapons "if used indiscriminately, will not do any better job of controlling violence or reducing resentment against 'police brutality' than the conventional billy club and pistol." The technical solution they offered was no substitute for training that mandated "discriminating" use.[78] Arnold and Louise Sagalyn drew attention to how other countries controlled unrest: extensive training in planning, operations, tactics, and specialized equipment at all personnel levels was required to do so effectively.[79] Yet even training was not enough, because the Army's domestic civil-disturbance training program SEADOC, for example, did not always distinguish between what Bertram Levine of the Community Relations Service called "vindictive and non-vindictive handling of specific stages of the control situation."[80]

REVERBERATIONS

Assiduous riot-control training and the adoption of nonlethal weapons did not lead to a decline in police killing of civilians. In fact, more civilians died at the hands of police in years after 1967 than before. From 1950 to 1967, the year Johnson appointed the Kerner Commission, police killed an average of 245 people annually. According to figures compiled at the time, from 1967 to 1973, police killed an average of 359 people annually.[81] What conditioned this paradoxical outcome? Nonlethal weapons were intended to be used in crowd control, to prevent political protest or more diffuse public expressions of anger from becoming destructive to people and property. The large-scale police adoption of CS in the United States followed from its use as a device to make killing easier in South Vietnam, far from the setting of crowd control. CS succeeded in making crowd-based, angry mass protest unpleasant. But the consequence was an increase in non–crowd-based political protest actions. These occurred alongside preemptive police attacks on radical political groups. As a result, although CS was supposed to prevent crowd-based violence, it came to be used in situations in which no crowds were present, just like in Vietnam, and was sometimes lethal, just like in Vietnam.

A review of the African American press is revealing: "tear gas" came to be used widely during the 1970s, and in a variety of situations other than "riot control." These uses contradicted what had been the best practices at the outset of the 1960s. After a decade of US experimentation in South Vietnam, warnings about the dangers of using chemicals in enclosed spaces, where they could asphyxiate and kill, were forgotten.

Police used gas against Black radical organizations across the country, including the Black Panther Party, Republic of New Africa, and MOVE. Gas tortured and incapacitated police targets, facilitating their capture in killing. In Detroit, for example, city and state officials "commended" police "restraint" after one of their own was shot in October 1970 while harassing Black people selling political literature: when fifteen people hid inside "a house described as a Black Panthers headquarters," three who refused to surrender faced "tear gas to flush them out." A few weeks later in Warren County, North Carolina, when teenage Black students protested their school board's cancellation of a dance and the postponement of student-government elections, two dozen highway patrolmen broke up the gathering with tear gas.

Soon, situations with no political angle saw the use of tear gas—or a political angle came to be added to the narrative after the deployment of tear gas. A suicidal "sniper" in Omaha, Nebraska, shot and killed a police officer in 1974 when he tried to enter a house in which the man was hiding. Meanwhile other, "combat-equipped" officers "hurled in canisters" of tear gas. These set the house on fire, and when a crowd gathered to protest, a police officer shot a young woman with his revolver. The crowd was not a target of the gas.

The same year three "armed Black [M]uslims" trying to elude the police hid in the studio of a radio station in Montgomery, Alabama, only to "be flushed out by . . . tear gas." An employee of the radio station, father of a supposed hostage, who exited the building peacefully, questioned the use of tear gas, but a US attorney praised the police. He brushed off the incident. In the father's eyes, the prosecutor had treated it "like hunting a bunch of niggers."

While searching for a suspect in a police officer's death in July 1974, Pittsburgh, Pennsylvania, officers ransacked a number of apartments, stealing money, eating food, smashing television screens, kicking holes in walls, and firing tear gas "without warning."

A suicidal "former mental patient" in Atlanta, Georgia, armed with a screwdriver, faced tear gas after he refused to leave his sister's house in March 1978.

Officers did not always need to become involved, though, for tear gas to be deployed: a Little Rock, Arkansas, bank installed "a new gas device" to prevent robberies, but when three "men dressed as women" robbed the bank, the device's activation failed to prevent their getaway.[82]

The violence of tear gas intended to preempt, prevent, retard, stanch, stem, and suppress other forms of violence that were in the weapons' conceptualization necessarily worse. These weapons aimed to preclude an expected immediate future of awful violence against property through less-awful violence against people. They were spectacular, showing force without killing crowd members. In protest situations to the present, this use persists, with crowd members almost never killed in the United States. The domestic introduction of CS for police allowed this shift. But gas weapons also would be used in distinctly nonspectacular ways. The police killings that occurred after 1967 tended to be outside the context of mass protest or crowds.[83] The use of nonlethal weapons beyond crowd control was licensed by their use in this way in Vietnam to force suspects from confined spaces. In turn, this use, in conjunction with traditional police arms, aided and abetted the continually rising levels of killing by police.

After 1968, social-movement repertoires shifted. Planned mass protests occurred during the first years of the Nixon administration, including gatherings of hundreds of thousands in Washington, DC. But the type of spontaneous, angry protests that led police to engulf crowds in tear gas became less common, especially in big cities. Instead, clandestine political activity grew more common. At the same time, the ranks of militants were decimated through legal and extralegal repression. Divisions and political factionalism led to exhaustion and fear, often sown by informants working for the FBI or other security agencies. At the same time, the state assented to some radical demands under Nixon.[84]

From wildcat strikes and sabotage to bombings and airplane hijackings, protest tactics shifted alongside police tactics. There was a move away from crowd-led unrest toward political actions that officials described in terms of disparate and apolitical criminality, and later "terrorism." In inchoate, tentative, experimental fashion, at the same time, security experts developed, tested, and stumbled into new modalities of policing, transforming the object of control from the criminal act, approached ex post facto, to the crime-inducing situation, approached preemptively. Police would now play an active role in controlling or choreographing the outcome of perceived crime-inducing situations, which to the policed in racially segregated, resource-deprived zones were often indistinguishable from everyday life.[85] If, as the Kerner Commission outlined, police actions could be liable to worsen the crime-inducing situation of crowd and mob action, control through dispersal and other means became paramount, forestalling destructive violence. Novel technologies enabled this reconfigured temporality, but they also legitimized it, leading to programmatic rather than discretionary reliance on weapons-based solutions to potentially crime-inducing situations. The result over the following decades was pre-judicial and prejudicial killing of many more people, disproportionately Black people, at the hands of security forces. Tear gas before riots was better than pistol fire after they had begun. But the ability to preempt crime or unrest with nonlethal weapons meant that police could treat political dissent as incipient rioting. Police tactics and technologies transformed political contention into risk management.

Categorical spatial distinctions—foreign/domestic, periphery/metropole—eroded in this context. Counterinsurgent knowledge evidenced, but also produced, this erosion through its comparative compulsion and its globe-spanning circuitry of expertise. The erosion registered in policing tactics domestically as a reshuffling or fracturing of traditional temporalities of policing. Collapse of spatial distance, then, produced a collapse of temporal distance. Now, counterinsurgency meant that the anticipation, prevention, and punishment of crime combined. The conjuncture midwifed through counterinsurgent prediction of and reaction to 1960s political-racial upheavals on a global scale was one in which the "temporal-hinge" of police between prevention and punishment closed.[86] The two came to coincide: police doctrine, rather than simply police discretion, as tradition had it, lurched toward meting out death penalties and "nonlethal" corporal punishments in the streets, rather than after criminal conviction. New technologies allowed, enabled, and vouchsafed this temporal shift. Along the continuum from crime-inducing situation to criminal act, investigation, arrest, further investigation, indictment, prosecution, trial, sentencing, and punishment, police activity came to subsume activities previously delegated to other aspects of the criminal justice system. Despite fears of some police officers and concerned citizens that nonlethal weapons would effectively disarm cops, they never replaced pistols, rifles, and shotguns; rather they supplemented them.

. . .

In 1969, President Nixon committed to a policy of no first use of chemical weapons. But CS was excluded. Six years later, however, President Gerald Ford responded to antiwar sentiment with an executive order banning the military use of "riot control agents" and herbicides in combat, except under special circumstances. Then, in 1993, the Chemical Warfare Convention superseded the Geneva Protocol to outlaw chemical weapons in war. The United States ratified the ban in 1997. This agreement did not cover domestic law-enforcement use of "riot control agents," however. As a result, the US military continues to uphold Ford's executive order today, while civilian law enforcement remained unfettered, still able to use CS when and where officers see fit.

If the circulation of counterinsurgent knowledge across borders appears to have proceeded easily, speedily, and with little modification needed or compelled—because of the isomorphism of social settings that Engle introduced in testimony to the Kerner Commission—this appearance may owe more to the situation of the present than to that of the 1960s. The free flow of policy expertise on a model of deregulated financial capital is a well-propagated nostrum today, despite its frequent mismatch with reality. Modular penal and policing practices, liberated to travel freely in order to shackle, encage, maim, and kill with alacrity—that is the conjunction of the day. Nonetheless, the current era of seemingly effortless circulation of security practices would have been impossible without the prior difficult labors, compulsive comparativism, threat inflation, and endless reassurances of the overcoming of future risks that constructed the institutions of law and order charted here.

EIGHT

Order Maintenance and the Genealogy of SWAT

AMONG STUDENTS OF POLICING, a story about the invention of the Special Weapons and Tactics (SWAT) unit in Los Angeles is repeated often. Daryl Gates sought advice on dealing with Black radical movements from US marines at Camp Pendleton near San Diego and the Naval Reserve Armory at Chavez Ravine in Los Angeles. Gates had been field commander of the LAPD during the Watts rebellion in 1965 and became police chief in 1978, serving into the mid-1990s. The threats he diagnosed in the late 1960s required that he revolutionize policing: "the streets of America's cities had become a foreign territory," and police were facing a spectrum of "disorder" from "urban riots" to "civil rights actions, sit downs, and student uprisings and protests of every kind." After consulting with marines and studying counterinsurgency theory, Gates created SWAT, believing existing methods of dealing with Black protest were inadequate.[1]

Though widely accepted, this account leaves out more than it reveals, however. The LAPD was already acting transnationally, but SWAT also drew on longstanding local policing ideas. Despite Gates's desire to change LAPD tactics, SWAT was not his agency's initial encounter with counterinsurgent knowledge.[2] Counterinsurgency was a police project, and SWAT represented less the militarization of that project than the distillation of its core commitment to maintaining order. This labor-intensive commitment was one already rehearsed frequently in Los Angeles. In turn, SWAT was one particularly capital-intensive iteration of the LAPD's consistent effort to undermine political opposition and agitation focused on revealing the racist core of policing. In Los Angeles, the attack on the police force's political antagonists had two prongs: surveillance and intelligence collection by the Law Enforcement Intelligence Unit and the Public Disorder Intelligence Division, and high-profile, aggressive SWAT operations like a 1969 assault on the Black Panthers. Fertilized locally, SWAT blended local policing practices and ideas, indigenous to the LAPD, into the already shifting transnational field of policing.

Deployed daily across the United States today—clad in body armor and helmets, carrying semi-automatic rifles, and riding in mine-resistant trucks— "paramilitary" SWAT teams symbolize the domestic repercussions of overseas warfare to many citizens, the infiltration of tools of state violence designed for overseas use onto American streets.[3] As US military tactics have come to rely more heavily on rapid-response special operations in the search for criminal suspects, SWAT replicates this image.

Gates himself constructed a transnational genesis story about the 1960s in his effort to legitimize SWAT in the 1990s, just as new federal subventions for local police forces were becoming available in the Democratic Party's second attempt to craft a crime-fighting federalism under President Bill Clinton. The US war in Vietnam was key to SWAT's branding. In 1991, after the first Gulf War, the country seemed finally to have kicked the so-called Vietnam Syndrome, which had made that war unmentionable. By tying SWAT to Vietnam, Gates set a mold that several subsequent tough-on-crime figures would adopt, designating himself as a maverick voice in law enforcement. The extraterritorial has often been the crucible in which this mold is cast. Yet at the time Gates turned to counterinsurgency theory, the field was in flux. His citations of the literature betrayed an ignorance of its leading edges. The transnational network of police-led counterinsurgency that SWAT supposedly realized already existed. Further, his particular deployment of the extraterritorial to find new ways to manage protests against racism shed the sense that US action in Vietnam was already a distended racializing project. Gates misrepresented what the United States was doing overseas—stabilizing racial order on a global scale through policing—as he localized it through SWAT.

Gates cultivated the image of a rebel. He believed that forming the first SWAT team was a radical act, subverting existing paradigms, even though it would have been impossible without LEAA funding and technology transfers.[4] His "gutty little ragtag outfit" was formed "without official authorization." His men "began reading everything we could get our hands on concerning guerrilla warfare." Yet "nobody" among the LAPD's brass "seemed interested in our pursuits." When Gates's squad "traded expertise" with marines stationed nearby, LAPD leaders were "offended," and his officers were "banished from everyday ... circles," forced to operate in secret and train in distant locations. With no budgetary support, "they cannibalized weapons they picked up off the streets." Gates had no choice but to use clandestine, unauthorized tactics to transform policing.[5]

This air of rebellion against entrenched police bureaucracies would prove valuable as Gates commenced his truly innovative work, which was not the invention of SWAT but rather its marketing and distribution. His memoir and other publications, lectures, interviews, and a radio call-in program built a platform. Most lucrative was his consultancy with a video-game company in the 1990s for the "Police Quest" series of games, which adopted the moniker "SWAT" in their subtitles. Although Gates ended his career as chief of the LAPD ignominiously, with scandal after scandal, he shaped an archetype that subsequent municipal police chiefs would embody. Many law-enforcement leaders, from August Vollmer on, had traveled widely to disseminate their expertise. Gates, in an incipient era of fast policy, became the top cop who debuted policy for the sake of its transfer.[6] Efficacy in its place of origin was a secondary concern. Administrative reorganization was a medium of his politics. After him came a generation of police celebrities in this mold, including William Bratton, Ray Kelly, Bernard Kerik, Gerry McCarthy, and others.

Policing in the United States has oscillated between expansion and contraction of police responsibilities beyond the domain of crime control. During the 1960s, a dispute arose among police professionalizers over whether policing should treat "order" as its ultimate goal. Some liberal experts favored entrusting police with the task of crime prevention through social services. In contrast, Gates's own mentor, William H. Parker, initiated a discourse of order maintenance in the 1950s, a proactive reconfiguration of the terms of policing as social control that would not violate civil rights law. The LAPD was already a transnational organization, and its officers traveled overseas in their commitment to order maintenance. In later decades, maintaining order became the dominant ethos and tactical disposition in urban policing. SWAT was symptom and expression of this reformatting of policing, not its cause or an anomaly, and it abutted the scandalous racist violence that subsequently marked the LAPD under Gates's tempestuous leadership.

"EFFECT, NOT CAUSES"

In 1923, the mayor of Los Angeles, Republican George Cryer, hired August Vollmer to lead his police force. The LAPD was supposed to be one of the first big-city forces to rein in corruption by creating new training and lines of command based on Vollmer's model. But entrenched resistance to reform stymied Vollmer's efforts.[7] Graft was too lucrative. He did manage to create a mobile rapid-response unit of elite crime-fighting officers, based on his experience with analogous counterguerrilla units in the Philippines.[8] When administrative reform came to the city, it drew more on O. W. Wilson than on Vollmer, repudiating the social-services model of police that the latter had once advocated. Its leader was William H. Parker III, an ambitious South Dakota–born cop. Alongside Arnold Sagalyn and Wilson, Parker worked to modernize and democratize the German police after World War II.[9] His grandfather, he claimed, had been "a colorful frontier law enforcement officer" (he had in fact been a US attorney and was elected to Congress),[10] but Parker's own career with the LAPD, beginning in 1927 and ending upon his death in 1966, can scarcely be called colorful. He was a stern, serious, moralistic man, whose hobbyhorse was standardization. Parkerism was proceduralism. The police procedural crime drama, a staple of US television, was a Parker creation. With de facto oversight of the 1950s television series *Dragnet,* Parker disseminated his vision of professionalized policing across the United States.

J. Edgar Hoover did not get along with many professionalizers, Parker included. Parker's flair for public relations and desire to create travel-ready models of policing, which his protégé Daryl Gates perfected with SWAT, represented an implicit challenge to Hoover's hegemony. Parker pursued organized crime. Hoover demurred. The abstemious Hoover did not like cops he considered drunks, and he accused Parker of overindulging.[11] The FBI's reluctance to share intelligence exacerbated Parker's difficulties with Hoover. A Parker subordinate responded by creating a rival intelligence-sharing network of law-enforcement agencies, the Law Enforcement Intelligence Unit.[12] But it was less Parker's habits, political orientation, or identification of scourges—like Hoover, he was a rigorous anticommunist—than his interpretation of the police function that distinguished him from the FBI director. Hoover trod a tightrope, tautened by the global great-power struggle against communism, between the massive powers at his disposal and his cherished belief that law enforcement should not fall to federal agencies. Parker had a more austere vision of policing. For him it was clear that the police should not and could not engage in a maximalist program of social engineering. He defined police narrowly. There was much they could never do. The challenge was to reconfigure social and political expectations of police so that the institution, now professionalized, did not get pulled into domains where it had no business (or experience) engaging. Once the police force extended its task to other areas of social life, it was bound to fail, discrediting itself and hampering its core anticrime and countersubversion mission, which came down to maintaining order.

Social upheaval provided the testing ground for Parker's theory of police. Los Angeles had experienced its fair share, and after Parker became LAPD chief, episodes of violence against Mexican Americans by the LAPD besmirched his reputation and forced a wedge between the police and the city's judiciary. One politically consequential incident was a wild and brutal police beating of seven young Mexican American men in 1951. Cops dragged them from their homes to a station house early on Christmas morning, where over a hundred drunken officers attacked the arrestees. In 1952, calls for civilian oversight in response roiled the LAPD and threatened Parker's program of professionalization. At stake was its institutionalization of autonomy from external intervention. Only an offensive smear campaign against those who demanded revision of the city charter and other interventions to rein in the police, followed by modest punishment of some officers involved, protected Parker. Once the imbroglio began to wane, Parker crystallized his position on how the police department should deal with controversy. He applied the metaphor of the "thin blue line" to police. For a time, the LAPD produced its own didactic television program about policing under that name. In Parker's view, the police separated two competing camps, civilized society and "the forces of chaos and iniquity." The latter included "not only organized crime but also racial minority groups, dissidents, especially communists, and anyone who supported these groups, which for Parker meant anyone who criticized the police."[13]

Parker developed a rationale for order-maintenance policing that disdained any sort of social intervention beyond crime prevention or attenuation. Such declarations were common in the police professional literature at the time, but Parker expressed the necessary commitment to order with particular insight into emergent sources of disorder: not simply protest against racist policing but the ensuing reconfiguration of racial meaning and, in time, legal architecture that would unsettle the social baseline for police decision-making. He initially elaborated on this way of thinking in a speech on police-community relations given at a conference at Michigan State University. In various versions, his speech was later republished in *The Police Chief,* the LAPD's Daily Training Bulletin, and *The Journal of Criminal Law, Criminology, and Police Science.* It was thus addressed to fellow police executives across the country and internationally, internally to Parker's officers, and to scholars.[14] The speech covered several topics. It discussed professionalization at length, but its main message actually belied its title, "The Police Role in Community Relations." Parker's position was that police-community relations should be minimized, if their extension meant involvement of police in affairs unrelated directly to the suppression of crime. Parker referred to the threat of nuclear holocaust that dramatized the Cold War. But he did not see the Cold War as an imposition on the common people from above. "Rather, the reverse is true," he argued. "Conflict begins not between nations or blocks [sic] of nations, but between men." Statesmen would not solve conflicts. Instead, the solution "will be found at the everyday level of social intercourse—in our homes, or on our streets, and in our individual consciences." This line of thinking was familiar. It underwrote all manner of litmus tests to tally loyalties, the insinuation of the first line of defense into everyday life, and even General Maxwell Taylor's call for a flexible response. "Community relations problems" were "a vital issue—a question of human weaknesses and society's failure to control that weakness." Remedying human weakness and "imperfection" was, however, impossible. "*Control,* not *correction,* is the key," he said. "Our job is to apply emergency treatment to society's surface wounds. We deal with effect, not causes."[15]

Racial desegregation compelled police to redefine their vocation carefully. Parker suggested that "hate" did not drive people's decisions. Habit did. The police themselves created habitual routines, including by preventing violence among mutually intolerant groups. Racial segregation, in his view, constituted peace, because it was "enforced order," even among enemies. Legal decisions that upset this order might have a salutary goal, given that segregation did "relegate some groups to second-class citizenship," but the "gentleman's agreements" and "intolerant" ideas that segregated the races would "never be eliminated so long as *conflict* keeps alive the beliefs that created them." As a result, a focus on social conflict itself, not the beliefs inciting it, was key: "We have not yet learned to control what men believe, but we can control what men do. I do not deny for a moment that the final solution is the perfection of human conscience. But in the interim, and it may be a long interim, we must have order." We must have order, he railed. Police could not control what was in people's minds. But they could constrain the "results of such beliefs."

In this statement, Parker identified a crucial practical departure from what would soon become dominant thinking on crime and its curtailment. Even if it were true that socioeconomic conditions led to crime, he held, police officers could not intervene to reshape them. All police could do was "repress" offenses or arrest perpetrators after the fact. Parker further elaborated a distinction between crime prevention and crime repression. Repression entailed police activities to "discourage" crime, whereas prevention entailed activities beyond policing per se.[16] Ideas about the social power of economic deprivation were coming into vogue at this time. These inchoate notions both relied on and informed social science to explain crime as much as revolution. The idea that ameliorating poverty might pacify the restive informed counterinsurgency. Less in refutation of this idea than as a practical response, Parker preemptively riposted that he would empower police to do whatever was necessary to maintain social order. "Root causes" were not on his agenda. To change root causes took too long. Police had to act quickly.

Parker did not shy away from addressing race. In contrast to many articles in *The Police Chief* in the 1950s, as public criticism of policing was increasing, he discussed the issue explicitly, without recourse to elaborate euphemisms. Yet his proposals did not outline a revanchist or recrudescent form of racism. He tentatively offered a flexible, debiologized race-thinking that prefigured future elaborations of racial liberalism. Certainly, LAPD officers were outwardly racist, and Parker has long been criticized for his own bigoted views and rumored links to the John Birch Society. Yet his statement contained a roadmap for order-maintenance policing recognizing no inherent racial inferiority that would nevertheless maintain racial hierarchy. He was explicit, reiterating the distinction between cause and effect:

> There is no inherent physical or mental weakness in any racial stock which tends it toward crime. But—and this is a "but" which must be borne constantly in mind—*police field deployment is not social agency activity.* In deploying to suppress crime, the police are not interested in why a certain group tends toward crime, they are interested in maintaining order. The fact that the group would not be a crime problem under different socio-economic conditions and might not be a crime problem tomorrow, does not alter today's tactical necessities. Police deployment is concerned with effect, not cause.

In maintaining order, the "unscientific breakdowns" of "Negro, Mexican, and Anglo-Saxon" were a "useful fiction," he argued. "The demand that the police cease to consider race, color, and creed is an unrealistic demand. *Identification is a police tool, not a police attitude.*" If the order that resulted retained its racial inequalities, the explanation was not to be found in the proclivities of the officer but in a panoply of social causes beyond his professional reach. After all, we have not yet learned to control what men believe.

Historians have been able to study Parker and Gates because they tried to shape how they would be remembered, but the risk is obscuring the larger transformations in which the LAPD was embedded, including the advance of civil rights and the linked procedural revolution in criminal law enforcement that attended the collapse of vagrancy law.[17] The LAPD at various points resisted and advanced professionalizing reforms, swaying with and against the offshore winds of US empire. What kept the LAPD grounded was its commitment to maintaining order. The narratives Parker and Gates crafted about their own fearlessness, independence, and ingenuity hid the constraints they faced. Social protest and focused legal activism challenged the LAPD, which responded through capital-intensive professionalizing reforms, intense policing of its political antagonists, and the rescripting of its racializing activities as race-independent order maintenance.

AMERICAN STREETS, FOREIGN TERRITORY

In his account of the origins of SWAT, Gates did not invoke the LAPD's actual transnational, Cold War connections. These were both more extensive than he revealed and less militaristic—because Engle's OPS facilitated them. Nor did he embed SWAT in Parker's demand for the maintenance of order. Yet both mattered, and each nourished the other. In Gates's memoir, his career proceeded as follows: chapter 7 of his life was "Watts," the next was "SWAT." A rebellion of Black people against police abuse, economic exploitation, and social marginalization demanded, in his self-aggrandizing narration, a revolutionary response of his own. He originally named his specialized squad the Special Weapons Attack Team. A colleague rejected the name's bellicosity. Gates rechristened it the Special Weapons and Tactics team or SWAT, retaining the implicit violence of the acronym, which would make Gates famous. Acronyms like it proliferated. In Los Angeles, there was also the special gang squad CRASH, or Community Resources Against Street Hoodlums, originally named TRASH, with the T standing for Total. Gates later invented DARE, or Drug Abuse Resistance Education. In Detroit, STRESS emerged: Stop The Robberies, Enjoy Safe Streets. These police initiatives were marked by wastefulness, abuse, and ineffectiveness.

SWAT's early history consisted of a series of shoot-outs, accompanied by copious clouds of CS, with the Black Panther Party and the Symbionese Liberation Army. In 1967, LAPD Chief Tom Reddin addressed the IACP at its annual meeting in Kansas City. Reliance on nonlethal weapons, especially zany, untested ones then earning press coverage, was, he believed, a mistake. Police needed their guns.[18] So it would be with SWAT. In the December 1969 siege on the Black Panther Party headquarters at 41st and Central in Los Angeles, SWAT used tear gas to burn and choke eleven party members over the course of five hours. The nominal reason for the SWAT mission was to serve warrants and make arrests, but the Panthers expected police to attack their base and had fortified its walls. LAPD officers realized, as had soldiers in South Vietnam, that CS used on people inside fortified spaces could make targeting their bullets easier. They fired 5,000 rounds at the incapacitated Panthers, shooting three and grievously wounding two.[19]

There is no way to know what the marines told Gates, but we can infer it from the LAPD's 1968 "Model Civil Disturbance Control Plan."[20] Gates commanded the LAPD's Tactical Operations Planning Group, which developed this plan, drawing upon departmental regulations in effect since August 1966. The plan created a blueprint for easy sharing with other municipalities. Civil unrest was the focus, but the plan choreographed emergency response to a wide range of cataclysmic events, from major fires and industrial accidents to earthquakes. After a discussion of the SWAT concept, the manual offered the subheading "The Rioters Tactics," followed by a single terse phrase: "Principle is to 'know thy enemy.'" Yet in counterinsurgency, the "know thy enemy" approach—fighting guerrillas with guerrillas—had been the aspect of the Kennedy program that Robert Komer repudiated. Although clandestine operations still occurred, police had become the centerpiece of US counterinsurgency. Gates's plan also featured a 22-item list of suggested readings, which included texts such as *Mao Tse-Tung on Guerrilla Warfare*, *La Guerra de Guerrillas* by Che Guevara, and *The Art of War* by Sun Tzu. The list mixed revolutionary catechism with US military tactical manuals. Some of the texts were decades old, others relatively recent. Many articles and books that Gates recommended elaborated an outdated, masculinist pro-guerrilla notion, with its emphasis on "seek out and destroy."[21] To the credulous, this emphasis sounded like SWAT. Gates portrayed himself as cutting-edge, but when it came to counterinsurgent knowledge, he was behind the times. There was no need for him to have called upon the marines for this information on guerrilla warfare. Whether on a military base or in a public library, however, he would have encountered a literature structured, not by a distinction between domestic law enforcement and overseas war making, but by their blurring.

Even before SWAT's initiation, Gates honed his reputation as a law-enforcement guru who could provide many agencies with solutions based on his own experience, particularly in riot control. Soon after Watts rebelled, Gates became a jet-setting consultant for police executives. He traveled around the country and created doctrinal manuals, imparting his wisdom to multiple audiences. He became an advisor to the Kerner Commission, one of dozens of reviewers who offered comments on its recommendations. Produced for the Commission's use, the LAPD "Model Civil Disturbance Control Plan" was officially published the same month as the Kerner *Report,* helping to disseminate the SWAT concept.[22] Development of this LAPD plan was secret, but it landed in journalists' hands prior to publication anyway.[23] Separately, the IACP also published a popular manual on riot-control techniques authored by two other experts in 1968. Gates was one of three primary advisors, and Sagalyn was another, on this publication.[24]

Gates carried riot-control expertise from the City of Angels elsewhere, but he also insisted that the LAPD needed to reconfigure its modes of operation. SWAT was the vehicle. LAPD leaders had been certain of their officers' skill in riot control and prevention. Parker praised his "special division" of "shock troops" in 1964.[25] The LAPD refused federal assistance in the months before the Watts rebellion.[26] Afterwards, less certain of the LAPD's capabilities but still cocksure, Gates found his calling as an expert in the unconventional, evolving from "Watts" to "SWAT." Gates recalled that a surprise shooting of police officers responding to a routine call a month after the Watts rebellion confirmed what he suspected: "we were going to have to devise another method for dealing with snipers or barricaded criminals other than our usual indiscriminate shooting." Gates's own officers, some of them military veterans, drew on the experience of colleagues in Delano, California, an agricultural locale that had developed a specialized, rapid-response policing unit to manage protests and job actions by the United Farm Workers.[27] This precedent, combined with Gates's sense of urgency about tactical reform, resulted in SWAT. He initially described SWAT as "essentially infantry type units," before its branding coalesced as unique and specialized.[28] SWAT hybridized tactical thrusts: relying on both heavy weapons and CS; proclaiming the importance of avoiding indiscriminate gunfire but nonetheless using "highly-trained anti-sniper teams" to rain bullets on targets. Overwhelming firepower, not the sly and deceptive tactics of the guerrilla fighting guerrillas, ruled the day on the streets of Los Angeles. On Gates's own terms—"If anybody gets killed or injured, the operation's a failure"—SWAT was a disaster.[29]

But like much of the era's policing reform, its failure led to it being tried again.

Gates bastardized common reformist approaches to inflate his maverick reputation. SWAT's heavy armaments contradicted much of counterinsurgent policing thinking in the 1960s, which emphasized de-escalation, demilitarization, and minimal force. The IACP civil-disorder guidelines issued in the wake of the Kerner *Report* juxtaposed Gates's advocacy of SWAT with Sagalyn's advocacy of CS in consecutive appendices.[30] Sagalyn himself may have sparked Gates's own thinking on the utility of a specialized tactical unit beyond what the LAPD had already developed with its D-Platoon in 1966. Arnold and Louise Sagalyn had recommended the development of standing rapid-response forces financed by the federal government's highway fund at the state, rather than municipal, level. They were to be trained for riot control as well as many other unpredictable emergency tasks. The experience of other countries also was a useful model.[31]

More generally, SWAT was not as new as Gates claimed. Several other big-city police forces had developed specialized emergency units throughout the 1960s, including San Francisco, Chicago, New York, and Philadelphia. Boston's tactical police unit formed as early as 1962, and once the national vogue for SWAT began, this preexisting unit became the city's SWAT equivalent.[32] The professional literature analyzed and bolstered this trend of centrally controlled, capital-intensive police units.[33] OPS also promoted the creation or revamping of specialized tactical teams in other countries.[34] Rather than the LAPD, the FBI was training municipal SWAT units across the United States in the early 1970s, 456 of them by 1975.[35]

Gates innovated in the realm of branding. Extant specialized units in other locales, including Los Angeles County, did not much change their personnel or gear when they adopted names like SWAT over the course of the 1970s and after. But the brand and its reputation mattered. For example, Gates himself told reporters he would be happy to send his men to rescue US hostages in Iran in 1979. President Carter demurred. Undertaken by soldiers, the mission ultimately was a disastrous failure, but because Gates had offered assistance before it failed, SWAT's reputation emerged untarnished on the global stage, if also untested.[36] This reputation relied an origins story, a contrast of fearless impudence with existing hamstrung LAPD practice. It also required a contrast with mainstream orthodoxy so that SWAT might itself become a new mainstream orthodoxy. Gates lamented the LAPD's "usual indiscriminate shooting" and "bazookas" approach, but the new SWAT team struggled to shake old LAPD habits.[37] The flaw in the origins story was how Gates rendered SWAT the bearer of knowledge from beyond borders. In fact, thanks to OPS, a new orthodoxy centered on police reform was already circulating beyond borders, and passing through Los Angeles as well. In turn, OPS also facilitated the circulation of those LAPD habits abroad.

THE GLOBAL LAPD

The LAPD was woven into the global circuit of police reform, providing personnel and modeling tactics. Overall, compared to all other states, California supplied the greatest percentage of public safety advisors, particularly after 1965, the year of the Watts rebellion.[38] At its peak, OPS counted 135 advisors from California (30.7 percent), compared to 51 from Virginia (11.6 percent) and 22 from New York (5 percent).[39] Byron Engle visited Los Angeles multiple times for recruitment, including of Spanish-speaking LAPD officers. He enrolled Stanley Sheldon, Parker's head of publicity, an important figure for a chief obsessed with his public image. Sheldon was the LAPD's liaison to the production of *Dragnet,* ensuring it represented Parkerism properly. LAPD badge 714, used in the credits as the show's emblem, sat on his desk. Engle recognized the centrality of police public relations to professionalization, as well as its importance to the delicate balancing act of counterinsurgency. Hiring a leader in the field allowed advisors to instill public relations protocols in many other countries even before police departments at home adopted them. The original *Dragnet* series ended in 1959. That year, Sheldon became a public safety advisor initially focused on recruitment, later visiting Pakistan and Brazil.[40]

The LAPD celebrated its international involvement. Under IACP contract and with Sheldon's help, many foreign police officers observed the city's police and trained at nearby universities. The department's internal newsletter, *The Beat,* printed photographs in June 1966 of a retired detective in a rice paddy in South Vietnam while working with OPS, for example.[41] Foreign dignitaries from OPS-assisted countries occasionally visited the LAPD, among them Nguyen Cao Ky, the controversial Vietnamese vice president, who lauded the force's "professional standards." Ky elicited a vivid comparison of LAPD standards to those of other forces. Unlike in Los Angeles, police in San Francisco used tear gas during protests of his visit.[42] Impressed with LAPD standards, OPS sought to translate the complete run of the

LAPD Daily Training Bulletin, produced under Parker, for overseas circulation.[43] Parker approved the public safety program's overseas dissemination of his "scientific method" for determining personnel needs, and in late 1964, AID sent Parker to India as a police consultant.[44] LAPD training films on topics like foot patrol became integrated into overseas police assistance beginning in 1957.[45]

Beyond Engle's persuasiveness, another OPS recruitment strategy was to hire popular, well-known officers like Frank Walton, who might then get their colleagues to join. Like his mentor, Michigan State's Ralph Turner, Walton was one of several nationally prominent cops who became an overseas advisor. He had previously worn the LAPD badge for twenty-one years, rising to the rank of deputy chief.[46] After public safety work in Laos and the Philippines, Walton directed the program in South Vietnam from 1959 to 1961 and again from 1969 to 1971. The author of several key planning and guidance documents for police and prisons in Vietnam, Walton had previously published in the professional policing literature on "selective distribution" of patrol, based on research in Los Angeles. He built explicitly on O. W. Wilson's doctrines. The Crime Commission echoed and refined Walton's recommendation of preemptive police patrol based on continuous monitoring of crime data and localized trends, which became common practice.[47]

As war intensified in Southeast Asia, Walton acted like a travel agent, encouraging current and former LAPD officers to take all-expenses-paid trips across the Pacific for the Agency for International Development. One of Walton's frequent correspondents was William W. Herrmann, a former LAPD detective with a PhD in public administration. Herrmann reinvented himself as a social scientist and counterinsurgency expert, working for the Institute for Defense Analyses, RAND, and its spin-off System Development Corporation. He offered his services to the Crime Commission and repeatedly to OPS. After conferring with Walton while both were in Washington in October 1966, Herrmann eventually won a contract, on behalf of System Development Corporation, to analyze the Thai National Police. Herrmann proposed an integrated intelligence, policing, and civic action program. His particular emphasis was on the benefits of using new computer technologies for information collection, processing, and management, though he predicted computerization would be time- and resource-intensive. The United States did build an integrated counterinsurgency program, minus the computerization, in Thailand, relying on the Border Patrol Police, a force the CIA helped create in 1951.[48] Stateside in 1968, Herrmann pivoted from information management to riot control.[49] The next year, he chaired California's Riots and Disorders Task Force, which LEAA appropriations funded. Gates was a member.[50] Critics such as Huey P. Newton, leader of the Black Panther Party, lambasted Herrmann's dual role working in Sacramento for state law enforcement and in Santa Monica for Pentagon-funded research firms. Herrmann's most notable proposal for California replicated his proposal for Thailand. The state would draw on $18.8 million in LEAA funds to support a computer-based "coordinated intelligence system." This statewide computer system was to be modeled on one the LAPD was already developing, designed to predict "civil disturbances" with mathematical precision, "based on social, political and economic information."[51] The LAPD eventually outsourced this computer system to put it beyond the reach of prying public eyes.

The most enduring imprint of the LAPD on another land, and of the Kennedy administration's zeal for "internal defense" on the LAPD, almost never occurred. In April 1962, in the Dominican Republic, it seemed that the police were losing control of the streets. Almost a year earlier, with CIA aid, assassins had felled Rafael Trujillo, the country's longtime military dictator. To Henry Dearborn, Washington's top official on the ground, Trujillo had become too erratic.[52] Even in his absence, calm was elusive. Now, after his demise, the National Police was hiring many officers in response to unrest, but it lacked the capacity to train them. There was no US public safety program in the country, and advisors were already stretched thin in the hemisphere. The chief of public safety assistance for Latin America made a quick assessment of local conditions and decided a program was needed. The formal inauguration of OPS in Washington was still several months away, but the volatility in Santo Domingo in the spring of 1962 made the new US ambassador, John Bartlow Martin, impatient. In a bind, Washington sought assistance from the LAPD, knowing it employed Spanish-speaking officers. At first, the brass refused. The State Department then floated the name of Joseph Lohman, an exemplary police reformer, who had succeeded O. W. Wilson as dean of the Berkeley School of Criminology. Like Parker, Lohman had overseen the production of a television program meant to disseminate his vision of professionalization.[53] But when the LAPD balked, Attorney General Kennedy contacted Parker directly.[54] He reconsidered, unhappy at the prospect of a competitor like Lohman getting the job. The LAPD assigned Sergeant Jesus Mejia and Patrolman Hector J. Guevara, members of its "Mexican squad" who shared their chief's policing creed, to the task of training Dominican police.[55]

Leftists planned a demonstration in Santo Domingo for June 14, 1962, commemorating the day a group of Dominican exiles had returned and unsuccessfully attempted to foment a revolution against Trujillo three years earlier. Mejia and Guevara arrived on June 2 and agreed to stay for a month. They found undisciplined local officers eager to use automatic weapons and "fragmentation type hand grenades" on crowds. Inadequate training facilities, lacking usable materials as basic as blackboards, hampered their efforts to instill Engle's vision. But they persevered, and on June 14, newly trained Dominican police, looking "confident and well-disciplined" and armed with batons, not guns, confronted some four thousand demonstrators. Mejia and Guevara had recommended encouraging the organizers of the demonstration to form their own peacekeeping units, whose members wore green arm bands that read *orden* ("order"). This approach seemed to work on June 14, but the LAPD officers warned that such a "committee of order" could degenerate into a "goon squad." In ensuing weeks, the retraining of local police was interrupted by a prison uprising and mass escape, further demonstrations, and a national strike, during which AID-supplied tear gas thwarted a march by a "leftist group." Mejia and Guevara translated an LAPD training film on riot-control formations and the 1944 LAPD riot-control manual into Spanish for their Dominican pupils. OPS's Latin America chief deemed their performance "outstanding." Their mission ended up lasting 105 days, burnishing the LAPD's credibility.[56] To a journalist, Parker dismissed allegations of police brutality at home by citing this deployment abroad. He bristled: how could officers qualified to export "democracy" be called brutal?[57]

After the LAPD team returned to Los Angeles, the new public safety program in the Dominican Republic struggled. In October 1962, Ambassador Martin requested a "token quantity" of CN grenades and gas masks to help "maintain enthusiasm" and the "confidence" of the Dominican government in the US commitment to its security.[58] A brief democratic opening in the country saw the election of Juan Bosch to the presidency in late 1962, and Vice President Lyndon Johnson attended Bosch's inauguration the following February, chauffeured in Santo Domingo by public safety advisor Anthony Ruiz, a retired LAPD captain of detectives.[59] Bosch's restoration of democracy quickly disintegrated, and there was a right-wing coup in September 1963. Public anger roiled the country. Journalists noted, however, that the Dominican police now used tear gas and truncheons, not "tommyguns," against protesters.[60] Police reform was palpable. AID helped the National Police open a new police training school in January 1964, directed by a graduate of the OPS Inter-American Police Academy.[61] The FBI legal attaché led classes on fingerprint identification and classification that year in Santo Domingo; one of his students wrote a textbook in Spanish on the topic and dedicated it to him.[62]

Then, in April 1965, a military counter-coup erupted into a brief civil war. Many AID-supplied weapons were stolen, and a number of OPS-trained Dominican police were killed. Their advisors felt endangered too. Public safety advisor Lee Echols recalled driving in Santo Domingo as unrest broke out. He came upon a roadblock manned by "Communist rebels," who stopped his car, but failed to take the wary defensive measures a well-trained cop would when approaching a suspicious vehicle. The rebel cradled his gun and told Echols to get out with his hands up. Instead, Echols shot him point blank, floored the pedal, and rammed his car into another rebel.[63] Contrary to his administration's proxy counterinsurgency stance in Latin America, President Johnson subsequently opted to send in US soldiers and marines to put down the rebellion, feeding anti-US sentiment in the hemisphere and across the globe.[64]

The public safety mission was at the center of US policymaking in the Dominican Republic, but internal politics within US-assisted security agencies threatened US strategy. A provisional government, installed in September 1965, tentatively resolved the crisis that broke out in April. McGeorge Bundy then convened a meeting to plan future steps in the country. Attendees included, among others, J. Edgar Hoover, CIA representatives, and Byron Engle and his deputy. Based on OPS and CIA findings, this group decided to continue bolstering the public safety program and monitoring propitious rifts among leftists. An OPS plan to consolidate all internal security responsibilities into the National Police, taking them away from the military, was proving impossible to implement. Instead, the United States would urge the creation of a "strike force" unit of three hundred paramilitaries, assisted by US Special Forces, to liaise with the National Police. It was, in effect, a huge SWAT team. The attendees at Bundy's meeting were heartened to learn that the Dominican Republic's provisional president, Héctor García-Godoy, had chosen an acceptable leader to head the national intelligence organization and reappointed the FBI-trained chief of the secret police, who had previously been transferred, after displeasing his boss. These moves laid the groundwork for ousting the Dominican attorney general, whom US intelligence considered a leftist. US-assisted security agencies claimed he was impeding the strengthening of the police and causing military officers to threaten to resign.[65]

The ongoing instability of the Dominican Republic solidified desires among US officials for extreme discretionary action. Ambassador Martin, who supported the training program developed by the LAPD team, reneged on his own prior commitments to civil liberties by advocating the type of "methods once used by the police in Chicago." In the Dominican Republic, police reportedly felt free to harass, illegally detain, and torture any "known hoodlum" they saw on the street.[66] Police shootings of demonstrators and striking workers also persisted.[67]

The Dominican experience nonetheless subsequently became the basis for a two-hour lecture that was part of required training for new public safety advisors, which contrasted the use of 23,000 US troops in 1965 with civilian police assistance after the civil war.[68] Through 1971, US public safety assistance to the Dominican Republic cost a total of $3.5 million, ranking it fourth in the hemisphere, behind Brazil, Colombia, and Guatemala.[69]

The LAPD's Caribbean adventure illustrated how flexible it could be under the right circumstances, and how comfortable officers already were, in 1962, transcending city limits. Mejia and Guevara taught OPS-endorsed riot control methods, rather than the type of indiscriminate violence that marked LAPD methods a few years later during the Watts rebellion. And they encountered OPS-endorsed surveillance and intelligence-gathering practices that resonated with Los Angeles's traditions of nativist anticommunism. They may have even learned new tricks. AID had helped the Dominican Republic develop "an elite, sophisticated intelligence service." OPS and the CIA considered this police division the most important, after riot control; the CIA provided over $190,000 for it in 1966.[70] Though their colleagues did not know it, six of the eighteen public safety advisors in the country in 1969 were CIA officers and taught intelligence techniques to the Dominican secret police, according to an AID employee.[71] President Joaquín Balaguer increased the power of the secret police, which was integral to his deeply repressive second term, which lasted until 1976. The role of the radical Left in the civil war was negligible, but it suffered mightily under Balaguer's subsequent autocracy.

Sergeant Mejia joined the LAPD's equivalent secret unit, the Public Disorder Intelligence Division, which like the Dominican secret police specialized in infiltrating radical groups. Formed in 1970, it was only the latest iteration of the most voracious municipal red squad in the United States. Soon it became the most secretive. The division embodied Gates's dictum to "know thy enemy." Through surveillance and informants, it gathered millions of pages of records on dissenters engaged in legal activities, including elected officials, organizations opposed to LAPD spying, and US–Central America solidarity groups. But it refrained from writing down its own briefings. The division relayed information to Gates verbally.[72] When scandal engulfed the division, Mejia was its commander. He retired and subsequently refused to be interviewed in departmental disciplinary proceedings.[73]

The final nail in the coffin of the LAPD's Public Disorder Intelligence Division was a revelation that officers had shared intelligence files instead of destroying them to preclude abuse of civil liberties as had been publicly announced. The recipient of these files was the Western Goals Foundation, a private right-wing aggregator of information on leftist and radical groups.[74] Western Goals, one of several private intelligence firms, stood out by reason of operating a novel computerized information management system of the kind William Herrmann had envisioned for both Bangkok and Sacramento. Board members of Western Goals included Roy Cohn, Senator Joseph McCarthy's assistant in the early 1950s, and John Singlaub, a former CIA officer in East Asia. By the 1980s, Singlaub was at the hub of paramilitary anticommunist efforts on three continents, as an arms dealer and bagman willing to lose money for the cause of turning up the Cold War's heat. Singlaub gained his greatest notoriety after the White House pinned blame on him for violating a congressional ban by shipping weapons to the Contras in Nicaragua—though Singlaub himself had collaborated with NSC and CIA officials to help find ways for the White House to circumvent the ban.[75] Fighting the revolutionary government of Nicaragua, the paramilitary Contras largely comprised former members of the Guardia Nacional, which OPS had assisted for a few years in the early 1970s.[76] Western Goals published encomia to the Contras and threw a party in Washington, DC, for Roberto D'Aubuisson, once a participant at the International Police Academy and by the 1980s a commander of death squads in El Salvador.[77] If Mejia had been in the vanguard of the transformation of riot-control techniques in the 1960s through his work overseas, he was also in the vanguard of the transformation of police intelligence techniques nearly two decades later when they were privatized to avoid public scrutiny and legal constraint, computerized for convenience, and globalized, amid mutations of US empire and protest against it.

Mobile LAPD veterans exported their agency's techniques and forged bonds across borders. On the principle that these techniques marked an improvement on indigenous policing practices in Latin America or Southeast Asia, these Angelenos shaped political outcomes in these regions for decades.

Yet strong as connections were between the LAPD and US foreign police assistance, they were of less consequence for Gates himself than was his relationship with his mentor, the longtime LAPD chief William Parker. Gates briefly studied counterinsurgency theory, but he was a lifelong student of LAPD practices. Gates rose in the department serving as Parker's personal driver. Throughout the 1950s, every morning, he wrote, Parker "engaged me in discussions on law enforcement and philosophical concepts." In time, the callow Gates "became totally smitten" with him.[78] Parker was unafraid to reveal the otherwise disavowed race-management content of police reformism. He had a vision for the LAPD, and he tried to propagate it widely. It was printed on the armbands of the peacekeepers of June 14, 1962, in Santo Domingo: *orden*, order. To explain the aggressive, militaristic form of policing Gates developed as SWAT, we need not, therefore, look overseas for its antecedents, but only as far as the back seat of the car Gates drove throughout the 1950s, where Chief Parker held forth on the need to compel compliance. Gates transformed this principle into SWAT. It was not a lesson learned in Vietnam. It was native to Los Angeles.

. . .

For Gates, counterinsurgency was the proper response to revolutionary Black organizing during the 1960s. Faced with a profound threat to the existing social order, he claimed, police drew on the overseas experience of the military in theaters of war to find ways to eradicate this threat. It is tempting to believe him. The claim dramatizes the challenge the Watts rebellion and Black political formations like the Black Panther Party posed to a racist social order. It also highlights the racial revanchism of empire. Yet this claim hypostatizes the transit of techniques of rule from a violent and debased imperial periphery to an otherwise untarnished domestic arena. In fact, the routes of transit for counterinsurgency and policing during the 1960s were more multidirectional, exorbitant to a vision of empire that, in its flattest variants, can let US imperialism off the hook for what happens overseas as long as those operations remain far afield and never boomerang homeward.

Such an account of how the violence of empire reverberates domestically relies on two implicit claims that can reassert the nationalism of the liberal creedal narrative of providential transcendence of the history of US racism. First, it suggests that techniques of rule in imperial peripheries are inherently more violent than actions elsewhere and thus corrode otherwise liberal, democratic polities at home when they return.[79] This claim, however, risks colluding in isolationist, nationalistic arguments against US empire that raise the specter of the degradation of US character through sexual, violent, and/or cultural encounters. There is reciprocity between this disavowal of overseas encounter and the pleasure-seeking, sadistic, and prurient desire to take part in violence ascribed to the peripheral other through its management. In this sense, skepticism abounded among technical advisors that modernized security forces of former colonies, still composed of members of the alien local population of racial others, could ever truly discard their savage ways. It exonerated the United States. Any tortures or abuses these forces enacted signaled their own barbarism, even if US advisors gave them tools to carry them out.

The second, related, claim implicit in Gates' repatriation story is that somehow the 1965 Watts rebellion, or the LAPD's response to it, was not already a transnational story, a sequence of global events. Smuggled in here is a notion that Black people, their grievances against state and capital, and their political mobilizations were inherently local or provincial, in contrast to the technocrats of US empire, whose work played out on an inherently transnational stage. Gates narrated his own learning process as if it were he who had discovered US empire, not the Black people in Los Angeles who saw themselves as struggling against it. Their reactions to police violence, like the violent arrest that ignited the Watts rebellion, were, for him, simply the latest in a long line of "protests of every kind," now with contours that he associated with an inherently foreign type of political activity. Yet he also knew it was not foreign. It was to him simply disorder.

William Parker's position on how to foster order marked less the maintenance of the racist status quo than the active reformatting of US racial rule. Under the sign of order, but within a new legal covenant, the despotism of the police power remained. This shifting terrain formed the context of SWAT more directly than its relationship to counterguerrilla warfare. With the advent of the LEAA and the War on Crime, military-surplus matériel made its way into the hands of police across the United States, regardless of whether agencies possessed specialized units called SWAT. Yet the LAPD initiation of SWAT also realized the inherent possibilities for experimentation allowed by the national-level state project of local autonomy for police. When Richard Nixon became President, aides floated Gates as a possible appointee to the troika leading the LEAA, but he chose to stick with the LAPD. The SWAT unit is important, not for what it reveals about the militarization of policing, but because of its self-conscious projection of the absolute necessity of maintaining order. It provided a rote lesson to police agencies across the country in the need to go to great lengths to maintain order. It further symbolized a vision of policing that repudiated social uplift as a means of crime prevention. Via overseas counterinsurgency, these contending approaches to crime control became fodder for much larger intellectual debates on political economy.

NINE

"The Discriminate Art of Indiscriminate Counter-Revolution"

TO TAKE STOCK: over the course of the 1960s, the US police assistance program was at the center of a deterritorialized state-building project, which beckoned and influenced a broad range of policing professionals, who, thanks to its work, developed new technical repertoires and political positions, among them facility with state-building itself. The Omnibus Crime Control and Safe Streets Act of 1968 adopted OPS as a tacit model of devolutionary state-building, of using law enforcement to reconfigure the state, while extending the reach of centralized security resources and expertise. The police power—characterized by the US Supreme Court in 1873 as "incapable of any very exact definition or limitation"—would finally be matched in its conceptual limitlessness by a functionally unlimited and interconnected set of police institutions.[1] Though often competitive with each other for resources, police agencies joined US city precinct to Southeast Asian rural hamlet, through a unified set of techniques and technologies. A unified disposition corresponded: security came first. But this period also saw a broad shift in political culture. Before elected officials latched onto cries for law and order, law-enforcement officials already found such demands to be politically feasible, drawing increased attention, legitimacy, and resources to their own agencies. Soon, law and order became a dominant, bipartisan theme of political campaigns, driving the state-building whose contours the project of global counterinsurgency had suggested.

But the reasoning within law and order discourse also shifted in the 1960s and 1970s. Concern about the causes of crime and social disorder that united liberals and some conservatives would be superseded with a new causal argument. Where poverty had been thought to cause crime, a new discourse reversed this causality to claim, in short, that crime and social nonconformity led to impoverishment and related deleterious social phenomena. As a result, intellectual perspectives on stopping crime transitioned from a focus on economic uplift to a more coercive focus on prevention of criminal acts, which coincided with a transition in the legal framework of policing from the control of status to the control of behavior. A broad consensus came to declare that the way to control crime was to raise the cost of crime, since deviant behavior had rational underpinnings.[2] This idea germinated in conservative circles, articulated in different veins by the economist Gary Becker and the political scientist James Q. Wilson, and it obtained practical reach beyond academic economics through field-testing in counterinsurgency.

Through the 1960s, the top-down professionalization of policing, reliant on capital-intensive repertoires and technologies, from tear gas to single-officer patrol cars, remained the orthodoxy. Cracks in this consensus emerged by decade's end. The most widely recognized form of the repudiation of dominant forms of management-led professionalization came with so-called "broken windows" policing, named for an article published in 1982 by George L. Kelling and James Q. Wilson.[3] This article has typically been seen as a prospectus for the future of policing, or even a prophecy, but its highly discretionary and coercive behavior-control model of policing was already nascent, ushered into the streets by William H. Parker and public safety advisors and explained in LAPD guidance and OPS textbooks. Contained within Kelling and Wilson's article was also a governing philosophy that corresponded to emergent social-scientific discourses of rationality premised on the individual rational actor.

By the 1980s, new trends in policing were congruent with the counterinsurgency theory of the preceding decades, particularly as theorists oscillated toward more avowedly coercive approaches and dispensed with economic-development components. The foundations of the law-and-order conservative intellectual edifice that dominated US policymaking for decades, thanks to figures like James Q. Wilson, were forged in transnational debates about counterinsurgency. These debates provided the platform for a reconfiguration of the broader conservative intellectual milieu, allowing the convergence of rational-choice economistic thinking with demands within policing for order maintenance. Conservative intellectuals who crafted a novel political dispensation of law and order that placed new forms of policing at its center echoed police-led counterinsurgency, primarily through the resources-control program outlined in the 1964 OPS textbook *The Police and Resources Control in Counter-Insurgency*. This elite intellectual shift, catalyzed by debates over why the United States could not change course in South Vietnam, tracked positions delineated within law-enforcement circles by figures who saw their task as stopping social revolution. The order-maintenance mode of policing that became dominant within a couple decades of the end of the public safety program replicated the primary lessons the program imparted across the globe. Order-maintenance policing replicated counterinsurgency.

FROM COUNTERINSURGENCY TO CRIME CONTROL

New resources available for counterinsurgency research, including from the Advanced Research Projects Agency (ARPA) in the Department of Defense, caused an expansion of scientific study of the topic throughout the 1960s. But research took time, and the focus of social concern shifted quickly. The war in Vietnam was a disaster, protests on US streets were persisting, crime rates were growing, and new forms of political violence or "terrorism" were emerging. Experts thus transposed many findings about overseas insurgency to control of domestic crime and political strife. Research fields on crime and insurgency proved incestuous, with far more transnational exchange of ideas than has typically been appreciated. Some research firms supplied their findings to congressional investigations or presidential commissions. For instance, among these research reports was one from 1966 by Simulmatics Corporation that integrated foreign and domestic analyses into a single research product. It included a detailed analysis of Algeria's revolution, an overview of 137 insurgencies in twenty-one Latin American countries in the post-1945 period, and an investigation of police communications and coordination in the Watts rebellion. Arnold Sagalyn's arm of the Kerner Commission acquired multiple such reports, including from the Army's Special Operations Research Office housed at American University in Washington, DC. Several were co-written by Adrian Jones, a retired African American military policeman. Jones testified before the House Committee on Un-American Activities on "the use of violence and subversive activities in the name of 'civil rights'" and would go on to work for the LEAA.[4]

When antiwar protest tightened the flow of money from the Pentagon as rapidly as it had opened, many firms diversified their research products domestically. The RAND Corporation and American Institutes for Research, for example, engaged in research on policing.[5] Law enforcement was a logical area for new grant proposals once money from the Pentagon became scarce. Not only had counterinsurgency researchers been interacting with public safety expertise throughout the period, now the LEAA was offering money that could fill the gap left by the Pentagon's shift. Diversification from overseas warfare into domestic policing was not accompanied by diversification in theory or methods, however. Some research firms made bold claims about the applicability to policing or counterinsurgency of their research on far-removed topics, a position underpinned by a commitment to methodological positivism and the universalism of modernization. For instance, American Institutes for Research identified "many important analogies" among "cross-cultural relations abroad . . . and subcultural relations here in the United States." Based on the firm's research on discord between US troops and locals in South Korea, researchers could generate a new approach to analyzing interactions among US police and urban residents. Not only was the survey instrument from Korea repurposed in San Francisco, the 1971 findings were similar: "Americans basically felt that we were giving money away to people who did not want to work and who were lazy. The analogous critical issue in the police-community relations context was welfare."[6] The racism of US troops toward Koreans was analogous to the racism of San Francisco police toward the city's nonwhite residents, researchers discovered.

In the 1960s, law-enforcement professional literature also began citing counterinsurgency theory. Experts found it to be an export-import bank, aiding exchange of ideas on racial difference. Scientific analyses of social turmoil overseas often refracted it through the lens of the historical experience of racial antagonism within the United States. Such analyses further anticipated and adumbrated technical solutions to domestic clashes between white supremacy and Black freedom movements in the mold of those field-tested in the Gray Areas. In the decade after the Harlem uprising of 1964, the professional policing literature, exemplified by *The Police Chief* and *Police,* published numerous articles that discussed counterinsurgency in addition to covering the public safety program.

Policing experts interpreted the new urban rebellion after the passage of the Civil Rights and Voting Rights Acts as a signal that political instability was here to stay and was continually going to intensify. They began to proselytize, citing social-scientific research funded by the Pentagon. For example, in 1966, *The Police Chief* published in two parts the entirety of a 1965 Air War College thesis titled "The Role of the Police in Counter-Insurgency," comprising nearly thirty magazine pages. It introduced readers to French counterinsurgency theory in vogue at organizations like RAND, as well as tenets of modernization theory, while also referring to standard policing texts by figures like O. W. Wilson and William Parker.[7] Subsequent articles directed at law-enforcement audiences, including one by Nicholas D. Rudziak, an Army colonel, drew upon OPS's *The Police and Resources Control in CounterInsurgency,* Special Operations Research Office case studies, and counterinsurgency theorists in Edward Lansdale's circle.[8] *The Police Chief* and *Police* also published a welter of more technically oriented articles on crowd control and new weapons, which frequently referred to overseas experience. In turn, scientific Army-funded studies, such as Carl F. Rosenthal's "Phases of Civil Disturbances: Characteristics and Problems," which explicitly focused on "Negro ghettos," cited articles in *The Police Chief* by Sagalyn and Gates. The Army's Limited War Laboratory published a summative technical report on riot control that relied on assistance from Rudziak and Rosenthal, as well as FBI and DOJ advisors.[9] Through sustained dialogue, a coterie of security experts developed a unitary, global field of vision and identified a single problem to solve.

Outside formal channels of research funding and grant applications, many individuals rebranded themselves as counterinsurgency experts in this period. And counterinsurgency experts became criminologists. Social-scientific analyses of urban guerrilla warfare became popular books that sold well.[10] For some, any experience overseas prepared them to give confident advice about countering guerrillas. Richard Sanger, for example, lectured in counterinsurgency courses for the State Department and subsequently applied his analyses to African American politics, including in testimony before Congress.[11] At President Kennedy's behest, most of the Foreign Service had received specialized education in modernization and counterinsurgency. In the process, they frequently applied generic, racialized analogies of crime and insurgency.

To label insurgency crime was to sap it of political legitimacy, to contend that the problems counterinsurgency faced did not rise to the level of formal politics. One British expert in Malaya, "preferred to call the insurgents 'bandits,' because if they were captured they would have no rights. If they were called prisoners of war," upon capture, it would be necessary to follow international legal conventions dictating their proper treatment.[12] As the journalist Robert Critchfield put it, drawing on police-led counterinsurgency in Malaya, South Vietnam's problems in 1968 were ones of "law and order."[13]

The Australian army advisor Ted Serong, who briefed the SGCI and offered advice to OPS, belittled the dedication of guerrillas in South Vietnam, calling them mere "juvenile delinquents" who had been duped into fighting with promises of adventure.[14] Even General Westmoreland considered the "Viet Cong" to be criminals engaged in "raiding, robbing, molesting, and killing."[15] Thus, insurgency's solution could be similarly prepolitical. Banditry fascinated counterinsurgency theorists, especially those who remained obsessed with the question of "who lost China?" References to banditry recurred because local community approval of such criminal activity—basically, banditry meant extracting an informal tax—represented a structure of feeling that was refractory to state power and official political authority. Agitators, it was believed, could easily plant and fertilize communism's magic beanstalks in such soil. At the center of the conflation of insurgency with crime, which typically referred to burglary and robbery, was the premise that external inputs and resources were essential to social protest movements, a widely shared notion that fed conservative skepticism of social welfare programming. The claim was that the War on Poverty fostered protest mobilization, even though its participatory mechanism was designed to rechannel it.[16]

The value for counterinsurgents to label insurgency crime, claiming that crime was tantamount to insurgency, was to introduce persistent threat inflation. It made their advice a necessity. As the 1960s wore on, "traditional youth gangs in the ghetto," which may have included criminals, seemed to be attaining "conscious political orientation."[17] Crime, or, as the former CIA officer James Cross called it, "non-directional urban rebellion," was not simply crime by this point.[18] And if crime was becoming directional, security forces needed to be prepared. Prior to release of the Kerner Commission's findings that no exogenous subversives had been responsible for the unrest of 1967, Robert Rigg, an Army officer, declared that guerrilla "warfare in alleys, streets, cellars, sewers and rooftops" needed "no prodding by Communists or other political movements. It could erupt simply from poverty or racial or local issues."[19] One experienced FBI agent analyzed urban unrest and found Rigg to be correct: "The primary troublemakers throughout the riots were not organized groups." The main offenders were not concerned about civil rights, but were simply "street-corner hoodlum gangs."[20] Moreover, crime was particularly worrisome if found in "the revolutionary environment," which might be in "California, Pennsylvania, Mississippi, or the rice paddies and jungles of Viet-Nam."[21] This sort of threat inflation and compulsive comparativism hindered sober assessments. Later social-scientific and historical research on urban unrest in the period showed the claim that criminals were responsible to be false.[22] Some conservative analyses also confirmed radical left-wing evaluations of "crime" as displaced revolutionary activity: "The urban crime rate that the government is unable to prevent is actually an individualized, unorganized form of guerrilla warfare conducted by people with little political consciousness but an overwhelming hatred for the circumstances under which they must live."[23] With crime scripted as incipient social revolution, crime control meant maintaining the sociopolitical status quo and opposing revolution reflexively.

In this pursuit, police seemed to possess the necessary toolkit. Military experts came to agree. Serong was committed to "police predominance," as were the conservative Hudson Institute's Frank Armbruster, Lansdale's colleague Charles Bohannan, and other experts on the ARPA-funded counterinsurgency circuit.[24] As Rudziak wrote in *The Police Chief*, hallowing US police assistance overseas and police-led countersubversion at home, "local police forces, whether in a typical mid-western town in the United States or in the heart of a jungle in Viet-Nam, are normally best suited to acquire and evaluate the type of intelligence that assists them to maintain law and order. Their intimate knowledge of the language, the customs, and the characters and personalities of the people in their communities gives them a capability which no other local force or agency possesses." In any case, for Rudziak, rather than political grievance or colonial exploitation, "insurgency begins with lawlessness and gangsterism."[25] Hardline Southern Democrats with no special expertise also contributed to this discourse, making its racist content more visible. Senator Robert Byrd (D-WV) argued that police "have a great deal of sympathy with the troops in Vietnam because they fight a similar type of dirty war in which the enemy is forever striking from the shadows. The police know guerrilla warfare because they fight it day in and day out with criminals on America's streets."[26]

Policing became imperative in discussions of counteirnsurgency that evoked street crime. Pacification, the journalist Gloria Emerson declared in a 1971 lament at US failures in South Vietnam, "is being able to walk down a country road at night, or drive on a highway, without risking your life."[27] Robert Rigg similarly insisted that "to keep our cities from becoming battlegrounds," preventive measures must be taken, including the establishment of an effective system of intelligence in the ghettos of urban America, which would include "penetration by police intelligence, application of military intelligence, and reliance on traditional FBI methods."[28] This intertwined surveillance effort was exactly what occurred, with CIA and FBI cooperation to spy on radicals, and even elected officials and their families, thought to have ties to organizations and governments overseas; military surveillance of the antiwar movement; and extensive local police spying. The CIA also liaised with local police. Municipal cops were for a spell afforded the same type of training public safety advisors received at a CIA facility.[29] This transnational exchange of ideas on crime and insurgency in the 1960s and 1970s reconfigured the discourse of law and order, raising the political importance of police control of crime and submerging concerns with socioeconomic causes of crime.

COST-BENEFIT COUNTERINSURGENCY

The RAND Corporation, the most prominent Pentagon-funded social-scientific research firm of the 1950s and 1960s, was central to reshaping how intellectuals understood the control of deviant behavior by the 1970s. *Rebellion and Authority: An Analytic Essay on Insurgent Conflicts,* a RAND book written collaboratively by the economist Charles Wolf Jr. and the Kremlinologist Nathan Leites, set out to discredit counterinsurgency as it had been practiced throughout the 1960s by introducing a new model: cost-benefit counterinsurgency. In the process, the book demonstrated that the type of economistic thinking that RAND had applied to strategic air defense could also be applied to social control of populations at home and abroad. It focused attention principally on the Gray Areas, but also drew extensively on examples of "urban and campus rebellions in the more developed countries."[30] In *Rebellion and Authority,* Leites and Wolf echoed what OPS was already practicing overseas, presenting order maintenance as a solution to the failures of counterinsurgency, without acknowledging that order maintenance was itself at the core of counterinsurgency.

RAND initially received funding from the Air Force, but it embraced the 1960s turn to counterinsurgency with gusto. After the installation of the Kennedy administration, strategic air defense lost some of its luster, all the more so when one of RAND's most respected thinkers, Albert Wohlstetter, showed flaws in the theory of massive retaliation. The doctrine of flexibility meant that strategic air defense became but one color on the new palette of defense priorities. The Army was rising. RAND's response was to start working for ARPA and the Office of the Secretary of Defense, which led directly to funding for research on Vietnam and counterinsurgency more generally.[31] Like lesser-known organizations, RAND issued numerous studies of insurgency threats that crossed the foreign-domestic divide, with figures like Albert and Roberta Wohlstetter assessing "inequalities and disorder at home and abroad," the Indonesia expert Guy Pauker evaluating "black nationalism and the prospects for violence in the ghetto," and a junior researcher, Brian M. Jenkins, developing multiple robust analyses of urban guerrilla warfare and eventually conceding that "the study of actual urban guerrilla warfare elsewhere was a surrogate for the study of potential urban guerrilla warfare at home."[32] RAND's prestige put the many other researchers who offered similar analyses on solid ground.

In the 1960s, Charles Wolf, a Harvard-trained economist who headed the Economics Department at RAND, applied rational choice theory, the approach RAND favored, to counterinsurgency. The firm's initial foray into researching the instabilities of the Gray Areas was the founding of its "Third Area Conflict Board," which included Wolf, Pauker, and Albert Wohlstetter, who had quietly advised the Kennedy campaign. Area expertise soon proved overrated. Pauker, the Asianist, clung to bromides.[33] Wolf was the first RAND employee to visit Vietnam under official auspices, though consultants had also visited. He accompanied William H. Draper to Saigon, during research for his eponymous committee, where Wolf met Ngo Dinh Diem, along with the ubiquitous Ed Lansdale. Wolf had little specific background in Vietnam, but his contributions to counterinsurgent knowledge overrode the particular. In much of RAND's contracted social-scientific research in Vietnam, however, local context was important. RAND circulated well-informed research, based on interviews with captured and defected National Liberation Front (NLF) members, through its "Viet Cong Motivation and Morale Project." This project's findings did not match many of Washington's demands, so they were ignored. In contrast, Wolf aspired to heed Washington's demands for counterinsurgency advice applicable across contexts.

In the mid-1950s, Wolf had advocated a structural-functionalist understanding of foreign aid consonant with the modernizers' dominant aim to direct and accelerate development. This earned him the position working with Draper. Then, after reading an excoriation of foreign aid by Milton Friedman, Wolf began to rethink its usefulness. He did not immediately change his mind, but in responding to Friedman, he began to qualify his support for foreign aid. By 1961, he admitted aid was limited in what it could achieve.[34] This ratcheting down of ambitions would prove crucial when he turned to counterinsurgency. Yet it was only with the confluence of Robert McNamara's application of Fordist management to the military, Rostow's urging of aggressiveness toward Vietnam, Taylor's flexible-response posture, and the Kennedys' obsession with guerrilla warfare that Wolf, with RAND now drawing funding for counterinsurgency research, began to shift toward marrying the methodologically individualist rational-choice perspective RAND had been cultivating to a ruthless, unsentimental view of insurgency.

Overall, RAND followed the political winds when it came to foreign aid. Kennedy's election signaled widespread approval for his ambition to expand civilian aid for modernization, but when the Johnson administration began to run into trouble in Southeast Asia, RAND intellectuals reconsidered. Starting in summer 1964, they argued for narrowing the goals of assistance to South Vietnam. Overall development was too hazy an objective amid the ongoing violence. Flipping likely NLF recruits was a better approach. Indiscriminate aid, spread across the country, meant that some resources would necessarily go to supporters of the NLF. But those who pledged allegiance should be rewarded. RAND experts recommended aid ranging from commodities to public housing, from expanding education to incentivizing entrepreneurship. The goal was simple: draw support away from the communists by offering a better, more targeted carrot and then continue to support those who took that carrot, to keep it from falling into the wrong hands. Further, let the areas under control of the enemy languish, so as to highlight the difference in quality of life for those in government-controlled areas.[35] "This approach," writes a RAND historian, "assumed that peasants would make a 'rational choice' based on economic benefits alone."[36] A cohort of RAND economists and natural scientists had developed the rational choice approach earlier. It found its most popular expression in game theory, which tried to calculate probabilities of how a nuclear-armed superpower standoff might play out.[37] Wolf picked up this perspective and ran with it, transforming an analytic frame for statecraft into an individualistic social ontology. He had support in RAND's Social Sciences Division, where Hans Speier had begun to question the link between economic deprivation and political rebellion, and thus the link between economic aid and pacification, influenced by the paterfamilias of 1960s conservative US intellectuals, Edward Banfield.[38]

This budding rational-choice approach deviated from most counterinsurgency theory. It dismissed the importance of popular support for the government or the insurgents. According to numerous counterinsurgency experts who believed that Mao offered a blueprint for insurgency, popular support was crucial. "The people are the sea in which the guerrilla swims," according to a Maoist aphorism. Security measures tried to separate the fish from the sea. Counterinsurgency also entailed, therefore, gaining influence over the sea, attracting the loyalty of the population. The common name for this approach was "hearts and minds," though "participatory development" is a more accurate way to characterize the mechanism of such pacification. After the US war in Vietnam, commentators used the phrase "hearts and minds" with chagrin, a sardonic recognition of what the Johnson administration had hoped, but failed, to win in Vietnam.

The proper response to insurgency was to be found, "not in pouring more troops into the jungle, but in the hearts and minds of the people," General Sir Gerald Templer had reasoned in Malaya in 1952.[39] Templer's protégé Sir Robert G. K. Thompson subsequently packaged the approach and brought it to Vietnam, where he sought to convince Diem that following the Malaya model was the best way to wage counterinsurgency. According to this model, Templer won the hearts and minds of the population in Malaya through the provision of amenities ranging from schools to potable water; the encouragement of elections; and the gradual isolation of areas of fighting to allow peaceful return to normalcy in many locations. Revisionist historical accounts, however, point out that Templer's efforts associated with winning hearts and minds postdated highly coercive phases of counterinsurgency begun in advance of Templer's arrival in Malaya.[40] Further, in Templer's 1955 "Report on Colonial Security," which summarized his thinking in flamboyant prose, he concluded, "There are two main ways of tackling Communism— economic action to prevent or check it at the source, and police action, to contain or suppress it. In the Colonies the emphasis has hitherto been on the first approach, which is obviously the only constructive one. But if Malaya had spent on law and order a fair proportion of the large sums she was devoting to welfare, the present emergency, with the attendant colossal expenses, might well have been avoided."[41] Security was the first order of the day. And Templer himself was unconvinced that winning hearts and minds was the best way to ensure security. Policing was more important.

Wolf's initial foray into applying rational-choice thinking to counterinsurgency came in a bracing 1965 report, "Insurgency and Counterinsurgency: New Myths and Old Realities." His approach was distinct. He questioned the role of popular support in the success of insurgencies. Wolf dispensed with the premise that counterinsurgency required winning hearts and minds through the provision of social welfare. He argued that to increase assistance to peasants in order to better their livelihood and thus assure their loyalty represented a misunderstanding of what was at stake, and what was needed to defeat insurgency. What insurgents needed was not amorphous popular political support but "certain inputs" including cheap food, information, and recruits. Cheap meant obtainable without spending much money *or* engaging in coercion. Wolf argued that the costs to insurgents of obtaining these inputs "may be 'reasonable' without popular support for the insurgents." Furthermore, "the costs may be raised considerably" by the government "*without* popular support" for the government. Wolf reassessed three pillars of common thinking behind pacification: the beliefs that insurgents and counterinsurgents vied for popular support because they both required it to succeed; that neutralizing popular support for insurgents could be achieved by providing economic and social benefits; and that socioeconomic aid was essential for counterinsurgency. The safest way to ensure that aid did not fall into the wrong hands and become an "input" for insurgency was to condition its provision upon the "the kind of behavior the government wants to promote among the people."

Within a system-theoretic framework, Wolf characterized insurgency as depending on the conversion of "inputs" into "outputs." Tangible inputs like food and intangible ones like intelligence led to outputs like "acts of sabotage, terror, public demonstrations, small scale attacks and eventually larger attacks and 'mobile warfare'" against state officials and infrastructure. For Wolf, curtailing outputs was labor- and capital-intensive. It was difficult. Focusing on inputs, which did not necessarily require military intervention, was a better approach.

Behind Wolf's sweeping reassessment was a certain modesty: behavior can be modified in the near term, whereas attitudes take a long time to change. Moreover, echoing Walt Rostow, he noted that "transitional societies" were strapped with "endemic and pervasive" fault lines and "antagonisms." Insurgency was not a departure from this situation but an extension of it. Insurgency was no mystery, but a "coherent operating system that needs to be understood structurally and functionally if it is to be effectively countered." A focus on matching counterinsurgency to rebels' beliefs and attitudes, as undertaken by Wolf's RAND colleagues conducting interviews with ex-guerrillas, was not helping counterinsurgency; in fact, it was delaying the needed action. When faced with political instability, authorities had little time to spare. They had little ability to sway attitudes if they themselves were the target of dissatisfaction. Wolf argued that "the operational problem, therefore, is how to increase the effectiveness of such counterinsurgency efforts directly; how to influence behavior and action in the short run, so that attitudes and loyalties can be altered in the long run."[42]

In 1966, Wolf partnered with Nathan Leites to update his views. Together, they clarified the emerging perspective. They concluded that policymakers needed "to separate the control of rebellion from *all* the other problems in the third world." Intellectually and practically, counterinsurgency was not synonymous with "modernization and development." The community-development aspect of pacification, or "democracy-in-action," might be fine, but it was not "the principal way to get at the problem of rebellion." Leites had even less prior knowledge of Southeast Asia than Wolf, though he followed the findings of the Motivation and Morale Project. On his own, Leites did not believe socioeconomic deprivation was to blame in catalyzing rebellion in South Vietnam, as many social scientists had concluded, using the "J-curve" to plot the distance between rising economic expectations and stagnant economic reality.[43] Rather, for Leites, the government was to blame. The rebellion resulted from a discrepancy between Vietnamese peasants' traditional cultural expectations and burdensome taxation and bureaucrats' extravagant lifestyles, for example. The NLF, in contrast, was frugal and honorable.[44]

Under Wolf's influence, however, this cultural explanation quickly went through a sieve, filtering out Leites's concern for government underperformance. Leites had long believed in psychological explanations for Bolshevism, but now subversives' commitment to a cause lost its status as a primary concern. Peasant behavior, not peasant psychology, became key. In miniature, their collaboration represented what would occur across the social sciences in ensuing decades: disciplinary autonomy undermined when ideas from economics swallowed other disciplines. For Leites and Wolf, focusing on government actions and the consequent attitudes of the populace remained "on the *demand* side of the insurgency problem." In contrast to this attention to "*preferences*," which was an intractable problem in underdeveloped areas, it was necessary to consider "*opportunities*"—the supply side, inputs.[45] Here, an appraisal of how the enemy operated was crucial. The NLF's "ruthless effectiveness" in dispensing "penalties and rewards to motivate compliant behavior," Wolf later reflected, impressed them both.[46]

Over the coming years, as the situation worsened in South Vietnam and rebellions occurred in other locales, Leites and Wolf developed their ultimate statement, issued for ARPA in 1970 as *Rebellion and Authority*, a book whose source base jumbled time periods, geographies, and political situations. It drew from a combination of RAND's ethnographic research, news stories on events from Queens, NY, to Luzon to Cuba to Greece, and the memoirs of T. E. Lawrence and other notable figures. The analysis cherry-picked data and made grandiose extrapolations. Leites and Wolf propounded a generalizable, positivist theory of how to compel behavioral compliance and stamp out rebellion. They also dispensed with ethical concerns, favoring a bloodless technical view. Yet blood was certainly on the agenda. Counterinsurgents were compelled to face the fact that insurgency succeeded through coercion. Counterinsurgency would too.

Leites and Wolf relied on simple renderings of the issues at hand, consistent with the vocabulary of mainstream economics. They maintained the input-output binary and put it within a broader dichotomous analytic framework of rebellion versus authority, or, as they termed it, "R and A." From hearts and minds, with its *demand-pull* view of insurgency, they elaborated "an alternative approach": *cost-push.* Demand tended to be less "elastic," impervious to dramatic change. Supply, in contrast, would be responsive to control techniques.[47] Out with demand, in with supply—but to counter rebellion, the beast of insurgency had to be starved of supply of recruits, food, intelligence, weapons, and so on.

Rebellion and Authority combined readability, as if revealing what should have been common sense, with the appurtenances of scientific rigor, including technical appendices, graphs, and equations. It presented its findings as tough truth-telling. "Some US economic aid projects in Vietnam have almost certainly helped the Viet Cong," they wrote, opening the door to non-modernizing austerity. The approach aligned theory, methodology, and ontology: the individual rational actor was to be the vessel of the maintenance of authority. In clarion prose, Leites and Wolf described the axis around which the alternative approach revolved: "Fundamental to our analysis is the assumption that the population, as individuals or groups, behaves 'rationally': that it calculates costs and benefits to the extent that they can be related to different courses of action, and makes choices accordingly." They alchemized population, rebellion, and authority into individual agents.

It followed, then, that cost-benefit counterinsurgency entailed four primary vectors aimed at rational actors. First, input-denial could include interdiction of materials, construction of barriers to movement, and preemptive buying of supplies. Second, impeding the transformation of input into output could make use of the black arts: disseminating misinformation, attracting defectors, sowing distrust among insurgents, and adding "noise" to "R's information system." Third was military "counterforce," reliant on sound intelligence to avoid "targeting error" where "targets are closely collocated with the people." Finally, passive and active defense measures composed the fourth vector: either improving fortifications or "strengthening local paramilitary and police units" for "local defense." In the political realm, Leites and Wolf recommended "certifying" with the government's "adherence to law and order in contrast to R" that "it *should* be governing because it *is* governing." Yet because it was difficult to determine what source of authority rebels preferred, all that could be analyzed was conduct. "As a source of inputs, the important characteristic for scrutiny . . . is behavior or conduct, not sympathies or preferences." The rational, and even profit-maximizing, decision became avoiding getting oneself killed, or as they put it, the decision to be "damage-limiting."[48] Yet there was no clear way to estimate the optimal amount of coercive force. Absent a benchmark minimum to induce potential rebels' cost-limiting behavior, there was only a maximum of death and desolation.

The work received a mixed reception, particularly among those trying to plot a course to US victory in Vietnam. Daniel Ellsberg mounted a vociferous critique in empirical, methodological, and theoretical terms.[49] Wolf had interviewed and hired Ellsberg at RAND, and Ellsberg's biographer Tom Wells speculates that a schism opened between them due to Ellsberg's scathing criticisms of the *Rebellion and Authority* manuscript. Wells implies that Ellsberg was so troubled by the new direction of RAND thinking on counterinsurgency and Wolf's defensiveness that he leaked the *Pentagon Papers* in part as a response.[50] In addition, Albert Wohlstetter registered disagreements in a chummy, unblinded peer review. He worried the manuscript might discredit the broader shift ongoing within RAND. Hearts and minds had been prominent at RAND, thanks to frequent consultation with Robert Thompson, but Wohlstetter was not fond of it, calling it "HAM." He appreciated maverick thinking but reasoned, "The fun you poke at HAM . . . tends to reinforce the impression that you don't put much importance on what people in a country engaged in a civil war actually want." Wolf and Leites did bracket what people wanted. Wohlstetter feared that despite the appearance of scientific rigor, the manuscript was fundamentally biased, taking "the side of the authority." Given "the present climate of partisan extremity," he reckoned that their commitment to authority would "identify your book as simply a contribution to the discriminate art of indiscriminate counter-revolution."[51]

Other thinkers, however, relished the perspective of *Rebellion and Authority*. It was consonant with a broader intellectual shift that was undermining tenets of the modernization paradigm and driving a deterioration in its status.[52] Most famously, this shift set the terms of a debate that unfolded between Samuel Popkin and James Scott, who elaborated two different interpretations of peasant life-worlds in Southeast Asia over the ensuing decade, one individualistic, the other communitarian, neither amenable to past modernization practice.[53] Both Popkin and Scott responded to a conjunctural debate, spawned from near-term political considerations, by positing relatively transhistorical explanations based on beliefs and routines observed in field research. Yet the debate had also been percolating for a while in the background, with an early entry in the form of a study of the "backward" Basilicata region of southern Italy by a dissonant character whose time had come by the early 1970s, Edward Banfield, mentor to James Q. Wilson and Samuel Huntington. Banfield reached the desultory conclusion that a change of "ethos" in a backward area was nigh impossible. It was important to introduce a gospel of industriousness. But it was more critical to implement "rapid devolution of as many government functions as possible" to enable "local bodies" to "demonstrate capacity for self-government." After all, the most plausible approach was to manipulate the behavior of actors themselves, rather than the broader "underlying situation" of uneven development.[54]

Although drafts of Wolf's work circulated in Saigon, the war was only one concern for Leites and Wolf. They developed the cost-benefit mode of counterinsurgency also to prove that rational-choice thinking could be applied beyond economics to the most important political issues of the day. Similarly, Gary Becker analyzed the economics of crime and punishment according to rational-choice theory in a widely cited 1968 article that he workshopped at RAND, building on the ideas of RAND's Kenneth Arrow.[55] The approach of Leites and Wolf was "by no means an aberration for the era," but "all the roads to rational choice theory lead from RAND."[56] Army officers debated hearts and minds in professional military periodicals, developing similar conclusions, while other Pentagon-funded researchers with the Hudson Institute offered "conservative" analyses of how "ideas, ideals or group and personal dissatisfactions are irrelevant."[57] These studies did not have a great impact on changing the course of the war but did solidify political convictions among their authors.

Leites and Wolf did not demonstrate whether, in refuting hearts and minds, they were actually addressing contemporary revolutionary practice.

Was it actually the case that hearts and minds, as a response to Mao-inspired guerrilla warfare, matched the threat it diagnosed? By 1970, revisions of Mao's approach were legion, among them the *foco* approach of Che Guevara and Régis Debray, which abjured the popular-support component central to Mao's approach as they understood it.[58] Leites and Wolf did not address this shift. Furthermore, they never proved it was actually true that guerrillas lived off resources drawn from the population at large. They took this presupposition for granted, even though other RAND researchers showed it was often untrue.[59] After 1968, when the NLF suffered severe losses, moreover, guerrilla insurgency no longer remained an apt characterization of what was occurring in South Vietnam, as regular troops from the North replaced dead or captured NLF cadres.

The coercive approach Leites and Wolf heralded as a repudiation of ongoing counterinsurgency practice was actually consistent with ongoing counterinsurgency practice. They represented pacification in stylized fashion, leading to two key inaccuracies that made it seem as though their coercive methods had never been tried. First, their claim that hearts and minds placed "primacy" on "politics over force" did not actually correspond to counterinsurgency in Malaya or South Vietnam.[60] Coercive measures to fabricate security took the prime place. Second, controlling inputs was not a new invention or radical solution to insurgency. Instead, resources control was literally the OPS textbook model of counterinsurgency in South Vietnam. The resources control textbook argued that controls on unauthorized mobility and smuggling would prevent more serious subversive and violent acts.[61] Moreover, OPS acknowledged that control of stocks of ammunition, clothing, and more built on practices devised in Malaya, where a "food denial program" was intended to starve guerrillas, obliging them either to surrender or attempt audacious raids that would reveal their location to authorities. "Party liners and other marginal operators heard the hunger pangs in their stomachs above the call of the Communist propaganda," OPS declared.[62] Soon, experiments with chemical defoliants in Malaya to destroy brush lining railways, roads, or canals that offered cover to guerrillas escalated into the destruction of food crops. One British diplomat approved of this shift when, influenced by British tactics in Malaya, it also occurred in Vietnam: "to deprive one's enemy of the means to carry on the war, even by destruction of his food supplies, seems to me to be a normal method of warfare."[63] Hearts? Minds? Or bellies? The distance between policing geared toward deprivation of basic foodstuffs and the genocidal imperative to starve a people to death was slim, particularly once the process became mechanized. But destruction of food to compel compliance or surrender was also an old US war-fighting tactic, with precedents in the westward expansion of the United States.[64] Only the rational-choice framing was novel.

The theory of behavior control through input control that Leites and Wolf offered was not new, though the vocabulary of their presentation was. "Control is historically a police function and there is nothing new or mysterious about it," OPS noted in 1964.[65] It was the baseline of the proxy-led counterinsurgency effort in South Vietnam. And it had failed by 1970.[66] Behavior control failed forward, however, avoiding rejection because it resonated so strongly with the rational-choice perspective that was achieving "paradigmatic privilege" in the social sciences.[67]

A repudiation of hearts and minds was consonant with a broader recoil from social welfare provisioning to reformat social landscapes and political attitudes that was ongoing within intellectual circles. What would replace it? Coercion to control behaviors. No hearts, just rational minds, responding to rewards and penalties. The strength of the analysis mounted by Leites and Wolf might have suffered from its insulation from practical evidence. Yet, in a counterintuitive way, that insulation enabled the analysis to retain salience it would not otherwise have acquired. The US war in Vietnam discredited the hearts and minds strategy, which many believed had failed, but cost-benefit counterinsurgency appeared untested. A better intellectual framework just might have succeeded. Popkin, for example, drew on his experience in Vietnam to develop such ideas and spent decades afterward promoting rational-choice theory. Yet cost-benefit counterinsurgency was not untried. Security practices in Southeast Asia transformed the so-called moral peasant into the rational peasant by eliminating any other options and shredding social bonds.[68] In contrast to their portrayal in academic debate, the figures of the moral or rational peasant were less static descriptors than contested outcomes of political processes. The intensity of coercion in Vietnam increased when the apparently moral actions of peasants correlated with insecurity. The condition of possibility for the rational actor was the impossibility of the moral actor, underwritten by the US war effort.

The same process occurred in law-enforcement expertise. A strong current, typified by William Parker's exhortations, was already shaping policing within the United States. This approach argued against changing beliefs and for controlling behaviors instead. Leites and Wolf's key conclusion would have fit easily in Parker's declarations, with all acknowledging coercion as the short-run answer, given the snail's pace of change from economic develop-ment: "When the population is the audience, the aim of communicating is to identify the kind of behavior that is sought and the kind of behavior that is discouraged, with clear indication of the consequences attached to each behavior: the carrot and the stick, each adequately publicized."[69] But intellectuals paid far more attention to the domestic equivalent of hearts and minds, the idea that crime might be reduced through provision of social resources. Those who influenced policymakers, like James Q. Wilson, considered this program a failure. Yet it barely got off the ground, with the War on Poverty curtailed almost as soon as it began to take effect. As with the RAND scientists' discovery of cost-benefit counterinsurgency, when it appeared that other approaches to crime control failed, police seemed to have stumbled accidentally into a rational-choice solution to social ills, lending legitimacy to an individualistic critique of more communitarian solutions and a focus on behavior control as the only way to stop crime. The War on Poverty, in this rendering, failed to bring about peace at home. Strict punish-ment, however, might.[70] Yet a narrow definition of effective punishment as entailing only supervised confinement blinded many commentators to the ways in which police were already eliding coercive behavior control and pun-ishment, whether in the application of CS or by commanding utility compa-nies to cut off gas or electricity services to the homes of Black radicals.[71]

A bipartisan gathering of law-and-order intellectuals and policymakers transformed the tough-on-crime wave into a broader political backlash against what they claimed to be failures of state policy of the 1960s. Some got their start overseas. For instance, the future criminologist and conservative intellectual Charles A. Murray entered the guild as a junior researcher of pacification in Thailand for the ARPA-funded American Institutes for Research, which urged crop destruction and resources control, reflecting the input-output, behavior-focused framework of Leites and Wolf.[72] Once crime was firmly on the agenda, these conservatives switched their attention, but not their framework, to other domains. For example, after his years of pub-lishing on riot control, Raymond Momboisse went on to support a range of conservative causes as an aide to Governor Ronald Reagan. He was an archi-tect of "welfare reform" and helped found the conservative/libertarian Pacific Legal Foundation.[73] Leites and Wolf's revision to counterinsurgent knowl-edge not only echoed the backlash formulation in its particulars but gave it further intellectual purchase under RAND's imprimatur by extending its geographic borders. Yet such intellectual maneuvers hid the deep family resemblances and practical connections between policing at home and counterinsurgency overseas. Both had actually been operating in the very shape of their later revisions at the time of supposed state failures. Black and brown radicals recognized these resemblances early on. When Leites and Wolf recommended resources control as a shift from old methods, the old methods already consisted of resources control, stop-and-frisk, and other coercive surveillance tools. These tools composed the materiality of the new law and order. The emergent frameworks of policing and counterinsurgency prompted by earlier failures, now buoyed by shifting and enlarging sources of funding, were not new. They were the building blocks of the failure to decrease crime and win the US war in Vietnam. They fueled the very rebellions they sought to curtail. It appeared that Leites and Wolf repudiated the methods that lost the war, but they actually replicated them.

Police executives like Parker mounted their critique of attempted social transformation by registering skepticism that beliefs might be mutable. Instead, they needed to maintain order. It was exactly what Leites and Wolf argued. In vogue among police professionals, as OPS evidenced, was not a hearts and minds–like attempt to refashion attitudes and beliefs. There was a broad agreement to issue narrow and targeted interventions to assure behavioral compliance. Against lofty demands for social transformation, ideologically and practically, on American streets, policing was, in Wohlstetter's phrase, the discriminate art of indiscriminate counterrevolution. It pinpointed individuals for coercion in scattershot, population-wide fashion as if each individual were, as Gary Becker suggested, a potential threat. This art was not an invention of social scientists vying to herald a new authoritative voice. It was in part a reaction formation to social revolution on the streets, in factories, on campuses, and in households. But it also predated many of these upheavals. An extensive apparatus for the suppression of inputs, without any sense of what type of outputs would result, had developed behind the backs of the rational-choice counterinsurgents. It was order-maintenance policing. This approach should have been the target of dismissal and reaction, but thanks to these intellectuals' superciliousness, it lived on, to shape the ensuing decades. If Leites and Wolf produced the clearest expression of cost-benefit counterinsurgency, Wilson and Kelling did the same for order-maintenance policing, or what might be called cost-benefit policing, with their "broken windows" theory. Wilson took the rational-choice perspective increasingly popularized in criminology by figures like Becker and joined it to policing's longer traditions of racialized social control, which Becker tried to skirt.[74]

Using the term "order-maintenance policing" to describe what Parker and his professionalizing ilk recommended, what OPS proposed as resources control, and what RAND scientists offered as the aim of rational action may seem an anachronism. Today, it means discretionary, proactive policing of misdemeanors. Yet the thinking behind such behavior-control policing originated long before the 1980s or 1990s, when that term came into vogue, along with its companion "broken windows." Kelling and Wilson's 1982 article "Broken Windows: The Police and Neighborhood Safety" described shifts in policing practice that had occurred on a limited scale in the 1970s under experimental auspices, but it also described them as the typical form of policing in decades past.[75] Kelling and Wilson argued that professionalization and new technologies, from the cruiser to the radio, had severed cops from the people they served. But Kelling and Wilson also subtly shifted the identity of who the police served. This newly dominant form of policing came to match an emerging political economy; police now primarily protected rentiers who profited from symbols of urban order. The era of secular increases in labor redundancy and surplus now had a policing theory and practice to match.[76] Whereas Engle's generation of professionalizers taught police to match patrol deployments to the rhythms of the working day, disciplining laborers or those in the penumbra of the Fordist labor force, order-maintenance policing assumed its object to be the permanently surplus, whose behavior signaled their economic marginalization and participation in informal economic circuits. This behavior could be detrimental to property owners, tourism, and real estate interests.

The prospective pendulum shift outlined by Kelling and Wilson was concordant with intellectual shifts that had occurred among counterinsurgency theorists, toward the rational-choice framework. The theory of broken windows relied on economistic, methodologically individualizing determinations of how behavior would be affected by punishment or reward, and it reduced social life to a dichotomous division of order/disorder, insider/outsider, and reputable/disreputable. Leites and Wolf deemed insurgency a system that automatically transformed inputs into outputs; the broken windows thesis had a similar structural-functional quality. Wilson's first reflections in this vein accompanied his attempt to destroy root-causes thinking in criminology and undermine the War on Poverty. He advanced arguments against an implicit moral-economy framework by promoting a supply-side system of penalties ("costs") to shape rational actors' behaviors.[77] For Kelling and Wilson, inputs of minor offenses—graffiti, public drinking, panhandling—transformed, "in a kind of developmental sequence," into outputs of greater harm. Crime itself constituted an autopoietic system. Strict enforcement of laws against minor offenses was sand in that system's gears. It could be based on observation, "reasonable suspicion" as *Terry v. Ohio* (1968) termed it, or "probable cause." Counterinsurgency that focused on resources control functioned the same way. Like the rational-choice approach that Leites and Wolf applied to preventing insurgent activities, broken windows is a theory of discretionary crime prevention, of stopping crimes that have yet to occur. A punitive response to a small offense, the theory suggested, would dissuade the rational actor from committing a greater offense.

Broken windows as a theory attempted to grapple with urban social life in a United States no longer structured by de jure segregation or by the vague control of status allowed by vagrancy laws, which the Supreme Court found unconstitutional in a series of decisions from the mid-1950s to the early 1970s.[78] James Wilson had once wagered that a cop would be at his best when he "reasserts community values," like wariness at a "teenager hanging out on a street corner late at night, especially one dressed in an eccentric manner" or "interracial couples."[79] Broken windows rendered such suspicions impersonal but concrete through reference to physical and aesthetic signifiers of the same supposed violations of community values. With the collapse of legal and cultural restrictions on racial integration, these criminologists sought new footing. It was not simply that people of color in a white neighborhood were necessarily outsiders and thus considered threatening, though of course that might have been true among some cops and residents. Instead, the problem was that homogeneity and the clear boundedness of neighborhoods had become scrambled. The stability that made communities congeal for Wilson was imperiled in theory and in law, if not in practice, by movements to end racial exclusion. These struggles were invisible in Kelling and Wilson's narrative, which blamed changes in patrol practice and new technologies for declining police legitimacy. Yet those reforms were themselves responses to the long history of police corruption, to punctual protest against racist police activity during the 1960s, and to the decomposition of vagrancy law as a police tool.

Although the country's failure to achieve racial desegregation in the decade and a half after it became the law of the land was already becoming visible by 1982 when the *Atlantic Monthly* "Broken Windows" article appeared, backers of the theory did then and continue today to insist that its dichoto-mous premise was not about race. In fact, it reworked the salience of race to policing, filling the void left by the outlawing of vagrancy arrests according to status with novel prognostic criteria for police intervention drained of racial meaning. Today, racialization works through such apparently nonracial forms of ascription of risk and threat potential, which achieve legitimacy because they are specifically not subtended by formal and explicit categorizations of heritability and color. After the legal erosion of the viability of racial catego-rization, cops were compelled to use other proxies, like reputable or disrepu-table. But the political economy and geographies of US cities would not easily be relieved of the historical racial inequity that shaped the terrain of policing. Crime might no longer be inherently blackening, but white crime became the stochastic blur around probabilistic definitions of Blackness as risk. Absent the strict control of status enabled by vagrancy law, conduct became status.

"Broken Windows" told cops, and everyone else, a story about police his-tory. It demanded a return to a fictive past when cops' jobs were easier, when they acted at their communities' behest, and the causes of fear were obvious. It also conjured up a past when race was superfluous to US social life in order to project a future when policing would be unencumbered by racism, though the authors acknowledged with resignation that police might remain "agents of neighborhood bigotry." The nostalgia Kelling and Wilson evoked was for a time when cops could apply easy dichotomies, when communities were, by law and custom, more apparently homogeneous. Lost between Parker's demands for order and Kelling and Wilson's article was one regime of racism. Its replacement was a more flexible one. What remained consistent through-out the decades was the technology of order maintenance: the discretionary despotism of policing. This was as true in Indochina as Indiana, Kinshasa as Kansas City. The form of policing that Kelling and Wilson described, which was also a political philosophy of social order, reproduced the mechanics of cost-benefit counterinsurgency that Leites and Wolf delineated. Both, in turn, were consonant with long-standing global policing practices pursued under the auspices of the public safety program.

. . .

One way to read the history of the rise of the carceral state, in light of its transnational connections, would be to say that counterinsurgency practices used in foreign territories were subsequently repatriated as policing practices on American streets. There is an element of truth to this claim. But the more robust and historically accurate accounting offered in this book shows that the experts involved in developing both did so simultaneously, mobilizing a unified field of vision that did not distinguish security practices used overseas from those used at home. This reframing matters, not simply for fidelity to the historical record, but because of the political demands that issue from misinterpretation. Repression was not the logical result of failures of liberal reformism. The conservative backlash against freedom movements and the expansion of social welfare operated through misrepresentation, acting as though its leaders had not already been seeking to thwart marginalized people's aspirations and practical gains all along. This bad faith was contiguous with the bad faith that misrepresented the hearts and minds strategy in order to discredit it. The backlash formulation relies on a narration of events that clings to analytic geographies that historical experience did not maintain. The order of events was not rebellion overseas, its smothering, rebellion at home like rebellion overseas, and then its smothering in the shape of overseas counterrevolution. Nor was rebellion at home followed by justifiable reaction. Rather, counterrevolution in both zones developed in advance of and simultaneously to insurgency in both zones. Policing was already global, already counterinsurgent. US empire operates according to an implacably expansive vision of its field of operations.

Conclusion

IN 1973, THE FILM *The Exorcist* captured a mixture of panic, malaise, and misanthropy that was gripping the American psyche. The film's title indicated that the upheavals of the 1960s, including the disasters of Southeast Asia, needed to be expunged from the United States' sense of itself in an act of radical purification. *The Exorcist* concluded with a famous horror scene that suggested the impossibility of that purification without drastic measures—in this case, suicide. *The Exorcist* depicted a lone man intentionally tumbling down a narrow, long staircase to his death in order to end a cycle of demonic possession. It was not quite the horror of the massacre on the wide steps in Odessa in Sergei Eisenstein's 1925 *Battleship Potemkin*, but both scenes had political resonances. The earlier one was clear: brutal Cossacks wantonly attacked men, women, and children. The Office of Public Safety's recommendations to avoid exactly that sort of violence might have had Eisenstein's film in mind. *Battleship Potemkin* clearly shows the tsarist regime in a bad light, providing fodder for the Bolshevik critique. The message of the scene in *The Exorcist* requires a bit more interpretative work. Fredric Jameson has written of the transformation evoked by this comparison: this film and others like it, "may ... be seen as expressing the nostalgia for a system in which Good and Evil are absolute black-and-white categories: they do not express a new Cold War psychology as much as they express the longing and the regret for a Cold War period in which things were still simple, not so much belief in Manichaean forces as the nagging suspicion that everything would be so much easier if we could believe in them."[1] The same could be said of OPS guidance. The building that provided the far wall of the long staircase in *The Exorcist* was the old trolley barn in Georgetown that housed the International Police Academy. Inside it, those Manichaean beliefs were alive, if only for a little while longer until Congress closed the academy (with final administrative actions and the publication of the last issue of the *IPA Review* early in 1975). Yet these beliefs also had long afterlives that shaped the transitional decade of the 1970s.

Critics of OPS believed it supported repressive regimes, including by teaching torture and other unsavory practices. Through public protest, the 1972 Costa-Gavras film *State of Siege,* which dramatized Dan Mitrione's kidnapping and assassination, investigative journalism, and congressional lobbying, these critics undermined the credibility of OPS, leading to two revisions to the Foreign Assistance Act that shut it down, first overseas in 1974 and then at home by closing the IPA in 1975. Though OPS would be no more, former public safety advisors did their best to keep the security infra-structure of the Manichaean beliefs intact. Some adventures stand out. One country sought a route around the defunding of police assistance well before OPS's closure was proposed in Congress. Saudi Arabia wanted to guarantee its ability to draw upon the expertise of OPS, regardless of the political winds in Washington. Beginning in 1968, Saudi Arabia's novel solution was that *it,* not the US federal purse, would provide all the funding for a police assistance program. Every expense US advisors incurred on behalf of the Agency for International Development, from salaries to housing to petty cash, would be funded through a special account Saudi Arabia opened. No other country's program received funding this way. Once the termination of OPS was on the horizon, Nicaragua and Venezuela joined Saudi Arabia in seeking ways to continue US police assistance. "Saudi Arabia decided to drastically increase the emphasis on internal security," and seventeen former public safety advi-sors began a massive survey "in the fields of records and identification, crimi-nalistics, disaster control, traffic, and corrections" on behalf of the Saudi Ministry of the Interior in early 1975.[2] Ultimately, the US Department of State and AID, in compliance with the new Section 660 of the Foreign Assistance Act of 1974, refused to allow continued US public safety pro-grams, even if funded by the countries in which they were based.

As a result, another option emerged: the privatization of internal-security training. Contracted corporations began employing former public safety advisors. Engle's successor, Lauren Goin, founded one. For $80 million, Saudi Arabia hired the California-based Vinnell Corporation to train its expanded National Guard, a paramilitary police force.[3] The left-leaning Senator James Abourezk (D-SD), who sponsored the amendments that ter-minated OPS activities, felt this contract violated the letter and spirit of his legislation.[4] At least two former public safety advisors joined Vinnell.[5] In addition to such contracting, private security consulting was a growth field. Arnold Sagalyn and Byron Engle became consultants, with Engle traveling to Rhodesia with a delegation from the American Conservative Union to monitor the risk of guerrilla attacks on polls during the high-stakes 1979 election to form the new government of Zimbabwe.[6] John Longan returned to Venezuela as a private consultant to help locate a kidnapped US corporate executive.[7] Some former public safety advisors sought new assignments in other federal agencies, like Charles Sloane, who tried to get a job with the CIA, or Herb Johnston, Weyland Walter, and over ten others who found employment directly with the Law Enforcement Assistance Administration or in positions funded by it.[8] Others became, in their own words, "soldiers of fortune."[9]

Under President Ronald Reagan, US training of foreign police resumed. Narcotics control was the primary reason. In time, it became an enormous operation, involving multiple US agencies, from the Department of Justice to the Pentagon to the Drug Enforcement Administration (DEA) and more, as well as private contractors. AID even got back in on the action too. In the early 1970s, an old argument had reappeared: Chinese communists were not only exporting subversion; they were exporting opium too. The claim was so flimsy that OPS prepared a standard memorandum template replying to the charge, but it would not convince true believers.[10] President Nixon's war on drugs nonetheless provided a new rationale for much of the professionalizing work OPS had already been conducting with police overseas. Even before Nixon's 1969 inauguration, OPS had begun to incorporate antinarcotics routines and training into its repertoires. In testimony before a House Subcommittee in 1973, Engle reflected on his own time in Turkey: "I took one of the first advisers overseas in 1951 in the field of narcotics to assist foreign governments in combating this evil."[11] After Nixon's landmark address in June 1971 on the prevention of drug abuse, public safety advisors worked to demonstrate how they could play a unique role.[12] OPS organized one of the first interagency meetings on narcotics in October 1971, gathering representatives from across the government to meet with counterinsurgency experts and public safety advisors.[13] In the early 1970s, furthermore, OPS advisors participated in newly formed coordinating bodies, like the East Asia Working Group on Narcotics. The OPS role was unique among agencies. As one report put it, OPS "supports, but is not to be confused with the overseas efforts of other US agency representatives, which are operational in character. Public Safety Advisors work in closest harmony with them," including narcotics and customs agents in the Treasury Department.[14]

This support of narcotics control was a prominent justification AID officials mobilized for continuing police assistance as controversies imperiled it beginning in 1970. When OPS operations in South Vietnam did conclude, the new DEA provided continuing assistance, as "narcotic suppression was not included in the legislative prohibition" against further police assistance. With no AID contribution, however, US support for narcotics control to South Vietnam was projected to decrease by more than half for fiscal year 1975.[15] Overall, in a few years, however, the US budget for overseas narcotics control increased by 600 percent.[16] The DEA, along with a new State Department program, became in many respects the successor to OPS.[17] Ultimately, five OPS advisors remained overseas in official capacities after the phase-out of police assistance, now as "narcotics advisors."[18] All they had to do was change signs on office doors from counterinsurgency to counternarcotics.

The LEAA, whose bureaucratic shape and purpose mimicked OPS, provided another way to maintain the technical-assistance mission to police overseas. To the astonishment of the activist researcher Nancy Stein, "LEAA acquired an international role at the same time that OPS was being phased out."[19] This push originated with Nixon's domestic law-enforcement advisory staff, overseen by Egil Krogh, not the NSC, State Department, or Pentagon, which were "dragged" "kicking and screaming" into narcotics control.[20] Congress amended the legislation governing the LEAA in 1973, in part to expand its scope. It authorized the agency to gather information on law enforcement outside the United States and to provide technical assistance abroad.[21] Categorical redefinition as well as invention of new crime categories enabled the LEAA to assume new responsibilities.

Think tanks helped LEAA bureaucrats envision how to expand its crime-fighting role. Funded by the LEAA, the Mitre Corporation issued an analysis of three domains into which LEAA officials believed their agency could expand: skyjacking, terrorism, and narcotics trafficking.[22] The first two were explicitly political tactics that radicals and revolutionaries increasingly used, as traditional social movements faced uncompromising repression. Control of narcotics was rapidly becoming the new purpose for long-standing rural counterguerrilla practice. No single agency bore responsibility for suppressing these activities, according to the Mitre Corporation, and the LEAA was already represented on working groups convened to strategize responses. The LEAA could assume a leadership role. Consultants understood skyjacking, terrorism, and narcotics trafficking to "transcend local boundaries" and hence jurisdictional restrictions. A newly created research institute within the LEAA was perfectly poised to become a "clearinghouse," recapitulating the function of the IPA's Reference Center, and to provide technical assistance. Although the Omnibus Crime Control and Safe Streets Act recognized that crime was a "local problem," it also insisted that "all levels of government" needed to be involved in the endless effort "to insure the greater safety of the people." Consultants seized upon this language. "Criminal activity has no respect for levels of government," they asserted. With its proactive research focus and support for experimental technologies and approaches, LEAA stood out: "no other Federal agency is apt to be engaged in research with international implication." Still, in contrast to OPS, it was important that LEAA not concern itself with reducing crime in other countries. All that mattered were efforts abroad that would reduce crime domestically. The thin ideological linkage between international development and crime control that underwrote three decades of overseas police assistance was finally severed. Private consultants estimated how much it would cost LEAA to issue grants or to use its own staff and resources to provide new international research, technical assistance, and coordination; they based their estimate of not more than $4 million on a review of OPS expenditures.[23]

Former public safety advisors cultivated their expertise in firearms in the 1970s, with some pushing for liberalization of gun laws. Although the War on Crime began with efforts to control the availability of some handguns, by the mid-1970s, gun possession within the United States was becoming a hot-button political issue in the other direction. Now, many who supported tough-on-crime legislation also demanded a loosening of controls on gun ownership. The largest gun-owners' organization, the National Rifle Association (NRA), had backed curtailment of some gun rights in the 1960s. Less than a decade later, its leadership was not ready to change its tune, despite the urging of many of its members. Members and former employees therefore staged a coup. Involved was a man who knew a few things about coups, and a lot about guns: Byron Engle.

In 1975, the NRA created a lobbying group, the Institute for Legislative Action. Its leader was Harlon B. Carter, who had formerly been the commander of the US Border Patrol and was once a president of the NRA. Carter was a gun-rights zealot who believed that harsh punishment, not gun control, was necessary to lessen violent crime. NRA veterans, including Engle, oversaw Carter's institute. Earlier, Engle had joined two other men in conducting the search that resulted in Carter's hiring to lead the lobbying effort.[24] The gulf between Carter and the mainstream NRA soon proved too great, however, and he was sacked, along with dozens of other employees who supported rapid and thorough liberalization of gun laws. In 1977, two years after the institute had been created, less than a year after it was closed, a phalanx of Carter's supporters took over the NRA's national meeting through parliamentary chicanery. The insurgents reinstated the institute, made him the (unelected) executive director of the organization, and changed the rules for appointments of members of the board of directors. They kicked out the old guard and dramatically reoriented the NRA. Harlon Carter—who as a teenage vigilante had shot and killed Ramón Casiano, a younger Mexican American teenager, whom he suspected of having helped to steal the Carter family car—shifted the NRA toward the far more extreme and fundamentalist gun-rights positions it has maintained over the past few decades.[25] He came back into the organization's fold because of Byron Engle.

What can we conclude about Engle's Zelig-like appearance in both NRA offices and the rural backcountry of Rhodesia during the 1970s? First, partisanship offers little guidance. Engle started a Democrat and ended a Republican, but he never for a second turned his eyes away from distant shores. In the 1960s, a few isolationists and interventionists switched party allegiances over some foreign-policy issues, but a bipartisan consensus shaped the commitment to underwriting the US economy through Keynesian countercyclical defense spending. Matching this spending commitment was a political one. It entrusted to an unelected military machine and the executive with the discretionary prerogative—the police power—to act offensively in the world to forever shore up the world-system Truman, Dean Acheson, and Paul Nitze had ushered into being. Engle's entire professional life can be traced back to a pragmatic linkage between Democrats, the right-place-right-time Harry Truman and the incorrigible, venal Tom Pendergast, without whose backing Truman might never have been later elected president. Likewise, without Pendergast's corrupt police and Kansas City's ensuing municipal reconstruction, Engle might never have found his purpose in life. Once in the White House, Truman gave centralized shape and infinite budgetary license to the national security state, ensuring the solidity of what one historian has called "global realm with no limit, global realm with no name," the consistently disavowed US empire.[26] There is a term for the art of government enacted as the limitless, the nameless, the enumerated but innumerable, the definitive but undefined—it is police. The pullulating American reformation of empire as such is police. There were many levels or modes of this new imperial dispensation, from the financial to the fine arts, all glued together or cemented by an ideological commitment, a mood, of anticommunism. Yet one level secured the everyday safety of the others, ensuring the reproduction of the whole: civilian policing.

Truman's global realm with no limit needed tutors who would educate its willing proxies in how to ensure material, practical fealty to it. Engle was one among hundreds. In turn, extraterritorial experiences and rehearsals fueled and sharpened state-formation at home, the if-you-build-it-threats-will-come construction of capacities of security. What police assistance aimed to do, even as it often focused on rooting out ideological opponents to a US-superintended world-system of capitalist accumulation, was to reformat the social terrain from which revolutionary impulses and organizations could grow. In its fostering of state connectivity across borders, it would sever organic, solidary connections of political fellowship. Policing, through its shaping of social subjects by preemptive, proactive insinuation into manifold realms of social regulation, aims to make insurgency impossible, not ideologically but practically. Repression may breed resistance. But OPS and professionalizers more broadly internalized criticisms of police violence, defanging them, if only momentarily. Furthermore, expansive, well-tuned police forces shorten the horizons of political possibility by actively recoding political deviance and social struggle against authority as disorder. Engle might once have been dependent on his Democratic Party bona fides, but he was far more loyal to order.

. . .

The shift from collective to individual action evoked by the comparison of the Odessa steps with the Georgetown steps, from preserving moral bonds to rational cost-benefit calculus, tracks an oscillation in horizons of political possibility and intellectual frameworks across the American Century. For too long the role of the police power in this shift, and the way the shift has registered within the police institution itself, has been held in a black box. Even in critical analysis, the police institution often appears static. It is ever a dependent variable, never the independent one. Yet as police have shifted toward behavior control as order maintenance, individualizing the collectively felt social precariousness of capitalism's icy compulsions, the people who compose these institutions have become ever more tightly bound together as a collective political actor, shifting away from individualistic competition for graft or opportunities to filch from the state purse (though these persist). Professionalization sundered political loyalties that previously organized the collective life of patrol officers. In turn, now independent and autonomous, they became political actors unto themselves, fighting not to line their individual pockets but their collective ones, whether through federal subventions or strong collective bargaining agreements. This process, set into motion with the War on Crime, snowballed afterward.

The history of OPS cannot be disentangled from the history of the professionalization of policing. The argument of *Badges Without Borders* has, however, been that the reverse was even more consequential: professionalization was a transnational project, OPS its chief organizer. Scholars generally have not appreciated the restless itinerary of professionalization. Unlike militarization, which is both an externally imposed category and, in substance, the adoption of external criteria, police executives and law-enforcement experts themselves used the term "professionalization." It was internal to their worldview, rather than a category developed externally. The history of OPS, moreover, shows that the worldview of the professionalizers was geographically expansive, and that it expanded geographically through confrontation with extraterritorial threats to national security. Police may narrate the institution as hermetic, static, and insulated from civil-society and social-movement pressures, but this history shows that the appearance of such achieved qualities requires strenuous efforts and political struggles within, against, and across the population—and within the state itself. Whereas the militarization metaphor implies contamination by alien and externally imposed pathogens, police professionalizers accepted the challenge of testing professionalization in foreign settings, to domesticate the foreign through modularity of practice.

OPS failures and frustrations owed not to incommensurability between the aims of professionalization and indigenous capacities and capabilities but more typically to the vertiginous contradiction between the empowerment of an autonomous institutional force at the edge of state power in independent postcolonial nations and the necessity of that force's and those nations' fealty to US political and economic designs. Yet police-led counterinsurgency also aimed to be a vehicle of commensuration, of creating a police institution that could liquidate social antagonism to capitalist order. Where modernization theory proposed widely applicable criteria of development and prescribed a set of blunt tools for their rapid achievement, police professionalization as OPS practiced it sought ways to bridge the socio-technical gap between US designs and on-the-ground realities. Modernization narrated this gap in terms of chronology, reliant on a schema that transposed spatial distance and (subjective) cultural strangeness from a conjured West in terms of a temporal lag.[27] The lag would be neutralized upon arrival at a stage of consumption-heavy capitalism. Professionalization did not posit a fully formed and reachable termination status, however. It would be an ever-unfinished process, which meant police within the United States were as eligible for it as police overseas.

Professionalization also diverged from modernization. Its itinerary and chronology were not "bonded to the nation-state," whereas moderniza-tion presupposed and hypostatized the nation-state as the container of its unfolding stages. This presupposition, however, occluded the relationship of modernization to capitalism, as the itinerary of capitalism intersected but exceeded the nation-state.[28] Unlike modernization, police professionalization addressed itself to a set of institutions and social problems at once smaller and greater than the nation-state. The police would remain eminently local in scale. US power would never relinquish its proxy status, thanks to the inter-vening operation of technical police assistance. Yet professionalization would mount the appropriate challenge to threats to social order that refused to be contained by the contingent boundaries of the historical invention called the nation-state. As Engle reflected upon his retirement, "Once the problem was local. The criminal was local. . . . Then as transportation and communications improved, so did the dimensions of the problem change from local to inter-city, from inter-county to interstate. Today, it's becoming international and intercontinental."[29] The expanded geographic orbit of policing relied on an expansive and expanding collection of threats, but also on the static singular-ity of the criminal. What should be clear in this review of the ambitions and actualities of the professionalization of policing is that it could antedate and then outlast the conjuncture that gave purpose and plausibility to moderniza-tion theory because the police power intersects with the nation and exceeds it—like capitalism. Furthermore, in its adequacy to capitalism, as lubricant to the formatting and reformatting of social terrain that policing takes as its object, the US vision of police professionalization also sought to adequate itself to challenges to capitalist social order that were themselves smaller and larger than the nation-state, such as, chiefly, Black radicalism.

At home, the transnational itinerary of police professionalization left multiple imprints. Among them were the devolutionary bureaucratic shape of the War on Crime's institutionalization; the coalescence of police as a specially endowed political actor; the enlargement and deepening of specialized training for police; the development of new weapons, communications, and data-management technologies; the creation of new markets for policing expertise and repertoires; and the creation and field-testing of individualizing police techniques that addressed and promoted the failure of social-welfare programming. Once counterinsurgency is understood as primarily a police project historically, it becomes possible to discern not simply linkages across borders but the unified field of vision that is security and the singular set of repertoires enacting this vision under the aegis of police. Between international security and interpersonal safety looms a single mediating factor—police.

Still, there remains a tendency to ascribe only grossly repressive activities to the reverberations of empire. The nub of this critique is the mismatch of these illiberal activities with liberal governance. Yet liberal governance is better understood as forged through the accommodation of illiberal practices. The cohabitation of the liberal and illiberal gives fuel to the internecine battles within the foreign-affairs apparatuses of the state that comfort the liberal outlook and sanctify its telos, by always demonstrating that improvement of liberalism is at last around the next bend. Furthermore, illiberal acts are necessitated by social threats that refuse the operational terms of liberalism. The small war is liberalism's well-spring. This process of illiberal detour appears as the proactive identification, and neutralization, of the threat whose realization otherwise will engender war of all against all. To avoid it, whatever measures may be necessary are necessary.

Racialized state repression did not disappear in the 1970s after public revelations of the numerous seamy and illegal forms it took. The eclipse of J. Edgar Hoover with the declaration of the War on Crime and his demise soon thereafter, however, opened the possibility for a structural transformation in policing American streets that tracked macroeconomic shifts. As red squads and industrial-security experts assured the security of production in a Fordist economy, everyday policing, particularly in its emergent order-maintenance guise, would come to ensure the realization of capital and its smooth circulation in space, necessary complements to, by the 1980s, increasingly pacified shop-floor antagonisms and financialized accumulation strategies. Repression continues. But the productive side of policing, its construction of particular social subjects, including through the fear of repression and the demonstrative training of the public in how to interact with police, remain salient under the long reign of professionalization. Where the zenith of US social-welfarism saw the wedding of policing to productive, participatory human development programming, in the wake of this conjuncture, with the annihilation of many of these state capacities of nonpunitive controlled uplift, policing has become the primary modality of pacification. Policing American streets, schools, workplaces, and consumption sites entails the process by which discrepant forms of habitus are eliminated, to create a particular bearing, a way of acting in the world, of rationally acting. This way of acting in the world is the object of order maintenance. It is order.

The critique of policing as increasingly repressive, the state as increasingly punitive, has been intertwined with a critique of US empire. Jack O'Dell, for a time an advisor to Martin Luther King Jr., offered a particularly cogent analysis in 1968: "Policemanship as a style of government is no longer confined to the Southern-way-of-life but is now becoming institutionalized on a national level. And the line between foreign and domestic policy is fading out as well, as militarism and the military presence become 'coextensive with the Star Spangled Banner.'"[30] Through a collision with Black radicalism, white New Left militancy, antiwar action, and anti-imperialist solidarity, this critique fixated on overseas police assistance and attracted the attention of Senator Abourezk. It was one of the most successful anti-imperialist movement efforts of the era, resulting in the legislative revisions that terminated OPS.

The enlargement of solidarities and the sharpening of the critique began the process. Opposition to police assistance cohered not long after the cruelest months for OPS, July and August 1970. First came a photo essay in *Life* magazine that depicted prisoners kept in inhumane, torturous conditions on Con Son Island off the coast of South Vietnam, in a prison under the advisory assistance of OPS.[31] Then came Dan Mitrione's kidnapping and assassination in Uruguay. These events confirmed suspicions at home—among public safety advisors. The police truly were the first line of defense, and occasionally the offense would come armed with a gun; at other times, it might be armed with a pen. News stories confirmed the suspicions of others, as radicals became aware of what OPS was doing. Researchers began to dig. Journalists and movement organizations like the North American Congress on Latin America, National Action/Research on the Military-Industrial Complex, the Center for Research on Criminal Justice, and others all engaged in activist research, combing through public records, charting connections, figuring out how US empire was built brick by brick. Newly engaged activists came together to stage a protest outside the IPA in November 1970.

An ad hoc group calling itself the Coalition Against Police Exploiters of Repression, or CAPER, organized the rally.[32] Was CAPER correct? A catchy acronym made for organizing purposes is not an analysis unto itself. Though it was pitch-perfect in its satire of the endless strings of acronyms that characterize and obfuscate US geopolitical power (and weave through this analysis of it), we can ask: was OPS a police exploiter of repression? Embedded in that awkward phrase is a theory of power. One way to read it is that the forces of repression—the CIA or other shadowy actors—used police assistance to hide their true aims. OPS thus strengthened authoritarian regimes that were friendly to US economic and political interests. This nonliteral reading would be consonant with the Tupamaros' take on OPS, justifying their killing of Mitrione. It would also be consonant with most New Left critiques, as well as more recent scholarly analyses of OPS.[33] Disaffected former public safety advisors often felt they also had been used.

Yet there is another, more literal way to read the phrase Police Exploiters of Repression. Even in its critique of this activity, CAPER recognized that police work is not confined to the post hoc apprehension of the criminal. Instead, police act in advance. Traditionally, "repression" was a term in English that referred to this future-oriented action, paired with backward-looking action. In 1780, according to the *Oxford English Dictionary,* this conjunction appeared in a Scottish tract: "The repression of disorders, and the punishment of crimes." Repression as such is the proactive, counterinsurgent function of police. But is policing actually repressive, meaning subtractive, not productive, meaning additive? And does it correspond only to the vernacular, critical identification of practices that comprise repression? These include infiltration of radical groups, disinformation campaigns, entrapment, trumped-up charges, torture, and assassination. The answer, *Badges Without Borders* cannot but conclude, is no. To elaborate this reading of CAPER, police forces often do resort to grossly repressive acts. But this set of practices is only one within a wider, more varied set of tools available to officers. To use repression is a choice available to police, and the police power is defined by that discretion. Other choices might not necessarily single out those who are outwardly, explicitly politically radical. Instead, typical police tactics are available, such as observation, conversation with community members, stop-and-frisk, and enforcement of traffic and other noncriminal laws and regulations. They compose what in 1780 was called repression insofar as they compose the forward-looking action of police to shape social subjects and make impossible the intricacies of rebellion.

This mode of governance tried to define Black life in the United States for a long time, but new civil rights legislation and changes to criminal-law procedure forced it to find new legitimacy. These came amid imperial reconfiguration. In the era of decolonization, social-scientific and counterinsurgent analogizing often attempted to slot the Black experience neatly within the boundaries of the nation and to see Black politics that reached beyond those boundaries as suspicious, unloyal, or subversive. But the nation-state as a form continually failed to provide durable redress for Black people. As a consequence, Black political identification frequently sculpted smaller-scale, localized forms of communalism and broader, transnational polities— adopting different geographies of analogy in response to the insufficiency of national belonging. Wary of the illiberalism of such geographies, to contain and enclose political demands, security experts fixed the limits of liberalism by inhabiting similar geographies. In their effort to protect the nation-state, they empowered the local white small-town despots who themselves disidentified with federal power; they also reached across the globe, seeking experiments in authoritarianism to hone the technics of security's assurance. This illiberalism summoned Black resistance that both reshaped the state and posed the question of liberalism's limits anew. But state violence can never eliminate resistance. In its attempt to do so, state violence, not resistance to it, imperils the civil society that is to be the ultimate manifestation of liberalism. The purpose of the professionalized civilian police is to draw the line between society and state, to define the state as the ultimate, legitimate arbiter of society's safety within the terms of liberalism. It also narrows those terms by narrowing the population that can access that safety and the civil society that it is to protect. To refuse that narrowing, while also recognizing the insufficiency of the nationally constrained civil society from which the narrowing excludes, is to enact a radical, internationalist antiracism.

The history of the professionalization of US policing is a transnational history in which the fear of resistance to liberalism from below, to which the labels "communist" and "subversive" were repeatedly attached, gave purpose and meaning to travel, to a search for experiences that might fit the analogy. When General Vo Nguyen Giap remarked to Robert F. Williams, after the Tet Offensive, "We learned from Detroit to go to the cities," he endorsed what counterinsurgent knowledge already presumed.[34] One worry was that Black people at home would learn from subversives overseas, but a greater one was that subversives overseas would become, through their actions, Black people such as existed at home. Not only would they confer upon civil society its inadequacy by probing its limits, but they would resist enclosure within a risk calculus the heuristic device of race would define. These worries—that the *legitimacy* of a monopoly on violence would erode, that racial demarcation was insufficient to render uncertainty measurable—energized the police power, giving it the limitlessness that the apparently fixed object of Blackness seemed to demand in its refusal to be fixed by ascriptive racism.

. . .

Transnational police assistance expanded dramatically after September 11, 2001. Contemporary forms of US security assistance exceed what Engle could have imagined, as do their domestic reverberations. Yet the consecration of security as governing paradigm, and the mobilization of executive discretion for this singular purpose, which mark the present, would be recognizable to Komer and Engle. It was a configuration initiated by a third key figure from the Show-Me State, Harry Truman. This present would also be recognizable to Huynh Van Tam, one of the NLF's overseas representatives, who responded to trumped-up charges against Bill Epton in the aftermath of the 1964 uprising in Harlem by proclaiming that repression against Black people in New York was the domestic version of the violation of the "rights to independence and freedom of other nations," like what was occurring in Vietnam. Tam continued, "the more aggressive is the foreign policy of a government, the more anti-democratic is its home policy and vice-versa."[35] Both sides of this vice versa, the perpetual motion machine of US empire, are what *Badges Without Borders* has uncovered. Hopes for a return from the austere, illiberal present to a bygone era of post-1945 plenitude, increasingly shared across the truncated US political spectrum, must grapple with this history, with the present as its product. The core aspiration of *Badges Without Borders* is to show that any assessment of the present's relationship to the past must hold foreign and domestic in a single frame, as indissolubly linked, as co-constituted. Any liberation effort to reconfigure security policy on one side must also reconfigure it on the other.

In the wake of Black Lives Matter, an upsurge of popular protest against policing tactics and violence unlike any seen in decades, the cable-news host Chris Hayes tried to assay what it is that police do when they maintain order, why the maintenance of order raises hackles and engenders street protest. Invoking the internal colony metaphor, he highlighted how solving crime is not what police do primarily. What police do, he found, is ensure order, which he differentiated from safety. And he offered an interpretation of why the prevention of crime and disorder has fueled protest movements. He wrote, thinking of the enforcement of quality-of-life regulations, "Order is a slippery thing: it's in the eyes of the beholder and the judgments of the powerful."[36] But order is not only about how people feel subjectively. The order that police have historically produced and maintained—conscripted us into—may feel like order to some and disorder to others. But that feeling of imbalance is not all that defines it. Instead, what defines it is its purpose, which is to create the conditions grounding the feeling. Imbalance is not simply an outcome; it is how, and why, order operates. Order is the systematic organization of the social to disorganize opponents of the present social synthesis. Order is the condition of insurgency-against-order countered. The order police on American streets have created, the order OPS would propagate by proxy abroad, the order the War on Crime facilitated is the order of capital, the order of white supremacy, the order of empire. Together these demand security, at home and abroad. Security is the protection of a sum that is greater than these parts. But security is not metaphysics. Security is the positing of a world governed by its metaphysics alone. It is forever expansive, forever unfinished, forever self-justifying. Security is, according to its own imperatives, simply forever. Until it is not.

ACKNOWLEDGMENTS

This book, like empire, goes in many directions. Unlike empire, it has a relatively simple origin point. A couple of sentences and a footnote in *Lockdown America: Police and Prisons in the Age of Crisis* by Christian Parenti sparked this project. I am grateful for another citation, which led me to Christian's sentences, in an article about my beloved Brooklyn by Forrest Hylton. Above all, this project stands upon a foundation built by Tracy Tullis, whose path-breaking dissertation taught me so much about the topic. My thanks go to several authors who blazed a trail by writing about the Office of Public Safety at a moment when the political stakes could not have been higher: Mike Klare, A.J. Langguth, and Tom Lobe. All three offered me encouraging words. I must also extend thanks and appreciation to the North American Congress on Latin America, whose political spirit this project aspires to honor. Among kindred analysts, my greatest debt is to Micol Seigel, comrade, great friend, and interlocutor.

The Program in American Studies at New York University was a wonderful place to grow intellectually and politically. I am so glad to have met everyone in the program. Zenia Kish and Emma Kreyche were particularly welcoming and supportive. Other brilliant folks who preceded me and extended collegial friendship include Andy Cornell, Eva Hageman, Rana Jaleel, Liz Mesok, Dacia Mitchell, and Zach Schwartz-Weinstein. Marisol LeBrón, for a time my international traveling buddy, has been a close friend and important interlocutor. I could not have been more fortunate than to share a cohort with Thulani Davis, Justin Leroy, Manijeh Moradian, and Claudia Sofía Garriga López, whose support, collegiality, and wisdom were formative and crucial. I also owe many thanks to AJ Bauer, honorary member of our cohort, for his wit and political insight, as well as to Sam Ng.

Beyond American Studies, my greatest thanks go to Hillary Angelo, Daniel Aldana Cohen, and David Wachsmuth. The adage that graduate students learn the most from their peers has never been more accurate. Their comradeship is unparalleled. I can only hope to indicate how robustly dialectical this journey has been by saying that I could not imagine wider discussions of the micro or more focused discussions of the macro. I extend deep thanks to the many historians who offered me a home department away from home, especially Jeannette Estruth, Joshua Frens-String, Laura Helton, Ebony Jones, David Klassen, Alex Manevitz, Max Mishler, Tej Nagaraja, Samantha Seeley, Shauna Sweeney, Geoff Traugh, Katy Walker, and Beatrice Wayne.

The Charles Warren Center was a wonderful place to land after completing my PhD, where I met a great big crew of formidable scholars. I am especially grateful to Megan Black for her camaraderie, kindness, level-headedness, and fellowship. I can't thank every other postdoc, professor, and fellow I met individually, but all of them helped along the way in different ways. For insights crucial to this project, I'm particularly grateful to Garrett Felber, Lily Geismer, Julilly Kohler-Hausmann, Donna Murch, Amy Offner, Timothy Stewart-Winter, and Heather Ann Thompson. Chris Clements provided great friendship. I'm glad I got to know Ella Antell, Tim Barker, Jonathon Booth, Sam Klug, and Jackie Wang, as well as numerous incredibly smart undergraduates. Indispensable support came from Vince Brown, Elizabeth Hinton, Arthur Patton-Hock, Walter Johnson, Lisa McGirr, Brandon Terry, and Kirsten Weld. Beverly Gage, Paul Kramer, Timothy Mitchell, and Richard White gave me lovely feedback and encouragement that shaped the book, in large and small ways. I'm grateful to Megan for sharing that amazing day with me in Cambridge.

The Tamiment Library provided essential resources in a moment of near desperation, and I'm grateful that this unique institution persists. I appreciate all of its staff, and I'm especially happy to have gotten to know Mike Koncewicz as a friend and interlocutor.

The relationship of historian to archivist can be vexed, particularly when the historian's questions do not hew to the categories that organize the archive itself. Nonetheless, I could not have had a better experience working with an archivist than I have had with Allen Fisher at the LBJ Library. His deep knowledge and willingness to go even more than the extra mile are unmatched. To single him out does not detract from the many other helpful archivists, volunteers, and staff members I have met along the way, who answered my occasionally bizarre questions with charity and smiles, including at the Johnson, Kennedy, Nixon, and Reagan Libraries, as well as at the Kansas City Municipal Library, Los Angeles Public Library Central Branch, and Walnut Creek Historical Society, among other repositories. Thanks very much to Naclista Fred Goff and the DataCenter for unique research assistance. Thanks also to the comrades at Bibliomania and Bolerium.

I have benefited from presenting portions of this work to audiences at Hampshire College, Harvard University, Johns Hopkins University, NYU, Towson University, and UC Santa Cruz. And I would not have been able to complete the research for this project without the generous support of several other institutions. Thank you to the American Council of Learned Societies, the Blum Center for Developing

Economies, the Lyndon Baines Johnson Foundation, the Mellon Foundation, the Social Science Research Council, the Society for Historians of American Foreign Relations, and Vassar College. For research and travel funding from NYU, thank you to the Department of Social & Cultural Analysis, the Graduate School of Arts & Sciences, and the Provost's Global Research Initiatives. Thank you also to the Charles Warren Center and the Provost's Professional Development fund at Harvard. And thanks to all the medical staff at the New York Eye and Ear Infirmary who repaired my failing eyes, enabling me to write a book.

Numerous people have welcomed me to Baltimore and to Johns Hopkins University, helping me to finish this book while also starting anew. Among them I am especially grateful to Andy Cherlin, Niki Fabricant, Casey Lurtz, James Lynch, Katrina McDonald, Beverly Silver, Lester Spence, and Vesla Weaver. Thanks also to Jessie Albee and Terri Thomas for all their help.

A wider family of my choosing has thankfully survived this crazy process intact, and I am so thankful for the love and support of Rob Buschgans, Holly Danzeisen, James Gatherer, Angela Gelso, Jill Hubley, Jen Ingles, Shannon Kearns, Dave and Libby McComb, Matt Smith, Erin Tomlinson, Nick Turner, Esmé Webb, and Thera Webb. When my brothers Clint Chapman and Francisco J. Aranda-Ortega and I finally settle down to our *vida comunale,* I know they'll be proud to put this thing on the shelf next to old issues of *Maximum Rocknroll, Raising Hell,* and *Final Curtain.* Thanks for reminding me always to sweat the small stuff. Thanks also to a great number of other friends in London, Austin, Los Angeles, Mexico City, Oakland, San Francisco, and Seattle. In New York and these cities a number of amazing little humans have entered our lives since I began working on this project, and I hope it contributes to making the world you will inherit more just and peaceful.

Many thanks are due to Emma Shaw Crane. I've cherished the conversation of Orisanmi Burton, Jordan T. Camp, Alex Elkins, Leif Fredrickson, Max Felker-Kantor, Adam Goodman, Christina Heatherton, Jessie Kindig, Brendan McQuade, Melanie Newport, Jack Norton, Lydia Pelot-Hobbs, Peter Pihos, David Stein, and Simon Toner. This generation of scholars is producing brilliant work that matches political acuity with analytic depth; I wish only that the material conditions to facilitate such work were not so shallow.

Crucial intellectual support for this project has come, in small and large ways, from Chris Capozzola, Nils Gilman, Fred Logevall, Aziz Rana, and Quinn Slobodian. Ananya Roy has practiced and modeled mentorship in indelible ways. I also have appreciated the intellectual support and friendship of Dan Berger, Danny Bessner, Bob Brigham, Ashley Dawson, Anne Eller, Andrew Friedman, Craig Gilmore, Julian Go, Alyosha Goldstein, Hannah Gurman, Daniel Immerwahr, Jeremy Kuzmarov, Jenna Loyd, Nick Mitchell, Naomi Murakawa, Lien-Hang Nguyen, Dara Orenstein, Tony Platt, Joy Rohde, Lisa Stampnitzky, Chris Taylor, Alex Vitale, and Tyler Wall. Special thanks for help in envisioning this project's future early on go to Brandon Proia. The reviewers of the manuscript helped me greatly, and I hope I haven't been too stubborn in how I dealt with your sharp feedback. Niels Hooper understood what I wanted to do with this book from our first conversation, and I'm grateful for his support and understanding throughout. Thanks also to Robin Manley for help in the final stages.

The faculty of NYU's Department of Social & Cultural Analysis is without peer intellectually and politically. I cannot express all the ways I am so lucky to have ended up learning from all of them, especially Lisa Duggan and Arlene Dávila. I must also single out Jennifer Morgan for her sage advice, empathy, and even-keeled leadership. Carolyn Dinshaw and Mary Louise Pratt were both also highly supportive. What a fortuitous treat to get to know Sukhdev Sandhu, whose Colloquium for Unpopular Culture showed how to merge eccentric interests with smart analysis. I'll never forget how he introduced me when I spoke to the Colloquium: kinder words about me have rarely been spoken.

Slightly further afield at NYU, I must thank Manu Goswami, Barbara Weinstein, and Marilyn Young. I'm terribly sad that Marilyn won't be able to read what resulted—she was the first professor I ever mentioned this project to. What Marilyn said that morning has guided it: counterinsurgents need insurgents. Thanks also to Karl Appuhn, Patrick Deer, Monica Kim, Andrew Needham, Molly Nolan, Guy Ortolano, Kristin Ross, and Alejandro Velasco. Kim Phillips-Fein has been a wonderful friend and interlocutor.

A more inspiring dissertation committee is difficult to envision. Thanks to Greg Grandin for his astute historical analysis, which never ceases to keep in view the stakes of the work we do. Without Andrew Ross none of this would have been possible. Andrew is the rarest of scholars, as inspiring off the page as on it. Many ideas herein germinated through ongoing dialogue with Ruth Wilson Gilmore, whose sharp analyses and political commitments continue to inspire me daily. Neil Brenner's warmth and encouragement have been incredibly valuable, outshined only by his intellect. I hope the imprint of his rigor shows in these pages. Finally, even before our earliest conversations, Nikhil Pal Singh's ideas and politics have shaped my own. I am so grateful for the way he has consistently sharpened my own thoughts by pulling out and relaying back with far greater clarity the key elements of what I have wanted to say. For many people, graduate school consists of little more than a series of infantilizing requirements, feelings of inadequacy, and solitary drudgery. For me, thanks to my friends and this committee, especially Nikhil, it was an incredibly rewarding journey of intellectual maturation.

My small family has always been supportive. Thank you to Juni Sudol and Cynthia and Richard Vallario. I am so sad that my grandmother Phyllis Waller is not here to witness the successes I have had, which she always believed were forthcoming. I am forever grateful for her love. Erica Vallario's death left us with a hole in our hearts that will never be filled. In this book, I analyze senseless, sudden death as group-differentiated, but I know that when it occurs it always occurs individually, in families and communities. To have lost my only cousin to a midnight single-car crash is incomparable to the massive scale of death the twentieth century witnessed, but the suddenness and inexplicability of Erica's passing shaped my understanding of how every death is local and personal, even if anonymous to the historian's best efforts.

I am so fortunate to have been accepted into the Gospodarek family, whose love and good cheer I cherish. Thanks to Dan Thornton for the laughs and the love. Gail Moody's illness and death near the outset of graduate school was immeasurably difficult. I will never forget her love and support, and I hope this book evidences the sense of justice she held in her heart and carried with her daily. Let these pages mark the historicity of the vengeful punitive turn, so that we might imagine a world that does not create the stigmatization and demonization that tears such good people up from the inside.

Writing as a vocation became imaginable to me at an early age from the example Mike Stoddard provided. His wit, flair for storytelling, and uncompromising bullshit detector have guided me. My life may never become the stuff of legendary anecdote, but it has been enriched thanks to Fidel's sister, who whispered in Mike's ear to get the hell out of Cuba before the revolution unfolded. I'm so sorry he won't be able to read these pages.

Jane Marie Schrader's unfailing support, pride, and sacrifice have made me who I am. Nothing can repay this debt, but neither would she ever ask for its repayment. All of my achievements are the direct result of her unconditional love and encouragement. This book—and all of my work, really—is dedicated to her.

Christy Thornton and I began our journey together before it became *this* journey. I cannot imagine having had to embark on all of its twists and turns without her. Christy's political acumen, ethical clarity, and sheer brilliance have shaped and improved every aspect of my life, which is our life. Christy, my gratitude that you are my best friend, my comrade, and my intellectual partner is boundless.

NOTES

INTRODUCTION

1. The literature on the carceral state is burgeoning. See, e.g., Jordan T. Camp, *Incarcerating the Crisis: Freedom Struggles and the Rise of the Neoliberal State* (Berkeley: University of California Press, 2016); Michael W. Flamm, *Law and Order: Street Crime, Civil Unrest, and the Crisis of Liberalism in the 1960s* (New York: Columbia University Press, 2005); Marie Gottschalk, *Caught: The Prison State and the Lockdown of American Politics* (Princeton, NJ: Princeton University Press, 2016); Elizabeth Hinton, *From the War on Poverty to the War on Crime: The Making of Mass Incarceration in America* (Cambridge, MA: Harvard University Press, 2016); Julilly Kohler-Hausmann, *Getting Tough: Welfare and Imprisonment in 1970s America* (Princeton, NJ: Princeton University Press, 2017); Ruth Wilson Gilmore, *Golden Gulag: Prisons, Surplus, Crisis, and Opposition in Globalizing California* (Berkeley: University of California Press, 2007); Naomi Murakawa, *The First Civil Right: How Liberals Built Prison America* (New York: Oxford University Press, 2014); Jonathan Simon, *Governing through Crime: How the War on Crime Transformed American Democracy and Created a Culture of Fear* (New York: Oxford University Press, 2007); Simon, "Rise of the Carceral State," *Social Research* 74, no. 2 (2007): 471–508; Joe Soss and Vesla M. Weaver, "Police Are Our Government: Politics, Political Science, and the Policing of Race–Class Subjugated Communities," *Annual Review of Political Science* 20, no. 1 (2017): 565–591; Heather Ann Thompson, "Why Mass Incarceration Matters: Rethinking Crisis, Decline, and Transformation in Postwar American History," *Journal of American History* 97, no. 3 (2010): 703–734; Jeremy Travis, Bruce Western, and Steve Redburn, eds., *The Growth of Incarceration in the United States: Exploring Causes and Consequences* (Washington, DC: National Academies Press, 2014); Loïc J. D. Wacquant, *Prisons of Poverty* (Minneapolis: University of Minnesota Press, 2009); Vesla Weaver, "Frontlash: Race and the Development of Punitive Crime Policy," *Studies in American Political Development* 21, no. 2 (2007): 230–265.

Emerging research has been previewed recently in edited sections of journals: "Historians and the Carceral State" in the *Journal of American History* in 2015; "Urban America and the Carceral State" in the *Journal of Urban History* in 2015 (*Journal of Urban History* has a scheduled forthcoming section on urban policing); "African Americans, Police Brutality, and the US Criminal Justice System: Historical Perspectives" and "Gendering the Carceral State: African American Women, History, and the Criminal Justice System" in the *Journal of African American History* in 2013 and 2015, respectively; and "Black Women and Police and Carceral Violence" in *Souls* in 2018.

Works that examine developments prior to 1945 include Sarah Haley, *No Mercy Here: Gender, Punishment, and the Making of Jim Crow Modernity* (Chapel Hill: University of North Carolina Press, 2016); Khalil Gibran Muhammad, *The Condemnation of Blackness: Race, Crime, and the Making of Modern Urban America* (Cambridge, MA: Harvard University Press, 2011); Bryan Wagner, *Disturbing the Peace: Black Culture and the Police Power after Slavery* (Cambridge, MA: Harvard University Press, 2009).

2. Marie Gottschalk, "Hiding in Plain Sight: American Politics and the Carceral State," *Annual Review of Political Science* 11 (2008): 235–260; Robert S. Hogg, Eric F. Druyts, Scott Burris, Ernest Drucker, and Steffanie A. Strathdee, "Years of Life Lost to Prison: Racial and Gender Gradients in the United States of America," *Harm Reduction Journal* 5 (2008): 4; Sarah K.S. Shannon, Christopher Uggen, Jason Schnittker, Melissa Thompson, Sara Wakefield, and Michael Massoglia, "The Growth, Scope, and Spatial Distribution of People with Felony Records in the United States, 1948–2010," *Demography* 54, no. 5 (2017): 1795–1818; Christopher Wildeman, "Incarceration and Population Health in Wealthy Democracies," *Criminology* 54, no. 2 (2016): 360–382; Emily Wirda, "Incarceration Shortens Life Expectancy," Prison Policy Initiative Blog, June 26, 2017.

3. On figure-ground movement, see Terence K. Hopkins, "World-Systems Analysis: Methodological Issues," in *World-Systems Analysis: Theory and Methodology*, ed. Terence K. Hopkins and Immanuel Wallerstein (Beverly Hills, CA: Sage, 1982), 145–158.

4. Daryl F. Gates with Diane K. Shah, *Chief: My Life in the LAPD* (New York: Bantam Books, 1993), 126.

5. Robert L. Allen, *Black Awakening in Capitalist America* (New York: Doubleday, 1969); Robert Blauner, "Whitewash over Watts," *Trans-Action*, March–April 1966; Blauner, "Internal Colonialism and Ghetto Revolt," *Social Problems* 16, no. 4 (1969): 393–408; Stokely Carmichael and Charles V. Hamilton, *Black Power: The Politics of Liberation in America* (New York: Vintage Books, 1967); Harold Cruse, "Revolutionary Nationalism and the Afro-American," *Studies on the Left* 2, no. 3 (1962): 12–25; George Jackson, *Soledad Brother: The Prison Letters of George Jackson* (1970; rev. ed., New York: Bantam Books, 1972); Huey P. Newton, "A Citizens' Peace Force," *Crime and Social Justice* 1 (1974): 36–39; Jack O'Dell, *Climbin' Jacob's Ladder: The Black Freedom Movement Writings of Jack O'Dell*, ed. Nikhil Pal Singh (Berkeley: University of California Press, 2010).

The literature on Black internationalism is extensive, revealing the intertwined character of anticommunism and racism, and of anti-imperialist and anti-racist movements. Books focused on this period include Joshua Bloom and Waldo E. Martin, *Black against Empire: The History and Politics of the Black Panther Party* (Berkeley: University of California Press, 2013); Ashley Farmer, *Remaking Black Power: How Black Women Transformed an Era* (Chapel Hill: University of North Carolina Press, 2017); Robeson Taj Frazier, *The East Is Black: Cold War China in the Black Radical Imagination* (Durham, NC: Duke University Press, 2015); Robin D. G. Kelley, *Freedom Dreams: The Black Radical Imagination* (Boston: Beacon Press, 2002); Sean T. Malloy, *Out of Oakland: Black Panther Party Internationalism During the Cold War* (Ithaca, NY: Cornell University Press, 2017); Brenda Gayle Plummer, *In Search of Power: African Americans in the Era of Decolonization, 1956–1974* (New York: Cambridge University Press, 2013); Nikhil Pal Singh, *Black Is a Country: Race and the Unfinished Struggle for American Democracy* (Cambridge, MA: Harvard University Press, 2004); and Cynthia A. Young, *Soul Power: Culture, Radicalism, and the Making of a U.S. Third World Left* (Durham, NC: Duke University Press, 2006).

6. Bobby Seale, "The 'Coming Long Hot Summer,'" *Black Panther Black Community News Service* 1, no. 3 (June 20, 1967).

7. For example, Center for Research on Criminal Justice, *The Iron Fist and the Velvet Glove: An Analysis of the US Police* (Berkeley, CA: Center for Research on Criminal Justice, 1975).

8. Kurt Jacobsen, *Pacification and Its Discontents* (Chicago: Prickly Paradigm Press, 2009), 5; Dan Berger, "Social Movements and Mass Incarceration," *Souls* 15, no. 1–2 (2013): 3–18.

9. Key precedents in this effort upon which I have relied are Tracy Tullis, "A Vietnam at Home: Policing the Ghettos in the Counterinsurgency Era" (PhD diss., New York University, 1999); Julilly Kohler-Hausmann, "Militarizing the Police: Officer Jon Burge, Torture, and War in the 'Urban Jungle,'" in *Challenging the Prison-Industrial Complex: Activism, Arts, & Educational Alternatives,* ed. Stephen John Hartnett (Chicago: University of Illinois Press, 2011), 43–71; and Christian Parenti, *Lockdown America: Police and Prisons in the Age of Crisis* (New York: Verso, 1999). On the carceral aspects of counterinsurgency, see Laleh Khalili, *Time in the Shadows: Confinement in Counterinsurgencies* (Stanford, CA: Stanford University Press, 2012).

10. Lyndon Johnson equated his "war on poverty" with a "war against crime and a war against disorder" in October 1964. He pointed out that the police were on the front lines of "our war against crime" in September 1965, and he demanded expansion of a "war on crime" in March 1966, only six months after he had signed federal legislation organizing a new anticrime infrastructure, the Law Enforcement Assistance Act. Lyndon B. Johnson, "Remarks on the City Hall Steps, Dayton, Ohio," October 16, 1964, by Gerhard Peters and John T. Woolley, *The American Presidency Project (TAPP)*; "Statement by the President Following the Signing of Law Enforcement Assistance Bills," September 22, 1965, *TAPP;* "Special Message to the Congress on Crime and Law Enforcement," March 9, 1966, *TAPP.*

Nixon used the war metaphor in his most important speech on narcotics control, in June 1971, though it was a "war against heroin addiction," geared toward protecting wayward white youth, but relying above all on "international cooperation." Richard Nixon, "Special Message to the Congress on Drug Abuse Prevention and Control," June 17, 1971, *TAPP*.

11. The most respected text of the backlash narrative is Thomas Byrne Edsall and Mary Edsall, *Chain Reaction: The Impact of Race, Rights, and Taxes on American Politics* (New York: Norton, 1992). In contrast, see Camp, *Incarcerating the Crisis;* Gilmore, *Golden Gulag;* Marie Gottschalk, *The Prison and the Gallows: The Politics of Mass Incarceration in America* (New York: Cambridge University Press, 2006); Joseph E. Lowndes, *From the New Deal to the New Right: Race and the Southern Origins of Modern Conservatism* (New Haven, CT: Yale University Press, 2008); Murakawa, *First Civil Right;* Simon, *Governing through Crime;* Singh, *Black Is a Country;* Weaver, "Frontlash." For early literature on the War on Crime, see Malcolm Feeley and Austin D. Sarat, *The Policy Dilemma: Federal Crime Policy and the Law Enforcement Assistance Administration* (Minneapolis: University of Minnesota Press, 1980); Thomas E. Cronin, Tania Z. Cronin and Michael E. Milakovich, *US v. Crime in the Streets* (Bloomington: Indiana University Press, 1981).

12. A recent overview of the historical literature on US empire, which plows aside a good deal of conceptual confusion, is Paul A. Kramer, "Power and Connection: Imperial Histories of the United States in the World," *American Historical Review* 116, no. 5 (2011): 1348–1391. For a sociological interpretation, see George Steinmetz, "Return to Empire: The New US Imperialism in Comparative Historical Perspective," *Sociological Theory* 23, no. 4 (2005): 339–367. I have relied on definitional work by Kramer and Steinmetz, particularly their advocacy of thinking "the imperial" as process and outcome. See also Perry Anderson, *American Foreign Policy and Its Thinkers* (New York: Verso, 2015); Andrew J. Bacevich, *Washington Rules: America's Path to Permanent War* (New York: Metropolitan Books, 2011); Greg Grandin, *Empire's Workshop: Latin America, the United States, and the Rise of the New Imperialism* (New York: Metropolitan Books, 2006); Harry D. Harootunian, *The Empire's New Clothes: Paradigm Lost, and Regained* (Chicago: Prickly Paradigm Press, 2004); Ann Laura Stoler, *Duress: Imperial Durabilities in Our Times* (Durham, NC: Duke University Press, 2016). There are dissenters from the term. Elizabeth Cobbs Hoffman, *American Umpire* (Cambridge, MA: Harvard University Press, 2013), argues that the unique federal structure of the US state has prevented it from becoming an empire. In contrast, I argue that the federal approach to governance is precisely the unique logic of US empire.

13. NACCD, *Report of the NACCD* (New York: Bantam Books, 1968), especially 323–332, 491–493, 502–504.

14. Byron Engle, Statement, September 20, 1967, series 1, *Civil Rights during the Johnson Administration, 1963–1969, Part V: Records of the NACCD (Kerner Commission)* online (*CRDJA*), 001346–003–0256, 1328–1335. The precirculated version of Engle's remarks differs: attachment to Byron Engle to Arnold Sagalyn, September 21, 1967, ser. 21, *CRDJA,* 001346–011–0264.

15. Robert H. Bruce, "Human Rights and US Training of Third World Police," *Conflict Quarterly* 8 (1988): 48–60; Bruce, "Impact of the Occupation of Japan on American Notions about US-Induced Reform in the Third World," *Indian Journal of American Studies* 75, no. 2 (1985): 123–127; Martha K. Huggins, *Political Policing: The United States and Latin America* (Durham, NC: Duke University Press, 1998); Michael T. Klare, *War without End: American Planning for the Next Vietnams* (New York: Knopf, 1972); Michael T. Klare and Cynthia Arnson, *Supplying Repression: US Support for Authoritarian Regimes Abroad* (Washington, DC: Institute for Policy Studies, 1981); Jeremy Kuzmarov, *Modernizing Repression: Police Training and Nation Building in the American Century* (Boston: University of Massachusetts Press, 2012); A.J. Langguth, *Hidden Terrors: The Truth about US Police Operations in Latin America* (New York: Pantheon Books, 1978); Thomas Lobe, "US Police Assistance for the Third World" (PhD diss., University of Michigan, 1975); Lobe, *United States National Security Policy and Aid to the Thailand Police* (Denver: University of Denver, Graduate School of International Studies, 1977); Lobe, "The Rise and Demise of the Office of Public Safety," *Armed Forces & Society* 9, no. 2 (1983) 187–213; Otwin Marenin, "United States' Aid to African Police Forces: The Experience and Impact of the Public Safety Assistance Programme," *African Affairs* 85, no. 341 (1986): 509–544; Michael McClintock, *Instruments of Statecraft: US Guerrilla Warfare, Counterinsurgency, and Counterterrorism, 1940–1990* (New York: Pantheon Books, 1992); Ethan Avram Nadelmann, *Cops across Borders: The Internationalization of US Criminal Law Enforcement* (University Park: Pennsylvania State University Press, 1993); Rodrigo Patto Sá Motta, "Modernizando a repressão: a Usaid e a polícia brasileira," *Revista Brasileira de História* 30, no. 59 (2010): 235–262; William Rosenau, *US Internal Security Assistance to South Vietnam: Insurgency, Subversion, and Public Order* (New York: Routledge, 2005); Micol Seigel, "Objects of Police History," *Journal of American History* 102, no. 1 (2015): 152–161; Seigel, *Violence Work: State Power and the Limits of Police* (Durham, NC: Duke University Press, 2018); and Kirsten Weld, *Paper Cadavers: The Archives of Dictatorship in Guatemala* (Durham, NC: Duke University Press, 2014).

The literature on other empires' policing efforts is large; see David Anderson and David Killingray, eds., *Policing and Decolonisation: Nationalism, Politics and the Police, 1917–65* (Manchester, England: Manchester University Press, 1992); Georgina Sinclair, *At the End of the Line: Colonial Policing and the Imperial Endgame 1945–80* (Manchester, England: Manchester University Press, 2006); Martin Thomas, *Violence and Colonial Order: Police, Workers and Protest in the European Colonial Empires, 1918–1940* (New York: Cambridge University Press, 2012).

16. Byron Engle, "AID Assistance to Civil Security," *The Police Chief* (henceforth cited as *TPC*), May 1972; "IPA Graduation," *International Police Academy Review* 9, no. 1 (January 1975); Lauren J. Goin, "Address," in *The Police Yearbook 1975* (Gaithersburg, MD: IACP, 1975), 227–230; James Angleton to deputy director for operations, March 27, 1973; CIA Family Jewels, National Security Archive Electronic Briefing Book 222, 601.

17. See Bruce Cumings, "'Revising Postrevisionism,' or, The Poverty of Theory in Diplomatic History" *Diplomatic History* 17, no. 4 (1993): 539–570, 565; Franz Schurmann, *The Logic of World Power* (New York: Pantheon Books, 1974).

18. The term "militarization of policing" incompletely captures this process. Literature using this concept, and sometimes also the term "counterinsurgency," includes Radley Balko, *Rise of the Warrior Cop: The Militarization of America's Police Forces* (New York: PublicAffairs, 2013); Tom Burghardt, ed., *Police State America: US Military 'Civil Disturbance' Planning* (San Francisco: Arm the Spirit/ Solidarity, 2001); Camp, *Incarcerating the Crisis;* Jordan T. Camp and Christina Heatherton, eds., *Policing the Planet: Why the Policing Crisis Led to Black Lives Matter* (New York: Verso, 2016); Peter B. Kraska, ed., *Militarizing the American Criminal Justice System: The Changing Roles of the Armed Forces and the Police* (Boston: Northeastern University Press, 2001); Kristian Williams, *Our Enemies in Blue: Police and Power in America* (Cambridge, MA: South End Press, 2007); Kristian Williams, Will Munger, and Lara Messersmith-Glavin, eds., *Life during Wartime: Resisting Counterinsurgency* (Oakland, CA: AK Press, 2013).

19. "The Role of AID Public Safety Programs during the Johnson Administration" (n.d. [1968]), Internal Defense and Public Safety [IPS] 21, Entry [E] 31, box 35, Records of the Agency for International Development, Record Group [RG] 286, National Archives and Records Administration [NARA], 2.

20. Beverly Gage, *The Day Wall Street Exploded: A Story of America in Its First Age of Terror* (New York: Oxford University Press, 2006); Michael J. Hogan, *A Cross of Iron: Harry S. Truman and the Origins of the National Security State, 1945–1954* (New York: Cambridge University Press, 1998); Lisa McGirr, *The War on Alcohol: Prohibition and the Rise of the American State* (New York: Norton, 2015); Schurmann, *Logic of World Power.*

21. On the linkage of the US national security state and global capitalism, see Thomas J. McCormick, *America's Half-Century: United States Foreign Policy in the Cold War* (Baltimore: Johns Hopkins University Press, 1989); Giovanni Arrighi, *The Long Twentieth Century: Money, Power, and the Origins of our Times* (New York: Verso, 1994); Leo Panitch and Sam Gindin, "Superintending Global Capitalism," *New Left Review* 2, no. 35 (2005): 101–123. On antecedents, see Neil Smith, *American Empire: Roosevelt's Geographer and the Prelude to Globalization* (Berkeley: University of California Press, 2003); Marilyn Blatt Young, ed., *American Expansionism: The Critical Issues* (Boston: Little, Brown, 1973). On military Keynesianism and the warfare-welfare state, see Arrighi, *Long Twentieth Century;* Ruth Wilson Gilmore, "Globalisation and US Prison Growth: From Military Keynesianism to post-Keynesian Militarism," *Race & Class* 40, nos. 2–3 (1998–1999): 171–188; James O'Connor, *The Fiscal Crisis of the State* (New York: St. Martin's Press, 1973). The term "Cold War" is a vexed one, but it seems impossible to dispense with it. I avoid attributing causal powers to the Cold War and tend to use the term as a temporal marker. Two recent essays demonstrate what is at stake in different interpretations of what exactly the Cold War was: Anders Stephanson, "Cold War Degree Zero," and Odd Arne Westad, "Exploring the Histories of the Cold War: A

Pluralist Approach," in *Uncertain Empire: American History and the Idea of the Cold War*, ed. Joel Isaac and Duncan Bell (New York: Oxford University Press, 2012), 19–49, 51–59. Their interpretations differ based on periodization, with Stephanson focused on events before 1963 and Westad on events after 1970, and based on the role of the Soviet Union, with Stephanson seeing it as reactive to US initiatives and Westad seeing it as equally a progenitor of the Cold War. See also Odd Arne Westad, *The Global Cold War: Third World Interventions and the Making of Our Times* (New York: Cambridge University Press, 2005), and Robert J. McMahon, ed., *The Cold War in the Third World* (New York: Oxford University Press, 2013). Ultimately, the impasse can be resolved through closer attention to how this "war" could be both hot and cold, extensive and intensive: via civilian policing. That the Cold War entailed the deaths of over twenty million people around the globe indicates the failure of the hope that preemptive policing could keep the peace; Paul Thomas Chamberlin, *The Cold War's Killing Fields: Rethinking the Long Peace* (New York: Harper, 2018).

22. On the catalytic effect of Khrushchev's speech on the Kennedy administration's view of the necessity of counterinsurgency, see Rosenau, *US Internal Security Assistance*, 81; Douglas S. Blaufarb, *The Counterinsurgency Era: US Doctrine and Performance, 1950 to the Present* (New York: Free Press, 1977), 18. It would be a mistake, however, to exaggerate the effect of a single speech, because unrest in Africa, Southeast Asia, and Latin America predated the speech; McClintock, *Instruments of Statecraft*, ch. 6. The speech was also directed at audiences in China.

23. David H. Bayley, *Patterns of Policing: A Comparative International Analysis* (New Brunswick, NJ: Rutgers University Press, 1985), 47. Classic studies of police professionalization include Robert M. Fogelson, *Big-City Police* (Cambridge, MA: Harvard University Press, 1977); Samuel Walker, *A Critical History of Police Reform: The Emergence of Professionalism* (Lexington, MA: Lexington Books, 1977); and Robert F. Wintersmith, *Police and the Black Community* (Lexington, MA: Lexington Books, 1974).

24. "The Agency for International Development Helps Brazilians Fight War on Crime," *Police*, March–April 1966.

25. The standard accounts are D. Michael Shafer, *Deadly Paradigms: The Failure of US Counterinsurgency Policy* (Princeton, NJ: Princeton University Press, 1988); Blaufarb, *Counterinsurgency Era;* Roger Hilsman, *To Move a Nation: The Politics of Foreign Policy in the Administration of John F. Kennedy* (New York: Doubleday, 1967). In contrast, the centrality of assistance to proxies in, and the global scope of, US internal-defense policy is analyzed in Jeffrey H. Michaels, "Managing Global Counterinsurgency: The Special Group (CI) 1962–1966," *Journal of Strategic Studies* 35, no. 1 (2012): 33–61. Other studies of the Kennedy turn to counterinsurgency useful to my understanding are Frank L. Jones, "The Guerrilla Warfare Problem: Revolutionary War and the Kennedy Administration Response, 1961–1963," in *The US Army War College Guide to National Security Issues: National Security Policy and Strategy*, vol. 2, ed. J. B. Bartholomees (Carlisle, PA: Strategic Studies Institute, US Army War College, 2010), 381–395; McClintock, *Instruments of Statecraft*. On

pre-1964 US assistance to police and paramilitaries in South Vietnam, see Rosenau, *US Internal Security Assistance;* John Ernst, *Forging a Fateful Alliance: Michigan State University and the Vietnam War* (East Lansing: Michigan State University Press, 1998); Jessica Elkind, *Aid under Fire: Nation Building and the Vietnam War* (Lexington: University Press of Kentucky, 2016).

26. A new historical literature on counterinsurgency focused on the military includes those who applied their scholarship practically in places like Iraq, authored doctrinal guidance for the US Army, and rose to prominence in the Donald J. Trump administration. David J. Kilcullen, *Counterinsurgency* (New York: Oxford University Press, 2010); H. R. McMaster, "Learning from Contemporary Conflicts to Prepare for Future War," *Orbis* 52, no. 4 (2008): 564–584; John Nagl, *Learning to Eat Soup with a Knife: Counterinsurgency Lessons from Malaya and Vietnam* (Chicago: University of Chicago Press, 2005); David Petraeus and James F. Amos, US Army/Marine Corps, *Counterinsurgency Field Manual FM 3–24* (Chicago: University of Chicago Press, 2007), which referenced James Mattis. As Michaels points out in "Managing Global Counterinsurgency," many recent accounts rely on Andrew F. Krepinevich Jr., *The Army and Vietnam* (Baltimore: Johns Hopkins University Press, 1986). Critics of this literature from within the military include Gian Gentile, *Wrong Turn: America's Deadly Embrace of Counterinsurgency* (New York: New Press, 2013), and Douglas Porch, *Counterinsurgency: Exposing the Myths of the New Way of War* (New York: Cambridge University Press, 2013).

27. President Kennedy had visited Fort Bragg, home to the Army's special forces, in 1961. David DiLeo, *George Ball, Vietnam, and the Rethinking of Containment* (Chapel Hill: University of North Carolina Press, 1991), 141; Arthur Schlesinger Jr., *Robert Kennedy and His Times* (New York: Ballantine Books, 1978), 730–731; *Noticias de la Academia Inter-Americana de Policia,* February 1963, ADM 6–2, E27, box 2, RG 286, NARA; Byron Engle, "Director's Message," *International Police Academy Review* 2, no. 3 (1968).

28. I develop this definition of civil violence based on Michael B. Katz, "Why Don't American Cities Burn Very Often?" *Journal of Urban History* 34, no. 2 (2008): 185–208.

29. United States Senate, "The Central Intelligence Group and the Central Intelligence Agency, 1946–1952," bk. 4, pt. 1, "Supplementary Detailed Staff Reports on Foreign and Military Intelligence," in *Final Report of the Select Committee to Study Governmental Operations with Respect to the Intelligence Activities* (Washington, DC: Government Printing Office [GPO], 1976), 31; David Rudgers, "The Origins of Covert Action," *Journal of Contemporary History* 35, no. 2 (2000): 249–262.

30. Jennifer Robinson, "Cities in a World of Cities: The Comparative Gesture," *International Journal of Urban and Regional Research* 35, no. 1 (2011): 1–23; Hopkins, "World-Systems Analysis"; Jamie Peck, "Geography and Public Policy: Mapping the Penal State," *Progress in Human Geography* 27, no. 2 (2003): 222–232.

31. "The Police Function, Its Scope and Limitations within Doctrinary Aspects," in Theodore D. Brown, "Report of the United States Delegation to the

First Inter-American Congress of Uniformed Police, Lima, Peru, August 25–September 3, 1966" (Washington, DC: OPS, 1966), annex H, 2.

32. William Blackstone, *Commentaries on the Laws of England,* vol. 4 (Oxford: Oxford University Press, 1769), 162; Mark Neocleous, *The Fabrication of Social Order: A Critical Theory of Police Power* (London: Pluto Press, 2000), 3.

33. Markus D. Dubber and Mariana Valverde, "Perspectives on the Power and Science of Police," in *The New Police Science,* ed. Dubber and Valverde (Stanford, CA: Stanford University Press, 2006), 1–16.

34. The distinction between uncertainty and risk has a long history in social theory, going back to Max Weber and his student Frank H. Knight. To use this distinction to theorize police is my own contribution. Jochen Runde, "Clarifying Frank Knight's Discussion of the Meaning of Risk and Uncertainty," *Cambridge Journal of Economics* 22 (1998): 539–546; Frank H. Knight, *Risk, Uncertainty and Profit* (Boston: Houghton Mifflin, 1921).

35. Wagner, *Disturbing the Peace,* 5.

36. On imperial reverberations, see Alfred W. McCoy, *Policing America's Empire: The United States, the Philippines, and the Rise of the Surveillance State* (Madison: University of Wisconsin Press, 2009); Alfred W. McCoy and Francisco A. Scarano, eds., *Colonial Crucible: Empire and the Making of the Modern American State* (Madison: University of Wisconsin Press, 2009); Ann L. Stoler, ed., *Haunted by Empire: Geographies of Intimacy in North American History* (Durham, NC: Duke University Press, 2006); Andrew Friedman, *Covert Capital: Landscapes of Denial and the Making of US Empire in the Suburbs of Northern Virginia* (Berkeley: University of California Press, 2013); and Katherine Unterman, *Uncle Sam's Policemen: The Pursuit of Fugitives across Borders* (Cambridge, MA: Harvard University Press, 2015).

37. Marc Becker, *The FBI in Latin America: The Ecuador Files* (Durham, NC: Duke University Press, 2017).

38. Acting secretary of state to consulate general at Batavia [Jakarta], June 8, 1949, US Department of State, *Foreign Relations of the United States [FRUS]* (Washington, DC: GPO), 1949), 7, pt. 1, 293; Secretary of state to US Embassy in Indonesia, September 13, 1941, *FRUS,* 1951, 6, pt. 1, 411.

39. Memo for the Record, OTR Requirements in Support of the 1290-d Program, March 21, 1956; CIA Records Search Tool [CREST], CIA-RDP62–00634A000200050001–2; Commission on CIA Activities within the United States, *Report to the President* (Washington, DC: GPO, 1975), 234–235.

40. This paragraph draws on Julian Go, "Imperial Returns: American Empire and Militarization at Home," paper presented at the 112th Annual Meeting of the American Sociological Association, Montréal, August 15, 2017.

41. Lauren Goin, quoted in Bruce, "Human Rights and US Training," 52.

42. I am grateful to Christopher Capozzola for help on this point.

43. Lauren J. Goin, memoir (oral history) by James D. Williams, April 1991, Institute of Inter-American Affairs Collection, Columbia University.

44. Byron Engle to U. Alexis Johnson, September 12, 1969, IPS 2, E31, box 25, RG 286, NARA.

45. Lobe, *US National Security Policy,* 10; Lobe, "Rise and Demise"; Nadelmann, *Cops across Borders,* 114. "Name Berkeley Man New Chief of Walnut Creek City Police," *Contra Costa Walnut Kernel,* January 10, 1957, Walnut Creek Historical Society, Walnut Creek, CA; "Public Safety Advisor—Police Field Forces" (n.d.[1967]), attachment A, NP/ORG, E525, box 14, Records of the US Forces in Southeast Asia, 1950–1975, RG 472, NARA.

46. "Public Safety Advisors: Experience by Geographical Areas" (n.d. [July 1966]); Josemarie Derenzo, Qualities of Public Safety Advisory Personnel, September 26, 1966, IPS 12–5, E31, box 33, RG 286, NARA.

47. "Guerrilla Acts of Sabotage and Terrorism in the United States 1965–1970," *Scanlan's Magazine,* January 1971, 26; "Mystery Explosion Rocks Walnut Creek," *San Francisco Chronicle,* January 20, 1969.

48. Frank Jessup, RTAC Special Textbook Program, July 21, 1961, ICATO circular XA-486, IPS 1, E26, box 88, RG 286, NARA.

CHAPTER 1. RETHINKING RACE AND POLICING IN IMPERIAL PERSPECTIVE

1. Joe R. Feagin and Harlan Hahn, *Ghetto Revolts* (New York: Macmillan, 1973), 89–90.

2. J. E. Weckler and Theo E. Hall, *The Police and Minority Groups: A Program to Prevent Disorder and to Improve Relations between Different Racial, Religious, and National Groups* (Chicago: International City Managers' Association, 1944), 1.

3. "Race Relations Course for Police," *Police Chiefs' News Letter,* March 1946; "Cincinnati's Race Relations Detail," ibid., April 1945.

4. Mary L. Dudziak, *Cold War Civil Rights: Race and the Image of American Democracy* (Princeton, NJ: Princeton University Press, 2000), from which these examples are drawn, offers the classic argument about Cold War imperatives overseas bolstering elite support for the fight for civil rights at home; see also Murakawa, *First Civil Right.* W. E. B. Du Bois, "The African Roots of War," *Atlantic Monthly,* May 1915.

5. Robert Vitalis, *White World Order, Black Power Politics: The Birth of American International Relations* (Ithaca, NY: Cornell University Press, 2015).

6. See Singh, *Black Is a Country,* especially 166–173; Penny M. Von Eschen, *Race against Empire* (Ithaca, NY: Cornell University Press, 1997); and Jodi Melamed, *Represent and Destroy: Rationalizing Violence in the New Racial Capitalism* (Minneapolis: University of Minnesota Press, 2011). Gunnar Myrdal, *An American Dilemma: The Negro Problem and Modern Democracy,* vols. 1 and 2 (New York: Harper & Brothers, 1944).

7. [Marion] Norton Hardesty, "Cooperation," *TPC,* November 1955, 12.

8. W. E. B. Du Bois, "The Present Outlook for the Dark Races of Mankind" (1900), in *The Problem of the Color Line at the Turn of the Twentieth Century: The Essential Early Essays,* ed. Nahum Dmitri Chandler (New York: Fordham Univer-

sity Press, 2013), 111–137, 112; Du Bois, "The Color Line Belts the World," *Collier's Weekly*, October 20, 1906.

9. James Forman, Jr., *Locking Up Our Own* (New York: Farrar, Straus and Giroux, 2017), 113.

10. W. E. B. Du Bois, *Color and Democracy: Colonies and Peace* (1945; repr., Millwood, NY: Kraus-Thomson Organization, 1975).

11. Eduardo Bonilla-Silva, *Racism without Racists: Color-Blind Racism and the Persistence of Racial Inequality in America* (Lanham, MD: Rowman & Littlefield, 2006).

12. Du Bois, *Color and Democracy*, v, 85.

13. W. E. B. Du Bois, "My Evolving Program for Negro Freedom" (1944), in *What the Negro Wants*, ed. Rayford Logan (South Bend, IN: University of Notre Dame Press, 2001), 44.

14. CIA, "The Break-Up of the Colonial Empires and Its Implications for US Security" (September 3, 1948), ORE 25–48, CREST, CIA-RDP78–01617 A003200020001–3.

15. Ibid.

16. See Kwame Nkrumah, *Neo-Colonialism, the Last Stage of Imperialism* (New York: International Publishers, 1966); Walter Rodney, *How Europe Underdeveloped Africa* (1972; Washington, DC: Howard University Press, 1982), 190–201.

17. E5045, box 1, General Records of the Department of State, RG 59, NARA. Few records of Komer's experience working for central intelligence are available. This lone, orphaned box held in College Park contains records otherwise unavailable in the bulk of his archives collected at the Kennedy and Johnson libraries, including some personal correspondence from his NSC days. Perhaps it would be an exaggeration to say this analysis is the key to decoding his thought over subsequent decades. Yet it is nonetheless notable that he carried this intelligence brief with him to the third floor of the Old Executive Office Building, though he did not author it. On Komer's CIA career, see Frank Leith Jones, *Blowtorch: Robert Komer, Vietnam, and American Cold War Strategy* (Annapolis, MD: Naval Institute Press, 2013), 19.

18. Joseph Lelyveld, "Ex-NY Policeman Aids Congo Force," *New York Times*, April 18, 1965; Reg Davis and Harry James, *The Public Safety Story* (Santee, CA: Public Safety Newsletter, 2001).

19. David Laughlin to Herbert Hardin, July 9, 1962, TRV 7–2, E27, box 9, RG 286, NARA.

20. Jeter Williamson, "Riot Control Training" (February 3–6, 1964), IPS 3, E31, box 27, RG 286, NARA.

21. Frank S. Tenny, "Law Enforcement in the Far East" *Police*, September–October 1963.

22. David Correia and Tyler Wall, *Police: A Field Guide* (New York: Verso, 2018); Alex S. Vitale, *The End of Policing* (New York: Verso, 2017).

23. Forman, *Locking Up Our Own*, ch. 3.

24. W. E. B. Du Bois, *The Philadelphia Negro: A Social Study* (1899; repr., New York: Schocken Books, 1967), 132.

25. Charles E. Coulter, *Take Up the Black Man's Burden: Kansas City's African American Communities, 1865–1939* (Columbia: University of Missouri Press, 2006), 122–123; W. Marvin Dulaney, *Black Police in America* (Bloomington: Indiana University Press, 1996); Kelly Lytle Hernández, *City of Inmates: Conquest, Rebellion, and the Rise of Human Caging in Los Angeles, 1771–1965* (Chapel Hill: University of North Carolina Press, 2017), 184–189.

26. Transcript, Robert S. McNamara Oral History, interview I, by Walt W. Rostow, January 8, 1975, Lyndon Baines Johnson Presidential Library, Austin, TX (LBJL), 50; Paul Bower to Arnold Sagalyn, November 2, 1967, Kerner Commission—Sagalyn Correspondence, box 3, Arnold Sagalyn Papers, American University, Washington, DC (ASP).

27. Leslie Gill, *The School of the Americas: Military Training and Political Violence in the Americas* (Durham, NC: Duke University Press, 2004), 26.

28. Holmes Alexander, "The Latinos Admire Valor and JFK Has Somehow Lost His White Plume," *New Orleans States-Item,* November 12, 1962, in INF 5–2, E27, box 3, RG 286, NARA.

29. By the 1960s, the FBI no longer relied on "Bertillonage," an anthropometric method of describing and recognizing facial features according to a typology, originally invented by Alphonse Bertillon in the late 1800s. Lauded by Cesare Lombroso, the method of pinpointing suspects fed into racial-criminal anthropology, including phrenology. Inaccuracy, rather than bad bedfellows, discredited Bertillonage. Fingerprinting superseded it. Yet AID retained Bertillonage and distributed pamphlets based on old FBI templates to participants, translated into multiple languages, detailing the method.

30. Robert Ihrie, memorandum from Byron Engle to the administrator on relocating the Inter-American Police Academy (n.d.), IAPA Admin. Files—Building Facilities/Space—1962–64, E27, box 1, RG 286, NARA.

31. Arthur M. Thurston, "Survey of Training Activities of the AID Police Assistance Program" (Washington, DC: AID, November 1962), 35.

32. E. H. Adkins Jr., "An Idea for a Foreign Police Academy" (n.d.); Jack Ryan to A. F. Brandstatter, December 22, 1960, folder 13, box 680, Vietnam Project Records, MSUA, 9.

33. One of the IPA's first mentions in the national press concerned twenty-two police officials from Africa who were to visit in July 1963 for training in "police operation and criminal investigation," with thirty more to follow in September for training in riot control. "Africans Training in US," *Miami Herald,* June 9, 1963, in INF 5–2, E27, box 3, RG 286, NARA.

34. "Cop Class," *New Yorker,* June 6, 1959.

35. Subcommittee on Inter-American Affairs, House, 88th Cong., 1st sess., *Castro-Communist Subversion in the Western Hemisphere,* March 4, 1963, 241, 243.

36. "Requirements for Police Women," *Public Safety Division Newsletter* 19 (November 1959), IPS 1, E31, box 21, RG 286, NARA. Women predominated in the program's large administrative and clerical staff in Washington and in missions overseas.

37. "IPA's First Woman Participant," *IPA Review* 6, no. 2 (April 1972).

38. Nikhil Pal Singh, *Race and America's Long War* (Berkeley: University of California Press, 2017); Singh, "Cold War," *Social Text* 100 (2009): 67–70; William Pietz, "The 'Post-Colonialism' of Cold War Discourse," *Social Text* 19–20 (1988): 55–75; "Totalitarianism and the Lessons of History: Reply to Stephanson," *Social Text* 22 (1989): 130–140; Gerald Horne, "Race from Power: US Foreign Policy and the General Crisis of White Supremacy," *Diplomatic History* 23, no. 3 (1999): 437–461.

39. Markus Dirk Dubber, *The Police Power: Patriarchy and the Foundations of American Government* (New York: Columbia University Press, 2005); Ann Laura Stoler, *Race and the Education of Desire: Foucault's History of Sexuality and the Colonial Order of Things* (Durham, NC: Duke University Press, 1995), 72.

40. Racialization, for Omi and Winant, entails "the extension of racial meaning to a previously unclassified relationship, social practice or group." Criminalization is analogous, but the two processes have proceeded on intersecting tracks historically in the United States. Michael Omi and Howard Winant, *Racial Formation in the United States: From the 1960s to the 1980s* (New York: Routledge, 1986), 64.

41. Some historians "place too much emphasis on the role of racism and too little on the role of security," Michael Flamm argues. "The unraveling of liberalism was therefore not simply the result of racism *per se.* It was, rather, due to the also widespread loss of popular faith in liberalism's ability to ensure personal security" (Flamm, *Law and Order,* 9). This analytic divide between racism and security is simply untenable without retention of biologistic definitions of race that are themselves the product of racism. Security is unthinkable without race.

42. Michelle Alexander, *The New Jim Crow: Mass Incarceration in the Age of Colorblindness* (New York: New Press, 2010), 130–131.

43. Alys Eve Weinbaum, *Wayward Reproductions: Genealogies of Race and Nation in Transatlantic Modern Thought* (Durham, NC: Duke University Press, 2004), 35; Thomas Holt, "Marking: Race, Race-Making, and the Writing of History," *American Historical Review* 100, no. 1 (1995): 1–20.

44. Gilmore, *Golden Gulag,* 247.

45. Singh, *Race and America's Long War,* 133.

46. Sonja Buckel, "The Juridical Condensation of Relations of Forces: Nicos Poulantzas and Law," in *Reading Poulantzas,* ed. Alexander Gallas, Lars Bretthauer, John Kannankulam, and Ingo Stützle (London: Merlin, 2011), 154–169, 163.

47. See Cedric J. Robinson, *Black Marxism: The Making of the Black Radical Tradition* (1983; Chapel Hill: University of North Carolina Press, 2000).

48. Paul Kramer argues that "absolutizing" understandings of race as "bodily, color-coded, and mental, scientized and segregating, fixed and fixing" constrain analysis of racism's persistence in foreign relations after World War II, which often took "civilizing" forms; Kramer, "Shades of Sovereignty: Racialized Power, the United States and the World," in *Explaining the History of American Foreign Relations,* ed. Frank Costigliola and Michael J. Hogan (New York: Cambridge University Press, 2016), 245–270, 264.

49. Nancy Fraser, "Expropriation and Exploitation in Racialized Capitalism: A Reply to Michael Dawson," *Critical Historical Studies* 3, no. 1 (2016): 163–178; Michael C. Dawson, "Hidden in Plain Sight: A Note on Legitimation Crises and the Racial Order," *Critical Historical Studies* 3, no. 1 (2016): 143–161.

50. I am grateful to Monica Kim for helping me think through this point.

51. Chris Chen, "The Limit Point of Capitalist Equality," *Endnotes* 3 (2013): 202–223.

52. Micol Seigel, "Beyond Compare: Comparative Method after the Transnational Turn," *Radical History Review* 91 (2005): 62–90; Ann Laura Stoler, "Tense and Tender Ties: The Politics of Comparison in North American History and (Post) Colonial Studies," *Journal of American History* 88, no. 3 (2001): 829–865.

53. Paul A. Kramer, *The Blood of Government: Race, Empire, the United States, & the Philippines* (Chapel Hill: University of North Carolina Press, 2006).

54. Thomas McCarthy, *Race, Empire, and the Idea of Human Development* (New York: Cambridge University Press, 2009).

55. Walt Rostow to the president, July 28, 1967, Riots (1), box 32, office files of Harry McPherson, LBJL; Tullis, "Vietnam at Home," 24–5.

56. Lyndon B. Johnson, "The President's Address to the Nation on Civil Disorders," July 27, 1967, *TAPP*.

57. Hannah Arendt, *The Origins of Totalitarianism* (1950; New York: Harcourt, Brace, Jovanovich, 1973), 206, 430; Aimé Césaire, *Discourse on Colonialism*, trans. Joan Pinkham (1950; New York: Monthly Review Press, 2000), 36; Jean-Paul Sartre, "Preface," in Frantz Fanon, *The Wretched of the Earth*, trans. Richard Philcox (1961; New York: Grove Press, 2004), liv; Michel Foucault, *"Society Must Be Defended": Lectures at the Collège de France, 1975–76*, trans. David Macey (New York: Picador, 2003), 103. Stephen Graham, *Cities under Siege: The New Military Urbanism* (New York: Verso, 2010), adopts the boomerang metaphor in the context of recent security practices.

58. Césaire was attuned to some of the specifics of US empire, which he called "American domination"; Césaire, *Discourse on Colonialism, 77*.

59. On exceptionalizing difference, see Kramer, "Shades of Sovereignty."

60. "Thefts Easy in Japan," *Kansas City Star,* August 6, 1948.

61. Huey P. Newton, "Intercommunalism (1974)," June 11, 2018, www.viewpointmag .com/2018/06/11/intercommunalism-1974.

62. Lothrop Stoddard, *The Rising Tide of Color against White World–Supremacy* (New York: Charles Scribner's Sons, 1921).

63. Patricia Owens, *Economy of Force: Counterinsurgency and the Historical Rise of the Social* (New York: Cambridge University Press, 2015). Owens explains the fundamental connection between the patriarchal despotism of the household—which had historically been considered the police power—and counterinsurgency, though without detailed attention to the practical role of policing in counterinsurgency.

64. Frank Walton, "National Police Plan for Vietnam" (Saigon: Public Safety Division, USOM, March 1964), Public Safety, box 20, Komer-Leonhart File, NSF, LBJL, 10.

65. Elbridge Colby, "How to Fight Savage Tribes," *American Journal of International Law* 21, no. 1 (1927): 279–288, 287. Colby concludes with the term "economy of force" to define why exactly law cannot be the ultimate guide in warfare: "The discretion and the decency of the commander are also factors. The really controlling element in the handling of a field force is economy. Economy of effort, economy of force, maintained by a well-knit and well-disciplined army directed toward the most direct and proper attainment of the end in view—these are the precepts by which the commander will govern his actions" (288).

Elbridge Colby was the father of William Colby, who oversaw South Vietnam's "highly specialized, largely police-type operation" of assassination and imprisonment called Phoenix, before becoming CIA director. This description of Phoenix comes from Robert Komer, whom William Colby succeeded as head of Civil Operations and Rural Development Support in South Vietnam; Robert W. Komer, "Texts of Ambassador Komer's News Conferences, 1 Dec. 1967, 24 Jan. & 18 Apr. 1968," Widener Library, Harvard University, IND 9476.246, 7.

66. Dubber, *Police Power.* Max Weber paradigmatically defines the modern state as "a human community that (successfully) claims the *monopoly of the legitimate use of physical force* within a given territory"; "Politics as a Vocation" (1921), in *From Max Weber: Essays in Sociology,* trans. and ed. H. H. Gerth and C. Wright Mills (New York: Oxford University Press, 1946), 77–128; Andrew Zimmerman, "'What Do You Really Want in German East Africa, Herr Professor?' Counterinsurgency and the Science Effect in Colonial Tanzania," *Comparative Studies in Society and History* 48, no. 2 (2006): 419–461, especially 428. I am grateful to Christopher Taylor for inspiration on this point.

67. The literature on French pacification expertise prior to World War II, and their influence on American experts, especially via David Galula, is large. See Anne Marlowe, *David Galula: His Life and Intellectual Context* (Carlisle, PA: US Army Strategic Studies Institute, 2010); Mark Neocleous, "Security as Pacification," in *Anti-Security,* ed. Mark Neocleous and George Rigakos (Ottawa: Red Quill Books, 2011), 24–56; Paul Rabinow, *French Modern: Norms and Forms of the Social Environment* (Chicago: University of Chicago Press, 1989); and Thomas Rid, "The Nineteenth Century Origins of Counterinsurgency Doctrine," *Journal of Strategic Studies* 33, no. 5 (2010): 727–758.

68. Quincy Wright, "The Bombardment of Damascus," *American Journal of International Law* 20, no. 2 (1926): 263–280, 265.

69. Susan Pedersen, *The League of Nations and the Crisis of Empire* (New York: Oxford University Press, 2015), 152.

70. Aziz Rana, "Settler Wars and the National Security State," *Settler Colonial Studies* 4, no. 2 (2014): 171–175; Rana, *The Two Faces of American Freedom* (Cambridge, MA: Harvard University Press, 2010).

71. Eyal Weizman, *The Least of All Possible Evils: Humanitarian Violence from Arendt to Gaza* (New York: Verso, 2012), 19; Owens, *Economy of Force,* 259n18.

72. Alexander "Clubber" Williams, nineteenth-century New York City's most infamous cop, highlighted the power of the nightstick, which contained more law than "a Supreme Court decision." Marilynn S. Johnson, *Street Justice: A History of Police Violence in New York City* (Boston: Beacon Press, 2004), 41.

73. Rana, *Two Faces of American Freedom*, especially 281–290.

74. John Grenier, *The First Way of War: American War Making on the Frontier, 1607–1814* (New York: Cambridge University Press, 2005); Paul A. Kramer, "Race-Making and Colonial Violence in the U.S. Empire: The Philippine-American War as Race War," *Diplomatic History* 30, no. 2 (2006): 169–210.

75. Micol Seigel, "Nelson Rockefeller in Latin America: Global Currents of US Prison Growth," *Comparative American Studies* 13, no. 3 (2015): 161–176.

76. David W. Samuels, Donald O. Egner, and Donald Campbell, *Riot Control: Analysis and Catalog* (Aberdeen Proving Ground, MD: US Army Limited War Laboratory, 1969), 2; Carl F. Rosenthal, *Phases of Civil Disturbances: Characteristics and Problems* (Washington, DC: Center for Research in Social Systems, 1969).

77. Singh, *Black Is a Country;* Étienne Balibar, "Racism and Nationalism," in *Race, Nation, Class: Ambiguous Identities,* ed. Balibar and Immanuel Wallerstein, trans. Chris Turner (New York: Verso, 1991), 37–67.

CHAPTER 2. BYRON ENGLE AND THE RISE OF
OVERSEAS POLICE ASSISTANCE

1. Wherry's line has been widely quoted but its original source is unclear. See Eric F. Goldman, *The Crucial Decade: America, 1945–1955* (Westport, CT: Greenwood Press, 1956); Michael E. Latham, "Introduction: Modernization, International History, and the Cold War World," in *Staging Growth: Modernization, Development, and the Global Cold War,* ed. David C. Engerman, Nils Gilman, Mark H. Haefele, and Michael E. Latham (Amherst: University of Massachusetts Press, 2003), 1–22.

2. "History of the Office of Public Safety (1955 to 1969)" (n.d.), IPS 6–1, E18, box 4, RG 286, NARA, 44.

3. Lobe, "US Police Assistance," 55; "AID Official Byron Engle Dies at Age 79," *Washington Post,* January 12, 1990.

4. This story appeared on a municipal website.

5. Landon Laird, "About Town," *Kansas City Times,* October 3, 1957; "Byron Engle Receives Citation," *TPC,* April 1958.

6. Robert H. Ferrell, *Truman and Pendergast* (Columbia: University of Missouri Press, 1999).

7. Correspondence–Byron Engle, Supreme Commander for the Allied Powers, Assistant Chief of Staff, G-2, Public Safety Division, Police Branch, Subject File, 1945–52, UD 1140 (L), box 328, Allied Operational and Occupation Headquarters, RG 331, NARA. Newspaper articles mention a wife (Ruth) and daughter (Betty Sue) from before he met Jelsch: e.g., "Thefts Easy in Japan," *Kansas City Star,* August 6,

1948. One article focused on Ruth, a nurse, who saved a young boy's life while visiting with fellow policemen's wives, during Engle's time in Japan: "Boy Saved By a Nurse" (n.p. [August 21, 1947]), F. 154, ser. 1, Clippings Scrapbook, 1939–1947, SC 122, Kansas City Police Historical Society (KCPHS), Missouri Valley Special Collections, Kansas City Municipal Library, Kansas City, MO.

8. "High Score Fails," *Christian Science Monitor*, September 15, 1942; this article also mentions that Engle's (unnamed) wife scored the highest in the women's competition (before he met Jelsch).

9. Lee E. Echols, *Hilarious High Jinks and Dangerous Assignments* (Washington, DC: National Rifle Association of America, 1990).

10. *Public Safety Newsletter* [*PSN*] 32 (October 1981). Issues 19, 30, 31, 32, and 34 of *PSN* are found in box 3 and 5; Charles F. Sloane Papers, Hoover Institution Archives, Stanford, CA (HIA). Indiana University recently accessioned a nearly complete run of the publication. See Seigel, *Violence Work*.

11. *PSN* 30 (June 1981).

12. Clipping attached to John Manopoli to Byron Engle, January 5, 1972, IPS 20–1, E31, box 296, RG 286, NARA.

13. Lobe, "US Police Assistance," 3.

14. Kuzmarov, *Modernizing Repression*, 11.

15. Harold Saunders to Robert W. Komer [RWK], June 9, 1965, Counter-Insurgency Police Program, 1964–1965–1966, box 15, files of RWK, NSF, LBJL.

16. "Municipal Mirror" (n.p. [August 1945]), F. 152, ser. 1, Clippings Scrapbook, 1939–1947, KCPHS.

17. Karen Leventhal, "Byron F. Engle First OPS Chief," *Front Lines*, May 31, 1973, in box 8, Charles F. Sloane Papers, HIA.

18. "Local Touch in Japan," *Kansas City Times*, September 19, 1950; "A Visit by Byron Engle," *Kansas City Star*, June 11, 1955.

19. Roy Wilkins with Tom Mathews, *Standing Fast: The Autobiography of Roy Wilkins* (New York: Da Capo, 1992), 60. Wilkins, the longtime Black political leader, was a journalist with the *Kansas City Call* for eight years beginning in 1923.

20. Lear B. Reed, *Human Wolves: Seventeen Years of War on Crime* (Kansas City, MO: Brown-White-Lowell Press, 1941), 202.

21. Dowdal H. Davis, "They Forced the Chief Out," *The Crisis* (October 1941); Sherry Lamb Schirmer, *City Divided: The Racial Landscape of Kansas City, 1900–1960* (Columbia: University of Missouri Press, 2002), 227.

22. Jack Anderson, "Trujillo Assassins Implicated CIA," *Washington Post*, May 15, 1975); telegram, Department of State to US Embassy in the Dominican Republic, October 13, 1963, US Department of State, *Foreign Relations of the United States* [*FRUS*], 1961–1963 (Washington, DC: GPO), 12: 360.

23. Statement of policy as police chief by Lear B. Reed, *Kansas City Times*, September 26, 1939, microfilm, roll 16, SC 52, Kansas City Municipal Library Mounted Newspaper Clippings (KCMNC), Missouri Valley Special Collections, Kansas City, MO.

24. "Reed Is 'Not Worried'" (n.p., n.d.), F. 152, series 1, Clippings Scrapbook 1939–1947, KCPHS; Reed, *Human Wolves*, ch. 22 and 23; "Call Editor Eues Former Police Chief in $20,000 Libel Suit," *The Plaindealer*, February 20, 1942.

25. Bruce, "Impact of the Occupation," 125.

26. Reed, *Human Wolves*, 293, 261.

27. "His FBI Diploma Near," *Kansas City Star*, July 11, 1943.

28. Rollin M. Perkins, ed., *Police Examinations* (Brooklyn, NY: Foundation Press, 1947).

29. Reed, *Human Wolves*, 287.

30. Richard J. Olive, "Police Academy Here Reaches Milestone," *Kansas City Star*, January 17, 1966; "Governor Greets Law Officers" *Iowa City Press-Citizen* (June 17, 1946).

31. Bruce, "Impact of the Occupation," 125; Christopher Aldous, *The Police in Occupation Japan: Control, Corruption and Resistance to Reform* (New York: Routledge, 1997).

32. Davis and James, *Public Safety Story*, 3; Lobe, "US Police Assistance," 56; Bishop, *Modernizing Repression*, 170, 204;. Russell A. Snook, "Report of the IACP Training Division," *TPC*, December 1956.

33. "Brighter World Faces Freed POW," *Daily Courier* [Connellsville, PA], November 1, 1950.

34. "Seek New Police Chief," *Kansas City Star*, July 6, 1952; "Relieves a Police Captain," *Kansas City Times*, July 31, 1951.

35. Landon Laird, "About Town," *Kansas City Times*, June 6, 1952, and October 3, 1957; Excerpts concerning the General Directorate of Security from the radio broadcast from Moscow on March 1, 1952, E19, box 25, Records of the Drug Enforcement Administration, RG 170, NARA.

36. Bruce, "Impact of the Occupation," 124.

37. "Local Touch in Japan"; "Thefts Easy in Japan."

38. Frank Sojat to Harry Anslinger, September 1, 1951, March 3, 1952, April 7, 1952, E19, box 25, RG 170, NARA.

39. Daniel Weimer, *Seeing Drugs: Modernization, Counterinsurgency, and US Narcotics Control in the Third World, 1969–1976* (Kent, OH: Kent State University Press, 2011).

40. Matthew R. Pembleton, "Imagining a Global Sovereignty: U.S. Counternarcotic Operations in Istanbul during the Early Cold War and the Origins of the Foreign 'War on Drugs,'" *Journal of Cold War Studies* 18, no. 2 (2016): 28–63.

41. Dankwart A. Rustow and Robert E. Ward, *Political Modernization in Japan and Turkey* (Princeton, NJ: Princeton University Press, 1964); Nathan J. Citino, "The Ottoman Legacy in Cold War Modernization," *International Journal of Middle East Studies* 40, no. 4 (2008): 579–597.

42. Davis and James, *Public Safety Story*.

43. Allen E. Wagner, *Good Order and Safety: A History of the St. Louis Metropolitan Police Department, 1861–1906* (St. Louis: Missouri History Museum, 2008), 15–48.

44. Christine Byers and Nick Pistor, "St. Louis Police Department Preparing for City Control," *St. Louis Post-Dispatch,* August 21, 2013; Ray Hartmann, "Think Again: Don't Know Much about History," *St. Louis Magazine,* November 8, 2010.

45. James Wunsch, "The Social Evil Ordinance," *American Heritage* 33, no. 2 (February–March 1982).

46. Lent D. Upson, "The International Association of Chiefs of Police and Other American Police Organizations," *Annals of the American Academy of Political and Social Science* 146 (1929): 121–127, 122. The IACP would not come into formal existence, however, until 1893, at the Chicago World's Fair. It returned to St. Louis the following year for its first conference. A history of the IACP appears in the October 1964 issue of *The Police Chief,* titled "The International Association of Chiefs of Police: Its History and Its Purpose," which built on a 1962 speech given at an IACP annual meeting by Quinn Tamm: Report from the Office of the Executive Director by Quinn Tamm, IACP 1962, E29, box 1, RG 286, NARA.

47. "A Depressed GOP"(n.p., n.d. [March 1932]), F. 116, ser. 1, Clippings Scrapbook, 1932, KCPHS. "As a Political Analyst Sees Kansas City's Boss," *Kansas City Star,* March 4, 1932, F. 116, ser. 1, Clippings Scrapbook. 1932, KCPHS. The *Kansas City Star* opposed Pendergast for almost half a century; Ferrell, Truman and Pendergast. Just a few weeks after Pendergast met Roosevelt, the Missouri Supreme Court restored municipal control of the police to the city—meaning to Pendergast. Until that point, he had cared greatly who the state's governor was. Then it ceased to matter.

48. Lawrence H. Larsen and Nancy J. Hulston, *Pendergast!* (Columbia: University of Missouri Press, 1997), 110–111; Jan Lelain Lorenzen, "Kansas City, Missouri, Newspapers of 1932 and the Pendergast Political Machine" (MA thesis, University of Missouri–Kansas City, 2003).

49. Reed, *Human Wolves,* 343.

50. Ferrell, *Truman and Pendergast.*

51. Curt Gentry, *J. Edgar Hoover: The Man and the Secrets* (New York: Norton, 1991).

52. Christina Heatherton, "University of Radicalism: Ricardo Flores Magón and Leavenworth Penitentiary," *American Quarterly* 66, no. 3 (2014): 557–581. The definitive account of Van Deman's experience and influence is McCoy, *Policing America's Empire.*

53. Charles F. Sloane, "The Police in Viet Nam," *TPC,* January 1958; "Viet Nam Continues to Reorganize," *TPC,* February 1958; "More About Viet Nam," *TPC,* March 1958.

54. Kuzmarov, *Modernizing Repression,* 143.

55. William J. Bopp, *"O. W.": O. W. Wilson and the Search for a Police Profession* (Port Washington, NY: Kennikat Press, 1977), 54.

56. J. E. Weckler, *Polynesians: Explorers of the Pacific* (Washington, DC: Smithsonian Institution, 1943); Harry Hoijer, "Joseph Edwin Weckler Jr. 1906–1963," *American Anthropologist* 66 (1964): 1348–1350.

57. "Theo Hall Receives Promotion," *TPC,* May 1949.

58. Kuzmarov, *Modernizing Repression*, 222; Allan Nairn, "Occupation Haiti: The Eagle is Landing," *The Nation,*(October 3, 1994; Stuart Schrader, "Nicaragua: Central America's Security Exception," *NACLA Report on the Americas* 49, no. 3 (2017): 360–365.

59. The official was August Vollmer. Herman Schwendiger and Julia Schwendinger, *Who Killed the Berkeley School?* (Brooklyn: Thought Crimes and Punctum Books, 2014), 125n4.

60. Bruce Cumings, *The Origins of the Korean War: Liberation and the Emergence of Separate Regimes, 1945–1947* (Princeton, NJ: Princeton University Press, 1981).

61. Kuzmarov, *Modernizing Repression*, 201; Theo Hall to Clyde Phelps, December 2, 1957, IPS 1–1, E30, box 62, RG 286, NARA.

62. Bopp, "*O. W.,*" 43, 63–64.

63. Walter E. Kreutzer, "A Simplified Method of Patrol Distribution," *TPC,* July 1968.

64. "Asks Old Police Blue" (n.p., November 29, 1945), "Limit to Stretch in Khaki" (n.p., n.d.), F. 152, ser. 1, Clippings Scrapbook, 1939–1947, KCPHS.

65. Alfred E. Parker, *Crime Fighter: August Vollmer* (New York: Macmillan, 1961), 23–37; Gene Carte, "Introduction," in *August Vollmer: Pioneer in Police Professionalism* (Berkeley: University of California, Bancroft Library, Regional Oral History Office, 1972), vi–xii; Willard M. Oliver, "August Vollmer," in *Icons of Crime Fighting: Relentless Pursuers of Justice,* vol. 1, ed. Jeffrey B. Bumgarner (Westport, CT: Greenwood Press, 2008), 83–115, 89–90. O. W. Wilson, "August Vollmer" *Journal of Criminal Law, Criminology, and Police Science* 44, no. 1 (1953): 91–103.

66. Oliver, "August Vollmer."

67. Parker, *Crime Fighter,* 144.

68. Oliver, "August Vollmer," 100.

69. Frederic Wakeman, "American Police Advisers and the Nationalist Chinese Secret Service, 1930–1937," *Modern China* 18, no. 2 (1992): 107–137.

70. Upon its founding, the permanent faculty of five trainers at the International Police Academy included two men with degrees from MSU, and the part-time faculty of eleven included two with degrees from Berkeley. Biography of International Police Academy Faculty, Tab E, Memorandum for the Special Group (CI) (n.d.), Special Group (CI) 6/20/63–8/1/63, E5206, box 3, RG 59, NARA.

71. Aldous, *Police in Occupation Japan,* 9.

72. "Police Start Drive on Obscene Books," *Nippon Times,* January 11, 1947.

73. "Tokyo Task for Engle" (n.p., August 1946), F. 152, ser. 1, Clippings Scrapbook, 1939–1947, KCPHS.

74. Byron Engle, Outline of a Lecture to Provost Marshals Conference, June 2, 1947, Schools and Training Publications, 1947, E149, box 9, Records of General Headquarters, Far East Command, Supreme Commander Allied Powers, and United Nations Command, RG 554, NARA, 353. I am grateful to Tejasvi Nagaraja for sharing this document.

75. Bopp, "*O. W.,*" 68.

76. Bruce, "Impact of the Occupation," 124.

77. Bopp, "*O. W.*," 72.

78. Eric H. Monkkonen, *Crime, Justice, History* (Columbus: Ohio State University Press, 2002), 160.

79. O. W. Wilson, "Report on the Public Safety Training Program of ICA," July 21–27, 1958, folder 9, box 679, Vietnam Project Records, Michigan State University Archives & Historical Collections, East Lansing, MI (MSUA).

80. TOAID A-29, January 26, 1962, IPS 1, E26, box 88, RG 286, NARA.

81. Theo Hall to O. W. Wilson, January 5, 1958, IPS 1–1, E30, box 62, RG 286, NARA.

82. Murakawa, *First Civil Right,* 47–48.

83. Bruce, "Impact of the Occupation"; H. Richard Friman, "The Impact of the Occupation on Crime in Japan," in *Democracy in Occupied Japan: The US Occupation and Japanese Politics and Society,* ed. Mark E. Caprio and Yoneyuki Sugita (Florence, KY: Routledge, 2007), 89–119.

84. "Police School—August Vollmer, Instructor," *Kansas City Star,* May 24, 1929, roll 15, KCMNC.

85. Foreign Affairs Association of Japan, *The Japan Year Book, 1946–48* (Tokyo, 1948), 452.

86. Harry Emerson Wildes, "The Postwar Japanese Police," *Journal of Criminal Law and Criminology* 43, no. 5 (1953): 655–671.

87. Aldous, *Police in Occupation Japan.*

88. "Valetine Is Likely to Go to Japan; Wants 10 Police Experts as Aides," *New York Times,* February 1, 1946; "Valentine and Aides Begin Trip to Tokyo to Reorganize Police," *New York Times,* March 2, 1946; Kuzmarov, *Modernizing Repression,* 64–65; Lewis J. Valentine, *Night Stick: The Autobiography of Lewis J. Valentine* (New York: Dial Press, 1947), ch. 18.

89. Lindesay Parrott, "Local Police Rule Proposed in Japan," *New York Times,* June 7, 1946.

90. Aldous, *Police in Occupation Japan;* Oscar G. Olander, *Michigan State Police: A Twenty-five Year History* (East Lansing: Michigan Police Journal Press, 1942); "Commissioner Olander Recommends Sweeping Reforms in Jap Rural Police System," *TPC,* September 1946.

91. McCoy, *Policing America's Empire;* F. C. Miller, "The State Police," in *Papers and Proceedings of the Third Annual Meeting of the Minnesota Academy of Social Sciences,* ed. William A. Schaper (Minnesota Academy of Social Sciences, 1910), 102.

92. A. F. Brandstatter, "The Genesis and Early History of Criminal Justice Studies at Michigan State University," presented at the Midwestern Criminal Justice Association Meeting, Chicago, October 11–13, 1989; interview with Arthur Brandstatter by Jeff Charnley, April 11, 2001, Sesquicentennial Oral History Project, MSUA.

93. OPS, "Assistance to Civil Security Forces, Republic of Vietnam" (Washington, DC: AID, September 1971; pdacs391); Elkind, *Aid under Fire;* Ernst, *Forging a Fateful Alliance;* Kuzmarov, *Modernizing Repression;* Rosenau, *US Internal Security Assistance.*

94. Arthur Brandstatter, James Denison, Charles Killingsworth, and Edward Weidner, "Report of the Special FOA Mission from Michigan State College for Public Administration, Public Information, Police Administration, and Public Finance and Economics," October 16, 1954, folder 16, box 677, Vietnam Project Records, MSUA.

95. Jack Ryan to MSU Department of Police Administration, November 9, 1955, folder 2, box 680, Vietnam Project Records, MSUA; "Resume of MSU-USOM Relationships" (n.d.), attached to Ralph Turner to Arthur Brandstatter, June 16, 1960, folder 3, box 1694, Ralph F. Turner Papers, MSUA.

96. Conference of Americans in Police and Security Work, Far East Asia, March 6, 7, 8, 1957, attached to Paul Lawrence to Byron Engle, March 19, 1957, IPS 1, E31, box 36, RG 286, NARA, 13.

97. "Terrorists Raid Plants in Strike" *New York Times,* December 2, 1948.

98. "Oklahoman Named Public Safety Leader," *Hartford Courant,* March 9, 1963.

99. Arthur Brandstatter to Ralph Turner, June 15, 1960, folder 3, box 1694, Ralph F. Turner Papers, MSUA.

100. Jack Ryan to Arthur Brandstatter, December 17, 1955, folder 2, box 680, Vietnam Project Records, MSUA; Ernst, *Forging a Fateful Alliance,* 70.

101. Quoted in Ronald H. Spector, *Advice and Support: The Early Years, 1941–1960* (Washington, DC: Center of Military History, 1985), 322.

102. Michigan State University Police Advisory Staff, "Report on the Proposed Organization of the Law Enforcing Agencies of the Republic of Vietnam" (Saigon: MSU, April 1956); Guy Fox, *Final Report Covering Activities of the Michigan State University Vietnam Advisory Group* (Saigon: MSU, June 1962); Rosenau, *US Internal Security Assistance.*

103. Jack Ryan to Arthur Brandstatter, January 11, 1956, folder 2, box 680, Vietnam Project Records, MSUA.

104. Howard Hoyt to Glenn Taggart, December 12, 1957, folder 1, box File Drawer, Ralph H. Smuckler Papers, MSUA.

105. Rosenau, *US Internal Security Assistance,* 124–125.

106. Pulliam quoted in Aldous, *Police in Occupation Japan,* 167.

107. For instance, in 1957, Engle visited Hong Kong, Japan, Korea, Cambodia, Laos, South Vietnam, Thailand, and pre-statehood Hawai'i, where he met Honolulu's chief of police Daniel S. C. Liu, who in the coming decade would become one of the strongest voices for police professionalization in the United States. Summary Report of Official Overseas Travel, attached to Herbert Rupard to Edwin Arnold, May 29, 1957, IPS 1, E31, box 21, RG 286, NARA.

108. Lloyd D. Musolf, Ralph F. Turner, and A. F. Brandstatter, "Report on the MSUG Police Participant Program" (East Lansing: MSU, 1960).

109. Alvin Roseman to Byron Engle, May 14, 1956, IPS 1, E31, box 21, RG 286, NARA.

110. "Byron Engle Receives Citation," *TPC,* April 1958.

111. This distinction between "a" world and "the" world, drawn from Fernand Braudel, is the basis for Immanuel Wallerstein's oeuvre, as he explains in the 2011

Prologue to the reissued *The Modern World-System I* (1974; Berkeley: University of California Press, 2011), xviii.

112. James Baldwin, "Fifth Avenue, Uptown," *Esquire,* July 1960; "A Report from Occupied Territory," *The Nation,* July 11, 1966; Robert Blauner, "Whitewash over Watts"; Blauner, "Internal Colonialism and Ghetto Revolt."

CHAPTER 3. HOW COUNTERINSURGENCY BECAME POLICING

1. *First Line of Defense* (OPS film), Moving Images, 286.235, RG 286, NARA.

2. The best monograph on President Kennedy's reconfiguration of the NSC, though with insufficient attention to these transformations, is Andrew Preston, *The War Council: McGeorge Bundy, the NSC, and Vietnam* (Cambridge, MA: Harvard University Press, 2010).

3. "Address of Allen Welsh Dulles, Director of Central Intelligence, to the International Association of Chiefs of Police at Philadelphia, Pennsylvania, 3 October 1955," box 7, Philip G. Strong Collection, Department of Rare Books and Special Collections, Princeton University Library, Princeton, NJ. Charles Cabell, Dulles, Richard Helms, Lyman Kirkpatrick, and Lawrence White, all of the CIA directorate, addressed the IACP from 1954 to 1960.

4. Daniel Breslau, "The American Spencerians: Theorizing a New Science," in *Sociology in America: A History,* ed. Craig Calhoun (Chicago: University of Chicago Press, 2007), 39–62, quotation on 61.

5. George Steinmetz, "American Sociology before and after World War II: The (Temporary) Settling of a Disciplinary Field," in *Sociology in America,* 314–266, quotation on 357.

6. Walt W. Rostow, "Guerrilla Warfare in the Underdeveloped Areas," June 28, 1961, Fort Bragg, North Carolina, Army, box 69a, President's Office Files, JFKL, 4.

7. Harry Harootunian, *Marx after Marx: History and Time in the Expansion of Capitalism* (New York: Columbia University Press, 2015).

8. A broader intellectual lineage of modernization theory that goes back to Talcott Parsons and structural-functionalism is detailed in Nils Gilman, *Mandarins of the Future: Modernization Theory in Cold War America* (Baltimore: Johns Hopkins University Press, 2003), especially ch. 3.

9. Proposal for an Institute of Modernization Studies, attached to Walt Rostow to U. Alexis Johnson, February 14, 1962, Special Group (CI) 1/1/62–7/31/62, E5206, box 1, RG 59, NARA.

10. Carol Clifford, "Police Academy under Fire for Aiding 'Foreign Dictatorships,'" *Los Angeles Times,* June 7, 1974.

11. Defense Research Corporation, *Workbook for Participants: Urban Insurgency Conference August 1–September 4, 1964* (Santa Barbara, CA: Defense Research Corporation, 1964), 14, in IPS 10A, E18, box 9, RG 286, NARA.

12. Kuzmarov, *Modernizing Repression;* Charles Maechling Jr., "Insurgency and Counterinsurgency: The Role of Strategic Theory," *Parameters* 14, no. 3 (1984): 32–41; Maechling, "Camelot, Robert Kennedy, and Counter-Insurgency: A Memoir," *Virginia Quarterly* 75, no. 3 (1999).

13. Michael E. Latham, *The Right Kind of Revolution* (Ithaca, NY: Cornell University Press, 2011).

14. "Report of the Interagency Committee on Police Assistance Programs in Newly Emerging Countries" (n.d. [July 20, 1962]), IPS 7–1, E18, box 5, RG 286, NARA, 2.

15. Allan Evans to U. Alexis Johnson, August 28, 1962, Special Group (CI) 8/1/62–10/31/62, E5206, box 1, RG 59, NARA.

16. Quoted in Kenneth R. Hansen to Robert W. Komer [RWK], September 18, 1961, Counterinsurgency Special Group 2/61–46/62 and undated, box 414, NSF, JFKL.

17. Defense Research Corporation, *Workbook,* 14.

18. Kuzmarov, *Modernizing Repression;* Dennis M. Rempe, "An American Trojan Horse? Eisenhower, Latin America, and the Development of US Internal Security Policy 1954–1960," *Small Wars & Insurgencies* 10, no. 1 (1999): 34–64.

19. Herbert Hoover Jr., memorandum for the record, July 20, 1956; Counterinsurgency Police Program; box 413; NSF; JFKL.

20. J. H. Smith Jr. to Allen Dulles, November 28, 1958; IPS 1; E31; box 22; RG 286; NARA; Lobe, *United States National Security Policy;* Gordon Young, *Journey from Banna: An Autobiography* (Xlibris, 2011).

21. RWK to Walt W. Rostow, May 4, 1961; RWK Chron File, January–June 1961, box 1, Papers of RWK, LBJL.

22. The positions found intellectual support in Max F. Millikan and Walt W. Rostow, *A Proposal: Key to an Effective Foreign Policy* (New York: Harper & Bros, 1957).

23. Marvin R. Zahniser and W. Michael Weis, "A Diplomatic Pearl Harbor? Richard Nixon's Goodwill Mission to Latin America in 1958," *Diplomatic History* 13, no. 2 (1989): 163–190, 183.

24. Fredric Jameson, "Periodizing the 60s," *Social Text* 9–10 (1984): 178–209.

25. Committee of the Judiciary, *Communist Anti-American Riots, Mob Violence as an Instrument of Red Diplomacy, Bogota, Caracas, La Paz, Tokyo,* Staff Study, 1960, Senate, 86th Cong., 2nd sess.

26. McClintock, *Instruments;* Willard F. Barber and C. Neale Ronning, *Internal Security and Military Power; Counterinsurgency and Civic Action in Latin America* (Columbus: Ohio State University Press, 1966); Rempe, "American Trojan Horse"; Seymour J. Deitchman, *Limited War and American Defense Policy* (1964), 2nd ed. (Cambridge, MA: MIT Press, 1969); Stephen G. Rabe, *Eisenhower and Latin America* (Chapel Hill: University of North Carolina Press, 1988), 106–108, 146–148; Burton I. Kaufman, *Trade and Aid* (Baltimore: Johns Hopkins University Press, 1982), 152–175.

27. Department of State, "Draper Committee Recommendations on Military and Economic Assistance" (n.d.), Declassified Documents Reference System [DDRS], CK3100332355.

28. Deitchman, *Limited War*, 3.

29. Quoted from a memorandum to G. A. Lincoln, a West Point professor and chum of Rostow's, in Rempe, "American Trojan Horse," 53.

30. David Apter and Maxwell D. Taylor, "Tape-Recorded Interview," December 12, 1955, Speeches, Addresses, etc., Maxwell D. Taylor Papers, National Defense University Library; Maxwell D. Taylor, *The Uncertain Trumpet* (New York: Harper, 1960).

31. John Lewis Gaddis, *The Cold War: A New History* (New York: Penguin Press, 2005), 165; McCormick, *America's Half-Century*.

32. NSC 68: United States Objectives and Programs for National Security; Paul H. Nitze, "Nitze's Commentary," in *American Cold War Strategy: Interpreting NSC 68*, ed. Ernest R. May (Boston: Bedford Books of St. Martin's Press, 1993), 29, 105.

33. National Security Action Memorandum (NSAM) 2, "Development of Counter-Guerrilla Forces," February 3, 1961, NSF, JFKL; enclosure with letter from Secretary of State Rusk to Secretary of Defense McNamara, February 4, 1961, *FRUS*, 1961–63, 8: 10.

34. Jones, *Blowtorch*, 48.

35. RWK to attorney general, November 6, 1962, Counterinsurgency Police Program, box 413, NSF, JKFL.

36. RWK to Walt W. Rostow, May 4, 1961, RWK Chron File, January–June 1961, box 1, Papers of RWK, LBJL.

37. Mircea Alexandru Platon, "'Protracted Conflict': The Foreign Policy Research Institute 'Defense Intellectuals' and Their Cold War Struggle with Race and Human Rights," *Du Bois Review: Social Science Research on Race* 12, no. 2 (2015): 407–439; John K. Galbraith, "A Positive Approach to Economic Aid," *Foreign Affairs* 39, no. 3 (April 1961): 444–457.

38. Transcript, Harold H. Saunders Oral History, by Thomas Stern, November 24, 1993, Foreign Affairs Oral History Project, Association for Diplomatic Studies and Training (ADST), 11.

39. RWK to Allen Dulles, March 7, 1961, Personal 1964, E5045, box 1, RG 59, NARA.

40. RWK to Dulles, March 7, 1961.

41. Saunders Oral History, 13, 16, 13.

42. Walt Rostow to Secretary Rusk and Secretary McNamara, March 27, 1967, RWK Chron File, January–March 1967, box 7, Papers of RWK, LBJL.

43. Komer wrote this phrase in pen when he signed a memorandum updating the president on the situation in Vietnam; RWK to the president, October 5, 1966, Komer, Washington Papers, E5045, box 1, RG 59, NARA.

44. Transcript, Peter R. Rosenblatt Oral History I, July 26, 1984, by Ted Gittinger, LBJL, 26; David Halberstam, *The Best and the Brightest* (1972; New York: Ballantine Books, 1992), 647.

45. RWK to Bernard Fall, February 3, 1967, RWK Chron File, January–March 1967, box 7, Papers of RWK, LBJL. In 1956–1957, he attended the National War

College while on leave from the CIA; Transcript, Robert W. Komer Oral History, January 30, 1970, by Joe B. Frantz, LBJL, 2.

46. RWK to N. A. Komer, September 18, 1964, Personal 1964, E5045, box 1, RG 59, NARA.

47. Jones, *Blowtorch,* 18.

48. Ibid., ch. 1.

49. Neil Sheehan, *A Bright Shining Lie* (New York: Random House, 1988), 654–655.

50. Duong Van Mai Elliott, *RAND in Southeast Asia* (Santa Monica, CA: RAND, 2010).

51. The author's name has been redacted from this memorandum, but all signs point to Komer as its author, including its location in his files. Its vituperation, too, is characteristic of his tendencies. [Redacted] to DD/I [deputy director of intelligence], October 21, 1960, RWK Chron File, 1958–1961, box 1, Papers of RWK, LBJL.

52. Thomas K. Finletter, *Power and Policy: US Foreign Policy and Military Power in the Hydrogen Age* (New York: Harcourt, Brace, 1954). The term "Gray Areas" saw use into the 1960s, including by military and academic counterinsurgency experts, like Lucian Pye; see, e.g., William A. Lybrand, ed., *Proceedings of the Symposium "The U.S. Army's Limited-War Mission and Social Science Research," March 26–28, 1962* (Washington, DC: Special Operations Research Office [SORO], American University, 1962), 85, 161. "Third World," invented at roughly the same time, for similar purposes, in the wake of the issuance of NSC 68, has survived it.

53. CIA, "Break-Up of the Colonial Empires," 11.

54. Notes of a Meeting, February 24, 1966, *FRUS, 1964–1968,* 4: 84.

55. No recording of this conversation exists. It has been reconstructed from Komer Oral History, January 30, 1970, 22; Frank L. Jones, "Blowtorch: Robert Komer and the Making of Vietnam Pacification Policy," *Parameters* 35, no. 3 (2005): 103–118, 104; Robert W. Komer, *Bureaucracy Does Its Thing: Institutional Constraints on U.S.-GVN Performance in Vietnam.* (Santa Monica, CA: RAND Corporation, 1972).

56. Quoted in Sheehan, *Bright Shining Lie,* 653. Komer and his team developed the concept in a detailed analysis of pacification in South Vietnam up to summer 1966: "Giving a New Thrust to Pacification," draft 3, August 7, 1966, Pacification, box 7, files of RWK, NSF, LBJL; Jones, *Blowtorch,* 113–115.

57. Report of Interdepartmental Technical Subcommittee on Police Advisory Assistance Programs, June 11,1962, IPS 1, E18, box 2, RG 286, NARA, 38.

58. Saunders Oral History, 16.

59. Jones, *Blowtorch,* 94–95.

60. RWK, memorandum to the president's special assistant for national security affairs (Bundy), March 27, 1961, *FRUS, 1961–1963,* 23: 156. A copy Komer sent to Rostow included a handwritten apology for insulting the acumen of some of Rostow's social-scientist friends, like Lucian Pye and Guy Pauker. See Robert B. Rakove, *Kennedy, Johnson, and the Nonaligned World* (New York: Cambridge University Press, 2013), 114.

61. Background of Counter-Guerrilla Task Force Report, February 2, 1962; CREST, CIA-RDP83–00036R000500150037–0.

62. RWK to Rostow, May 4, 1961.

63. Krepinevich, *Army and Vietnam*, 47–53.

64. RWK to Walt W. Rostow, May 23, 1961, RWK Chron File, January–June 1961, box 1, Papers of RWK, LBJL.

65. Walt Rostow, "Guerrilla Warfare in the Underdeveloped Areas"; Rostow,"Countering Guerrilla Attack," in *Modern Guerrilla Warfare: Fighting Communist Guerrilla Movements, 1941–1961,* ed. Franklin Mark Osanka (New York: Free Press of Glencoe, 1962), 464–471.

66. NSAM 28, "Guerrilla Operations in Viet-Minh Territory," March 9, 1961, NSF, JFKL.

67. An American Officer [Edward Lansdale], "The Report the President Wanted Published," *Saturday Evening Post,* May 20, 1961; NSAM 9, "re: General Lansdale's Story of the Counter-Guerrilla Case Study," February 6, 1961, NSF, JFKL.

68. Bureau of Intelligence and Research, "Internal Warfare and the Security of the Underdeveloped States," PRS-1, November 20, 1961, Counterinsurgency, box 98, President's Office Files, JFKL, I, 46, 47–48. This report built on a prior Policy Planning Council report, which explicitly discussed the Overseas Internal Security Program and emphasized modernization, half a year before Rostow joined the Policy Planning Council; "Internal Defense of the Less Developed World," PPC 61–5, June 16, 1961, box 303, NSF, JFKL.

69. Robert H. Johnson to Carl Kaysen, December 1, 1961, Counterinsurgency Special Group 2/61–4/62 and undated, box 414, NSF, JFKL.

70. Transcript, William P. Bundy Oral History II, March 6, 1972, by William W. Moss, JFKL Oral History Program, 70.

71. Albert L. Fisher, "How to Beat the Guerrillas at Their Own Game," *Military Review* 43, no. 12 (December 1963), 81–86, quotations on 83, 82. A widely circulated book by an Army lieutenant colonel would reprise this postulate in 1966, even after it had begun to fall from favor: "the most logical solution does lie in developing a counterrevolutionary strategy which applies revolutionary strategy and principles IN REVERSE to defeat the enemy with his own weapons on his own battlefield." John J. McCuen, *The Art of Counter-Revolutionary War: The Strategy of Counter-Insurgency* (Harrisburg, PA: Stackpole Books, 1966), 78.

72. Samuel E. Belk to Walt W. Rostow (n.d. [June 28, 1961]), Counterinsurgency Special Group 2/61–4/62 and undated, box 414, NSF, JFKL.

73. Thomas L. Ahern Jr., *The Way We Do Things: Black Entry Operations into North Vietnam, 1961–1964* (Washington, DC: Center for the Study of Intelligence, May 2005), 3, National Security Archive Electronic Briefing Book.

74. Spector, *Advice and Support,* 164.

75. Eqbal Ahmad, "Revolutionary War and Counter-Insurgency," *Journal of International Affairs* 25, no. 1 (1971): 1–47, 32n41.

76. NSAM 162, Development of US and Indigenous Police, Paramilitary and Military Resources, June 7, 1962, NSF, JFKL; Jefferson P. Marquis, "The Other

Warriors: American Social Science and Nation Building in Vietnam," *Diplomatic History* 24, no. 1 (2000): 79–105.

77. Circular telegram from the Department of State, February 27, 1963, *FRUS, 1961–1963*, 12: 106.

78. RWK to Walt W. Rostow, February 28, 1961, Counterinsurgency Special Group 7/61–5/63, White House Memoranda, box 414, NSF, JFKL.

79. Cross was the author of *Conflict in the Shadows: The Nature and Politics of Guerrilla War* (Garden City, NY: Doubleday, 1963).

80. RWK to Walt W. Rostow, August 11, 1961, RWK Chron File, June–December 1961, box 1, Papers of RWK, LBJL.

81. On the counterinsurgent and racist origins of the term "boondocks" from the Tagalog *bundok* (mountain), see Kramer, *Blood of Government,* 33.

82. "US Counter-Guerrilla Operational and Training Capabilities," attached to George McGhee to Maxwell D. Taylor, August 7, 1961, DDRS, CK3100435843.

83. RWK to Maxwell Taylor, August 7, 1961, RWK Chron File, June–December 1961, box 1, Papers of RWK, LBJL.

84. RWK, "Revamping the MAP," August 29, 1961, attached to RWK to Dick Bissell, August 29, 1961, RWK Chron File, June–December 1961, box 1, Papers of RWK, LBJL.

85. Untitled (n.d.), 24–53, Counterinsurgency Special Group 2/61–4/62 and undated, Bx 414, NSF, JFKL, 41.

86. "Counter-Guerrilla Warfare Task Force, Elements of US Strategy to Deal with 'Wars of National Liberation,'" December 9, 1961, CREST, CIA-RDP83–00036R001100160001–1, i.

87. RWK to Maxwell Taylor, August 7, 1961.

88. NSAM 124, "Establishment of the Special Group (Counter-Insurgency)," January 18, 1962, NSF, JFKL; RWK to McGeorge Bundy, January 31, 1962, RWK Chron File, January–June 1962, box 2, Papers of RWK, LBJL.

89. Transcript, Robert W. Komer Oral History V, December 22, 1969, by Dennis J. O'Brien, JFKL Oral History Program, 95.

90. Memorandum for the record, June 21, 1962, Special Group (CI) 1/1/62–7/31/62, E5206, box 1, RG 59, NARA.

91. RWK to McGeorge Bundy, April 10, 1962, RWK Chron File, January–June 1962, box 2, Papers of RWK, LBJL. Jones, "Guerrilla Warfare Problem"; Maechling, "Camelot"; McClintock, *Instruments;* Michaels, "Managing Global Counterinsurgency."

92. NSAM 165, "Assignment of Additional Responsibility to the Special Group (CI)," June 16, 1962, NSF, JFKL. The original draft of NSAM 124, which mentions Colombia, is: McGeorge Bundy, "Establishment of the Special Group (Counter-Insurgency)," January 2, 1962, Special Group (CI) 4/6/61–6/7/62, box 319, NSF, JFKL.

93. Gaddis Smith, *The Last Years of the Monroe Doctrine, 1945–1993* (New York: Hill & Wang, 1994), 118–119.

94. Attachment to CSAM 218–65, April 21, 1965, Counter-Insurgency Police Program 1964–1965–1966, box 15, files of RWK, NSF, LBJL.

95. RWK to McGeorge Bundy, January 21, 1966, Counter-Insurgency Special Group 1964–1965–1966, box 15, files of RWK, NSF, LBJL.

96. US OIDP, September 1962, IPS 7–2, E18, box 5, RG 286, NARA; Maechling, "Insurgency and Counterinsurgency."

97. Andrew J. Birtle, *US Army Counterinsurgency and Contingency Operations Doctrine, 1942–1976* (Washington, DC: Center of Military History, 2006), 237.

98. Ibid., 239.

99. Komer, *Bureaucracy Does Its Thing*, 30–36; Edward G. Miller, *Misalliance* (Cambridge, MA: Harvard University Press, 2013).

100. RWK to Dave Bell, February 28, 1963, RWK Chron File, January–June 1963, box 3, Papers of RWK, LBJL.

101. McGeorge Bundy to Maxwell Taylor, December 16, 1961, Oral History Kennedy, box 10, Papers of RWK, LBJL

102. Maechling, "Camelot"; Transcript, Victor H. Krulak Oral History, November 19, 1970, by William W. Moss, JFKL Oral History Program, 5; Blaufarb, *Counterinsurgency Era*, 69.

103. John A. McCone, memorandum of discussion, August 17, 1962, *FRUS*, 1961–1963, 7–9, microfiche supplement, 277.

104. Transcript, Thomas L. Hughes Oral History, by Charles Stuart Kennedy, July 7, 1999, ADST, 113, 43, 106.

105. William Beecher, "US Effort to Counter Red Insurgency Guided by Little-Known Group," *Wall Street Journal*, June 27, 1963.

106. Memorandum for the record, January 18, 1962, Special Group (CI) 1/1/62–7/31/62, E5206, box 1, RG 59, NARA.

107. RWK to McGeorge Bundy, Maxwell Taylor, January 31, 1962, Counterinsurgency Police Program, box 413, NSF, JFKL; RWK to McGeorge Bundy, February 7, 1962, RWK Chron File, January–June 1962, box 2, Papers of RWK, LBJL.

108. McGeorge Bundy to the president, February 14, 1962, with attached draft memo to Hamilton; RWK to McGeorge Bundy, February 14, 1962, RWK Chron File, January–June 1962, box 2, Papers of RWK, LBJL.

109. NSAM 132, "Support of Local Police Forces for Internal Security & Counter-Insurgency Purposes," February 19, 1962, NSF, JFKL.

110. Maxwell D. Taylor to the president, June 2, 1962, Special Group (CI) 1/1/62–7/31/62, E5206, box 1, RG 59, NARA.

111. NSAM 146, "Improvement of Police Training and Equipment in Newly Emerging Countries," April 20, 1962, NSF, JFKL.

112. RWK to [McGeorge Bundy], April 28, 1962, Special Group (CI) Meetings 6/8/61–11/2/1962, box 319, NSF, JFKL.

113. Memorandum for the record, April 26, 1962, Special Group (CI) 1/1/62–7/31/62, E5206, box 1, RG 59, NARA; Agenda for Friday Police Committee Meeting, April 25, 1962, RWK Chron File, January–June 1962, box 2, Papers of RWK, LBJL.

114. RWK to the president, June 11, 1962; RWK to McGeorge Bundy, May 16, 1962; RWK to McGeorge Bundy, April 24, 1962, RWK Chron File, January–June 1962, box 2, Papers of RWK, LBJL.

115. Report of Interdepartmental Technical Subcommittee, 54.

116. RWK to Carl Kaysen, June 22, 1962, RWK Chron File, January–June 1962, box 2, Papers of RWK, LBJL; Report of Interdepartmental Technical Subcommittee, 14.

117. Final Report of the Vietnam Task Force, July 1, 1962, *FRUS,* 1961–1963, 2: 233.

118. CIA, "Counter-Insurgency Critical List," July 25, 1962, CREST, CIA-RDP80B01676R000600090002–7.

119. Memo for the record, June 7, 1962, Special Group (CI) 1/1/62–7/31/62, E5206, box 1, RG 59, NARA.

120. RWK to McGeorge Bundy, July 14, 1962, RWK Chron File, July–December 1962, box 2, Papers of RWK, LBJL.

121. Memorandum for the president, July 20, 1962, attached to Report of the Interagency Committee on Police Assistance Programs in Newly Emerging Countries, IPS 7–1, E18, box 5, RG 286, NARA.

122. NSAM 177, "Police Assistance Programs," August 7, 1962, NSF, JFKL; Department of State, Police Assistance Programs, August 21, 1962, DDRS, CK3100583202.

123. Hal H. Saunders to RWK, October 29, 1962, Counterinsurgency Police Program White House Memoranda 5/61–10/63, box 413, NSF, JFKL; AID General Notice, Office of Public Safety (O/PS), November 1, 1962, IPS 1, E18, box 2, RG 286, NARA. When OPS opened, sixteen other "free world" countries, including France, Germany, Israel, the United Kingdom, and the Philippines, offered police assistance around the globe, mainly training. US evaluators considered these programs too inconsistent and small to substitute for OPS programming. Much of the assistance from European powers went to their former colonies. OPS advisors generally found these programs to be competition, even if the official diplomatic line touted cooperation and coordination. Competition and mutual disregard marked the relationship between OPS in South Vietnam and the small British Advisory Mission, run for a time by Robert G. K. Thompson. East Germany provided overseas police assistance in North Vietnam, as did the Soviet Union in Afghanistan, in the 1960s. See Report of Interdepartmental Technical Subcommittee, 49–53.

124. RWK to attorney general, November 6, 1962, Counterinsurgency Police Program White House Memoranda 5/61–10/63, box 413, NSF, JFKL. Robert Kennedy's late push to make OPS a reality has led some, such as Maechling, to overemphasize his role in its conceptualization, which was the work primarily of Komer, Engle, and their aides.

125. AID General Notice, Office Public Safety—Amendment to AID General Notice dated November 1, 1962, November 30, 1962, DDRS, CK3100583449.

126. RWK to Bill Gaud, February 18, 1965, Counter-Insurgency Police Program 1964–1965–1966, box 15, Files of RWK, NSF, LBJL.

127. Byron Engle to RWK, March 31, 1967, RWK Chron File. January–March 1967, box 7, Papers of RWK, LBJL.

128. Memorandum from the secretary of defense (McNamara) to the president, August 8, 1962, *FRUS,* 1961–1963, 2: 262.

129. Komer, *Bureaucracy Does Its Thing;* "Impact of Pacification on Insurgency in South Vietnam," *Journal of International Affairs* 25, no. 1 (1971): 48–69; *Impact of Pacification on Insurgency in South Vietnam* (Santa Monica, CA: RAND Corporation, 1970).

130. Jones, *Blowtorch;* Amy Austin Holmes, *Social Unrest and American Military Bases in Turkey and Germany since 1945* (New York: Cambridge University Press, 2014).

CHAPTER 4. BRINGING POLICE ASSISTANCE HOME

1. Joseph Lukban, "International Policing and Global Peace," *Police,* March–April 1965.

2. Murakawa, *First Civil Right,* 205.

3. Congressional Budget Office, *Federal Law Enforcement Assistance: Alternative Approaches* (Washington, DC: GPO, 1978), 9; Virginia Gray and Bruce Williams, *The Organizational Politics of Criminal Justice* (Lexington, MA: Lexington Books, 1980); Joel R. Kramer, "Criminal Justice R&D: New Agency Stresses Police over Corrections," *Science* 166, no. 3905 (1969): 588–590.

4. Leigh David Benin, *The New Labor Radicalism and New York City's Garment Industry: Progressive Labor Insurgents in the 1960s* (New York: Garland, 2000), 15.

5. Baldwin, "Report from Occupied Territory"; Feagin and Hahn, *Ghetto Revolts;* Louis Hyman, *Debtor Nation: The History of America in Red Ink* (Princeton, NJ: Princeton University Press, 2011), 173–190; Thomas J. Sugrue, *Sweet Land of Liberty* (New York: Random House, 2008); Keeanga-Yamahtta Taylor, "Back Story to the Neoliberal Moment: Race Taxes and the Political Economy of Black Urban Housing in the 1960s," *Souls* 14, no. 3–4 (2012): 185–206. Feagin and Hahn write that Black people's "ghetto rioting" can be understood as their "first major effort . . . to employ the principles of federalism to their own advantage" (320).

6. "Interview with J. Edgar Hoover," *US News & World Report,* December 21, 1964.

7. Lyndon B. Johnson, "Statement by the President upon Making Public an FBI Report on the Recent Urban Riots," September 26, 1964; "Special Message to the Congress on Crime and Law Enforcement," March 9, 1966; "Statement by the President upon Signing the Omnibus Crime Control and Safe Streets Act of 1968," June 19, 1968, *TAPP.*

8. Edward Scheidt, "Civil Rights Legislation: Testimony in Opposition to H. R. 2145, 85th Congress, 1st Session," *TPC,* May 1957, 10–12, 10.

9. Timothy Conlan, *From New Federalism to Devolution: Twenty-Five Years of Intergovernmental Reform* (Washington, DC: Brookings Institution Press, 1998), 4.

10. Richard M. Flanagan, "Lyndon Johnson, Community Action, and Management of the Administrative State," *Presidential Studies Quarterly* 31, no. 4 (2001): 585–608, quotation on 585–586.

11. Weaver, "Frontlash," 247.

12. Murakawa, *First Civil Right,* 12.

13. Lyndon B. Johnson, "Special Message to the Congress on Law Enforcement and the Administration of Justice," March 8, 1965, *TAPP.*

14. Lisa L. Miller, *The Perils of Federalism: Race, Poverty, and the Politics of Crime Control* (New York: Oxford University Press, 2008), 27.

15. William Thomas Allison, review of *Modernizing Repression,* by Jeremy Kuzmarov, *Journal of American History* 100, no. 1 (2013): 300–301.

16. "Text of FBI Report to President on Summer Riots in 9 Cities over Country" *New York Times,* September 27, 1964.

17. Lyndon B. Johnson, "Statement by the President on the Riots in New York City," July 21, 1964, *TAPP.*

18. Bradford M. Crittenden, "Federal Intervention—Are We Heeding the Warning Signals?" *TPC,* September 1963.

19. O. W. Wilson, *Police Administration* (New York: McGraw-Hill, 1950), 82.

20. "Riot Toll in Cities with Major Incidents, 1964–1967," Reports and Memos Related to Racial Riots 1967, box 5, personal papers [PP] Sherwin J. Markman, LBJL.

21. NACCD, *Report,* 35–37.

22. Cater was Sagalyn's direct contact. Cater's responsibilities originally centered on foreign policy but shifted toward domestic policy over time. He was interested in using the new Community Relations Service, initiated by the Civil Rights Act, rather than the FBI to investigate the cause of the Harlem unrest. Cater was already looking for alternatives to traditional routines of law enforcement. David C. Carter, *The Music Has Gone Out of the Movement: Civil Rights and the Johnson Administration, 1965–1968* (Chapel Hill: University of North Carolina Press, 2009), 166.

23. Arnold Sagalyn, "Creation of a Federal Technical Police Assistance Program for Local and State Police Departments" (n.d.), attached to Sagalyn to Douglass Cater, September 9, 1964, Law Enforcement—Police Matters 11/22/63–10/22/65, Ex JL6, box 39, White House Central File [WHCF], LBJL.

24. Dwight D. Eisenhower, "Annual Message to the Congress on the State of the Union," January 6, 1955, *TAPP.*

25. The Commission in 1961 recommended grants-in-aid for police recruiting and training, including in the constitutional rights of citizens; Murakawa, *First Civil Right,* 74, 231n14. In the early 1960s, Senator Philip Hart (D-MI) had unsuccessfully tried to develop legislation in this vein, likely influenced by MSU's Brandstatter. MSU's president, John A. Hannah, chaired this Commission (MSU faculty were training police in South Vietnam at the same time); President Nixon later appointed Hannah administrator of AID, a position he held during the period of OPS's closure.

26. Arnold Sagalyn, "Lawlessness and the Police" (n.d.), attached to Sagalyn to Lee White, September 15, 1964; Sagalyn to Lee White, September 15, 1964, Law Enforcement—Police Matters 11/22/63–10/22/65, Ex JL6, box 39, WHCF, LBJL.

27. Johnson, "Special Message," March 8, 1965.

28. Bopp, "*O. W.,*" 64.

29. Sagalyn self-published a memoir, *A Promise Fulfilled: The Memoir of Arnold Sagalyn*, in 2010. A copy of it is held in ASP. Quotation about Wilson on 104.

30. Max D. Phillips, "A Study of the Office of Law Enforcement Coordination, US Treasury Department," *Journal of Criminal Law and Criminology* 54, no. 3 (1963): 369–377.

31. Sagalyn, *Promise Fulfilled*, 223.

32. Interagency Police Group Charter, December 18, 1962, IPS 7–3, E18, box 7, RG 286, NARA.

33. Douglas Dillon to Fowler Hamilton, November 8, 1962, IPS 7–3, E18, box 8, RG 286, NARA.

34. Eventually all representatives other than Engle rotated off the membership roster; Interagency Police Group Members, October 1968, IPS 7–3, E18, box 8, RG 286, NARA.

35. Byron Engle to Eugene Rossides, May 6, 1969, IPS 7–3, E18, box 8, RG 286, NARA.

36. Sagalyn, *Promise Fulfilled*, 223, 229.

37. George Edwards, *The Police on the Urban Frontier* (New York: Institute of Human Relations Press, 1968).

38. Transcript, Krulak Oral History, 6.

39. Memo for the record, Minutes of Meeting of Special Group (CI), 10 May 1962, May 14, 1962, IPS 7–2, E18, box 5, RG 286, NARA.

40. Memo for the record, Minutes of Meeting of Special Group (CI), 15 March 1962, March 16, 1962, Special Group (CI) Meetings, box 319, NSF, JFKL.

41. Hal Saunders to RWK, February 24, 1964; Saunders to RWK, June 9, 1965, Counter-Insurgency Police Program, 1964–1965–1966, box 15, files of RWK, NSF, LBJL.

42. D. Van Buskirk, AIDTO circular XA-413, October 30, 1962, IPS 6–4, E18, box 4, RG 286, NARA; Joseph J. Wolf, memo for Special Group (CI) Assistants, March 27, 1963, Special Group (CI) 3/14/63–4/18/63, E5206, box 2, RG 59, NARA.

43. Byron Engle, "Director's Message," *IPA Review* 2, no. 2 (April 1968).

44. AIDTO circular A-30 (draft), November 30, 1961, IPS 6–4, E18, box 4, RG 286, NARA; J. Edgar Hoover, "The Role of the FBI in American Law Enforcement," *IPA Review* 2, no. 2 (April 1968).

45. J. Edgar Hoover appointment and phone logs, September 24, 1965, pt. 41 of 44, FBI Records: The Vault online.

46. Attachment to Byron Engle to U. Alexis Johnson, September 12, 1969, IPS 2, E31, box 25, RG 286, NARA.

47. Henry A. Fitzgibbon, "Police Procedure against Sniper Attack," *IPA Review* 2, no. 3 (July 1968).

48. Walter Burch to Byron Engle, May 15, 1967; Jeter Williamson to Lauren Goin, June 6, 1967, IPS 1, E31, box 23, RG 286, NARA.

49. Sagalyn, *Promise Fulfilled*, 310–313.

50. Sagalyn, "Creation of a Federal Technical Police Assistance Program."

51. Russell Snook to Theo Hall, February 14, 1958, IACP (General), E29, box 1,

RG 286, NARA; Subcommittee on Inter-American Affairs, Committee on Foreign Affairs, House, 88th Cong., 1st sess., Castro-Communist Subversion in the Western Hemisphere, March 4, 1963.

52. Jeter Williamson to Thomas Cahill, March 30, 1967, IPS 1, E31, box 23, RG 286, NARA. OPS sent this letter to chiefs in San Francisco, Chicago, Detroit, Honolulu, Los Angeles, New York City, and Philadelphia.

53. Committee on Internal Security, House, 91st Congress, 2nd sess., Black Panther Party, pt. 4, October 15, 1970, 4902.

54. Quinn Tamm, report from the Office of the Executive Director, October 8, 1962, IACP (1962), E29, box 1, RG 286, NARA.

55. Police Administration Division, *Minutes of Staff Meetings, 1955–1960*, March 7, 1959 (Saigon: MSU Vietnam Advisory Group, n.d.).

56. Edward Kennelly, memo for the record, December 29, 1962, E29, box 1, RG 286, NARA.

57. See, e.g., A. F. Brandstatter to Ralph Turner, November 6, 1959, folder 2, box 1694, Ralph F. Turner Papers; MSUA.

58. J.J. Daunt to [Cartha] De Loach, April 29, 1965; De Loach to [John] Mohr, May 6, 1965, FBI 62–94062. Thanks to Garrett Felber for sharing this source, Parker's FBI file.

59. "Legion Is Warned of 'War' in Streets," *New York Times*, August 28, 1966.

60. George W. O'Connor, "IACP Testimony of H. R. 6508," *TPC*, August 1965, 22.

61. "Surplus Equipment for Police Emergency Preparedness," *TPC*, December 1965; "Purchase of Surplus Military Equipment" *TPC*, April 1969.

62. On the relationship between police reform and municipal politics at mid-century, see Chris Lowen Agee, *The Streets of San Francisco* (Chicago: University of Chicago Press, 2014).

63. Gerald Caplan, "Reflections on the Nationalization of Crime, 1964–1968," *Law and the Social Order* 3 (1973): 583–635.

64. Barry Mahoney, "The Politics of the Safe Streets Act, 1965–1973: A Case Study in Evolving Federalism and the National Legislative Process" (PhD diss., Columbia University, 1976), 90.

65. For recent reinterpretations of crime-rate data, see Committee on Causes and Consequences of High Rates of Incarceration, *The Growth of Incarceration in the United States: Exploring Causes and Consequences,* ed. Jeremy Travis, Bruce Western, and Steve Redburn (Washington, DC: National Academies Press, 2014), chap. 4; Murakawa, *First Civil Right*, 72; Hinton, *From the War on Poverty;* Weaver, "Frontlash."

66. Public Law 90–351, June 19, 1968.

67. Quinn Tamm, "Justice—*Now!*" *TPC,* July 1968.

68. Hinton, *From the War on Poverty,* 104.

69. Robert F. Diegelman, "Federal Financial Assistance for Crime Control: Lessons of the LEAA Experience," *Journal of Criminal Law & Criminology* 7, no. 3 (1982): 994–1011.

70. John Price to Charles Rogovin, April 3, 1970, Ex FG 17–7, FG 17, box 5, WHCF, Richard M. Nixon Presidential Library, Yorba Linda, CA (RMNL).

71. Vesla Weaver, "The Significance of Policy Failures in Political Development: The Law Enforcement Assistance Administration and the Growth of the Carceral State," in *Living Legislation: Durability, Change, and the Politics of American Law-making*, ed. Jeffery A. Jenkins and Eric M. Patashnik (Chicago: University of Chicago Press, 2012), 221–251.

72. Feeley and Sarat, *Policy Dilemma*, 41–43.

73. Daunt to De Loach, April 29, 1965.

74. Mahoney, "Politics of the Safe Streets Act," 138.

75. Weaver, "Significance of Policy Failures."

76. Cronin, Cronin, and Milakovich, *US v. Crime in the Streets;* Feeley and Sarat, *Policy Dilemma;* Flamm, *Law and Order;* Weaver, "Significance of Policy Failures."

77. Republican Coordinating Committee, "The Restoration of Federalism," 113 Cong. Rec. (April 10, 1967), 8815–8818. On this blueprint for revisions to federalism enacted by Nixon and President Ronald Reagan, see Mahoney, "Politics of the Safe Streets Act." Because most historiography of the rise of the New Right focuses on movement conservatives, little attention has been paid to staid and unglamorous policy efforts to reshape federal-state relations, even though they have been consequential. The first block grants came with the 1966 Partnership for Health Act, but they were minuscule in comparison to what the LEAA budgeted and did not give rise to an entirely new administrative agency. See also Republican Coordinating Committee, "Crime and Delinquency—A Republican Response" (Washington, DC: Republican National Committee, May 1968).

78. Gray and Williams, *Organizational Politics of Criminal Justice*, 110.

79. Donald E. Santarelli to Richard M. Nixon, June 4, 1974, Ex FG 17–7/A, FG 17, box 5, WHCF, RMNL; "IPA Graduation" *IPA Review* 8, no. 3 (July 1974).

80. Hinton, *From the War on Poverty.*

CHAPTER 5. POLICING AND SOCIAL REGULATION

1. Seigel, *Violence Work.*

2. "Plans Made for Policing Training" *Yuma Daily Sun,* January 8, 1961; "In Choosing a Sheriff," ibid., August 29, 1960.

3. D. E. Bordenkircher and S. A. Bordenkircher, *Tiger Cage: An Untold Story* (Cameron, WV: Abby Publishing, 1998); *Pappy's Rendition: Corrections & Detention Iraq 2005–2009* (Cameron, WV: Abby Publishing, 2012).

4. Roger Morris, "Thirty-Six Hours at Santa Fe," *Playboy,* March 1981; "West Virginia Inmates Take 14 Hostages in Riot," *New York Times,* January 2, 1986.

5. Michael Mann, "The Autonomous Power of the State: Its Origins, Mechanisms and Results," *European Journal of Sociology* 25, no. 2 (1984): 185–213.

6. US Embassy Montevideo to secretary of state, September 7, 1970, "Mitrione Kidnapping," CREST, CIA-RDP78–04491A000100030003–8; Jeffrey L. Gould, "Solidarity under Siege: The Latin American Left, 1968," *American Historical Review* 114, no. 2 (2009): 348–375.

7. Andrew Best Sr., *Bad Cop No Doughnut* (n.p., 2011); Bordenkircher and Bordenkircher, *Tiger Cage;* Lee E. Echols, *Hilarious High Jinks and Dangerous Assignments* (Washington, DC: National Rifle Association of America, 1990); Morris Grodsky, *The Home Boy's Odyssey: The Saga of the Journey from Orphan Boy to Criminalist* (n.p., 2004); David L. Laughlin, *Gringo Cop* (New York: Carlton Press, 1975); Adolph Saenz, *The OPS Story* (San Francisco: Robert D. Reed, 2002); Young, *Journey from Banna.*

8. Schrader, "Nicaragua."

9. Bob Jessop, "Fordism and Post-Fordism," in *Beyond the Regulation Approach: Putting Capitalist Economies in Their Place,* ed. Bob Jessop and Ngai-Ling Sum (Northampton, MA: Edward Elgar, 2006), 58–89, 60; Neocleous, *Fabrication of Social Order.*

10. I am inspired here by Gavin Walker, *The Sublime Perversion of Capital: Marxist Theory and the Politics of History in Modern Japan* (Durham, NC: Duke University Press, 2016).

11. Langguth, *Hidden Terrors;* Lobe, "Rise and Demise."

12. Mark Neocleous, *War Power, Police Power* (Edinburgh: Edinburgh University Press, 2014); Neocleous, "Security as Pacification" and George Rigakos, "'To Extend the Scope of Productive Labour': Pacification as a Police Project," in *Anti-Security,* ed. Neocleous and Rigakos (Ottawa: Red Quill Books, 2011), 57–83, and, more broadly, the essays in *Socialist Studies / Études socialistes* 9, no. 2 (2013); Neocleous, "Security, Liberty and the Myth of Balance: Towards a Critique of Security Politics," *Contemporary Political Theory* 6, no. 2 (2007): 131–149; Stuart Schrader, "To Secure the Global Great Society: Participation in Pacification," *Humanity* 7, no. 2 (2016): 225–253; Mariana Valverde, "Questions of Security: A Framework for Research," *Theoretical Criminology* 15, no. 1 (2011): 3–22; Tyler Wall, Parastou Saberi, and Will Jackson, eds., *Destroy, Build, Secure: Readings on Pacification* (Ottawa: Red Quill Books, 2017).

13. Theodore J. Curtis, *A Brief History of USOM Support to the Thai National Police Department* (Bangkok: AID, July 1973; pdacs802).

14. William E. Colby and Peter Forbath, *Honorable Men: My Life in the CIA* (New York: Simon & Schuster, 1978), 256; Schrader, "To Secure the Global Great Society."

15. Charles F. Sloane, "History of Police," June 1957, box 8, Charles Francis Sloane Papers; HIA.

16. Stuart Hall, Chas Critcher, Tony Jefferson, John Clarke, and Brian Roberts, *Policing the Crisis: Mugging, The State, and Law and Order* (London: Macmillan, 1978), 319; Nicos Poulantzas, *State, Power, Socialism,* trans. Patrick Camiller (New York: Verso, 1980).

17. Richard T. McCormack Oral History, by Charles Stuart Kennedy, January 2, 2002, ADST; "Thai Local Administration" (Fort Washington, PA: Philco-Ford Corporation, June 1968).

18. Rex Applegate, *Kill or Get Killed: Riot Control Techniques, Manhandling, and Close Combat, for Police and the Military* (1943; new ed., Boulder, CO: Paladin Press, 1976); Paul Gutierrez to Theodore D. Brown, November 21, 1963, IAPA Administrator Files, E27, box 1, RG 286, NARA.

19. Aaron W. Navarro, *Political Intelligence and the Creation of Modern Mexico, 1938–1954* (University Park: Pennsylvania State University, 2010).

20. Albert F. Robinson, "Policing Vietnam: The Public Safety Program," *Vietnam* 16, no. 6 (2004): 26–32.

21. OPS, *Worldwide Police Casualty Study, CY69/CY71* (Washington, DC: AID, 1972).

22. Office of Public Safety Casualty Summary, June 6, 1968, IPS 14–3, E18, box 9, RG 286, NARA.

23. News clippings from Robert Kimball case, 1965, folder 55, box 1699, Ralph F. Turner Papers, MSUA.

24. Transcript, John Sylvester Jr. Oral History, by Laura M. Calkins, August 4, 2004, ADST, 104.

25. James A. Bower to Robert C. Lowe, April 11, 1966; Hoang Van Niem, Information Report, April 1, 1966, Propaganda/Security, E525, box 6, RG 472, NARA.

26. Debrief of a Prison Advisor (Public Safety), Phuoc Tuy, Thua Thien, and Gia Dinh, Vietnam, 1960–1967 (Honolulu: Asia Training Center, n.d.; pdabz912), 10.

27. Saenz, *OPS Story*, 121–122.

28. Lindsey Churchill, *Becoming the Tupamaros: Solidarity and Transnational Revolutionaries in Uruguay and the United States* (Nashville, TN: Vanderbilt University Press, 2014).

29. Stuart Schrader, "When NACLA Helped Shutter the US Office of Public Safety," *NACLA Report on the Americas* 48, no. 2 (2016): 181–187; "In Memoriam" *IPA Review* 5, no. 4, October 1971; "Fourth Memorial Mass for Dan A. Mitrione," *IPA Review* 7, no. 4, October 1973; Ernest W. Lefever, *U.S. Public Safety Assistance: An Assessment* (Washington, DC: Brookings Institution, 1973), 58.

30. Lauren J. Goin, "Director's Message" *IPA Review* 8, no. 4, October 1974, 2. The *IPA Review* described new training curricula, such as the emergence of narcotics control as a focal point in the early 1970s; subsequent promotions, accolades, and deaths of graduates; and new approaches to policing that advisors, attendees, and graduates were developing or researching. Originally, OPS printed 4,000 and 3,000 copies in English and Spanish, respectively, but after two years OPS increased the Spanish-language print-run to 3,500; Role of AID Public Safety Programs, 8. The IAPA, during its short existence, published its own newsletter in Spanish; ADM 6–2, E27, box 1, RG 286, NARA.

31. Robinson, "Policing Vietnam."

32. David E. Bell, memorandum for the Special Group (CI), April 5, 1965, DDRS, CK2349123115.

33. *Evaluation Report of Public Safety Advisor Training Program* (Washington, DC: AID, 1970; pdacs387), app. 3 (n.p.), 61–62.

34. Technician Interview No. 50, September 25, 1962, GU00095, Digital National Security Archive, 1.

35. David Jickling, Oral History, by W. Haven North, September 15, 1998, ADST, 23; Davis and James, *Public Safety Story*, 21.

36. Paul Katz, "Central American International Security Telecommunications Survey Report" (Washington, DC: AID, February 1964; pnadw966); Byron Engle to Gordon Chase, March 23, 1964, DDRS, CK3100292500.

37. Ted Brown, Jack Ellis, and Rex Morris, *Survey Report of the Special Security Corps* (Washington, DC: AID, May 1965; pnadw942).

38. John P. Longan to Arnold Sagalyn, October 26, 1967; "America's Global Police Officers," *Kiwanis Magazine,* April 1969, annexes to John P. Longan Memoir (oral history), by James D. Williams, November 1984, The Institute of Inter-American Affairs Collection, Columbia University; Manuel A. Cohen Zabala, "Caracas Communications Center," *IPA Review* 1, no. 2, April 1967.

39. Sagalyn, *Promise Fulfilled,* 246–249

40. Raymond Knickel, "Electronics Equipment Associated with the Police Car," app. E to PCLEAJ, *Task Force Report: Science and Technology* (Washington, DC: GPO, 1967), 139; NACCD, *Report,* 329, 487; Lefever, *U.S. Public Safety Assistance,* 71.

41. Rex Applegate, "Weapons for Riot Control," *Ordnance,* May–June 1967.

42. Photo 8, "Private Industry Adaptation of OPS-Designed Hand-Held Transceiver," attached to "The Role of AID Public Safety Programs during the Johnson Administration" (n.d. [1968]), IPS 21, E31, box 35, RG 286, NARA; History of the Office of Public Safety (1955 to 1969).

43. Jeter Williamson, "Riot Control Training," February 3–6, 1964, IPS 3, E31, box 27, RG 286, NARA.

44. Lefever, *U.S. Public Safety Assistance,* 40.

45. Anthony A. Ruiz to Byron Engle, June 12, 1964, IPS 1, E26, box 43, RG 286, NARA.

46. Frank Walton, meeting with commander, National Police Command, March 16, 1971, folder 6, box 31, Dale W. Andrade Collection, TTU.

47. Maechling, "Camelot."

48. Leonard Friesz to Lauren Goin, January 24, 1973, IPS 11–1, E18, box 9, RG 286, NARA.

49. Comptroller General of the United States, *Phaseout of US Assistance to South Vietnam in Support of Police Organizations, Law Enforcement, and Public Safety Related Programs* (Washington, DC: GPO, 1975; 47112); OPS, *Assistance to Civil Security Forces: Republic of Vietnam* (Washington, DC: AID, 1971; pdacs391).

50. Joint USAID Public Administration and Public Safety Conference, December 11–15, 1963, INF 7, E27, box 4, RG 286, NARA, 80–81. By the summer of 1964, the SGCI was monitoring events in Venezuela closely, with CIA director Helms noting that "big operational sweeps" by security forces were ineffective. More finely targeted, the disappearance might have been better able to achieve goals Washing-

ton had set. Memorandum for the record, Minutes of the Meeting of the Special Group (CI), July 16, 1964, IPS 7–2, E18, box 6, RG 286, NARA.

51. John P. Longan Memoir, 20, 29, 50. Greg Grandin, *The Last Colonial Massacre: Latin America in the Cold War* (Chicago: University of Chicago Press, 2004), 74, 96–99; Grandin, "Living in Revolutionary Time: Coming to Terms with the Violence of Latin America's Cold War," in *A Century of Revolution: Insurgent and Counterinsurgent Violence during Latin America's Long Cold War*, ed. Greg Grandin and Gilbert M. Joseph (Durham, NC: Duke University Press, 2010), 1–42, 34n12; Kirsten Weld, "Because They Were Taken Alive," *ReVista: Harvard Review of Latin America* 13, no. 1 (2013): 8–11; Weld, *Paper Cadavers,* 103–105.

52. Paul G. Bower to Louise Sagalyn, November 8, 1967, Kerner Commission—Sagalyn Correspondence (1967–1968), box 3, ASP.

53. Huggins, *Political Policing.*

54. Subcommittee on Western Hemisphere Affairs, Committee on Foreign Relations, Senate, 92nd Cong., 1st sess., United States Policies and Programs in Brazil, May 4, 1971 (Testimony of Theodore D. Brown), 45–46.

55. Irwin Goodwin, "Dominican Police Using Gang to Subdue Leftists," *Washington Post,* September 7, 1971, in IPS 1–17, E26, box 47, RG 286, NARA; Irwin Goodwin, "Balaguer Launches Breakup of Gang Terrorizing Left," *Washington Post,* September 15, 1971.

56. Clifford, "Police Academy Under Fire."

57. Byron Engle, information memorandum for the deputy administrator, April 10, 1964, IPS 7–3, E18, box 7, RG 286, NARA.

58. Terri Shaw, "Police and Politics Abroad: AID Center Under Fire in Wake of Mitrione Murder," *Washington Post,* November 10, 1970.

59. Lobe, *United States National Security Policy,* 82.

60. E. H. Adkins Jr., *The Police and Resources Control in Counter-Insurgency* (Saigon: Public Safety Division, USOM, 1964), 1, 6–7, 12, 13, 5.

61. Ibid., 115.

62. Foreword by Frank E. Walton, ibid.

63. Ibid., 1, 41.

64. OPS, *Assistance to Civil Security Forces;* OPS, *The Role of Public Safety in Support of the National Police of Vietnam* (Washington, DC: AID, 1969; pnadw984), 11.

65. Leigh Brilliant, Utilization of National Police Records System to Identify and Apprehend Criminals, August 9, 1972, folder 6, box 31, Dale W. Andrade Collection, TTU.

66. Alan Hunt, "Police and the Regulation of Traffic: Policing as a Civilizing Process?" in *New Police Science,* ed. Dubber and Valverde, 168–184.

67. Saenz, *OPS Story,* 71.

68. Hal H. Saunders to RWK, April 9, 1964, Counter-Insurgency Special Group 1964–1965–1966, box 15, Files of RWK, NSF, LBJL.

69. Malcolm R. Alma, "East and West Meet—On Problem of Traffic" (n.p., November 20, 1957), box 3, Charles Francis Sloane Papers, HIA.

70. Public Law 89–583, September 19, 1966; For a more extensive discussion of participation and pacification, including the parallels between Title IX of the Foreign Assistance Act and Title II of the Economic Opportunity Act, see Schrader, "To Secure the Global Great Society."

71. William E. Colby, "Title IX and Vietnam," March 24, 1971, folder 25, box 3, William Colby Collection, TTU.

72. John Prados, *Lost Crusader: The Secret Wars of CIA Director William Colby* (New York: Oxford University Press, 2003).

73. Charles Bohannan, "Counter-Insurgency Terms, Objectives and Operations," October 23, 1964, Photocopies of Memoranda and Reports on Vietnam, 1963–1964, box 1, Charles T. R. Bohannan Papers, HIA.

74. David Lazar, Oral History, by W. Haven North, March 20, 1997, ADST, 46.

75. Jickling, Oral History, 13; Stephen M. Streeter, "Nation-Building in the Land of Eternal Counterinsurgency: Guatemala and the Contradictions of the Alliance for Progress," *Third World Quarterly* 27, no. 1 (2006): 57–68.

76. Comptroller General of the United States, *Stopping US Assistance to Foreign Police and Prisons* (Washington, DC: GPO, 1976; 098291), 32; Weld, *Paper Cadavers;* Grandin, *Last Colonial Massacre.*

77. "Honorary Membership Presented to President Castillo in Guatemala," *TPC,* April 1955.

78. History of the Office of Public Safety (1955 to 1969), 40.

CHAPTER 6. RIOT SCHOOL

1. Sidney Harring, "Taylorization of Police Work: Prospects for the 1980s," *Insurgent Sociologist* 11, no. 1 (1981): 25–32, 25; "The OLEA Fellowship Program," *TPC,* April 1968.

2. "'Hot Summer': Race Riots in the North," *New York Times,* July 26, 1964.

3. Francis X. Clines, "Policemen Exhaust Their Ammunition in All-Night Battle," *New York Times,* July 20, 1964. On these events in Harlem, see also Paul L. Montgomery and Francis X. Clines, "Thousands Riot in Harlem Area; Scores Are Hurt" *New York Times,* July 19, 1964; Mariame Kaba, "An (Abridged) History of Resisting Police Violence in Harlem" (Chicago: Project NIA, 2012); Janet L. Abu-Lughod, *Race, Space, and Riots in Chicago, New York, and Los Angeles* (New York: Oxford University Press, 2007); and Fred C. Shapiro and James W. Sullivan, *Race Riots: New York, 1964* (New York: Crowell, 1964), a sensationalist account lacking documentary citations. Adrian Jones and James M. Dodson, *A Selected Bibliography of Crowd and Riot Behavior in Civil Disturbances* (Washington, DC: SORO, 1965), a Pentagon-funded catalog, later collected by the Kerner Commission, notably cited Shapiro and Sullivan; see for it ser. 23, box 1, Records of the NACCD; LBJL.

4. George Kentera, "Policy on Unrest Could Help LBJ," *Newark Evening News,* July 23, 1964, clipping in Law Enforcement—Police Matters 11/22/63–10/22/65, Ex JL 6, box 39, WHCF, LBJL.

5. President Lyndon Johnson, telephone conversation with Robert Wagner, July 22, 1964, 8:39 am, 4304, White House Telephone Recordings and Transcripts (WHTRT), LBJL.

6. Flamm, *Law and Order*, 37–38; Flamm, *In the Heat of the Summer: The New York Riots of 1964 and the War on Crime* (Philadelphia: University of Pennsylvania Press, 2017), 147–148.

7. President Lyndon Johnson, telephone conversation with J. Edgar Hoover, July 21, 1964, 1:06 pm, 4295, WHTRT, LBJL.

8. LEAA, *Safe Streets at Work* (Washington, DC: GPO, 1971), 15–17.

9. J. Edgar Hoover to Walter W. Jenkins, October 1, 1964; J. Edgar Hoover to Bill D. Moyers, January 8, 1965, Law Enforcement—Police Matters 11/22/63–10/22/65, Ex JL 6, box 39, WHCF, LBJL.

10. Charles B. Saunders Jr., *Upgrading the American Police: Education and Training for Better Law Enforcement* (Washington, DC: Brookings Institution, 1970), 141.

11. Daniel L. Skoler to Courtney A. Evans, February 23, 1967, 1968 Budget (Congressional), E11, box 2, Records of the Law Enforcement Assistance Administration, RG 423, NARA.

12. J. Edgar Hoover to Mildred Stegall, August 31, 1967, JL 6 8/25/67–1/24/68, Ex JL 6, box 39, WHCF, LBJL.

13. United States Army Engineer Center and Fort Belvior, Riot Control Demonstration Press Kit, October 4, 1967, Civil Disturbances 1967 #2, box 11, PP Warren Christopher, LBJL; Paul Bower to Arnold Sagalyn, October 5, 1967, ser. 21, *CRDJA*, 001346–011–0176.

14. O'Reilly, "FBI," 113.

15. O'Reilly, "FBI," 98–99; NACCD, *Report*, 323–336. A copy of the 1967 publication can be found in Civil Disturbances 1967 #2, box 11, PP Warren Christopher, LBJL.

16. Office of Law Enforcement Assistance Projects Approved—Fiscal 1966 (n.d. [1966]), JL 6 10/23/65–9/15/66, Ex JL 6, box 39, WHCF, LBJL.

17. Gentry, *J. Edgar Hoover*, 417.

18. Lyman B. Kirkpatrick Jr., "Target: Free World Police," *TPC*, November 1960, 37.

19. Robert Wasserman to Stephen Kurzman, September 27, 1967, Kerner Commission—Sagalyn Correspondence (1967–1968), box 3, ASP.

20. Urban America, Inc., and The Urban Coalition, *One Year Later: An Assessment of the Nation's Response to the Crisis Described by the National Advisory Commission on Civil Disorders* (Washington, DC: Urban America; Urban Coalition, 1970?), 67–68.

21. "A Need: Recognized and Fulfilled," *TPC*, May 1968.

22. Transcript, McNamara Oral History Interview I; Ben A. Franklin, "Restraint in Riot Control Result of Long Planning," *New York Times*, April 14, 1968; Engle, Statement, September 20, 1967.

23. "IACP Board of Officers Holds First 1968 Meeting," *TPC*, March 1968.

24. Don R. Derning, "Year's Achievements Present A Challenge." *TPC,* September 1973.

25. Carl C. Turner, "The Use of the National Guard in Coping with Civil Disturbances," *TPC,* December 1967.

26. NACCD, *Report,* 84–108, especially 107.

27. FBI, "Racial Disturbances 1967," August 1967, Reports and Memos Related to Racial Riots 1967, box 5, PP Sherwin Markman, LBJL, 13a.

28. Interview of Former Special Agent of the FBI Patrick D. Putnam, May 8, 2005, by Susan Rosenfeld, FBI Oral History Heritage Project, National Law Enforcement Officers Memorial Fund, 12–13.

29. Christopher H. Pyle, *Military Surveillance of Civilian Politics, 1967–1970* (New York: Garland, 1986), 80, 104; Birtle, *US Army Counterinsurgency and Contingency Operations Doctrine, 1942–1976.*

30. Albert Rabida to Byron Engle, October 18, 1965, IPS 7–3, E18, box 8, RG 286, NARA; A Model Police Force for Developing Nations, E22, box 1, RG 286, NARA.

31. Paul J. Scheips, *The Role of Federal Military Forces in Domestic Disorders, 1945–1992* (Washington, DC: Center of Military History, 2012), 362.

32. "Gen. Turner Named Chief US Marshal" *Washington Post,* March 19, 1969; "Chief US Marshal Forced Out after Study of NCO Club Fund," *New York Times,* September 5, 1969; Robert M. Smith, "Senate Panel to Hear Testimony on Arms Deals by High Officer," *New York Times,* October 5, 1969; Martin Waldron, "Panel Told General Asked Gun Receipts' Destruction: Arms Linked to 'Agency,'" *New York Times,* October 14, 1969.

33. Paul G. Edwards, "Ex-General Gets 3 Years in Guns Theft," *Washington Post,* May 11, 1971; "Ex-Army Law Chief Is Granted Parole," *New York Times,* June 28, 1972.

34. G. R. Mather, Senior Officers Civil Disturbance Orientation Course, October 1968, HU 2 8/1/68–10/10/68, Ex Hu 2, box 9, WHCF, LBJL; Tullis, "Vietnam at Home," 158–159.

35. Paul Estaver to W. Bryce Hill, August 31, 1970, OLEP 13–2, E10, box 56, RG 423, NARA.

36. Turner, "Use of the National Guard."

37. Jack E. Ryan, "Vietnamese Police and Security Services Participant Observations Regarding Pre-Departure Training and the Program at Ft. Gordon, Georgia" (East Lansing, MSU, May 1960), folder 28, box 882, Vietnam Project Records, MSUA.

38. David E. McGiffert to Warren Christopher, February 3, 1968, Civil Disturbance 1968 #1, box 11, PP Warren Christopher, LBJL.

39. United States Army Military Police School, Program of Instruction for Civil Disturbances Orientation Course, January 1968, Civil Disturbance 1968 #1, box 11, PP Warren Christopher, LBJL; Homer Bigart, "Army Helps Police Learn about Riots," *New York Times,* (March 22, 1968).

40. Interview with Patrick D. Putnam, 14.

41. James W. Ewing, Fact Sheet (n.d.) attached to James D. Hughes to Bud Krogh, June 8, 1970, SEADOC, Egil Krogh Files, box 19, White House Special Files, RMNL.

42. Scheips, *Role of Federal Military Forces,* 413. Thanks to Andrea Miller.

43. Clark McPhail, David Schweingruber, and John McCarthy, "Policing Protest in the United States: 1960–1995," in *Policing Protest: The Control of Mass Demonstrations in Western Democracies,* ed. Donatella della Porta and Herbert Reiter (Minneapolis: University of Minnesota Press, 1998), 49–69, 62, 63.

44. Robert Carlson to Byron Engle, July 2, 1971; "Hazardous Devices Training Course," attached to M. Thomas Clark, LEAA Posture for the Coming Summer, June 11, 1971, OLEP 9–18, E10, box 48, RG 423, NARA.

45. Bertram Levine to the director [Roger Wilkins], February 15, 1968, Civil Disturbance 1968 #1, box 11, PP Warren Christopher, LBJL.

46. Bayley Pike, report on visit to USA and Canada, June 26, 1972, A/BR/513, WO 188/2756, National Archives, Kew, United Kingdom (TNA).

47. Daniel L. Skoler to Warren Christopher, February 16, 1968, Civil Disturbance 1968 #1, box 11, PP Warren Christopher, LBJL.

48. McGiffert to Christopher, February 3, 1968.

49. Levine to the director, February 15, 1968.

50. McPhail, Schweingruber, and McCarthy, "Policing Protest."

51. Ibid., 62; Scheips, *Role of Federal Military Forces,* 413n33.

52. "IPA Graduation," *IPA Review* 9, no. 1 (January 1975), 17; Comptroller General of the United States, *Stopping US Assistance,* 15.

53. South Vietnam trained as many as 140,000 police officers under US advisement; History of the Office of Public Safety (1955 to 1969), 19, 10; Engle, "AID Assistance to Civil Security," 28. A retrospective AID estimate of police "trained and equipped" by OPS around the world is 500,000: Heather S. McHugh, "Key Issues in Police Training: Lessons Learned from USAID Experience" (Washington, DC: AID, September 1994; PN-ABY-304), 13.

54. Arthur Thurston to William Gaud, May 17, 1968, IPS 7–3, E18, box 7, RG 286, NARA.

55. Marenin, "United States' Aid to African Police Forces," 529.

56. Roger Robinson to James Bower, March 31, 1966, Propaganda/Security, E525, box 6, RG 472, NARA.

57. William Phillips to Frank Walton, October 23, 1970, folder 9, box 33, Dale W. Andrade Collection, TTU.

58. Rio Bravos in San Martin was also the city depicted in OPS's training film, *First Line of Defense.*

59. Thomas K. Fitzpatrick, "The POCC Story," *IPA Review* 1, no. 1 (January 1967), 15; David Sanford, "Agitators in a Fertilizer Factory," *New Republic,* February 11, 1967; Otwin Marenin, "From IPA to ILEA: Change and Continuity in US International Police-Training Programs," *Police Quarterly* 1, no. 4 (1998): 93–126.

60. "Shelves of Knowledge: Reference Center," *IPA Review* 1, no. 4 (October 1967).

61. Fitzpatrick, "POCC Story," 15.

62. History of the Office of Public Safety (1955 to 1969), 36.

63. [Paul Bower], "Summary of the Suggestions from November 1st and 2nd Conference of Police Chiefs," November 7, 1967, Kerner Commission—Sagalyn Correspondence (1967–1968), box 3, ASP.

64. Thomas Finn to John Barrows, March 14, 1972, Mil. Assist. Programs–AID/OPS Coordination 1969–1972, E22, box 1, RG 286, NARA.

65. Morris Janowitz, *Social Control of Escalated Riots* (Chicago: University of Chicago Center for Policy Studies, 1967), 24–25.

66. Taylor Branch and John Marks, "Tracking the CIA," *Harper's Weekly,* January 24, 1975; OPS, *Program Guide: Public Safety Training* (Washington, DC: AID, March 1967); Bell, Memorandum for the Special Group (CI).

67. Weld, *Paper Cadavers,* ch. 4.

68. Nepalese, South Vietnamese, Zairian, and Colombian IPA graduates advocated what most interpreters considered to be torture. "Notes from Theses Written by Students at the IPA" (n.d.); Torem—notes (n.d.); Jimmy Kolker, typescript memo, May 30, 1974, Notes from Reports Written at the IPA, box Ab832, James G. Abourezk Papers; Richardson Collections, University of South Dakota, Vermillion, South Dakota (USD); Center for Research on Criminal Justice, *Iron Fist, Velvet Glove: An Analysis of the US Police* (Berkeley: Center for Research on Criminal Justice, 1975), 91; Huggins, *Political Policing,* 114.

69. Robert H. Jackson, "Thesis Program," *IPA Review* 3, no. 4 (October 1969), 13.

70. Technician Interview No. 50, September 25, 1962, GU00095, Digital National Security Archive, 11.

71. Transcript, Harvey E. Gutman, interviewed by Stuart Van Dyke, August 26, 1997, Foreign Affairs Oral History Project, Association for Diplomatic Studies and Training, 19–20.

72. OPS, IPA Graduates Follow-Up, June 30, 1974, B7E, E21, box 1, RG 286, NARA; OPS, IPA, June 1974, IPS 1, E18, box 2, RG 286, NARA; "U.S. Public Safety Advisor—Colombia, An Interview," *NACLA's Latin America & Empire Report* 6, no. 1 (1971): 18–20.

73. Two Iraqi police officials participated in IACP-contracted training in 1961, visiting cities like Chicago, Mobile, and Dallas, and became high-ranking officials after the coup in Iraq in late 1963. Weldon C. Matthews, "The Kennedy Administration, Counterinsurgency, and Iraq's First Ba'thist Regime," *International Journal of Middle East Studies* 43, no. 4 (2011): 635–653.

74. Jim Garbolino to Molly Sturges [*sic:* Sturgis], August 2, 1974, Legal Affairs—Military Department, Governor's Office Files, box GO 191, Gubernatorial Papers, Ronald Reagan Presidential Library, Simi Valley, CA (RRL).

75. Herbert E. Ellingwood, who was a member of the California Council on Criminal Justice, the State Planning Agency that worked with the LEAA, visited SEADOC and, as a close aide to Governor Reagan, was responsible for bringing Giuffrida to the new CSTI. Herbert Ellingwood, oral history by Gabrielle Morris, *Law Enforcement and Criminal Justice in California, 1966–1974*, Regional Oral History Office, Bancroft Library, University of California, Berkeley, 1985, 34.

76. Committee on Governmental Affairs, Senate, 97th Cong., 1st sess., Nomination of Louis O. Giuffrida, May 6, 1981, 22, 16.

77. "Observations Relative to Chapter 5 of the Commission Report" (n.d. [1970]), attached to John McCoy to Herbert Ellingwood, October 21, 1970, "Analysis of Scranton Report on Campus Unrest '70," Legal Affairs Unit, Governor's Office Files, box GO 78, Gubernatorial Papers, RRL.

78. [Undated document with name "Neil Algood" written at top; probably meeting minutes], CA Specialized Training, 57, Organization Files, box 2, Governor's Task Force on Civil Rights, California State Archives, Sacramento, CA (CSA). This document also echoed the IPA ethos: "Next y[ea]r = Planning for planners."

79. Win Adams, Management Evaluation Charge Sheet: Policing Training, October 31, 1969, Business Transportation Agency to Ronald Reagan, October 21, 1969, Police Training; Cabinet Office Files, Governor's Office Files, box GO 10, Gubernatorial Papers, RRL.

80. Committee on Governmental Affairs, Nomination of Louis O. Giuffrida, May 6, 1981, 1; L.O. Giuffrida, "Training for Trouble," *Emergency Management Magazine,* October 1979, in CA Specialized Training, 57, Organization Files, box 2, Governor's Task Force on Civil Rights, CSA.

81. Derek Peters, "Notes Relating to a Visit to the United States of America, October 26, 1978," ADRIS/103/8, WO 188/2756, TNA.

82. Course Evaluation (n.d.), CA Specialized Training, 57, Organization Files, box 2, Governor's Task Force on Civil Rights, CSA.

83. Garbolino to Sturges [*sic*], April 2, 1974.

84. Peters, "Notes Relating to a Visit."

85. Ken Lawrence, "The New State Repression," *CovertAction Information Bulletin* 24 (Summer 1985): 3–11, 6.

86. Thomas Finn to Louis Giuffrida, March 21, 1972, Mil. Assist. Programs–AID/OPS Coordination 1969–1972, E22, box 1, RG 286, NARA.

87. Stephen Hess to Bud Krogh, November 18, 1969; Jerris Leonard to Charles Rogovin, August 12, 1969, Civil Disorder, Egil Krogh Files, box 85, White House Special Files, RMNL.

88. Edward M. Davis, "Professional Police Principles," *The Beat* 24, no. 5 (December 1969), 6. Thanks to Emma Shaw Crane for help obtaining this source.

CHAPTER 7. THE IMPERIAL CIRCUIT OF TEAR GAS

1. C.R. Weinert, "The Proper Use of Tear Gas as a Police Weapon," *TPC,* January 1961; Thompson S. Crockett, "Riot Control Agents: V. Tactical Use of Riot Agents," *TPC,* May 1969.

2. Engle, Statement, September 20, 1967.

3. J. Edgar Hoover, "'Police Brutality'—How Much Truth . . . How Much Fiction?" *US News & World Report,* September 27, 1965.

4. Arnold Sagalyn, "The Policeman's Gun Is Backfiring," National Symposium on Law Enforcement Science and Technology, March 19, 1967, Biographical-Publications / Articles by AS (1963–1969), box 1, ASP. On "fleeing felons," see, Paul Chevigny, *Police Power* (New York: Pantheon Books, 1969), 236–242.

5. Walter L. Miller, "Chemicals vs. Guerrillas," *Marine Corps Gazette* 48, no. 7 (1964).

6. Record of the Eleventh Meeting of the Interagency Police Group, November 13, 1963, IPS 7–3, E18, box 8, RG 286, NARA; Arnold Sagalyn and Joseph Coates, "Wanted: Weapons That Do Not Kill," *New York Times,* September 17, 1967; Joseph F. Coates, *Nonlethal and Nondestructive Combat in Cities Overseas* (Arlington, VA: Institute for Defense Analyses, May 1970; P-569).

7. Arnold Sagalyn to Nick [Katzenbach], September 17, 1965, NCC—Police—Public Safety, series 1, box 34, Records of the PCLEAJ, LBJL.

8. Paul Bower, List of Consultants and Advisors on Public Safety and Police-Community Relations, January 17, 1968, Kerner Commission—Sagalyn Correspondence (1967–1968), box 3, ASP.

9. Engle, Statement, September 20, 1967.

10. Seymour Deitchman to Arnold Sagalyn, November 30, 1967, Riot Control, ser. E1, box E5, Records of the NACCD, LBJL.

11. NACCD, *Report,* 492.

12. Joseph C. Goulden, "Cops Hit the Jackpot," *The Nation,* November 23, 1970.

13. Public Law 90–500, September 20, 1968, Title IV, Sec. 403 (a); Edwin Schriver to George W. O'Connor, October 9, 1969; George W. O'Connor to Paul Woodard, October 9, 1969, Surplus Weapons, E12, box 4; Alfred J. Hayes, "Procedures for the Sale of Surplus Equipment," June 11, 1971, OLEP 9–13, E10, box 48, RG 423, NARA.

14. "DOJ Activities Concerning the Prevention and Control of Civil Disorders" (n.d.), Civil Disturbances 1968 #3, box 12; PP Warren Christopher; LBJL.

15. Thompson S. Crockett, *Police Chemical Agents Manual* (Washington DC: IACP, 1969).

16. Professional Standards Division, IACP, Riot Control Agent Information Series (n.d.), folder 6, E9, box 56, RG 423; NARA, 5. The IACP's *Police Chemical Agents Manual* superseded guidance documents in this series.

17. Anthony Harrigan, "The Case for Gas Warfare," *Royal United Services Institution Journal* 108, no. 632 (1963): 356–357.

18. Wil D. Verwey, *Riot Control Agents and Herbicides in War: Their Humanitarian, Toxicological, Ecological, Military, Polemological, and Legal Aspects* (Leyden: A. W. Sijthoff, 1977), 8. A perceptive undergraduate essay deals with some of these issues and uses similar sources: Thomas Dethlefs, "Tear Gas and the Politics of Lethality: Emerging from the Haze," *Yale Historical Review* 2, no. 3 (2013): 83–118.

19. Miller, "Chemicals vs. Guerrillas."

20. The "free-fire zone" became the US Army's central spatial modality of targeting in its operations after 1965, at the time Washington tried to discard the term. Nick Turse, *Kill Anything That Moves* (New York: Metropolitan, 2013), 59–64; James William Gibson, *The Perfect War* (New York: Vintage Books, 1988), 186.

21. CS is named after its inventors, Ben Corson and Roger Stoughton. Its chemical name is 2-chlorobenzylmalononitrile.

22. Editorial Note, *FRUS,* 1958–1960, 3: 114.

23. Like CS, CN was originally a military technology that gained wider use by civilian forces. Daniel P. Jones, "From Military to Civilian Technology: The Introduction of Tear Gas for Civil Riot Control," *Technology and Culture* 19, no. 2 (1978): 151–168; Anna Feigenbaum, *Tear Gas* (New York: Verso, 2017). On CN's phase-out: AIDTO Circular XA-710, January 8, 1964, Training–IAPA (General Correspondence), 1962–1964, E27, box 8, RG 286, NARA. CN's chemical name is chloroacetophenone. It was sometimes combined with DM, or adamsite, an arsenic-based agent that caused vomiting (some reports suggested its effects lasted days).

24. "Characteristics of Riot Control Agent CS" (n.d. [1967?]), ser. 23, box 1, Records of the NACCD, LBJL.

25. Milt Machlin, "Front-line Report: Viet-Nam" *Argosy,* October 1966, 79–80.

26. AIDTO Circular XA-1344, June 1, 1963, Training–IAPA (General Correspondence), 1962–1964, E27, box 8, RG 286, NARA.

27. Department of State cable, April 26, 1965, DDRS, CK234906730.

28. L. W. McNaught, "Use of CR in Hong Kong," August 31, 1977, WO 188/2759, TNA; W. H. Marshall, "Exercise Cloud View in Hong Kong" (n.d.); Abraham to secretary of state, January 29, 1974; clipping: Robert Jones, "Gas and the Gunmen," *New Scientist,* January 3, 1974; R. J. E. Abraham, "Exercise Gentle Rain," October 5, 1973, DEFE 24/1915, TNA. The chemical name of CR is dibenzoxazepine.

29. Max Frankel, "US Reveals Use of Nonlethal Gas against Vietcong," *New York Times,* March 23, 1965.

30. George Bunn, "Banning Poison Gas and Germ Warfare: Should the United States Agree?" *Wisconsin Law Review* 2 (1969): 375–420, particularly 401.

31. Jack Raymond, "Decision on Gas Not President's, White House Says," *New York Times,* March 24, 1965.

32. Frankel, "US Reveals Use"; President's Special Assistant for National Security Affairs (Bundy) to President Johnson, March 23, 1965, *FRUS,* 1964–1968, 2: 210.

33. Frankel, "US Reveals Use." Issued in 1967, 1970, 1973, and 1980, the US Marine Corps manual *Counterinsurgency Operations* (FMFM 8–2) formalized the recommendation of using "riot control agents" when "insurgents may be found close to or mingled among a noncombatant population" (124). A March 1964 US Army manual, *Combat in Fortified and Built-Up Areas* (FM 31–50), mentioned "toxic chemical agents" like CS that could be deployed in maneuvers against "fortifications."

34. Bundy to Johnson, March 23, 1965. Johnson asked McNamara to acquire precise, bullet-pointed information on the issue from Bundy. This type of communication was Bundy's specialty. McNamara, in turn, gave this information to the press in a background briefing the same day; "Discussion on the Use of Riot Control Agents in South Vietnam," March 23, 1965, folder 13, box 8, George J. Veith Collection, TTU; Johnson, telephone conversation with Robert McNamara, March 23, 1965, 10:36 am, 7138, WHTRT, LBJL.

35. D. Hank Ellison, *Chemical Warfare during the Vietnam War: Riot Control Agents in Combat* (New York: Routledge, 2011), 12–17.

36. "Excerpts from Transcript of Rusk News Parley on Use of Gas in Vietnam," *New York Times,* March 25, 1965.

37. Johnson, telephone conversation with Drew Pearson, March 23, 1965, 11:35 am, 7139, WHTRT, LBJL.

38. Raymond, "Decision on Gas Not President's."

39. Lyndon B. Johnson, "The President's News Conference," April 1, 1965, *TAPP.*

40. Johnson telephone conversation with Pearson, March 23, 1965. Johnson also urged Rusk to tell the press that DC's chief of police would use tear gas, which would be far preferable to guns, the very next day if protesters were to storm the Capitol. Johnson telephone conversation with Dean Rusk, March 23, 1965, 11:20 am, 7144, WHTRT, LBJL.

41. Rex Applegate, "Smoke vs. The Mob Cancer," *TPC,* October 1963; "New Riot Control Weapons," *Ordnance,* July–August 1964; Raymond M. Momboisse, *Riots, Revolts, and Insurrections* (Springfield, IL: C. C. Thomas, 1967). A deputy attorney general from California, Momboisse published several books and many articles with his recipes for riot control and "industrial security," a Cold War euphemism for suppression of worker militancy. Beginning in its January–February 1965 issue, *Police* published a series on "Crowd Control and Riot Prevention" based on Momboisse's writings. Over five hundred pages long, *Riots, Revolts and Insurrections* included a lengthy final chapter titled "Counter-Insurgency Operations" that summarized a range of counterinsurgent knowledge, focusing on urban operations, though many of its empirical examples came from rural Vietnam.

42. Robert McNamara to McGeorge Bundy, September 22, 1965, folder 12, box 8, George J. Veith Collection, TTU.

43. Gibson, *Perfect War.*

44. Johnson, News Conference, April 1, 1965.

45. J. B. Neilands, "Gas Warfare in Vietnam in Perspective," in *Harvest of Death: Chemical Warfare in Vietnam and Cambodia,* ed. Neilands et al. (New York: Free Press, 1971), 3–101, 56. On US scientists and tear gas in this period more generally, see Sarah Bridger, *Scientists at War: The Ethics of Cold War Weapons Research* (Cambridge, MA: Harvard University Press, 2015), 81–87.

46. Chemical Mace appeared on the market in 1965, with assistance from Rex Applegate, who devoted an entire chapter of his book to it; *Riot Control—Materiel and Techniques* (Harrisburg, PA: Stackpole Books, 1969), ch. 12. He received a 5 percent royalty on its sales. A few years after its introduction, a formulation using CS instead of CN emerged, but this version, inspired by the US Army, was considered less effective simply because liquid CN took effect more quickly. Gary Wills, *The Second Civil War: Arming for Armageddon* (New York: New American Library, 1968).

47. AIDTO Circular XA-710.

48. "Excerpts from Transcript of Rusk News Parley."

49. Ellison, *Chemical Warfare during the Vietnam War*, 144; Klare, *War without End*, 139. National Action Research on the Military Industrial Complex, *Weapons for Counterinsurgency* (Philadelphia: NARMIC, 1970), 33.

50. The IACP manual on chemical munitions included specifications for several such dispersers; Crockett, *Police Chemical Agents Manual*, 168–176. Some were depicted in a collection the US Army provided to the Kerner Commission: enclosure 1 to James Hebbeler to chief of staff, Army, August 9, 1967, ser. 23, box 2, Records of the NACCD; LBJL.

51. Donald Hornig to McGeorge Bundy, September 17, 1965, folder 12, box 8, George J. Veith Collection, TTU.

52. Secretary of Defense McNamara to President Johnson, September 22, 1965, *FRUS, 1964–1968*, 3: 147; McNamara to Bundy, September 22, 1965; Ellison, *Chemical Warfare*, 15.

53. Memo for the record, September 29, 1965, *FRUS, 1964–1968*, 3: 155.

54. Bundy to President Johnson, September 23, 1965, *FRUS, 1964–1968*, 3: 150.

55. Moyers, memo for the record, September 29, 1965.

56. Verwey, *Riot Control Agents*, 166.

57. Enclosure 1 to James A. Hebbeler to chief of staff.

58. Verwey, *Riot Control Agents*, 60.

59. 1st Infantry Division, "Combat Operation after Action Report: Operation Birmingham," 30, 39, www.dtic.mil/dtic/tr/fulltext/u2/387622.pdf.

60. Coates, "Nonlethal and Nondestructive Combat," 103.

61. The estimate of thirty different delivery methods is from Milton Leitenberg, "America in Vietnam: Statistics of a War," *Survival* 14, no. 6 (1972): 268–274. For a compilation of excerpted contemporaneous news accounts of the use of chemical munitions in Vietnam, see Seymour Melman et al., *In the Name of America* (New York: Clergy and Laymen Concerned about Vietnam, 1968), 117–130.

62. Verwey, *Riot Control Agents*, 65; George C. Wilson, "CS Gas Purchase for Vietnam Increased 16-fold since '64," *Washington Post*, July 24, 1969.

63. Coates, "Nonlethal and Nondestructive Combat," 83.

64. Ellison, *Chemical Warfare*, 84–85.

65. Proceedings of the Conference on Chemical and Biological Warfare, American Academy of Arts and Sciences and the Salk Institute, July 25, 1969, Boston, MA, "Chemical-Biological Warfare: US Policies and International Effects," November–December 1969, Subcommittee on National Security Policy and Scientific Developments, Committee on Foreign Affairs, House, 91st Cong., 1st sess., app. E, 464.

66. Coates, "Nonlethal and Nondestructive Combat," 107.

67. Donald O. Enger, *The Evaluation of Less-Lethal Weapons* (Aberdeen, MD: US Army Human Engineering Laboratory, 1977).

68. Lobe, "US Police Assistance," 448n51; Applegate, *Riot Control—Materiel and Techniques*, 174.

69. Applegate, *Riot Control—Materiel and Techniques,* ch. 10; Aircraft Armaments, Inc., "Multi-Purpose Grenade System" (n.d.), Kerner Commission—Civil Disorder Reports—Riot Control (1967–1968), box 2, ASP.

70. Ellison, *Chemical Warfare,* 73.

71. Scheips, *Role of Federal Military Forces,* 337, 175.

72. Paul Bower to Warren Christopher, May 23, 1968, Civil Disturbances 1968 #2, box 12, PP Warren Christopher, LBJL.

73. "California National Guard's Support to Law Enforcement and Civil Authorities" (n.d.), attached to Glenn Ames to James Jenkins, April, Research File—Legal Affairs—Military Department, box GO 191, Governor's Office Files, Gubernatorial Papers, 1966–75, RRL; Officer of the Governor, "The 'People's Park': A Report on a Confrontation at Berkeley, California," July 1, 1969, Proclamations—Berkeley Riots, box GO 73, Governor's Office Files, Gubernatorial Papers, 1966–75, RRL.

74. Heather Ann Thompson, *Blood in the Water: The Attica Prison Uprising of 1971 and Its Legacy* (New York: Pantheon Books, 2016), 185.

75. Bordenkircher and Bordenkircher, *Tiger Cage,* 160.

76. Richard W. Wilsnack et al, "Comprehensive Law & Order Assistance Research and Development Program Final Report" (Aberdeen Proving Ground, MD: US Army Land Warfare Laboratory, March 1971; Technical Report 71–04), 22.

77. I am grateful to discussions with Daniel Immerwahr about tear gas in the Philippines and Puerto Rico.

78. Deitchman to Sagalyn, November 30, 1967.

79. Arnold Sagalyn and Louise Sagalyn, "The Control of Group Violence: Past, Present, and Future Aspects," October 1968, Publications/Articles by AS, 1965–1974, box 1, ASP, 16–17.

80. Bertram Levine to the director [Roger W. Wilkins], February 15, 1968, Civil Disturbance 1968 #1, box 11, PP Warren Christopher, LBJL.

81. Overall the proportion of people killed by police nationally who were Black remained constant: 50 percent. Bertram J. Levine, *Resolving Racial Conflict: The Community Relations Service and Civil Rights, 1964–1989* (Columbia: University of Missouri Press, 2005), 146.

82. "Arrests Follow 8-Hour Siege: 15 Held in Detroit Patrolman's Murder," *Boston Globe,* October 26, 1970; "Police Gas NC Marchers," *Chicago Daily Defender,* November 17, 1970; "Sniper, Cop Slain; 10 Hurt in Battle," *Chicago Defender,* June 8, 1974; Bessie Ford, "Police Chief Defends Firing into Building," *Atlanta Daily World,* October 18, 1974; Robert Flipping Jr., "Blacks Accuse Police of Gestapo Tactics," *New Pittsburgh Courier,* July 13, 1974; "Police Subdue Ex–Mental Patient after Long Deal," *Atlanta Daily World,* March 31, 1978; "Gas Fails to Halt Escaping Little Rock Bank Robbers," *Baltimore Afro-American,* January 31, 1976.

83. Notable exceptions include the shootings near South Carolina State University in 1968 and at Kent State University in 1970.

84. Bloom and Martin, *Black against Empire.*

85. Paul Gilroy, "You Can't Fool the Youths . . . Race and Class Formation in the 1980s," *Race & Class* 23 (1981): 207–222; Poulantzas, *State, Power, Socialism,* 186–87.

86. The term "temporal-hinge" is from Markus D. Dubber and Mariana Valverde, "Policing the Rechtsstaat," in *Police and the Liberal State,* ed. Markus D. Dubber and Mariana Valverde (Stanford, CA: Stanford University Press, 2008), 1–13, 4.

CHAPTER 8. ORDER MAINTENANCE AND
THE GENEALOGY OF SWAT

1. Balko, *Rise of the Warrior Cop,* 53, 60, 62; Camp, *Incarcerating the Crisis,* 41; Max Felker-Kantor, *Policing Los Angeles: Race, Resistance, and the Rise of the LAPD* (Chapel Hill: University of North Carolina Press, 2018), 52–54; Flamm, *Law and Order,* 119; Gerald Horne, *Fire This Time: The Watts Uprising and the 1960s* (Charlottesville: University of Virginia Press, 1995), 165; Tullis, "Vietnam at Home," 160–161; Williams, *Our Enemies in Blue,* 199; Daryl F. Gates with Diane K. Shah, *Chief: My Life in the LAPD* (New York: Bantam Books, 1993), 126.

2. Los Angeles also has a transnational history of incarceration. See Hernández, *City of Inmates.*

3. Peter B. Kraska, "Militarization and Policing—Its Relevance to 21st Century Police," *Policing* 1, no. 4 (2007): 501–513.

4. Hinton, *From the War on Poverty,* 206–207.

5. Gates with Shah, *Chief,* 125, 130, 131, 132. Diane K. Shah, Gates's amanuensis, was also an author of crime thrillers and an actor. She originally met Gates when she interviewed him for *Playboy* (August 1991).

6. Jamie Peck and Nik Theodore, *Fast Policy: Experimental Statecraft at the Thresholds of Neoliberalism* (Minneapolis: University of Minnesota, 2015).

7. Joseph Gerald Woods, "The Progressives and the Police: Urban Reform and the Professionalization of the Los Angeles Police" (PhD diss., University of California, Los Angeles, 1973); Alisa Sarah Kramer, "William H. Parker and the Thin Blue Line: Politics, Public Relations and Policing in Postwar Los Angeles" (PhD diss., American University, 2007).

8. Thanks to Julian Go for help on this point.

9. *Parker on Police,* ed. O. W. Wilson (Springfield, IL: Charles C. Thomas, 1957).

10. Ibid., "Introduction," x.

11. John T. Donovan, "'I Have No Use for This Fellow Parker': William H. Parker of the LAPD and His Feud with J. Edgar Hoover and the FBI," *Southern California Quarterly* 87, no. 2 (2005): 171–198.

12. Frank Donner, *Protectors of Privilege: Red Squads and Police Repression in Urban America* (Berkeley: University of California Press, 1990), 79–85, 245–254.

13. Edward J. Escobar, "Bloody Christmas and the Irony of Police Professionalism: The Los Angeles Police Department, Mexican Americans, and Police Reform in the 1950s," *Pacific Historical Review* 72, no. 2 (2003): 171–199, 195.

14. W. H. Parker, "The Police Role in Community Relations," *Journal of Criminal Law, Criminology, and Police Science* 47, no. 3 (1956): 368–379; *TPC,* January 1956. The versions differ slightly. Quotations herein come from the version published in the *Journal of Criminal Law.* The publisher Charles C. Thomas collected and issued bound volumes of the LAPD's Daily Training Bulletin to disseminate the LAPD's expertise nationally. Vollmer authored a preface, and Parker's essay on community relations appeared as the first chapter of one. It also appeared in Wilson, *Parker on Police.*

15. LAPD Annual Report, 1952, quoted in Kramer, "William H. Parker and the Thin Blue Line," 49.

16. W. H. Parker, "Can We Attain Total Prevention? Remove Shackles of Outmoded Tradition," *TPC,* December 1956.

17. Murakawa, *First Civil Right,* Risa Goluboff, *Vagrant Nation: Police Power, Constitutional Change, and the Making of the 1960s* (New York: Oxford University Press, 2016).

18. Ronald J. Ostrow, "Nonlethal Weapons No Substitute for Guns, Reddin Says," *Los Angeles Times,* September 13, 1967.

19. Bloom and Martin, *Black against Empire,* 221–225.

20. LAPD, "Model Civil Disturbance Control Plan," March 1968, attachment to Daryl Gates to Arnold Sagalyn, October 27, 1967, *CRDJA,* 001346–010–0736.

21. Fisher, "How to Beat the Guerrillas at Their Own Game," 82; Benjamin A. Cowan, "Rules of Disengagement: Masculinity, Violence, and the Cold War Remakings of Counterinsurgency in Brazil," *American Quarterly* 66, no. 3 (2014): 691–714.

22. Arnold Sagalyn to Daryl Gates, February 19, 1968, Kerner Commission—Sagalyn Correspondence, box 3, ASP.

23. John Dreyfuss, "Secret Program to Put Down Riots Drafted by LA Police," *Los Angeles Times,* February 15, 1968.

24. Gates with Shah, *Chief,* 122. R. Dean Smith and Richard W. Kobetz, *Guidelines for Civil Disorder Mobilization and Planning* (Washington, DC: IACP, September 1968), in IACP, E9, box 55, RG 423, NARA.

25. "A Police Chief Talks of 'Police Brutality,'" *The Beat* 19, no. 1 (September 1964).

26. James W. Button, *Black Violence: Political Impact of the 1960s Riots* (Princeton, NJ: Princeton University Press, 1978), 119.

27. Paul Clinton, "Daryl Gates and the Origins of LAPD SWAT," *Police,* April 16, 2010.

28. LAPD, "Model Civil Disturbance Control Plan," 112.

29. Gates with Shah, *Chief,* 125, 131.

30. Smith and Kobetz, *Guidelines.*

31. Arnold Sagalyn and Louise Sagalyn, "The Control of Group Violence: Past, Present, and Future Aspects," October 1968, Publications/Articles by A.S., 1965–1974, box 1, ASP.

32. Agee, *Streets of San Francisco,* 205–206. Nicholas Bookout, "A Movement towards Militarization: The History of Tactical Policing in Boston," *Tempus: The Harvard College History Review* 17, no. 2 (2106): 13–25.

33. Glenford S. Leonard, "Our Tactical Police Unit," *TPC,* April 1962.

34. Federico L. Smith Ibarra, "The Mobile Unit," *IPA Review* 3, no. 4 (October 1969).

35. Philip Agee, "Exposing the CIA," *CounterSpy* 2, no. 2 (Winter 1975).

36. Gates with Shah, *Chief,* 132; Lee Harris, "SWAT Team Could Free Hostages, Gates Says," *Los Angeles Times,* November 21, 1979.

37. Gates with Shah, *Chief,* 125, 131.

38. Public Safety Advisors: State from which Hired (n.d. [1966]), IPS 12–5, E31, box 33, RG 286, NARA.

39. Geographic Source of Personnel Recruitment (n.d. [1972]), IPS 2, E31, box 25, RG 286, NARA.

40. Huggins, *Political Policing,* xvii; Kramer, "William H. Parker and the Thin Blue Line," 84–85; Davis and James, *Public Safety Story;* "Personnel," *Public Safety Division Newsletter* 12 (January–February 1959), folder 36, box 679, Vietnam Project Records, MSUA.

41. "Visiting Police Officials Study US Methods," *TPC,* July 1961; "This Is Retirement?" *The Beat* 20, no. 11 (June 1966), 13; see also Robert Pell, "Former California Policeman Plies His Trade in Vietnam," *Police* (January–February 1966).

42. Nguyen Cao Ky, "Thank You, LAPD!" *The Beat* 28, no. 1 (January 1971); "Ky Heckled in California," *New York Times,* December 2, 1970.

43. Frank Jessup, TOAID A-29, January 26, 1962, IPS 1, E26, box 88, RG 286, NARA.

44. "Study of Police Officer Personnel Requirements." *Public Safety Division Newsletter* 12 (January–February 1959), folder 36, box 679, Vietnam Project Records, MSUA; Howard Hertel, "Chief Parker Solves a Crime on India Trip," *Los Angeles Times,* January 17, 1965.

45. "Police Training Films Available for Loan from ICA/W," *Public Safety Division Newsletter* 6 (November 1957), folder 36, box 679, Vietnam Project Records, MSUA.

46. Myrna Oliver, "Frank Walton; Athlete, LAPD Deputy Chief," *Los Angeles Times,* November 27, 1993.

47. Frank E. Walton, "Selective Distribution of Police Patrol Force: History, Current Practices, Recommendations," *Journal of Criminal Law, Criminology, and Police Science* 49, no. 1 (1958): 165–171; PCLEAJ, *The Challenge of Crime in a Free Society* (Washington, DC: GPO, 1967), 95–96, 257.

48. William Herrmann to James Vorenberg, March 16, 1966, Misc on Riots, ser. 13, box 274, Records of the PCLEAJ, LBJL; Herrmann to Frank Walton, February 8, 1966, IPS 7, E31, box 28; Herrmann to Walton, December 2, 1966, IPS 1, E31, box 23, RG 286, NARA; Herrmann, "Report to United States Agency for International Development, Office of Public Safety" (Santa Monica, CA: System Development Corporation, July 12, 1967); Tullis, *Vietnam at Home,* 116–118; Lobe, *United States National Security Policy.*

49. William W. Herrmann, "Riot Prevention and Control: Operations Research Response" (Santa Monica, CA: System Development Corporation, April 8, 1968).

50. Riots and Disorders Task Force, January 8, 1969, Meeting Files, January–February 1969, box 2, California Council on Criminal Justice, CSA.

51. Huey P. Newton, "A Citizens' Peace Force," *Crime and Social Justice* 1 (1974): 36–39; William Drummond, "State Intelligence System: Stigma of a 'Big Brother,'" *Los Angeles Times,* March 18, 1970.

52. Stephen G. Rabe, "The Caribbean Triangle: Betancourt, Castro, and Trujillo and U.S. Foreign Policy, 1958–1963," *Diplomatic History* 20, no. 1 (1996): 55–78.

53. Melanie Newport, "Men Whose Lives Are Always Public" (presentation, May 3, 2018, Cold War Seminar, Tamiment Library, New York).

54. Herbert Hardin to the ambassador, April 13, 1962, IPS 1–2, E26, box 45; W. H. Parker to Hardin, April 27, 1962; William Bateman to Joel Sterns, May 10, 1962, IPS 1, E26, box 43, RG 286, NARA.

55. John Bartlow Martin, *Overtaken By Events* (New York: Doubleday, 1966), 122; Lobe, "US Police Assistance"; Davis and James, *Public Safety Story.*

56. [Herbert Hardin], Public Safety Monthly Report—June 1962, July 6, 1962, IPS 1, E26, box 43; Hector Guevara and Jesus Mejia to Fowler Hamilton, Terminal Report, (n.d. [October 24, 1962]), IPS 1–2, E26, box 45, RG 286, NARA.

57. Kramer, "William H. Parker and the Thin Blue Line"; Wesley Marx, "Parker: The Cop As Crusader," *Los Angeles,* August 1962.

58. [John] Martin to secretary of state, October 23, 1962, CU00619, Digital National Security Archive.

59. Jacob Jackson, TOAID A-469, March 6, 1963, IPS 1, E26, box 43, RG 286, NARA.

60. Robert Berrellez, "Santo Domingo Police Use Clubs and Gas to Quell Demonstration," October 21, 1963 (n.p.), INF 5–2, E27, box 3, RG 286, NARA.

61. Rafael Guzman Acosta, "Senior Education Seminar," *IPA Review* 1, no. 4 (October 1967).

62. *Society of Former Special Agents of the FBI,* 2nd ed. (Paducah: Turner Publishing, 1998), 128.

63. Echols, *Hilarious High Jinks,* 228–229.

64. Alan McPherson, *Yankee No! Anti-Americanism in US-Latin American Relations* (Cambridge, MA: Harvard University Press, 2003).

65. W. G. Bowdler, memorandum of meeting, September 16, 1965, DDRS, CK3100480177; L. J. Goin and L. T. Shannon to director, OPS, May 20, 1965, DDRS, CK2349122530; memorandum from the deputy director for coordination of the Bureau of Intelligence and Research (Koren) to the director (Hughes), December 8, 1965, *FRUS,* 1964–1968, 32: 147; Anthony Ruiz to Byron Engle, January 20, 1964, IPS 1, E26, box 43, RG 286, NARA; CIA, President's Daily Brief [PDB], September 6, 1965, CIA Electronic Reading Room.

66. Martin, *Overtaken by Events,* 100; Fred Goff and Mike Klare, "How US AID Shapes the Dominican Police," *NACLA Newsletter* 5, no. 2 (1971): 19–20.

67. PDB, October 30, 1965; PDB, February 9, 1966, CIA Electronic Reading Room.

68. Evaluation Report of Public Safety Advisor Training Program (Washington, DC: AID, 1970; pdacs387), 16.

69. Report of Audit of Public Safety USAID/Dominican Republic (Washington, DC: AID, March 15, 1972; pdacs401); Joseph E. Mulligan, "Policing the Dominican Republic," *The Nation*, March 1, 1975.

70. Byron Engle and David Powell, "Report of Observations in Dominican Republic" (n.d. [January 1965]), IPS 1, E26, box 43, RG 286, NARA; Lauren J. Goin, William Broe, and L. T. Shannon, "Dominican Republic: The Civil Security Development Plan" (Washington, DC: AID, September 13, 1965; pnadn991). US and Dominican officials denied a CIA role, but the declassified version of the latter report reveals the CIA budgetary contribution, supporting accusations first published by NACLA.

71. Fred Goff and David Fairchild, "U.S. AID in the Dominican Republic—An Inside View," *NACLA Newsletter* 4, no. 7 (1970): 1–11, 8.

72. Joe Domanick, *To Protect and Serve: The LAPD's War in the City of Dreams* (New York: Pocket Books, 1994): 294–295.

73. "LAPD Accused of Political Spying," *Los Angeles Times*, June 14, 1978; Joel Sappel, "Paul's Ex-Boss Won't Testify at Police Hearing," ibid., February 22, 1984.

74. Donner, *Protectors of Privilege*, 255–289.

75. Kyle Burke, *Revolutionaries for the Right: Anticommunist Internationalism and Paramilitary Warfare in the Cold War* (Chapel Hill: University of North Carolina Press, 2018); Malcolm Byrne, *Iran-Contra: Reagan's Scandal and the Unchecked Abuse of Presidential Power* (Lawrence: University Press of Kansas, 2014).

76. Schrader, "Nicaragua."

77. Translated transcript of televised interview with Roberto Santiváñez [*sic.* Santibáñez] (n.d.), folder 22, box 17, Philip Agee Papers, Tamiment Library, New York. D'Aubuisson also attended the US Army's School of the Americas.

78. Gates with Shah, *Chief*, 37, 39.

79. George Steinmetz, "Decolonizing German Theory: An Introduction," *Postcolonial Studies* 9, no. 1 (2006): 3–13.

CHAPTER 9. "THE DISCRIMINATE ART OF
INDISCRIMINATE COUNTER-REVOLUTION"

1. Dubber, *Police Power*, xi; Slaughter-House Cases, 83 US 36, 49 (1873).

2. Diana R. Gordon, *The Justice Juggernaut: Fighting Street Crime, Controlling Citizens* (New Brunswick, NJ: Rutgers University Press, 1990); David Garland, *The Culture of Control: Crime and Social Order in Contemporary Society* (New York: Oxford University Press, 2001).

3. George L. Kelling and James Q. Wilson, "Broken Windows," *Atlantic Monthly*, March 1, 1982; Samuel Walker, "'Broken Windows' and Fractured History: The Use and Misuse of History in Recent Police Patrol Analysis," *Justice Quarterly* 1, no. 1 (1984): 75–90.

4. Adrian H. Jones and Andrew R. Molnar, "Internal Defense against Insurgency: Six Cases" (Washington, DC: Center for Research in Social Systems, December 1966); Jones and Molnar, "Combating Subversively Manipulated Civil Disturbances" (Washington, DC: Center for Research in Social Systems, October 1966); John L. Sorenson, *Urban Insurgency Cases* (Santa Barbara, CA: Defense Research Corporation, 1965); *Report on Urban Insurgency Studies* (New York: Simulmatics Corporation, 1966), ser. 23, box 4, Records of the NAACD, LBJL. Richard [B.] Holcomb to Milan Miskovsky, October 25, 1967, *CRDJA*, 001346–021–0286; Button, *Black Violence*, 194.

5. David I. Sheppard and Albert S. Glickman, *A Method for Constructing Career Paths to Meet Requirements of Tomorrow's Police Force* (Washington, DC: American Institutes for Research, July 1971); Elliott, *RAND in Southeast Asia*, 615–626; Joy Rohde, *Armed with Expertise: The Militarization of American Social Research during the Cold War* (Ithaca, NY: Cornell University Press, 2013).

6. Terry Eisenberg, Robert H. Fosen, and Albert S. Glickman, *Project PACE: Police and Community Enterprise; A Program for Change in Police-Community Behaviors, Final Report* (Washington, DC: American Institutes for Research, August 1971), 2; Rohde, *Armed with Expertise*, 139–141.

7. Theodore J. Newnam, "The Role of Police in Counter-Insurgency, Part I," *TPC*, February 1966; "The Role of Police in Counter-Insurgency, Part II," *TPC*, March 1966.

8. Nicholas D. Rudziak, "Police-Military Relations in a Revolutionary Environment," *TPC*, September 1966; David G. Epstein, "The Police Role in Counterinsurgency Efforts," *Journal of Criminal Law, Criminology, and Police Science* 59, no. 1 (1968): 148–151.

9. Rosenthal, *Phases of Civil Disturbances*; Samuels et al, *Riot Control*.

10. Martin Oppenheimer, *The Urban Guerrilla* (Chicago: Quadrangle Books, 1969); Robert Moss, *The War for the Cities* (New York: Coward, McCann & Geoghegan, 1972); Sam C. Sarkesian, ed., *Revolutionary Guerrilla Warfare* (Chicago: Precedent, 1975).

11. Richard H. Sanger, *Insurgent Era: New Patterns of Political, Economic, and Social Revolution* (Washington, DC: Potomac Books, 1967). I am grateful to Robert Vitalis for bringing Sanger to my attention.

12. Elliott, *RAND in Southeast Asia*, 27n49; David French, *The British Way in Counter-Insurgency, 1945–1967* (New York: Oxford University Press, 2011), 61–62.

13. Richard Critchfield, *The Long Charade: Political Subversion in the Vietnam War* (New York: Harcourt, Brace & World, 1968), 208; quoted in Timothy Mitchell, *Rule of Experts: Egypt, Techno-Politics, Modernity* (Berkeley: University of California Press, 2002), 126.

14. Elliott, *RAND in Southeast Asia*, 39, 40; interview with Richard J. Brockett, by Anne Blair, March 11, 1999, Vietnam Archive Oral History Project, OH0226, TTU; Michaels, "Managing Global Counterinsurgency."

15. Gibson, *Perfect War*, 227.

16. Schrader, "To Secure the Global Great Society."

17. Rosenthal, *Phases of Civil Disturbances,* 44.

18. Cross, *Conflict in the Shadows,* 56.

19. Robert B. Rigg, "A Military Appraisal of the Threat to US Cities," *US News & World Report,* January 15, 1968.

20. Quoted in Kenneth O'Reilly, "The FBI and the Politics of the Riots, 1964–1968," *Journal of American History* 75, no. 1 (1988): 91–114, 105.

21. Rudziak, "Police-Military Relations."

22. Button, *Black Violence;* Sugrue, *Sweet Land of Liberty.*

23. Nicholas Von Hoffman, "The Great Panther Hunt," *Washington Post,* December 5, 1969, cited in Alvin Charles Turner, "The Police Role in Counterinsurgency Operations: Analysis of Alternatives" (MPA Thesis, John Jay College of Criminal Justice, 1970), 151. The thesis can be found in Subject File, 1943–1987, box 13, Edward Geary Lansdale Papers, HIA; Fred Moten, "The Subprime and the Beautiful," *African Identities* 11, no. 2 (2013): 237–245.

24. Frank E. Armbruster, *A Military and Police Security Program for South Vietnam* (Croton-on-Hudson, NY: Hudson Institute, 1967; HI-881/2-RR). Bohannan offered an extremist revision of the police "mission": "best described as the establishment and maintenance of peace and order, rather than the prevention or punishment of violations of the law"; "Comments on the HSR 'Police' Proposal," February 2, 1965[?], MAAG, box 2, Charles T. R. Bohannan Papers, HIA.

25. Rudziak, "Police-Military Relations," 32, 30.

26. Robert Byrd, "Police Brutality or Public Brutality?" *TPC,* February 1966, 10.

27. Gloria Emerson, "Pacification: It's Being Able to Walk Down a Road Safely," *New York Times,* April 18, 1971.

28. Rigg, "Military Appraisal."

29. Frank J. Donner, *The Age of Surveillance* (New York: Knopf, 1980); Donner, *Protectors of Privilege;* Hinton, *From the War on Poverty,* 145–146; Pyle, *Military Surveillance;* Tullis, "Vietnam at Home," ch. 3. Instances of CIA training of US police officers are found in CIA Family Jewels, National Security Archive Electronic Briefing Book 222; David E. Bell to John McCone, April 24, 1963, CREST, CIA-RDP80BO1676R002800040002–8.

30. Nathan Leites and Charles Wolf Jr., *Rebellion and Authority: An Analytic Essay on Insurgent Conflicts* (Santa Monica, CA: RAND, February 1970; R-462-ARPA), v.

31. Elliott, *RAND in Southeast Asia;* Alex Abella, *Soldiers of Reason* (New York: Harcourt, 2008); S. M. Amadae, *Rationalizing Capitalist Democracy* (Chicago: University of Chicago Press, 2003).

32. Albert and Roberta Wohlstetter, "Metaphors and Models: Inequalities and Disorder at Home and Abroad" (Santa Monica: RAND, August 1968; D-17664-RC/ISA); Guy J. Pauker, "Black Nationalism and Prospects for Violence in the Ghetto" (Santa Monica: RAND, June 1969; P-4118); Brian M. Jenkins, "Soldiers versus Gunmen: The Challenge of Urban Guerrilla Warfare" (Santa Monica: RAND, 1974; P-5182), 1–2.

33. Guy J. Pauker "Notes on Non-Military Measures in Control of Insurgency" (Santa Monica: RAND, October 1962; P-2642).

34. Charles Wolf Jr. "Economic Aid Reconsidered" (Santa Monica: RAND, February 14, 1961; P-2217).

35. Charles J. Zwick, Charles A. Cooper, Hans Heymann, and Richard H. Moorsteen, *US Economic Assistance in Vietnam: A Proposed Reorientation* (Santa Monica: RAND, July 1964; R-430-AID)

36. Elliott, *RAND in Southeast Asia,* 87. Although Elliott's history of RAND is compendious and insightful, it focuses on the more ethnographic research RAND conducted in Vietnam, giving short shrift to the work Wolf and others undertook. The fullest accounts of the rise of the rational-choice perspective among RAND counterinsurgency thinkers are Ron Robin, *The Making of the Cold War Enemy: Culture and Politics in the Military-Intellectual Complex* (Princeton, NJ: Princeton University Press, 2001), 189–205, and Robin, *The Cold World They Made: The Strategic Legacy of Roberta and Albert Wohlstetter* (Cambridge, MA: Harvard University Press, 2016).

37. I am grateful to Daniel Bessner for help on this point.

38. Robin, *Making,* 190; Edward C. Banfield, *American Foreign Aid Doctrines* (Washington, DC: American Enterprise Institute for Public Policy Research, 1963).

39. Paul Dixon, "'Hearts and Minds'? British Counter-Insurgency from Malaya to Iraq," *Journal of Strategic Studies* 32, no. 2 (2009): 353–381, 362n27; Simon Smith, "General Templer and Counter-Insurgency in Malaya: Hearts and Minds, Intelligence, and Propaganda," *Intelligence and National Security* 16, no. 3 (2001): 60–78.

40. Karl Hack, "Malaya—Between Two Terrors: 'People's History' and the Malayan Emergency," in *Hearts and Minds: A People's History of Counterinsurgency,* ed. Hannah Gurman (New York: The New Press, 2013), 17–49; Hack, "The Malayan Emergency as Counter-Insurgency Paradigm," *Journal of Strategic Studies* 32, no. 3 (2009): 383–414.

41. Gerald Templer, "Report on Colonial Security," April 23, 1955, CAB 21/2925, pt. 1 of 2, TNA, 11.

42. Charles Wolf Jr., "Insurgency and Counterinsurgency: New Myths and Old Realities" (Santa Monica: RAND, July 1965; P-3132-1), 5, 22, 11, 8, 25, 8. Wolf disseminated the argument more widely in the *Yale Review,* where he had previously published his rejoinder to Friedman.

43. James C. Davies, "The J-Curve of Rising and Declining Satisfactions as a Cause of Some Great Revolutions and a Contained Rebellion," in *Revolutionary Guerrilla Warfare,* ed. Sarkesian, 117–141.

44. Robin, *Making,* 190–191.

45. Nathan Leites and Charles Wolf Jr., "Rebellion and Authority: Myths and Realities Reconsidered" (Santa Monica, CA: RAND, August 1966; P-3422), 14, 13, 6, 13, 5, 6.

46. James Digby, "Early RAND: Personalities and Projects as Recalled in *The Alumni Bulletin*" (Santa Monica: RAND, March 2001; P-8055), 12.

47. Leites and Wolf, *Rebellion and Authority,* 28, 29.

48. Ibid., 19, 29, 36–37, 42, 43.

49. Daniel Ellsberg, "Revolutionary Judo" (Santa Monica: RAND, January 1970; 06-M-0006).

50. Tom Wells, *Wild Man: The Life and Times of Daniel Ellsberg* (New York: Palgrave Macmillan, 2001), 293–294.

51. Albert Wohlstetter, "Comments on the Wolf-Leites Manuscript: 'Rebellion and Authority'" (Santa Monica: RAND, August 30, 1968; D(L)-17701-ARPA/ AGILE).

52. Gilman, *Mandarins*.

53. Samuel L. Popkin, *The Rational Peasant: The Political Economy of Rural Society in Vietnam* (Berkeley: University of California Press, 1979); James C. Scott, *The Moral Economy of the Peasant: Rebellion and Subsistence in Southeast Asia* (New Haven, CT: Yale University Press, 1977).

54. Edward C. Banfield, *The Moral Basis of a Backward Society* (New York: Free Press, 1958), 162–163.

55. Gary S. Becker, "Crime and Punishment: An Economic Approach," *Journal of Political Economy* 76, no. 2 (1968): 169–217.

56. Robin, *Cold World*, 148; Amadae, *Rationalizing Capitalist Democracy*, 11.

57. Birtle, *US Army Counterinsurgency and Contingency Operations Doctrine, 1942–1976*, 436–437; Boyd Bashore, "The Parallel Hierarchies, Part I," *Infantry Journal* 58 (May–June 1968): 5–8; "The Parallel Hierarchies, Part II," ibid. (July–August 1968): 11–15; William J. Buchanan and Robert A. Hyatt, "Capitalizing on Guerrilla Vulnerabilities," *Military Review* 43, no. 8 (1968): 3–40; Raymond D. Gastil, "A Conservative, Decentralized Approach to Pacification in South Vietnam" (Croton-on-Hudson, NY: Hudson Institute, August 8, 1967; HI-878–2/1-RR), I-30.

58. Edward Friedman, "Neither Mao, Nor Che: The Practical Evolution of Revolutionary Theory," in *Revolutionary Guerrilla Warfare*, ed. Sarkesian, 421–428.

59. David W. P. Elliott, *The Vietnamese War: Revolution and Social Change in the Mekong Delta, 1930–1975*, vol. 2 (Armonk, NY: M. E. Sharpe, 2003), 803.

60. Leites and Wolf, *Rebellion and Authority*, 71.

61. Adkins, *Police and Resources Control*, 3, 21.

62. Ibid., 136–137.

63. J. K. Blackwell to D. F. Murray, May 14, 1963, DV1192/23, FO 371/170130, TNA.

64. Andrew J. Birtle, *US Army Counterinsurgency and Contingency Operations Doctrine 1860–1941* (Washington, DC: Center of Military History, 2006), 67; Grenier, *First Way of War*.

65. Adkins, *Police and Resources Control*, 2.

66. Richard Shultz, "Coercive Force and Military Strategy: Deterrence Logic and the Cost-Benefit Model of Counterinsurgency Warfare," *Political Research Quarterly* 32, no. 4 (1979): 444–466.

67. Josh Whitford, "Pragmatism and the Untenable Dualism of Means and Ends: Why Rational Choice Theory Does Not Deserve Paradigmatic Privilege," *Theory and Society* 31, no. 3 (2002): 325–363.

68. Elliott, *Vietnamese War.*

69. Leites and Wolf, *Rebellion and Authority,* 140.

70. James Q. Wilson, *Thinking about Crime* (New York: Basic Books, 1975); Timothy Crimmins, "Incarceration as Incapacitation: An Intellectual History," *American Affairs* 2, no. 3 (2018): 144–166.

71. Judson L. Jeffries, "Black Radicalism and Political Repression in Baltimore: The Case of the Black Panther Party," *Ethnic and Racial Studies* 25, no. 1 (2002): 64–98.

72. American Institutes for Research, *The Impact of Economic, Social, and Political Action Programs: Semi-Annual Progress Report (March 1969–August 1969)* (Bangkok: American Institutes for Research, 1969).

73. Ronald A. Zumbrun, Raymond M. Momboisse, and John H. Findley, "Welfare Reform: California Meets the Challenge," *Pacific Law Journal* 4 (1973): 739–785.

74. On Becker, see Bernard E. Harcourt, *The Illusion of Free Markets: Punishment and the Myth of Natural Order* (Cambridge, MA: Harvard University Press, 2011).

75. Kelling and Wilson, "Broken Windows." Among the experiments was one in Kansas City in the early 1970s that set out to repudiate the standards O. W. Wilson and Theo Hall had developed for single-officer patrol in cars.

76. Christina Heatherton, "U.S. Police: Broken Windows Neoliberalism," *The Funambulist* 8 (2016): 28–33.

77. Wilson, *Thinking about Crime.*

78. On vagrancy law, see Goluboff, *Vagrant Nation.*

79. James Q. Wilson, *Varieties of Police Behavior* (Cambridge, MA: Harvard University Press, 1968), 40, 39.

CONCLUSION

1. Fredric Jameson, "*The Shining,*" *Social Text* 4 (1981): 114–125, 124.

2. Davis and James, *Public Safety Story,* 23.

3. Comptroller General of the United States, *Stopping US Assistance to Foreign Police and Prisons* (Washington, DC: GPO, 1976; 098291), 17–18; Hannu Kyröläinen, "An Analysis of New Trends in the US Military Training and Technical Assistance in the Third World," *Instant Research on Peace and Violence* 7, no. 3–4 (1977): 167–183.

4. James Abourezk to Elmer Staats, February 19, 1975, Vinnell and Arms Training, box Ab685, James G. Abourezk Papers, USD.

5. Seigel, *Violence Work.*

6. Hearings before the Subcommittees on Africa and International Organizations, Committee on Foreign Affairs, House of Representatives, 96th Cong., 1st sess., Byron Engle, "A Unity of Purpose," in "Preliminary Report of the American Conservative Union Observer Delegation to the Rhodesian Elections," April 25, 1979, app. 10, 423–426.

7. John P. Longan Memoir, 4–8.

8. Charles Sloane to Central Intelligence Agency, March 6, 1974, box 4; OPS, Personnel Roster, October 1973, box 9, Charles Francis Sloane Papers, HIA; "XPSA Now Police Chief," *PSN* 30 (June 1981); Seigel, *Violence Work.*

9. "Soldier of Fortune Heard From," *PSN* 31 (August 1981).

10. East Asian Interagency Working Group on Narcotics Control Meeting, April 18, 1972; People's Republic of China, April 1972; Standard Reply to Charge That PRC Is Engaged in Narcotics Traffic (n.d.), IPS 12, E31, box 31, RG 286, NARA.

11. Subcommittee on Foreign Operations and Related Agencies, Committee on Appropriations, House, 92nd Congress, 2nd sess., Byron Engle, testimony, May 3, 1972, 799.

12. Nixon, "Special Message to the Congress on Drug Abuse Prevention and Control."

13. Attendees included Nixon's domestic "law and order" advisor Egil Krogh, AID Administrator John Hannah (previously president of MSU), counterinsurgency expert Ogden Williams (now a narcotics expert), Defense and CIA representatives, over twenty public safety advisors, and others. OPS, *Seminar on Narcotics: Summary of Report Proceedings, October 12–19, 1971* (Washington, DC: AID, 1971).

14. The Role of AID's Office of Public Safety in Overseas Narcotics Control (n.d.), IPS 16–1, E18, box 10, RG 286, NARA, 2.

15. Comptroller General of the United States, *Phaseout of US Assistance to South Vietnam in Support of Police Organizations, Law Enforcement, and Public Safety Related Programs* (Washington, DC: GPO, 1975; 47112), 4, 28, 32.

16. Klare and Arnson, *Supplying Repression,* 29.

17. In its first fifteen years, the DEA would train more foreign police officers than OPS had: Martha Cottam and Otwin Marenin, "Predicting the Past: Reagan Administration Assistance to Police Forces in Central America," *Justice Quarterly* 6, no. 4 (1989): 589–618. Nadelmann, *Cops across Borders,* 119–121; Weimer, *Seeing Drugs.*

18. Comptroller General, *Stopping US Assistance,* 11.

19. Nancy Stein to Tom Daschle, April 25, 1975, Nancy Stein—LEAA, box Ab685, James G. Abourezk Papers, USD.

20. Exit Interview with Geoffrey C. Shepard, September 11, 1974, by Terry Good, RMNL, 19.

21. Public Law 93–83, August 6, 1973.

22. Mitre Corporation, "Potential LEAA/NILECJ Activities Related to the International Aspects of Skyjacking, Terrorism, and Illegal Narcotics Traffic," March 8, 1974, Nancy Stein—LEAA, box Ab685, James G. Abourezk Papers, USD.

23. Executive Management Service, Inc., "International Role and Objectives of LEAA," July 1974, Nancy Stein—LEAA, box Ab685, James G. Abourezk Papers, USD, 16, 3, 7, 9, 23.

24. Hearings before the Subcommittee on Crime, Committee on the Judiciary, House of Representatives, 1975, 94th Congress, 1st sess., 2984.

25. Steven Rosenfeld, "The Surprising Unknown History of the NRA," *Alternet,* January 13, 2013.

26. Bruce Cumings, "Global Realm with No Limit, Global Realm with No Name," *Radical History Review* 57 (1993): 46–59.

27. Harootunian, *Empire's New Clothes.*

28. Ibid., 25.

29. Leventhal, "Byron F. Engle"; Goin, "Address."

30. Jack O'Dell, "The July Rebellions and the 'Military State,'" *Freedomways* 7, no. 4 (1967): 288–301.

31. "The Tiger Cages of Con Son," *Life,* July 17, 1970; Bordenkircher and Bordenkircher, *Tiger Cage.*

32. Terri Shaw, "Police and Politics Abroad: AID Center under Fire in Wake of Mitrione Murder," *Washington Post,* November 10, 1970.

33. Kuzmarov, *Modernizing Repression.*

34. Maxwell C. Stanford, "Revolutionary Action Movement (RAM): A Case Study of an Urban Revolutionary Movement in Western Capitalist Society" (MA thesis, Atlanta University, 1986), 72; Kalamu ya Salaam, "Robert Williams: Crusader for International Solidarity," *Black Collegian* 8, no. 3 (January–February 1978), 54–58. Although it is possible Giap made such a claim to Williams, Hanoi's chief military strategist, Le Duan, had already been considering, planning, training for, and executing urban operations prior to the Detroit uprising in summer of 1967 (Elliott, *Vietnamese War,* 978–989, 1038).

35. *We Accuse: Bill Epton Speaks to the Court* ([Brooklyn, NY: Progressive Labor Party],1966), Frame-Ups I, Reference Center for Marxist Studies Pamphlet Collection, box 38, Tamiment Library, New York.

36. Chris Hayes, *A Colony in a Nation* (New York: Norton, 2017), 216. A similar assessment is found in Nick Pinto, "The Point of Order," *New York Times Sunday Magazine,* January 18, 2015.

SELECTED BIBLIOGRAPHY

ARCHIVES AND ELECTRONIC COLLECTIONS

US Agency for International Development, Development Experience Clearinghouse

The American Presidency Project, by Gerhard Peters and John T. Woolley, Santa Barbara, CA *(TAPP)*

Archives/Special Collections, American University, Washington, DC
Arnold Sagalyn Papers (ASP)

California State Archives, Sacramento, CA
California Council on Criminal Justice
Governor's Task Force on Civil Rights
Organization Files

Central Intelligence Agency (CIA)
CIA Electronic Reading Room
CIA Records Search Tool (CREST)

Civil Rights during the Johnson Administration, 1963–1969, Part V: Records of the National Advisory Commission on Civil Disorders (NACCD) online database *(CRDJA)*

Declassified Documents Reference System, Farmington Hills, IL (DDRS)

Federal Bureau of Investigation (FBI) Records: The Vault online

Hoover Institution Archives, Stanford, CA (HIA)
Charles T. R. Bohannan Papers
Edward Geary Lansdale Papers
Charles Francis Sloane Papers

John F. Kennedy Presidential Library, Boston, MA (JFKL)
National Security File (NSF)
President's Office Files

Special Collections, Michigan State University, East Lansing, MI (MSUA)
Ralph H. Smuckler Papers
Ralph F. Turner Papers
Vietnam Project Records

Missouri Valley Special Collections, Kansas City Municipal Library, Kansas City, MO
  Kansas City Police Historical Society (KCPHS)
  Mounted Newspaper Clippings, microfilm (KCMNC)
Lyndon B. Johnson Presidential Library, Austin, TX (LBJL)
  National Security File (NSF)
  Office Files of Harry McPherson
  Papers of Robert W. Komer (RWK)
  Personal Papers (PP) of Sherwin Markman
  Personal Papers of Warren Christopher
  Records of the National Advisory Commission on Civil Disorders
  Records of the President's Commission on Law Enforcement and Administration
    of Justice (PCLEAJ)
  White House Central File (WHCF)
  White House Telephone Recordings and Transcripts (WHTRT)
The National Archives, Kew, United Kingdom (TNA)
  Records of the Cabinet Office
  Records of the Foreign Office
  Records of the Ministry of Defence
  Records of the War Office
National Archives and Records Administration II, College Park, MD (NARA)
  RG 59, General Records of the Department of State
  RG 170, Records of the Drug Enforcement Administration
  RG 286, Records of the Agency for International Development
  RG 331, Allied Operational and Occupation Headquarters
  RG 423, Records of the Law Enforcement Assistance Administration
  RG 472, Records of the US Forces in Southeast Asia, 1950–1975
  RG 559, Records of General Headquarters, Far East Command, Supreme
    Commander Allied Powers, and United Nations Command
National Defense University Library, Washington, DC
  Maxwell D. Taylor Papers
The National Security Archive, Washington, DC
  Digital National Security Archive
  Electronic Briefing Books
Department of Rare Books and Special Collections, Princeton University Library,
    Princeton, NJ
  Philip G. Strong Collection
Richard M. Nixon Presidential Library, Yorba Linda, CA (RMNL)
  White House Central File
  White House Special Files
Richardson Collections, University of South Dakota, Vermillion, South Dakota
    (USD)
  James G. Abourezk Papers
Ronald Reagan Presidential Library, Simi Valley, CA (RRL)
  Gubernatorial Papers

Tamiment Library, New York, NY
  Philip Agee Papers
  Reference Center for Marxist Studies Pamphlet Collection
US Department of State, *Papers Relating to the Foreign Relations of the United States*
  (*FRUS*)
The Vietnam Center and Archive, Texas Tech University, Lubbock, TX (TTU)
  Dale W. Andrade Collection
  William Colby Collection
  George J. Veith Collection
Walnut Creek Historical Society, Walnut Creek, CA
  Newspaper Collection

INTERVIEWS AND ORAL HISTORIES

Arthur Brandstatter, by Jeff Charnley, April 11, 2001, Sesquicentennial Oral History Project, MSUA.

Richard J. Brockett, by Anne Blair, March 11, 1999, The Vietnam Archive Oral History Project, OH0226, TTU.

William P. Bundy, Oral History II, March 6, 1972, by William W. Moss, Oral History Program, JFKL.

Herbert Ellingwood, by Gabrielle Morris, 1985, *Law Enforcement and Criminal Justice in California, 1966–1974*, Berkeley: University of California, Bancroft Library, Regional Oral History Office.

Lauren J. Goin, Memoir (oral history), by James D. Williams, April 1991, The Institute of Inter-American Affairs Collection, Columbia University.

Harvey E. Gutman, by Stuart Van Dyke, August 26, 1997, Foreign Affairs Oral History Project, The Association for Diplomatic Studies and Training (ADST).

Thomas L. Hughes, by Charles Stuart Kennedy, July 7, 1999, ADST.

David Jickling, by W. Haven North, September 15, 1998, ADST.

Robert W. Komer, Oral History V, by Dennis J. O'Brien, December 22, 1969, Oral History Program, JFKL.

Robert W. Komer, by Joe B. Frantz, January 30, 1970, LBJL.

Victor H. Krulak, by William W. Moss, November 19, 1970, Oral History Program, JFKL.

David Lazar, by W. Haven North, March 20, 1997, ADST.

John P. Longan, Memoir (oral history), by James D. Williams, November 1984, The Institute of Inter-American Affairs Collection, Columbia University.

Geoffrey C. Shepard, Exit Interview, by Terry Good, September 11, 1974, RMNL.

Sherwin Markman, Oral History Interview I, by Dorothy Pierce McSweeny, May 21, 1969, LBJL.

Richard T. McCormack, by Charles Stuart Kennedy, January 2, 2002, ADST.

Robert S. McNamara, Oral History Interview I, by Walt W. Rostow, January 8, 1975, LBJL.
Patrick D. Putnam, by Susan Rosenfeld, May 8, 2005, FBI Oral History Heritage Project, National Law Enforcement Officers Memorial Fund.
Peter R. Rosenblatt, Oral History I, by Ted Gittinger, July 26, 1984, LBJL.
Harold H. Saunders, by Thomas Stern, November 24, 1993, ADST.
John Sylvester Jr., by Laura M. Calkins, August 4, 2004, ADST.

SECONDARY SOURCES

Abella, Alex. *Soldiers of Reason: The RAND Corporation and the Rise of the American Empire*. New York: Harcourt, 2008.
Agee, Chris Lowen. *The Streets of San Francisco*. Chicago: University of Chicago Press, 2014.
Ahmad, Eqbal. "Revolutionary War and Counter-Insurgency." *Journal of International Affairs* 25, no. 1 (1971): 1–47.
Aldous, Christopher. *The Police in Occupation Japan: Control, Corruption and Resistance to Reform*. New York: Routledge, 1997.
Alexander, Michelle. *The New Jim Crow: Mass Incarceration in the Age of Colorblindness*. New York: New Press, 2010.
Allen, Robert L. *Black Awakening in Capitalist America: An Analytic History*. New York: Doubleday, 1969.
Amadae, S.M. *Rationalizing Capitalist Democracy: The Cold War Origins of Rational Choice Liberalism*. Chicago: University of Chicago Press, 2003.
Anderson, Perry. *American Foreign Policy and Its Thinkers*. New York: Verso, 2015.
Applegate, Rex. *Kill or Get Killed: Riot Control Techniques, Manhandling, and Close Combat, for Police and the Military*. 1943. New ed. Boulder, CO: Paladin Press, 1976.
———. *Riot Control—Materiel and Techniques*. Harrisburg, PA: Stackpole Books, 1969.
Arendt, Hannah. *The Origins of Totalitarianism*. 1950. New York: Harcourt, Brace, Jovanovich, 1973.
Arrighi, Giovanni. *The Long Twentieth Century: Money, Power, and the Origins of Our Times*. New York: Verso, 1994.
Bacevich, Andrew J. *Washington Rules: America's Path to Permanent War*. New York: Metropolitan Books, 2011.
Baldwin, James. "Fifth Avenue, Uptown." *Esquire*, July 1960.
———. "A Report from Occupied Territory." *The Nation*, July 11, 1966.
Balko, Radley. *Rise of the Warrior Cop: The Militarization of America's Police Forces*. New York: PublicAffairs, 2013.
Balibar, Étienne. "Racism and Nationalism." In *Race, Nation, Class: Ambiguous Identities*, trans. Chris Turner, ed. Étienne Balibar and Immanuel Wallerstein, 37–67. New York: Verso, 1991.

Barber, Willard F. and C. Neale Ronning. *Internal Security and Military Power; Counterinsurgency and Civic Action in Latin America.* Columbus: Ohio State University Press, 1966.

Bayley, David H. *Patterns of Policing: A Comparative International Analysis.* New Brunswick, NJ: Rutgers University Press, 1985.

Becker, Marc. *The FBI in Latin America: The Ecuador Files.* Durham, NC: Duke University Press, 2017.

Berger, Dan. "Social Movements and Mass Incarceration." *Souls* 15, nos. 1–2 (2013): 3–18.

Best, Andrew, Sr. *Bad Cop No Doughnut.* N.p., 2011.

Birtle, Andrew J. *US Army Counterinsurgency and Contingency Operations Doctrine, 1942–1976.* Washington, DC: Center of Military History, 2006.

Blaufarb, Douglas S. *The Counterinsurgency Era: US Doctrine and Performance, 1950 to the Present.* New York: Free Press, 1977.

Blauner, Robert. "Internal Colonialism and Ghetto Revolt." *Social Problems* 16, no. 4 (1969): 393–340.

———. "Whitewash over Watts." *Trans-Action,* March–April 1966.

Bloom, Joshua, and Waldo E. Martin. *Black against Empire: The History and Politics of the Black Panther Party.* Berkeley: University of California Press, 2013.

Bonilla-Silva, Eduardo. *Racism without Racists: Color-Blind Racism and the Persistence of Racial Inequality in America.* Lanham, MD: Rowman & Littlefield, 2006.

Bookout, Nicholas. "A Movement towards Militarization: The History of Tactical Policing in Boston." *Tempus: The Harvard College History Review* 17, no. 2 (2106): 13–25.

Bopp, William J. *"O. W.": O. W. Wilson and the Search for a Police Profession.* Port Washington, NY: Kennikat Press, 1977.

Bordenkircher, D. E., and S. A. Bordenkircher, *Pappy's Rendition: Corrections & Detention Iraq 2005–2009.* Cameron, WV: Abby Publishing, 2012.

———. *Tiger Cage: An Untold Story.* Cameron, WV: Abby Publishing, 1998.

Bridger, Sarah. *Scientists at War: The Ethics of Cold War Weapons Research.* Cambridge, MA: Harvard University Press, 2015.

Bruce, Robert H. "Human Rights and US Training of Third World Police." *Conflict Quarterly* 8 (1988): 48–60.

———. "Impact of the Occupation of Japan on American Notions about US-Induced Reform in the Third World." *Indian Journal of American Studies* 75, no. 2 (1985): 123–127.

Buckel, Sonja. "The Juridical Condensation of the Relations of Forces: Nicos Poulantzas and Law." In *Reading Poulantzas,* edited by Alexander Gallas, Lars Bretthauer, John Kannankulam, and Ingo Stützle, 154–169. London: Merlin, 2011.

Burke, Kyle. *Revolutionaries for the Right: Anticommunist Internationalism and Paramilitary Warfare in the Cold War.* Chapel Hill: University of North Carolina Press, 2018.

Butler, Brian E. "Title IX of the Foreign Assistance Act: Foreign Aid and Political Development." *Law & Society Review* 3, no. 1 (1968): 115–152.

Button, James W. *Black Violence: Political Impact of the 1960s Riots*. Princeton, NJ: Princeton University Press, 1978.

Calhoun, Craig, ed. *Sociology in America: A History*. Chicago: University of Chicago Press, 2007.

Camp, Jordan T. *Incarcerating the Crisis: Freedom Struggles and the Rise of the Neoliberal State*. Berkeley: University of California Press, 2016.

Caplan, Gerald. "Reflection on the Nationalization of Crime, 1964–1968." *Law and the Social Order* 3 (1973): 583–635.

Carmichael, Stokely, and Charles V. Hamilton. *Black Power: The Politics of Liberation in America*. New York: Vintage Books, 1967.

Carter, David C. *The Music Has Gone Out of the Movement: Civil Rights and the Johnson Administration, 1965–1968*. Chapel Hill: University of North Carolina Press, 2009.

Center for Research on Criminal Justice. *Iron Fist, Velvet Glove: An Analysis of the US Police*. Berkeley: Center for Research on Criminal Justice, 1975.

Césaire, Aimé. *Discourse on Colonialism*. 1950. Translated by Joan Pinkham. New York: Monthly Review Press, 2000.

Chamberlin, Paul Thomas. *The Cold War's Killing Fields: Rethinking the Long Peace*. New York: Harper, 2018.

Chen, Chris. "The Limit Point of Capitalist Equality." *Endnotes* 3 (2013): 202–223.

Chevigny, Paul. *Police Power*. New York: Pantheon Books, 1969.

Conlan, Timothy. *From New Federalism to Devolution: Twenty-Five Years of Intergovernmental Reform*. Washington, DC: Brookings Institution Press, 1998.

Correia, David, and Tyler Wall. *Police: A Field Guide*. New York: Verso, 2018.

Cottam, Martha, and Otwin Marenin. "Predicting the Past: Reagan Administration Assistance to Police Forces in Central America." *Justice Quarterly* 6, no. 4 (1989): 589–618.

Cronin, Thomas E., Tania Z. Cronin, and Michael E. Milakovich, *US v. Crime in the Streets*. Bloomington: Indiana University Press, 1981.

Cumings, Bruce. "Global Realm with No Limit, Global Realm with No Name." *Radical History Review* 57 (1993): 46–59.

———. *The Origins of the Korean War: Liberation and the Emergence of Separate Regimes 1945–1947*. Princeton, NJ: Princeton University Press, 1981.

———. "'Revising Postrevisionism,' or, The Poverty of Theory in Diplomatic History." *Diplomatic History* 17, no. 4 (1993): 539–570.

Cruse, Harold. "Revolutionary Nationalism and the Afro-American." *Studies on the Left* 2, no. 3 (1962): 12–25.

Dawson, Michael C. "Hidden in Plain Sight: A Note on Legitimation Crises and the Racial Order." *Critical Historical Studies* 3, no. 1 (2016): 143–161.

Deitchman, Seymour J. *Limited War and American Defense Policy*. 1964. 2nd ed. Cambridge, MA: MIT Press, 1969.

Dethlefs, Thomas. "Tear Gas and the Politics of Lethality: Emerging from the Haze." *Yale Historical Review* 2, no. 3 (Spring 2013): 83–118.

Diegelman, Robert F. "Federal Financial Assistance for Crime Control: Lessons of the LEAA Experience." *Journal of Criminal Law & Criminology* 7, no. 3 (1982): 994–1011.

Dixon, Paul. "'Hearts and Minds'? British Counter-Insurgency from Malaya to Iraq." *Journal of Strategic Studies* 32, no. 2 (2009): 353–381.

Donner, Frank J. *The Age of Surveillance.* New York: Knopf, 1980.

———. *Protectors of Privilege: Red Squads and Police Repression in Urban America.* Berkeley: University of California Press, 1990.

Donovan, John T. "'I Have No Use for This Fellow Parker': William H. Parker of the LAPD and His Feud with J. Edgar Hoover and the FBI." *Southern California Quarterly* 87, no. 2 (2005): 171–198.

Dubber, Markus D. *The Police Power: Patriarchy and the Foundations of American Government.* New York: Columbia University Press, 2005.

Dubber, Markus D., and Mariana Valverde, eds. *The New Police Science.* Stanford, CA: Stanford University Press, 2006.

Du Bois, W. E. B. *Color and Democracy: Colonies and Peace.* 1945. Millwood, NY: Kraus-Thomson Organization, 1975.

———. "The Color Line Belts the World." *Collier's Weekly,* October 20, 1906.

———. "My Evolving Program for Negro Freedom." In *What the Negro Wants,* ed. Rayford Logan. 1944. South Bend, IN: University of Notre Dame Press, 2001.

———. *The Philadelphia Negro: A Social Study.* 1899. Reprint. New York: Schocken Books, 1967.

———. "The Present Outlook for the Dark Races of Mankind." In *The Problem of the Color Line at the Turn of the Twentieth Century: The Essential Early Essays,* ed. Nahum Dmitri Chandler, 111–137. 1900. New York: Fordham University Press, 2013.

Dudziak, Mary L. *Cold War Civil Rights: Race and the Image of American Democracy.* Princeton, NJ: Princeton University Press, 2000.

Dulaney, W. Marvin. *Black Police in America.* Bloomington: Indiana University Press, 1996.

Echols, Lee E. *Hilarious High Jinks and Dangerous Assignments.* Washington, DC: National Rifle Association of America, 1990.

Elkind, Jessica. *Aid under Fire: Nation Building and the Vietnam War.* Lexington: University Press of Kentucky, 2016.

Elliott, David W. P. *The Vietnamese War: Revolution and Social Change in the Mekong Delta, 1930–1975.* Vol. 2. Armonk, NY: M. E. Sharpe, 2003.

Elliott, Duong Van Mai. *RAND in Southeast Asia: A History of the Vietnam War Era.* Santa Monica, CA: RAND, 2010.

Ellison, D. Hank. *Chemical Warfare during the Vietnam War: Riot Control Agents in Combat.* New York: Routledge, 2011.

Ernst, John. *Forging a Fateful Alliance: Michigan State University and the Vietnam War.* East Lansing: Michigan State University Press, 1998.

Escobar, Edward J. "Bloody Christmas and the Irony of Police Professionalism: The Los Angeles Police Department, Mexican Americans, and Police Reform in the 1950s." *Pacific Historical Review* 72, no. 2 (2003): 171–199.

Fanon, Frantz. *The Wretched of the Earth*. 1961. Translated by Richard Philcox. New York: Grove Press, 2004.

Farmer, Ashley. *Remaking Black Power: How Black Women Transformed an Era*. Chapel Hill: University of North Carolina Press, 2017.

Feagin, Joe R., and Harlan Hahn. *Ghetto Revolts: The Politics of Violence in American Cities*. New York: Macmillan, 1973.

Feeley, Malcolm, and Austin D. Sarat. *The Policy Dilemma: Federal Crime Policy and the Law Enforcement Assistance Administration*. Minneapolis: University of Minnesota Press, 1980.

Feigenbaum, Anna. *Tear Gas: From the Battlefields of World War I to the Streets of Today*. New York: Verso, 2017.

Felker-Kantor, Max. *Policing Los Angelese: Race, Resistance, and the Rise of the LAPD*. Chapel Hill: University of North Carolina Press, 2018.

Ferrell, Robert H. *Truman and Pendergast*. Columbia: University of Missouri Press, 1999.

Finletter, Thomas K. *Power and Policy: U.S. Foreign Policy and Military Power in the Hydrogen Age*. New York: Harcourt, Brace, 1954.

Flamm, Michael W. *In the Heat of the Summer: The New York Riots of 1964 and the War on Crime*. Philadelphia: University of Pennsylvania Press, 2017.

———. *Law and Order: Street Crime, Civil Unrest, and the Crisis of Liberalism in the 1960s*. New York: Columbia University Press, 2005.

Flanagan, Richard M. "Lyndon Johnson, Community Action, and Management of the Administrative State." *Presidential Studies Quarterly* 31, no. 4 (2001): 585–608.

Fogelson, Robert M. *Big-City Police*. Cambridge, MA: Harvard University Press, 1977.

Forman, James, Jr. *Locking Up Our Own: Crime and Punishment in Black America*. New York: Farrar, Straus & Giroux, 2017.

Foucault, Michel. *"Society Must Be Defended": Lectures at the Collège de France, 1975–76*. Translated by David Macey. New York: Picador, 2003.

Fraser, Nancy. "Expropriation and Exploitation in Racialized Capitalism: A Reply to Michael Dawson." *Critical Historical Studies* 3, no. 1 (2016): 163–178;

Frazier, Robeson Taj. *The East Is Black: Cold War China in the Black Radical Imagination*. Durham, NC: Duke University Press, 2015.

French, David. *The British Way in Counter-Insurgency, 1945–1967*. New York: Oxford University Press, 2011.

Friedman, Andrew. *Covert Capital: Landscapes of Denial and the Making of US Empire in the Suburbs of Northern Virginia*. Berkeley: University of California Press, 2013.

Friman, H. Richard. "The Impact of the Occupation on Crime in Japan." In *Democracy in Occupied Japan: The US Occupation and Japanese Politics and Society*, ed. Mark E. Caprio and Yoneyuki Sugita, 89–119. Florence, KY: Routledge, 2007.

Gaddis, John Lewis. *The Cold War: A New History*. New York: Penguin Press, 2005.

Gage, Beverly. *The Day Wall Street Exploded: A Story of America in Its First Age of Terror*. New York: Oxford University Press, 2006.

Garland, David. *The Culture of Control: Crime and Social Order in Contemporary Society*. New York: Oxford University Press, 2001.

Gates, Daryl F., with Diane K. Shah. *Chief: My Life in the LAPD*. New York: Bantam Books, 1993.

Gentile, Gian. *Wrong Turn: America's Deadly Embrace of Counterinsurgency*. New York: New Press, 2013.

Gentry, Curt. *J. Edgar Hoover: The Man and the Secrets*. New York: Norton, 1991.

Gibson, James William. *The Perfect War: The War We Couldn't Lose and How We Did*. New York: Vintage Books, 1988.

Gill, Leslie. *The School of the Americas: Military Training and Political Violence in the Americas*. Durham, NC: Duke University Press, 2004.

Gilman, Nils. *Mandarins of the Future: Modernization Theory in Cold War America*. Baltimore: Johns Hopkins University Press, 2003.

Gilmore, Ruth Wilson. "Globalisation and US Prison Growth: From Military Keynesianism to Post-Keynesian Militarism." *Race & Class* 40, nos. 2–3 (1998–1999): 171–188.

———. *Golden Gulag: Prisons, Surplus, Crisis, and Opposition in Globalizing California*. Berkeley: University of California Press, 2007.

Gilroy, Paul. "You Can't Fool the Youths ... Race and Class Formation in the 1980s." *Race & Class* 23 (1981): 207–222.

Goldstein, Alyosha. *Poverty in Common: The Politics of Community Action during the American Century*. Durham, NC: Duke University Press, 2012.

Goluboff, Risa. *Vagrant Nation: Police Power, Constitutional Change, and the Making of the 1960s*. New York: Oxford University Press, 2016.

Gordon, Diana R. *The Justice Juggernaut: Fighting Street Crime, Controlling Citizens*. New Brunswick, NJ: Rutgers University Press, 1990.

Gottschalk, Marie. *Caught: The Prison State and the Lockdown of American Politics*. Princeton, NJ: Princeton University Press, 2016.

Grandin, Greg. *Empire's Workshop: Latin America, the United States, and the Rise of the New Imperialism*. New York: Metropolitan Books, 2006.

———. *The Last Colonial Massacre: Latin America in the Cold War*. Chicago: University of Chicago Press, 2004.

———. "Living in Revolutionary Time: Coming to Terms with the Violence of Latin America's Cold War." In *A Century of Revolution: Insurgent and Counterinsurgent Violence during Latin America's Long Cold War*, ed. Greg Grandin and Gilbert M. Joseph, 1–42. Durham, NC: Duke University Press, 2010.

Gray, Virginia, and Bruce Williams. *The Organizational Politics of Criminal Justice*. Lexington, MA: Lexington Books, 1980.

Grenier, John. *The American Way of War: American War Making on the Frontier, 1607–1814*. New York: Cambridge University Press, 2005.

Grodsky, Morris. *The Home Boy's Odyssey: The Saga of the Journey from Orphan Boy to Criminalist*. Bloomington, IN: 1st Books Library, 2004.

Gurman, Hannah, ed. *Hearts and Minds: A People's History of Counterinsurgency*. New York: New Press, 2013.

Hack, Karl. "Malaya—between Two Terrors: 'People's History' and the Malayan Emergency." In *Hearts and Minds: A People's History of Counterinsurgency,* ed. Hannah Gurman, 17–49. New York: New Press, 2013.

———. "The Malayan Emergency as Counter-Insurgency Paradigm." *Journal of Strategic Studies* 32, no. 3 (2009): 383–414.

Halberstam, David. *The Best and the Brightest.* 1972. New York: Ballantine Books, 1992.

Haley, Sarah. *No Mercy Here: Gender, Punishment, and the Making of Jim Crow Modernity.* Chapel Hill: University of North Carolina Press, 2016

Hall, Stuart, Chas Critcher, Tony Jefferson, John Clarke, and Brian Roberts, *Policing the Crisis: Mugging, the State, and Law and Order.* London: Macmillan, 1978.

Harcourt, Bernard E. *The Illusion of Free Markets: Punishment and the Myth of Natural Order.* Cambridge, MA: Harvard University Press, 2011.

Harootunian, Harry D. *The Empire's New Clothes: Paradigm Lost, and Regained.* Chicago: Prickly Paradigm Press, 2004.

———. *Marx after Marx: History and Time in the Expansion of Capitalism.* New York: Columbia University Press, 2015.

Hayes, Chris. *A Colony in a Nation.* New York: Norton, 2017.

Heatherton, Christina. "University of Radicalism: Ricardo Flores Magón and Leavenworth Penitentiary." *American Quarterly* 66, no. 3 (2014): 557–581.

———. "U.S. Police: Broken Windows Neoliberalism." *The Funambulist* 8 (2016): 28–33.

Hernández, Kelly Lytle. *City of Inmates: Conquest, Rebellion, and the Rise of Human Caging in Los Angeles, 1771–1965.* Chapel Hill: University of North Carolina Press, 2017.

Hinton, Elizabeth. *From the War on Poverty to the War on Crime: The Making of Mass Incarceration in America.* Cambridge, MA: Harvard University Press, 2016.

Hogan, Michael J. *A Cross of Iron: Harry S. Truman and the Origins of the National Security State, 1945–1954.* New York: Cambridge University Press, 1998.

Holt, Thomas. "Marking: Race, Race-making, and the Writing of History." *American Historical Review* 100, no. 1 (1995): 1–20.

Hopkins, Terence. "World-System Analysis: Methodological Issues." In *Social Change in the Capitalist World Economy,* ed. Barbara Hockey Kaplan, 199–217. Beverly Hills, CA: Sage, 1978.

Horne, Gerald. *Fire This Time: The Watts Uprising and the 1960s.* Charlottesville: University of Virginia Press, 1995.

———. "Race from Power: US Foreign Policy and the General Crisis of White Supremacy." *Diplomatic History* 23, no. 3 (1999): 437–461.

Huggins, Martha K. *Political Policing: The United States and Latin America.* Durham, NC: Duke University Press, 1998.

Hyman, Louis. *Debtor Nation: The History of America in Red Ink.* Princeton, NJ: Princeton University Press, 2011.

Jackson, George. *Soledad Brother: The Prison Letters of George Jackson.* 1970. Rev. ed. New York: Bantam Books, 1972.

Jacobsen, Kurt. *Pacification and Its Discontents.* Chicago: Prickly Paradigm Press, 2009.

Jameson, Fredric, "Periodizing the 60s." *Social Text* 9–10 (1984): 178–209

———. "*The Shining.*" *Social Text* 4 (1981): 114–125.

Jessop, Bob. "Fordism and Post-Fordism." In *Beyond the Regulation Approach: Putting Capitalist Economies in Their Place,* ed. Bob Jessop and Ngai-Ling Sum, 58–89. Northampton, MA: Edward Elgar, 2006.

Jones, Frank L. "Blowtorch: Robert Komer and the Making of Vietnam Pacification Policy." *Parameters* 35 (2005): 103–118.

———. *Blowtorch: Robert Komer, Vietnam, and American Cold War Strategy.* Annapolis, MD: Naval Institute Press, 2013.

———. "The Guerrilla Warfare Problem: Revolutionary War and the Kennedy Administration Response, 1961–1963." In *The US Army War College Guide to National Security Issues: National Security Policy and Strategy,* ed. J.B. Bartholomees, 2: 381–395. Carlisle, PA: Strategic Studies Institute, US Army War College, 2010.

Kaba, Mariame. "An (Abridged) History of Resisting Police Violence in Harlem." Historical Moments of Policing, Violence & Resistance, vol. 3. Chicago: Project NIA, 2012.

Katz, Michael B. "Why Don't American Cities Burn Very Often?" *Journal of Urban History* 34, no. 2 (2008): 185–208.

Kaufman, Burton I. *Trade and Aid: Eisenhower's Foreign Economic Policy, 1953–1961.* Baltimore: Johns Hopkins University Press, 1982.

Kelley, Robin D. G. *Freedom Dreams: The Black Radical Imagination.* Boston: Beacon Press, 2002.

Kelling, George L., and James Q. Wilson. "Broken Windows: The Police and Neighborhood Safety." *Atlantic Monthly,* March 1, 1982.

Khalili, Laleh. *Time in the Shadows: Confinement in Counterinsurgencies.* Stanford, CA: Stanford University Press, 2012.

Klare, Michael T. *War without End: American Planning for the Next Vietnams.* New York: Knopf, 1972.

Klare, Michael T., and Cynthia Arnson. *Supplying Repression: US Support for Authoritarian Regimes Abroad.* Washington, DC: Institute for Policy Studies, 1981.

Knight, Frank H. *Risk, Uncertainty and Profit.* Boston: Houghton Mifflin, 1921.

Kohler-Hausmann, Julilly. *Getting Tough: Welfare and Imprisonment in 1970s America.* Princeton, NJ: Princeton University Press, 2017.

———. "Militarizing the Police: Officer Jon Burge, Torture, and War in the 'Urban Jungle.'" In *Challenging the Prison-Industrial Complex: Activism, Arts, & Educational Alternatives,* ed. Stephen John Hartnett, 43–71. Chicago: University of Illinois Press, 2011.

Komer, Robert W. *Bureaucracy Does Its Thing: Institutional Constraints on U.S.-GVN Performance in Vietnam.* Santa Monica, CA: RAND, 1972.

———. "Impact of Pacification on Insurgency in South Vietnam." *Journal of International Affairs* 25, no. 1 (1971): 48–69.

Kramer, Alisa Sarah. "William H. Parker and the Thin Blue Line: Politics, Public Relations and Policing in Postwar Los Angeles." PhD diss., American University, 2007.

Kramer, Paul A. *The Blood of Government: Race, Empire, the United States, & the Philippines*. Chapel Hill: University of North Carolina Press, 2006.

———. "Power and Connection: Imperial Histories of the United States in the World." *American Historical Review* 116, no. 5 (2011): 1348–1391.

———. "Shades of Sovereignty: Racialized Power, the United States and the World." In *Explaining the History of American Foreign Relations*, ed. Frank Costigliola and Michael J. Hogan, 245–270. New York: Cambridge University Press, 2016.

Kraska, Peter B. ed., *Militarizing the American Criminal Justice System: The Changing Roles of the Armed Forces and the Police*. Boston: Northeastern University Press, 2001.

Krepinevich, Andrew F., Jr. *The Army and Vietnam*. Baltimore: Johns Hopkins University Press, 1986.

Kuzmarov, Jeremy. *Modernizing Repression: Police Training and Nation Building in the American Century*. Boston: University of Massachusetts Press, 2012.

Langguth, A. J. *Hidden Terrors: The Truth about US Police Operations in Latin America*. New York: Pantheon Books, 1978.

Laughlin, David L. *Gringo Cop*. New York: Carlton Press, 1975.

Larsen, Lawrence H., and Nancy J. Hulston. *Pendergast!* Columbia, MO: University of Missouri Press, 1997.

Latham, Michael E. *The Right Kind of Revolution: Modernization, Development, and US Foreign Policy from the Cold War to the Present*. Ithaca, NY: Cornell University Press, 2011.

Leites, Nathan, and Charles Wolf Jr. *Rebellion and Authority: An Analytic Essay on Insurgent Conflicts*. Santa Monica, CA: RAND, February 1970. R-462-ARPA.

Levine, Bertram J. *Resolving Racial Conflict: The Community Relations Service and Civil Rights, 1964–1989*. Columbia: University of Missouri Press, 2005.

Lobe, Thomas. "The Rise and Demise of the Office of Public Safety." *Armed Forces & Society* 9, no. 2 (1983) 187–213;

———. *United States National Security Policy and Aid to the Thailand Police*. Denver: University of Denver, Graduate School of International Studies, 1977.

———. "US Police Assistance for the Third World." PhD diss., University of Michigan, 1975.

Maechling, Charles, Jr. "Camelot, Robert Kennedy, and Counter-Insurgency: A Memoir." *Virginia Quarterly* 75, no. 3 (1999).

———. "Insurgency and Counterinsurgency: The Role of Strategic Theory." *Parameters* 14, no. 3 (1984): 32–41.

Mahoney, Barry. "The Politics of the Safe Streets Act, 1965–1973: A Case Study in Evolving Federalism and the National Legislative Process." PhD diss., Columbia University, 1976.

Malloy, Sean T. *Out of Oakland: Black Panther Party Internationalism during the Cold War.* Ithaca, NY: Cornell University Press, 2017.

Mann, Michael. "The Autonomous Power of the State: Its Origins, Mechanisms and Results." *European Journal of Sociology* 25, no. 2 (1984): 185–213.

Marenin, Otwin. "From IPA to ILEA: Change and Continuity in US International Police-Training Programs." *Police Quarterly* 1, no. 4 (1998): 93–126.

———. "United States' Aid to African Police Forces: The Experience and Impact of the Public Safety Assistance Programme." *African Affairs* 85, no. 341 (1986): 509–544.

Marquis, Jefferson P. "The Other Warriors: American Social Science and Nation Building in Vietnam." *Diplomatic History* 24, no. 1 (2000): 79–105.

May, Ernest R., ed. *American Cold War Strategy: Interpreting NSC 68.* Boston: Bedford Books of St. Martin's Press, 1993.

McCarthy, Thomas. *Race, Empire, and the Idea of Human Development.* New York: Cambridge University Press, 2009.

McClintock, Michael. *Instruments of Statecraft: U.S. Guerrilla Warfare, Counterinsurgency, and Counterterrorism, 1940–1990.* New York: Pantheon Books, 1992.

McCormick, Thomas J. *America's Half-Century: United States Foreign Policy in the Cold War.* Baltimore: Johns Hopkins University Press, 1989.

McCoy, Alfred W. *Policing America's Empire: The United States, the Philippines, and the Rise of the Surveillance State.* Madison: University of Wisconsin Press, 2009.

McCoy, Alfred W., and Francisco A. Scarano, eds. *Colonial Crucible: Empire in the Making of the Modern American State.* Madison: University of Wisconsin Press, 2009.

McGirr, Lisa. *The War on Alcohol: Prohibition and the Rise of the American State.* New York: Norton, 2015.

McMahon, Robert J., ed. *The Cold War in the Third World.* New York: Oxford University Press, 2013.

McPhail, Clark, David Schweingruber, and John McCarthy. "Policing Protest in the United States: 1960–1995." In *Policing Protest: The Control of Mass Demonstrations in Western Democracies,* ed. Donatella della Porta and Herbert Reiter, 49–69. Minneapolis: University of Minnesota Press, 1998.

Melamed, Jodi. *Represent and Destroy: Rationalizing Violence in the New Racial Capitalism.* Minneapolis: University of Minnesota Press, 2011.

Michaels, Jeffrey H. "Managing Global Counterinsurgency: The Special Group (CI) 1962–1966." *Journal of Strategic Studies* 35, no. 1 (2012): 33–61.

Miller, Edward G. *Misalliance: Ngo Dinh Diem, the United States, and the Fate of South Vietnam.* Cambridge, MA: Harvard University Press, 2013.

Miller, Lisa L. *The Perils of Federalism: Race, Poverty, and the Politics of Crime Control.* New York: Oxford University Press, 2008.

Mitchell, Timothy. *Rule of Experts: Egypt, Techno-Politics, Modernity.* Berkeley: University of California Press, 2002.

Monkkonen, Eric H. *Crime, Justice, History.* Columbus: Ohio State University Press, 2002.

Moten, Fred. "The Subprime and the Beautiful." *African Identities* 11, no. 2 (2013): 237–245.

Motta, Rodrigo Patto Sá. "Modernizando a repressão: a Usaid e a polícia brasileira." *Revista Brasileira de História* 30 (2010): 237–266.

Muhammad, Khalil Gibran. *The Condemnation of Blackness: Race, Crime, and the Making of Modern Urban America.* Cambridge, MA: Harvard University Press, 2011.

Murakawa, Naomi. *The First Civil Right: How Liberals Built Prison America.* New York: Oxford University Press, 2014.

Nadelmann, Ethan Avram. *Cops across Borders: The Internationalization of US Criminal Law Enforcement.* University Park: Pennsylvania State University Press, 1993.

National Action Research on the Military Industrial Complex. *Weapons for Counterinsurgency.* Philadelphia, PA: NARMIC, 1970.

Neilands, J. B. "Gas Warfare in Vietnam in Perspective." In *Harvest of Death: Chemical Warfare in Vietnam and Cambodia,* edited by J. B. Neilands, Gordon H. Orians, E. W. Pfeiffer, Alje Vennema, and Arthur H. Westing, 3–101. New York: Free Press, 1971.

Neocleous, Mark. *The Fabrication of Social Order: A Critical Theory of Police Power.* London: Pluto Press, 2000.

———. "Security as Pacification." In *Anti-Security,* ed. Mark Neocleous and George Rigakos, 24–56. Ottawa: Red Quill Books, 2011.

———. "Security, Liberty and the Myth of Balance: Towards a Critique of Security Politics." *Contemporary Political Theory* 6, no. 2 (2007): 131–149;

———. *War Power, Police Power.* Edinburgh: Edinburgh University Press, 2014.

Newton, Huey P. "A Citizens' Peace Force" *Crime and Social Justice* 1 (1974): 36–39.

Nkrumah, Kwame. *Neo-Colonialism, the Last Stage of Imperialism.* New York: International Publishers, 1966.

O'Connor, James. *The Fiscal Crisis of the State.* New York: St. Martin's Press, 1973.

O'Dell, Jack. *Climbin' Jacob's Ladder: The Black Freedom Movement Writings of Jack O'Dell.* Edited by Nikhil Pal Singh. Berkeley: University of California Press, 2010.

———. "The July Rebellions and the 'Military State.'" *Freedomways* 7.4 (1967): 288–301.

Omi, Michael, and Howard Winant. *Racial Formation in the United States: From the 1960s to the 1980s.* New York: Routledge, 1986.

O'Reilly, Kenneth. "The FBI and the Politics of the Riots, 1964–1968." *Journal of American History* 75, no. 1 (1988): 91–114.

Owens, Patricia. *Economy of Force: Counterinsurgency and the Historical Rise of the Social.* New York: Cambridge University Press, 2015.

Panitch, Leo, and Sam Gindin. "Superintending Global Capitalism." *New Left Review* 2, no. 35 (2005): 101–123.

Parenti, Christian. *Lockdown America: Police and Prisons in the Age of Crisis.* New York: Verso, 1999.

Parker, Alfred E. *Crime Fighter: August Vollmer.* New York: Macmilllan, 1961.

Peck, Jamie. "Geography and Public Policy: Mapping the Penal State" *Progress in Human Geography* 27, no. 2 (2003): 222–232.

Peck, Jamie, and Nik Theodore. *Fast Policy: Experimental Statecraft at the Thresholds of Neoliberalism.* Minneapolis: University of Minnesota, 2015.

Pietz, William. "The 'Post-Colonialism' of Cold War Discourse." *Social Text* 19–20 (1988): 55–75.

———. "Totalitarianism and the Lessons of History: Reply to Stephanson." *Social Text* 22 (1989): 130–140.

Plummer, Brenda Gayle. *In Search of Power: African Americans in the Era of Decolonization, 1956–1974.* New York: Cambridge University Press, 2013.

Porch, Douglas. *Counterinsurgency: Exposing the Myths of the New Way of War.* New York: Cambridge University Press, 2013.

Poulantzas, Nicos. *State, Power, Socialism.* Translated by Patrick Camiller. New York: Verso, 1980.

Prados, John. *Lost Crusader: The Secret Wars of CIA Director William Colby.* New York: Oxford University Press, 2003.

Preston, Andrew. *The War Council: McGeorge Bundy, the NSC, and Vietnam* Cambridge, MA: Harvard University Press, 2010.

Pyle, Christopher H. *Military Surveillance of Civilian Politics, 1967–1970.* New York: Garland, 1986.

Rabe, Stephen G. "The Caribbean Triangle: Betancourt, Castro, and Trujillo and US Foreign Policy, 1958–1963." *Diplomatic History* 20, no. 1 (1996): 55–78.

———. *Eisenhower and Latin America: The Foreign Policy of Anticommunism.* Chapel Hill, NC: University of North Carolina Press, 1988.

Rakove, Robert B. *Kennedy, Johnson, and the Nonaligned World.* New York: Cambridge University Press, 2013.

Rana, Aziz. "Settler Wars and the National Security State." *Settler Colonial Studies* 4, no. 2 (2014): 171–175.

———. *The Two Faces of American Freedom.* Cambridge, MA: Harvard University Press, 2010.

Rempe, Dennis M. "An American Trojan Horse? Eisenhower, Latin America, and the Development of US Internal Security Policy 1954–1960." *Small Wars & Insurgencies* 10, no. 1 (1999): 34–64.

Rigakos, George. "'To Extend the Scope of Productive Labour': Pacification as a Police Project." In *Anti-Security,* ed. Mark Neocleous and George Rigakos, 57–83. Ottawa: Red Quill Books, 2011.

Robin, Ron. *The Cold World They Made: The Strategic Legacy of Roberta and Albert Wohlstetter.* Cambridge, MA: Harvard University Press, 2016.

———. *The Making of the Cold War Enemy: Culture and Politics in the Military-Intellectual Complex.* Princeton, NJ: Princeton University Press, 2001.

Robinson, Albert F. "Policing Vietnam: The Public Safety Program" *Vietnam* 16, no. 6 (2004): 26–32.

Robinson, Cedric J. *Black Marxism: The Making of the Black Radical Tradition.* 1983. Chapel Hill: University of North Carolina Press, 2000.

Robinson, Jennifer. "Cities in a World of Cities: The Comparative Gesture." *International Journal of Urban and Regional Research* 35, no. 1 (2011): 1–23.

Rodney, Walter. *How Europe Underdeveloped Africa.* 1972. Washington, DC: Howard University Press, 1982.

Rohde, Joy. *Armed with Expertise: The Militarization of American Social Research during the Cold War.* Ithaca, NY: Cornell University Press, 2013.

Rosenau, William. *US Internal Security Assistance to South Vietnam: Insurgency, Subversion, and Public Order.* New York: Routledge, 2005.

Rudgers, David. "The Origins of Covert Action." *Journal of Contemporary History* 35, no. 2 (2000): 249–262.

Runde, Jochen. "Clarifying Frank Knight's Discussion of the Meaning of Risk and Uncertainty." *Cambridge Journal of Economics* 22 (1998): 539–546.

Saenz, Adolph. *The OPS Story.* San Francisco: Robert D. Reed, 2002.

Sanford, David. "Agitators in a Fertilizer Factory." *New Republic,* February 11, 1967.

Sarkesian, Sam C., ed. *Revolutionary Guerrilla Warfare.* Chicago: Precedent, 1975.

Scheips, Paul J. *The Role of Federal Military Forces in Domestic Disorders, 1945–1992.* Washington, DC: Center of Military History, 2012.

Schurmann, Franz. *The Logic of World Power.* New York: Pantheon Books, 1974.

Scott, James C. *The Moral Economy of the Peasant: Rebellion and Subsistence in Southeast Asia.* New Haven, CT: Yale University Press, 1977.

Seigel, Micol. "Beyond Compare: Comparative Method after the Transnational Turn." *Radical History Review* 91 (2005): 62–90.

———. "Nelson Rockefeller in Latin America: Global Currents of US Prison Growth." *Comparative American Studies* 13, no. 3 (2015): 161–176.

———. "Objects of Police History." *Journal of American History* 102, no. 1 (2015): 152–161.

———. *Violence Work: State Power and the Limits of Police.* Durham, NC: Duke University Press, 2018.

Shafer, D. Michael. *Deadly Paradigms: The Failure of U.S. Counterinsurgency Policy.* Princeton, NJ: Princeton University Press, 1988.

Sheehan, Neil. *A Bright Shining Lie: John Paul Vann and America in Vietnam.* New York: Random House, 1988.

Simon, Jonathan. *Governing through Crime: How the War on Crime Transformed American Democracy and Created a Culture of Fear.* New York: Oxford University Press, 2007.

———. "Rise of the Carceral State." *Social Research* 74, no. 2 (2007): 471–508.

Singh, Nikhil Pal. *Black Is a Country: Race and the Unfinished Struggle for Democracy.* Cambridge, MA: Harvard University Press, 2004.

———. "Cold War." *Social Text* 100 (2009): 67–70.

———. *Race and America's Long War* Berkeley: University of California Press, 2017.

Smith, Neil. *American Empire: Roosevelt's Geographer and the Prelude to Globalization.* Berkeley: University of California Press, 2003.

Smith, Simon. "General Templer and Counter-Insurgency in Malaya: Hearts and Minds, Intelligence, and Propaganda" *Intelligence and National Security* 16, no. 3 (2001): 60–78.

Steinmetz, George. "Decolonizing German Theory: An Introduction." *Postcolonial Studies* 9, no. 1 (2006): 3–13.

———. "Return to Empire: The New US Imperialism in Comparative Historical Perspective." *Sociological Theory* 23, no. 4 (2005): 339–367.

Stephanson, Anders. "Cold War Degree Zero." In *Uncertain Empire: American History and the Idea of the Cold War,* ed. Joel Isaac and Duncan Bell, 19–49. New York: Oxford University Press, 2012.

Stoler, Ann L. *Duress: Imperial Durabilities in Our Times.* Durham, NC: Duke University Press, 2016.

———. *Race and the Education of Desire: Foucault's History of Sexuality and the Colonial Order of Things.* Durham, NC: Duke University Press, 1995.

———. "Tense and Tender Ties: The Politics of Comparison in North American History and (Post) Colonial Studies." *Journal of American History* 88, no. 3 (2001): 829–865.

———, ed., *Haunted by Empire: Geographies of Intimacy in North American History* Durham, NC: Duke University Press, 2006.

Sugrue, Thomas J. *Sweet Land of Liberty: The Forgotten Struggle for Civil Rights in the North.* New York: Random House, 2008.

Taylor, Keeanga-Yamahtta. "Back Story to the Neoliberal Moment: Race Taxes and the Political Economy of Black Urban Housing in the 1960s." *Souls* 14, no. 3–4 (2012): 185–206.

Thompson, Heather Ann. *Blood in the Water: The Attica Prison Uprising of 1971 and Its Legacy.* New York: Pantheon Books, 2016.

———. "Why Mass Incarceration Matters: Rethinking Crisis, Decline, and Transformation in Postwar American History." *Journal of American History* 97, no. 3 (2010): 703–734.

Travis, Jeremy, Bruce Western, and Steve Redburn, eds. *The Growth of Incarceration in the United States: Exploring Causes and Consequences.* Washington, DC: National Academies Press, 2014.

Tullis, Tracy. "A Vietnam at Home: Policing the Ghettos in the Counterinsurgency Era." PhD diss., New York University, 1999.

Turse, Nick. *Kill Anything That Moves: The Real American War in Vietnam.* New York: Metropolitan, 2013.

United States. National Advisory Commission on Civil Disorders. [Kerner] *Report.* Washington, DC: Government Printing Office, 1968.

Valverde, Mariana. "Questions of Security: A Framework for Research." *Theoretical Criminology* 15, no. 1 (2011): 3–22.

Verwey, Wil D. *Riot Control Agents and Herbicides in War: Their Humanitarian, Toxicological, Ecological, Military, Polemological, and Legal Aspects.* Leyden: A. W. Sijthoff, 1977.

Vitale, Alex S. *The End of Policing.* New York: Verso, 2017.

Vitalis, Robert. *White World Order, Black Power Politics: The Birth of American International Relations.* Ithaca, NY: Cornell University Press, 2015.

Von Eschen, Penny M. *Race Against Empire: Black Americans and Anticolonialism, 1937–1957.* Ithaca, NY: Cornell University Press, 1997.

Wacquant, Loïc J. D. *Prisons of Poverty.* Minneapolis: University of Minnesota Press, 2009.

Wagner, Bryan. *Disturbing the Peace: Black Culture and the Police Power after Slavery.* Cambridge, MA: Harvard University Press, 2009.

Wagner, Allen E. *Good Order and Safety: A History of the St. Louis Metropolitan Police Department, 1861–1906.* St. Louis: Missouri History Museum, 2008.

Wakeman, Frederic. "American Police Advisers and the Nationalist Chinese Secret Service, 1930–1937." *Modern China* 18, no. 2 (1992): 107–137.

Walker, Gavin. *The Sublime Perversion of Capital.* Durham, NC: Duke University Press, 2016.

Walker, Samuel. *A Critical History of Police Reform: The Emergence of Professionalism.* Lexington, MA: Lexington Books, 1977.

———. "'Broken Windows' and Fractured History: The Use and Misuse of History in Recent Police Patrol Analysis." *Justice Quarterly* 1, no. 1 (1984): 75–90.

Wallerstein, Immanuel. *The Modern World-System I.* 1974. Berkeley: University of California Press, 2011.

Weaver, Vesla. "Frontlash: Race and the Development of Punitive Crime Policy." *Studies in American Political Development* 21, no. 2 (2007): 230–265.

———. "The Significance of Policy Failures in Political Development: The Law Enforcement Assistance Administration and the Growth of the Carceral State." In *Living Legislation: Durability, Change, and the Politics of American Lawmaking,* ed. Jeffery A. Jenkins and Eric M. Patashnik, 221–251. Chicago: University of Chicago Press, 2012.

Weimer, Daniel. *Seeing Drugs: Modernization, Counterinsurgency, and US Narcotics Control in the Third World, 1969–1976.* Kent, OH: Kent State University Press, 2011.

Weinbaum, Alys Eve. *Wayward Reproductions: Genealogies of Race and Nation in Transatlantic Modern Thought.* Durham, NC: Duke University Press, 2004.

Weld, Kirsten. *Paper Cadavers: The Archives of Dictatorship in Guatemala.* Durham, NC: Duke University Press, 2014.

Wells, Tom. *Wild Man: The Life and Times of Daniel Ellsberg.* New York: Palgrave Macmillan, 2001.

Westad, Odd Arne. "Exploring the Histories of the Cold War: A Pluralist Approach." In *Uncertain Empire: American History and the Idea of the Cold War,* ed. Joel Isaac and Duncan Bell, 51–59. New York: Oxford University Press, 2012.

———. *The Global Cold War: Third World Interventions and the Making of Our Times.* New York: Cambridge University Press, 2005.

Williams, Kristian. *Our Enemies in Blue: Police and Power in America.* Cambridge, MA: South End Press, 2007.

Wills, Garry. *The Second Civil War: Arming for Armageddon.* New York: New American Library, 1968.

Wilson, James Q. *Thinking about Crime.* New York: Basic Books, 1975.
———. *Varieties of Police Behavior: The Management of Law and Order in Eight Communities.* Cambridge, MA: Harvard University Press, 1968.
Wilson, O. W., ed. *Parker on Police.* Springfield, IL: Charles C. Thomas, 1957.
Wintersmith, Robert F. *Police and the Black Community.* Lexington, MA: Lexington Books, 1974.
Woods, Joseph Gerald. "The Progressives and the Police: Urban Reform and the Professionalization of the Los Angeles Police." PhD diss., University of California, Los Angeles, 1973.
Young, Cynthia A. *Soul Power: Culture, Radicalism, and the Making of a U.S. Third World Left.* Durham, NC: Duke University Press, 2006.
Young, Gordon. *Journey from Banna: An Autobiography.* Xlibris, 2011.
Young, Marilyn Blatt, ed. *American Expansionism: The Critical Issues.* Boston: Little, Brown, 1973.
Zahniser, Marvin R., and W. Michael Weis. "A Diplomatic Pearl Harbor? Richard Nixon's Goodwill Mission to Latin America in 1958." *Diplomatic History* 13, no. 2 (1989): 163–190.
Zimmerman, Andrew. "'What Do You Really Want in German East Africa, Herr Professor?' Counterinsurgency and the Science Effect in Colonial Tanzania." *Comparative Studies in Society and History* 48, no. 2 (2006): 419–461.

INDEX

Certain persons are identified in subheadings by their initials. For example, John F. Kennedy, Robert F. Kennedy, and Lyndon B. Johnson are referred to as JFK, RFK, and LBJ, respectively, in subheadings.

When two or more people share the same last name, the relevant person's full name appears in subheadings uninverted and alphabetized on the first name. For example, there are two Wilsons. 'Wilson, O. W.' in main headings becomes 'O. W. Wilson' in subheadings.

Abourezk, James, 260–61, 269
Abu Ghraib (Iraqi prison), 66
Acheson, Dean, 89, 265
Advanced Research Projects Agency (ARPA), 147, 237, 243, 247, 253
Africa, 4, 28, 30, 33, 36, 95, 100, 152, 183. *See also* Congo/Zaire
African Americans. *See* Black people
AID (Agency for International Development): Bertillonage retained by, 292n29; chemical weapons purchased by, 206–7; vs. the CIA, 109; DC training facility for, 36; and the Dominican Republic, 228–29, 230; and Engle, 58; foreign graduates of, 186; Hannah as administrator of, 312n25, 341n17; and the IACP, 6, 134; ICA as predecessor of, 55; IPG created by, 129; Jelsch in, 62; vs. *Kill or Get Killed*, 147; and LEAA funding, 175; narcotics control mission of, 261–62, 341n17; in Nixon era, 341n17; and OPS, 111, 134, 260; pacification resisted by, 162; in the Panama Canal Zone, 108; and Paraná, 157; Philco funded by, 147; and the POCC, 184; and

police assistance, 108, 110, 113, 132; public safety programs curtailed by, 260; in South Vietnam, 150; and training of foreign men of color, 36–37; in Uruguay, 149; War on Crime internationalized by, 12. *See also* Guatemala; *headings under police professionalization;* Inter-American Police Academy; International Police Academy; SGCI
Airlie House meetings, 174–75
Alabama, 169, 202
Alexander, Holmes, 36
Algeria, 237
American Conservative Union, 261
An American Dilemma (Myrdal), 27–28
American Indian Movement, 179
American Institutes for Research, 237–38, 253
Anslinger, Harry, 61–62, 128, 133
anticolonialism, 3, 6, 19, 30, 38, 42, 96
anticommunism: and Black internationalism, 282–83n5; of Engle, 68; of Hoover, 113, 217; and internal security, 90; and law enforcement, 174; in Los Angeles, 230; of Parker, 217; and racism, 28; of

anticommunism *(continued)*
Singlaub, 231; social regulation oriented toward, 69; and US empire, 28, 265. *See also* liberalism; right-wing politics and policies

anti-imperialism, 19, 31, 116, 269

Applegate, Rex, 147, 202, 328n46

Apter, David, 88

Arendt, Hannah, 43

Argentina, 7 *map,* 176

Arkansas, 169

Armas, Carlos Castillo, 163

Armbruster, Frank, 241

Army (US). *See* chemical weapons; CS tear gas; Military Police; riot-control training; SEADOC

Army's Directorate for Civil Disturbance Planning and Operations (US Army), 179

ARPA (Advanced Research Projects Agency), 147, 237, 241–43, 247–48, 253

Arrow, Kenneth, 250

Ashworth, Ray, 69

Asia, 4, 30, 107, 126, 183

atomic weapons. *See* nuclear weapons

Attica State Prison (New York), 208

Balaguer, Joaquín, 230

Baldwin, James, 78

Baltimore, 183, 209

banditry, 240

Banfield, Edward, 244, 250

Battleship Potemkin (Eisenstein film), 259

Bay of Pigs invasion (Cuba), 11, 96, 98–99, 101, 108

Becker, Gary, 236, 250, 254

behavior control: broken windows policing as, 48, 255; coercive behavior control, 252–54; conduct as status in, 257; counterinsurgency tactics of, 157–60; by CS, 253; and discretionary police power, 236; by input control, 252; order-maintenance police power as, 265; origins of, 255; police power as, 20, 145; and rational-choice theory, 250, 252–53; and socioeconomic determinants of behavior, 255; in US empire, 157; Wolf advocating, 246–47. *See also* social control/regulation

Belgian empire, 146

Bell, David, 105

Berkeley, California police department, 67

Bertillonage (facial feature typology), 36, 42, 292n29

Birmingham, Alabama, 204

Bissell, Richard, 102–3, 111

Black communities/neighborhoods: Black police officers in, 34–35; in CSTI riot control planning, 189; and federalism, 72, 118–20, 311n5; grassroots achievement of, 120; and LEAA funding, 141; Levine urging cooperation with, 176; police occupation of, 3, 78; police power vs., 27, 28; politics of, 239; SWAT units in, 24; tear gas used in, 192, 194; unrest in, 168–71, 191; white police vs., 63. *See also* Harlem; Watts (Los Angeles)

Black internationalism, 282–83n5

Black Lives Matter movement, 272

Black Muslims, 210

Black nationalism, 243

Black Panther Party, 3, 45, 139, 210, 215, 221–22, 227, 232, 282–83n5

Black people: accused of communism, 59; ascriptive racism rejected by, 41–42, 272; civil rights of, 118; and decentralized police despotism, 72; Giuffrida's mass internment plans for, 188; governments' failure to redress, 271; vs. LAPD police abuses, 221; LAPD response to, 232; life expectancy of, lost to incarceration, 2; newspapers owned by, 59, 210; as police officers, 29–30, 34–35, 139, 237; police protection lacking for, 34; police shootings of, 197, 209, 212, 330n81; police violence against, 4, 27–28; preemptive killing of, 212; racist violence against, 8, 169; rights of, violated, 119; socioeconomic living conditions of, 116; vs. US empire, 232; viewed as imperial subjects, 42; voting rights demanded by, 116; in white neighborhoods, 256. *See also* freedom/justice demands and movements

Black political networks, 45, 115, 117, 271

Black political radicals: the CIA vs., 169; the FBI vs., 169; Gates vs., 232; overseas counterinsurgency techniques recognized by, 254; penal apparatus critiqued by, 3, 282–83n5; and social-welfare programming, 170; surveillance of, 176; and SWAT's origins, 214; tactics of, 197; utilities cut off in homes of, 253

Black politics, 113, 116–17, 271

Blackstone, William, 16

Blauner, Robert, 78

block grants, 114, 120, 139–40, 172, 187, 315n77

Bohannan, Charles, 241, 337n24

Bolivia, 184, 191

Bordenkircher, Donald, 142–43, 208

Bosch, Juan, 156–57, 228

Brandstatter, Arthur, 74, 76–77, 135, 167–68, 196, 312n25

Bratton, William, 216

Braudel, Fernand, 302n111

Brazil: brutal repression of demonstrations in, 166; Crisostomo in, 150; death squads in, 156; Draper in, 104; Mitrione in, 158; POCC replicated in, 184; police assistance to, 230; repression of demonstrations in, 155; Rocker in, 181; and SGCI, 104; Sheldon in, 225. *See also* Paraná

"The Break-Up of the Colonial Empires and Its Implications for US Security" (CIA report), 31, 80, 94, 96, 306n51

Brilliant, Leigh, 21

British counterinsurgency activities: chemical defoliants used in, 251; in competition with OPS, 310n123; CR developed for, 199; CS tear gas used by, 199; international prisoner-of-war conventions evaded in, 239; in Malaya, 77, 156, 198, 239, 251; and Northern Ireland, 180, 188; trainers trained in British foreign facilities, 77

British Guiana, 199

Britton, Dudley, 57

broken windows policing, 24, 48, 236, 256

Brooklyn, New York, 169

Brown v. Board of Education of Topeka (US Supreme Court), 11

Buckel, Sonja, 40

Bundy, McGeorge: on casualty reduction, 204; as communication specialist,

327n34; and the Dominican Republic, 229; guerrilla operations advocated by, 100; and JFK, 98, 106; and Komer, 106–8; and LBJ, 200, 327n34; in the NSC, 90; police programs' retention advocated by, 107; and RFK, 106; and SGCI, 106; on tear gas use, 200, 204, 327n34

Bundy, William P., 100

Bureau of Intelligence and Research (State Department). *See* INR

Burma, 100, 110, 113

Burundi, 32

Butchers, Ralph, 129

Byrd, Robert, 241

Cabell, Charles P., 96, 303n3

Cable Splicer civil-disturbance plan, 187

California, 187–92, 225, 227. *See also* CSTI

California Specialized Training Institute. *See* CSTI

The Call (KC African American Newspaper), 59

Cambodia, 7 *map*, 77, 113, 207, 302n107

Cambridge, Maryland, 202

Cameroon, 110

CAPER (Coalition Against Police Exploiters of Repression), 270

capitalism: internal security as guarantor of, 41; minority group control in, 34; and modernization, 82, 267; and the national security state, 286n21; police assistance as protector of, 265; and police-led counterinsurgency, 266; and police power, 144; and police professionalization, 267; and police reform, 143; security practices motivated by, 213; and social control, 144

Capone, Al, 64

carceral state: archival research on, 3; and law and order politics, 18; literature on, 281n1; and the national security state, 24; origins of, 2, 4–5, 167; and overseas counterinsurgency techniques repatriated to the US, 257–58; and overseas police assistance, 113; police professionalization and, 121; as racialized social control, 3, 49; and riot-control training,

carceral state *(continued)*
166; transnationalism of, 257–58; and the War on Crime, 119; and welfare programs, 125
Carter, Harlon, 264
Carter, Jimmy, 224
Castro, Fidel, 96
Cater, S. Douglass, 124, 312n22
Césaire, Aimé, 43, 294n58
Chad, 32
The Challenge of Crime in a Free Society (PCLEAJ report), 174
Chemical Mace, 203, 328n46
Chemical Warfare Convention, 213
chemical weapons: Army's use of, 209; and China, 200; countries recommended as targets of, 209; defoliants, 112, 198, 205, 251; Elbridge Colby on, 46; and the Geneva Protocol, 200; in guerrilla warfare, 198; indiscriminate use of, 209; LBJ justifying, 195; and Nixon, 213; as riot-control agents, 198–200; in South Vietnam, 112, 151, 195, 198, 205; and the Soviet Union, 200; US's no-first-use policy, 213; in the Vietnam War, 198. *See also* CN tear gas; CS tear gas; tear gas
Chicago police force, 70, 224, 230
Chicago rebellion, 177
Chile, 184
China, 35, 74, 97, 106, 200, 261
Church, Frank, 156
CIA (Central Intelligence Agency): and the 1290d program, 85; AID vs., 109; vs. Black political radicals, 169; and counterinsurgency goals, 13; covert infiltration tactics of, 13; Cuban failure of, 96; vs. direct colonial rule, 80; and the Dominican Republic, 58, 227, 229–30, 335n70; Eisenhower guided by, 11; Engle in, 60–62; vs. the FBI, 18; foreign police trained in US by, 18; and the global color line, 31–32; in Guatemala, 163–64; guerrilla warfare advocated by, 100; Hoover's resentment of, 64; in Indochina, 100; International Police Services as front for, 185; and the IPA, 186; Jelsch in, 61–62; and Komer, 88, 94, 96, 291n17; mercenaries hired by, 165; and

nationalism, 95–96; and OISP, 109; and police assistance, 163, 269; and public safety advisors, 133; radical groups under surveillance by, 240–41; security threats in foreign countries investigated by, 110; and South Vietnam, 77; Truman as creator of, 18, 64; US police advisors sent abroad by, 18; and US world leadership, 95; William Colby as director of, 295n65
Cincinnati, Ohio, 3, 184
Civil Disturbances and Disasters (Army riot-control manual), 176
civil disturbance training program (US Army), 178
civil rights: activism, 214; of Black people, 118; civil rights actions and the police, 214; civil rights leaders, 181; civil rights movement, 4; and the Cold War, 28, 290n4; Commission on Civil Rights (US), 125; foreign support for, 28; Hoover's failure to pursue violations of, 118; and the LAPD, 216; legislation enabling, 271; and Sagalyn, 114; Southern police crackdowns on, 8; white backlash against, 4, 120, 284n11
Civil Rights Act, 11, 43, 120, 122, 137, 139, 216, 312n22
Clinton, Bill, 215
CN/DM lachrymator/emetic agent, 199, 201–2, 327n23
CN tear gas, 195, 199, 205–6, 206 *fig. 12*, 208, 229, 327n23, 328n46
Coalition Against Police Exploiters of Repression (CAPER), 270
Coast Guard Training Center (US), 185
Coates, Joseph, 196, 205
Cohn, Roy, 231
Colby, Elbridge, 46–47, 49, 295n65
Colby, William, 46, 90–91, 101, 145, 161, 295n65
Cold War: and civil rights, 28, 290n4; and counterinsurgency, 14, 38, 45–51, 52; and decolonization, 31–32, 35, 38, 271; disappearance as tactic in, 155; interpretations of, 286n21; justifying police power in US, 5; and national security, 10; and the national security state, 10;

nostalgia for, 259; and NSC 68, 89, 306n52; Parker's views of, 219; police assistance programs of, 49, 54, 163; and racialization, 41; and riot control, 167; and the Soviet Union, 91, 286n21; terminology for, 286n21; and US imperial governance, 5

Colombia, 31, 104, 110, 159, 230, 324n68

colonialism, 3–4, 19–20, 30–31, 43, 49, 80, 245, 272, 282–83n5. *See also* neo-colonialism

Commission on Civil Rights (US), 125, 312n25

Committee on Police Assistance Programs (U. Alexis Johnson), 110, 129

communism: Black people accused of, 59; and centralization of police forces, 123; communist-led instability, 79; CORDS vs., 97; counterinsurgency vs., 82; crime equated with, 10, 113–14; and *First Line of Defense*, 79; IACP vs., 134; in Indonesia, 18; in Los Angeles, 229; and modernization, 82; and national security, 10; OPS vs., 97; penal/police apparatus justified by, 6; police assistance vs., 50; political sovereignties vs., 12; and public safety advisors overseas, 148; Reed on, 59; SGCI vs., 97; shifting tactics of, 88; in Southeast Asia, 113; sympathizers with, banned from police service by Vollmer, 66; Templer's views on combating, 245; vs. repression in US-backed regimes, 166; War on Crime vs., 8. *See also* Khrushchev, Nikita; Soviet Union

communist revolution, 5, 6, 74, 96–97

communist subversion: and crime, 115; Engle's reports on, 37, 109, 160; FBI vs., 131–32; first lines of defense against, 81, 107; Hoover on, 182; JFK vs., 11; Kerner Commission vs., 207; LBJ vs., 122; police assistance overseas vs., 51, 72, 88, 110; police work vs., 8

Community Relations Service (DOJ), 180, 189, 209, 312n22

compulsive comparativism, 9, 12, 42, 212–13, 240

Congo/Zaire, 32–33, 42, 95, 97, 324n68

Congress of Racial Equality, 28

conservatives and conservativism: and block grants, 139–40, 315n77; and the carceral state, 4; and crime as revolutionary activity, 241; vs. demands of freedom and justice, 258; and federalism, 120, 140, 172, 315n77; and law-and-order policies, 236–37; and the omnibus bill, 139; and order-maintenance policing, 236; and police reform as a necessity, 167; and sociological conditions underlying unrest, 235–36; vs. the War on Poverty, 140; vs. welfare programs, 170, 240, 252–53, 258

Con Son Island (prison), 269

Contras (Nicaraguan paramilitary force), 231

CORDS (Civil Operations and Revolutionary Support), 90, 97, 111–12

Corson, Ben, 327n21

Costa-Gavras (film director), 260

Costa Rica, 109

cost-benefit counterinsurgency, 24, 47–48, 242, 248–49, 253, 257

Côte d'Ivoire, 32

counterinsurgency: overview, 79–112; and African American politics, 239; as American governance, 48; archival research on, 15; behavior-control tactics of, 157–60; vs. Black radicals, 3, 232; centralized command lacking for, 85; characteristics of, 3, 14, 195; as civic action, 87; and coercion, 248, 251; and crime control, 237–42; development of, 19–20; domestication of, 7, 9, 23, 25, 45, 51, 74, 113, 118, 121, 125, 143, 238; economic aid as component of, 244, 246; as economy of force, 47–48; of Engle, 7–9, 72; food deprivation as weapon in, 251–52; foreign/domestic divide obliterated by, 9, 195, 212, 258; French counterinsurgency theory, 239, 295n67; global reach of, 106–7, 143, 258; goals of, debated, 13; hearts and minds theory of, 245; insurgency preceded by, 258; international legal limits of, 46; JFK's advocacy of, 198; literature on, 288n26; and military assistance, 87, 100; and order-maintenance policing, 237, 242; overseas,

counterinsurgency *(continued)*
applied in the US, 7, 9, 23, 25, 45, 51, 74, 113, 176; in the Philippines, 19; *The Police and Resources Control in Counter-Insurgency,* 158; and police assistance, 14, 22, 84–85, 96, 107; as police project, 14, 108–11, 268; and police reform, 19; and political participation, 161–62; popular support as central to, 245–46, 249; preemptive, 13–14, 91, 110, 212; by proxy, 50, 252; and race-making, 45; racial idioms of, 44–45; research studies on, 237–39, 243; RFK's commitment to, 13; "The Role of the Police in Counter-Insurgency," 239; security imperatives of, 45, 46; and social regulation, 157–60; socioeconomic causes of unrest downplayed by, 242; and the status quo, 82; Taylor on, 107; terminology of, 13–14; in Third World countries, 9; unforeseen effects of, 84; veterans of, recruited into state police, 74; and Vollmer in the Philippines, 67; and the Watts rebellion, 166. *See also* China; Cold War; cost-benefit counterinsurgency; crime control; Cuba; *headings under police professionalization;* insurgency; modernization; OPS; Philippines; police-led counterinsurgency; SGCI; social control/regulation; South Vietnam; Venezuela; War on Crime
counterinsurgent knowledge: and anticolonialism, 42; across borders, 213; comparative compulsion in, 212, 328n41; defined, 15; as domestic policing, 194; export of, 45; foreign/domestic divide reduced by, 212; and Gates, 214, 222, 225; Giap's affirmation of, 271; in prison administration, 143; Wolf and Leites's contributions to, 243, 253
counter-revolution overview, 235–58
covert operations, 11, 13–14, 18, 84–85, 105, 110, 129
CRA. *See* Civil Rights Act
Crime Commission (PCLEAJ), 127, 151–52, 174, 196, 226
crime control, 216, 233, 235–42, 253, 263. *See also* Omnibus Crime Control and Safe Streets Act

crime rates, 8, 137, 150, 237, 314n65
Crisostomo, Desiderio L. (Dey), 150
Critchfield, Robert, 239
CR lachrymatory agent, 199, 327n34
Cross, James Eliot, 102, 240
Cryer, George, 216–17
CS tear gas: advertised, 206, 206 *fig. 12;* the Army's use of, 197–98, 202, 208; in Attica Prison uprising, 208; in Baltimore, 209; behavior control by, 253; Black women exposed to, 209; British colonial forces' use of, 199; in Chemical Mace, 328n46; and China, 200; civilian law enforcement's use of, 212, 253, 327n23; and CN, 195, 202–3, 205; CS-1/CS-2 variants, 205; delivery systems of, 203; domestic use of, 195, 197–98, 207–11; effects of, 194, 199, 203, 205–6, 206 *fig. 12;* Engle's advocacy of, 194; excluded from chemical weapons ban, 213; expanding uses of, 210–12; fatalities resulting from, 210; foreign/domestic divide reduced by use of, 195, 211–12; and the Geneva Protocol, 200; and the IACP, 197; indiscriminate use of, 208; inventors of, 327n21; Kerner Commission as conduit of, 195–98; and LBJ, 195, 200–204; as a military weapon, 212; naming of, 327n21; National Guard's use of, 198, 202; open market sales of, prohibited, 202–3; OPS early recommendations against, 199, 203; physical substance of, 199; police gunfire reduced by use of, 208; preemptive use of, 194; public responses to, 200–204; as a riot-control agent, 202, 208; Sagalyn's advocacy of, 224; in South Vietnam, 23, 200–208, 210–11, 222; and the Soviet Union, 200; on UC Berkeley campus, 208; in urban unrest, 198
CSTI (California Specialized Training Institute), 23, 187–90
Cuba, 35, 68, 74, 96, 151. *See also* Bay of Pigs invasion
Cuban missile crisis, 104, 111–12
Cyprus, 199

D'Aubuisson, Roberto, 231, 335n77
DEA (Drug Enforcement Administration), 261–62, 341n17

Dearborn, Henry, 227
death squads, 156–57, 231
Debray, Régis, 251
decolonization, 5, 11, 22, 31, 38, 50, 191, 271
Deitchman, Seymour, 169, 196–97, 209
Democrats and the Democratic Party:
crime-fighting federalist legislation of,
137–40, 215; and Engle, 264–65; on
federal funding of local police forces,
140; and flexible response, 89; and
foreign aid, 87, 161; and Komer, 92, 95;
and military assistance, 86; and Pendergast, 63–64; and racial integration of
police forces, 140; Sagalyn's loyalty to,
127; Southern Democrats' racist policies, 241; Southern Democrats vs.
federalism, 138–40; in St. Louis, 63; and
Truman, 56, 71; urban municipalities
led by, 140; War on Crime created by,
140–41
denazification, 65, 127
Department of Defense. See DOD;
Pentagon
deterritorialized state-building, 2, 17–18,
52, 77–78, 235, 265
Detroit: Army riot control restraint in,
179–80; command chaos in, 180; CS
tear gas used in, 198; Giap on, 271;
National Guard in, 179; rebellion in, 3,
27, 43, 166, 173, 176, 332n34; riot-control
in, 210; STRESS program in, 221; tear
gas used in, 210; Vance restoring order
in, 174
Dewey, Thomas, 64
Diem, Ngo Dinh. See Ngo Dinh Diem
Directorate for Civil Disturbance Planning
and Operations (US Army), 171
disappearance of political opponents, 14,
143, 155–57, 186, 318n50
discretionary employment of police power:
and behavior control, 236; and broken-
windows police power, 236, 256; and
cost-benefit counterinsurgency, 257;
despotism of, 48, 257; at intrastate level,
10; as kill, jail, control, 46; and the
LEAA, 141; of minor offenses, 255; in
order-maintenance policing, 257; police
autonomy leading to, 66; police profes-

sionalization advancing, 155; and police
self-understanding, 17; and racism, 34,
41, 257; as repression, 270; responsibility
in, 11; in shooting, 57; standardization
of, 146–55; in Third World countries,
41; and US discretionary empire, 24,
34; violence in, 143; worldwide, 264
DOD (Department of Defense), 6, 198, 237,
242–43
DOJ (Department of Justice): civil unrest
discussion meetings organized by, 174;
and crowd control, 6; and CS tear gas,
207–8; Kerner Commission's nonle-
thal-weapons recommendations
accepted by, 207–8; Levine's report to,
on police violence, 180; narcotics control mission of, 261; OPS as example for,
113; riot-control assistance provided by,
239; and Sagalyn, 113; SEADOC
reviewed by, 180; and Turner, 177;
Vance's ideas on riot control conveyed
to, 174. See also Community Relations
Service
Dominican Republic, 58, 154, 156–57, 174,
227–30, 335n70
Donovan, William, 142
Dorsey, George, 28
Do Van Gioi, 148
Dragnet (TV police series), 217, 225
Draper, William H., 87, 104, 243
Draper Committee, 86–88, 90, 98, 102
Drug Enforcement Administration (DEA),
261–62, 341n17
Du Bois, W. E. B., 28–30, 34
Dudziak, Mary L., 290n4
Dulles, Allen, 81, 303n3
Dulles, John Foster, 55
Dutch empire, 146

Eastland, James O., 87, 173
Echols, Lee, 142, 229
Echols, O. P., 68
Economic Opportunity Act (EOA), 117,
120, 161
economy of force, 45–48, 295n65
Eisenhower, Dwight D.: atomic weapons
deterrence policies of, 89; and the Bay
of Pigs invasion, 96; and chemical

Eisenhower, Dwight D. *(continued)*
weapons, 204; and the Draper Committee, 86–87; federal assistance program of, 125; geopolitical power strategies of, 11; hierarchical management approach of, 91; and the ICA, 85; Japanese protests against, 87; and militarized responses to civic unrest, 169; Military Assistance Program of, 86; and the NSC, 86; and OISP, 99; Taylor vs., 89

Eisenstein, Sergei, 259

Ellingwood, Herbert E., 324n75

Ellsberg, Daniel, 249

El Salvador, 148, 231

Emerson, Gloria, 241

empire (US). *See* US empire

England. *See* British counterinsurgency activities

Engle, Byron: overview, 52–78; anticommunism of, 68; chemical munitions advocated by, 5, 196–97; as CIA representative, 85; CORDS police assistance advocated by, 111; counterinsurgency policies and programs of, 7, 9, 72; crime prevention goals of, 80; and domestic police apparatus, 166–67; and the Dominican Republic, 229; family of, 296–97n7; as father of foreign police assistance, 53; as firearms expert, 56, 263; flexible-response policies of, 194; foreign police capabilities assessed by, 77, 109, 129, 154, 302n107; global police reform by, 80; and global supremacy in law enforcement, 128; and Hall, 65; and the IACP, 37, 134; influence of, 5; as intelligence gathering advocate, 100; international police trainee statistics cited by, 181; and Interpol, 128; in the IPG, 128–29; in Japan, 60–62, 65, 68–69, 72–73; and the Kerner Commission, 196–97, 213; LBJ's empowerment of, 169; and MacArthur, 60; methodologies of, 68–69; and the NRA, 264; OPS impact on police officers estimated by, 181; and overseas police apparatus, 5–6, 69, 112, 166, 196–97; and Pendergast, 264; personal profile of, 54–62, 296–97n7; photo of, 38 *fig. 2*, 55 *fig. 3*; vs.

police centralization, 73, 77; and police professionalization, 71, 166, 225, 255; on police/public relations, 225; police reform measures of, 115, 127; as police technical assistance advocate, 53; political party affiliations of, 264–65; and preemptive counterinsurgency, 91; racial views of, 36, 44; as recruiter, 58; in Rhodesia, 261; as riot-control specialist, 60, 196–97; social regulation theories of, 68–69; subordinates of, 80; tear gas advocated by, 5, 192–94; technical subcommittee of, 131; torture accusations against, 61; on traffic control as crowd control, 160; and Truman, 265; in Turkey, 61–62, 128, 261; and U. Alexis Johnson, 109; and US global law-enforcement supremacy, 129; and Walton, 76. *See also* CS tear gas; Dominican Republic; federalism; Hall, Theo E.; Harlem; *headings under police professionalization;* Hoover, J. Edgar; IACP; IAPA; Johnson, Lyndon B.; Kansas City, Missouri; Komer, Robert W.; modernization of police forces; MSU; OPS; Reed, Lear B.; Sagalyn, Arnold; SCAP; SCGI; South Vietnam; Turner, Ralph F.

EOA (Economic Opportunity Act), 117, 120, 161

Epton, Bill, 116, 272

Evans, Courtney, 129, 132, 137

The Exorcist (Friedkin film), 259

extraterritorial state-formation, 265

Fall, Bernard, 93–94

FBI (Federal Bureau of Investigation): vs. Black political radicals, 169; CIA vs., 18; and CSTI, 189; in the Dominican Republic, 229; General Intelligence Division of, 65; informants of, vs. radical groups, 211; and the IPG, 131–32; and Latin America, 18; local police chiefs vs., 136; National Academy of, 60, 132, 172, 178, 186, 190; and OPS, 131, 132–33; and Pendergast, 64; *Prevention and Control of Mobs and Riots,* 173; public safety advisors in, 133; radical groups infiltrated by, 182; radical groups under surveillance by, 240–41; and riot-control training, 167, 172–73, 239; SWAT teams trained by, 224; vs. Treasury law-enforcement agencies, 133; and the VBI of South Vietnam, 77

federalism: and Black civil rights, 118; vs. Black communities, 72, 118–20; Black people taking advantage of, 311n5; and the CSTI, 187; devolution as, 120, 141, 167, 189, 235; and Engle, 121, 123; fiscally conservative federalism, 172; Hoover vs., 118; and the IACP, 122, 133–34, 175; and Komer, 121; in law enforcement, 117–22, 131–34; New Federalism, 141; and Nixon, 315n77; and OPS, 121; and police assistance, 121; police embodiment of, 123; police executives acceptance of, 9–10; and political battles for law-enforcement, 141; and the Republican Coordinating Committee, 315n77; social groups disempowered by, 121; in Southern states, 119; states' rights vs., 119; vs. the War on Poverty, 120; training of trainers funding under, 187; and urban unrest, 167; and the War on Crime, 49, 117–20, 141

Federal Laboratories, Inc., 192, 202
felony records, 2
figure-ground movement, 1–2
Finletter, Thomas K., 94
first line of defense: applicability of, expanding, 81; and CIA, 80, 158; and coercion, 158; first responders, 151; functionalism of, 81–84; at grassroots level, 219; and Hoover, 80; and JFK, 79; and the Johnson administration, 79; and Komer, 84, 88, 105, 107; and law enforcement on a global scale, 129; and LBJ administration, 79; local police as, 79, 118, 139–40; and OIDP, 105; police power as, 81, 105, 107, 269; public safety programs as, 142; against subversion, 79; in Third World countries, 79

First Line of Defense (OPS training film), 79
Fishel, Wesley, 74–75

Flamm, Michael, 170, 293n41
flexible-response policies, 14, 86–90, 194, 219, 244, 306n52
Ford, Gerald, 140, 213
Fordism, 143, 146, 244, 255, 268–69
Foreign Assistance Act, 161–64, 260, 320n70. *See also* Title IX
Fort Gordon, Georgia, 177, 185
Fort Leavenworth, Kansas, 65
Foucault, Michel, 43
France: chemical weapons used by, 201; CIA as advisor to, 100; counterinsurgency theory of, 239; extralegal police power used by, 46; imperial inheritance from, 77; as imperial power, 11; and OPS, 310n123; order restoration by, post-WWII, 47; pacification efforts of, 46; police techniques in, 108; public safety advisors in former colonies of, 146; Syria bombed by, 46; and Vietnam, 47, 75
freedom/justice demands and movements: by Black people in US, 11, 28, 115–16, 238; and crowd control in South Vietnam, 160; defined as lawlessness, 115; in Harlem, 115–16, 168; police power resisting, 143; tear gas used against, 192; transnationalism of, 51
Friedman, Milton, 243
Fulbright, J. William, 87

García-Godoy, Héctor, 229
Garden Plot civil-disturbance plan, 176
Gates, Daryl: vs. Black rebellions against police abuse, 221; as consultant, 223; and counterinsurgent knowledge, 214, 222, 225; and Iran hostage crisis, 224; and the Kerner Commission, 223; and the LEAA, 233; militarization of police advocated by, 214; military manuals recommended by, 222; and Nixon, 233; and Parker, 217, 232; on riot control, 175, 222–23; scandals involving, 216; and SWAT's origins, 214, 221; unorthodox methods of, 215; and the Watts rebellion, 214, 221, 223, 232
Gathoni, Gladys Philip, 38
Geneva Protocol (1925), 200, 213

Georgetown (Washington, DC), 36, 259–60
Georgetown University, 183, 185
Germany, 65–66, 68–71, 73–74, 77, 217, 310n123
Giap, Vo Nguyen. *See* Vo Nguyen Giap
Gilligan, Thomas, 115, 168
Gilmore, Ruth Wilson, 40
Giuffrida, Louis O., 186–89, 191, 324n75
Goin, Lauren, 20, 260, 317n30
Goldwater, Barry, 140, 169
Gray Areas, 94, 97, 111–12, 242, 306n52
Great Britain/the British. *See* British counterinsurgency activities
Great Society (LBJ social programs), 43, 97, 120, 124, 170
Gross, H. R., 37
Guatemala: AID in, 150, 163; Armas assassinated in, 163; the CIA in, 163–64; disappearance originating in, 155; Operación Limpieza in, 156, 163; police assistance to, 155–56, 230; Rocker in, 181; SGCI threat assessment of, 110; surveillance and repression in, 186; trust-building in, 150
guerrilla warfare: banditry in, 240; and Bissell, 98–99, 102–3; Bundy as advocate of, 100; chemical weapons used in, 198; CIA advocacy of, 100; in the Civil War, 19; counterguerrilla warfare, 19, 47, 85, 89, 104; and counterinsurgency, 84; failure of, 101; foreign/domestic divide crossed by, 243; guerrillas used in, 100, 102, 222, 223, 307n71; and JFK, 89, 100, 244; Komer on, 99; in Latin America, 143; local support as essential to, 100, 245, 251; Maoist conceptions of, 74, 91, 101, 111, 245–46, 251; military approaches to, 103; and narcotics control, 262; in *The Police and Resources Control in Counter-Insurgency,* 158; police assistance vs., 111; research studies on, 239; and social regulation, 158; in South Vietnam, 158–59; and SWAT, 233; urban guerrilla warfare, 239, 243; in the US, 176, 243; US forces in, 84; US vs. Soviet, 84
Guevara, Che, 222, 251

Guevara, Hector J., 227–28, 230
Gulf of Tonkin incident, 100

Haiti, 18, 50
Hall, Theo E.: and Engle, 68, 71; minority hiring advocated by, 29; and O. W. Wilson, 69–70; as police modernizer, 71; as police reformer, 127; and preemptive counterinsurgency, 91; on race management abroad, 29; on riots, 27, 29; unrest report issued by, 65; as US police assistance overseer, 142; and Weckler, 65; and Wilson, 66, 70, 340n75; and women public safety advisors, 38. *See also* "The Police and Minority Groups"
Hamilton, Fowler, 107
Hannah, John, 312n25, 341n17
Harlem, 112–13, 115–17, 166–68, 198
Harlem rebellion: and the Civil Rights Act, 312n22; counterinsurgency predictions following, 238; and Epton, 117, 272; equated with US actions in South Vietnam, 272; insurgency predictions following, 238; and law and order, 122; and LBJ, 169–70, 190; NLF's response to, 272; police gunfire in, 168, 320n3; police reform stimulated by, 190–91; police violence in, 168–70; severity of, 123
Harriman, Averell, 106
Hart, Philip, 312n25
Hayes, Chris, 272–73
hearts and minds theory, 245, 249–54
Herrmann, William W., 226–27, 231
Hilsman, Roger, 13, 91–92, 100–101
Hitler, Adolf, 69
Holcomb, Richard L., 70
Honduras, 151
Hong Kong police, 199
Hoover, J. Edgar: vs. Anslinger, 133; anti-communism of, 217; and the Army, 176; Carl Turner vs., 177; vs. centralized police authority, 123; changes affecting, 131; and the CIA, 64; civil rights violations ignored by, 118; defectors from, 171; and the Dominican Republic, 229; and Engle, 60, 133; vs. Evans, 137; vs. federal police force, 131; and the Harlem

rebellion, 170; and the IACP, 134; and LBJ, 170, 173; local police autonomy supported by, 170; *Masters of Deceit*, 182; vs. national police system, 133; and organized crime, 118, 217; vs. Parker, 217; and police causing urban unrest, 194; and police reform, 62; and Reed, 58, 60; and RFK, 132–33; and riot-control training, 172–73; and Sagalyn, 133; states' rights advocated by, 118; on subversives in urban unrest, 122; and Tamm, 135, 171, 173–75; vs. the Law Enforcement Assistance Act, 137; War on Crime vs., 268

Hoyt, Howard W., 65–66, 70–71, 75, 91, 127

Hudson Institute, 241, 250

Human Wolves (Reed), 59

Huntington, Samuel, 250

Huynh Van Tam, 272

IACP (International Association of Chiefs of Police): Africans warned against southern travel by, 37; AID's termination of contract with, 134–36, 175; as anticommunist, 134; and block grants, 140; civil-disorder guidelines issued by, 224; on CS tear gas, 197; and Engle, 134; federal intervention in urban unrest advocated by, 124; and federalism, 122, 133, 175; foreign officers trained by, 19; and Gates, 223–24; and Hoover, 134; and the ICA, 134; and interagency friction, 175; local police chiefs vs., 136; mission of, 134; and MSU, 135; and OISP, 109; omnibus crime bill supported by, 175; origins of, 299n46; and Pentagon military gear, 136; "The Police and Minority Groups" distributed by, 28; and *The Police Chief*, 5, 134, 173, 175, 197; and police professionalization, 135; politicization of, 114, 134–36; Professional Standards Division of, 197; public safety advisors in, 134; racial disturbance preparedness survey, 133–34; and riot control, 167, 171–72, 174–75, 223; Sagalyn as advisor to, 223; and St. Louis, 63, 299n46; Tamm as director of, 9,

134–35, 171–74, 299n46; training of foreign men of color, 36–37; Vollmer as president of, 67; vs. 911 system, 151; and the War on Crime, 10, 135

IAPA (Inter-American Police Academy), 13, 19, 36–37, 108, 229

ICA (International Cooperation Administration), 19, 55, 62, 70, 85, 134

Immigration and Nationality Act, 182–83

imperialism (US). *See* US empire

incarceration, 2–5, 114, 314n65, 331n2

India, 7 *map*, 94, 113, 226

Indian Wars (US), 19, 49, 253

indigenous security forces, 45, 77, 84–85, 88, 98–100, 105, 158, 231

Indonesia, 18, 85, 96, 243

INR (Bureau of Intelligence and Research) (State Department), 83, 100

Institute for Defense Analyses, 173, 196, 205–6, 226

Institute for Policy Studies, 3

insurgency: anticolonial insurgency, 30; Black political insurgency, 113; communist insurgency, 41, 100; counterrevolution developing transnationally in advance of, 258; crime equated with, 51, 237–42; and JFK, 10–11; in Nicaragua, 68; in the Philippines, 68; racialization of, 239; RAND studies of, 242; Rostow on, 102; in rural South Vietnam, 75, 77, 91, 251; as threat to LBJ, 117; Wolf on, 246–48. *See also* counterinsurgency; Wolf, Charles, Jr.

"Insurgency and Counterinsurgency" (Wolf), 245

Insurgency Critical. *See* SGCI

integration, 49, 119, 139

intelligence gathering: across borders, 138, 151; and colonial intelligence databanks, 19; computer-based, 226; and Interpol, 128; in IPA training, 182; and the IPG, 130; and Jerry Jelsch Engle, 62; by Komer, 91, 94, 291n17; by the LAPD, 214–15, 217, 230–31; in Latin America, by FBI, 18; LEAA funding of, 227; Leites and Wolf on, 246–49; by local police forces, 100, 145–50, 186, 226, 241–42; methodological nationalism in,

intelligence gathering *(continued)*
95; in national security state, 14; by
OPS, 151; by Philco-Ford, 147; *The
Police Chief*'s advocacy of, 175; as police
power, 215; by police vs. military forces,
100; in police work, 186; by SCAP, 72;
in SEADOC training, 178, 180; in
South Vietnam, 160; by the State
Department, 83, 100; on subversives, 72;
by torture, 66. *See also* CIA
Interagency Police Group (IPG), 129–32,
196
Inter-American Police Academy. *See* IAPA
"Internal Warfare and the Security of the
Underdeveloped States" (INR), 100
International Association of Chiefs of
Police. *See* IACP
International Criminal Police Organiza-
tion. *See* Interpol
internationalism, 44, 149, 271, 282–83n5
International Police Academy. *See* IPA
International Police Services (Inpolse), 185
Interpol (International Criminal Police
Organization), 128–30, 133–34, 185
IPA (International Police Academy):
Africans trained in, 292n34; and the
CIA, 186; closure of, 260; and CSTI,
189; and D'Aubuisson, 231; doctrines
taught in, 17 *fig. 1,* 17–18; and the FBI,
133, 185; foreign graduates of, 186,
324n73; in Georgetown, 36–37, 56–57,
259–60, 265; *International Police Acad-
emy Review,* 149, 157, 260, 317n30; and
MSU, 300n70; protests against, 269;
RFK's commitment to, 13; riot-control
training by, 182–86; Sagalyn addressing,
130 *fig. 7;* seminar at, 185 *fig. 10;* and
torture, 186; trainees' statistics in, 181;
training of, replicated, 182; Tupamaros
infiltration of, 149
Iran, 11, 109, 166, 184, 224
Iraq, 7 *map,* 66, 71, 143, 288n26, 324n73
Israel, 101, 310n123
Italy, 69, 108, 250

Janowitz, Morris, 185
Japan: Burma invaded by, 100; chemical
weapons recommended for use in, 209;

Engle developing police forces of,
60–61, 68–69, 72, 77–78; Engle's view
of Japanese people, 44; federalized
policing model in, 73; and Germany, 77;
nationalism in, 73; and the New Left,
87; police assistance program developed
in, 18, 73; police forces decentralized in,
73; as a police state, 73; political protests
in, 87; Public Safety Division in, 18, 68,
72–73; SCAP's reforms in, 89; US at
war with, 13; US empire's western flank
secured by, 71–72; US occupation of, 18,
68, 72; and US policing model, 71–72;
Valentine in, 74; and white superiority,
31
Jelsch Engle, Geraldine L. "Jerry," 55,
60–62, 85, 296–97n7
Jenkins, Brian M., 243
JFK. *See* Kennedy, John F.
Jickling, David, 150
Jim Crow racism, 34, 58
Johnson, Lyndon B. (LBJ): anticrime
programs privileged over welfare, 127;
and Army riot-control training, 176;
and Black urban unrest, 169; block
grants vs. grants-in-aid by, 140; chemical weapons justified by, 195; and counterinsurgent police assistance programs,
96; CS tear gas approved by, 194, 200–
204, 207; Detroit riot's impact on, 43;
in the Dominican Republic, 228–29;
and Engle, 8, 109, 169; federal and local
priorities balanced by, 169; and the
Federal Law Enforcement Training
Center, 182; federal/local priorities
balanced by, 119; and the first line of
defense, 79; foreign assistance under the
control of, 111; Goldwater's political
challenge to, 169; and the Harlem
rebellion, 169–70, 190; and hearts and
minds, 245; and Hoover, 170, 173; and
the Kerner commission, 4, 43; and
Komer, 98, 112; law enforcement officials' influence on, 8; and the LEAA,
113, 139; local police autonomy supported by, 118, 123, 139, 170; vs. military
response to urban unrest, 169; other war
in Vietnam of, 96–98, 104, 144–45,

160–63; overseas and domestic problems of, 117; PCLEAJ created by, 127; photo of, 93 *fig. 6;* on police violence, 169–70; riot-control gas information demanded by, 200, 327n34; and Rostow, 42–43; tear gas advocated by, 195; TV address of July 1967, 43; unrest, on subversives in urban, 122; war on poverty in South Vietnam, 97. *See also* Crime Commission (PCLEAJ); Economy Opportunity Act; Engle, Byron; Foreign Assistance Act; Great Society; Komer, Robert W.; War on Crime; War on Poverty

Johnson, U. Alexis, 83, 90, 106, 108–10

Jones, Adrian, 237

justice demands. *See* freedom/justice demands and movements

Kansas City, Missouri (KC), 52, 56, 64–65, 67, 71–72, 78, 222, 264

Kansas City police department, 34, 52–54, 55 *fig. 3,* 58–60, 65–67, 72, 78, 264, 299n47, 340n75

Kelling, George L., 236, 256, 257

Kelly, Ray, 216

Kennedy, John F. (JFK): and the Bay of Pigs invasion, 96; and chemical weapons, 198; and civilian foreign aid, 244; vs. communist subversion, 11; and counterinsurgency, 13; economic-development foreign policy of, 86; and the first line of defense, 79; flexible response policies of, 89; Foreign Service counterinsurgency training instituted by, 239; and guerrilla warfare, 222, 244; and Hilsman, 100; vs. insurgency, 10–11; and the IPG, 129; and the juvenile delinquency, 125, 137; and Komer, 88, 91, 98, 107–8; and militarized responses to civic unrest, 169; and military assistance, 86; Military Assistance Program reevaluated by, 101–2; military power in South Vietnam expanded by, 47; and modernization, 81; New Frontier program of, 11, 88; NSAMs issued by, 89, 107–8; NSC reorganized by, 303n2; and overseas police assistance, 14, 103; and

Sagalyn, 128; security as priority for, 90; and the SGCI, 107; strategic air defense downplayed by, 243; and Taylor, 86; and Vietnam, 13; Vietnamese struggle vs. France supported by, 47; Wohlstetter as advisor to, 243

Kennedy, Robert F. (RFK): assassination of, 137; counterinsurgency supported by, 13; and the FBI, 132–33; and Hilsman, 100; and Hoover, 132–33; and Komer, 90, 91; and OPS, 310n124; and overseas police assistance, 14; and Parker, 227; and Rostow, 132; and the SGCI, 106–7, 111, 131–32

Kennelly, Edward, 133

Kerik, Bernard, 216

Kerner Commission (NACCD): vs. communist subversion reports, 207; creation of, 4, 43; and CS tear gas, 195–98, 206; DOJ adopting recommendations of, 6; Engle's ideas adopted by, 6, 213; federal domestic spending urged by, 4; Gates as advisor to, 223; and LBJ, 4; LBJ's creation of, 43; vs. lethal riot-control weaponry, 197; Longan as advisor to, 156; nonlethal weapons advocated by, 195–97; on non-violent crowd control, 212; and OPS, 6, 189; and the PCLEAJ report, 174; on police killings of Black protesters, 197; vs. police overreaction, 212; vs. racism, 4; racism as concern of, 192, 195–96; on riot-control methods, 197, 213; and riot-control training, 173–75, 189; rioter/bystander distinctions made by, 207; and Sagalyn, 8, 130, 173–74, 196, 224, 237; Vance's ideas on riot control conveyed to, 174; and the War on Crime, 4, 286n21

Keynesianism, 10–11, 264, 268n21

Khrushchev, Nikita, 11, 83, 287n22

Kill or Get Killed (Applegate), 147

Kimberling, Arthur, 60

King, Martin Luther, Jr., 176, 208, 269

Komer, Robert W.: as ambassador to Turkey, 111–12; and the CIA, 32, 80, 88, 91, 94–95, 291n17; CORDS overseen by, 97, 112; and counterinsurgency's global reach, 106–7; and counterinsurgent

Komer, Robert W. *(continued)*
police assistance programs, 96; and the
Draper Committee, 98; and Engle, 13,
78, 80, 88, 89, 94, 108, 128; fall of, 92;
Focus concept of, 94–95, 106–7; global
fundamentals of, 88–96; vs. guerrilla
warfare, 99, 222; on indigenous forces,
105; intelligence gathering by, 91, 100,
291n17; and JFK, 88, 91, 98, 107–8; and
LBJ, 93 *fig. 6*, 96, 98, 112; Middle East
mandate of, 98; vs. militarization, 99,
102, 111–12, 145; and the Military Assistance Program, 101–2; in military intelligence, 94; modernization of police
forces by, 85, 92; nationalism as focus of,
89; and the national security state,
89–90; on the NSC, 96; as OPS overseer, 80, 89–90, 111, 310n124; and pacification czar, 97, 98; personal profile of,
91–94; and Phoenix, 295n65; photo of,
93 *fig. 6;* and police assistance, 52, 84,
109, 117; and preemptive counterinsurgency, 91; and Rostow, 84, 99, 102,
306n60; in SCGI meetings, 104; South
Asian mandate of, 98; and Taylor,
102–3; and U. Alexis Johnson, 108, 110;
US-centered world as objective of, 90;
and US war in Vietnam War, 92, 112;
and Vance, 174. *See also* CIA; first line
of defense; national security state;
OIDP; OISP; RAND Corporation;
SGCI; South Vietnam
Korea, 66, 74, 166, 238, 302n106
Krogh, Egil, 262, 341n17
Krulak, Victor, 90–91, 100
Ku Klux Klan, 169

La Banda death squad, 156–57
Lansdale, Edward G., 87, 90–91, 100, 161,
239, 243
Laos, 77, 85, 95, 104, 113, 154, 207, 226,
302n107
LAPD. *See* Los Angeles Police Department
Latin America: chemical weapons recommended for use in, 209; disappearances
in, 143–44; and the FBI, 18; IPA trainees from, 183; LAPD techniques in, 231;
LBJ's counterinsurgency efforts in, 229;

Longan in, 155–56, 251; military assistance to, 101–2; nationalist revolution in,
95; Nixon in, 86–87, 112; North American Congress on Latin America, 3, 262,
269; police assistance in, 143; police
training in, 36; Simulmatics Corporation's analyses of insurgencies in, 237;
unrest in, 86; US military in, 229; US
police power in, 30
Latinos and Latino populations, 2, 36. *See
also* Mexican Americans
law and order: bipartisan support for, 113; vs.
Black political insurgency, 113; and the
carceral state, 18; and compulsive comparativism, 213; conservative advocacy of,
236–37; in cost-benefit counterinsurgency, 249; domestic and foreign, 43;
global reach of, 24; in the Great Society,
124; imperial institutions of, 116; in
Indonesia, 18; *Law and Order* magazine,
141; and local autonomy, 116, 119; local
police benefitting from, 141; multiplicity
of agencies involved in, 131; and national
security, 116; origins of, 8; overseas,
applied in the US, 253; and police professionalization, 113–14; political discourse
on, 116; and racialized fear of crime, 121;
and resources control, 254; security
practices resulting from, 254; in South
Vietnam, 239; in state-building, 2, 235;
vs. urban unrest, 136; and the US carceral
state, 1; and US police power, 114
Law Enforcement Assistance Act, 127,
136–37, 172, 283–84n10
Law Enforcement Assistance Administration. *See* LEAA
Law Enforcement Intelligence Unit, 214,
217
Lazia, Johnny, 64
LBJ. *See* Johnson, Lyndon B.
LEAA (Law Enforcement Assistance
Administration): and AID, 175; block
grants issued by, 139, 315n77; computer-
based intelligence systems funded by,
227; congressional expansion of, 262;
creation of, 137–40; crime-related
appropriations by, 138; CSTI funded by,
187; and discretionary police power, 141;

domestic vs. foreign law enforcement funded by, 238; federal law enforcement funds distributed by, 113; intelligence gathering funded by, 227; and the IPA, 182; and LBJ, 113; local police autonomy supported by, 139; and the New Federalism, 141; and Nixon, 140; and OLEA, 137; and OPS, 9, 24; origins of, 131; overseas police assistance continued by, 261–63; police as primary recipients of funds from, 114; and the racialization of lawlessness, 141; and riot control, 167, 172, 190, 197; and SEADOC, 179; SWAT units funded by, 215; troika system of, 140, 233; as War on Crime centerpiece, 9. *See also headings under police professionalization*

League of Nations, 47, 77

Leavenworth prison, 65

Le Duan, 332n34

leftists and left-wing politics, 18, 19, 66, 116, 131, 228–30. *See also* New Left; radicals and radical groups

Leites, Nathan, 242, 247–50. *See also* Wolf, Charles, Jr.

Levine, Bertram, 180–81, 189, 209

liberalism: and Black resistance movements, 271; and the carceral state, 4; and chemical weapons, 209; on crime as revolutionary activity, 241; failure of reforms in, 258; illiberal practices accommodated by, 268; and modernization, 88; and pacification, 145; on police reform as a necessity, 167; racial liberalism, 22, 28, 34, 48–49, 220; and racism, 293n41; socioeconomic causes of unrest emphasized by, 216, 235–36; and the socioeconomic conditions of Black areas, 124; and Vollmer, 68

Limited War Laboratory (US Army), 239

Lindquist, John A., 70

Liu, Daniel S. C., 302n107

Lohman, Joseph, 227

Longan, John P., 155–57, 261

Los Angeles, 27, 184, 214, 216, 221–26, 230, 331n2. *See also* Watts (Los Angeles)

Los Angeles Police Department (LAPD): and the Civil Rights Act, 216; and civil

rights advancement, 221; corruption in, 216–17; CRASH program of, 221; Daily Training Bulletin of, 218–19, 226, 332n14; DARE program of, 221; and the Dominican Republic, 227, 230; and Engle, 221; federal assistance refused by, 223; Model Civil Disturbance Control Plan of, 222; and OPS, 221; and racist violence, 216; Reddin as chief of, 221–22; and South Vietnam, 225; Tactical Operations Planning Group of, 222; transnationalism of, 214, 216, 225, 231, 233; and Vollmer, 67, 216–17. *See also* Parker, William H.

Lukban, Jose, 113, 115

MacArthur, Douglas, 60, 68, 73

Mace (Chemical Mace), 203, 328n46

Machado y Morales, Gerardo, 67

Maechling, Charles, Jr., 104–6, 154, 310n124

Malaya: British counterinsurgency in, 77, 158; chemical weapons used in, 198, 251; counterinsurgency in, 251; Engle and, 77; hearts and minds theory in, 245; pacification in, 159; police-led counterinsurgency in, 239; social control in, 158–59; Southeast Asian police instructors sent to, 77

Malcolm X, 116

Manopoli, John F., 32–33, 42, 57

Mao Zedong, 72, 74, 91, 100, 112, 222, 245, 251

marginalized communities, 24, 120, 143, 221, 255, 258

Martin, John Bartlow, 227, 230

Marx, Karl, 40

Masters of Deceit (Hoover), 182

McCann, Michael, 133

McCarthy, Gerry, 216

McCarthy, Joseph, 231

McClellan, John, 173

McCone, John A., 106

McDonough, James, 63

McNamara, Robert, 34, 89, 103, 112, 174, 200, 204, 244, 327n34

Mejia, Jesus, 227–28, 230–31

Meselson, Matthew, 205

Mexican Americans, 29, 189, 218
Michigan State Police, 74
Michigan State University. *See* MSU
militarization of policing, 66–67, 69,
    233–34, 266, 268n18
military assistance, 14, 47, 86–87, 101–2,
    154
Military Assistance Command Vietnam,
    97, 207
Military Intelligence Division (US Army),
    65
Military Police: and Adrian Jones, 237;
    Brandstatter in, 74; Carl Turner in
    charge of, 173; Fort Gordon, Georgia
    training facility for, 178, 185; and OPS,
    33, 176–77, 185; riot-control training
    by, 173, 177, 185, 208; tear gas stockpiled
    by, 208
Miranda v. Arizona (US Supreme Court),
    138
Mississippi, 169, 202
Mitrione, Dan, 158, 260, 269–70
Mity Mite delivery system, 203, 208
modernization: and Black-white US divide,
    42; and capitalism, 267; and commu-
    nism, 82; and counterinsurgency, 81, 99,
    104; as counterrevolutionary revolution,
    47; destabilizing effects of, 82, 113;
    failure of, 161; and foreign aid, 243;
    goals of, 84; JFK as advocate of, 88;
    Leites and Wolf vs., 247, 250; non-com-
    munist, 62; and OISP, 307n68; and
    OPS, 85, 266–67; and Parsons, 303n8;
    "The Police and Minority Groups"
    pre-figuring, 42; and police profession-
    alization, 266–67; promises vs. realities
    of, 84; and race management, 50; and
    revolution, 61; Rostow on, 44, 81–82,
    99, 102, 104, 132, 246; and structural-
    functionalism, 81–84, 303n8; in Turkey,
    62; and US-centered world, 41–42; US
    vs. Soviet visions of, 91
modernization of police forces: by Engle,
    52, 78; in Germany, 69, 74, 217; and the
    Great Society, 124; with Komer's sup-
    port, 84, 92; and modernization theory,
    88, 109; and national security, 12; by
    Parker, 217; police violence resulting in,

169; and state-formation, 52; as univer-
    sal, 238; in the US, 115; and US hegem-
    ony, 50; and the War on Crime, 115
Momboisse, Raymond, 202, 253, 328n41
Moses, Abe J., 129
MOVE (Black liberation group), 210
Moyers, Bill, 172, 204
MSU (Michigan State University): and
    Brandstatter, 74, 76–77, 196; CIA
    funding for, 74; and the Diem regime,
    74–76, 75*fig. 5*, 133; and Hannah,
    312n25; Hoyt at, 65; and the IPA,
    300n70; Parker at, 218–19; police train-
    ing facilities at, 65, 74, 167–68; and
    South Vietnam, 74–77, 135, 160, 192, 193
    fig. 11, 312n25
multi-purpose grenades, 197, 207
Munroe, Johnson, 60
Murray, Charles A., 253
Myrdal, Gunnar, 27–29

NACCD (National Advisory Commission
    on Civil Disorders). *See* Kerner Com-
    mission (NACCD)
narcotics control, 61–62, 128, 261–62,
    283–84n10, 317n30
National Advisory Commission on Civil
    Disorders. *See* Kerner Commission
    (NACCD)
National Association for the Advancement
    of Colored People, 28
National Guard (US), 6, 123, 175–76, 178–
    79, 187–88, 194, 197–98
nationalism: Black nationalism, 243; CIA
    analysis of, 96; in the Congo, 95; in
    decolonizing zones, 89; in Indonesia,
    96; as Komer's focus, 89; methodologi-
    cal nationalism, 95; vs. nuclear stale-
    mate, 96; in South Vietnam, 96; vs. the
    national security state, 97; in Turkey,
    61; and US overseas police assistance,
    113; vs. US world leadership, 94
National Liberation Front. *See* NLF
    (National Liberation Front)
National Rifle Association, 263–64
national security: archival research on, 15;
    as bipartisan priority, 5; and the Cold
    War, 10; globalization of, 12; impera-

tives of, across the foreign/domestic divide, 41, 45; and imperialism, 16–17; justifying penal apparatus in US and abroad, 4, 8; and law and order, 116; and modernization of police forces, 12; motility of, 10; and police professionalization, 113; risks and threats determined by, 16; and WWII, 10

National Security Council. *See* NSC

national security state: ambitions of, 94; and the carceral state, 4, 24; and the Cold War, 10; as global, 24, 265, 286n21; intelligence gathering in, 14; and Komer, 89, 92; nationalism's destabilizing of, 94; and Nixon, 141; Truman as creator of, 56, 265; and US global hegemony, 35; and the War on Crime, 8

Nazis, 66, 128

neo-colonialism, 96

Nepal, 110, 324n68

Ness, Eliot, 127–28

Newark, New Jersey, 3, 166, 173, 180, 198, 207

New Left, 3, 87, 186, 195, 262, 269

New International Economic Order, 11

Newton, Huey P., 45, 227

New York City, 29, 117, 170, 272

New York City police department, 65, 73, 168, 224

New York State, 33, 208, 225. *See also* Rochester, New York

Ngo Dinh Diem, 74–77, 110, 133, 164, 243, 245

Nguyen Cao Ky, 225

Nguyen Thi Hai, 147

Nicaragua, 18, 32, 66, 68, 109, 144, 231, 260

Nitze, Paul H., 89, 264

Nixon, Richard: block grants favored by, 140; chemical weapons no-first-use agreement of, 213; and federalism, 140–41, 315n77; and Gates, 233; and Hannah, 312n25; JFK vs., 89; in Latin America, 86–87, 112; and the LEAA, 9, 141; and the national security state, 141; and overseas police assistance, 144, 262; police assisted despotism under, 144; political protests during term of, 211; and the Republican Coordinating

Committee, 188, 315n77; riot-control training evaluated by, 190; security imperatives of, 141; and Vietnamization, 97–98; war metaphors used by, 283–84n10; and the War on Crime, 9; and the War on Drugs, 261

Nkrumah, Kwame, 31

NLF (National Liberation Front) (South Vietnam), 243, 247, 251, 272

nonlethal weapons. *See* CN tear gas; CS tear gas; DOJ; Engle, Byron; Johnson, Lyndon B.; Kerner Commission (NACCD); OPS; riot control (nonlethal); South Vietnam

North American Congress on Latin America, 3, 269, 335n70

North Carolina, 210

Northern Ireland, 188, 199

North Vietnam, 101, 159, 202, 310n123

Northwestern University, 185

NRA (National Rifle Association), 263–64

NSAM (National Security Action Memorandum): concerning counterinsurgency, 91; JFK's issuing of, 92, 143; No. 2, 89; No. 124, 103; No. 132, 108; No. 162, 101; No. 177, 111–12, 129, 131; as policy statements, 91, 106

NSC (National Security Council): 1290d action of, 18, 85; chemical weapons approved by, 198; and communications systems built overseas, 151; and counterinsurgency goals, 13; JFK reorganization of, 303n2; Kennedy's reorganization of, 103; Komer on, 13, 80, 88, 90, 96; and modernization, 81; and OPS, 11; police assistance programs requested by, 18; and the SGCI, 103

NSC 68, 88–89, 306n52

nuclear weapons, 10, 81, 86, 88, 96, 104, 219, 244

Oakland, California, 3

occupation forces (domestic), 1, 3, 78

occupation forces (foreign). *See* Germany; Japan

O'Dell, Jack, 269

Office of Law Enforcement Administration (OLEA). *See* OLEA

Office of Public Safety. *See* OPS (Office of Public Safety)

OIDP (Overseas Internal Defense Policy), 104

OISP (Overseas Internal Security Program): 1290d program renamed as, 18, 85; Bissell vs., 98; centralization of, 109; deficiencies in, 108; as Eisenhower-era program, 99; and Engle, 85; enlargement of, 88, 99; global reach of, 85; inter-agency conflicts in, 85; and Komer, 18, 88, 97, 99, 102; mission of, 85; and modernization, 307n68; and the SGCI, 104

Olander, Oscar G., 74

OLEA (Office of Law Enforcement Assistance), 137–38, 167, 170, 172–74, 181

Omnibus Crime Control and Safe Streets Act: overview, 137–41; and FBI funding, 173; IACP's support for, 175; an international crime control, 263; and the LEAA, 9, 131; and OPS, 235; and riot-control funding, 197; and State Planning Agencies, 139–40; and War on Crime funding, 187

1290d (NSC police assistance program), 18, 85

Operación Limpieza (Guatemala), 156, 163

Operation Birmingham, 204

OPS (Office of Public Safety): advisors' backgrounds, 20–21, 150; authoritarian regimes strengthened by, 270; as behavior-control force, 20; and Carl Turner, 177; centralization in, 72; civil society shaped by, 144; closure of, 11, 14, 19, 143, 165, 269–70; communications systems built overseas by, 151–52, 153 *fig. 8;* vs. communist revolution, 39; and Con Son prison, 269; creation of, 11, 19, 108–12, 129, 132–33; CS recommendations issued by, 199; and CSTI, 189; and death squads, 156; as devolutionary state-building model, 235; and disappearance, 155; doctrine flow chart of, 17 *fig. 1;* doctrines taught by, 17–18; and the Dominican Republic, 228–30; enforcement powers of, 20; and Engle, 36, 57–58, 111, 134, 221, 225, 226, 310n124; failures of, 266; and federalism, 121;

First Line of Defense training film of, 79; internationalism vs., 19; and international police trainee statistics, 181, 323n53; and the Kerner Commission, 6; and Komer, 58, 80, 97, 104, 111, 310n124; and the LAPD, 221, 225; leftists vs., 19, 186, 269–70; and Malaya, 158–59, 251; manpower peak of, 20–21; marksmanship training of, 57 *fig. 4,* 57–58; and modernization, 85, 160, 266–67; and NACCD, 189; narcotics control missions of, 261–62; in Nicaragua, 32, 66, 144, 231; nonlethal chemical munitions developed by, 192; numbers of police officers exposed to training by, 181; officers trained by, vs. the DEA, 341n17; and Paraná, 157; peak years of, 20–21; in Peru, 15; *The Police and Resources Control in Counter-Insurgency* textbook by, 158; and police professionalization, 69, 266; and police reform, 122; recruitment to, 21, 36, 58, 76, 134, 174, 225–26; responsibilities of, 109; and RFK, 13, 111, 310n124; security force connectivity established by, 157; and the SGCI, 104, 108–11; social subjects created by, 144; and the Special Warfare Center, 114, 185; as state-building model, 9; and *State of Siege,* 260; strategies of, 80; and SWAT teams, 221, 224; tear gas developed by, 207; in Thailand, 145; in Third World countries, 6, 9, 19, 79, 115, 194; torture allegations against, 260; and traffic control, 132, 148, 160, 182; and the Tupamaros, 149; and the United Kingdom, 310n123; US proxy status maintained by, 113, 252; and Vance, 174; violence rejected by, 259. *See also* AID; Engle, Byron; *headings under police professionalization;* IPA; NSC; POCC; riot-control training; Sagalyn, Arnold; South Vietnam; torture; War on Crime

order-maintenance policing: as behavior control, 265; conservatives' advocacy of, 236; counterinsurgency replicated by, 237, 242; current state of, 255–58; and labor redundancy, 255; of minor offenses, 255; nature of, questioned,

272–73; order as the object of, 269; and overseas wartime military experience, 232; Parker's rationale for, 218; and police professionalization, 269; vs. protests against racist police, 218; racialization of, 221; racism at the core of, 214; and rational-choice counterinsurgency theory, 237; socioeconomic conditions underlying unrest ignored in, 219–20; and SWAT, 216

Organization of American States, 31

Overseas Internal Security Program. *See* OISP

overseas police assistance overview, 52–78. *See also headings under OPS; headings under police assistance*

Owens, Patricia, 45, 294n63

Oxford, Mississippi, 202

pacification: by Britain in Malaya, 159; and coercion, 145, 162–63; and economic aid, 244; as economy of force component, 48; Emerson on, 241; as expansionist violence, 49; French pacification, 46, 295n67; Komer as czar of, 97, 98; limitations on, 162; participation in, 161–65; in the Philippines, 34; and police power, 145, 269; and policing, 145–46; and racial repression, 30; resistance to, 162; and revenge, 48–49; as social tutelage, 48–49; in South Vietnam, 96–97; Wolf vs., 247, 251

Pacific Legal Foundation, 253

Pakistan, 225

Panama, 109, 174

Panama Canal Zone, 19, 36–37, 79, 108

paramilitary police: and the Civil Guard of South Vietnam, 75, 85; in cost-benefit counterinsurgency, 249; as death squads, 156; in the Dominican Republic, 229; in Nicaragua, 231; Pentagon support for, 109; in Saudi Arabia, 260; and Singlaub, 231; in St. Louis, 63; SWAT teams as, 215; in Thailand, 145; in Third World countries, 177; and Turner, 177

Paraná (Brazilian state), 157–58

Parker, William H.: vs. Black Panther Party, 232; and *Dragnet*, 217; and Gates, 217, 232; in Germany, 217; Hoover vs., 217; in India, 226; as LAPD police chief, 218–21; LAPD's Daily Training Bulletin produced by, 226; at MSU, 218–19; and order-maintenance policing, 216, 257; and organized crime, 217; police brutality denied by, 228; as police professionalizer, 217; "The Police Role in Community Relations," 219; and police violence against Mexican Americans, 218; racial views of, 218–20; and rational-choice counterinsurgency, 252–53; and RFK, 227; socioeconomic conditions ignored by, 218; and SWAT, 221

Parsons, Talcott, 81, 303n8

Pauker, Guy, 243, 306n60

PCLEAJ (President's Commission on Law Enforcement and Administration of Justice). *See* Crime Commission

Pearson, Drew, 201

Pendergast, Tom, 63–65, 67, 264, 299n47

Pentagon: Advanced Research Projects Agency of, 147; antiwar protests at, 177; and Bissell, 99; CN tear gas phased out by, 199; and counterinsurgency goals, 13; CS tested by, 199; Komer vs., 99; military gear distributed to police by, 136; and narcotics control, 261–62; paramilitary-support programs funded by, 109; Philco funded by, 147; Project PROVOST of, 203; racial crime analysis of, 51; RAND Corporation funded by, 242; riot-control agent budget of, 204; South Vietnam civilian projects funded by, 97; specialized training by, 110–11. *See also* DOD

People's Park (Berkeley), 188, 208

Peru, 15

Philadelphia, 30, 34, 81, 123, 224

Philco-Ford company, 146–47

Philippines: chemical weapons recommended for use in, 209; communism as crime in, 113; counterinsurgency in, 19, 67; counterinsurgency veterans from, 74; insurgency in, 68; and OPS, 310n123; pacification in, 34; police assistance in, 18; riot groups in, 176; Vollmer in, 67, 217; Walton in, 226

Phoenix program (South Vietnam), 144, 161–62, 295n65
POCC (Police Operations Control Center of the IPA), 183–85, 184 *fig. 9*
police action, 12
Police Administration (Wilson), 70–71
"The Police and Minority Groups" (Hall and Weckler), 27–28, 42
The Police and Resources Control in Counter-Insurgency (OPS textbook), 158, 236–37
police assistance (non-US), 310n123
police assistance (overseas): AID funding of, 107, 113; autonomous funding of, 110; to Brazil, 230; brutality of, 143; budgets for, 154; capital investment in, 17; civilian management of, 110; to Colombia, 230; vs. communist subversion, 51, 72, 88, 110; and counterinsurgency, 14, 85, 96, 107; and crime control, 263; and democracy enhancement overseas, 163; destructive vs. constructive modes of, 161; development of, 18, 19–20; and dissent, 162, 164; to the Dominican Republic, 227–30; flexible-response policies of, 88, 260; funding issues of, 108, 113, 260; and global police fraternity, 32–33, 142; global reach of, 90; to Guatemala, 155–56, 230; vs. guerrilla warfare, 111; humanitarian spin in, 21; IACP contract cancelled, 175; in Indonesia, 18; intelligence gathering through, 186; and Komer, 84, 96; labor organizing as target of, 143; material aid in, 20; and military intervention, 98–100, 102; military intervention in, 87; narcotics control mission of, 261; as non-priority, 86; origins of, 18–19, 85; and the POCC, 183–85; as preemptive, 110; as preventive medicine, 102, 107; privatization of, 260; public responses to, 210; and racialization, 32–38; as repressive, 163; RFK's interest in, 13; as riot control, 85; as self-rule instrument, 100; as service-oriented, 16; in South Vietnam, 45, 90, 158–62; as state-building project, 80, 235; technological expertise in, 20–21, 28–30, 39, 108–9,

149–51, 161–62, 164–65, 169, 186, 262, 266; termination of, 24, 260, 269; in Third World countries, 115; time span of, 11; and torture, 186; training assistance domain of, 20, 39; and U. Alexis Johnson, 110, 129; urban focus of, 13; and the US discretionary empire, 20; as US security by proxy, 113, 252, 267; and the War on Crime, 114, 124. *See also* CIA; *headings under police professionalization;* JFK; 129od; OPS; RFK; SGCI; War on Crime
police assistance (transnational), 145, 242, 265, 267–68, 272
police assistance (in the US): and the Great Society, 124; as state-building project, 235; technological expertise in, 262; training for public safety advisors, 150. *See also* civil rights; Civil Rights Act; discretionary employment of police power; *headings relating to Black people; headings under race; headings under riot control; headings under unrest;* LEAA; OLEA; police power; riots; War on Crime; War on Poverty
The Police Chief (IACP monthly magazine): and AID, 134; CN and CS advertisements in, 206 *fig. 12;* on communism, 123; counterinsurgency articles published in, 238; overseas police executives subscribing to, 78; Parker's views published in, 218, 220; riot-control tactics published in, 234, 238; Tamm as editor of, 173; tear gas information in, 192, 197, 206. *See also* IACP
Police Executive Research Forum, 11
Police Foundation, 11
police-led counterinsurgency, 13–14, 78, 194, 215, 236, 239, 241, 266
police modernization. *See* modernization of police forces
police power: overview, 113–41; archival research on, 15; and assassination, 270; as behavior control, 20, 145, 236; Black people as fixed target of, 272; and capitalism, 16–17, 144; characteristics of, 143–50; and civil unrest, 4; and colonialism, 4; constructive vs. destructive

aspects of, 143, 165, 195–96; and the criminalization of racial difference, 39; vs. demands of freedom and justice, 143; despotic vs. infrastructural aspects of, 143; as discretionary, 16, 34, 46–47; and economy of force, 47; expansion of, 4, 47; vs. federal intervention, 117; fictional past histories of, 257; global reach of, 258; and grassroots community development, 116; infrastructural aspects of, 144; insecurities created by, 46; international legal limits of, 46; as interstate and intrastate, 10; limitlessness of, 15–16, 24, 235, 272; local autonomy of, 116–17; local scope of, 267; macroeconomic shifts tracked by, 268; militarization of, 69, 139, 214, 232, 265, 286n18; and pacification, 145–46; post-WWII realization of, 47; as preemptive, 212; protesters as targets of, 143; and race-making, 21; racial cause and effect relationships in, 39; and racial profiling, 40; and racism, 3–4, 51; as repression, 269, 270; and slavery, 4, 34; as social control, 46; and social regulation, 16, 143–46; social subjects created by, 268–69, 270; southern, becoming a national institution, 34, 269; surveillance and intelligence gathering as, 214, 238–39; transnationalism of, 235; unaccountability of, 115; unprepared for urban unrest, 170–71. *See also* broken windows policing; communism; discretionary employment of police power; *headings under riot control;* Kerner Commission (NACCD); national security; police assistance (overseas); racial violence; riots; SWAT units

police professionalization (general): and capitalism, 267; and the carceral state, 121; and civilians killed by police, 209; components of, 11–12; and discretionary police despotism, 48; foreign/domestic divide obliterated by, 212; global reach of, 12; vs. militarization, 266; and modernization, 266–67; and OPS, 266; police political actors created by, 266; significance of, 113; technological expertise in, 11; training required for, 190; vs. subversives, 11. *See also* Engle, Byron

police professionalization (overseas): and Army counterinsurgency efforts, 19; basic police equipment provided by, 155; vs. collective police political loyalties, 266; and counterinsurgency, 19; as crisis management tool, 166; and democracy enhancement overseas, 163; development of, 71; discretionary police power advanced by, 155; discretion standardized in, 148; and the KC police department, 65–66; Komer's belief in, 113, 115–16, 164–65; and the LEAA, 11; and modernization, 266–67; and nonlethal riot control, 194; nonlethal weapons as component of, 194; and OPS, 12, 72; O. W. Wilson on, 69; vs. police killings of civilians, 155, 166; political unrest intensified by, 194; racialized, 148; replicability of, 69; and state formation, 17–18, 53–54, 77–78; and state monopolization of police power, 46–47; in Third World countries, 6, 11, 194; training required for, 185; and tyranny vs. democracy, 11; US-centered world as objective of, 78, 302n111; in Vietnam, 225. *See also* Engle, Byron

police professionalization (transnational): and colonialism, 19–20; and counterinsurgency, 116; development of, 12; dominance of, 11; effects deriving from, 266–69; and Engle, 115–16; firearms training in, 19; and the IACP, 11; labor- vs. capital-intensive modes of, 214; police political actors created by, 267–68

police professionalization (in the US): appropriations for, increased, 155; bigotry in, 30, 35; and Black populations, 27, 116; capital-intensive repertoires of, 236; and civil unrest, 27, 191; class distinctions in, 255; Committee on Civil Rights' recommendations of, 71; criminalization increased by, 155; development of, 166–67; discretionary police power advanced by, 155; effects of, 191; and federalism, 124, 170; and Harlem,

police professionalization *(continued)*
167–71; and Liu, 302n107; as modernization practice, 6; needs for, 167; and
order-maintenance policing, 269; by
O. W. Wilson, 66; and pacification, 269;
as police reform, 113–15; police violence
necessitating, 190–91; by Sagalyn, 130;
and state power, 271; successes of, 171;
and tear gas, 236; training required for,
185. *See also* IACP; Parker, William H.;
War on Crime; Wilson, Orlando W.
Police Records and *Police Planning* (Wilson), 70
police reform: AID-assisted, in the Dominican Republic, 228–29; and capitalism,
143; counterinsurgency as purpose of,
19; and foreign police assistance, 88,
146; and the global LAPD, 225; goals of,
24; Kerner Commission on, 197; LAPD
resistance to, 217, 221; LEAA's funding
of, 191; necessity of, 4, 8, 122–23; and
race management, 29, 232; riot-control
training as, 191; top-down, 236; and
Valentine, 74. *See also* Harlem; *headings
under police professionalization*
"The Police Role in Community Relations"
(Parker's MSU speech), 219, 332n14
police violence: against Black people, 27–28,
169; Black rebellions against, 221; civilians killed by, 210; erosion of legitimized
police monopoly, 272; escalating, 167; in
Harlem rebellion, 115, 167–69; of the
LAPD, 230; LBJ on, 169–70; police
modernization in response to, 169;
precipitating unrest, 25, 115, 117, 166, 180;
and random killings, 207–8; resulting
in death vs. criminal conviction, 212;
Sagalyn on, 209; severity of, 167; vs.
transnational US legitimacy, 167. *See
also* riots; Watts (Los Angeles)
political protests: changing characteristics
of, 211–12; and counterinsurgency, 9;
defined as rioting, 27, 39, 173, 212; in the
Dominican Republic, 228; in Japan, 87;
in Latin America, 86–87; local police
unprepared for, 171; nonlethal weapons
used in, 210; OPS's spin on, 21; overseas
police assistance ended by, 24; and police

killings of Black people, 197; police
suppression of, 190; in the present day,
272; race management of, 27; and socio-
economic deprivation, 244; in South
Vietnam, 182–83; tear gas used against,
192, 208, 210; violent police responses to,
8; and the War on Poverty, 239
Polynesia, 65
Popkin, Samuel, 250
Portuguese empire, 146
Postal Service Scientific Identification
Laboratory (US), 185
Powell, James, 115–16, 168. *See also* Harlem
rebellion
President's Commission on Law Enforcement and Administration of Justice
(PCLEAJ). *See* Crime Commission
Prevention and Control of Mobs and Riots
(FBI), 173
prison. *See* carceral state; incarceration
Prohibition, 10, 127
Project PROVOST, 203
public safety advisors: budgets for, 154; and
disappearances, 155; domestic police
training of, 150, 242; in the Dominican
Republic, 228–30; killed on duty, 147–
48; in Paraná, 157–58; reforms proposed
to, 182; regime legitimacy as task of,
164; retrained in the US, 150; returning
overseas, 186; in SEADOC, 179; in
South Vietnam, 147–48, 182; tools of,
151–55; trust-building by, 150; working
conditions of, 143–50
Public Safety Division. *See* Japan
public safety programs: in Bolivia, 191;
cancellation of, 149; vs. communism,
148; global reach of, 7 *map*, 12; and Gray
Areas' internal security, 113; Hall as
acting director of, 27; and police power,
15–16, 143–46; of riot prevention, 27; in
South Vietnam, 133; and training of
foreign men of color, 35–36; universality
of, 142
Puerto Rico, 209
Pulliam, Howard E., 68–69, 73, 77

race-making, 21, 34–35, 41, 45. *See also*
racialization

race management: overview, 28–51; abroad, 29–30; of American settlers, 48–49; and the CIA, 31–32; via communism, 50; and the Congress on Racial Equality, 28; and counterinsurgency, 45–51; via criminalization, 50; and decolonization, 30; and domestic technical police assistance, 50, 66; Du Bois on, 28–30, 34; and the global color line, 31–32; Hall and Weckler on, 27, 29; and the IACP, 133–34; and the killing of Black people, 27; by Manopoli in Africa, 32–33; of McNamara, 34; men of color conscripted into, 30, 34–35; Myrdal on, 27–29; and the National Association for the Advancement of Colored People, 28; by Parker, 232; in "The Police and Minority Groups," 27; and police assistance, 32–38; and police professionalization, 27, 34; and police reform, 29, 232; of political protests, 27; post-WWII, 34; as preemptive, 212; racial demarcation in, 39–40, 49–50; via racial difference, 50; and racialized hierarchies, 34–35; as racial rule, 34; of rational actors, 48, 236; and rioting, 27; State Department assisting in, 29; and US leadership image, 28; by violence, 48–49, 296n72; and white supremacy, 30. See also Cold War; pacification; racism; riot control; riots

racial demarcation, 33, 39, 49–50, 272
racial desegregation, 219, 256
racial discrimination, 36, 116–17, 119
racial equality, 49, 71, 119. See also Congress of Racial Equality
racial inequality, 28, 39
racial integration, 49, 119, 139, 256
racialization: in carceral states, 3; confirmation bias of, 146; of crime, 35, 38–39; in CSTI riot control planning, 189; defined, 39–41, 293n40; of the fear of crime, 121; of insurgency as crime, 239; law and order creating, 121; of lawlessness, 121, 141; of neighborhood boundaries, 189; non-racial disguises of, 257; of order-maintenance policing, 221; in police professionalization abroad, 148;

and re-racialization, 41; as risk assessment, 257; of social control, 202, 255; of social inequality, 39; of state oppression, 268; of subversion, 35, 38–39. See also race-making; racial demarcation
racial justice. See freedom/justice demands and movements
racial power, 63, 121
racial profiling, 40
racial/racist violence, 27–29, 65, 166, 216
racism: and anticommunism, 28, 282–83n5; vs. Black freedom movements, 28; and Black internationalism, 282–83n5; as the criminalization of race, 39; and Cuba, 35; definitions and characteristics of, 39–41; and discretionary police power, 34, 41, 257; in education, 39, 116–17; effects of, 38–45; elimination of, as a geopolitical necessity, 28, 42, 45; foreign police officers confronted by, 29–30; in health care, 39; in housing, 39, 116–17; imperial racism, 42, 44, 157, 232; in incarceration, 2–4; internationalism vs., 271; Jim Crow racism, 34, 58; in jobs, 39; Kerner Commission vs., 4; and liberalism, 27–29, 34, 42–45, 219–20, 271, 293n41; and order-maintenance policing, 214, 216, 218; and police power, 21, 256; and police professionalization, 35; in police ranks, 30; protests against, 9; race as product of, 39–41, 293n41; radicalism vs., 271; sanitized, 30; of Southern Democrats, 241; and South Vietnam police, 76; and US foreign policy, 28; US reputation for, 28–29, 31; without racists, 30
radicals and radical groups: and anticolonial racial assertion by, 42, 116; Black Power militants, 197; CAPER, 270; CIA surveillance of, 241; among European immigrants, 59; global law enforcement vs., 115; infiltration of, 146, 182, 230, 270; internationalist antiracism enacted by, 271; in Japan, 87; in labor organizations, 190; left-wing, 7–8, 231, 241; MOVE, 210; New Left, 3, 87, 186, 195, 262, 269; police reform vs., 24; vs. police repression, 190; preemptive

radicals and radical groups *(continued)* strikes against, 210; Progressive Labor, 115–17; as public safety advisors' target, 146; vs. repression by US-backed regimes, 166; Republic of New Africa, 210; resisting state limitations on civil protections, 271; surveillance of, 146, 241; Symbionese Liberation Army, 221; terrorism accusations against, 212. *See also* Black Panther Party; Black political radicals; New Left

RAND Corporation: Air Force funding of, 242; and ARPA, 242–43; cost-benefit counterinsurgency developed at, 253, 255; and the DOD, 242–43; Ellsberg vs., 249; on foreign aid, 244; and French counterinsurgency theory, 239; guerrilla warfare studies of, 251; hearts and minds theory at, 249; Herrmann employed by, 226; Komer in, 112; literature on, 338n36; Pentagon funding of, 242; policing research by, 237–38; rational-choice theory developed at, 244, 250, 252–53; *Rebellion and Authority* published by, 242, 247–48; and South Vietnam, 244; and strategic air defense theories, 242–43; Third Area Conflict Board of, 243; Viet Cong Motivation and Morale Project of, 243, 247; Wolf on Third Area Conflict Board of, 243

rational-choice counterinsurgency theory, 24, 48, 236, 243–45, 250, 252–56, 338n36

Reagan, Ronald, 187–90, 208, 253, 261, 315n77

rebellion. *See* insurgency

Rebellion and Authority (Leites and Wolf), 242, 248–50

Reddin, Tom, 221–22

Reed, Lear B., 58–60, 64–65, 67, 71, 75–77

Republican Coordinating Committee, 138, 140, 315n77

Republicans and the Republican Party, 64, 86, 138, 140, 169, 264

Republic of New Africa, 210

Reuther, Walter, 103

revolution and revolutionary activity: by Black people, 232; and Congolese nationalist revolution, 95; crime defined as, 241; in Cuba, 96; modernization as tool of, 82; as the permanence of crime, 50–51; police actions against, 41; and police power, 8, 11, 24; public safety programs vs., 22. *See also* communist revolution

RFK. *See* Kennedy, Robert F.

Rhodesia, 261, 264

Rigg, Robert, 240–41

right-wing politics and policies, 101, 116, 177, 231, 242. *See also* conservatives and conservatism

riot control: Army's Garden Plot plan, 176; and the carceral state, 166; and the Cold War, 167; as Engle's specialty, 60; failures of, 167; foreign police assistance as, 85; and the Great Society, 124; Kerner Commission on, 197; LEAA's funding of, 197; by Military Police, 173; overseas, applied in the US, 167; police violence in, 167; reforms in, 8; restrictions on military in, 213; tear gas grenades used in, 207; Vance on, 174; and worker militancy, 328n41. *See also* CN/DM lachrymator/emetic agent; CN tear gas; CS tear gas

riot control (lethal), 115, 147, 166, 173, 176, 194

riot control (nonlethal): CS tear gas as, 192, 194, 195, 210; Engle's advocacy of, 5; foreign, applied in the US, 5; foreign/domestic divide reduced in use of, 195; and the Geneva Protocol, 200; and noncombatant populations, 327n34; tear gas as, 192, 194–95

riot-control training: overview, 166–91; by the Army, 172–73, 175–82; in California, 172, 187–92; by the DOJ, 239; evaluation of, 190; by the FBI, 172–73, 239; and Hoover, 172–73; by the IACP, 172, 174, 197; by the IPA, 182–86, 189; LEAA funding increases enabled by, 191; by Military Police, 173, 177, 185, 208; multiplicity of agencies involved in, 172; by OPS, 167, 172, 182–87; police assistance in, 20; as police reform, 191; and SEADOC, 189; technological advancements enabled by, 191

riots, 27, 115, 122, 173. *See also* Black communities/neighborhoods; Black people; *headings under unrest*
Rochester, New York, 123, 169, 202
Rocker, Sidney, 174, 181
Rodney, Walter, 31, 174
"The Role of the Police in Counter-Insurgency" (Air War College thesis), 239
Rolling Thunder bombing campaign, 202
Roosevelt, Franklin D., 18, 64, 299n47
Rosenthal, Carl F., 239
Rostow, Walt W.: Bissell report redrafted by, 102; counterinsurgency advocated by, 90; on counterinsurgency and modernization, 82–83; on foreign/domestic parallels in LBJ's policies, 44–45, 45 *Table;* Institute of Modernization Studies proposed by, 82; on insurgency, 102; and Komer, 80, 92, 99, 102, 306n60; and LBJ, 42–43, 98; on modernization and counterinsurgency, 99, 104, 132; and OIDP, 104; and OISP, 99, 307n68; and police assistance in counterinsurgency, 84; and the Policy Planning Council, 307n68; and RFK, 132; on South Vietnam, 244
Rudziak, Nicholas D., 239, 241
Ruiz, Anthony, 228
Rusk, Dean, 89, 106, 111, 201, 203, 209, 328n40
Rwanda, 32
Ryan, Jack, 76, 133, 147

Saenz, Adolph, 142
Sagalyn, Arnold: career of, 127–31; and the civil rights movement, 114; "Control of Disorder" chapter authored by, 196; counterinsurgency programs of, 9; and the Crime Commission, 127, 130, 151; CS tear gas advocated by, 224; Democratic Party loyalties of, 127; and the DOJ, 113–14; domestic police assistance originating with, 124; and Engle, 6, 127, 128, 196; and Evans, 137; and federalism, 121; and Gates, 224; in Germany, 128, 217; and the Great Society, 124; and the Harlem rebellion, 122, 166–67; and Hoover, 133; and Interpol, 130; and the

IPG, 130; and the Kerner Commission, 8, 130, 174–75; and law-enforcement assistance, 114; LBJ's empowerment of, 169; and the LEAA, 9, 113, 130–31, 206; on lethal force used against Black people, 259; and Longan, 156; and modernization of police forces, 124, 130; and the 911 system, 151; nonlethal weapons advocated by, 195–96; and OPS, 9, 113–14, 130; and overseas police assistance supported by, 124; and O. W. Wilson, 127–28; photo of, 130 *fig. 7;* on police causing urban unrest, 194; and police legitimacy, 196; vs. police militarization, 125; on police/public relations, 175; as police reformer, 127; and police upgrading privileged over welfare programs, 125; as private police assistance consultant, 261; riot-control training observed by, 173; and social-welfare assistance, 114; on unrest overseas, 209; and the War on Crime, 114, 127. *See also* War on Crime
Sagalyn, Louise, 128, 209
Sanger, Richard, 239
Santarelli, Donald, 140–41
Sartre, Jean-Paul, 43
Saudia Arabia, 71, 260
Saunders, Harold H., 58, 110
SCAP (Supreme Commander for the Allied Powers), 60, 72–73, 119
School of Criminology (UC Berkeley), 68, 70, 227
Scott, James, 250
SEADOC (Senior Officers Civil Disturbance Orientation Course) (US Army), 178–82, 184–85, 187, 189, 209
Seale, Bobby, 3–4
segregation (racial), 4, 34, 36, 87, 219, 256
Selden, Armistead I., Jr., 37
Senior Officers Civil Disturbance Orientation Course (US Army). *See* SEADOC
Serong, Ted, 240
settlerism, 3–4
SGCI (Special Group Counter-Insurgency): accomplishments of, 107; and AID, 103, 108; and Brazil, 104; budget of, 110; and China, 106; and the CIA,

SGCI (Special Group Counter-Insurgency) (continued)
103, 107, 110; and Colombia, 104; counterinsurgency as priority of, 104; Engle in, 106; expansion of territory by, 104; interagency character of, 103; and JFK, 107, 129; and Komer, 32, 97, 103, 105–8; and Laos, 104; and the national security state, 89–90; non-violent maintenance of order investigated by, 108; and the NSC, 103; and the OIDP, 104; and OPS, 104; origins of, 103–8; police assistance in, 107; police violence studied by, 108; and RFK, 106–7, 111, 131; security threats in countries supported by, 110; in South Vietnam, 104; and the Soviet Union, 106; strategies of, 80; and Taylor, 104; and Thailand, 104; U. Alexis Johnson's subcommittee report to, 110; and Vance, 174; and Venezuela, 318n50

Shannon, Lyle, 129
Sheehan, Neil, 94
Sheldon, Stanley, 225
Simulmatics Corporation, 237
Singh, Nikhil Pal, 40
Singlaub, John, 231
Siragusa, Charles, 61, 129
slavery, 3–4, 34, 63
Sloane, Charles, 160, 261
social control/regulation: overview, 142–65; and capitalism, 144; cost-benefit counterinsurgency applied to, 242; by counterinsurgency, 157–60, 265; crime control as, 241–42; Engle's theories of, 68–69; labor- vs. capital-intensive modes of, 214; in the Nixon administration, 144; O. W. Wilson's advocacy of, 69; Parker's views on, 216–21, 232; by police, 16, 143–46, 252; in *The Police and Resources Control in Counter-Insurgency*, 158; and police assistance, 163–64; racialization of, 3, 23, 202; in South Vietnam, 158–60; traffic control's significance to, 69, 160; in US empire, 49. *See also* behavior control; police power
social regulation. *See* social control/regulation

social welfare. *See headings under welfare programs*
Somalia, 184, 261
Southern Illinois University, 185
South Vietnam: AID in, 150; aid withheld from, 105; Bordenkircher as OPS public safety advisor in, 142, 208; Bureau of Investigation (VBI) of, 77; chemical weapons used in, 195; Civil Guard of, 75 *fig. 5*, 75–76; communications systems developed for, 151; vs. Communist People's War, 161; counterinsurgency in, 98, 101, 112, 144–45, 158, 161–62, 207, 252; Crisostomo in, 150; crop destruction in, 112; CS tear gas used in, 23, 200–204, 210–11, 222; DEA replacing OPS in, 262; demonstrations repressed in, 166; domestic intelligence gathering in, 160; and Engle, 77, 302n107; French occupation of, 75; guerrilla warfare in, 158–59; insurrectionary movements in, 104; Komer in, 90, 96–97, 104, 145; law and order problems in, 239; LBJ's War on Poverty in, 97, 104; Manopoli in, 32; material assistance provided to, 151; and McNamara, 112; military personnel under civilian supervision in, 97; and MSU, 65, 74–77, 75 *fig. 5*, 160, 192, 193 *fig. 11*, 312n25; narcotics control missions in, 262; National Identity Registration Project of, 159–60; nationalism in, 96; National Police of, 57, 154–55, 159–60, 182–83; and OISP, 109; Operation Birmingham in, 204–5; OPS abuses in, 269; OPS and the Phoenix program in, 144; OPS assets created in, 150; OPS/British competition in, 310n123; OPS budget for, 154; OPS creating repressive bureaucracies in, 186; OPS/LAPD connections in, 225–26; OPS national-identity card program in, 159; OPS resources control in, 158, 251–52; OPS riot-control methods in, 23; OPS-trained National Police in, 57, 155, 183; OPS training and equipping of police in, 57, 148, 155, 183, 323n53; pacification in, 90, 96–97, 145; and the Philco-Ford company, 147; Phoenix program in,

144, 161–62; police assistance in, 45, 85, 158–62; police centralization in, 145; police forces in, trained by MSU, 65, 76, 193 *fig. 11;* police forces trained by, 323n53; police power in, 90; police professionalization in, 225; and political participation, 160–61; Popkin-Scott debates on, 250; proxy-led counterinsurgency in, 252; public safety program, 74–77, 133, 148–49, 154, 158, 160; and the RAND corporation, 243, 244; Ryan in, 76, 133; SGCI in, 104; social control in, 77, 158–59; socioeconomic deprivation in, 247; surveillance of citizens in, 159; tear gas delivery systems in, 208; tear gas tactics developed in, 192; tear gas used in, 194–95, 198, 200–208, 210; technical assistance provided to, 75 *fig. 5,* 76, 109; threat increases in, 155; torture in, 324n68; US failure to change course in, 237; US nation-building in, 101; and US policing apparatus, 3; and US racism, 76. *See also* MSU; NLF; Wolf, Charles, Jr.

Soviet Union: in the Cold War, 91, 286–87n21; guerrillas backed by, 84; Komer and, 95; policing methods of, 186; and the SGCI, 104; social transformation advocated by, 83; and US racism, 28, 31, 35; and US use of CS, 200. *See also* Khrushchev, Nikita

Spanish empire, 146

Special Operations Research Office (US Army), 237

Special Warfare Center (Fort Bragg), 185

Special Weapons and Tactics. *See* SWAT units

Speier, Hans, 244

state-building, 2, 17–18, 52, 77–78, 235, 265

State Department. *See* US State Department

state-formation, 17–18, 52, 54, 77, 265

State of Siege (Costa-Gavras film), 260

State Planning Agencies, 139

Stein, Nancy, 262

Stevenson, Adlai, 128

St. Louis police department, 63–64, 133

Stoddard, Lothrop, 45

Stoughton, Roger, 327n21

subversives and subversion: and China, 261; and civil rights, 237; countries most active in, 85; and crime, 35, 38, 50–52, 71, 73, 78, 80, 82, 150, 160; and Cuba, 151; democratic participation vs., 161; domestic-foreign alliances in, 12; Engle on, 72; first lines of defense against, 79, 107; input/output theories vs., 247; intelligence on, 72; Kerner report on, 240; local police vs., 9, 59, 72, 79, 100–104, 145; and modernization, 81; OPS vs., 6; overmilitarized responses to, 126; and Paraná, 157; in POCC training, 183; police-led countersubversion, 241; and police professionalization, 11; and protests for racial justice, 160; and race, 35, 39; and racial inequality, 39; racialization of, 35, 38–39; resource control vs., 252; in South Vietnam, 158–60; subversives fighting subversives, 101; technological expertise vs., 145, 151; Wolf on, 247. *See also* communist subversion

Sun Tzu (military strategist), 222

Supreme Commander for the Allied Powers. *See* SCAP

surplus military matériel (for police), 136, 197, 233

surveillance: of Black political radicals, 176; coercive surveillance, 254; as countersubversion technique, 158; court-mandated, 1; in Kansas City Police Department, 59; by the LAPD, 230–31; military surveillance of antiwar movement, 240, 242; police assistance as, 20, 85; as police power, 176; of political protests, 146; political surveillance as, 138; of radicals and radical groups, 146, 230; repatriation of, 65

SWAT (Special Weapons and Tactics) units: overview, 214–34; adopted in other US cities, 224; vs. Black rebellions against police abuse, 221; as capital-intensive, 214; CS used by, 221, 223; failure of, 223–24; FBI training of, 224; as foreign state-violence tool repatriated, 215; Gates's branding of, 224; and guerrilla warfare, 222, 223; vs. indis-

SWAT (Special Weapons and Tactics) units *(continued)* criminate gunfire, 223; LEAA funding of, 215; lethal weaponry of, 223; and the Marines, 214–15, 222; and the militarization of policing, 233–34; as order-maintenance policing, 214–34; origins of, 214–15, 221–24; and Parker, 221; in racially marginalized communities, 24; transnationalism of, 214, 221; and US war in Vietnam, 215

Symbionese Liberation Army, 221

Syria, 46

Tamm, Quinn: and AID, 135; and Carl Turner, 180; counterinsurgency programs of, 9; and Hoover, 135, 171, 173–75; and the IACP, 9, 135–37, 173–74, 299n46; LBJ's empowerment of, 169; and the omnibus bill, 137; as *Police Chief* editor, 173

Tampa, Florida, 3

Taylor, Maxwell: and counterinsurgency, 14, 90; vs. Eisenhower, 89; flexible-response doctrine of, 14, 86, 88; and Insurgency Critical, 104; and JFK, 13, 86, 98; and Komer, 102–3; and LBJ, 98; on police assistance in counterinsurgency, 107; replacement of, 106; and RFK, 106; as SGCI director, 104; *The Uncertain Trumpet,* 88

tear gas: overview, 192–213; AID as supplier of, 228; arguments against, 192; delivery systems of, 205, 329n50; discretionary employment of, 174; in domestic non-riot conditions, 225; domestic use of, 202; used in the Dominican Republic, 228; Engle's advocacy of, 192–94; Federal Laboratories, Inc. as manufacturer of, 192; as nonlethal riot control, 192; and police professionalization, 236; used in racially marginalized communities, 24; and targeting ineffectiveness, 209; tear gas grenades, 192, 202–3, 207–8, 229; in Vietnam, 192, 198, 200–201, 204–95. *See also* CN/DM tear gas; CN tear gas; CR tear gas; CS tear gas; Johnson, Lyndon B.; nonlethal weapons; South Vietnam

Templer, Gerald, 245

terrorism, 5, 179, 188, 212, 237, 262

Terry v. Ohio (US Supreme Court), 256

Thailand, 104, 145, 155, 175, 226–27, 253, 302n107

Thompson, Robert G. K., 245, 249, 310n123

Tillman, Lafayette, 34

Title IX (Foreign Assistance Act), 161–64, 320nn70–71. *See also* Foreign Assistance Act

torture, 61, 66, 143–44, 149, 165, 186, 270, 324n68

transnationalism. *See* carceral state; Los Angeles Police Department; police assistance (transnational); police power; police professionalization (transnational); police violence; SWAT

transnational method, 15–16

Treasury Department, 128, 133, 182, 262

Trujillo, Rafael, 58, 227–28

Truman, Harry S.: CIA created by, 18; and civil rights, 64; and the Cold War, 88; Committee on Civil Rights established by, 71; and Engle, 265; FBI and, 64, 76; globalization advocated by, 88, 264; and Komer, 94; national security state created by, 64, 265, 272; and NSC 68, 88; and Pendergast, 64, 264; and Roosevelt, 64, 71

Tupamaros (Uruguayan militants), 149, 270

Turkey, 61–62, 112, 128, 261

Turner, Carl C., 175–80, 191, 208

Turner, Ralph F., 75–77, 102, 136, 167

The Uncertain Trumpet (Taylor), 88

United Farm Workers, 223

United Kingdom (UK), 310n123. *See also* British counterinsurgency activities

United Nations, 31, 50, 115

United States v. Brignoni-Ponce (US Supreme Court), 40

University of California at Berkeley (UC Berkeley), 68, 70, 208, 227. *See also* School of Criminology (UC Berkeley)

unrest (civil/urban): chemical weapons to be used against, 192; and communist subversion, 122; compulsive comparativism hindering assessment of, 240; CS tear gas used in, 197; in Detroit, 3, 27, 43, 210; and federalism, 167; Hall and Weckler's report on, 65; law and order vs., 124, 136; and LBJ, 43, 122, 169; militarized responses to, 125, 139, 169; in northern states, 123–24; OPS simulations of, 185; and police crises, 9, 114, 124–26, 136; and police professionalization, 27; and police upgrading, 4; socioeconomic causes of, ignored, 51, 235–36; trending up, 118; as urban guerrilla warfare, 239; and white racist violence, 169

unrest (global), 86, 112, 122

Uruguay, 148–49, 269

US empire: and anticommunism, 265; behavior control modes in, 157; Black people viewed as imperial subjects in, 42; characteristics of, 43–44; and the Cold War, 5; and counterinsurgency, 14; and CS tear gas, 194–99, 204–7; as discretionary, 11, 20, 24, 30, 43–44, 50, 264–65; and Engle's's work in Japan, 72; and Gates, 232; and Harlem, 117; and Japan, 71–72; and Latin America, 30; literature on, 284n12; local police as protectors of, 30; local proxies required for, 49; overseas techniques of, repatriated, 232–33; in the Panama Canal Zone, 36; and police assistance, 20; and police power, 16–17; and post WWII occupation, 78; and previous imperial regimes, 40; and racism, 49, 157, 232; radicals vs., 42; and repressive policing, 269; social control in, 49; state coercive powers linked in, 49; and tear gas, 192–213; violence of, 208, 232; and Watts, 232; and West Germany, 71

US State Department: and African American politics, 239; aiding maintenance of US racial order, 29; Bureau of Intelligence and Research of, 83, 100; countries identified for special attention by, 110; on Geneva protocol and riot control agents, 200; Indonesia's appeal to, 18; LAPD assisted by, 227; narcotics control mission of, 262; US public safety programs discontinued by, 260

vagrancy law, 221, 256

Valentine, Lewis J., 65, 73–74

Vance, Cyrus R., 174

Van Deman, Ralph, 65

Venezuela, 151, 155, 159, 184, 260–61, 318n50

Vietnam, US war in: brought home to the US, 195, 198; chemical defoliants used in, 112, 198, 205, 251; and counterinsurgency studies, 237; Harlem rebellion equated with, 272; hearts and minds theory discredited by, 252; and the Kennedy administration, 13; and Komer, 92, 112; protests against, 115, 116, 237; as a race war, 41; and SWAT, 215; Tet offensive in, 92; Vietnam War Syndrome, 215; and William Colby, 46. *See also* Gulf of Tonkin incident; North Vietnam; South Vietnam

Vietnamization, 97–98

Vinnell Corporation, 260

Vollmer, August: and the Berkeley police department, 67; Berkeley's School of Criminology founded by, 68; in Cuba, 67; in Germany, 68; as IACP director, 67; in Kansas City, 67, 72; and the LAPD, 67, 216–17; and LAPD Daily Training Bulletin, 332n14; methodologies of, 70; military tactics of, 67; and O. W. Wilson, 70; in the Philippines, 67, 70, 78, 217; and police professionalization, 62–63, 166–67; as police reformer, 216–17; and Pulliam, 68; social liberalism of, 67–68

Vo Nguyen Giap, 100, 272, 332n34

Voting Rights Act, 43, 120, 137, 238

Wallerstein, Immanuel, 302n111

Walnut Creek, California, 21

Walton, Frank E., 45–46, 76, 154, 226

War on Crime: and AID, 12; block grants for, 187; carceral state created by, 119; vs. the civil rights movement, 4; and the Cold War, 8; vs. collective political participation, 120; and CSTI, 189; as Democratic Party initiative, 140; and domestic technical police assistance, 140; emergence of, 120; federal and local autonomy balanced in, 119; and federal-

War on Crime *(continued)*
ism, 49, 167–69; and gun regulation, 263; and the IACP, 135; and the Kerner Commission, 4; and LBJ, 63; local power unconstrained in, 120; and the national security state, 8; in the Nixon administration, 283–84n10; and the omnibus bill, 137; and OPS, 12, 23, 113–14, 124; and police as political actors, 266, 267–68; police assistance as a model for, 9; and police professionalization, 115, 267–68; and Sagalyn, 9, 114; states' carceral apparatus funded via, 8; and the War on Poverty, 120, 140, 283–84n10. *See also* Democrats and the Democratic Party; federalism; Harlem

War on Poverty: conservatives vs., 140; failings of, 253; federalism vs., 120; and Harlem unrest, 170; James Q. Wilson on, 255–56; LBJ on, 283–84n10; local power curtailed in, 120; and protest mobilization, 239; and the War on Crime, 120, 140, 283–84n10

Washington, DC, 36–37, 57, 211, 328n40

Washington, DC police department, 208

Watts (Los Angeles), 78

Watts rebellion: CS tear gas used in, 198; Gates as field commander during, 214; Gates's views on, 232; and People's Park, 188; police violence during, 230; racist social order threatened by, 232; severity of, 166; Simulmatics Corporation's analysis of, 237

Weber, Max, 295n66

Weckler, Joseph E., 27, 29, 42, 65

welfare programs: and the carceral state, 4, 125; conservative skepticism of, 170, 240; crime as social pathology vs., 50; failures of, promoted by police technologies, 268; police spending privileged over, 125, 141; Reagan's reform of, 253; and Sagalyn, 114; and the warfare-welfare state, 10

Western Goals Foundation, 231

West Germany, 71

Westmoreland, William, 201, 204, 240

Wherry, Kenneth, 52

White, Lee C., 124

white populations, 27, 118, 271

white supremacy/superiority, 30, 31, 45, 139, 238, 273

Wichita, Kansas, 63, 65, 69

Wichita police department, 66, 69

Williams, Alexander, "Clubber," 296n72

Williams, Ogden, 341n13

Williamson, Jeter L., 70, 152, 154

Wilson, James Q., 236, 250, 253, 255–57

Wilson, Orlando W.: as Berkeley School of Criminology dean, 227; as Chicago police commissioner, 70; and Engle, 68, 71; in Germany, 69, 71, 78, 217; and Hall, 69–70; influence of, 70–71; and KC's single-officer patrol car proposal, 340n75; in Los Angeles, 217; methodologies of, 69, 70; militarization of police by, 69; and Ness, 127–28; and Parker, 217; patrol tactics of, 66, 226, 256, 340n75; *Police Administration,* 70–71; and police professionalization, 62–63, 69, 71; *Police Records* and *Police Planning,* 70; *Public Safety Manual of Procedures,* 69; and Sagalyn, 127–28; training methods of, 182; and Vollmer, 70; and the Wichita police, 65–66

Wohlstetter, Albert, 242–43, 249, 254

Wohlstetter, Roberta, 243

Wolf, Charles, Jr.: behavior control advocated by, 246–47; on causes of counterinsurgency, 246–47; coercive counterinsurgency methods of, 246, 248–49, 251–54; cost-benefit counterinsurgency policies developed by, 242, 246; counterinsurgent knowledge contributions by, 243; demand-pull/cost-push insurgency paradigm of, 248; on democracy's limitations, 247; and discretionary police despotism, 257; and Ellsberg, 249; and foreign aid, 243; vs. hearts and minds theory, 158, 245; input-control counterinsurgency tactics of, 246–49, 251–55; "Insurgency and Counterinsurgency," 245; and Leites, 247–53; vs. pacification, 247, 251; and rational-choice counterinsurgency, 243–45, 250,

252–56; *Rebellion and Authority,* 248–50; on rebellion control as world priority, 247

women: as AID staff, 292n36; in the IPA, 38; job discrimination against, 37–38; and legalized prostitution, 63; noncombatant women killed by settlers, 49; as public safety advisors, 37–38; as tear gas victims, 209

Wright, Quincy, 46

Zaire. *See* Congo/Zaire

AMERICAN CROSSROADS

Edited by Earl Lewis, George Lipsitz, George Sánchez, Dana Takagi, Laura Briggs, and Nikhil Pal Singh

1. *Border Matters: Remapping American Cultural Studies,* by José David Saldívar

2. *The White Scourge: Mexicans, Blacks, and Poor Whites in Texas Cotton Culture,* by Neil Foley

3. *Indians in the Making: Ethnic Relations and Indian Identities around Puget Sound,* by Alexandra Harmon

4. *Aztlán and Viet Nam: Chicano and Chicana Experiences o f the War,* edited by George Mariscal

5. *Immigration and the Political Economy of Home: West Indian Brooklyn and American Indian Minneapolis, 1945–1992,* by Rachel Buff

6. *Epic Encounters: Culture, Media, and U.S. Interests in the Middle East since 1945,* by Melani McAlister

7. *Contagious Divides: Epidemics and Race in San Francisco's Chinatown,* by Nayan Shah

8. *Japanese American Celebration and Conflict: A History of Ethnic Identity and Festival, 1934–1990,* by Lon Kurashige

9. *American Sensations: Class, Empire, and the Production of Popular Culture,* by Shelley Streeby

10. *Colored White: Transcending the Racial Past,* by David R. Roediger

11. *Reproducing Empire: Race, Sex, Science, and U.S. Imperialism in Puerto Rico,* by Laura Briggs

12. *meXicana Encounters: The Making of Social Identities on the Borderlands,* by Rosa Linda Fregoso

13. *Popular Culture in the Age of White Flight: Fear and Fantasy in Suburban Los Angeles,* by Eric Avila

14. *Ties That Bind: The Story of an Afro-Cherokee Family in Slavery and Freedom,* by Tiya Miles

15. *Cultural Moves: African Americans and the Politics of Representation,* by Herman S. Gray

16. *Emancipation Betrayed: The Hidden History of Black Organizing and White Violence in Florida from Reconstruction to the Bloody Election of 1920,* by Paul Ortiz

17. *Eugenic Nation: Faults and Frontiers of Better Breeding in Modern America,* by Alexandra Stern

18. *Audiotopia: Music, Race, and America,* by Josh Kun

19. *Black, Brown, Yellow, and Left: Radical Activism in Los Angeles,* by Laura Pulido

20. *Fit to Be Citizens? Public Health and Race in Los Angeles, 1879–1939,* by Natalia Molina

21. *Golden Gulag: Prisons, Surplus, Crisis, and Opposition in Globalizing California,* by Ruth Wilson Gilmore

22. *Proud to Be an Okie: Cultural Politics, Country Music, and Migration to Southern California,* by Peter La Chapelle

23. *Playing America's Game: Baseball, Latinos, and the Color Line,* by Adrian Burgos, Jr.

24. *The Power of the Zoot: Youth Culture and Resistance during World War II,* by Luis Alvarez

25. *Guantánamo: A Working-Class History between Empire and Revolution,* by Jana K. Lipman

26. *Between Arab and White: Race and Ethnicity in the Early Syrian-American Diaspora,* by Sarah M. A. Gualtieri

27. *Mean Streets: Chicago Youths and the Everyday Struggle for Empowerment in the Multiracial City, 1908–1969,* by Andrew J. Diamond

28. *In Sight of America: Photography and the Development of U.S. Immigration Policy,* by Anna Pegler-Gordon

29. *Migra! A History of the U.S. Border Patrol,* by Kelly Lytle Hernández

30. *Racial Propositions: Ballot Initiatives and the Making of Postwar California,* by Daniel Martinez HoSang

31. *Stranger Intimacy: Contesting Race, Sexuality, and the Law in the North American West,* by Nayan Shah

32. *The Nicest Kids in Town:* American Bandstand, *Rock 'n' Roll, and the Struggle for Civil Rights in 1950s Philadelphia,* by Matthew F. Delmont

33. *Jack Johnson, Rebel Sojourner: Boxing in the Shadow of the Global Color Line,* by Theresa Rundstedler

34. *Pacific Connections: The Making of the US-Canadian Borderlands,* by Kornel Chang

35. *States of Delinquency: Race and Science in the Making of California's Juvenile Justice System,* by Miroslava Chávez-García

36. *Spaces of Conflict, Sounds of Solidarity: Music, Race, and Spatial Entitlement in Los Angeles,* by Gaye Theresa Johnson

37. *Covert Capital: Landscapes of Denial and the Making of U.S. Empire in the Suburbs of Northern Virginia,* by Andrew Friedman

38. *How Race Is Made in America: Immigration, Citizenship, and the Historical Power of Racial Scripts,* by Natalia Molina

39. *We Sell Drugs: The Alchemy of US Empire,* by Suzanna Reiss

40. *Abrazando el Espíritu: Bracero Families Confront the US-Mexico Border,* by Ana Elizabeth Rosas

41. *Houston Bound: Culture and Color in a Jim Crow City,* by Tyina L. Steptoe

42. *Why Busing Failed: Race, Media, and the National Resistance to School Desegregation,* by Matthew F. Delmont

43. *Incarcerating the Crisis: Freedom Struggles and the Rise of the Neoliberal State,* by Jordan T. Camp

44. *Lavender and Red: Liberation and Solidarity in the Gay and Lesbian Left,* by Emily K. Hobson

45. *Flavors of Empire: Food and the Making of Thai America,* by Mark Padoongpatt

46. *The Life of Paper: Letters and a Poetics of Living Beyond Captivity,* by Sharon Luk

47. *Strategies of Segregation: Race, Residence, and the Struggle for Educational Equality,* by David G. García

48. *Soldiering through Empire: Race and the Making of the Decolonizing Pacific,* by Simeon Man

49. *An American Language: The History of Spanish in the United States,* by Rosina Lozano

50. *The Color Line and the Assembly Line: Managing Race in the Ford Empire,* by Elizabeth D. Esch

51. *Confessions of a Radical Chicano Doo-Wop Singer,* by Rubén Funkahuatl Guevara

52. *Empire's Tracks: Indigenous Peoples, Racial Aliens, and the Transcontinental Railroad,* by Manu Karuka

53. *Collisions at the Crossroads: How Place and Mobility Make Race,* by Genevieve Carpio

54. *Charros: How Mexican Cowboys are Remapping Race and American Identity,* by Laura R. Barraclough

55. *Louder and Faster: Pain, Joy, and the Body Politic in Asian American Taiko,* by Deborah Wong

56. *Badges Without Borders: How Global Counterinsurgency Transformed American Policing,* by Stuart Schrader

Founded in 1893,
UNIVERSITY OF CALIFORNIA PRESS
publishes bold, progressive books and journals
on topics in the arts, humanities, social sciences,
and natural sciences—with a focus on social
justice issues—that inspire thought and action
among readers worldwide.

The UC PRESS FOUNDATION
raises funds to uphold the press's vital role
as an independent, nonprofit publisher, and
receives philanthropic support from a wide
range of individuals and institutions—and from
committed readers like you. To learn more, visit
ucpress.edu/supportus.

CPSIA information can be obtained
at www.ICGtesting.com
Printed in the USA
BVHW030917190919
558888BV00001B/11/P